Study Guide and Problems

to accompany

LIPSEY/STEINER/PURVIS

ECONOMICS

Eighth Edition

Dascomb R. Forbush
Emeritus, Clarkson University

Fredric C. Menz
Clarkson University

1817

HARPER & ROW, PUBLISHERS, New York
Cambridge, Philadelphia, San Francisco, Washington,
London, Mexico City, São Paulo, Singapore, Sydney

Study Guide and Problems to accompany Lipsey/Steiner/Purvis: ECONOMICS, Eighth Edition

ISBN: 0-06-042122-3

87 88 89 90 9 8 7 6 5 4 3 2 1

Contents

PART ONE
The Nature of Economics 1

1 The Economic Problem 1
2 Economics as a Social Science 10
3 An Overview of the Economy 21

Cases
1 *The 97.5 Percent Zinc Cent 28*
2 *Energy Use and GNP 30*

PART TWO
A General View of the Price System 34

4 Demand, Supply, and Price 34
5 Elasticity of Demand and Supply 46
6 Supply and Demand in Action: Price Controls and Agriculture 58

Cases
3 *Maintaining an All-Volunteer Armed Force* 72
4 *Pricing Congestion in Singapore* 76
5 *The Oscillating Avocado* 78

PART THREE Consumption, Production, and Cost 81

7 Household Consumption Behavior: The Marginal Utility Approach 81
8 Household Consumption Behavior: The Indifference Curve Approach 93
9 The Role of the Firm 105
10 Production and Cost in the Short Run 115
11 Production and Cost in the Long and Very Long Run 128

Cases
6 *Sapphires for Rent* 139
7 *The Costs of Driving an Automobile in the Mid-1980s* 140
8 *Supermammoth Supertankers* 142
9 *Choices Between A and B* 144

PART FOUR Markets and Pricing 146

12 Pricing in Competitive Markets 146
13 Pricing in Monopoly Markets 156
14 Competition and Monopoly Compared 168
15 Oligopoly 183
16 Public Policies About Monopoly and Competition 193
17 Who Runs the Firm and for What Ends? 202

Cases
10 *Adams and Brown* 210
11 *The Mountain Doctor* 212
12 *Are Diamonds (Valuable) Forever?* 213
13 *The Cigarette Industry: An Enduring and Beleaguered Oligopoly* 215
14 *Breakfast Cereals: A Shared Monopoly?* 219

PART FIVE The Distribution of Income 222

18 Factor Mobility and Factor Pricing 222
19 More on Factor Demand and Supply 232
20 Wages, Unions, and Discrimination 246
21 The Problem of Poverty 256

Cases
15 *"The Average Guy Takes It on the Chin" (After 1973)* 263
16 *Are the Rich Getting Richer?* 266
17 *Who Gets the Economic Surplus in Professional Baseball and Football?* 268

PART SIX
The Market Economy: Problems and Policies 271

22 Benefits and Costs of Government Intervention 271
23 Taxation and Public Expenditure 284

Cases
18 *Acid from the Skies* 292
19 *Taxing the Cigarette Habit in the Most Profitable Way* 293
20 *Government Regulation of Worker Safety: Valuing Human Lives* 296
21 *The Tax Reform Act of 1986* 297

PART SEVEN
National Income and Fiscal Policy 300

24 An Introduction to Macroeconomics 300
25 Measuring Macroeconomic Variables 308
26 National Income and Aggregate Demand 317
27 Changes in National Income I: The Role of Aggregate Demand 327
28 Changes in National Income II: The Role of Aggregate Supply 341
29 Business Cycles: The Ebb and Flow of Economic Activity 352
30 Fiscal Policy 364

Cases
22 *The Bottom Line: DPI Over Three Generations (1929–1985)* 376
23 *Multipliers and the Marginal Propensity Not to Spend* 378
24 *Investment Expenditures and Fluctuations in Economic Activity* 379
25 *How a Fiscal Shot in the Arm Would Work* 381

PART EIGHT
Money, Banking, and Monetary Policy 383

31 The Nature of Money and Monetary Institutions 383
32 The Role of Money in Macroeconomics 391
33 Monetary Policy 409

Cases
26 *Did the Silver Make the Quarter Valuable?* 421
27 *A Bond Boom: May 1984 to May 1986* 423

PART NINE
Issues and Controversies 426

34 Inflation 426
35 Employment and Unemployment 439
36 Economic Growth 448
37 Macroeconomic Controversies 457

Cases
28 *Controversy over the Federal Deficit* *464*
29 *Are the Worst Problems with High Unemployment Almost Over?* *466*
30 *Legislating Macroeconomic Goals* *468*

PART TEN
International Trade and Finance 470

38 The Gains from Trade 470
39 Barriers to Free Trade 479
40 Foreign Exchange, Exchange Rates, and the Balance of Payments 488
41 International Monetary Systems 500

Cases
31 *Breaking Through the Production-Possibilities Frontier with Trade* *509*
32 *Continued Protection for the Automobile Industry?* *513*
33 *Le Franc à $.20255 et la Gloire de la France* *516*

PART ELEVEN
Economic Growth and Comparative Systems 519

42 Growth and the Less-Developed Countries 519
43 Comparative Economic Systems: The Economies of China and the USSR 527

Cases
34 *The Hesitant MDCs and the Aspiring LDCs* *534*
35 *A Little Adam Smith in the Little Red Book* *535*

To the Student

The purpose of this book is to help you study and review independently the basic material in Lipsey, Steiner, and Purvis, *Economics,* Eighth Edition. Each chapter in this *Study Guide* corresponds to a chapter in the text and contains several sections: learning objectives, review and self-test, exercises, and short problems. At the end of each part are several cases.

The review and self-test section of each chapter contains matching concepts and multiple-choice questions, with answers provided at the end of the section. Each chapter also contains exercises to reinforce your learning of economics. The exercises are a quick way to test your ability to work with graphs, solve basic problems, analyze certain hypotheses, and demonstrate your understanding of important concepts. Answers to exercise questions are provided at the end of each chapter.

Most chapters also have at least one short problem, while some chapters, particularly those with substantial analytical content, have several. The short problems often build on material presented in the exercises. Your instructor has answers to the short problems.

The cases, which follow the chapters comprising the parts of the text, often provide empirical data and other illustrative material on a particular economic problem. Some of the cases are quite challenging to a beginning economics student; you may not fully understand them until after class discussion. We hope you will be challenged by such problems as "Acid from the Skies," "Who Gets the Economic Surplus in Professional

Baseball and Football?," and "Pricing Congestion in Singapore." Suggested answers to the cases are also provided to the instructor.

Students will differ in how they use this book. All of you should find the learning objectives useful for a succinct review, the self-test sections helpful in assessing your grasp of the material, and the exercises important in verbal and graphical expression of analytical concepts. Your use of the short problems and cases will be more selective depending on your interests and the requirements of your instructor.

Acknowledgments

In revising this edition of the *Study Guide,* we have benefited from comments of four reviewers of the seventh edition: Mary E. Deily (Texas A&M University), Frank A. Scott, Jr. (University of Kentucky), David C. Craig (Westark Community College), and E. O. Price, III (Oklahoma State University). Many of their suggestions have been incorporated in this revision.

We also thank those individuals who helped us during preparation of this revision: Mary Lou Mosher for her editorial advice; our students Michelle Altpeter, Jim Blake, Mary Kaufman, Don Napier, and David Rood; Anita Sampier for her excellent efforts in preparing the manuscript; and Dorothy Fitts Forbush (1919–1978), the coauthor of the first four editions of the *Study Guide and Problems*. To our wives, Janet and Eleanor, we express our appreciation for their direct and indirect contributions to the completion of the eighth edition.

Dascomb R. Forbush
Fredric C. Menz

PART ONE

The Nature of Economics

1

The Economic Problem

Learning Objectives

After reading this chapter, you should be able to

—understand the problem of scarcity and the need for choice;

—illustrate the relationship between scarcity, choice, and opportunity cost with a production possibility boundary;

—understand why resource allocation is a key economic problem;

—explain why unemployed resources force the economy inside its production possibility boundary;

—describe how growth in productive capacity makes it possible to have more of all goods and services;

—explain how alternative economic systems may differ in terms of public versus private ownership of resources, market versus command systems for decision-making, and incentive structures.

Review and Self-Test

Matching Concepts

______ 1. central problem of economics

______ 2. resource allocation

______ 3. attainable combinations of goods with efficient production and full employment

______ 4. unemployment of resources

______ 5. opportunity cost

______ 6. macroeconomics

______ 7. economic system characterized by decentralized decision making

______ 8. study of the allocation of resources and the distribution of income as affected by the price system and government policies

______ 9. cause of outward shift of production possibility boundary

______ 10. basic differences among economic systems

(a) process of choosing an economy's product mix

(b) ownership of resources, decision process, and incentive system

(c) amount of one commodity given up to obtain another

(d) situation of production inside production possibility boundary

(e) growth in productive capacity

(f) microeconomics

(g) scarcity of resources relative to (unlimited) human wants

(h) production possibility boundary

(i) study of the determination of economic aggregates such as the price level, total employment, total output, and the rate of economic growth

(j) market economy

Multiple-Choice Questions

1. The fundamental problem of economics is, in short,
   (a) too many poor people.
   (b) finding jobs for all.
   (c) the scarcity of resources relative to wants.
   (d) constantly rising prices.

2. Which of the following would *not* be classified as a factor of production?
   (a) natural resources
   (b) commodities
   (c) human services (labor)
   (d) manufactured capital equipment

3. Drawing a production possibility boundary for military and civilian goods will help us to
   (a) estimate how much it is necessary to spend on defense.
   (b) estimate the amount of unemployment that is likely to result from a given federal expenditure on housing.
   (c) illustrate the cost of defense in terms of the expenditure on nondefense commodities that will have to be forgone.
   (d) show the relative desires of the public for military and civilian goods.

4. Opportunity cost
   (a) is measured by how much of one commodity must be forgone in order to get some stated amount of another commodity.
   (b) measures how many different opportunities you have to spend your money.
   (c) applies to production choices but not to consumption choices.
   (d) refers to unattainable combinations above the production possibility boundary.

5. Concerning resource ownership in an economy, which of the following statements best reflects the points in the chapter?
   (a) Actual economies usually rely solely on either public or private investment.
   (b) In Great Britain, privatization involves nationalizing key industries.
   (c) The United States has the highest percentage of private to total investment of any major country in the world.
   (d) Most, if not all, countries exhibit a mixture of public and private ownership of productive assets.

6. If tuition plus other expenses of going to college come to $10,000 per year, and you could have earned $12,500 per year working instead, the opportunity cost of your college year is
   (a) $10,000.
   (b) $12,500.
   (c) $22,500.
   (d) $2,500.

7. If a commodity can be obtained without sacrificing the production or consumption of anything else,
   (a) its opportunity cost is zero.
   (b) the economy is on its production possibility boundary.
   (c) the opportunity cost concept is irrelevant and meaningless.
   (d) its opportunity cost equals its money cost.

8. Points to the left of the current production possibility boundary
   (a) are currently unattainable and are expected to remain so.
   (b) will be attainable only if there is economic growth.
   (c) will result if some factors of production are unemployed or used inefficiently.
   (d) have higher opportunity costs than points on the boundary itself.

9. A country's production possibility boundary shows
   (a) what percentage of its resources is currently unemployed.
   (b) what choices in production are currently open to it.
   (c) what it is actually producing.
   (d) the available methods of production.

10. A shift outward in the production possibility boundary
    (a) would result if more of one product and less of another were chosen.
    (b) could reflect higher prices for goods.
    (c) could reflect increased unemployment.
    (d) could result from increased productivity of resources.

11. The process of determining the relative quantities of various goods and services to be produced is referred to by the term
    (a) resource allocation.
    (b) macroeconomics.
    (c) consumption.
    (d) scarcity.

12. The study of economic aggregates such as total output, total employment, and the price level falls within
    (a) microeconomics.
    (b) opportunity costs.
    (c) macroeconomics.
    (d) production possibilities.

13. Specific government policy measures have "opportunity costs," which means
    (a) higher taxes will be necessary.
    (b) moving toward one policy goal may require moving away from another policy goal.
    (c) government action is usually inefficient.
    (d) government action provides new opportunities.

14. Which one of the following would not be a source of differences among alternative types of economic systems?
    (a) ownership of resources (public, private)
    (b) the process for making economic decisions (market, planned)
    (c) incentive systems
    (d) the need to determine what is produced and how to produce it

15. The opportunity cost of attending a movie instead of studying is
    (a) the admission price.
    (b) the lost study time.
    (c) both (a) and (b).
    (d) none of the above.

Self-Test Key

Matching Concepts: 1–g; 2–a; 3–h; 4–d; 5–c; 6–i; 7–j; 8–f; 9–e; 10–b

Multiple-Choice Questions: 1–c; 2–b; 3–c; 4–a; 5–d; 6–c; 7–a; 8–c; 9–b; 10–d; 11–a; 12–c; 13–b; 14–d; 15–c

Exercises

1. Four key economic problems are identified in Chapter 1:
   (1) What is produced and how (resource allocation)?
   (2) What is consumed and by whom (distribution)?
   (3) How much unemployment and inflation is there (total employment and the price level)?
   (4) How is productive capacity changing (economic growth)?

   After each of the topics listed below, place the appropriate number indicating which type of problem applies. Use each classification only once.
   (a) Rises in oil prices during the 1970s induced a switch to alternative energy sources. (1)
   (b) The standard of living in the United States, measured by real output per capita, has risen steadily over the last century. (4)
   (c) Large harvests worldwide lower grain prices, helping consumers but hurting farmers. (2)
   (d) The unemployment rate of January 1986 was 6.9 percent. (3)

2. The following data show what combinations of corn and beef can be produced annually from a given piece of land.

Corn (bushels)	Beef (pounds)
10,000	0
8,000	900
6,000	1,200
4,000	1,400
2,000	1,450
0	1,500

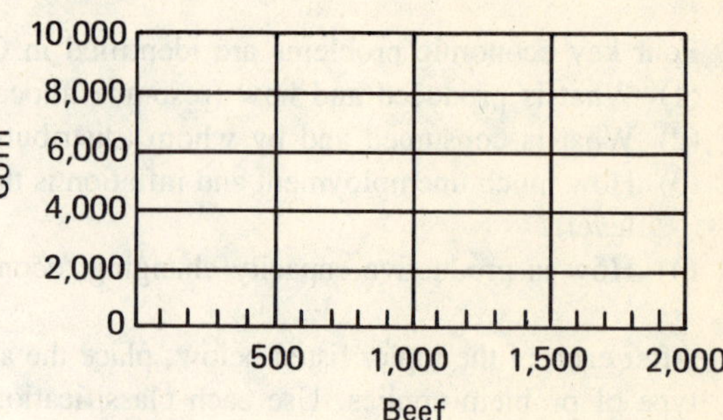

(a) On the graph above, draw the production possibility boundary for this piece of land.

(b) Can this acreage produce the combination of 5,000 bushels of corn and 500 pounds of beef? What does this combination suggest about the use of this acreage?

(c) Can this acreage produce the combination of 8,000 bushels of corn and 1,200 pounds of beef?

(d) What is the opportunity cost of expanding beef production from 900 to 1,200 pounds per annum, assuming the land is fully utilized?

(e) What happens to the opportunity cost of producing beef as this economy expands its production of beef?

(f) What would be the cost of producing 400 additional pounds of beef if this economy were currently producing 8,000 bushels of corn and 500 pounds of beef? Explain.

3. "Price of Candy Bars to Go to $.30," reads a 1985 headline. Assume that soda is $.60 a can and that $6.00 is available to spend.
   (a) Graph the consumption possibilities (later this will be called a *budget line*).
   (b) What is the opportunity cost of a can of soda?

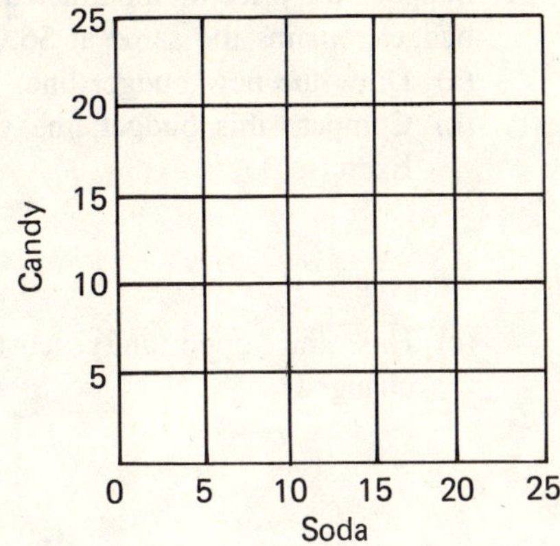

   (c) What does the straight downward-sloping line imply, compared to the production possibility boundary that is usually concave to the origin?

4. Suppose you have to wait in line to purchase a soft drink at a baseball game. The drink costs one dollar. While waiting in line, you hear the crowd roar as someone hits a home run. While running back to your seat, you fall and spill your drink on another spectator.
   (a) What is your money cost for the drink?
   (b) What is your opportunity cost for the drink? Explain.
   (c) What are the costs to others from your drink?
   (d) What are the full opportunity costs to you and the other spectator? (These will later be termed *social* costs.)

Short Problems

1. Suppose the price of soda increases to $.75 and that of a candy bar to $.40, but the budget remains the same at $6.00. (See Exercise 3.)
   (a) Draw the new budget line.
   (b) Compare this budget line with that in Exercise 3.
   (c) Has the opportunity cost of soda changed?

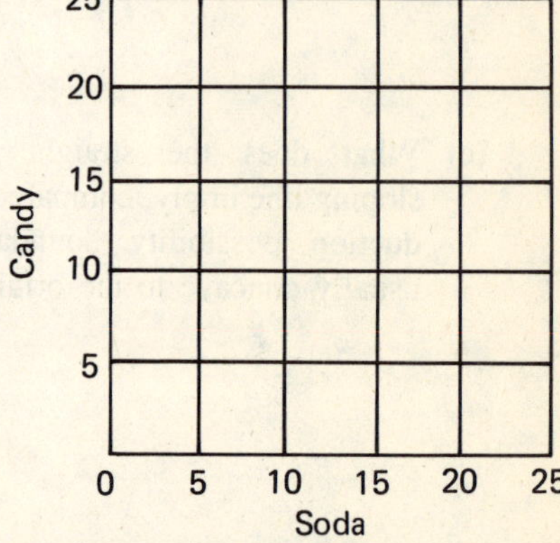

2. Consider the production possibilities for two totally dissimilar goods, such as apples and machine tools. Some resources are suitable for apple production and some for the production of machine tools. However, there is no possibility to shift resources from one product to another. In this case, what does the production possibility boundary look like? Explain and show graphically.

Answers to the Exercises

1. (a) 1 (b) 4 (c) 2 (d) 3

2. (a)

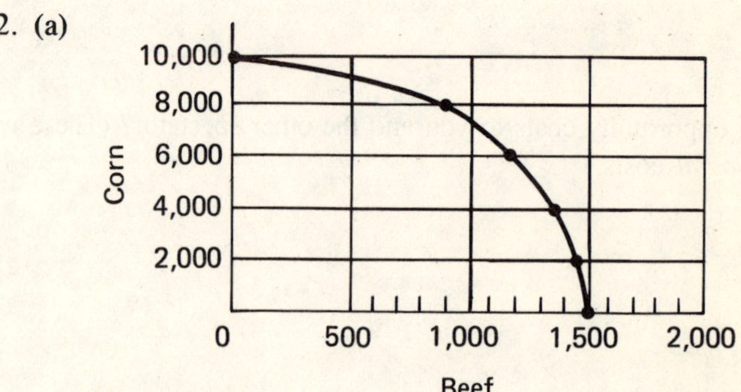

   (b) Yes. In fact, this combination is inside the production possibility boundary, indicating that resources are either not being used efficiently or are unemployed.
   (c) No, this combination lies outside the production possibility boundary.
   (d) Two thousand bushels of corn are lost.

(e) The opportunity cost increases. The opportunity cost of increasing beef production from 900 to 1,200 is 6.67 bushels of corn per unit increase in beef. If beef production is increased from 1,200 to 1,400, the opportunity cost per unit increase in beef is 10.0 bushels of corn.

(f) The cost would be zero, since no corn would be foregone.

3. (a) The possibilities can be represented as a straight line with candy intercept at 20, soda intercept at 10.

(b) two candy bars

(c) The straight line indicates a constant relative price ratio of candy bars and soda. That is, the opportunity cost of candy in terms of soda stays constant, no matter how much is consumed. The concave boundary line shows the increasing costs of producing either commodity.

4. (a) one dollar

(b) The opportunity cost to you is one dollar plus any benefits forgone as a result of missing the home run. (You also miss the benefits of drinking the soda!) Note that individuals may place different values on the cost of missing a hit (as they may on giving up one dollar).

(c) such costs as laundry bills, psychological trauma, and so on

(d) total of (b) and (c)

2

Economics As a Social Science

Learning Objectives

After studying the material in this chapter you should be able to

—distinguish between positive and normative statements;

—explain how the "law" of large numbers allows successful predictions about group behavior;

—understand the roles of variables, assumptions, and predictions in developing and testing theories;

—distinguish between endogenous and exogenous variables and between stocks and flows;

—give an example of a functional relation;

—explain the differences in the information provided by scatter diagrams, cross-classification tables, and regression analysis;

—understand that statistical testing methods accept or reject hypotheses only with degrees of probability.

Review and Self-Test

Matching Concepts

_______ 1. substance of a positive statement

_______ 2. substance of a normative statement

_______ 3. one reason for successful predictions about group behavior

_______ 4. method consisting of relating questions to evidence

_______ 5. regression analysis

_______ 6. endogenous variable

_______ 7. two-dimensional graph of the observations

_______ 8. proportion of variance in one variable explained by the changes in another

_______ 9. random sample

_______ 10. sole motivation of firms as profit maximization

(a) the law of large numbers

(b) coefficient of determination

(c) kind of variable determined within a theory or model

(d) the importance of import quotas because of fairness to certain producers

(e) selection process giving each member of the population an equal chance to be chosen

(f) the effect of government budget deficits on interest rates

(g) assumption frequently underlying economic theory of the firm

(h) scientific approach

(i) quantitative measure of the relationship among variables

(j) scatter diagram

Multiple-Choice Questions

1. Normative statements concern
   (a) what was.
   (b) what is the normal situation.
   (c) what will be.
   (d) what ought to be.

2. In an economic theory, endogenous variables
   (a) have no influence on the theory.
   (b) are always constant.
   (c) are determined by considerations outside of the theory.
   (d) are explained within the theory.

3. We do not want value judgments directly incorporated into scientific theories because
   (a) they are too complex.
   (b) they are too unrealistic to be tested.
   (c) they cannot be tested by an appeal to evidence.
   (d) they cannot be expressed mathematically.

4. A theory contains all but which one of the following?
   (a) a set of variables with their definitions
   (b) a set of assumptions about the conditions under which the theory is to apply
   (c) an hypothesis about the relationships among certain variables
   (d) a normative statement expressed as a functional relation

5. If a time dimension is required to give a particular variable meaning, then that variable is considered
   (a) a stock variable.
   (b) an endogenous variable.
   (c) an exogenous variable.
   (d) a flow variable.

6. The "law" of large numbers asserts that
   (a) random actions of a large number of individuals tend to offset each other.
   (b) what is true of large numbers is also true of a few individuals.
   (c) too many observations result in an unacceptable number of errors.
   (d) the range of errors of measurement increases with the number of observations.

7. Which of the following statements regarding economic theories is most appropriate?
   (a) The inability to conduct laboratory experiments makes economic theories unscientific.
   (b) The best kind of theory is worded so that it can pass any test to which it could be put.
   (c) The most important thing about the scientific approach is that it uses mathematics and diagrams.
   (d) We expect our theories to hold only with some margin of error.

8. In the statement, "the higher the price of carrots, the greater the quantity of carrots supplied,"
   (a) the quantity of carrots supplied is an exogenous variable.
   (b) the price of carrots and the quantity of carrots supplied are positively related.
   (c) the price of carrots is an endogenous variable.
   (d) both variables are exogenously determined.

9. A scientific prediction is a conditional statement because
   (a) it takes the form, "if this is done, then a particular result will follow."
   (b) it is impossible to test.
   (c) it can never be based on enough observations.
   (d) it is usually eventually shown to be false.

10. Which one of the following statements is incorrect?
    (a) Economists use theories to explain relationships among economic variables.
    (b) Economists use theories to predict economic events.
    (c) The best test of an economic theory is the realism of its assumptions.
    (d) An economic theory has certain logical implications that must be true if the theory is true.

11. Economic hypotheses are generally accepted only when
    (a) the evidence indicates that they are true with a high degree of probability.
    (b) they have been proven beyond a reasonable doubt.
    (c) they have been established with certainty.
    (d) the evidence is consistent with them in a majority of cases.

12. The relationship between two variables on a scatter diagram
    (a) may be obscured by the movement of another variable.
    (b) cannot be significant because of errors of observation.
    (c) will show a wavelike pattern if the variables are related to time.
    (d) will usually be a straight line.

13. Suppose a scatter diagram indicates that imports are on an average directly related to national income over time. If in one year imports fall when national income increases, the observation
    (a) disproves the direct relationship between the two variables.
    (b) suggests that other factors also influence the quantity of imports.
    (c) proves an inverse relationship between the two variables.
    (d) suggests that a measurement error has necessarily been made.

14. In statistical testing of a theory, choosing a random sample of observations is important because
    (a) it reduces the chance that the sample will be unrepresentative of the entire group.
    (b) it allows the calculation of the likelihood that the observed characteristics of the sample do not exist for the whole group.
    (c) economic theories cannot be tested using scientific methods.
    (d) both (a) and (b).

15. The statement that the quantity produced of a commodity and its price are positively related is
    (a) an assumption economists usually make.
    (b) a testable hypothesis.
    (c) a normative statement.
    (d) not testable as currently worded.

16. Which of the following equations is consistent with the hypothesis that federal income tax payments (*T*) are positively related to family income (*Y*) and negatively related to family size (*F*)?
    (a) $T = -733 + 0.197Y + 344F$
    (b) $T = -733 - 0.197Y - 344F$
    (c) $T = -733 + 0.197Y - 344F$
    (d) none of the above

17. Suppose that a regression analysis relates imports (*M*) and national income (*Y*) by the expression $M = 100 + 0.15Y$. This means that
    (a) imports are inversely related to national income.
    (b) when national income is zero, imports are zero.
    (c) imports are 15 percent of national income.
    (d) other things equal, for every $1.00 increase in national income, imports will rise by $.15.

Self-Test Key

Matching Concepts: 1–f; 2–d; 3–a; 4–h; 5–i; 6–c; 7–j; 8–b; 9–e; 10–g

Multiple-Choice Questions: 1–d; 2–d; 3–c; 4–d; 5–d; 6–a; 7–d; 8–b; 9–a; 10–c; 11–a; 12–a; 13–b; 14–d; 15–b; 16–c; 17–d

Exercises

1. After each phrase below, write P or N to indicate whether a positive or normative statement is being described.
    (a) a statement of fact that is actually wrong ______
    (b) a value judgment ______
    (c) a prediction that an event will happen ______
    (d) a statement about what the author thinks ought to be ______
    (e) a statement that can be tested by evidence ______
    (f) a value judgment based on evidence known to be correct ______
    (g) a hurricane forecast ______

2. Are the italicized variables endogenous (N) or exogenous (X) in the statements below?
   (a) *Market price* and *equilibrium quantity* of a commodity are determined by demand and supply. ______
   (b) The number of sailboats sold annually is a function of the *national income*. ______
   (c) The *condition of forest ecosystems* can be affected by regional air pollutants. ______
   (d) The quantity of housing services purchased is determined by the *relative price of housing, income,* and *household characteristics*. ______
   (e) Other things being equal, *consumer expenditures* are negatively related to interest rates. ______

3. Are the following variables stocks (S) or flows (F)?
   (a) the federal government's current budget deficit ______
   (b) the money supply ______
   (c) the total capital in the form of plant and equipment ______
   (d) personal income tax payments ______
   (e) an economy's annual total output ______
   (f) your bank balance at the end of the month ______
   (g) quarterly sales of U.S. automobiles ______

4. Given the relation between saving (S) and income (Y), $S = -\$100 + 0.10Y$, what is the amount of S for each of the indicated values of Y? Plot S on the graph.

Y	*S*
0	______
500	______
1,000	______
1,500	______
2,000	______

300
200
S 100
0
-100
0 1,000 2,000
Y

5. (a) Many economic variables are not distributed according to a normal curve, equally balanced on each side of the central point, but are skewed to one side or the other. Draw on the graph below how you would expect the curve to appear for persons distributed by income size. Take $25,000 as median family income.

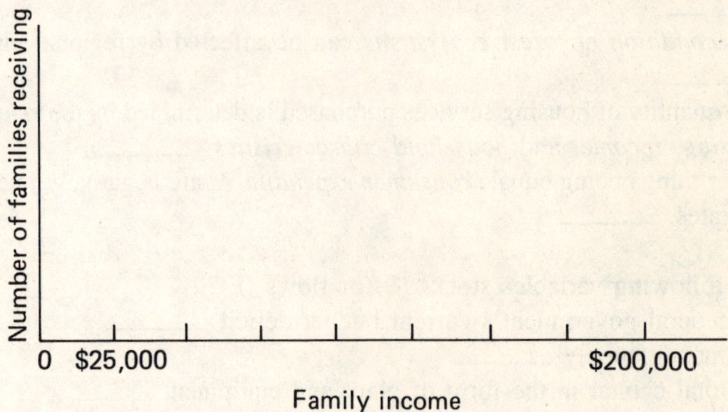

(b) Why is the assumption of a normal curve not appropriate here?

Short Problems

1. Classify the following statements as either positive (P) or normative (N). For the positive statements, comment on whether you think the statements are accurate and indicate how they might be tested. For the normative statements, indicate whether you agree and explain the basis for your position.
   (a) "My administration will balance the federal budget by 1983." (Ronald Reagan, campaign promise, 1980)

   (b) "Depression in energy industry pushes office vacancy rate in Houston to nearly 20%." (*Wall Street Journal,* June 1985)

   (c) "It is an economic contradiction for airline passengers to pay higher fares to fly shorter distances than longer ones." (Hobart Rowen, *Washington Post,* 1985)

   (d) "Value of one human life? From \$8.37 to \$10 million." (*New York Times,* June 25, 1985)

   (e) "Inflation makes everyone worse off by lowering the purchasing power of people's incomes."

   (f) "Rent controls are preferable to income grants for assisting low-income families."

2. Suppose that an economist hypothesizes that the quantity demanded of personal computers (Q_d) over some time period is determined by the price of each computer (P) and the average income of consumers (Y). The specific functional relationship among these three variables is hypothesized to be the expression $Q_d = 1Y - 4P$.
   (a) Which of these variables will be determined in the market for personal computers? Are these variables considered endogenous or exogenous?

   (b) Which of these variables will be determined outside the market for personal computers? Are these variables considered endogenous or exogenous?

   (c) What does the negative sign before the term $4P$ imply about the relationship between Q_d and P? What does the (implicit) positive sign before the term $1Y$ imply about the relationship between income and quantity demanded?

   (d) Which of the three variables are stock variables and which are flow variables? Explain.

   (e) Suppose for the moment that average income is constant at a level of 8,000. Write the expression for the demand relationship.

   (f) Assuming $Y = 8{,}000$, calculate the values of Q_d when $P = 500$, $P = 1{,}000$, $P = 2{,}000$, and $P = 0$.

(g) Plot the relation between P and Q_d (assuming $Y = 8{,}000$) on the graph below. Indicate the intercept values on both axes.

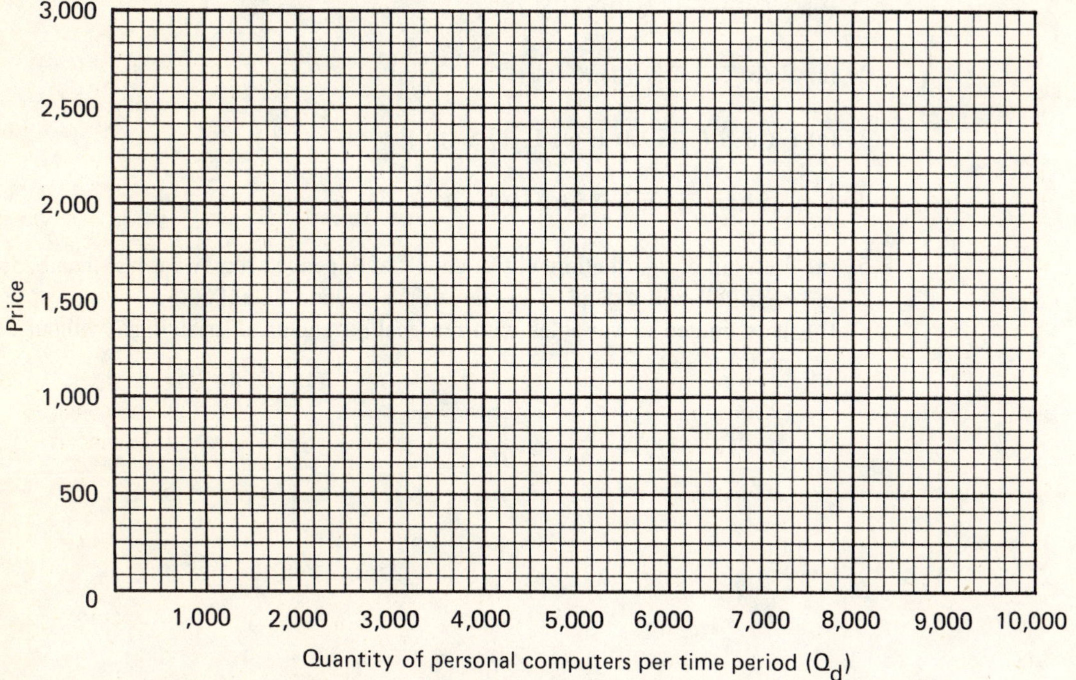

(h) Assuming $Y = 8{,}000$, calculate the change in the quantity demanded when the price increases from 1,000 to 2,000. Do the same for a price increase from 500 to 2,000. Call the change in the quantity demanded ΔQ_d and the change in the price ΔP. Form the ratio $\Delta Q_d / \Delta P$. Is this ratio constant?

(i) Suppose that there is evidence that the relationship in subsequent time periods has changed to $Q_d = 9{,}000 - 4P$. Plot the new relationship and indicate the intercept values on each axis. What has happened to the relation between the two variables? Why do you think the relationship changed over the two time periods?

Answers to the Exercises

1. (a) P (b) N (c) P (d) N (unless it is a prediction rather than opinion based on value judgment) (e) P (f) N (g) P

2. (a) N (b) X (c) N (d) X (e) N

3. (a) F (b) S (c) S (d) F (e) F (f) S (g) F

4. S = –$100; –$50; 0; $50; $100

5. (a) Left tail of distribution will be cut off at 0; peak at somewhat less than $25,000; right tail will extend at low levels far beyond $200,000.
   (b) It is limited to variables with reasonably random distributions (without cutoff point).

3

An Overview of the Economy

Learning Objectives

After studying the material in this chapter, you should be able to

—understand how modern economies are based on specialization and the division of labor;

—explain how three kinds of economic decision makers—households, firms, and government—interact in a market economy;

—explain the distinction between market and nonmarket sectors and between the private and public sectors;

—understand how the price system serves as a social control mechanism;

—explain the relation between microeconomics and macroeconomics;

—illustrate the circular flow of income.

Review and Self-Test

Matching Concepts

______ 1. division of labor

______ 2. criterion assumed for economic decision making by households

______ 3. public sector

______ 4. free-market economy

______ 5. change in demand

______ 6. product market

______ 7. change in supply

______ 8. components of household income not spent on consumption

______ 9. circular flow of income

______ 10. study of such aggregates as national output and the average price level

(a) part of economy dominated by government production

(b) income taxes and household savings

(c) decentralized decision making by individual households and firms

(d) macroeconomics

(e) consumer expenditures from households to firms; factor payments from firms to households

(f) specialization within the production process of a particular commodity

(g) altered willingness to purchase a commodity at all prices

(h) altered willingness to sell a commodity at all prices

(i) maximization of satisfaction, well being, or utility

(j) locus for the exchange of a commodity between buyers and sellers

Multiple-Choice Questions

1. Specialization of labor
   (a) is generally less efficient than self-sufficiency in production.
   (b) must be accompanied by trade to satisfy material desires.
   (c) resulted in a shift of resources from industry to agriculture in early societies.
   (d) was more common in nomadic societies.

2. In a free-market economy, the allocation of resources is
   (a) determined by central authorities or other government agencies.
   (b) completely independent of initial resource endowments.
   (c) determined only by producers who purchase factors of production.
   (d) a result of decisions made by producers and consumers in markets.

3. A household, as defined in economics, is
   (a) assumed to make decisions without regard to its resource limitations.
   (b) a home owner rather than an apartment dweller.
   (c) assumed to make consistent decisions as if it were composed of a single individual.
   (d) the principal user of the services of factors of production.

4. The price system in a free-market economy works in all but which of the following ways?
   (a) Price is a determinant of a firm's profits and therefore encourages or discourages production.
   (b) Prices signal to consumers how much they must sacrifice to obtain a commodity.
   (c) Prices indicate relative scarcities and costs of production.
   (d) Prices allocate resources equally among sectors of the economy.

5. A shift in consumer preferences from pork to chicken may be predicted to cause
   (a) a shift of resources into the production of chickens.
   (b) a fall in the price of chicken products.
   (c) a rise in the price of pork products.
   (d) none of the above.

6. Which one of the following is not usually a market sector activity?
   (a) municipal fire protection services
   (b) the production and sale of agricultural commodities
   (c) the sale of automobiles
   (d) an amusement park with fees to cover costs

7. The circular flow of income refers to
   (a) the flow of goods and services from sellers to buyers.
   (b) the flow of money in and out of the banking system.
   (c) the flow of money incomes from buyers to sellers.
   (d) both (a) and (c).

8. The price system is effective in allocating resources because
   (a) nobody understands how it works.
   (b) it is easy for central planners to manipulate consumer desires.
   (c) it coordinates individual, and apparently unrelated, decisions.
   (d) shortages and surpluses tend to be eliminated automatically by prices falling and rising, respectively.

9. Macroeconomics is concerned with aggregate flows within the entire economy, whereas microeconomics
   (a) looks at only the money flows in the aggregate economy.
   (b) is concerned with the total flow of payments to firms.
   (c) deals with the determination of prices for individual commodities.
   (d) concerns only money flows in the economy.

10. The circular flow of income is not a completely closed system because
   (a) households do not spend all of their income.
   (b) there are elements of aggregate demand that do not arise from household spending.
   (c) firms pay taxes and may also retain earnings.
   (d) of all of the above.

11. An increase in the supply of compact disc players (CDs), with no change in demand, will lead to
    (a) a glut of CDs at the existing price.
    (b) a fall in the market price of CDs.
    (c) an increase in consumer purchases of CDs at the lower price.
    (d) all of the above.

12. The two major types of markets in the circular flow of income are
    (a) public markets and private markets.
    (b) product markets and factor markets.
    (c) free markets and controlled markets.
    (d) goods markets and services markets.

13. Which one of the following is not an underlying assumption economists make about economic decision making in market economies?
    (a) Firms are assumed to act as profit maximizers.
    (b) The goal of households is to maximize satisfaction or utility.
    (c) The government always acts in a consistent fashion, as though it were a single individual.
    (d) Firms are the principal users, and households the principal owners, of the factors of production.

14. In the circular flow of income, firms
    (a) produce and sell commodities in product markets.
    (b) purchase the services of productive resources in factor markets.
    (c) are the major source of household income.
    (d) do all of the above.

15. Which of the following are components of aggregate demand?
    (a) investment by firms in equipment
    (b) taxes paid by firms
    (c) government expenditures
    (d) both (a) and (c)

Self-Test Key

Matching Concepts: 1–f; 2–i; 3–a; 4–c; 5–g; 6–j; 7–h; 8–b; 9–e; 10–d

Multiple-Choice Questions: 1–b; 2–d; 3–c; 4–d; 5–a; 6–a; 7–d; 8–c; 9–c; 10–d; 11–d; 12–b; 13–c; 14–d; 15–d

Exercises

1. Indicate whether or not the following events would occur in a market economy with a shift in interest from snowmobiling to skiing. Explain.
   (a) Initially, a shortage of ski equipment and a surplus of snowmobiles will develop.

   (b) Prices of snowmobiles will be increased to maintain profit levels.

   (c) Profits of ski equipment producers and retailers will rise; profits of snowmobile producers and dealers will tend to fall.

   (d) Central authorities will shift resources from production of skis to snowmobiles.

   (e) Production of skis will be expanded.

   (f) Resources will shift from production of snowmobiles to skis.

   (g) Resources particularly suited to producing snowmobiles will earn more, obtaining a greater relative share of national income.

2. Indicate whether the following economic transactions would occur in product markets (P) or factor markets (F).
   (a) retail sales of electronic equipment _______
   (b) payment of wages to McDonalds' employees _______
   (c) tenants' rent payments to landlords _______
   (d) dividends paid to shareholders of firms _______
   (e) expenditures for concerts, movies, and athletic events _______
   (f) grain sales to the Soviet Union _______

3. The events (a) through (f) will have economic consequences in certain markets. Match the consequences (in the right column below) with the most likely cause.

	Cause		Consequence
______	(a) growth in "high-tech" industries causes migration to Boston region	i.	reduction of jobs in oil production
______	(b) swift and drastic fall in price of oil on world markets	ii.	price of coffee increases
______	(c) grain producers have large excess stocks	iii.	earnings of computer programmers increase
______	(d) population of college-age students declines	iv.	camera workers' earnings decrease
______	(e) drought in major coffee-producing areas	v.	demand for college teachers decreases
______	(f) shift in preferences from cameras to VCRs	vi.	housing prices rise
______	(g) increased demand for computer software	vii.	price of grain falls

4. (a) Through a biological quirk, the avocado, regardless of when or where the tree is planted, yields crops that are far greater in odd years of harvest than in even years. Under a market system, we would predict that the potential gluts in good crop years would result in ________________ prices and that the potential shortages in poor crop years would lead to ______________ prices.
   (b) In the 1965–1977 period, the prices of avocados tended to increase more rapidly than the general price level. We would predict that this increase would result in ________________ land and other resources being dedicated to avocado production.
   (c) In fact, avocado production more than doubled. The reasonable inference is that consumer demand had substantially ______________.
   (d) Relative prices of avocados dropped significantly in 1978 and 1979 as compared with the previous poor and good crop years. What could this signal mean to growers and potential growers?

Answers to the Exercises

1. (a) likely to occur if shift takes place rapidly
   (b) No, lower prices are likely.
   (c) likely to occur
   (d) No, changing prices and profits will signal the shift automatically.
   (e) likely to occur as profits rise
   (f) likely to occur as profits rise in skis and fall in snowmobiles
   (g) No, exactly the opposite will occur.

2. (a) P (b) F (c) P (d) F (e) P (f) P (g) P

3. (a) vi (b) i (c) vii (d) v (e) ii (f) iv (g) iii

4. (a) lower; higher
   (b) more
   (c) increased (increased popularity in salads, in Mexican food, and greater familiarity with an unusual fruit could be reasons).
   (d) to be wary of expanding output further; present and prospective profits have almost certainly been reduced

CASES FOR PART ONE

CASE 1: The 97.5 Percent Zinc Cent

In 1982 the U.S. Bureau of the Mint commenced production and circulation of a cent comprised of 2.5 percent copper and 97.5 percent zinc. Before that, the cent was 95 percent copper and 5 percent zinc. The new coin, identical in appearance to the old, has a zinc alloy core (0.8 percent copper) with the outer surface electroplated with copper. It weighs 2.5 grams (181 cents to a pound) as against 3.11 grams (146 cents to a pound). Zinc has the virtues of being lower in price, \$.35 per pound at the start of 1986 compared to copper's \$.70 per pound, and of having much less volatility in price. The Bureau rapidly switched to production of only the "mostly zinc" coins, with a total of 13.7 billion produced in 1984.

The composition of the cent had been of concern to the Mint since the early 1970s. In 1973 the London price of copper had temporarily reached \$1.41 per pound, and shortages of cents had occurred periodically prior to 1982. The Mint estimated that at a price of \$1.20 a pound for copper, the standard cent would cost more to make than it would be worth in monetary transactions, and that at \$1.50 per pound of copper the recoverable metal alone would be worth more than one cent.

In March 1974, the Bureau of the Mint had proposed that the copper penny be replaced with an aluminum cent. One pound of aluminum, costing \$.29 then (\$.60 at the start of 1986), would make about 500 pennies. Other alternatives that had been proposed were the elimination of all coinage below \$.05, replacement of the penny with a 2-cent piece, and the use of a 30 percent zinc, 70 percent copper alloy that would give coins a whitish cast. Legislation was needed for all but the last of these alternatives, and none was adopted. While some groups such as copper producers felt that the authority to produce a copper/zinc alloy cent had been abused by the Bureau of the Mint, the action was allowed by Congress to stand.

Questions

1. As the price of copper rises above $1.50 a pound, what are the opportunity costs to a consumer of using pre-1982 copper cents for purchases? Why would even an approach to this price have made it difficult for the Bureau of the Mint to provide adequate coinage for circulation? How would the switch to the 97.5 percent zinc cent reduce this opportunity cost?

2. (a) Cash outlays represent opportunity costs since an expenditure forecloses the opportunity of using these funds for something else. Calculate the cost savings to the Mint from use of aluminum instead of the pre-1982 cent and the 97.5 percent zinc cent. For simplicity assume an annual production of 14 billion cents and 100 percent content of a single metal.

   (b) From your answer to (a) it is clear that the government has rejected the cost-minimizing alternative; what policy goals and other considerations could have resulted in this decision?

3. In 1939 the general consumer price level was approximately 40 percent of its level in 1967. In 1985 it was roughly 320 percent of its level in 1967. How did the purchasing power of a 1985 cent compare with that of a 1939 cent? (Keep in mind the reciprocal relationship: the higher the price level, the lower the purchasing power of a monetary unit.)

4. Predict the conditions under which the cent (mostly zinc or otherwise) will vanish from use in the United States.

CASE 2: Energy Use and GNP

This case is designed to illustrate an economist's approach to testing hypotheses by the use of such analytic methods as the scatter diagram. The hypothesis to be tested is that nations with high per capita production and income are high energy users. The data are from the International Comparisons sections of the *Statistical Abstract of the United States*. The production/income measure used was the 1980 gross national product (GNP) of each country, expressed in constant 1978 dollars and divided by the nation's population.[1] For energy use it was necessary to convert all forms (oil, electricity, etc.) to a common unit, which we call "Energy."[2] The student should recognize, as does the economist, that arbitrary judgments and measurement errors are made in calculating both variables. The twelve countries were chosen because they are representative of countries in various stages of development.

	Per capita energy use	Per capita GNP		Per capita energy use	Per capita GNP
United States	10,870	9,869	Japan	3,690	8,901
Argentina	1,818	2,532	Mexico	1,770	1,481
China	619	433	Sweden	5,269	10,814
Canada	10,241	8,864	Taiwan	2,111	1,613
Greece	2,137	3,602	Yugoslavia	2,049	2,665
India	191	169	Zaire	67	221

[1]GNP has not been defined yet in the text but can be understood as essentially consisting of consumer expenditures in the circular flow plus investment expenditures by firms and government payments for goods and services (see Chapter 3). The inflation of recent decades means that the dollar has decreased in purchasing power. It is important to use its real worth at a particular time as a constant yardstick when comparisons with physical figures are being made.

[2]The use of the energy equivalent of kilogram of coal rather than BTUs is suitably international and gives figures of the same magnitude as GNP.

Questions

1. Draw a scatter diagram that relates per capita GNP to per capita energy use.

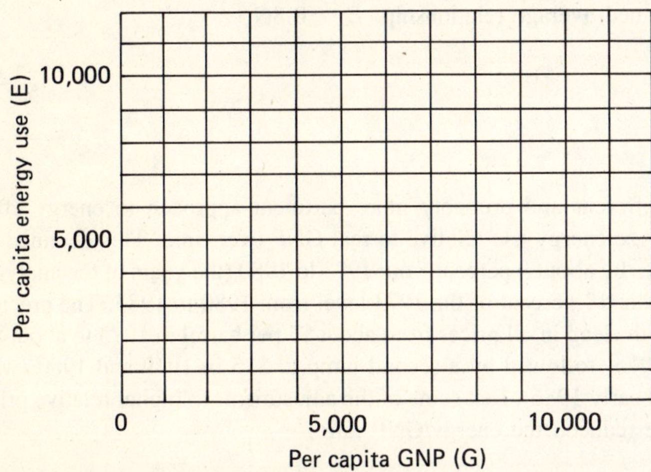

(a) Is the general relationship shown by the diagrams consistent with the hypothesis that high energy use is associated with high GNP?

(b) To express this relationship as a linear equation, draw a straight line that keeps the sum of the vertical distances from the observations as small as possible. $E = 0.8G$ is the approximate equation for such a line. Use this equation to "predict" the energy consumption of United States and Japan, and compare these with actual energy consumption.

(c) Clearly, using only the GNP to predict energy consumption leads to mediocre results for these two countries. By highlighting observations that deviate from the general relationship, the scatter diagram helps to indicate that other relevant variables may be important in explaining energy use. Three obvious contrasts between Japan and the United States are identified below. How could the inclusion of variables related to them improve the explanation of energy use?

(i) Japan had a population density of 822 per square mile over an area of 147,740 square miles in 1984. The United States had a population density of 64 over a land area of 3,539,000 square miles.

(ii) The United States has a continental climate with extremes of hot and cold (for example, the average January temperature in Minneapolis is –12°C, the average July temperature in Phoenix is 33°C). Japan has a moderate island climate (the January average in Tokyo is 3°C and the July average is 24°C).

(iii) The United States had abundant oil reserves (and was an exporter throughout the 1950s) and has enormous coal reserves. Japan produces negligible amounts of both oil and coal.

2. (a) The scatter diagram in (1) was cross sectional in that it dealt with data at one time (1980). It indicated that the United States was less "energy efficient" than average and consumed far more energy per unit of GNP than Japan. Calculate the amount of energy per unit of GNP for the United States, for Japan, and for the assumed average relationship, $E = 0.8G$.

(b) A different and probably more pertinent approach to energy efficiency is to analyze energy use relative to real GNP over time. This declined in the United States by about 9 percent from 1973 to 1980 (the years of the analysis above) and another 17 percent of the 1973 level from 1980 to 1985. The precipitating event was the leap in oil prices from about \$3 per barrel in 1973 to about \$12 per barrel in 1975, followed by a second jump to \$35 in 1979 and 1980 (where it stayed until early 1986). List some of the adjustments to higher relative prices that could have reduced the energy/GNP ratio.

(c) Why would the greatest decline in the ratio come after 1980, during a period in which oil prices were declining modestly? (In your answer, recognize the time dimension in the adjustments you listed.)

3. (Optional) This section illustrates the Chapter 3 concepts of regression, variance, and the coefficient of determination. The total variance in energy use of the sample of 12 countries is the sum of squares of the deviations from the average or mean energy use of the 12 countries in the sample, which is 3403. To illustrate, the deviation of Japan's energy use is 3690 – 3403 = 287. The square of 287 is approximately 82,000. For practice, work out the deviation squared for the United States: ______________________________. The total variance from the mean for the 12 countries is 145,393,000.

   Linear regression is a statistical technique for finding the equation of the linear relationships that has the minimum total variance. The line for $E = 0.8G$ represented a graphic approximation of a linear regression equation. The U.S. energy consumption predicted by this equation is 0.8(9869) = 7895. The contribution of the United States to the total variance from the regression estimate is the deviation (7895 – 10870) squared, or 8,850,000. Work out Japan's contribution to the total variance of the regression estimate: ______________________________.

   The total variance from the equation $E = 0.8G$ adds up to 45,468,000 for all 12 countries.

   The coefficient of determination (r^2) is simply that fraction of the original total variance that has been eliminated by using the regression equation rather than the mean as a predictor of energy consumption. It may be estimated by this equation:

$$r^2 = \frac{\text{variance from mean} - \text{variance from regression estimate}}{\text{variance from mean}}$$

   In this case we are willing to accept the importance of GNP in explaining energy use because $r^2 = 0.70$. We also stressed the importance of variables such as climate, density of population, and energy prices. Had we included such variables in the model, we would have been using multiregression analysis.

PART TWO

A General View of the Price System

4

Demand, Supply, and Price

Learning Objectives

After studying the material in this chapter, you should be able to

—distinguish the concepts: quantity demanded, quantity supplied, and quantity exchanged;

—explain demand schedules and demand curves as methods for showing the relation between quantity demanded and price;

—explain supply schedules and supply curves as methods for showing the relation between quantity supplied and price;

—explain the difference in movements along a curve and shifts in the curve;

—distinguish the differences in changes in quantity demanded from changes in demand and changes in quantity supplied from changes in supply;

—use comparative static analysis to illustrate the "laws" of supply and demand;

—explain how price theory is concerned with changes in relative prices.

Review and Self-Test

Matching Concepts

______	1. *ceteris paribus*	(a)	increase in quantity demanded
______	2. amount actually bought and sold	(b)	price at which quantity demanded equals quantity supplied
______	3. excess demand	(c)	quantity exchanged
______	4. results of "law" of supply and demand	(d)	carrot price increase of 20 percent; price level increase of 10 percent
______	5. rise in the relative price of carrots	(e)	results of "law" of supply and demand
______	6. cause of a shift in the supply curve	(f)	cause of a shift in the demand curve
		(g)	change in technology
______	7. change in consumer tastes and preferences	(h)	holding all other variables constant
______	8. equilibrium price	(i)	greater quantity demanded than quantity supplied at a given price
______	9. fall in equilibrium price and quantity following an increase in supply	(j)	rise in equilibrium price and quantity following an increase in demand
______	10. response to a lower price		

Multiple-Choice Questions

1. Which of the following does not influence the demand curve for a commodity?
   (a) amount of supply
   (b) amount of household income
   (c) tastes of consumers
   (d) size of population

2. A fall in the price of commodity *X* will cause, *ceteris paribus,*
   (a) a rightward shift of the demand curve for *X*.
   (b) an increase in the quantity of *X* demanded.
   (c) a leftward shift of the supply curve for *X*.
   (d) all of the above.

3. Which of the following will not cause the demand curve for Toyotas to shift?
   (a) a change in the price of gasoline
   (b) a change in the price of Nissans (a substitute)
   (c) a change in consumer tastes
   (d) a change in the price of Toyotas

4. A leftward shift in the demand curve for corn flakes would result from
   (a) a fall in the price of Wheaties.
   (b) a change in tastes away from hot cereals.
   (c) a rise in the price of corn flakes.
   (d) an increase in the cost of making corn flakes.

5. According to the "laws" of supply and demand, a rise in demand causes
   (a) a decrease in both the equilibrium price and the equilibrium quantity exchanged.
   (b) an increase in the equilibrium price and a decrease in the equilibrium quantity exchanged.
   (c) an increase in both the equilibrium price and the equilibrium quantity exchanged.
   (d) a rightward shift of the supply curve.

6. The supply curve of houses would probably shift leftward if
   (a) construction workers' wages increased.
   (b) cheaper methods of prefabricating homes were developed.
   (c) the demand for houses showed a marked decrease.
   (d) the population stopped growing.

7. Cost savings from mass production of compact disc players (CDs) have resulted in
   (a) increased demand for CDs.
   (b) increased supply of CDs.
   (c) an increase in the market price of CDs.
   (d) both (a) and (b).

8. Shifts of demand curves for food could be caused by
   (a) changes in prices of food.
   (b) changes in food processing methods.
   (c) crop failures or successes.
   (d) changes in tastes, income, and population.

9. Quantity supplied will be increased by
   (a) a rise in the cost of factors of production.
   (b) a rise in price.
   (c) a fall in demand.
   (d) a decline in expected profits.

10. The position of the supply curve would be unaffected by a change in
    (a) average household income.
    (b) prices of factors of production.
    (c) technology.
    (d) prices of related commodities.

11. The equilibrium price of a commodity is
    (a) higher than that which would induce excess demand.
    (b) the price at which there is neither excess demand nor excess supply.
    (c) the price at which there is neither shortage nor surplus.
    (d) all of the above.

12. In price theory, which of the following represents a relative price increase for strawberries, assuming the average price level is rising by 10 percent?
    (a) an increase in price from $1.00 to $1.05 per quart
    (b) an increase in price from $1.00 to $1.10 per quart
    (c) an increase in price from $1.00 to $1.15 per quart
    (d) both (b) and (c)

13. Excess demand for a commodity is ordinarily eliminated through market forces by
    (a) price rising, demand decreasing, and quantity supplied increasing.
    (b) price rising, quantity demanded decreasing, and supply increasing.
    (c) price rising, quantity demanded decreasing, and quantity supplied increasing.
    (d) price rising, demand decreasing, and supply increasing.

14. Assuming the demand curve is given, an increase in supply will cause all of the following except
    (a) a movement along the demand curve.
    (b) a decrease in equilibrium price.
    (c) an increase in quantity demanded.
    (d) a decrease in quantity exchanged.

15. Comparative statics
    (a) refers to unchanged prices and quantities.
    (b) is the analysis of demand without reference to time.
    (c) is the analysis of market equilibria under different sets of conditions.
    (d) describes the time path of equilibrium prices.

Use the diagram below to answer questions 16 to 18 (assume that the price can fluctuate according to market forces):

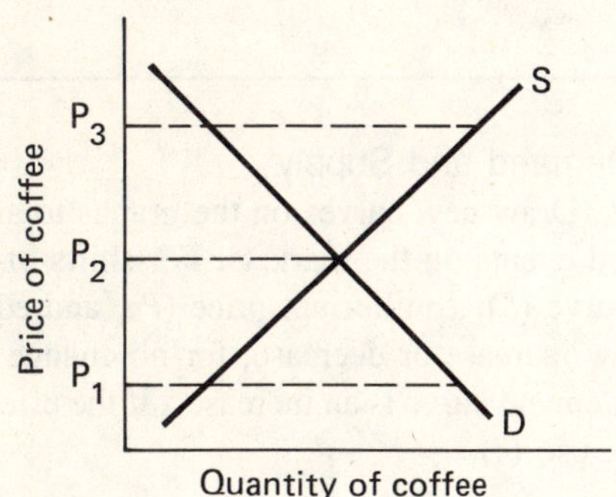

16. In the diagram, at price P_1,
    (a) there would be an excess supply of coffee.
    (b) there would be excess demand for coffee.
    (c) sellers would tend to accumulate a surplus of coffee.
    (d) the quantity actually exchanged would exceed quantity supplied.

17. At price P_3,
    (a) there would be a shortage of coffee.
    (b) the quantity actually exchanged would equal quantity supplied.
    (c) excess supply would exert downward pressure on price.
    (d) the coffee market would be in equilibrium.

18. Starting from equilibrium at price P_2, assume a drought reduces the yield of coffee beans. As a result,
    (a) supply will decrease, shifting the supply curve rightward.
    (b) equilibrium price will fall toward P_1.
    (c) the demand curve will shift leftward.
    (d) equilibrium quantity exchanged will decrease as the price rises.

The following multiple-choice questions refer to the exercises.

19. Assuming a seating capacity of 2,500, the equilibrium price for a ticket to the concert in Exercise 3 would be
    (a) $6. (c) $2.
    (b) $4. (d) $8.

20. (See Exercise 4.) If the quantity demanded at each price were to double while supply remained unchanged, the equilibrium price would
    (a) also exactly double.
    (b) rise to approximately $4.22.
    (c) remain unchanged because the supply curve has a positive slope.
    (d) eventually fall because of an increase in supply.

Self-Test Key

Matching Concepts: 1–h; 2–c; 3–i; 4–j; 5–d; 6–g; 7–f; 8–b; 9–e; 10–a

Multiple-Choice Questions: 1–a; 2–b; 3–d; 4–a; 5–c; 6–a; 7–b; 8–d; 9–b; 10–a; 11–d; 12–c; 13–c; 14–d; 15–c; 16–b; 17–c; 18–d; 19–a; 20–b

Exercises

1. The Hypothesis of Demand and Supply

Fill in the table below. Draw new curves on the graphs to aid you. Show the initial effects of the indicated events on the markets. For shifts of the demand curve (*D*), shifts of the supply curve (*S*), equilibrium price (*P*), and equilibrium quantity (*Q*), use (+) or (–) to show increase or decrease; for no change, use (*O*). (A rightward shift of the supply or demand curve is an increase.) If the effect cannot be determined from the information, use (?).

Market	Events		*D*	*S*	*P*	*Q*
a. Video cassette recorders (VCRs)	Technological advances reduce costs of producing VCRs.	D S Price Quantity	____	____	____	____
b. Wood-burning stoves (1970s)	The price of heating with oil and natural gas triples.	D S Price Quantity	____	____	____	____

Market	Events		D	S	P	Q
c. Florida citrus products	Frost destroys 50 percent of the Florida crop.	D S Price Quantity	___	___	___	___
d. Cigarettes	Increased publicity concerning health hazards of smoking occurs, and there is a doubling of the federal tax on tobacco.	D S Price Quantity	___	___	___	___
e. Bicycles	There is increasing concern about physical fitness, and the price of gasoline rises.	D S Price Quantity	___	___	___	___
f. Hospital services	Substantially higher wages are paid to hospital employees with no increase in their productivity.	D S Price Quantity	___	___	___	___
g. Rental apartments	Prices of owner-occupied housing rise; apartments are increasingly converted to condominiums.	D S Price Quantity	___	___	___	___

2. The demand and supply schedules for good X are hypothesized to be as follows, where quantities refer to units per time period:

(1) Price per unit	(2) Quantity demanded	(3) Quantity supplied	(4) Excess demand (–) Excess supply (+)
$1.00	1	25	______
.90	3	21	______
.80	5	19	______
.70	8	15	______
.60	12	12	______
.50	18	9	______
.40	26	6	______

(a) Using the grid below, plot the demand and supply curves (approximately). Indicate the equilibrium price and quantity of X by P_x and Q_x.

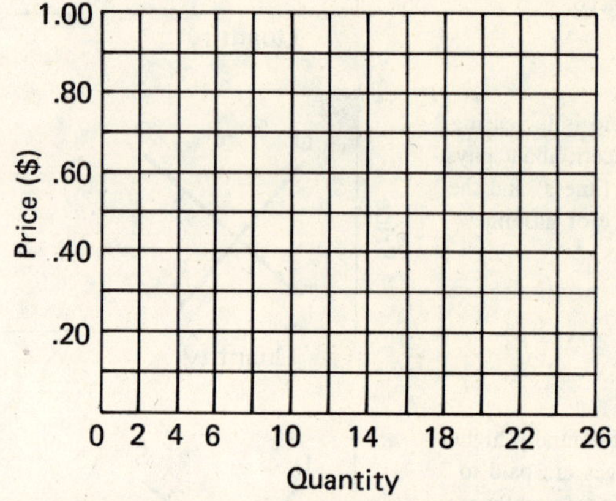

(b) Fill in column (4) for values of excess demand and excess supply. What is the value of excess demand (supply) at equilibrium? ______

(c) Indicate and explain the likely direction of change in the price of X if excess demand exists. Do the same for excess supply.

3. Suppose that student demand for tickets to a concert is as follows:

Price	Quantity demanded
$2	8,000
4	5,000
6	2,500
8	1,500

(a) With seating capacity fixed at 5,000 seats, would there be either excess demand or excess supply at a ticket price of $6? ______

(b) What ticket price should be set to insure that all seats are taken (so that there is neither a surplus nor shortage of seats)? ______

(c) The demand schedule above may apply to an "average" concert. Suppose that a very popular performer is booked and the quantity of tickets demanded at each price doubles. What is the new equilibrium price? ______

4. Assume the following demand and supply functions:

$Q_d = 28 - 4p \qquad Q_s = 18 + p$

(a) Determine the equilibrium price and equilibrium quantity.

(b) Plot the demand and supply curves on the graph and confirm your answer.

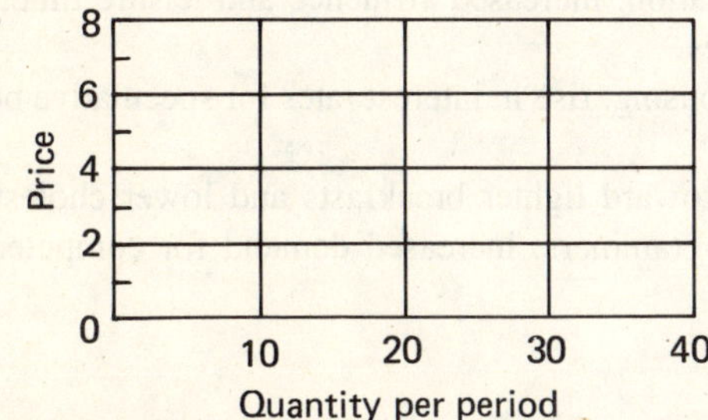

(c) Suppose that supply shifts to $Q_s = 8 + p$, with no change in demand. Determine the new equilibrium price and quantity.

(d) Suppose that price had been held constant at its original level in (b). Predict the effects if supply shifts as in (c).

5. Interpret the following statements using the economic theory of demand, supply, and price.

(a) Oil prices drop as the OPEC cartel is unable to restrict total supply.

(b) Retail prices of personal computers steadily fall despite rising demand.

(c) An apartment shortage spurs conversion of factory buildings to residential lofts.

(d) Lower airfares spark busiest-ever air travel over a holiday period.

(e) Corn prices plummet to 13-year lows on poor demand, excellent growing conditions.

Short Problems

1. Using the approach of Exercise 1, draw curves and predict the changes in demand, supply, and equilibrium price and quantity of the events in the following markets:
   (a) Microcomputers: increased availability of "user-friendly" software and a reduction in the cost of silicon chips.
   (b) Hospital services: higher wages paid to hospital employees accompanied by more than proportional increases in output per labor hour.
   (c) Outdoor recreation: increased affluence and leisure time; reduction in available recreation sites.
   (d) One-family housing: rise in interest rates for speculative builders and prospective homeowners.
   (e) Eggs: trends toward lighter breakfasts and lower cholesterol diets.
   (f) Computer programmers: increased demand for computer software.

2. In Exercise 3(c), suppose that in the interest of "fairness" ticket prices were held to $4 regardless of the popularity of the performing artist. Would you expect excess demand or excess supply to occur and, if so, under what circumstances?

3. Assume the demand and supply curves for a commodity are $Q_d = 40 - P$ and $Q_s = \frac{1}{2} P - 5$, respectively.
   (a) Estimate the equilibrium price and equilibrium quantity exchanged.

   (b) Draw a graph showing (i) the original demand and supply curves; (ii) the situation with the demand curve shifting to $Q_D = 70 - P$; and (iii) the excess demand at the original price.

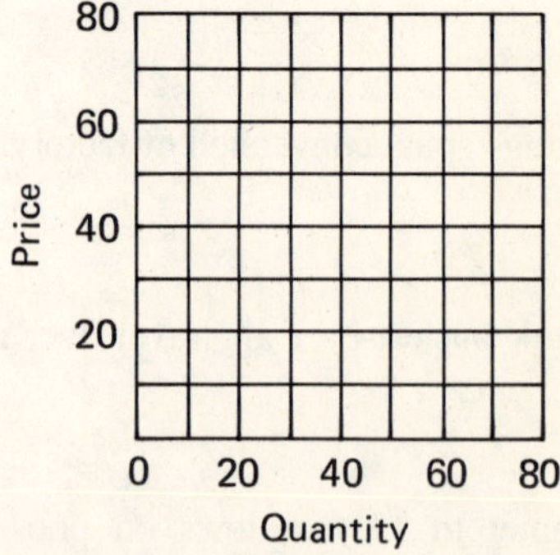

   (c) Explain how excess demand at the original price forces a new equilibrium.

4. Interpret the following statements using the economic theory of demand, supply, and price.

   (a) A strengthened dollar shrinks export market for California wines, causing price cuts.

   (b) Super Bowl tickets, with a face value of $60, sell at scalped prices of $600 to $800.

   (c) An office glut is a bonanza for tenants as landlords cut rents and add perks.

   (d) Oil prices plunge in early 1986 as Saudi Arabia doubles its output to 4.5 million barrels a day.

   (e) Marginal oil wells in the U.S. Southwest cease production with oil price drop to $15 per barrel.

Answers to the Exercises

1.

	D	*S*	*P*	*Q*	
(a)	0	+	–	+	(greater familiarity with VCR probably shifted demand as well)
(b)	+	0	+	+	(price of substitutes rise, so their quantities demanded decrease)
(c)	0	–	+	–	(decrease in supply is a leftward shift of the supply curve.)
(d)	–	–	?	–	(adverse publicity likely to decrease demand; tax causes leftward shift of supply curve)
(e)	+	0	+	+	(tastes change in favor of bicycles and the cost of using automobiles rises)
(f)	0	–	+	–	(if employee productivity had increased at the same rate as their pay, unit costs would *not* have increased)
(g)	+	–	+	?	(price of a substitute increases; also supply decreases)

2. (a)

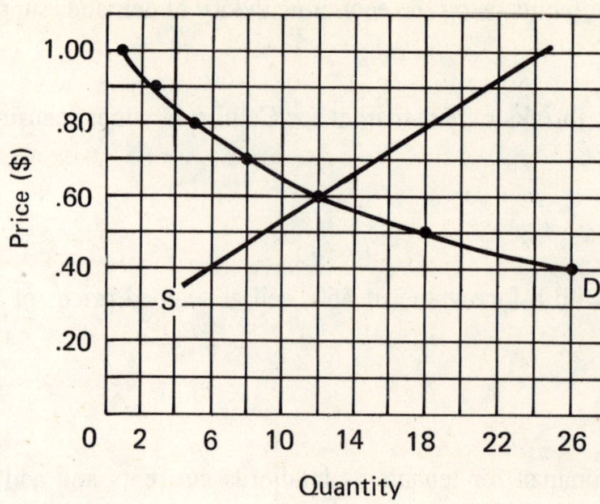

(b) It is zero.

Price	Excess demand (–) Excess supply (+)
$1.00	+24
.90	+18
.80	+14
.70	+ 7
.60	0
.50	– 9
.40	–20

(c) If excess demand exists, price is likely to rise; in the event of excess supply, price is likely to fall.

3. (a) excess supply (2,500 seats)
(b) ticket price of $4
(c) $6

4. (a) $Q_d = Q_s$: equilibrium price is 2 and equilibrium quantity is 20.
(b)

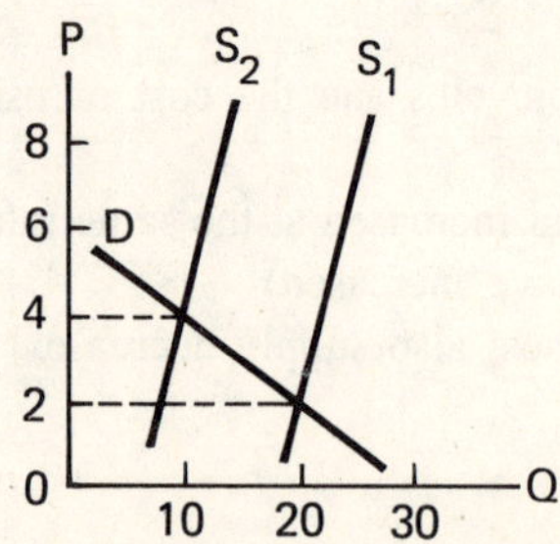

(c) $Q_d = Q_s$; equilibrium price is 4 and equilibrium quantity is 12.
(d) A shortage of 10 would result from the price control. At $p = 2$, only 10 would be supplied ($Q_s = 8 + p$), whereas 20 would be demanded ($Q_d = 28 - 4p$).

5. (a) rightward supply curve shift, demand curve constant, lowers equilibrium price.
   (b) increase in supply of computers offsets increase in demand, causing equilibrium price to fall; both curves are shifting rightward.
   (c) apartment "shortage" indicates high market price for residential living space; with higher prices, conversion of lofts becomes worthwhile. (Quantity supplied increases as price increases.)
   (d) movement along demand curve that shifted rightward on holidays.
   (e) leftward shift of demand curve; rightward shift of supply curve (This situation occurred in July 1986 when U.S. prices for corn futures dropped below $2 a bushel on sluggish export demand and excellent growing conditions in the Midwest.)

5

Elasticity of Demand and Supply

Learning Objectives

Understanding the material in this chapter should enable you to

—explain the meaning of elasticity of demand (also called price elasticity) and how it is measured;

—explain the significance of elastic and inelastic demands;

—distinguish between inelastic and perfectly inelastic demands;

—understand the relation between elasticity and total expenditure (total revenue);

—distinguish between income-elastic and income-inelastic demands;

—explain the meaning of cross-elasticity of demand and why substitute commodities have positive cross-elasticities while complements have negative ones;

—explain the meaning of elasticity of supply.

Review and Self-Test

Matching Concepts

______ 1. inelastic demand		(a) positive cross-elasticity of demand
______ 2. income elasticity of demand		(b) constant revenue with changing price
______ 3. infinite elasticity of demand		(c) change in quantity demanded from zero to an indefinitely large amount with small price decrease
______ 4. inferior goods		(d) negative income elasticity of demand
______ 5. goods in fixed supply		(e) negative cross elasticity of demand
______ 6. substitute goods		(f) reduction in total revenue with a rise in price
______ 7. complementary goods		(g) percentage change in quantity divided by percentage change in income
______ 8. elasticity of demand of unity		(h) zero elasticity of supply
______ 9. income-elastic demand		(i) quantity demanded changes by a smaller percentage than does price
______ 10. elastic demand		(j) income elasticity greater than one

Multiple-Choice Questions

1. The price elasticity of demand refers to
   (a) how the quantity demanded of a commodity changes when the price of that commodity changes, other things equal.
   (b) the response of price to a supply change.
   (c) how the quantity demanded of a commodity responds to a change in the price of a substitute commodity.
   (d) how rapidly price changes when the demand curve shifts.

2. Price elasticity of demand is measured by
   (a) the change in quantity demanded divided by the change in price.
   (b) the change in price divided by the quantity demanded.
   (c) the percentage change in quantity demanded divided by the percentage change in price.
   (d) the percentage change in price times the percentage change in quantity demanded.

3. If a small rise in the price of downhill ski tickets caused a decrease in total dollar sales, it could be concluded that
   (a) demand was inelastic.
   (b) demand was infinitely elastic.
   (c) demand was elastic.
   (d) the price rise caused a shift in demand for the tickets, so it is impossible to say.

4. Price elasticity of demand for a commodity tends to be greater
   (a) the more of a necessity it is.
   (b) the better substitutes there are for it.
   (c) over shorter time periods.
   (d) the lower the price.

Use these diagrams to answer questions 5 to 8:

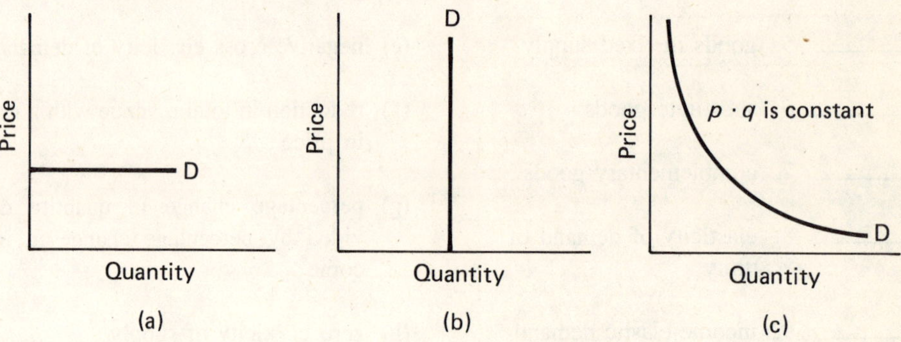

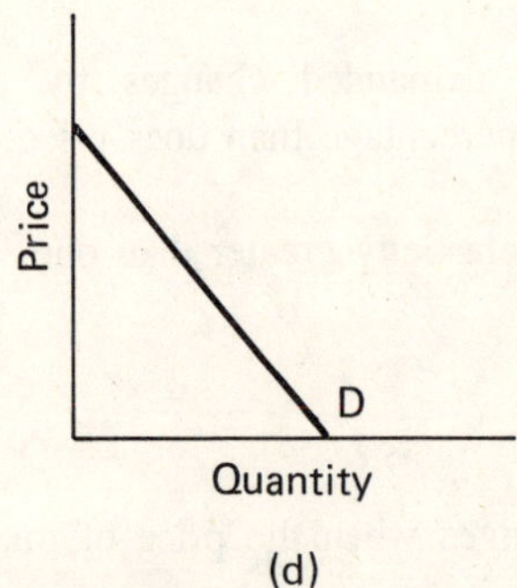

5. The demand curve with an elasticity of zero is
   (a) a. (c) c.
   (b) b. (d) d.

6. The demand curve with unitary elasticity is
   (a) a. (c) c.
   (b) b. (d) d.

7. The demand curve with an elasticity varying from zero to infinity depending on price is
   (a) a. (c) c.
   (b) b. (d) d.

8. The demand curve with an elasticity of infinity is
   (a) a. (c) c.
   (b) b. (d) d.

9. Inferior goods have
   (a) zero income elasticities of demand.
   (b) negative cross-elasticities of demand.
   (c) negative elasticities of supply.
   (d) negative income elasticities of demand.

10. When the demand is elastic,
   (a) a fall in price is more than offset by an increase in quantity demanded, so that total revenue rises.
   (b) the good is probably a necessity.
   (c) a rise in price will increase total revenue, even though less is sold.
   (d) buyers are not much influenced by prices of competing products.

Questions 11 and 12 refer to the schedule below:

Price per unit	Quantity offered for sale
$10	400
8	350
6	300
4	200
2	50

11. The supply curve implied by the schedule is
   (a) elastic for all price ranges.
   (b) inelastic for all price ranges.
   (c) of zero elasticity for all price changes.
   (d) of variable elasticity, depending on initial price chosen.

12. As price rises from $6 to $10 per unit, the supply response is
   (a) elastic.
   (b) of unit elasticity.
   (c) of zero elasticity.
   (d) inelastic.

13. If, when incomes rise by 5 percent, the quantity demanded of a commodity rises by 10 percent, income elasticity is
   (a) –2.
   (b) 2.
   (c) –(1/2).
   (d) 1/2.

14. If price elasticity of demand for a product is 0.5, this means that
   (a) any change in price changes demand by 50 percent.
   (b) a 1 percent increase in quantity demanded is associated with a 0.5 percent fall in price.
   (c) a 1 percent increase in quantity demanded is associated with a 2 percent fall in price.
   (d) a 0.5 percent change in price will cause a 0.5 percent change in quantity demanded.

15. If a 100 percent rise in the membership fee of a club causes the number of members to decline from 600 to 450,
    (a) demand was inelastic.
    (b) demand was infinitely elastic.
    (c) demand was elastic.
    (d) the price rise caused a shift in demand for membership, so it is impossible to say.

16. In a certain market, when the price of hot dogs rose from $1.52 per pound to $1.68 per pound, the quantity of hot dog rolls sold went from 11,000 to 9,000. Indicated cross-elasticity of demand is
    (a) 1/2.
    (b) –1/2.
    (c) 2.
    (d) –2.

17. Margarine and butter probably have
    (a) the same income elasticities of demand.
    (b) very low price elasticities of demand.
    (c) negative cross-elasticities of demand with respect to each other.
    (d) positive cross-elasticities of demand with respect to each other.

18. Which one of the following is least likely to be a determinant of the price elasticity of a commodity?
    (a) the closeness of substitutes
    (b) the current amount of total expenditures on the commodity
    (c) how widely or narrowly the commodity is defined
    (d) the time period over which the elasticity is considered

19. Total revenues will rise with a price increase when demand is inelastic (Exercise 1) because
    (a) the percentage decrease in quantity exceeds the percentage increase in price.
    (b) quantity increases with a price increase when demand is inelastic.
    (c) quantity demanded falls by a smaller percentage than the price rises.
    (d) of none of the above.

20. The results in Exercise 2 confirm which of the following propositions regarding a negative-sloped, straight-line demand curve?
    (a) Elasticity equals the slope of the demand curve.
    (b) Elasticity depends on the ratio of price change to quantity change, in absolute terms.
    (c) Elasticity varies along the demand curve from zero at the quantity axis to infinity at the price axis.
    (d) Total revenues always increase as price rises along a demand curve.

Self-Test Key

Matching Concepts: 1–i; 2–g; 3–c; 4–d; 5–h; 6–a; 7–e; 8–b; 9–j; 10–f

Multiple-Choice Questions: 1–a; 2–c; 3–c; 4–b; 5–b; 6–c; 7–d; 8–a; 9–d; 10–a; 11–d; 12–d; 13–b; 14–c; 15–a; 16–d; 17–d; 18–b; 19–c; 20–c

Exercises

1. Fill in the following table:

	Price elasticity	Change in price	Change in total revenue (up, down, or none)
(a)	2	up	——
(b)	1	down	——
(c)	——	up	none
(d)	0	down	——
(e)	0.6	——	up

2. Calculate the numerical values of price elasticity along the demand curve below. Use the four price-quantity segments indicated by the dots on the demand curve.

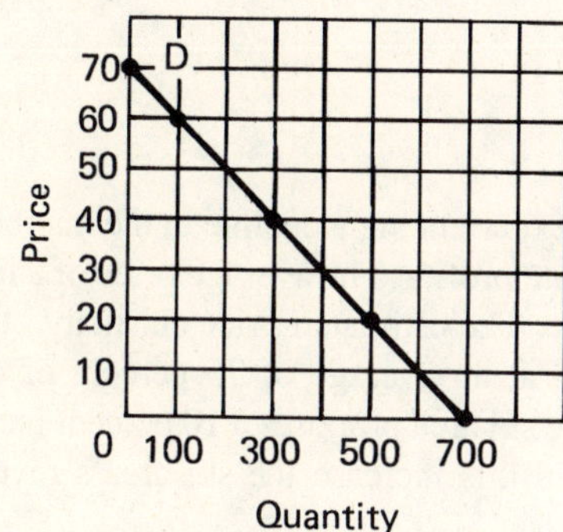

(a) Confirm that the elasticity declines as price decreases.

(b) What is the elasticity of demand when the price falls from $40 to $30? What is happening to total revenue as the price falls further?

3. The table below provides data on income and demand schedules for goods X and Y.

Period	Income	P_x	QD_x	P_y	QD_y
(i)	$10,000	$25	10	$10	42
(ii)	10,000	28	9	10	40
(iii)	10,000	28	8	15	35
(iv)	11,000	28	9	15	36
(v)	11,500	34	7	20	32

(a) Why should no elasticities be calculated between periods (iv) and (v)?

(b) Calculate the following elasticities, selecting appropriate periods and using arc formulas: price, for x ______; price, for y ______; income, for x ______; income, for y ______; cross, (i) to (ii) ______; cross, (ii) to (iii) ______.

4. A downhill ski area is experiencing a decline in the number of lift tickets sold, falling revenues, and inadequate profits. The average price of a lift ticket is $20 and there are 2,500 tickets sold daily. The estimated price elasticity of demand is 1.5 and the lifts are currently operating at an average of 75 percent of capacity.

(a) The manager of the ski area proposes a 10 percent increase in the average price of a lift ticket. Would this increase the ski area's revenues and profits? Explain.

(b) What would you recommend to the manager regarding lift ticket prices? Explain.

5. Given the two supply schedules S_1 and S_2 shown below, demonstrate that the elasticity of supply equals 1.0 throughout the ranges shown.

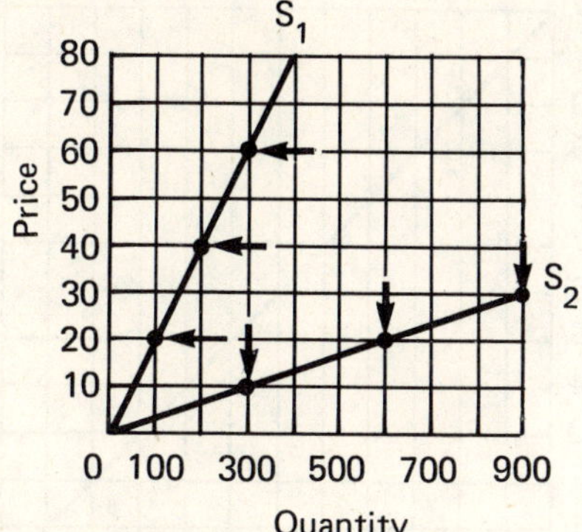

6. (Consult the appendix to Chapter 5 for the distinction between arc elasticity and point elasticity to do this exercise.)

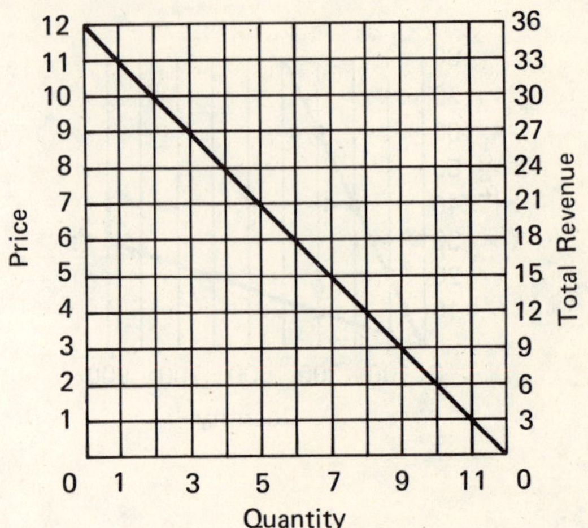

(a) You are given the demand curve in the diagram above, for which several points are contained in the table below. Its equation can be written $Q = 12 - P$. Note that $\Delta Q/\Delta P = -1$. Calculate the arc elasticities for the segments between the points, the point elasticities, and the total revenue. Draw in the total revenue curve on the diagram above using the right-hand scale, and enter the elasticities along the demand curve. For the arc elasticities use the proportion of ΔQ/ave.Q to ΔP/ave.P; for the point elasticities use $\Delta Q/\Delta P \times P/Q$. (Express elasticities as positive numbers as in the text.)

P	*Q*	Arc elasticity	Point elasticity	*TR*
$11	1		______	______
		______		
9	3		______	______
		______		
7	5		______	______
		______		
5	7		______	______
		______		
3	9		______	______
		______		
1	11		______	______

(b) What is the relationship between total revenue and price elasticity of demand?

Short Problems

1. For the following quotations, indicate (a) the relevant elasticity concept(s); (b) the implied elasticity (see Box 5-1 in the text); and (c) your interpretation or explanation of the quotation. The date of the quotation is in parentheses.
   (a) "Oil-price cuts appear unlikely to bring back old levels of consumption." (March 1986)

   (b) "Cost of TV sports commercials prompts cutbacks by advertisers." (August 1985)

   (c) "IBM's price cuts on personal computers are seen hurting some lookalike PC makers." (1984)

   (d) "Higher consumer incomes, lower prices increase sales and profits for U.S. wineries." (November 1982)

   (e) "Chicago's troubled transit system takes unorthodox steps to attract riders: reduces fares." (January 1984)

   (f) "Rising prices for seafood encourage fishermen to catch more fish." (1986)

2. (a) (See Exercise 3.) Predict the percentage changes in the quantity of X that would occur between the last two periods in the table because of the price increase to \$34, the income increase to \$11,500, and the price increase for product Y to \$20. Consider these as separate events (assume other things are unchanged) and then consider whether the drop in quantity from 9 to 7 is consistent with the three taking place simultaneously.

   (b) (See Exercise 4.) Ski areas typically charge higher prices for weekend and holiday skiing than for lift tickets purchased midweek. Is this practice consistent with the elasticity concepts discussed in this chapter?

3. Wines produced in foreign countries, particularly in Italy and France, significantly increased their share of the U.S. wine market during the early 1980s. Italian wines alone accounted for nearly 15 percent of U.S. wine market sales (in dollars), while imports from all foreign countries comprised approximately 25 percent of the \$7.6 billion total retail wine sales in 1982, up from 22 percent in 1981.
   (a) One explanation for the increase in imports was the falling value of the lira, which declined by approximately 10 percent during 1982 (from 1225 per dollar in January, 1982 to 1375 per dollar in January 1983). Use the elasticity concept to explain how the falling exchange rate for the lira might account for increased expenditures on Italian wine in the United States.

   (b) Predict how increased imports will affect prevailing prices of wine. Who gains and who loses as a result of increased imports?

4. Assume that the demand curve in Exercise 6 shifts to the right with two more units sold at every price. Calculate two or three elasticities to illustrate the general proposition that the new demand curve is less elastic than the old at each price.

Answers to the Exercises

1. (a) down (b) none (c) 1 (d) down (e) up

2. (a) Elasticity measures are

$$\frac{100/50}{10/65} = 13.0; \quad \frac{200/200}{20/50} = 2.5; \quad \frac{200/400}{20/30} = 0.75; \quad \frac{200/600}{20/10} = 0.167$$

   (b) $\dfrac{100/350}{10/35} = 1.0$

   At this point total revenue is constant. With further declines in price, total revenue will decline as we move into the inelastic portion of the demand curve.

3. (a) Elasticity measures are calculated under the *ceteris paribus* assumption, that other factors affecting demand are unchanged. Between periods (iv) and (v) not only has income changed, but so have the prices of *x* and of *y*.
   (b) Remember to calculate percentage changes using midpoints of intervals as the base. The answers are: price, *x* (–)0.93; price, *y* (–)0.33; income, *x* (+)1.24; income, *y* (+)0.30; cross, (i) to (ii), (–)0.43; (ii) to (iii), (–)0.29.

4. (a) Revenues (and profits) would decrease with the proposed price increase. With elasticity of 1.5, a 10 percent price increase would cause ticket sales to drop by 15 percent (to 2,125) and revenues to fall from \$50,000 to \$46,750. Costs of operating the ski area are likely to remain unchanged, so profits would fall.
   (b) Prices should be lowered. With an elastic demand, decreases in price will cause total revenues to rise. Assuming that costs to the ski area of additional skiers is nearly zero, the lifts should be run at or near their capacity. To achieve 100 percent capacity, lift ticket prices would have to be reduced by 22 percent (33 percent divided by 1.5).

5. Starting from the origin for S_1, the elasticities are

$$\frac{100/50}{20/10} = \frac{100/150}{20/30} = \frac{100/250}{20/50} = 1$$

and for S_2, the elasticities are

$$\frac{300/150}{10/5} = \frac{300/450}{10/15} = \frac{300/750}{10/25} = 1$$

6. (a)

			Elasticities	
P	*Q*	*TR*	Point	Arc
\$11	1	\$11	11	
				5
9	3	27	3	
				2.0
7	5	35	1.4	
				1.0
5	7	35	0.7	
				0.5
3	9	27	0.3	
				0.2
1	11	11	0.1	

Note the relationship between the two elasticity measures.

   (b) Demand is elastic when *TR* rises with falling price, is unitary at peak of *TR*, and is inelastic when *TR* falls with decreasing price.

6

Supply and Demand in Action: Price Controls and Agriculture

Learning Objectives

Working the material in this chapter should enable you to

—comprehend the patterns of shifts in and elasticities of supply and demand that lead to pressures for government market intervention;

—understand and explain the effects of government controls on prices;

—predict the consequences of rent controls (a form of price ceiling);

—be aware of the historical problems that have confronted U.S. agriculture as distinguished from other sectors of the economy;

—show the importance of elasticity concepts in explaining the "farm problem";

—describe the objectives and economic implications of government intervention in agricultural markets.

Review and Self-Test

Matching Concepts

_______ 1. black market

_______ 2. agricultural price supports to maintain relative level of base period price

_______ 3. quantity of commodity exchanged at controlled price

_______ 4. most likely long-run effect of rent controls

_______ 5. rising productivity and low-income elasticity of demand

_______ 6. price inelastic demand; fluctuating supply

_______ 7. government measure to reduce supply

_______ 8. "ever normal granary"

_______ 9. consequence of "effective" price floors

_______ 10. consequence of "effective" price ceilings

(a) reduction in available rental housing

(b) fundamental causes of long-term agricultural surpluses

(c) acreage restrictions

(d) attempt at price stabilization by storage in high-crop years and sale in low-crop years

(e) illegal sales of price-controlled commodities

(f) excess demand

(g) excess supply

(h) price parity

(i) the lesser of quantity demanded or supplied

(j) causes of large year-to-year changes in farm prices

Multiple-Choice Questions

1. In a free-market economy, the rationing of scarce goods is done by
   (a) the price mechanism.
   (b) the government.
   (c) business managers.
   (d) consumers.

Questions 2 to 6 are based on the following:

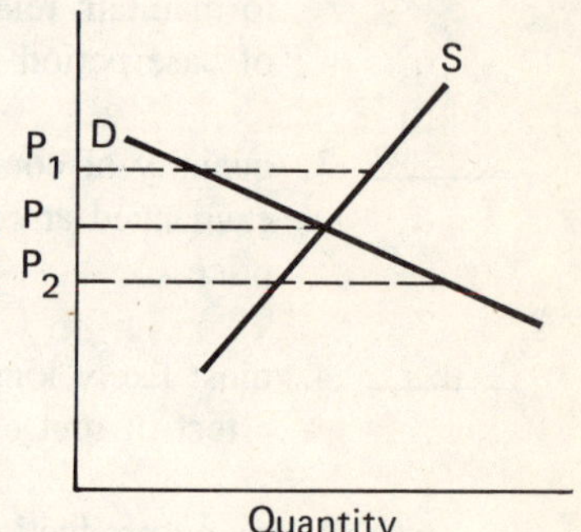

2. On the diagram, if p_1 were set by the government as a minimum price, it would
   (a) have no effect.
   (b) lead to shortages.
   (c) lead to surpluses and possibly to undercutting of the minimum price.
   (d) lead to government rationing.

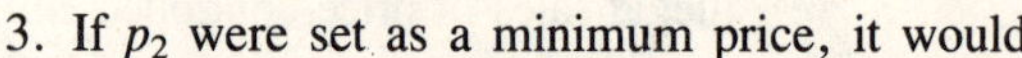

3. If p_2 were set as a minimum price, it would
   (a) have no effect.
   (b) lead to shortages and probably to black-market activity.
   (c) lead to surpluses and possibly to undercutting of the minimum price.
   (d) lead to government rationing.

4. Both maximum and minimum price controls, when effective, lead to
   (a) production controls.
   (b) rationing.
   (c) a drop in quality.
   (d) a reduction in quantity bought and sold.

5. On the diagram, if p_1 were a ceiling price, it would
   (a) have no effect.
   (b) lead to shortages and probably to black-market activity.
   (c) lead to surpluses and possibly to undercutting of the minimum price.
   (d) lead to government rationing.

6. If p_2 were a ceiling price, it would
   (a) have no effect.
   (b) lead to shortages and possibly to black-market activity.
   (c) lead to surpluses and possibly to undercutting of the minimum price.
   (d) lead to higher profits for sellers.

7. Black markets
   (a) make sense in theory but not in practice.
   (b) are effective in holding down a commodity's price.
   (c) almost inevitably accompany government price ceilings below equilibrium prices.
   (d) lead to a higher price, but also a greater quantity, than would have occurred without the ceiling price.

8. Allocating a commodity according to sellers' personal preferences
   (a) is more likely with price ceilings than with a market-determined price.
   (b) will usually improve the chances for a minority group to obtain the good.
   (c) can be discouraged through the use of effective price ceilings.
   (d) is more likely to occur with price floors set by the government than with price ceilings.

9. Rent controls in the United States have generally caused
   (a) an increase in the supply of rental accommodations.
   (b) a decrease in the availability of rental housing in localities with rent controls.
   (c) an improvement in the quality of rental apartments.
   (d) a permanent housing shortage to become a temporary one.

10. The rental housing market is characterized by
    (a) long- and short-run supply elasticities of equal magnitude.
    (b) price elasticity of demand equal to zero.
    (c) short-run inelastic supply and long-run elastic supply.
    (d) short-run elastic supply and long-run inelastic supply.

11. Bumper wheat crops
    (a) will probably increase wheat farmers' incomes.
    (b) ease the problems for price-support programs.
    (c) are likely to reduce wheat farmers' incomes.
    (d) are not likely to occur in the future because of soil erosion problems.

12. Unplanned fluctuations in the supply of agricultural produce
    (a) cause larger price changes when demand is elastic than when it is inelastic.
    (b) cause price variations that are in the same direction as the fluctuations.
    (c) make the supply more elastic.
    (d) cause price fluctuations that will be larger the more inelastic the demand.

13. A price completely stabilized by government's buying surpluses and selling its stocks when there are shortages means that
    (a) poor farmers will benefit the most.
    (b) government has imposed a perfectly inelastic demand curve on farms.
    (c) farmers' revenues will be proportional to output.
    (d) all farms will have satisfactory incomes and receipts will be stabilized.

14. Agricultural output in the United States has increased substantially since World War II mainly because
    (a) many people are going back to farming.
    (b) productivity and yields have risen.
    (c) rising demand has kept prices steadily increasing.
    (d) there has been unusually good growing weather.

15. Price changes tend to be large given unexpected changes in agricultural output because
    (a) the demand for agricultural output is elastic.
    (b) the demand for agricultural output is inelastic.
    (c) the long-run and short-run supplies are the same.
    (d) buyers' incomes change when output changes.

16. Government agricultural policies have included all but which one of the following?
    (a) price supports for agricultural products
    (b) a guaranteed annual income for farmers
    (c) acreage restrictions
    (d) gifts of food to the needy

17. Given the demand curve, a price ceiling below equilibrium results in a greater shortage
    (a) the less elastic the supply curve.
    (b) the more elastic the supply curve.
    (c) in the short run than in the long run.
    (d) the more inelastic the demand curve.

The following questions refer to certain exercises that follow:

18. Eliminating controls on rents [Exercise 2(c)] would
    (a) provide additional incentives for providing rental housing.
    (b) tend to increase the quantity of rental housing demanded.
    (c) have no effect on the demand for other forms of housing.
    (d) have no effect on either quantity demanded or quantity supplied of rental housing.

19. Government attempts to support farm prices above equilibrium levels (Exercise 5) will
    (a) cause quantity supplied to be less than equilibrium quantity.
    (b) have effects similar to any other price ceiling.
    (c) inevitably lead to an accumulation of unsold agricultural output.
    (d) have none of the above effects.

20. With an inelastic demand, technological improvements cause (Exercise 4)
    (a) supply and total farm revenues to rise.
    (b) farm incomes to rise.
    (c) increased demand for farm land.
    (d) farm revenues and incomes to fall.

Self-Test Key

Matching Concepts: 1–e; 2–h; 3–i; 4–a; 5–b; 6–j; 7–c; 8–d; 9–g; 10–f

Multiple-Choice Questions: 1–a; 2–c; 3–a; 4–d; 5–a; 6–b; 7–c; 8–a; 9–b; 10–c; 11–c; 12–d; 13–c; 14–b; 15–b; 16–b; 17–b; 18–a; 19–c; 20–d

Exercises

1. The diagram below illustrates two situations: (a) a short-run situation with the supply of a commodity relatively inelastic; and (b) a long-run situation with a more elastic supply. The subscripts for the demand curves indicate demand for subsequent periods of time within either the short or long run.

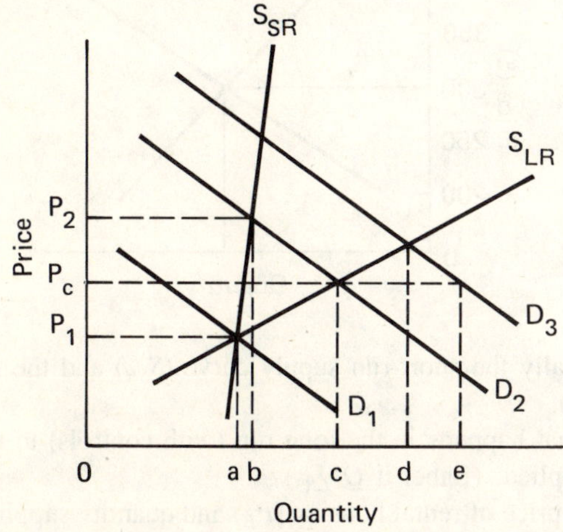

1. (a) Suppose demand shifts from D_1 to D_2. In the short run, price would be expected to increase from ______ to ______, and the equilibrium quantity from ______ to ______.

(b) (i) Assume the predicted sharp increase in price alarms the public, so the government sets the price at P_c. Is this rent control an effective price ceiling? Explain.

(ii) In the long run, quantity supplied will increase to ______ and P_c will be the ______ price. The main effects of the price control will be a short-run shift of income from (landlords, tenants) to (landlords, tenants). The long-run allocation of resources will have been (efficient, inefficient), given P_c.

(c) If P_c is maintained in the face of a further shift of the demand curve to D_3, P_c becomes a price (floor, ceiling), and the excess quantity demanded in the long run will be ______.

2. The diagram below illustrates the rental housing market at a certain point in time. The government decides that the current "average" rent of \$300 per month is socially desirable and fixes rents at that price. Subsequently, the costs of supplying rental housing (fuel, maintenance, etc.) rise permanently by \$50 per month.

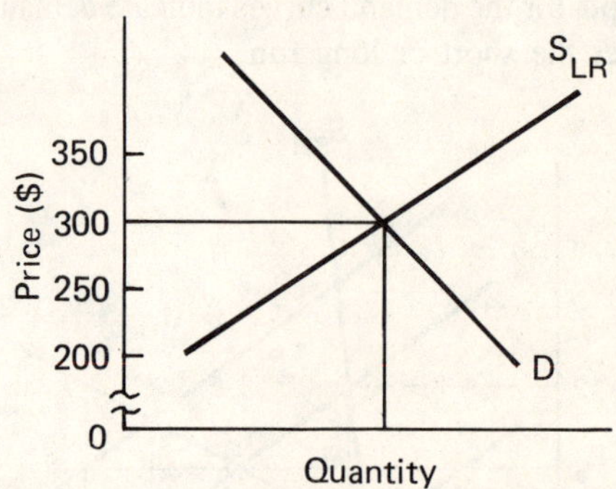

(a) Draw vertically the short-run supply curve (S_{SR}) and the new long-run supply curve (S'_{LR}).
(b) Illustrate what happens in the long run (with controls) to the quantity of rental housing supplied. (Label it Q'_{LR}.)
(c) Indicate the price of rental housing (P_E) and quantity supplied (Q_E) if there were no controls.

3. Use economic analysis in commenting on each of the following statements:
(a) "Ticket prices for college concerts should be constant, rather than varying according to the popularity of the performer(s)."

(b) "The drop in U.S. energy prices in the mid-1980s reduced the incentive to conserve energy and discourages domestic energy production."

(c) "The government should set an effective ceiling on interest rates for home mortgages since home ownership is part of the 'American dream.' "

(d) "In 1986 the minimum wage, constant at \$3.35 since 1981, is no longer an 'effective price floor' since fast food stores, long noted for paying the minimum, in many regions must pay more to attract sufficient help."

4. Show the following by drawing new curves on the graph:
   (a) a large shift in agricultural products due to population growth
   (b) a small shift in demand for agricultural products due to population growth
   (c) farmers' total revenue before and after these shifts

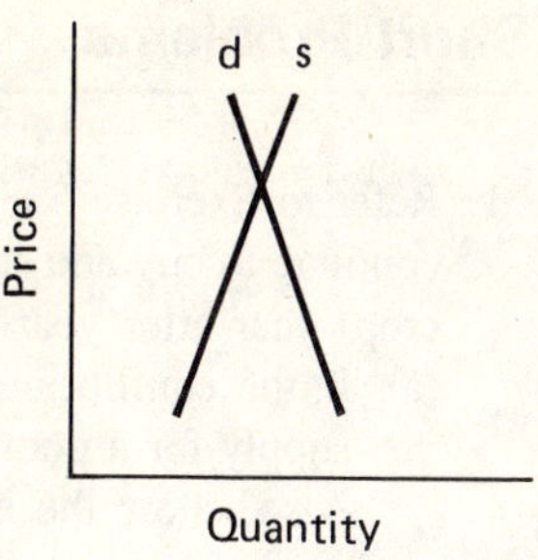

Use the graph to confirm these newspaper quotes:

   (d) "Consumers to bear brunt of poor wheat harvest."
   (e) "Good weather, record crop cause collapse of farm incomes."

5. Assume the agricultural market described in the figure below and determine the following:

	No price support	*$4 price floor*
(a) Total revenue of farmers	______	______
(b) Expenditures by consumers	______	______
(c) Expenditures by government	______	______
(d) Units purchased by government	______	______

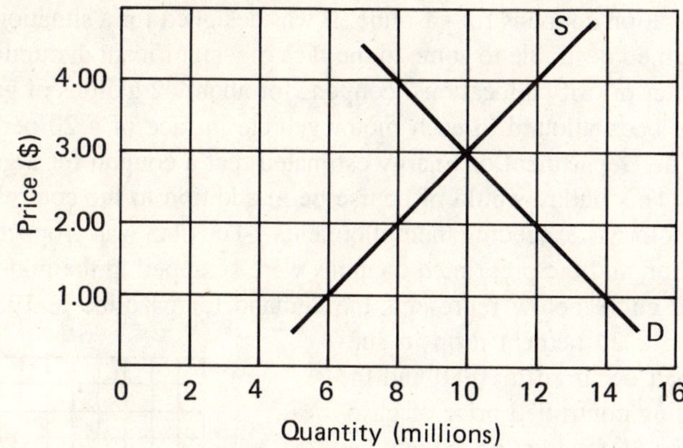

Short Problems

1. Refer to Exercise 5 above and assume a price floor of $4. The government will not continue to buy and store 4 million bushels a year (one-third of the 12-million bushel crop) year after year.
   (a) If the equilibrium is interpreted as that for a bumper year, show the shift in supply for a poor year that would enable the government to eliminate its stock. Also, show the normal supply if the long-run equilibrium price is $4.

   (b) Consider these ways of eliminating the stock buildup, whether and how they could be shown graphically, and potential problems with them.
      (i) acreage quotas
      (ii) marketing quotas
      (iii) domestic or foreign giveaways
      (iv) sale at low price for other uses (grain for gasohol)
      (v) producer fees to support advertising
      (vi) dropping price support level

2. "White" Market for Gasoline
   In 1980 the Carter administration prepared a standby plan that included freely marketable ration coupons for gasoline. It was designed for a situation in which price controls seemed desirable to some in the face of a significant disruption in petroleum imports. After priority allocations, coupons for about 42 gallons of gasoline a month would have been allotted to each motor vehicle in face of a 20 percent cutback in supplies. The Department of Energy estimated that a coupon for a gallon might sell for $1.70. (This outlay would of course be in addition to the controlled price at the pump for motorists exceeding their allotments.) The plan was dropped by the Reagan administration and the preprinted coupons were scrapped in the mid-1980s. Assume the demand curve below represents the demand for gasoline in 1980.
   (a) Assume a 20 percent drop in supplies had occurred in 1980 and the prevailing controlled price of gasoline was $1.50 a gallon. Show diagrammatically the excess demand at $1.50.

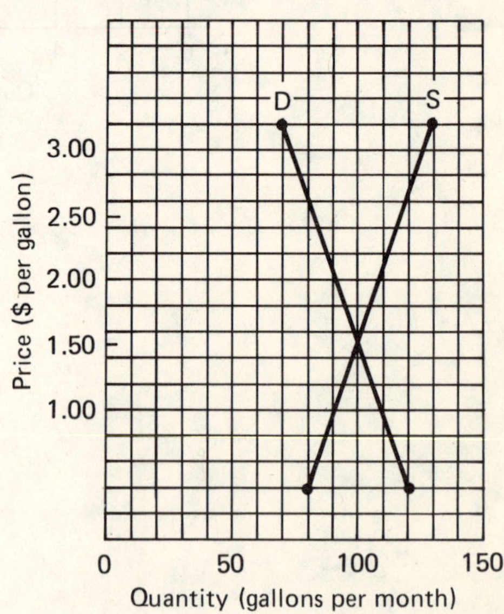

(b) Assume the prediction of a price of $1.70 for coupons is correct. What is the effective price that faces the motorist for gasoline under the plan? Explain why it is the same whether or not the motorist is working within the coupon allocation. (Remember the concept of opportunity costs.)

(c) What assumption has been made as to the elasticity of demand for gasoline in the prediction of total price, including that of the coupon, in (b)?

(d) If the elasticity of supply were greater than zero, how would the free-market price compare with the price in (b)? (Refer to diagram.)

(e) Compare this "white market" scheme with other possible price control arrangements (no ration coupons or nontransferable ration coupons). Stress its main advantage(s).

(f) What does it accomplish as compared to a free market? What is its major failing, one that is likely to become more serious the longer the period of supply curtailment?

3. Too Much Cheese

From 1979 through 1983, the Commodity Credit Corporation's annual purchase of dairy products increased from 3 billion to 22 billion pounds at a cost of nearly $3 billion in 1983. These purchases were required to maintain the floor price of $12.60 per hundredweight (cwt) mandated by agricultural legislation. Milk production, abetted by an average annual increase of 1.9 percent in milk produced per cow, was increasing by 2.7 percent per year after 1978. This rate of expansion at a time when many dairy farmers were apparently suffering financial hardship suggested that the support level was above the long-run equilibrium price.

The government program had put no limits on the output of farmers and the 1980s experience suggested that the quantities supplied at support levels was about 10 percent above demand. The government had run out of ways to dispose of surplus milk (school lunch program, foreign giveaways, and the cheese-for-the-poor program discussed in Box 6-3 of the text).

To drop the support program entirely or to lower the support price sufficiently to eliminate the milk surplus would be politically impossible. Thus, in 1983 the government embarked on a program to pay $10 per (cwt) for reductions in production below a 1981–1982 base. The program proved to have little appeal to the lower-cost farmers who had already expanded production beyond that of 1981–1982, particularly because it required culling of efficient cows at meat prices that would curtail farmers' long-run capacity to produce. It fell substantially short of its goals.

In 1985, after this program expired, Congress came up with another output-reducing approach starting April 1, 1986. It included a slight reduction in support levels, but its main feature was to buy out whole dairy herds and provide for their use as meat. Participating farmers would have to agree to leave dairying and not return for five years. The price paid by the government was determined by farmers' low bids on what they would accept per cwt for their past milk production levels.

(a) Is the 1985–1986 program in accord with the last paragraph of Chapter 6, which states, in part, "it would be more efficient to subsidize farm workers to change occupations and farm producers to change products rather than to subsidize them to stay where they are not needed"?

(b) What makes it so difficult for Congress to allow market forces to eliminate the excess capacity in many branches of agriculture?

(c) This program upset the beef industry, particularly when the Secretary of Agriculture estimated that the number of cows to be "diverted" would be 1.5 million (instead of the expected 930,000). Why?

(d) What have been subsequent developments for this program and for dairy support prices and surpluses?

5. Farm Price Supports: Price Versus Income

D represents the demand curve for an agricultural commodity whose normal supply curve is *S* (the supply available for marketing would be S_n); in poor crop years the supply actually available for marketing is S_1; in bumper crop years it is S_2. The dashed line labeled η = 1 has unitary elasticity.

In answering the following questions, use letters to designate line segments, such as *oc* for price and *oi* for the corresponding quantity.

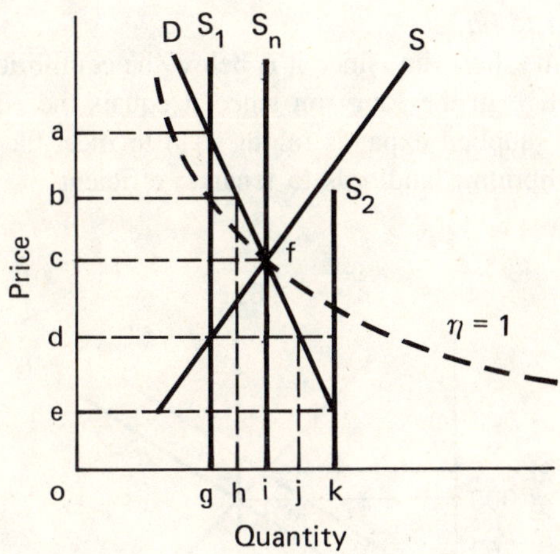

1. First assume that no price or income maintenance controls are used.
   (a) In a normal year the predicted price is ________________; the predicted quantity is ________________.
   (b) In a year of bumper crops the predicted price is ________________; the predicted quantity is ________________; farmers' revenues will be (greater than/less than) normal because the demand curve is (elastic/inelastic).

2. Now assume that the government seeks to maintain the price that in a normal year would just clear the market.
   (a) Why will it not be enough for the government simply to specify that no sales below that price are legal?

   (b) In a bumper crop year the government will have to (purchase/sell) quantity ____.
   (c) In a poor crop year it will have to (purchase/sell) quantity ________________.

3. An alternative policy is to maintain farmers' total revenues, rather than to maintain one fixed price.
   (a) In this case, in a bumper crop year the price could be allowed to drop to ________________ and the government would have to (purchase/sell) quantity ________________.
   (b) In a poor year the price could rise to ________________ and the government would (purchase/sell) quantity ________________.
   (c) Why might the government actually make money under this arrangement? Why in any case will the government's expenses be less under (3) than under (2)?

Answers to the Exercises

1. (a) $0P_1$ to $0P_2$; $0a$ to $0b$
   (b) (i) Yes, in the short run, since it is below the equilibrium price. [It would not be effective in the long run since it equals the equilibrium price as the quantity supplied expands (along S_{LR}) to meet the demand, $0c$, on D_2.]
   (ii) $0c$; equilibrium; landlords to tenants; efficient
   (c) ceiling; *ce*

2.

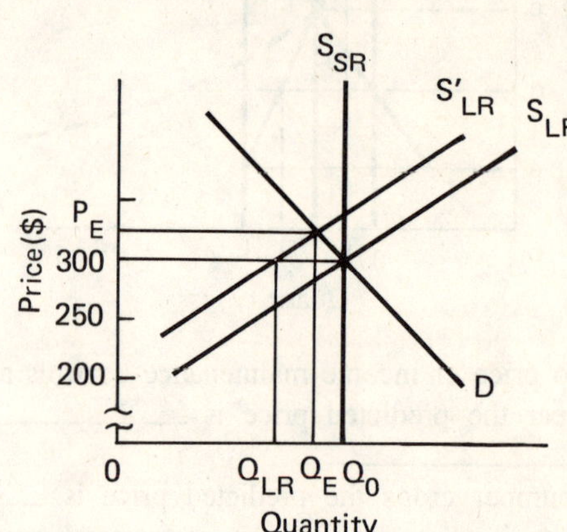

3. (a) There is likely to be a shortage of seats for the most popular entertainment (and perhaps scalping of tickets and long lines) and a surplus of seats for the less popular groups (unutilized resources).
   (b) Small increases in quantity demanded and reductions in quantity supplied would be expected. Measures to conserve energy tend to be long term (insulation, energy efficient equipment) and irreversible. Expectations of higher future prices could keep conservation incentives alive.
   (c) An effective ceiling on interest rates implies excess demand and means the thwarting of house ownership for many unless the government supplied the mortgage money.
   (d) The suggestion is clear that in many areas the equilibrium wage for the inexperienced and unskilled is above the minimum wage and that it, rather than the minimum, is the effective floor.

4. (a) large rightward shift in the supply curve
   (b) small rightward shift of the demand curve
   (c) extent of decline in *TR* depends on relative magnitudes of shifts
   (d) large leftward shifts in supply raises farmer revenues (buyer expenditures)
   (e) large rightward shift in supply lowers farm revenues

5.

	No price support	*$4 price floor*
(a)	$30,000,000	$48,000,000
(b)	$30,000,000	$32,000,000
(c)	0	$16,000,000
(d)	0	$ 4,000,000

CASES FOR PART TWO

CASE 3: Maintaining an All-Volunteer Armed Force

Authority to draft men for the armed forces expired July 1, 1973, after 33 years of almost uninterrupted dependence on conscription and 6 months of no draft calls. The switch to a volunteer force was partially based on the recommendations of a presidential commission which, after studying the problem, concluded that despite increased budgetary expenses to the government, the actual costs of an all-volunteer force would be lower than with the draft. One reason is that draftees' artificially low pay does not reflect true opportunity costs to either themselves or to society. Also, volunteer costs (both budget expenditures and real costs) would be lower because the turnover rate among military personnel would tend to decrease. Inductees generally do not reenlist, whereas volunteers frequently do; and the terms of voluntary enlistments are three to four years, not the two years under the draft. In addition, artificially low pay distorts decisions about the use of resources within the military.

Despite these arguments, however, the volunteer armed force has its critics. One of the most frequent arguments is that volunteer recruits come disproportionately from the ranks of the poor and nonwhites. Some critics vehemently suggest that this is a racist policy[1]; others suggest that a broader cross section of the population is needed (intellectually, racially, and socially) for purposes of acculturating less well-educated men and women recruits in military and other environments.

The army volunteers of 1974 contained a smaller percentage of high school graduates than the draftees of earlier years, but also had a smaller percentage of recruits with scores in the lowest third on the armed forces qualification test (AFQT). However, by the late 1970s the qualifications of enlisted personnel, as measured by scores on the AFQT, had dropped significantly, with 45 percent of enlistments coming from the bottom third of AFQT scores. The percentage of blacks had more than doubled and female enlisted personnel were 10 percent of the total.

While Congress had lifted monthly pay for recruits in 1973 from the draft level of $134 to $326 (exclusive of living costs), military pay rates have not always kept pace with civilian pay rates. In addition, Congress mandated that a minimum of 65 percent of first-term enlisted personnel be high school graduates and limited the proportion of enlistees with test scores in the bottom third to 20 percent. Special enlistment incentives,

[1]These critics may have varying political orientations. Participation of almost 30 percent of blacks in combat positions today is a great contrast to the minuscule percentages permitted blacks in the two world wars. What is seen as a threat of future black ascendancy by some is seen by others as injustice to blacks. The poor and blacks who serve will be less poor under the market wages paid in a volunteer army.

including enhanced educational benefits and more recruiting funds, were provided to reach these goals.

The President's Military Manpower Task Force in late 1982 expressed confidence "that the higher active and reserve strengths planned for the next five years can be achieved without a resumption of the draft," and that possible difficulties for the army by 1985 "can be overcome by enlistment incentives." The only significant shortage in quality enlistments seen by the Task Force was anticipated in the combat branches of the army (the infantry and armored forces). In order to eliminate this prospective shortfall, the Task Force recommended more intensive use of special incentives to steer personnel into hard-to-fill slots.

Questions

1. In this question our major interest is using demand-and-supply analysis to illuminate economic issues in all-volunteer U.S. armed forces. The quantity variable in the diagram below is the number of new first-term enlisted personnel required per year. *D,* the demand curve, slopes downward even though the strength of the force needed can be taken as a constant determined by political forces. The downward slope of the demand curve reflects that at lower pay rates soldiers may be substituted for civilians and equipment, reenlistments are less likely, and the period of first enlistment may be shorter. The position of the supply curve *(S)* is determinated by the population of potential enlistees that meet current military standards, the nonmonetary advantages of serving in the military as compared with alternative occupations, and the monetary compensation available elsewhere. The upward slope of the supply curve postulates that increases in the military wage, with all other supply determinants constant, will result in a greater quantity of military enlistees.

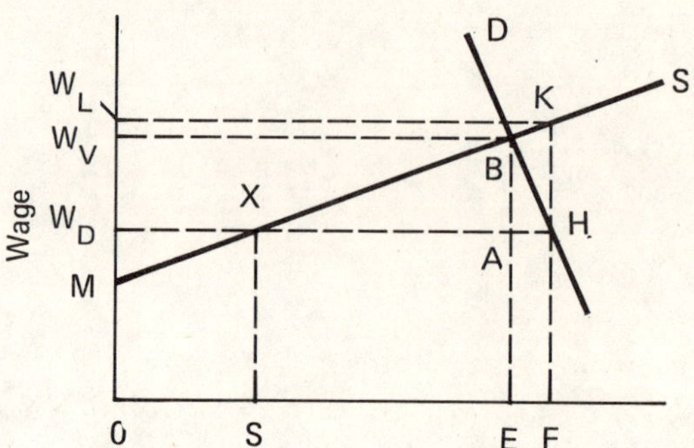

(a) The equilibrium wage in the diagram for an all-volunteer force (AVF) is ________________. (Use boundary letters for this and other questions.)

(b) W_D, the wage under a hypothetical draft, is an "effective maximum" price since it is (above, below) the equilibrium wage.

(c) The excess demand at W_D is ________________; with a draft, it would be met by ________________.

(d) Budget expenditure under the AVF for the first-term enlisted personnel is the area ________________ and is (greater/less) than that under the draft, which is shown by the area ________________.

(e) The number of true volunteers under the draft would be ________________; under the AVF, ________________.

(f) The total opportunity cost of volunteer recruits can be measured by the area under the supply curve and is ________________. Under the draft such opportunity costs would at least be ________________ (but almost certainly would be far greater since many draftees would be taken from the supply to the right of *K*).

2. Most students reading this case either are or have been in the prime age group (17 to 20) constituting the pool from which the supply of new enlistees is drawn. Take the current wage for recruits as an approximation of W_V (in 1986 it stood at $639 per month plus living allowances, along with educational benefits and "kickers" for its less popular branches that are cited below). Consider where you are (or were) located on the supply curve and the reasons for this location.

3. Consider the problem of the AVF during the late 1980s and the early 1990s posed by demographic trends. The number of births in the United States dropped from 3.95 million per year in the 1965–1970 period to 3.15 million per year in the early and mid-seventies (with a subsequent recovery to 3.625 million per year in the 1980–1985 period).
   (a) What does this signify for supply and for the wage necessary to meet the demand for recruits of the same quality as those of the early 1980s?

   (b) Colleges and the AVF are in potential competition for a reduced pool of people. Assess the strategy of the army in 1985 with its "new GI Bill" and supplemental kicker, the "new Army College Fund." The new GI Bill entitled recruits after June 30, 1985 to receive from $9,000 to $10,800 in educational assistance following their enlistment, with a contribution of $1,200 during their enlistment term. The new Army College Fund provides extra kickers to those scoring in the top 50 percent of the AFQT who enlist in one of eighty selected Army occupational specialties. The kickers can result in an additional $8,000 to $14,400 in educational benefits, depending on the enlistment term (two to four years).

   (c) Explain why W_V, the equilibrium price, would fluctuate between recession and prosperity. Since military compensation is likely to be a sticky price requiring congressional action for changes, how can the armed forces adjust to temporary disequilibrium positions?

CASE 4: Pricing Congestion in Singapore

Major cities such as Brussels, London, Paris, Singapore, and Tokyo have recently implemented policies designed to reduce traffic congestion.[1] The policies in most cities have emphasized *physical* measures, such as promoting public transport systems, expanding or improving highway capacity, developing off-street parking facilities, and providing areas limited to pedestrian traffic. Certain *regulatory* measures have also been used, including on-street parking controls, time restrictions, and exclusive lanes for certain types of vehicles. Economists have long argued that there should be more emphasis on *economic* measures, such as changing prices to influence both the amount of travel and its mode.

In June 1975 the city of Singapore introduced a road pricing scheme, the first of its kind in the world. The Singapore government considered various policy options to counteract increasing congestion, particularly in the city center. The government finally decided that solution of the long-term congestion problem required fundamental changes in travel behavior that could best be achieved through a system of pricing measures for traffic restraint.

There are three major components to the Singapore traffic restraint scheme: area licenses, requiring the purchase and display of a special supplementary license if a motorist wishes to enter a designated restricted area; parking surcharges in congested areas, designed to disperse parking more evenly throughout the city; and a park-and-ride scheme to provide an alternative mode of transport for motorists who are discouraged from driving into the city by the new policy.

The restricted zone was chosen to minimize the number of entry points to be policed, permit escape routes for motorists who were about to enter the zone mistakenly, and take advantage of existing facilities that could be used for fringe car parks. Entry into the zone is restricted only during certain times of the day, initially from 7:30 to 9:30 A.M. but later extended to 10:15 A.M. after congestion developed at 9:30 A.M. when the plan was first implemented. The supplementary license fee was initially set at $26.00 a month or $1.30 a day.[2] In December 1975 the fee was increased to about $35.00 a month, and the rates for company-registered cars were doubled. The only vehicles required to display area licenses are private cars carrying fewer than four persons (including taxis and company cars). Commercial vehicles, buses, motorcycles, private cars with four or more passengers, and emergency vehicles are exempt from the requirements. Licenses can be purchased at 16 curbside booths or at post offices.

Analysis of vehicle traffic flows (shown in the following table) shows that the licensing scheme has had a greater effect in changing the time than the place of travel, although both have been influenced. Of the reduction in traffic flow between 7:30 and 10:15 A.M., a much larger fraction make their journeys before 7:30 A.M. than bypass the restricted zone on peripheral roads.

[1]For discussion of these policies, see *Managing Transport* (Paris: Organization for Economic Cooperation and Development, 1979).

[2]All monetary values are in U.S. dollar equivalents. For purposes of comparison, GNP per capita in Singapore in 1977 was U.S. $2,880, while GNP per capita in the United States was $8,520.

Figures for traffic entering the restricted zone are as shown below (percentage change from March 1975 in parentheses):

	Private cars				*Total vehicles*			
	Mar. 1975	Aug. 1975	Dec. 1975	Mar. 1976	Mar. 1975	Aug. 1975	Dec. 1975	Mar. 1976
7:00–7:30	5,384	7,078 (+32.3)	4,866 (–9.6)	6,836 (+27)	9,800	12,097 (+23.3)	9,382 (–4.3)	11,212 (+14.4)
7:30–10:15	42,790	11,130 (–74.0)	12,106 (–71.1)	10,616 (–75.2)	74,014	42,897 (–42.0)	43,252 (–41.6)	40,172 (–45.7)
10:15–10:45	N.A.	7,375	6,529	6,449	N.A.	15,159	13,604	13,505

In addition, the number of cars in car pools doubled by December 1975, and there was increased use of public transportation. Overall, the reduction in number of vehicles entering the restricted zone between 7:30 and 10:15 A.M. was the combined effect of a modest shift from cars to public transport, a staggering of journey times, a diversion of travel routes, and a marked increase in car occupancy rates.

Questions

1. The goal of the Singapore pricing policy was to reduce traffic congestion in the center city. How well would you say it met this goal?

2. Compare the new parking rate policy with the old. Why would the new policy favor short-term parking? Explain why location would also be affected.

3. Compare the pricing measures that Singapore extensively relied on with the following alternative policy measures with respect to (1) their potential effectiveness in altering the time and place of vehicle use; (2) their potential effectiveness in reducing the overall rate of vehicle use (rather than their use at a particular time or place); and (3) costs of administration and enforcement.
   (a) higher registration fees for motor vehicles
   (b) continuous road charging by on-vehicle meters or tollbooths
   (c) higher fuel taxes
   (d) expansion of highway capacity
   (e) expanding mass transit facilities and lowering their money price

4. Consider the equity of Singapore's pricing policies. How does it compare with other measures in its "fairness"? Could equity considerations possibly have been a reason for exempting car pools from area license fees?

5. Suggest reasons why the Singapore pricing policy may or may not be as effective in other cities that experience similar traffic congestion problems.

CASE 5: The Oscillating Avocado

The avocado tree grows in southern California and Florida and possesses the interesting biological quirk that no matter when or where the tree is planted it yields abundantly only when the harvest year is an odd number. The table below gives the quantity (in tons) and the average price per ton (column 4) for the eleven crop years 1968–1969 through 1978–1979. (Column 5 (P^*) will be explained later.)

(1) Period	(2) Crop year	(3) Quantity (tons)	(4) Price (dollars)	(5) P^* (constant 1972 dollars)
0	1968–1969	73,700	$289	$342
1	1969–1970	45,700	561	635
2	1970–1971	85,800	357	386
3	1971–1972	45,400	691	716
4	1972–1973	89,300	499	499
5	1973–1974	73,700	672	636
6	1974–1975	127,400	450	387
7	1975–1976	87,400	827	660
8	1976–1977	141,100	567	431
9	1977–1978	117,700	733	527
10	1978–1979	152,400	488	327

This should represent an ideal situation for measuring the elasticity of demand, assuming the demand curve for avocados has not shifted over the time period. Under this assumption of unchanging demand, the alternate shifts in supply to the right and left should yield good measures of elasticity. At this point do question 1 below.

Your answers to question 1, with one elasticity measure more than three times the other for nearly the same range of prices, suggests that the demand curve has shifted. Part of the problem is that the general price level was rising over the time period. The theory of demand is a theory of *relative* prices; the absolute drop in price from $691 in 1971–1972 to $499 for a ton of avocados the following season understates the drop in avocado prices relative to all other prices. Column 5 corrects this problem by expressing all avocado prices in "constant 1972 dollars," monetary units whose purchasing power in terms of consumer goods remains the same.

The numbers in column 5 are determined by dividing the column 4 figures by the "implicit price deflator for personal consumption," an index with 1972 as the base year when the index equaled 100 percent or 1. For the years used in question 1, the adjustment was modest since the price index rose from 96.5 in 1971 to 105.7 in 1973 (the index value for the first year in a period was used in the deflation). In the whole period encompassed by this table, consumer prices rose from an index of 85.5 in 1968 to 149.2 in 1978, an increase of over 75 percent.

It becomes clear from the terminal periods (0 and 10) that a substantial rightward shift in the demand for avocados had taken place. The quantity had more than doubled though the real, relative price had scarcely changed—$342 in 1968–1969 and $327 in 1978–1979. The variables involved in the demand curve shift almost certainly include population, real income, and a shift in consumer preferences to favor a somewhat exotic ingredient for salads. These changes could be expected to occur gradually throughout the period. The evidence, both before and after the three years emphasized, suggest a rightward demand curve shift of about 7,000 tons a year. (The student may want to consider the data and whether another estimate is more reasonable.) At this point, do question 2 below.

The results of question 2 are consistent with our hypothesis above. We would expect the first measurement to be somewhat higher than the second since the average price, $607.50, is higher than for the second, $567.50. The first measurement is along a 1972–1973 demand curve and the second on the shifted 1973–1974 demand curve. You should remember that elasticities decline along a linear demand curve and are less in the same price range for a demand curve further right with the same slope. Do questions 3, 4, and 5 at this point.

Questions

1. Calculate the elasticity using the arc concept, in which the percentage changes in quantity and price are measured from midpoints of intervals, for the changes between 1971–1972 and 1972–1973, and between 1972–1973 and 1973–1974. Use quantities in column 3 and prices in column 4 for making calculations.

2. Recalculate the elasticities requested in question 1 using these adjusted price (P^*) and quantity changes (preparing a diagram of three parallel demand curves separated by 7,000 in quantity should make the adjustments clear).

	Relative price change	Quantity change attributed to price change
1971–1972 to 1972–1973	$716 to 499	52,400 to 89,300
1972–1973 to 1973–1974	$499 to 636	96,300 to 73,700

3. Compare this avocado elasticity with that of other agricultural commodities whose bumper crops can be a disaster for farmers and where government has often intervened to regulate supply.

4. The years 1973–1977 may well have encouraged expansion of, and entry into, avocado growing, but 1978–1979 may have checked some of the enthusiasm for such entry. Explain.

5. Make a final elasticity calculation for the change from 1977–1978 to 1978–1979. Use the P^* figures but use unadjusted quantities since evidence suggests no continued shift in demand. On the basis of your calculation, does a bumper crop now pose more of a financial threat to the avocado farmer? Compare the elasticity in the 1977–1979 period with that in earlier periods.

PART THREE

Consumption, Production, and Cost

7

Household Consumption Behavior: The Marginal Utility Approach

Learning Objectives

After completing the material in this chapter, you should be able to

—distinguish between marginal utility and total utility;

—explain how individuals can maximize total utility by comparing a commodity's marginal utility and price;

—explain how marginal utility theory can be used to derive a demand curve;

—explain how diminishing marginal utility and consumers' surplus are related;

—resolve the paradox of value.

Review and Self-Test

Matching Concepts

	Concepts		Definitions
______	1. consumers' surplus	(a)	MU_A/MU_B
______	2. marginal utility	(b)	high (low) total utilities accompanied by low (high) prices
______	3. commodity with a marginal utility of zero	(c)	law of diminishing marginal utility
______	4. scarce good	(d)	increase in total utility with consumption of one more unit of a good
______	5. paradox of value	(e)	free good
______	6. marginal disutility	(f)	commodity for which quantity demanded exceeds quantity supplied at a price of zero
______	7. allocation of expenditures so that the utility for the last dollar spent on each is equal	(g)	negative marginal utility
______	8. hypothesis that additional consumption will increase total utility at a decreasing rate	(h)	excess of price consumers are willing to pay over price actually paid
		(i)	condition for maximization of utility
______	9. market demand (curve)	(j)	horizontal summation of household demand curves
______	10. P_A/P_B		

Multiple-Choice Questions

1. In the utility theory of consumer demand, the term *utility* is best defined as
   (a) the satisfaction someone receives from consuming commodities.
   (b) the value of a commodity to society.
   (c) the usefulness of a product.
   (d) individual demand for a commodity.

2. The hypothesis of diminishing marginal utility states that
   (a) the less of a commodity one is consuming, the less the additional utility obtained by an increase in its consumption.
   (b) the more of a commodity one is consuming, the more the additional utility obtained by an increase in its consumption.
   (c) the more of a commodity one is consuming, the less the additional utility obtained by an increase in its consumption.
   (d) marginal utility cannot be measured, but total utility can.

3. Diamonds have a higher price than water because
   (a) the total utility of diamonds is greater than that of water.
   (b) the total utility of water is greater than that of diamonds.
   (c) the marginal utility of water is greater than that of diamonds.
   (d) the marginal utility of diamonds is greater than that of water.

4. According to utility theory, a consumer will maximize total satisfaction when *A* and *B* are consumed in quantities such that MU_A/MU_B
   (a) equals the ratio of the price of *A* to the price of *B*.
   (b) equals the ratio of total utility of *A* to that of *B*.
   (c) equals the ratio of the price of *B* to the price of *A*.
   (d) exceeds P_A/P_B.

5. The "paradox of value" is that
   (a) people are irrational in consumption choices.
   (b) the total utilities yielded by commodities do not directly relate to their market values.
   (c) value has no relationship to utility schedules.
   (d) free goods are goods that are essential to life.

6. All consumers facing the same prices in a market system will, according to utility theory,
   (a) have the same ratio between marginal utilities for goods that are purchased.
   (b) have the same marginal utilities.
   (c) have the same ratios between total utilities of goods consumed.
   (d) achieve the same total utilities.

7. If the total utility of 11 units is 100 and that of 10 units is 95, then the marginal utility of the eleventh unit is
   (a) 1.
   (b) 100.
   (c) –5.
   (d) 5.

8. According to utility theory, the quantity of candy demanded will decrease if its relative price rises because
   (a) purchasing fewer units will increase total utility.
   (b) the marginal utility of candy is higher when less candy is consumed.
   (c) marginal utility of a good is determined by its price.
   (d) marginal and total utilities must be equated to maximize satisfaction.

9. If the relative prices of *X* and *Y* became 2:1, and an individual was consuming *X* and *Y* such that MU_X/MU_Y was 3:2, then to achieve maximum utility
   (a) the individual must consume more of *X* and less of *Y*.
   (b) the price of *X* must rise.
   (c) the individual must consume less of *X* and more of *Y*.
   (d) the individual's income must rise.

10. Consumers' surplus derived from the consumption of a commodity
    (a) is the difference between the total value placed on a certain amount of consumption and the total payment made for it.
    (b) will always be less than the total amount paid for the commodity.
    (c) will always be more than the total amount paid for the commodity.
    (d) equals the total value of that commodity to consumers.

11. If a utility-maximizing individual is prepared to pay $3 for the first unit of a commodity, $2 for the second unit, and $1 for the third unit, and the market price is $1 per unit,
    (a) consumers' surplus is $3.
    (b) the demand schedule for the commodity is negatively sloped.
    (c) the individual will purchase three units of the commodity.
    (d) all of the above.

12. The provision of a "scarce" good to consumers free of charge
    (a) ensures that the commodity will be used where it yields the highest marginal utility.
    (b) is likely to result in some consumption with a marginal utility of zero.
    (c) results in the same allocation of resources as when a positive price is charged.
    (d) allocates resources to their highest-valued uses.

13. Marginal utility theory implies that all consumers in the same market have, for the products they consume,
    (a) the same marginal utilities.
    (b) the same ratio between marginal utilities.
    (c) different ratios between marginal utilities reflecting differences in income.
    (d) no relationship between marginal utilities because of changing tastes.

14. Consumer surplus can be measured as
    (a) the area between the demand curve and the quantity axis.
    (b) the area between the demand curve and the supply curve.
    (c) the area between the demand curve and a horizontal line at the market price.
    (d) the distance along the horizontal axis.

15. The prediction of the aggregate behavior of all households illustrated by a market demand curve requires that
    (a) all households act rationally all of the time.
    (b) all households act rationally some of the time.
    (c) most households act rationally much of the time.
    (d) some households act rationally some of the time.

16. That the voters in a town could respond in a poll that an excellent school system is an important public asset, and then vote down a school bond issue,
    (a) is clearly irrational behavior because of the high total utility of education.
    (b) suggests bias in the poll that led to an overassessment of the importance given to public education.
    (c) indicates a low voter turnout except for antitaxers.
    (d) could be quite consistent since low marginal utility in ranges of high expenditure is often associated with high total utility.

17. The most appropriate economic reason for water meters for individual households is
    (a) to require that all water users, even the poor, pay something.
    (b) to provide employment for meter readers and manufacturers.
    (c) to prevent usage that has very low marginal utility of a good that is becoming increasingly scarce.
    (d) invalid since so vital a necessity should be financed from tax revenues rather than by user charges.

18. When the price of commodity *X* triples, all other prices and income remaining constant, then for an individual consuming *X*,
    (a) the quantity of *X* consumed must fall to one-third its previous level.
    (b) the quantity of *X* consumed must fall until the marginal utility of *X* has tripled.
    (c) the individual must increase his or her consumption of *X*.
    (d) the consumption of all other commodities must fall.

The following questions refer to certain exercises that follow:

19. What should be the rates of consumption for two items, J and K, whose prices are equal (Exercise 1)?
    (a) J and K in equal amounts
    (b) quantities of each sufficient to provide the same total utility
    (c) the quantities of each which provide equal marginal utilities
    (d) amounts equalizing the total and marginal utilities of J and K

20. Consumers' surplus will result from an individual's consumption of cola (Exercise 3)
    (a) only if marginal utility exceeds total utility.
    (b) only if price times quantity exceeds marginal utility times quantity.
    (c) as soon as diminishing marginal utility occurs.
    (d) when willingness to pay for cola exceeds the amount actually paid.

Self-Test Key

Matching Concepts: 1–h; 2–d; 3–e; 4–f; 5–b; 6–g; 7–i; 8–c; 9–j; 10–a

Multiple-Choice Questions: 1–a; 2–c; 3–d; 4–a; 5–b; 6–a; 7–d; 8–b; 9–c; 10–a; 11–d; 12–b; 13–b; 14–c; 15–c; 16–d; 17–c; 18–b; 19–c; 20–d

Exercises

1. (a) The following are hypothetical total utility schedules for products *J* and *K*. Compute the marginal utilities.

Units per week	*TU* (*J*)	*MU* (*J*)	*TU* (*K*)	*MU* (*K*)
0	0	______	0	______
1	30	______	20	______
2	50	______	32	______
3	60	______	40	______
4	65	______	47	______
5	65	______	50	______

(b) At what amounts of consumption does diminishing marginal utility occur for *J* and *K*?

(c) Does disutility occur for either good? Explain.

(d) What rate of consumption would maximize utility if *J* were a free good? Explain.

(e) Assuming no budget constraint and an equal price (greater than zero) for *J* and *K*, identify which commodity will be consumed first, which unit second, and so on. When should additional consumption cease?

2. Suppose an individual was willing to pay the amounts shown in the table below for bottles of cola.

Bottles of cola per day	Amount individual is willing to pay for this incremental bottle
1st	$.90
2nd	.75
3rd	.50
4th	.10

(a) At a price of $.50 per bottle of cola, how many per day would the person consume? ______ Explain.

(b) At a price of $.50, what would be the total value of cola consumed? What would be the consumers' surplus?

(c) If price rises to $.75 per bottle, what will be the effect on quantity demanded and consumers' surplus?

3. Assume a utility function of the form $TU = 10X - X^2$, where TU is total utility and X is units of X consumed per week.

   (a) What is the equation for determining marginal utility?

   (b) After what rate of consumption does diminishing total utility begin? How is it determined?

   (c) Compute the total and marginal utilities ($TU = 10X - X^2$) and plot them on the graph.

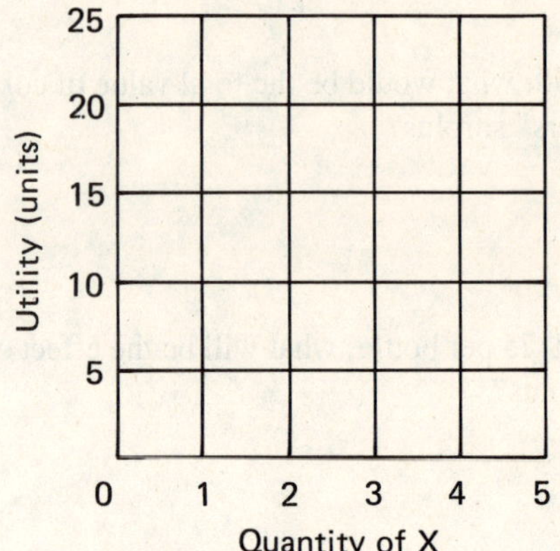

   (d) If price per unit of X were \$6, how many units should be purchased (assuming the marginal utility/price ratios for all other commodities consumed is one)? Explain.

4. Ezra Grundig, a college student, finds himself with a total of only five hours a week for outdoor recreation. The two activities that appeal to him are canoeing and hiking. Estimated marginal utility schedules are shown below. Assume that the time constraint is serious enough so that additional utility drops to zero after five hours in either or both activities.

Hours (per week)	Marginal utility: Hiking	Marginal utility: Canoeing
1	20	20
2	18	19
3	16	18
4	14	17
5	12	16

(a) First, assuming no significant costs, how should Ezra allocate his leisure time between canoeing and hiking to maximize his total utility?

(b) Now assume that the cost of canoeing is $1.00 per hour and for hiking is $.75 an hour, and that, at the margin in the consumption of other goods, Ezra's ratio (*MU/P*) is 16 utility units per dollar. To maximize total utility, how should Ezra reallocate his time between hiking and canoeing? Explain.

(c) Ezra now discovers that the *MU/P* ratio for other goods has risen to 20 utility units per dollar. What adjustments does this call for in his outdoor recreation program? What could have caused this rise in the *MU/P* ratio?

5. In June 1970, the village of Potsdam, New York, raised the price of water from $.60 to $1.20 per 1,000 gallons to pay for a new sewage treatment plant. The village administrator predicted water revenues would double from $180,000 to $360,000 with volume remaining at approximately 300 million gallons. In fact, revenue was only $340,000 for about 283 million gallons.
   (a) What did the actual experience imply about the shape of marginal utility functions for water and about its elasticity of demand?

   (b) What did the *prediction* imply about the shape of the marginal utility functions for water and about its elasticity of demand?

Short Problems

1. Given the demand curve $P = 9 - 0.01Q$, estimate the consumer surplus at $P = 6$ and at $P = 3$. Show diagrammatically.
   (a) At $P = 6$: ______
   At $P = 3$: ______

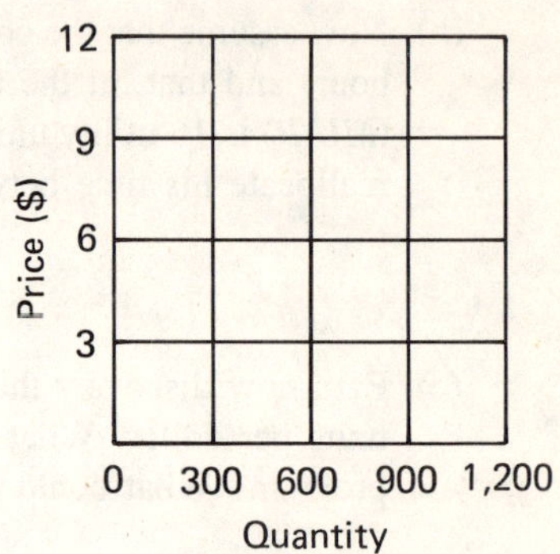

   (b) Explain why consumers' surplus increases as price decreases.

2. Assume two commodities, *A* and *B*, with marginal utilities as follows:

Marginal Utility from the Consumption of Product *A* and Product *B*

	Units of A or B									
	1	2	3	4	5	6	7	8	9	10
MU_A	10	9	8	7	6	5	4	3	2	1
MU_B	20	18	16	14	12	10	8	6	4	2

(a) Determine the quantities of the two goods that maximize satisfaction for each of the budget and price combinations shown below. This can be done by the procedure followed in Exercise 2. Units are selected in order of *MU* per dollar until the budget is exhausted.

	Budget	P_A	P_B	Q_A	Q_B	MU_B/MU_A
(a)	$43	$3	$7.00	______	______	______
(b)	43	3	3.50	______	______	______
(c)	15	5	5.00	______	______	______
(d)	40	5	5.00	______	______	______
(e)	50	5	5.00	______	______	______

(b) What do you note about the relationship between P_B/P_A and MU_B/MU_A? Is this what the chapter would have led you to expect?

Answers to the Exercises

1. (a) $MU(J)$ = 30; 20; 10; 5; 0 $MU(K)$ = 20; 12; 8; 7; 3
   (b) For both commodities, marginal utility begins to diminish after the first unit.
   (c) No; marginal utility is never less than zero.
   (d) Five; consume additional units until marginal utility equals zero.
   (e) Start with 1 unit of *J*. The second and third units would be another *J* and the first *K* (*MU* = 20). The rest would be consumed as follows: *K*2 (*MU* = 12); *J*3 (*MU* = 10); *K*3 (*MU* = 8); *K*4 (*MU* = 7); *J*4 (*MU* = 5); *K*5 (*MU* = 3). Do not consume *J*5 (*MU* = 0).

2. (a) 3, since the individual values the third bottle just at $.50 while valuing the first and second bottles at higher amounts. (b) $2.15; $.65 (c) quantity demanded will be reduced to 2 bottles; consumer surplus falls to $.15

3. (a) $10 - 2X$ (the first derivative of the utility function), which gives the rate at which utility is being added as the consumption of a unit is finished.
   (b) $X = 5$ [Find the value of *X* where the first derivative ($10 - 2X$) equals zero.]
   (c) Plot points for *X* of 1 to 5 for *TU* are 9, 16, 21, 24, 25, respectively; for *MU*, the points are 8, 6, 4, 2, 0 (using the equation, $10 - 2X$). (The *MU*s plotted at unit midpoints would be 9, 7, 5, 4, 3, and 1.)
   (d) Consume 2 units per week to maximize utility when *P* = $6. Marginal utility is being gained at the rate of 5 when consumption of the second unit is completed, so *MU*/*P* ratio equals that for other commodities.

4. (a) Three hours of canoeing and two hours of hiking will maximize total utility at 95.
   (b) The third hour of canoeing yields only 18 utility units per dollar; the third hour of hiking yields 21.3 units per dollar and should be substituted for it. This new combination will yield 93 units of total utility plus 4 units from the extra $.25 used elsewhere. For the same money outlay ($4.50), the old combination yielded only 95.
   (c) The second unit of canoeing dollar should be dropped since the marginal utility is only 19 per dollar. Perhaps Ezra will use that extra hour of leisure time jogging around the neighborhood at no cost. Available income may have dropped (another rise in tuition?), forcing cutbacks in consumption; prices of other goods may have dropped.

5. (a) The implication was that the marginal utility function was decreasing steeply in this price range (similar to U_2 in Figure 7-5 of the text, though in other price ranges it may resemble U_1 in Figure 7-5), and that the demand was very inelastic, less than 0.1.
   (b) The prediction assumed a fixed quantity of water (with high marginal utility), terminating in a perpendicular to the axis so that the elasticity would be zero.

8

Household Consumption Behavior: The Indifference Curve Approach

Learning Objectives

After completing the material in this chapter, you should be able to

—use price and income data to construct a budget line;

—explain the characteristics of indifference curves;

—explain why household equilibrium will occur at the tangency of the budget line to an indifference curve;

—draw a price-consumption line and income-consumption line;

—derive a demand curve using indifference analysis;

—distinguish between the income and substitution effects of a price change;

—distinguish among normal goods, inferior goods, and Giffen goods.

Review and Self-Test

Matching Concepts

_______ 1. locus of maximum amounts of commodities available given real income and prices

_______ 2. marginal rate of substitution

_______ 3. goal achieved at tangency of an indifference curve with the budget line

_______ 4. locus of all combinations of two goods that yield the same satisfaction

_______ 5. change in relative prices

_______ 6. normal good

_______ 7. Giffen good

_______ 8. commodities valued for their ability to confer status on purchasers

_______ 9. altered indifference map

_______ 10. shift in budget line

(a) change in real income

(b) maximum consumer satisfaction

(c) commodity with reinforcement of substitution effect of price change by income effect

(d) budget line

(e) commodity with upward-sloping demand curve

(f) conspicuous consumption goods

(g) change in slope of budget line

(h) slope of indifference curve

(i) indifference curve

(j) changes in consumer preferences

Multiple-Choice Questions

1. Indifference curve theory requires that
   (a) consumers can measure satisfaction in precise units.
   (b) consumers can identify preferred combination of goods.
   (c) consumers always behave consistently.
   (d) all consumers have the same preference patterns.

2. An increase in money income accompanied by the same percentage increase in all prices
   (a) leaves the position of the budget line unchanged.
   (b) changes the slope of the budget line.
   (c) causes a parallel outward shift of the budget line.
   (d) causes a parallel inward shift of the budget line.

3. A change in household money income will always shift the budget line for two commodities parallel to itself if
   (a) money prices of the two commodities stay constant.
   (b) relative prices stay constant, but money prices change by the same percentage as income.
   (c) real income stays constant.
   (d) money prices change in the same direction and proportion for the two commodities.

4. Halving all absolute prices, other things constant, has the effect of
   (a) halving real income.
   (b) halving money income.
   (c) changing relative prices.
   (d) doubling real income.

5. A change in one commodity's price, other things constant, will
   (a) shift the budget line parallel to itself.
   (b) change money income.
   (c) cause a change of slope in the budget line.
   (d) have no effect on real income.

6. An indifference curve indicates
   (a) constant quantities of one good with varying quantities of another.
   (b) the prices and quantities of two goods that can be purchased for a given sum of money.
   (c) all combinations of two goods that will give the same level of satisfaction to the household.
   (d) combinations of goods whose marginal utilities are always equal.

7. Households may attain consumption on a higher indifference curve by all but which one of the following?
   (a) an increase in money income
   (b) a reduction in absolute prices
   (c) a proportionate increase in money income and in absolute prices
   (d) a change in relative prices caused by a reduction in one price

8. The slope of the budget line with product Y on the vertical axis and product X on the horizontal axis is
   (a) $-(P_y/P_x)$.
   (b) -1.
   (c) $-(X/Y)$
   (d) $-(P_x/P_y)$.

9. The relative prices of two goods can be shown by
   (a) the slope of the budget line.
   (b) the slope of an indifference curve.
   (c) the marginal rate of substitution.
   (d) the price-consumption line.

10. At the point where the budget line is tangent to an indifference curve,
    (a) equal amounts of goods give equal satisfaction.
    (b) the ratio of prices of the goods must equal the marginal rate of substitution.
    (c) the prices of the goods are equal.
    (d) a household cannot be maximizing its satisfaction.

11. The consumption choice that will maximize satisfaction occurs
    (a) when the slope of the budget line exceeds that of an indifference curve.
    (b) when the slope of the budget line is the same as that of an indifference curve.
    (c) when the slope of the budget line is less than that of an indifference curve.
    (d) when the two slopes are reciprocals.

12. The substitution effect can be graphically shown
    (a) with a change in slope of the budget line.
    (b) with a rightward shift of the budget line.
    (c) with a leftward shift of the budget line.
    (d) by the switch to dentures for those neglecting to floss regularly.

13. A Giffen good can be characterized
    (a) by an upward-sloping demand curve.
    (b) by a negative income effect that outweighs the substitution effect.
    (c) as one type of inferior good.
    (d) by all of the above.

14. If household money income rises by 10 percent and all prices rise by 5 percent,
    (a) household purchasing power will increase by 10 percent.
    (b) the household budget line will shift outward to the right.
    (c) household real income has declined.
    (d) the budget line shifts to the left and inward.

15. The income effect of a decline in price for a commodity
    (a) will be small unless expenditure on the good is very important in the consumers' budget.
    (b) implies that consumers' real income has also declined.
    (c) can be predicted to increase purchases of an inferior good.
    (d) can be predicted to decrease purchases of a normal good.

16. Demand curves for normal goods slope downward because
    (a) the substitution effect is greater than the income effect.
    (b) substitution and income effects work in the same direction.
    (c) the income effect is greater than the substitution effect.
    (d) none of the above; the demand curves slope upward.

17. The average money income of U.S. households was about the same in 1920 and 1940, a period with significant decline in consumer prices (see Exercise 4 for details). We may reasonably predict
    (a) a rightward shift of most budget lines.
    (b) a leftward shift of most budget lines.
    (c) no change in budget lines.
    (d) nothing at all about budget lines without evidence concerning consumer preferences.

18. In the United States, relative energy prices declined in the post World War II period until 1972 and increased to 1981. The slope of the budget lines comparing energy-related commodities (electricity, gasoline, etc.) with all other consumer goods (vertical axis)
    (a) decreased to 1972 and then increased.
    (b) increased to 1972 and then decreased.
    (c) did not change.
    (d) shifted without a change in slope.

Self-Test Key

Matching Concepts: 1–d; 2–h; 3–b; 4–i; 5–g; 6–c; 7–e; 8–f; 9–j; 10–a

Multiple-Choice Questions: 1–b; 2–a; 3–a; 4–d; 5–c; 6–c; 7–c; 8–d; 9–a; 10–b; 11–b; 12–a; 13–d; 14–b; 15–a; 16–b; 17–a; 18–a

Exercises

1. Assume that a household has a budget of $600 per year to spend on two recreation activities: skiing (at $20 per day) and golf (at $12 per 18-hole round).
    (a) Draw the budget line for recreation expenditures on the graph below.

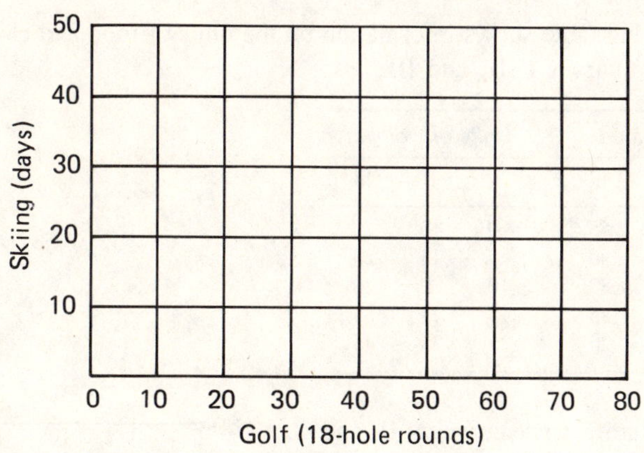

    (b) Is a combination of 20 units of skiing and 20 rounds of golf attainable? Explain.

    (c) Suppose an increase in income allowed a 50 percent increase in the recreation budget. Plot the new budget line, assuming the prices of golf and skiing are unchanged.

2. Refer to the budget line in Exercise 1(c). Suppose now that the price of skiing increases to $30 per day, other things constant.
   (a) Draw the new budget line on the graph.

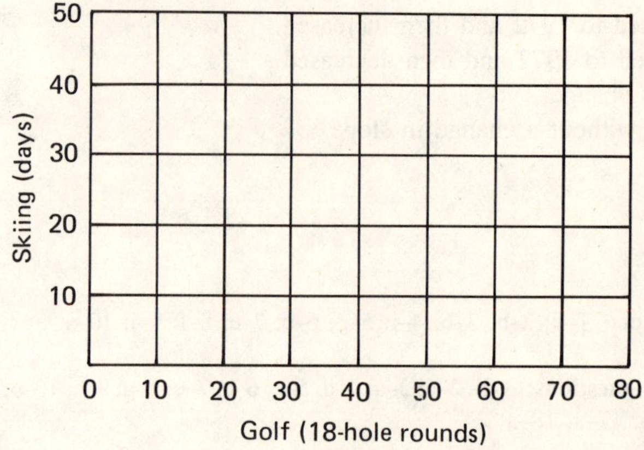

   (b) Suppose now that the price of a round of golf increases to $18. Draw in the new budget line.
   (c) Compare the new budget line in (b) with the budget line in Exercise 1(a). Explain your findings.

3. The following table shows information on the units of food and clothing that are on indifference curves I, II, and III.

Units of food			*Units of clothing*		
I	II	III	I	II	III
45	50	55	0	10	20
30	35	40	5	15	25
20	25	30	10	20	30
15	20	25	15	25	35
10	15	20	25	35	45

   (a) Draw indifference curves I, II, and III on the graph.
   (b) Draw a budget line on the graph that represents a budget constraint of $350 and food and clothing per unit costs of $10 and $15, respectively.
   (c) Given (a) and (b) above, what combination of food and clothing will maximize consumer satisfaction? Explain.

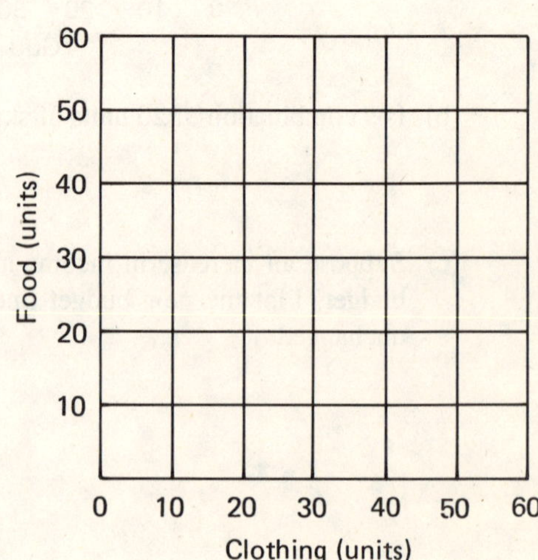

4. In marked contrast to the performance of recent years, consumer prices were generally declining or stable from 1920 to 1940. Food prices declined more than others during the period, and the money income of the average household declined slightly.

   The budget line is an excellent tool to indicate the change in household purchasing power. On the following graph, each unit on the horizontal axis is the amount of food that could be purchased for one dollar in 1967 with the consumer price index defined as 1.00 or 100 percent; the unit on the vertical axis is the amount of "all items except food" that could be purchased for one dollar in 1967. By dividing by the price index expressed as a decimal (i.e., 60 percent = 0.60), you can estimate the units that could be purchased in 1920 and 1940.

	Price indexes		Household	Food	"Other"
	Food	Other	income	intercepts	intercepts
1920	60	60	$2,200	______	______
1940	35	47	2,100	______	______

(a) Draw the budget lines for 1920 and 1940 after completing the table.

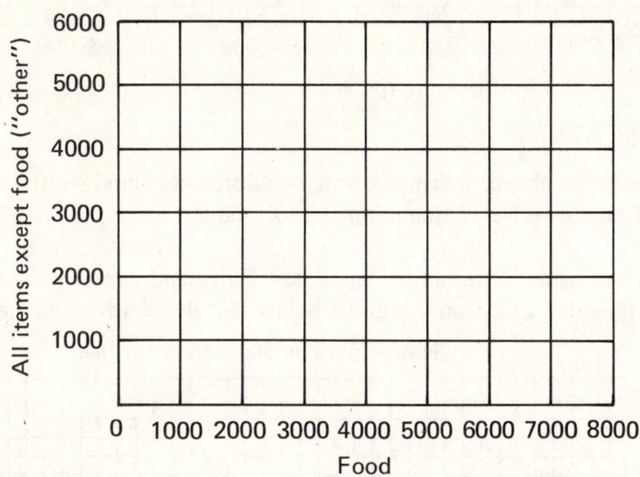

(b) Does your graph indicate that price declines can produce a rise in real income? Explain.

(c) How is the relatively greater decline of food prices shown on the graph? Draw indifference curves that show that a family spending a large percentage of income on foods would have had a greater rise in real income over the 1920–1940 period.

5. Deriving Household Demand Curves from Indifference Maps

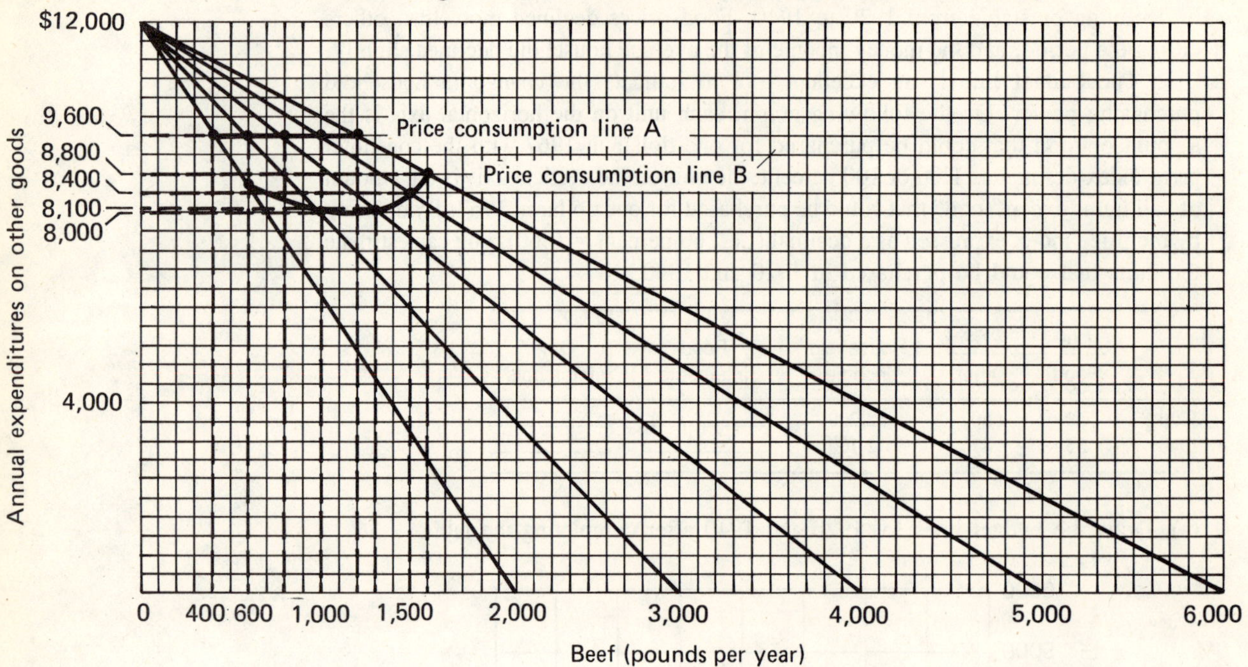

(a) On the graph above, sketch in (using two different colors) indifference maps that could lead to price-consumption lines *A* and *B*.

(b) From the price-consumption lines, derive demand curves *A* and *B* and enter quantities demanded on the graph below and the chart on the next page.

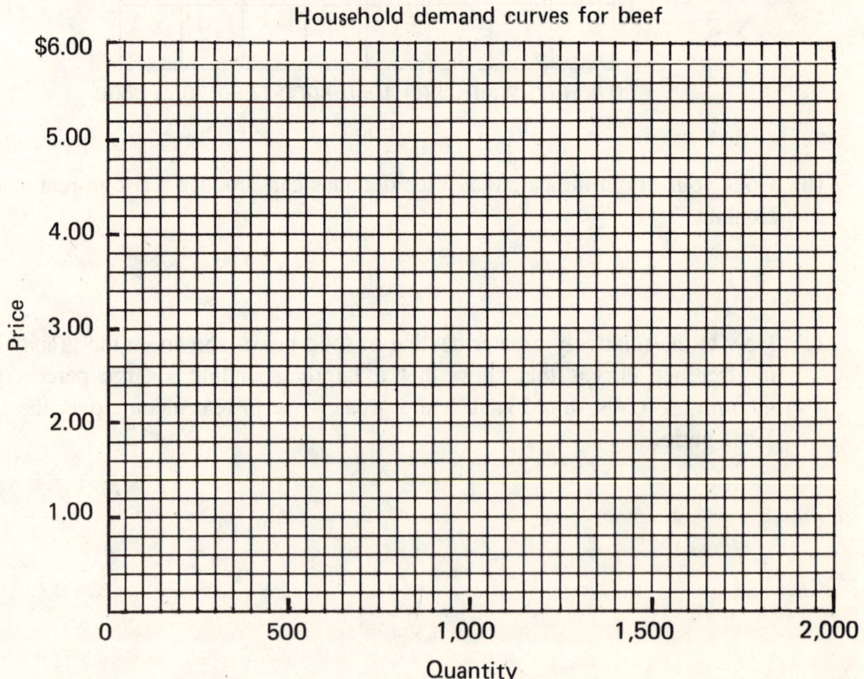

			Expenditure on beef	
P	Q_A	Q_B	*A*	*B*
$6.00	______	______	______	______
4.00	______	______	______	______
3.00	______	______	______	______
2.40	______	______	______	______
2.00	______	______	______	______

(c) What is price elasticity of demand for household *A?* At what price does elasticity of demand for household B approach unit elasticity?

Short Problems

1. Before doing this problem you will find it helpful to work Exercise 4. On the diagram below, each unit on the horizontal axis is the amount of energy (including motor fuels and electricity) that could be purchased for one dollar in 1967; the unit on the vertical axis is the amount of "all items except energy" that could be purchased in 1967 (when CPI = 100).

	CPI total	CPI for energy	CPI for all items except energy	Personal disposable income
1958	84	90	84	$1830
1972	125	114	126	3860
1981	272	410	257	8830

(a) Draw the budget lines for 1958, 1972, and 1981.

(b) 1972 represented the end of a long-term relative decline in energy prices. How is this shown by the budget lines?

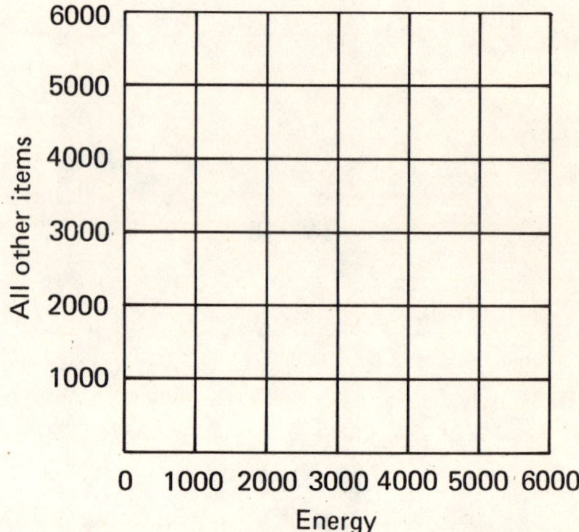

(c) While 1981 showed a slight increase in real income over 1972, individuals with tastes toward much driving and large homes to heat could be worse off. Show an indifference map for an individual that indicates a fall in real income between 1972 and 1981.

(d) What kind of adjustments could individuals make to minimize or avoid such a loss in real living standards? (The CPI assumed fixed-quantity weights and thus overstated the proportion of 1981 income spent on energy.)

(e) Relative energy prices started declining in 1982. In the first quarter of 1986, the drop in the absolute price of oil was so rapid as to reduce the total CPI. How does this relative decline affect the slope, and the absolute decline, the position, of the budget line?

2. Extend the analysis and use the same graph in Exercise 3 to show the derivation of a demand curve for clothing by proceeding as follows (assume that "clothing" stands for "everything consumed except food").
   (a) Change the price of clothing so that a budget line with the same food intercept (35) is tangent to each of the indifference curves I, II, and III. Extend the X-axis as necessary.
   The X-intercepts for budget lines tangent to indifference curves I, II, and III are approximately ______________________________, respectively.
   The prices of clothing represented by the budget lines are approximately ______________________________, respectively.
   (b) Draw the price-consumption line on the graph.
   (c) Describe how the information on the price-consumption line can be used to derive a demand curve for clothing.

Answers to the Exercises

1. (a) Intercepts on the graph are 30 days of skiing and 50 rounds of golf.
   (b) The combination of 20 units of each activity is unattainable; it is outside the budget line.
   (c) Intercepts would now be at 45 days of skiing and 75 rounds of golf.

2. (a) Intercept for golf would not change; skiing intercept would change to 30 days.
   (b) Skiing intercepts would remain at 30 days; golf intercept would shift to 50 rounds.
   (c) The intercepts are identical because absolute prices and money income changed in exactly the same proportions (50 percent).

3. (a) Draw a graph from information in the table, as below.
   (b) Draw budget line on the graph, as below.
   (c) $F = 20$; $C = 10$. Given the budget constraint, this is the highest indifference curve attainable.

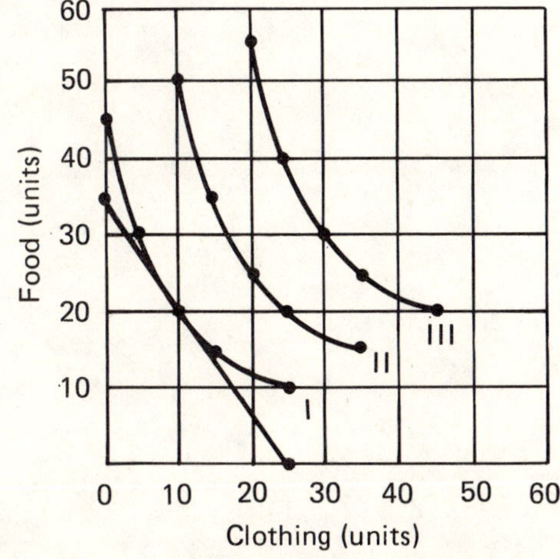

4. (a) The 1920 budget line would intercept the food axis and the "other" axis at 3,667 units; the 1940 line would intersect at 6,000 units for food and 4,468 units for "other."
   (b) The 1940 line is above the 1920 line, so that attainable combinations of all commodities have increased.
   (c) By a flatter slope. The farther right the indifference map on the diagram, the greater the distance between 1920 and 1940 points of tangency.

5. (a) The indifference maps drawn will have curves that are tangent to the budget lines at the price-consumption lines *A* and *B*, respectively.
   (b)

P	Q_A	Q_B	Exp. *A*	Exp. *B*
$6.00	400	600	$1,200	$1,800
$4.00	600	1,000	$1,200	$2,000
$3.00	800	1,300	$1,200	$1,950
$2.40	1,000	1,500	$1,200	$1,800
$2.00	1,200	1,600	$1,200	$1,600

   (c) Unity for *A*; at $2 for *B*

9

The Role of the Firm

Learning Objectives

After completing the material in this chapter, you should be able to

—identify the major differences among single proprietorships, partnerships, and corporations;

—list the advantages of the corporate form of organization;

—distinguish between debt and equity financing;

—understand the role of inputs, or factors of production, in the production process;

—explain the meaning of economic efficiency;

—explain the meaning of opportunity cost, particularly in the context of decision making by the firm;

—distinguish economic profits from other definitions of profits;

—explain how profits provide important signals for the allocation of resources.

Review and Self-Test

Matching Concepts

_______ 1. economic efficiency (in production)

_______ 2. dividends

_______ 3. debt financing

_______ 4. a firm's physical assets comprised of plant, equipment, and inventories

_______ 5. land, labor, and capital

_______ 6. imputed returns to capital and risk taking necessary to keep firm in industry

_______ 7. proprietorship

_______ 8. loss in value of an asset over time

_______ 9. limited liability

_______ 10. imputed costs

(a) real capital

(b) method of raising financial capital by selling bonds or borrowing from financial institutions

(c) firm with one owner responsible for its actions and debts

(d) factors of production

(e) payments to stockholders

(f) depreciation

(g) advantage of a corporation

(h) costs of using factors already owned by a firm

(i) normal profits

(j) achievement of least-cost method of production

Multiple-Choice Questions

1. In the operation of a firm, real capital is
   (a) financing provided by the owners.
   (b) money borrowed from banks to run the firm.
   (c) the outstanding obligations of the firm to others.
   (d) comprised of plant, equipment, and inventories.

2. Which of the following groups of claimants would be the last to have its claims honored in a bankruptcy?
   (a) bondholders
   (b) commercial creditors
   (c) common stockholders
   (d) employees who are owed back wages

3. A major assumption in the economic theory of the firm is that
   (a) decisions within the firm are made by consensus between labor and management.
   (b) regardless of their size, firms are assumed to act as a single consistent decision-making unit.
   (c) every firm behaves in a fundamentally different and unpredictable way.
   (d) objectives of firms depend on the size of the firm.

4. A roundabout process of production is one
   (a) using heavy labor such as roustabouts.
   (b) inherently more inefficient than a direct process.
   (c) using capital goods.
   (d) involving a circular assembly line as in the Volvo plants in Sweden.

5. The difference between economic profits and normal profits is that normal profits
   (a) are always smaller.
   (b) are necessarily larger for all firms.
   (c) are part of opportunity costs, whereas economic profits are returns in excess of opportunity costs.
   (d) take into account monopoly power; economic profits do not.

6. For an owner-manager,
   (a) economic profits will invariably be large because the costs will be low.
   (b) imputed costs of management and capital must be included to estimate economic profits.
   (c) economic and accounting profits will be equal.
   (d) economic profits will invariably exceed accounting profits.

7. Applying the concept of opportunity cost to the firm is difficult
   (a) because it requires imputing certain costs when a resource is not directly hired.
   (b) because most of a firm's costs are monetary costs.
   (c) to the extent that the modern firm borrows money from banks.
   (d) all of the above.

8. The major role of economic profits, as seen in this chapter, is to
   (a) provide income for shareholders.
   (b) provide income for entrepreneurs.
   (c) act as a signal to firms concerning the desirability of devoting additional resources to a particular activity.
   (d) encourage labor to reform the system.

9. "Profits are necessary for the survival of the U.S. textile business." This chapter
   (a) disagrees with this viewpoint entirely.
   (b) accepts this viewpoint but defines the necessary profits as opportunity costs.
   (c) accepts this viewpoint without qualification or clarification.
   (d) would say that this statement is an exaggeration.

10. Which of the following would most likely represent an *imputed cost* for a firm?
    (a) monetary payments to current employees
    (b) interest paid on borrowed funds
    (c) dividends paid to shareholders
    (d) interest that could have been received on money currently invested in inventory

11. Economic theory usually assumes that firms try to maximize profits because
    (a) firms always maximize profits.
    (b) firms ought to maximize profits to be fair to their stockholders.
    (c) use of this simple assumption has frequently led to accurate predictions.
    (d) firms never have other objectives.

12. Depreciation, defined as the loss of value of an asset associated with its use in production,
    (a) is clearly a monetary cost.
    (b) is a function only of wear and tear in use.
    (c) is not an economic cost if the asset has no market value or alternative use.
    (d) does not apply to used equipment.

13. Normal profits refer to
    (a) what all firms, on average, obtain as a return on investment.
    (b) the base used by the tax authorities to levy business taxes.
    (c) the imputed return to capital and risk-taking required to keep owners in the business.
    (d) the level of profits necessary to ensure that the firm covers its day-to-day operating costs.

14. Opportunity costs for a firm should include
    (a) monetary outlays alone.
    (b) imputed costs alone.
    (c) monetary outlays plus imputed costs.
    (d) neither monetary outlays nor imputed costs.

15. "Sunk" costs are
    (a) the costs to a firm of using its own money capital.
    (b) costs incurred in the past that involve no current opportunity cost.
    (c) costs that must be accounted for only if the firm is currently producing output.
    (d) all of the above.

16. An *economically efficient* method of production is one that
    (a) uses the smallest number of resource inputs.
    (b) necessarily involves the use of roundabout methods of production.
    (c) costs the least.
    (d) cannot also be technologically efficient.

17. Interest on invested capital should be included as an opportunity cost (Exercises 1 and 2) because
    (a) the money could have earned interest if left in the bank.
    (b) it represents the cost of funds invested in the business.
    (c) it represents the cost of the next best alternative use of those funds.
    (d) all of the above.

18. The imputed cost of a factor of production
    (a) is not part of the economic cost of producing something.
    (b) is the value of a purchased input.
    (c) should not be included as a component of opportunity cost.
    (d) is the amount the factor of production could earn in its next best use.

Self-Test Key

Matching Concepts: 1–j; 2–e; 3–b; 4–a; 5–d; 6–i; 7–c; 8–f; 9–g; 10–h

Multiple-Choice Questions: 1–d; 2–c; 3–b; 4–c; 5–c; 6–b; 7–a; 8–c; 9–b; 10–d; 11–c; 12–c; 13–c; 14–c; 15–b; 16–c; 17–d; 18–d

Exercises

1. After five years of working, Mary Kaufman left a $25,000 job to start her own business with the use of $20,000 she had saved. She charged the business with $15,000 a year for her services but made no allowance for the 10 percent she might have earned on her savings in an investment of equal risk. In 1986 her accounting profits were $10,000. Had the business been economically profitable to that point? What needs to be known to decide whether it is economically profitable to continue the business?

2. The exhibit below represents an annual income statement for Harry's Hardware Store. Harry worked full time at the store. He had used $25,000 of his savings to furnish and stock the store (included in costs). He had recently been offered a $20,000 annual salary to work in another hardware store.

Annual Income Statement

Revenues		Costs	
Sales	$90,000	Wholesale purchases	$60,000
Increase in inventory	5,000	Store supplies	2,000
		Labor costs (hired)	10,000
		Utilities	1,000
		Rent	5,000
		Depreciation on fixtures	2,000
Total revenues	$95,000	Total costs	$80,000

(a) Calculate the accounting profits for Harry's Hardware Store.

(b) What are some *imputed* costs that Harry should include in estimating the total costs of owning his business?

(c) Assume an interest rate of 10 percent. What are the total costs of Harry's owning this business?

(d) Calculate his *economic* profits.

3. Assume that there are two methods for making 100 widgets per month with capital and labor requirements as shown below. Assume that the cost of these factors of production are $5 per unit of labor and $20 per unit of capital.

	Method A	Method B
Capital	10 units	5 units
Labor	50 units	100 units

(a) Can you determine which method (A or B) is technologically efficient? Explain.

(b) Can you distinguish the economically efficient method? Explain.

(c) Suppose the price of capital increased to $50 per unit. Would this change your answer to (b)?

4. (a) A student at Universal University had the following budget for the college year (the alternative was a job away from home with an annual wage that was $12,000 greater than the summer earnings consistent with college attendance):

Tuition, fees, books—$7,000; dormitory—$1,500; board—$2,000; car expense—$1,200; all other expenses—$1,200

Estimate the economic costs for this student of attending Universal University. (Students might well consider the costs they are incurring in their particular circumstances.)

(b) In a 5-course, 40-meetings-a-semester arrangement, about 400 class meetings were held per year. What is the opportunity cost of attending a single class meeting after college comittment has been made and all fees paid? What would be the cost of not attending a particular lecture?

5. (a) For $10,000 a firm purchases a machine with an estimated 10 years of economic life and zero salvage value. What is the straight-line depreciation per year?

(b) At the end of five years; this firm finds the machine has a market value of only $1000, which is expected to decline to zero after the five remaining years. What is the economically relevant depreciation per year now?

6. Arrange the following items and use the information below to obtain (a) net profit before income taxes; (b) economic profit before taxes; and (c) economic profit after income taxes. (*Hint:* See Table 9-1 in the text.)
   1. Revenue from sale of goods = $5 million
   2. Tax rate = 50 percent of net profit before tax
   3. Depreciation = $500,000
   4. Salaries, cost of raw materials = $3 million
   5. Required return to capital and risk-taking = $500,000

(a) Net profit before income tax ________________

(b) Economic profit before tax ________________

(c) Economic profit after tax ________________

Short Problems

1. Skiing at Whiteface

In fall 1986, Don Napier, who was an avid skier, was looking forward to the coming ski season at Whiteface Mountain near Lake Placid, New York. He obtained a lift fee schedule and was trying to determine whether to purchase a season pass for $350. The pass would allow unlimited skiing at no additional daily charge for lift tickets. The alternative was to purchase lift tickets on a daily basis, at an average price of $20 per day. (Multiple-day packages were also available, yet were not considered because they had to be used on consecutive days.) Don attended Clarkson University, which was about a two-hour drive from Whiteface.

(a) Don was unsure of how many days he would actually get to ski. Should he purchase a season pass if he expects to ski 20 days? What if he expects to ski only 15 days?

(b) Suppose he has purchased a season pass and is considering skiing on a particular day during the season. What would be the opportunity cost of a day of skiing? Should the cost of the season pass enter into the decision to ski on a particular day?

(c) Assume that Don had decided against purchasing the season pass. On a particular day, he and a friend decide to ski at Whiteface and both purchase an all-day pass for $20 each. After a few runs, Don is tired and cold and wants to sit in the lodge for the rest of the day. His friend suggests that this would be just like throwing $20 "down the drain" and that Don should continue skiing. Is Don's decision sensible? Explain.

2. The Case of the Economically Efficient Chinese Airstrip
The name off this case comes from the building of airstrips in China during World War II using extremely primitive methods—baskets, shovels, and other hand tools. The following table outlines the requirements for three production methods for an airstrip: the manual method (A); a method using trucks and bulldozers (B); and a highly sophisticated method involving heavy earthmovers, pavers, and other machinery (C). The factors used are designated as *M* (capital—machinery), *T* (capital—simple tools), *U* (unskilled labor), and *S* (skilled labor). Capital is measured in arbitrary units that take time into account; labor is measured in work days. Units of factors required are given in the columns headed "Req." Prices are given for three types of economy: the underdeveloped economy under war conditions; the developing nation; and the industrialized nation. Your job is to uncover the economically efficient method for each economy.
(a) Fill in the worksheet.
(b) By filling in the worksheet, you can ascertain the economically efficient method for each economy:
Underdeveloped (war) ____________
Developing nation ____________
Industrial nation ____________

Cost Analysis Worksheet

Factor	Price of factor	Method A Req.	Method A *TC*	Method B Req.	Method B *TC*	Method C Req.	Method C *TC*
Underdeveloped (war)							
M	$5,000	0	______	20	______	100	______
T	5	2,000	______	500	______	200	______
U	1	100,000	______	20,000	______	2,000	______
S	50	0	______	200	______	1,000	______
Total cost			______		______		______
Developing nation							
M	300	0	______	50	______	100	______
T	5	2,000	______	500	______	200	______
U	1	100,000	______	20,000	______	2,000	______
S	15	0	______	200	______	1,000	______
Total cost			______		______		______
Industrial nation							
M	100	0	______	20	______	100	______
T	5	2,000	______	500	______	200	______
U	25	100,000	______	20,000	______	2,000	______
S	50	0	______	200	______	1,000	______
Total cost			______		______		______

Answers to the Exercises

1. No, she would have been $2,000 better off to this point by working and investing separately. This is past history and could be expected in starting a business. Prospective profits must be estimated; current alternatives are what count—can she get $25,000 in the old (or another) job? Can she sell business assets for $20,000 and reasonably expect a $2,000 return? Will sales increase next year and tend to greater future profits?

2. (a) $15,000
   (b) He should include imputed costs for (1) annual interest on $25,000 investment (assuming he could recover it); and (2) $20,000 opportunity cost for his own salary.
   (c) Total costs would be accounting costs of $80,000 plus interest of $2,500 and $20,000 salary.
   (d) A *loss* of $7,500 is indicated for the past year (but it is the firm's prospective profitability that should determine his decision to work for someone else).

3. (a) Both could be technologically efficient. A is capital intensive; B is labor intensive.
   (b) Method A is economically efficient. Method A costs $450; B costs $600.
   (c) Yes. The two methods each cost $750, so they are equally efficient from an economic standpoint.

4. (a) $19,000 tuition and earnings forgone. (Dormitory and travel costs could be appropriate for students whose alternative was to live at home.)
   (b) Opportunity cost of attendance would involve no dollars and would simply be the utility of alternative activity, such as recreation, sleep, studying for another course, and so on. Opportunity cost of nonattendance would be knowledge forgone (or ultimately attempts to rectify this deficit by further study) or conceivably having to make up for failed courses.

5. (a) $1,000
   (b) $200, the amount of market value given up by using machine one more year

6. | | | |
|---|---|---|
| Revenue from sales | = $ 5.0 | million |
| less salaries, and so on | = $ 3.0 | million |
| less depreciation | = $ 0.5 | million |
| Net "profit" before tax | = $ 1.5 | million Answer (a) |
| less cost of capital | = $ 0.5 | million |
| Economic profit | = $ 1.0 | million Answer (b) |
| less taxes | = $ 0.75 | million (0.5 times $1.5 million) |
| Economic profit after tax | = $ 0.25 | million Answer (c) |

10

Production and Cost in the Short Run

Learning Objectives

After studying the material in this chapter, you should be able to

—explain how the different time horizons (short, long, and very long run) affect decision making by firms;

—explain the hypothesis of diminishing marginal returns;

—show how the marginal and average product curves and marginal and average cost curves are related;

—relate the production function to the cost concepts;

—explain the economic definitions of capacity and excess capacity.

Review and Self-Test

Matching Concepts

_______ 1. short run

_______ 2. hypothesis of eventual decreases in marginal product as units of a variable input are used with fixed inputs

_______ 3. very long run

_______ 4. total fixed cost

_______ 5. inputs whose quantities may be altered in the short run

_______ 6. production function

_______ 7. increase in total cost when output increases by one unit

_______ 8. variable costs

_______ 9. marginal product

_______ 10. level of output at which short-run average total costs are minimum

_______ 11. cost curve that always declines with more output

_______ 12. period of time in which all inputs can be varied in quantity, but basic technology of production is unchanged

(a) marginal cost

(b) change in total product with an increase of one unit of a variable input

(c) plant capacity

(d) period of time over which some inputs cannot be varied in quantity

(e) long run

(f) set of all technologically efficient combinations of inputs and outputs for a specified commodity

(g) average fixed cost

(h) cost curve that is horizontal as output increases

(i) "law" of diminishing returns

(j) costs whose total changes with output

(k) variable inputs

(l) period during which technology available to firm changes

Multiple-Choice Questions

1. The production function relates
   (a) cost to inputs.
   (b) cost to output.
   (c) wages to profits.
   (d) outputs to inputs.

2. The short run is a period of time
   (a) long enough for a firm to change its fixed inputs.
   (b) of insufficient length to vary its output.
   (c) in which at least one input is fixed.
   (d) in which all factors of production may be varied.

3. Short-run average total costs eventually rise because of
   (a) rising overhead costs.
   (b) rising factor prices.
   (c) diminishing marginal and average productivity of the variable input(s).
   (d) reduced incentives to work in large plants.

4. The hypothesis of diminishing returns
   (a) predicts that marginal products will eventually decline.
   (b) refers to reductions in total product that result as additional variable inputs are employed.
   (c) makes intuitive sense but has not often been confirmed empirically.
   (d) applies only when all inputs are used in fixed proportions.

5. The marginal or incremental cost associated with adding another rider on a weekend car trip home from college
   (a) is always the same as the average total cost.
   (b) is always equal to zero once the trip is planned.
   (c) is small but positive, due to additional variable costs associated with each passenger.
   (d) declines continuously, due to "spreading" the overhead costs.

6. Long-run decisions
   (a) do not affect short-run decisions.
   (b) can consider all factors variable in quantity.
   (c) are not very important because the long run is a succession of short runs.
   (d) are taken with fewer alternatives open than in the case of short-run decisions.

Use the table below to answer questions 7 through 9:

Units of capital	Units of labor	Output
2	0	0
2	1	20
2	2	50
2	3	75
2	4	80

7. The time period these data refer to is
   (a) the short run.
   (b) the long run.
   (c) the very long run.
   (d) indeterminate from the data provided.

8. The marginal product of the second unit of the variable factor is
   (a) 20.
   (b) 25.
   (c) 30.
   (d) 50.

9. The point of diminishing marginal returns commences with the addition of which unit of labor?
   (a) first
   (b) second
   (c) third
   (d) fourth

10. Which of the following statements is true?
   (a) There will be a different set of marginal, average, and total product curves for each specified quantity of a fixed input.
   (b) Marginal and average products are equal at the minimum marginal product.
   (c) Average product is total product per unit of fixed input.
   (d) Marginal product is total product per unit of variable input.

11. Which of the following necessarily declines continuously in the short run as output increases?
   (a) marginal cost
   (b) average fixed cost
   (c) average variable cost
   (d) total fixed cost

12. When average total cost is declining as output increases, marginal cost must be
   (a) declining.
   (b) above average total cost.
   (c) below average total cost.
   (d) rising.

13. Marginal cost
   (a) is the increase in fixed costs that results from increasing production by one unit.
   (b) equals average total cost multiplied by the number of units produced.
   (c) can be calculated by multiplying average product by the variable factor's cost.
   (d) is the change in total cost associated with a small change in output.

14. A firm's short-run average variable cost curve is at its minimum at the quantity where
   (a) average product is at its maximum.
   (b) fixed costs are at their lowest level.
   (c) marginal costs have just begun to rise.
   (d) average total costs are at their maximum level.

15. At any particular level of output, a firm's total costs equal
   (a) average total cost minus average variable cost.
   (b) average variable cost times output.
   (c) average total cost times output.
   (d) average imputed cost plus average variable cost.

16. Plant capacity is
   (a) the output at which short-run average total costs are at their minimum level.
   (b) the maximum output possible for a firm.
   (c) where short-run average total costs are at their maximum level.
   (d) where marginal costs begin to rise.

17. Average total cost is
    (a) total fixed cost plus total variable cost divided by the number of units of output.
    (b) total fixed cost minus total variable cost.
    (c) total cost divided by the number of units of the fixed factor.
    (d) always constant if fixed cost is constant.

18. Total cost is $30 at 10 units of output and $32 at 11 units of output. In this range of output, marginal cost is
    (a) equal to average total cost.
    (b) greater than average total cost.
    (c) less than average total cost.
    (d) indeterminate with the information provided.

19. If the difference between average total cost (ATC) and average variable cost (AVC) at 100 units of output is $1.00, then at 200 units of output the difference between ATC and AVC must be
    (a) $2.00.
    (b) $1.00.
    (c) $.50.
    (d) indeterminate from the information provided.

20. The short-run average variable cost curve is often drawn U-shaped to reflect the assumption of
    (a) a negatively sloped demand curve.
    (b) increasing followed by diminishing average productivity.
    (c) constantly changing technology.
    (d) rising fixed costs over the short-run period.

Self-Test Key

Matching Concepts: 1–d; 2–i; 3–l; 4–h; 5–k; 6–f; 7–a; 8–j; 9–b; 10–c; 11–g; 12–e

Multiple-Choice Questions: 1–d; 2–c; 3–c; 4–a; 5–c; 6–b; 7–a; 8–c; 9–c; 10–a; 11–b; 12–c; 13–d; 14–a; 15–c; 16–a; 17–a; 18–c; 19–c; 20–b

Exercises

1. The table below relates the quantities of a variable input to units of output.
   (a) Calculate the average and marginal products to complete the table below.

Variable input	Output	Average product	Marginal product
0	0		
1	10	_____	_____
2	30	_____	_____
3	60	_____	_____
4	80	_____	_____
5	90	_____	_____
6	96	_____	_____

   (b) Graph the marginal and average products (remember to plot the marginal product at midpoint of quantity interval).

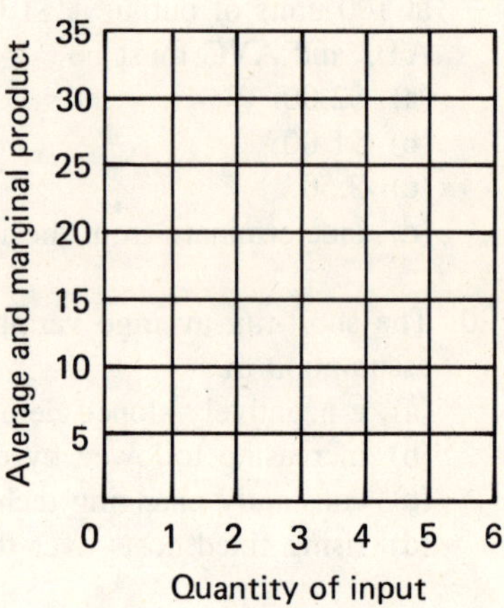

2. This problem is designed to illustrate the relationship between productivity and cost with very few figures. Take $30 as the costs associated with the fixed factors and $10 as the cost of each variable unit. Consider, for example, an agricultural situation with the variable factors being seed, labor, fertilizer, and equipment of various forms and the fixed factor as land.
   (a) Complete the table below.

Units of variable factor	Total product	Marginal product	Average product	Total cost	Marginal cost	Average cost
0	0		0	$30		∞
		2			$5	
1	2		2	$40		$20
		_____			_____	
2	5		_____	_____		_____
		_____			_____	
3	7		_____	_____		_____
		_____			_____	
4	8		_____	_____		_____
		_____			_____	
5	8		_____	_____		_____

(b) Show the total, average, and marginal product graphically on diagram (a) and the three cost curves on graph (b). To emphasize the inverse relationship between product and cost, number each point plotted with the number of variable factor units used. Remember that these "marginal" points are plotted at the midpoints of the intervals on the horizontal axis.

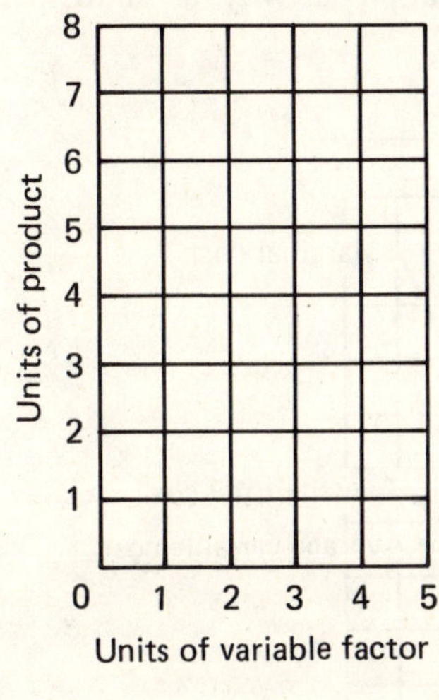

(a)

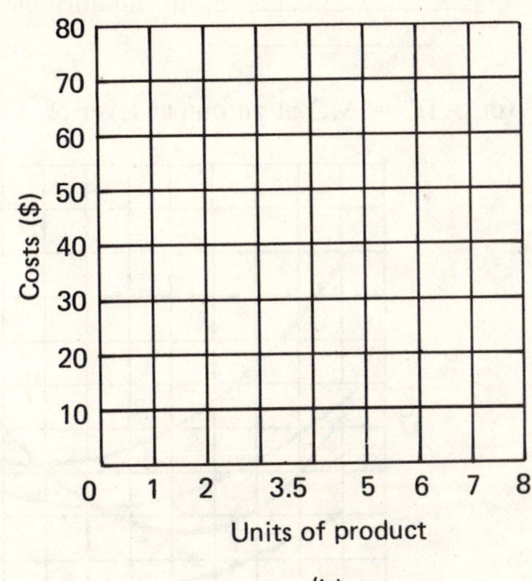

(b)

3. Marginal costs for a firm are shown below. Assume fixed costs are $100.
   (a) Calculate total costs and average total costs and complete the table.

Output	Marginal costs	Total costs	Average total costs
0		______	______
	$ 50		
1		______	______
	40		
2		______	______
	50		
3		______	______
	100		
4		______	______
	200		
5		______	______

(b) Plot the average total cost curve on the graph.
(c) What is the plant capacity? ____________

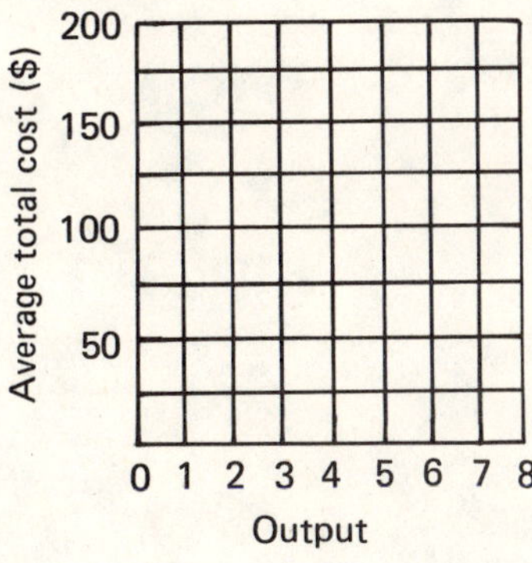

4. Given the cost curves of a hypothetical firm shown below, answer the following questions:
   (a) The capacity of the firm occurs at an output of ______________.
   (b) The effect of diminishing marginal productivity occurs at an output level of ______________; of diminishing average productivity at an output of ______________.
   (c) ATC = MC at an output level of ______________.

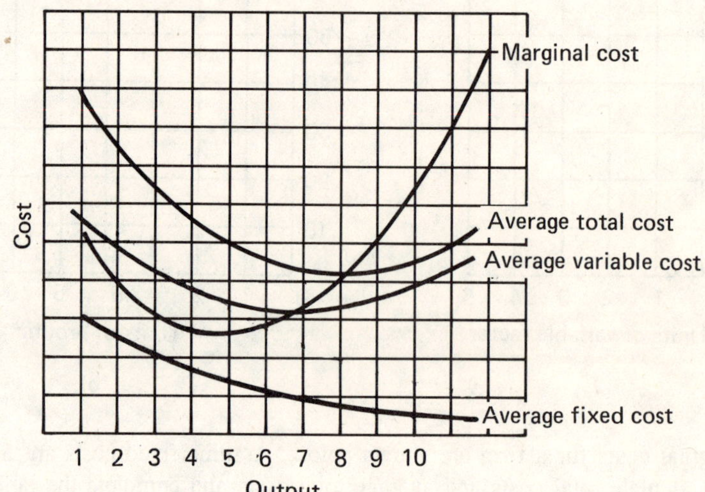

5. Assume you are in the business of producing a commodity for which the short-run cost function is

$$TC = 30 + 3Q + Q^2$$

where Q is output of the commodity and TC represents total costs.

(a) Fill in the following table:

Q	Total variable costs	Total fixed costs	Total costs	Average total costs	Marginal costs
0	______	______	______	______	
					______
1	______	______	______	______	
					______
2	______	______	______	______	
					______
3	______	______	______	______	
					______
4	______	______	______	______	
					______
5	______	______	______	______	
					______
6	______	______	______	______	
					______
7	______	______	______	______	
					______
8	______	______	______	______	
					______
9	______	______	______	______	
					______
10	______	______	______	______	

(b) At what output level are average total costs (*ATC*) at a minimum?

(c) What is the marginal cost at this output?

(d) Assume total fixed costs were zero instead of 30. Would this affect the marginal costs? Explain.

(e) Explain why *ATC* declines to a minimum and then rises.

Short Problems

1. Use the output information in Exercise 1 to determine short-run costs. Assume fixed costs of $100 and variable input costs of $50 per unit. Determine total costs, average total costs, and marginal costs. Draw a graph and plot the marginal and average total cost curves. (*Hint:* Use outputs of 0, 10, 30, 60, 80, 90, 96, as in the exercise.)

2. The precise answers cited for (b) and (c) of Exercise 5 can be determined with calculus. The average total cost (ATC) is obtained by dividing the cost function by Q to get $30/Q + 3 + Q$. To get the minimum ATC take the first derivative and set it equal to zero. The marginal cost is the first derivative of TC or $3 + 2Q$. Note why MCs are plotted at midpoints: At an output of 5 the MC is _______; at an output of 6 the MC is _______. The difference of 14 in the total cost of six and five units is the level of MC being incurred at a production rate of 5.5. Check this with your answers to Exercise 5, (b) and (c).

3. This short problem is similar to Exercise 1 but slightly more advanced. We start with a production function and develop the various output relationships through mathematical concepts.

   Suppose that a small manufacturing plant has just been completed and its production function is

   $$Q = 10L + 6L^2 - L^3$$

   where Q stands for the quantity of hammers produced per day and L refers to the units of labor employed. Assume also that there are two units of a fixed factor of production, such as assembly equipment.

   The total product that results from the utilization of a certain number of labor units can be determined by plugging that number of labor units into the production function and solving for Q.

   The average product for any particular quantity of labor can be determined by dividing the production function by L, and solving for AP. That is,

   $$AP = \frac{Q}{L} = \frac{10L + 6L^2 - L^3}{L} = 10 + 6L - L^2$$

   The marginal product for any particular quantity of labor refers to the incremental change in output as the quantity of labor is changed. Thus MP is the first derivative of the production function with respect to the variable factor. In this particular example,

   $$MP = \frac{dQ}{dL} = 10 + 12L - 3L^2$$

   The marginal product for a particular amount of L can be determined by plugging that L into the MP formula. [Actually, the MP obtained by using the derivative is the continuous marginal product that is being added for minuscule changes in inputs (much less than a full-unit change), so that the marginal product estimated by taking a derivative will deviate somewhat from the differences in total product when one whole unit of input is added.]

Questions

(a) What is the total output when three units of labor are employed?

(b) What is the marginal product when two units of labor are employed?

(c) What happens to the marginal product of labor as additional units are employed? Calculate MP at $Q_L = 3$, 4, and 5 to verify your answer.

(d) What is the average product if four units of labor are employed?

(e) Can you determine the point of diminishing average productivity? (*Hint:* Recall that $MP = AP$ where AP is at its maximum.)

(f) The point where MP is at its maximum can be determined by setting the first derivative of the MP equal to zero. At what quantity of labor employed does this occur?

4. Suppose that you were able to determine the following short-run total cost function, where Q refers to the number of bicycles produced per day in a small plant. This cost function is based, of course, on a certain production function and costs per unit for the fixed and variable factors.

$$TC = 1000 + 10Q - 6Q^2 + Q^3$$

(a) What are the total fixed costs if 10 bicycles are produced? What if 20 were produced?

(b) Compute the average fixed costs if 10 are produced. What if 20 were produced?

(c) How much would the average variable costs be if output were 10 bicycles per day?

(d) What would the marginal cost be if output were 10 bicycles per day? (*Hint: MC* can be estimated by taking the first derivative of the total cost function with respect to Q.)

(e) How much are average total costs at an output rate of 10 bicycles per day?

Answers to the Exercises

1. (a) Average product: 10, 15, 20, 20, 18, 16
   Marginal product: 10, 20, 30, 20, 10, 6

   (b)

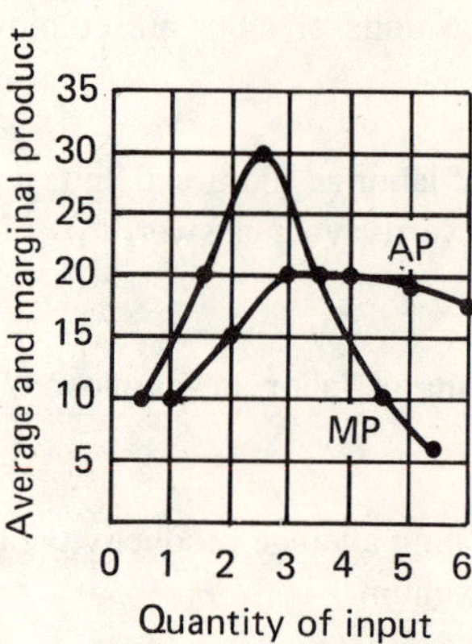

2. (a) Blanks should be filled as follows:

MP	*AP*	*TC*	*MC*	*AC*
3	2.5	$50.00	$ 3.33	$10.00
2	2.3	60.00	5.00	8.57
1	2.0	70.00	10.00	8.75
0	1.6	80.00	∞	10.00

   (b)

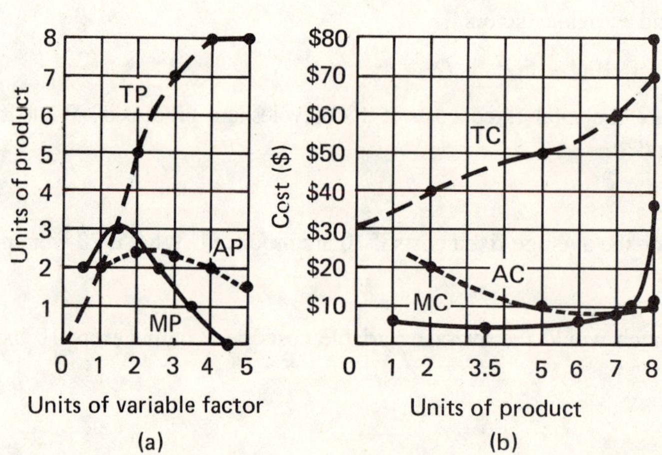

3. (a) Total costs: 100, 150, 190, 240, 340, 540
   (b) Average total costs: ∞, 150, 95, 80, 85, 108
   (c) Plant capacity is at minimum ATC; output = 3

4. (a) 8 (b) 4 to 5; 6 to 7 (c) 8

5. (a)

Q	*TVC*	*TFC*	*TC*	*ATC*	*MC*
0	0	30	30	—	
1	4	30	34	34	4
2	10	30	40	20	6
3	18	30	48	16	8
4	28	30	58	14.5	10
5	40	30	70	14	12
6	54	30	84	14	14
7	70	30	100	14.3	16
8	88	30	118	14.8	18
9	108	30	138	15.3	20
10	130	30	160	16	22

(b) A tolerable estimate is 5.5, the midpoint of the output range of 5 to 6 (5.477 by minimizing *ATC* function).* Either 5 or 6 are correct if only integer quantities are possible.

(c) 14 (13.954 by taking first derivative of TC function at 5.477)*

(d) No, marginal costs depend only on variable costs.

(e) Average fixed costs (*AFC*) decline at a decreasing rate as output increases, causing *ATC* to fall. The steady rise in *AVC* exceeds this decline in *AFC* after an output of about 5.5 units, so *ATC* must then rise.

*For these more precise answers to (b) and (c), go to Short problem 2.

11

Production and Cost in the Long and Very Long Run

Learning Objectives

After studying the material in this chapter, you should be able to

—distinguish the long run and very long run from the short run;

—list the sources of economies of scale and diseconomies of scale;

—describe the possible shapes of the long-run average cost curve;

—understand the distinction between invention and innovation;

—recognize causes of change in the rate of productivity growth.

Review and Self-Test

Matching Concepts

_______ 1. $MP_K/MP_L = P_K/P_L$

_______ 2. principle of substitution

_______ 3. MP_K/MP_L

_______ 4. P_K/P_L

_______ 5. long-run average cost curve

_______ 6. cause of shift of cost curves

_______ 7. new production techniques, innovative products, improved quality of inputs

_______ 8. shift in demand from manufactured goods to services

_______ 9. introduction of an invention into use

_______ 10. productivity

(a) ratio of contribution to output of last units of factors

(b) envelope curve for *SRAC*s

(c) cause of decline in productivity level of an economy

(d) rise in factor prices

(e) innovation

(f) output produced per unit of input

(g) condition for cost minimization

(h) changes affecting production functions in very long run

(i) relative prices of factors of production

(j) proposition that changes in relative factor prices change methods of production

Multiple-Choice Questions

1. The long-run average cost curve
   (a) shows total output related to total input.
   (b) assumes constant factor proportions throughout.
   (c) reflects the least-cost method for producing each output level.
   (d) continuously decreases because of the "law" of diminishing returns.

2. Constant long-run average costs for a firm mean that
   (a) there are greater advantages to small- than to large-scale plants.
   (b) an unlimited amount of output will be produced.
   (c) any scale of production is as cheap per unit as any other.
   (d) no additional inputs are being used.

3. Decreasing average costs for a firm as it expands plant size and output
   (a) result from decreasing returns to scale.
   (b) result usually from the effects of increased mechanization and specialization.
   (c) result from the increased complexity and confusion of rapid expansion.
   (d) are very rare and often caused by exogenous events.

4. If the marginal product of capital is six times that of labor and the price of capital is three times that of labor, for costs to be minimized,
   (a) capital should be substituted for labor.
   (b) labor should be substituted for capital.
   (c) the price of capital will fall.
   (d) twice as much capital as labor should be employed.

5. The long-run average cost curve is determined by
   (a) long-run demand.
   (b) long-run supply.
   (c) population growth and inflation.
   (d) technology and input prices.

6. If for a given combination of labor and capital, the ratio of their marginal productivities is 2:1, then for cost minimization
   (a) the ratio of their prices must be 2:1.
   (b) two units of labor are combined with one unit of capital.
   (c) the ratio of their prices must be 1:2.
   (d) there is more capital being used than labor.

7. A rise in labor costs relative to capital costs in an industry, *ceteris paribus,* will
   (a) lead to replacement of some workers by machines where possible.
   (b) cause the industry to be unprofitable.
   (c) necessarily increase long-run costs.
   (d) always be offset by rising labor productivity.

8. A firm with long-run increasing returns that chooses to expand output should do so by
   (a) substituting labor for capital.
   (b) replication.
   (c) building smaller plants.
   (d) building a larger plant.

9. A major source of the large increase in the U.S. standard of living in this century has been
   (a) population growth.
   (b) advertising.
   (c) an increase in output per unit of labor input.
   (d) increases in production keeping pace with population growth.

10. Innovation can be defined as
    (a) any particularly important invention.
    (b) an invention whose source is endogenous to the firm.
    (c) a change in output per unit of input.
    (d) the initial introduction of a significant change in a production function.

11. Increasing productivity in the very long run can be attributed to all but which one of the following causes?
    (a) declining average fixed costs
    (b) invention and innovation
    (c) improved quality of labor
    (d) improved quality of machines and materials

12. The lowering of the rate of growth in labor productivity during the 1970s and early 1980s was associated with all but which of the following?
    (a) a lower proportion of firms' resources spent on research and development
    (b) greatly increased energy prices
    (c) a reduced proportion of the population with college degrees
    (d) chronic operation of the economy at below full capacity

13. Which of the following is a measure of productivity?
    (a) bushels of corn per acre
    (b) production of wheat
    (c) labor hours
    (d) tons of steel

14. The very long run
    (a) is necessarily longer than the long run.
    (b) always involves a greater range of output than the short run or long run.
    (c) applies to a period in which new production methods are introduced.
    (d) extends long-run analysis to higher production levels.

15. The decision of a firm to increase its research and development budget is primarily a question for
    (a) very short-run analysis.
    (b) short-run analysis.
    (c) long-run analysis.
    (d) very long-run analysis.

16. Economies of scope
    (a) are identical with economies of scale.
    (b) refer to efficiencies achievable with greater size in such functions as marketing and finance.
    (c) apply only to single-product firms.
    (d) are unrelated to the size of the firm.

Appendix

17. If the marginal rate of substitution is –2 at a point on an isoquant involving two factors,
    (a) the ratio of factor prices is +1:2.
    (b) the ratio of marginal productivities is –1:2.
    (c) the ratio of marginal productivities is –2.
    (d) one factor of production has negative marginal productivity.

18. An isocost line for two factors C and L (their respective prices are P_C and P_L) could have which of the following equations?
    (a) $LC = \$100$
    (b) $\$100 = P_C + P_L$
    (c) $\$100 = P_L L + P_C C$
    (d) $\$100 = P_L P_C$

19. If two factors C and L are graphed in the same unit scale with C on the vertical axis, and an isocost line has a slope = –2, then
    (a) $P_L = 2P_C$.
    (b) $P_C/P_L = 2$.
    (c) $C = 2L$.
    (d) $L = 2C$.

20. At the point of tangency of the isocost line in question 19 with an isoquant,
    (a) the desired factor combination has $2C$ for each L.
    (b) the marginal product of labor is twice that of capital.
    (c) the desired factor combination has $2L$ for each C.
    (d) the marginal product of capital is twice that of labor.

Self-Test Key

Matching Concepts: 1–g; 2–j; 3–a; 4–i; 5–b; 6–d; 7–h; 8–c; 9–e; 10–f

Multiple-Choice Questions: 1–c; 2–c; 3–b; 4–a; 5–d; 6–a; 7–a; 8–d; 9–c; 10–d; 11–a; 12–c; 13–a; 14–c; 15–d; 16–b; 17–c; 18–c; 19–a; 20–b

Exercises

1. Below is a table showing hypothetical costs for a firm as it expands output and plant size. Complete the table by computing total and average costs.

Output (units)	100,000	200,000	300,000	400,000	500,000
Materials	$ 50,000	$100,000	$150,000	$200,000	$250,000
Labor	$100,000	$180,000	$260,000	$340,000	$440,000
Capital (interest and depreciation)	$ 50,000	$ 90,000	$130,000	$170,000	$220,000
Total cost	______	______	______	______	______
Average cost	______	______	______	______	______

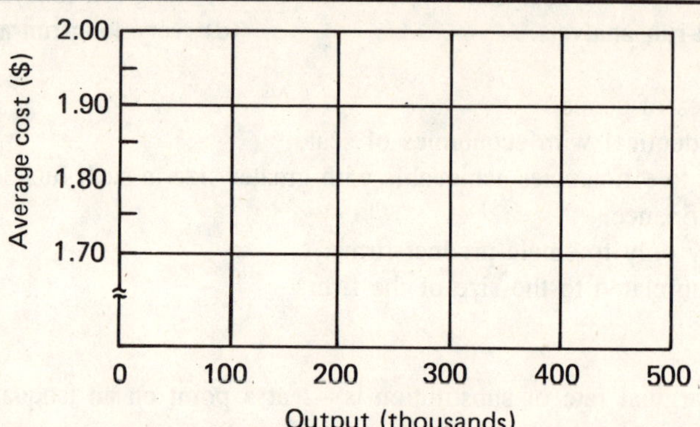

(a) Calculate the average cost for each level of output above and plot it on the graph.
(b) Returns to scale continue until what output is reached?
(c) Would you say that there seems to be substitution occurring or not? Explain.
(d) Judging from these figures, what would you recommend that this firm do in the long run to produce output of 800,000 units?

2. Assume that because of indivisibilities only two sizes of plant are available to a firm. Each plant type can produce 500,000 units per year. Plant A would have annual total costs equal to $500,000 + 5Q$, and plant B would have total costs equal to $1,000,000 + 3Q$, where Q is quantity produced. Draw *LRAC*, i.e., the lowest average cost available for each output with plant size variable.

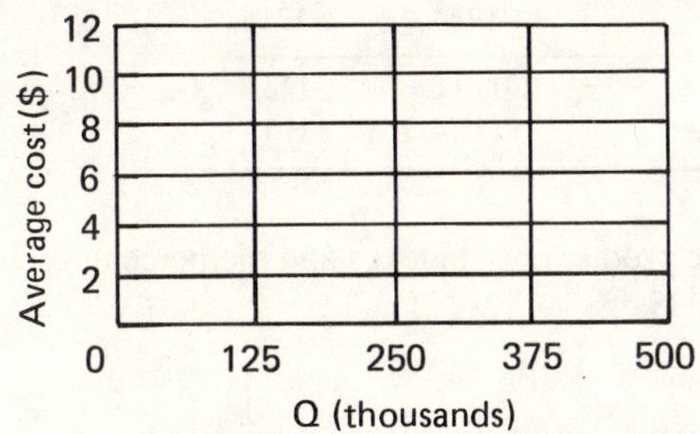

Which plant would be selected if sales were expected to be 125,000? ________
Which plant if expected sales were 375,000 units?________________

3. At the beginning of some time period, it is observed that a firm producing 1,000 bottles of wine per month uses the following inputs of capital (K) and labor (L) per month: $K = 5$ units and $L = 100$ units. The price of capital is $20 and the price of labor is $4 per unit.

As the firm increases its output over a period of time, the following changes in the use of capital and labor are observed:

Output per month	K	L
2,000	10	180
4,000	18	300
6,000	25	400
8,000	40	720
10,000	60	1,000

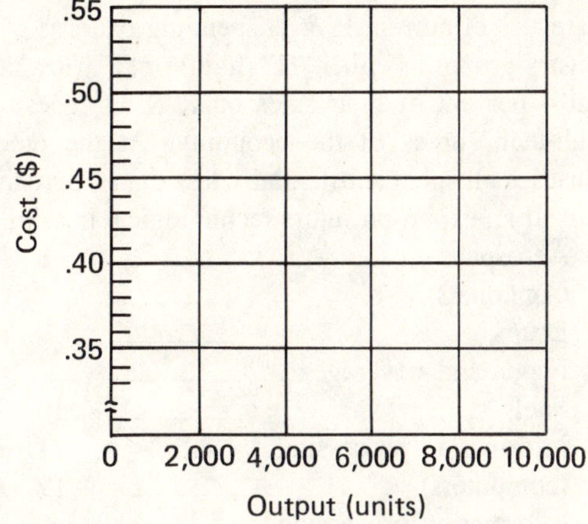

(a) Calculate and graph the long-run average cost curve. (Ignore the cost of materials which are assumed proportional to output, so they affect the level but not the shape of the curve.)
(b) At what output level do increasing returns come to an end?

4. Table 11-1 in the text showed productivity increases in the United States from 1950 to 1984. The underlying indexes for outputs (output originating in the business sector in 1972 dollars) and inputs (hours of all persons in the sector) showed the following values (1977 = 100) for 1984 and 1985. Data are from the 1986 *Economic Report of the President*.

	1984	1985
Index of output	119.0	122.3
Index of hours worked	113.4	116.1

(a) Calculate the productivity indexes and the percentage change in productivity for 1984 and 1985.

(b) How does this change compare with the annual rates of change in Table 11-1?

5. In its R & D scoreboard for 1983, *Business Week* reported on the research and development expenditures of 776 companies with sales of at least $35 million that spend at least $1 million or 1 percent of their sales on R & D. As a share of the U.S. gross national product, R & D appeared to be turning upward in 1983. Figures rose from 2.2 percent in 1977 to 2.4 percent in 1981 and 2.7 percent in 1982. Test your awareness of current R & D spending patterns by designating each of the following industry groups as either "H" (high) or "L" (low). The high R & D groups all spent at least 4 percent of their sales on R & D. These industries are often referred to as "high-tech" areas of the economy. At the other extreme, the five low R & D industries all spent substantially less than 1 percent of their sales on R & D. Consider yourself an expert on future technological possibilities if you miss no more than one.

1. Aerospace ______
2. Containers ______
3. Drugs ______
4. Foods and beverages ______
5. Fuels ______
6. Information processing (computers) ______
7. Information processing (office equipment) ______
8. Information processing (peripherals, services) ______
9. Leisure (including photography) ______
10. Semiconductors ______
11. Steel ______
12. Tires, rubber ______

Appendix

6. The table below shows six methods of producing 100 widgets per month using capital and labor.

Method	Units of capital	Units of labor	ΔCapital	ΔLabor	Estimated *MRS* of capital for labor
A	10	80			
B	15	58	______	______	______
C	25	40	______	______	______
D	40	24	______	______	______
E	58	15	______	______	______
F	80	9	______	______	______

(a) Complete the last three columns in the table.

(b) On the graph below, plot the isoquant indicated by the data in the table. (Assume these are the only feasible methods and connect points by dotted line segments.)

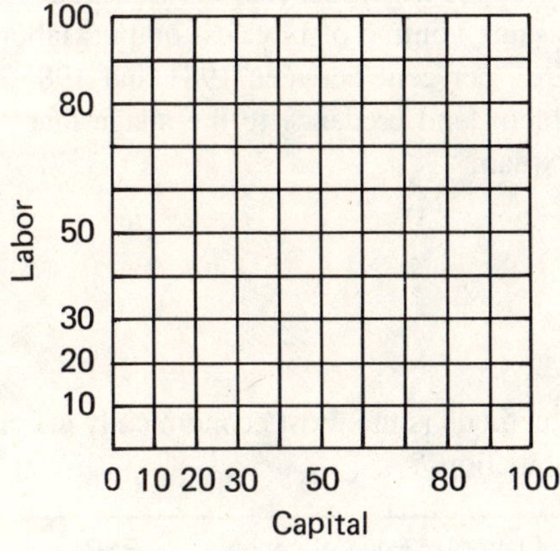

Short Problems

1. Inco's Bulk Mining

Well into the post-World War II period Inco (then International Nickel) possessed great monopoly power based on its then unique nickel ore body around Sudbury, Ontario. However, discoveries in Cuba, New Caledonia, and elsewhere gradually eroded its power to control prices. During the metals slump of the early 1980s Inco posted net losses of $1 billion (1981–1984). Starting in 1981, Inco developed and introduced a technique of "bulk mining" of columns of ore 300 feet high. Only two tunnel shafts were required: The upper shaft was used for crews to drill the ore column and deposit explosives; the lower shaft, 300 feet below, was used to load the fallen ore. This replaced a technique of drilling out 20-foot sections. Inco made a modest profit of $45 million in 1985 (although nickel prices remained depressed and volume static) with 21,000 employees as compared with 35,000 in 1981.

(a) The economist would term this a ______ run development. It would result in ______ shifts of the ______ run and ______ run cost curves.

(b) Assuming the same volume of physical output, labor productivity increased by roughly ______ per cent between 1981 and 1985.

(c) Does this problem lend credence to the adage that "necessity is the mother of invention"? Explain.

2. (Refer to Exercise 6.)

(a) Which of the methods is the most economically efficient for each of the following price combinations?

	Price of labor	Price of capital	P_L/P_K	Method
(1)	$1000	$ 500		
(2)	$1000	$1000		
(3)	$1000	$2000		

(b) Draw minimum isocost lines, with slope indicated by P_L/P_K, on the diagram for Exercise 6. Choose the most efficient method for each set of factor prices (for case 1, two efficient combinations are indicated).

3. How Agriculture Has Become More Productive

In the following table all columns are indexes with 1977 = 100.

	(1) Farm production	(2) Crop production per acre	(3) Total inputs	(4) Hours of farm labor	(5) Agricultural chemicals[a]	(6) Mechanical power and machinery
1940	50	53	97	417	9	36
1950	61	59	102	310	19	72
1960	76	77	98	207	32	83
1970	84	88	97	126	75	86
1980	103	100	103	92	123	101
1985	117	118	100	80	120	88

[a]Includes fertilizer, lime, and pesticides. Columns 4, 5, and 6 show 1984 figures. *Sources:* U.S. Department of Agriculture; reported in *Economic Report of the President,* 1986.

Questions

(a) Which of the columns is a productivity index? ________

(b) Between 1940 and 1985, agricultural production more than doubled and labor input decreased to slightly less than one-fifth of that of 1940. Therefore, labor productivity in agriculture in 1985 was over ________ times as great as in 1940.

(c) What evidence is there in the data above of the technological changes responsible for this?

(d) Why would it be misleading to say that overall productivity in agriculture increased more than 10 times between 1940 and 1985 without specifying labor productivity?

(e) Using columns 1 and 4, construct a labor productivity index for agriculture (1977 = 100).

1940 ________ 1970 ________
1950 ________ 1980 ________
1960 ________ 1985 ________

Answers to the Exercises

1. (a) Total costs: $200,000; $370,000; $540,000; $710,000; $910,000
Average costs: $2.00, $1.85, $1.80, $1.78, $1.82
(b) 400,000
(c) No, proportions of labor and capital are constant.
(d) Build two plants to produce 400,000 each.

2. To draw *LRAC*, first find output at which costs are equal:

   $\$500{,}000 + 5q = \$1{,}000{,}000 + 3q$

   $q = 250{,}000$ with average costs of $7. At 125,000 output, Plant A will be used with average costs of $9; at 375,000, Plant B with average costs of $5.67. *LRAC* can now be plotted (at 500,000, Plant B will have cost of $5) using these four points and recognizing that average costs will rise rapidly at low outputs. There will be a discontinuity of slope at 250,000 where the cost curve of A is replaced by that of B as the *LRAC*.

3. (a) At the 6 output levels (beginning with 1,000), the *LRAC* are: $.50, $.46, $.39, $.35, $.46, $.52.
   (b) 60,000

4. (a) productivity indexes: 1984, 119.0/113.4 = 1.0494; 1985, 122.3/116.1 = 1.0534 percentage change: 0.0040/1.0494 = 0.38%
   (b) The increase was small even compared with lower rates after 1965.

5. Percent spent on R & D are in parentheses: 1–H (5.1); 2–L (0.7); 3–H (6.0); 4–L (0.7); 5–L (0.5); 6–H (6.8); 7–H (5.1); 8–H (7.2); 9–H (4.8); 10–H (7.8); 11–L (0.7); 12–L (0.5)

6.

Method	ΔCapital	ΔLabor	Rate of substitution
A			
B	+ 5	−22	−0.23
C	+10	−18	−0.55
D	+15	−16	−0.94
E	+18	− 9	−2.00
F	+22	− 6	−3.67

CASES FOR PART THREE

CASE 6: Sapphires for Rent

In the early 1980s, Alex Sapphire located his jewelry store adjacent to a suburban shopping center. He spent $150,000 for land and store and enjoyed substantial profits. His stated profits increased and his 1986 income statement showed:

Gross margin (sales less cost of goods sold)		$175,000
Wages and salaries (including $25,000 for self)	$100,000	
Taxes, depreciation, and insurance on store	15,000	
Interest on mortgage—$100,000 at 8 percent	8,000	
Other expenses	25,000	148,000
Income before taxes		$ 27,000

In early 1987 a national jewelry chain offered Sapphire $50,000 a year rent under a long-term lease. (Sapphire would have to meet taxes, depreciation, and insurance on the store plus the interest on mortgage.) The chain would pay $150,000 for inventory and fixtures, and Sapphire estimated he could get a real return of 8 percent on the proceeds and take a job at $35,000 as manager of a department store jewelry department.

Sapphire estimated that his future results would be similar to those in 1986 with both revenues and costs reflecting inflation. Although business had been growing, he feared possible competition from the chain in another location and saw risks in the rise of gold, silver, and precious stone prices.

Revise his income statement to estimate the economic profits of continuing his business. Make a recommendation to Alex—should he sell the store? Explain.

CASE 7: The Costs of Driving an Automobile in the Mid-1980s

In early 1986, the Hertz Corporation (one of the nation's leading car rental firms) published an estimate of the cost of owning and operating an automobile. Information such as this is published annually by Hertz, the American Automobile Association, or the U.S. Federal Highway Administration.

Actual costs differ dramatically from model to model, place to place, and among drivers. For a 1985 compact-sized car like the Ford Tempo, Hertz estimates were based on a "sticker" price of $9,798 for a car with normal options—including power steering, power brakes, air conditioning, and automatic transmission. Assuming an approximate 5 percent discount for "bargaining," the final purchase price (including a 6 percent sales tax) was $9,834.

Expenses for owning and operating a car are usually classified as either "fixed" or "variable" costs, depending on whether the item relates primarily to the vehicle's ownership or to its operation. Fixed expenditures stay substantially the same regardless of the number of miles the car is driven in any one year. These fixed costs include insurance, interest, license fees, taxes and depreciation. Variable expenses are for items that depend primarily on the number of miles an auto is driven, such as gasoline and oil, and maintenance expenses, including tires, service, and repairs, parking fees, and highway tolls. Fixed and variable costs for the 1985 compact-sized car, assumed to be driven 10,000 miles annually for five years (then traded), are as follows:

Variable costs (1985, cents per mile)	
Gasoline and oil*	$.0456
Maintenance, repairs, and service	.0430
Miscellaneous	$.0272
	$.1158
Fixed costs (annual costs)	
Depreciation	$1,564
Insurance	1,102
Interest	849
License, fees and other charges	91
	$3,606

*Assumes fuel-efficiency of 24.5 miles per gallon and a per-gallon fuel price of $1.117.

Several things should be noted concerning these estimates. The 10,000 annual mileage assumption is important. As the number of miles driven annually increases, fixed costs may increase somewhat (additional mileage may lower a car's resale value, thus increasing annual depreciation). Depreciation, which is the decline in market value with use of the automobile, ranges from 27 to 32 percent of a car's purchase price in the first year to 1 to 2 percent in the tenth year. On a 1985 compact, the assumed five-year depreciation rate was 1.325 percent a month, producing annual depreciation of $1,564, or $.1564 a mile at the 10,000 mile annual average. Cost of interest includes both loan interest paid and interest lost on down-payment. The $849 in the table assumes a typical new-car buyer pays one-third down and finances the remaining two-thirds of the purchase price for five years.

Questions

1. Why should interest *lost* on the down-payment be included as a cost of automobile ownership? Would there be an interest cost if the automobile were a gift?

2. Assume that total variable costs (*TVC*) vary directly with mileage driven and that annual fixed costs (*TFC*) remain the same within the mileage ranges shown below. Complete the following table to compute the average per mile costs of owning and operating a compact 1985 automobile.

Miles/year	*TFC* (dollars)	*TVC* (dollars)	Total costs (dollars)	*AFC*	*AVC* = *MC* (cents per mile)	*ATC*
5,000	$3,606					
10,000	3,606	1,158				
11,000	3,606					

3. Suppose you occasionally use your 1985 compact car for business travel and are reimbursed at a rate of $.25 per mile. Is this sufficient compensation, assuming that you would be driving 10,000 miles for personal use and 1,000 miles for business use? Explain. Would your answer change if the mileages driven for personal and business use were 1,000 miles and 10,000 miles, respectively?

4. What do you consider to be the relevant cost of driving an extra mile? Is this amount consistent with the Hertz estimate? What do you consider the be the cost of carrying an additional passenger to your home town on a college vacation?

5. How and why does the text discussion of "lemons" suggest a different pattern of depreciation than that used by Hertz? How would the decision to own and operate older used cars produce a different mix of fixed and variable costs for automobile operation?

CASE 8: Supermammoth Supertankers

The largest supertanker operating at the start of 1969 was the *Universe Iran* rated at 326,933 deadweight ton-carrying capacity, a few hundred tons more than four sister ships of the same design. This was over 14 times as large as the largest tanker of 1945, but the end was not in sight. Even in 1967, *Fortune* noted negotiations for a 500,000-ton tanker and quoted a U.S. expert as seeing "no objection or technical difficulty in the way of the one-million-ton tanker."

In 1981, the largest registered tanker was the *Seawise Giant,* at 565,000 deadweight tons. Its length of 1,504 feet exceeded that of the *Universe* group by 465 feet; its beam of 209 feet was 30 feet greater.

The following table summarizes the data from 1945 to 1985:

	Number of tankers registered	Deadweight capacity (tons)	Largest supertanker size (tons)	Tanker mean size (tons)
1945	1,911	24,000,000	23,000	12,500
1956	2,778	45,000,000	45,000	16,000
1966	3,524	103,000,000	210,000	29,000
1976	5,311	302,000,000	550,000	56,900
1981	5,359	346,000,000	565,000	64,600
1984	5,497	315,000,000	565,000	57,800

What are the advantages of large tankers? As listed in *Fortune* in September 1967, they include the following:

1. The size and expense of the instrument-packed and expensive deck-house remain largely unchanged as the size of the tanker increases.
2. Frequent repetition of steel shapes for cargo tanks allows mass-production techniques.
3. Steel thickness in big ships does not increase with size of vessel, partly because the danger of sitting on the top of a single wave with consequent strain to ship midsection is reduced.
4. Longer ships do not require proportionally more power to move through the water, so increases in engine size are far less than proportional.
5. In the highly automated, low-cost shipyards of Japan these considerations add up to a cost of $200 per deadweight ton for a 25,000-ton vessel, $104 for a 50,000-tonner, and $75 for tankers of 150,000 tons and up.
6. Large tankers are much more economical to operate. The 30-member crew of an automated 150,000-ton tanker is the same size as that of an older 25,000-ton tanker and, as suggested above, the fuel-cost increases are less than proportional.

What are the limits to the scale of tankers?

1. The limited ocean routes available to them. The Suez Canal could handle only 80,000-ton ships full and 200,000-ton ships empty (its closing in 1956 set off the size explosion). One oil executive has stated that "the 300,000-tonners are too inflexible; you have to dredge oceans for them." Many harbors and even such ocean channels as the Malacca Straits are too shallow.
2. The lack of harbor and offshore loading facilities for them. For example, the United States has no facilities on either the East or West Coasts and only a Louisiana offshore port on the Gulf Coast.

3. Large tanker spills involved environmental and aesthetic damage of such extent that commercial insurance companies have declined to offer oil disaster insurance, forcing tanker operators to establish their own insurance pools. In 1979, a freak accident to Amoco's *Cadiz* deposited 220,000 tons of oil along 100 miles of the northwest French coast. (But even such an accidental spill is a small fraction of the 5 to 10 million tons of petroleum deposited in the oceans each year.)
4. The glut of supertanker capacity that developed by 1979 discouraged any new building of larger tankers. Almost half of 764 tankers of over 200,000-ton capacity were idle; excess capacity so large in face of reduced oil use meant that little building of any supertankers (including still bigger ones) was likely for the foreseeable future.

Questions

1. (a) Supertankers seem to be a clear illustration of what kind of economies? What will be the general shape of the *LRAC* curve?

   (b) Why do both labor and capital productivity increase with the size of the tanker? What other factor is used more effectively with increased size?

2. From the table it is apparent that many small tankers are still operating; why may they still be able to compete?

3. It seemed unlikely in the 1980s that the United States would develop deep-water port facilities on the Atlantic coast to handle supertankers. Proposals for developing a deep-water harbor in Machiasport, Maine, and for an offshore unloading facility on the Delaware coast had been rejected by the state governments. What are the arguments for and against such developments?

4. The *World Almanac* is a convenient source for checking for a possible new size leader and for changes in the world tanker fleet. You may wish to do so. (As of 1986, the scrapping and downsizing of supertankers was continuing. Your findings may show a further reduction in capacity and average size of tanker. What could change this trend?)

CASE 9: Choices Between A and B

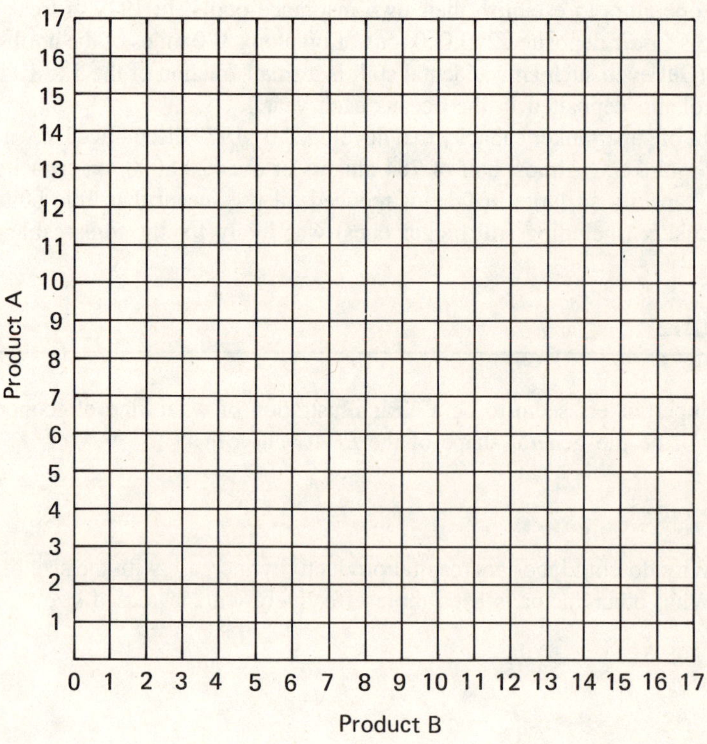

Questions

1. Draw on the figure above the indifference curves for levels of satisfaction indicated by 54, 108, and 144 units in the total utility table that follows. Label the indifference curves with letters.

Total Utility from the Consumption of Product *A* and Product *B*

	Product B										
Product A	0	1	2	3	4	5	6	7	8	9	10
0	0	20	38	54	68	80	90	98	104	108	110
1	10	30	48	64	78	90	100	108	114	118	120
2	19	39	57	73	87	99	109	117	123	127	129
3	27	47	65	81	95	107	117	125	131	135	137
4	34	54	72	88	102	114	124	132	138	142	144
5	40	60	78	94	108	120	130	138	144	148	150
6	45	65	83	99	113	125	135	143	149	153	155
7	49	69	87	102	117	129	139	147	153	157	159
8	52	72	90	106	120	132	142	150	156	160	162
9	54	74	92	108	122	134	144	152	158	162	164
10	55	75	93	109	123	135	145	153	159	163	165

2. (a) Plot budget lines on the figure for each budget and price combination in the table below.

	Budget	P_A	Q_A	P_B	Q_B
(a)	$43	$3	______	$7.00	______
(b)	43	3	______	3.50	______
(c)	15	5	______	5.00	______
(d)	40	5	______	5.00	______

(b) Determine graphically the combination of goods A and B that maximizes satisfaction for each budget and price combination and enter in the table.

3. To see that the same combinations of A and B are obtained by the marginal utility and indifference theories, compare your answers with those for Short problem 2, Chapter 9.

[As to why they are the same, remember that the slope of the budget line is the ratio of relative price P_B/P_A. At the tangency point this equaled the slope of the indifference curve, which is the marginal rate of substitution of A for B: $\Delta A/\Delta B$ (or dA/dB). When less A and more B is consumed along an indifference curve, the amount of satisfaction given up ($\Delta A \times MU_A$) must equal the amount of satisfaction gained ($\Delta B \times MU_B$) and thus $\Delta A/\Delta B = MU_B/MU_A$. Therefore, at the point of tangency we have the equivalent of $P_B/P_A = MU_B/MU_A$.]

The Indifference Map as a Production Function

(Prerequisite Appendix, Chapter 11)

4. The indifference map above can be conceived of as a set of ________________. The units of product A can be thought of as units of factor A (capital) and units of factor B could represent ________________.

5. The budget lines are now ________________ lines. The tangencies represent the maximum output that can be obtained for a given total cost or the ________________ cost of producing a particular output.

6. Cases 2(a) and 2(d) illustrate the "principle of substitution." When relative prices (P_A/P_B) switch from 3/7 to 1, ________________ units of the relatively cheaper factor B are substituted for ________________ of factor A to produce an output of ________________ units.

7. If long-run output is expanded from 54 to 108 units when the prices of factors are $5, total costs of production will rise from ________________ to ________________. The change in long-run average costs from ________________ to ________________ indicates (economies, diseconomies) of scale. (Using figures which show diminishing marginal utility give this curious result immediately.)

8. If the short-run output now drops to the previous level of 54, the combination of factors used will be ________________ units of fixed capital (A) and ________________ units of labor (B).

PART FOUR

Markets and Pricing

12

Pricing in Competitive Markets

Learning Objectives

After studying the material in this chapter, you should be able to

—understand why economists say that individual firms in a competitive market structure do not behave like rivals;

—explain the behavioral rules for a profit-maximizing firm;

—understand why individual competitive firms are price takers and face a horizontal demand curve;

—define average revenue, marginal revenue, and price under perfect competition;

—explain how the short-run industry supply curve can be derived;

—describe the role of entry and exit of firms in achieving long-run market equilibrium;

—distinguish short-run and long-run equilibrium of competitive firms and industries.

Review and Self-Test

Matching Concepts

______ 1. conditions of short-run equilibrium output for a firm

______ 2. response to short-run profits in competitive industry

______ 3. price taker

______ 4. production at minimum point of *LRAC* curve

______ 5. short-run market supply curve

______ 6. reduction of productive capacity

______ 7. marginal revenue

______ 8. $P < AVC$ at output where $MR = MC$

(a) condition for shutdown of competitive firm in short run

(b) condition for long-run equilibrium for a firm

(c) $P = MC$; $P \geqslant AVC$

(d) symptom of a declining industry

(e) firm acting as if demand curve is perfectly elastic

(f) horizontal summation of firms' *MC* curves

(g) change in firm's total revenue as sales increase by one unit

(h) entry of new firms

Multiple-Choice Questions

1. Which of the following best characterizes a competitive market structure?
   (a) Each firm advertises unique attributes of the product.
   (b) Individual firms set prices so as to maximize profits.
   (c) Existing firms restrict entry of new firms into the market.
   (d) Firms are price takers.

2. Which of the following is not a required characteristic of a perfectly competitive industry?
   (a) Consumers have no reason to prefer one firm's product to another.
   (b) There are enough firms so that none can influence market price.
   (c) Any firm can enter or leave the industry.
   (d) Industry demand is highly elastic.

3. A perfectly competitive firm does not try to sell more of its product by lowering its price below the market price because
   (a) this would be considered unethical price chiseling.
   (b) its competitors will not permit it.
   (c) its demand curve is inelastic, so total revenue will decline.
   (d) it can sell whatever it chooses to produce at the existing market price.

4. A firm should not produce at all in the short run if
   (a) the loss in revenue is less than the total fixed cost.
   (b) average variable cost at the current output level is less than average revenue.
   (c) total revenue does not cover total cost.
   (d) the average revenue from selling its output is less than the average variable cost of producing it.

5. A firm will increase profits by expanding output as long as
   (a) $MC = MR$.
   (b) $MC > MR$.
   (c) $MR > MC$.
   (d) $MR - MC$ is at a maximum level.

6. The demand curve facing a single firm in perfect competition
   (a) is virtually horizontal over the normal range of production.
   (b) usually exhibits a slightly upward slope.
   (c) equals market demand divided by the number of firms.
   (d) has the same slope as the market demand curve.

7. If the market demand curve for wheat has price elasticity of 0.25, and the market is competitive,
   (a) an individual wheat farmer can increase revenue by reducing output.
   (b) nothing can be said about the elasticity of demand for an individual wheat farmer.
   (c) revenue from wheat sales will rise with an increase of industry production.
   (d) each wheat farmer, nevertheless, faces a highly elastic demand.

8. The perfectly competitive firm's demand curve coincides with
   (a) both its marginal and average revenue curves.
   (b) its average revenue curve and total revenue curve.
   (c) both its marginal and total revenue curves.
   (d) its total revenue curve.

9. In the short run, a profit-maximizing firm will produce additional units of a product as long as
   (a) price at least covers average fixed cost.
   (b) additional revenue per unit exceeds additional cost per unit.
   (c) total revenue is increasing.
   (d) elasticity of demand is infinite.

10. The output where economic profits are zero occurs when
    (a) $P = AVC$.
    (b) $P = MC = AVC$.
    (c) $P = ATC$.
    (d) $P > MC < ATC$.

11. The short-run supply curve of a firm in a perfectly competitive market
    (a) is identical to the firm's *AVC* curve above its *MC* curve.
    (b) is derived from the market supply curve.
    (c) is identical to the firm's *MC* curve above its *AVC* curve.
    (d) is the same line as the firm's demand curve.

12. Long-run economic profits will not exist in a perfectly competitive industry because
    (a) new firms will enter the industry and eliminate them.
    (b) corporate income taxes eliminate such excess profits.
    (c) competitive industries are too inefficient to be profitable.
    (d) long-run increasing costs eliminate profits.

13. In long-run equilibrium in an industry of perfectly competitive, profit-maximizing firms,
    (a) price will equal average variable cost.
    (b) price will exceed marginal cost.
    (c) price will equal average total cost.
    (d) average fixed cost will be at a minimum.

14. Equilibrium price and output in a market
    (a) are established when the amount people wish to buy equals the amount people wish to sell.
    (b) depend entirely on cost.
    (c) depend entirely on demand.
    (d) are best described as the price and output existing at a particular time.

15. If there were a steady decrease in demand for a product produced in a competitive market, we would predict that
    (a) firms will gradually leave the industry and the productive capacity of the industry will shrink.
    (b) firms will modernize capital equipment in order to increase efficiency.
    (c) existing firms will increase output levels to recover losses.
    (d) the industry will expand as new, more efficient firms enter.

Questions 16 to 18 refer to the diagram below, which applies to a firm in a perfectly competitive market:

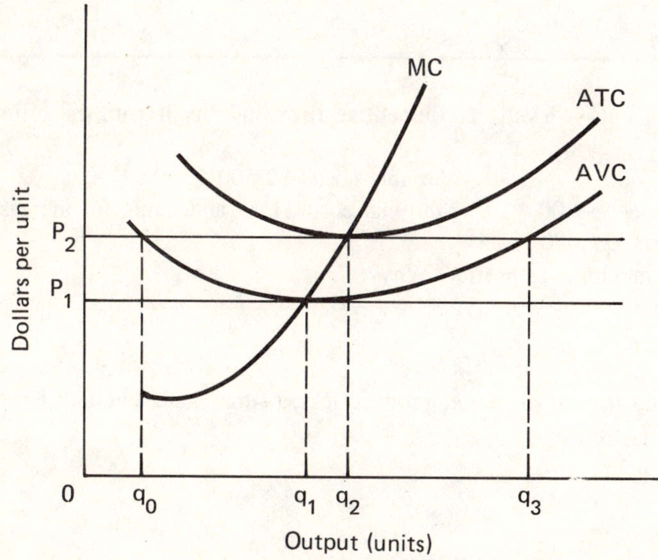

16. Assuming market price is P_2, which output maximizes the firm's profits?
    (a) q_0
    (b) q_1
    (c) q_2
    (d) q_3

17. If market price fell to P_1, what should the profit-maximizing firm do in the short run?
(a) cease production entirely
(b) continue to produce q_2
(c) reduce output level to q_1
(d) either (a) or (c)

18. Which of the following best describes the behavior of a profit-maximizing competitive firm in the short run?
(a) produce q_3 regardless of price, since $P > AVC$ for all units between q_0 and q_3
(b) do not produce at all unless market price exceeds P_2
(c) produce output q_1 at price P_2
(d) produce output levels where $P = MC$ as long as price exceeds AVC at that output

The next two multiple-choice questions refer to certain exercises that follow:

19. In long-run competitive equilibrium (Exercise 2), market price will normally tend to equal the minimum point on
(a) the average variable cost curve.
(b) the average total cost curve.
(c) the marginal cost curve.
(d) the average fixed cost curve.

20. The condition for a firm to maximize profits in all of the exercises that follow is to produce the output where
(a) $MC < MR$
(b) $MC = MR$
(c) $MC > MR$
(d) none of the above

Self-Test Key

Matching Concepts: 1–c; 2–h; 3–e; 4–b; 5–f; 6–d; 7–g; 8–a

Multiple-Choice: 1–d; 2–d; 3–d; 4–d; 5–c; 6–a; 7–d; 8–a; 9–b; 10–c; 11–c; 12–a; 13–c; 14–a; 15–a; 16–c; 17–d; 18–d; 19–b; 20–b

Exercises

1. At present output levels, a competitive firm finds itself with the following:

Output: 5,000
Market price: $1.00
Fixed costs: $2,000
Variable costs: $2,500
Marginal cost: $1.25 and rising for increases in output

(a) Is it maximizing profits? Why?

(b) Should it produce more, produce less, or the same amount? Explain.

2. The graph below shows the short-run cost situation of a hypothetical perfectly competitive, profit-maximizing firm. Fill in the blanks below.

If market price is	\$10.00	\$7.50	\$5.50
(a) equilibrium output will be	___	___	___
At this output,			
(b) total revenue is	___	___	___
(c) total cost is	___	___	___
(d) total profit is (+ or −)	___	___	___
(e) marginal revenue is	___	___	___
(f) marginal cost is	___	___	___
(g) average total cost is	___	___	___
(h) profit per unit is	___	___	___

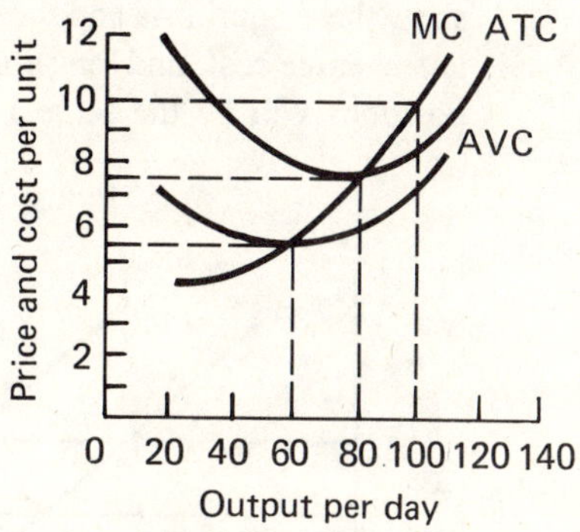

(i) Why is neither \$10.00 nor \$5.50 the long-run market price?

3. Another competitive firm has the following:
Output: 80 units
Market price: \$10
Average total costs are at their minimum level and are equal to \$7.50

(a) What is marginal cost at this output? ______________
(b) Is the firm making profits? ______________
(c) Is it making maximum profits? ______________
(d) Should it change its output? ______________
(Refer to the diagram accompanying Exercise 2.)

4. Suppose you are considering harvesting and selling firewood on a part-time basis. You would be operating within a competitive market with no influence over price. Assume the current price for firewood is \$70 per cord and the following short-run total cost function, where q represents cords per month: $TC = 800 + 16q + q^2$.
(a) What is the profit-maximizing output? (Remember: $MC = dTC/dq$)

(b) Calculate the estimated short-run profits (or losses).

(c) Based on the rule that a firm should produce only if it covers its variable costs of production, should you produce? Explain.

5. In graph A, the industry demand and short-run and long-run supply curves are shown. The initial equilibrium output of *X* is disturbed by a shift in demand to *D'D'*. The new short-run equilibrium output is *Y* and long-run equilibrium output is *Z*. On graph B show these equilibria and the adjustments for a firm. Use demand, short-run marginal and average cost, and long-run average cost curves. (*Note:* The firm's initial and final positions will be the same.)

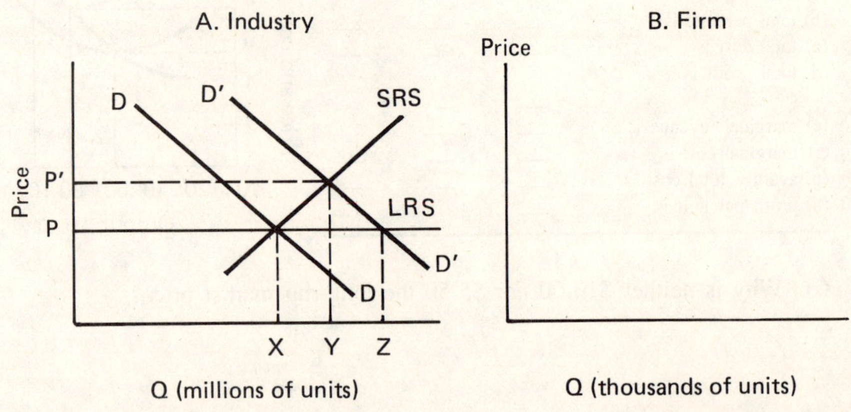

6. Output of peanuts in the United States, it is assumed, is two million tons in a given year. One of the many producers, Mr. Shell, has experienced a doubling of his output over his previous year's output of 40 tons. All other firms report no change in their output. The market elasticity of demand is estimated to be 0.20.
   (a) Calculate the effect on the world price of peanuts of Mr. Shell's increase in output (in percentage terms).

   (b) Calculate the elasticity of demand facing Mr. Shell's firm.

   (c) Does your answer for (b) indicate that the firm is likely to act as a price taker? Explain.

Short Problems

1. In the table below are output and cost data for three firms that are representative of those in a perfectly competitive market. Assume that all costs in the table are variable costs. Minimum average variable costs are as follows for the three firms: firm A, \$4 at output of 30; firm B, \$2.71 at output of 35; firm C, \$4.15 at output of 40.
   (a) Complete the table.

Firm A			*Firm B*			*Firm C*		
Output	Total cost	Marginal cost	Output	Total cost	Marginal cost	Output	Total cost	Marginal cost
30	120		25	80		36	150	
40	160	____	30	82.5	____	40	166	____
50	210	____	35	95	____	44	186	____
60	280	____	40	135	____	48	214	____
70	380	____	45	195	____	52	254	____
80	520	____	50	285	____	56	310	____

   (b) On the graphs, plot (at the intervals of output) the short-run supply curve for each firm and a portion of the industry supply curve. (The industry supply curve will be only a "rough" approximation given the format of the data.) Recall that only after its intersection with the minimum point on the *AVC* is the *MC* a short-run supply curve.

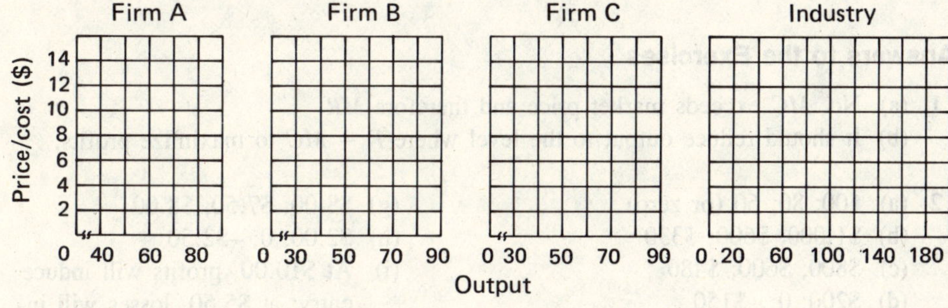

2. The diagram below illustrates the cost position of firms operating in a perfectly competitive market immediately following the introduction of a cost-saving innovation.

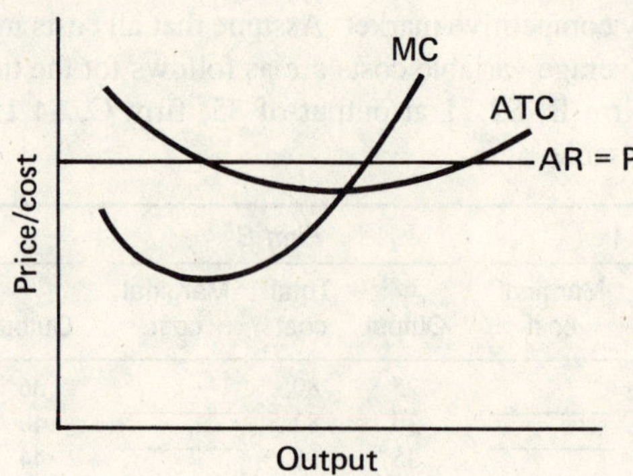

(a) What initial advantage are the firms enjoying from the innovation?

(b) Can this advantage remain? Justify your answer by noting what will be taking place in the industry in the long run.

Answers to the Exercises

1. (a) No. *MC* exceeds market price and therefore *MR*.
   (b) It should reduce output to the level where $P = MC$ to maximize profits.

2. (a) 100; 80; 60 (or zero)
   (b) $1,000; $600; $330
   (c) $800; $600; $480
   (d) $200; 0; –$150
   (e) $10.00; $7.50; $5.50
   (f) $10.00; $7.50; $5.50
   (g) $8.00; $7.50; $8.00
   (h) $2.00; 0; –$2.50
   (i) At $10.00, profits will induce entry; at $5.50, losses will induce exit of firms, so industry supply curve shifts.

3. (a) $7.50 (b) yes (c) no (d) Yes, it should increase output to 100.

4. (a) $16 + 2q = 70$, $q = 27$
   (b) $TR - TC = \$1,890 - 1,961 = -\$71$
   (c) Yes, because $TR > TVC$; $\$1,890 - 1,161 = \$729$

5.

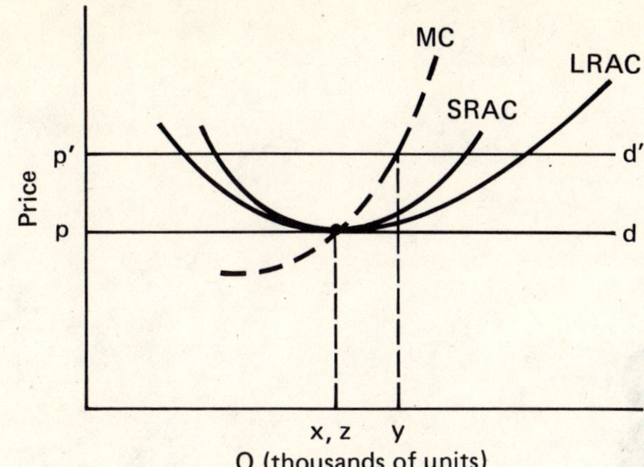

6. (a) The market elasticity of demand (E_m) is given by the formula

$$E_m = \frac{\text{percentage change in output}}{\text{percentage change in price}}$$

Here: $0.20 = \dfrac{40/2{,}000{,}000}{\text{percentage change in price}}$; percentage change in price $= 0.0001$

(b) The firm's elasticity of demand is the percentage change in the output of the firm divided by the percentage change in the price [calculated in (a)]. This is equal to

$$\frac{40/60}{0.0001} = 6{,}667$$

(c) Yes. For practical purposes the elasticity is (negative) infinity and the firm has no effect on price.

13

Pricing in Monopoly Markets

Learning Objectives

Careful study of the material in this chapter should enable you to

—explain the relationship of price and marginal revenue for a monopolist;

—relate marginal revenue, total revenue, and elasticity;

—illustrate potential monopoly profits in any competitive equilibrium;

—distinguish between natural and created barriers to entry;

—identify two measures of monopoly power;

—define price discrimination and identify conditions that make price discrimination both possible and profitable.

Review and Self-Test

Matching Concepts

	Concept		Definition
_______	1. price discrimination	(a)	barriers to entry
_______	2. short-run profit-maximizing position of a monopolist	(b)	requisites for price discrimination
		(c)	rate of output where $MR = MC$
_______	3. $P > MC$	(d)	concentration ratio
_______	4. long-continuing profits greater than opportunity costs	(e)	market demand curve for product
		(f)	evidence of monopoly power
_______	5. cartel	(g)	differences in prices not associated with differences in costs
_______	6. control over supply and ability to prevent resale	(h)	characteristic of monopoly price
_______	7. impediments to the production of a commodity by additional firms	(i)	grouping of firms to limit competition among themselves
		(j)	inadequate measure of the market power of those firms
_______	8. fraction of total market sales made by a specified number of an industry's largest firms		
_______	9. number of firms in an industry		
_______	10. monopoly firm's demand curve		

Multiple-Choice Questions

1. Whether a firm is a monopolist or competitor, to maximize profits it should produce the rate of output where
   (a) marginal cost is less than average total cost.
   (b) marginal revenue exceeds marginal cost.
   (c) average total costs are at a minimum.
   (d) marginal revenue is equal to marginal cost.

2. A monopolist has a downward-sloping demand curve because
   (a) it has an inelastic demand.
   (b) typically, it sells only to a few large buyers.
   (c) its demand curve is the same as the industry's demand curve.
   (d) consumers prefer that product.

3. At the profit-maximizing output for a single-price monopolist, price
   (a) equals marginal cost.
   (b) exceeds marginal cost.
   (c) always exceeds average total cost.
   (d) equals marginal revenue.

4. In a monopolized industry,
   (a) other firms have no incentive to enter.
   (b) profits are inevitable.
   (c) there must be barriers to entry if the monopoly is to persist.
   (d) there will be less incentive to lower costs than under competition.

5. Monopoly power of a firm or group of firms
   (a) can be adequately measured as the number of firms in an industry.
   (b) will always vary inversely with the concentration ratio.
   (c) is often measured by concentration ratios and high profit rates.
   (d) is easily and precisely measured by economists.

6. Concentration ratios have been found to
   (a) have considerable correlation with profit rates.
   (b) have little usefulness in industries where there are more than two firms.
   (c) have little relevance in measuring the degree of monopoly power in an industry.
   (d) be very low in the great majority of manufacturing industries.

7. Price discrimination is possible
   (a) in all cases where firms have complete monopoly power.
   (b) if firms keep it a secret.
   (c) only if firms conspire with competitors.
   (d) if buyers of the commodity can be prevented from reselling a monopolized commodity.

8. A monopoly firm will not have more than normal profits unless
   (a) it practices price discrimination.
   (b) its price exceeds average total cost.
   (c) its marginal revenue exceeds marginal cost.
   (d) it faces an inelastic demand curve.

9. Which statement best describes the behavior of a profit-maximizing, single-price monopolist?
   (a) It picks a price known to give a profit and sells as much as it can.
   (b) It produces as much as it can and sets whatever price is necessary to sell it all.
   (c) It seeks to select a price at which the additional revenue associated with one more unit just equals the addition to cost.
   (d) It sets price equal to marginal cost at its most profitable output.

10. Output under price discrimination will
   (a) generally be larger than under single-price monopoly.
   (b) be produced at higher average cost than under single-price monopoly.
   (c) usually be the same as under perfect competition.
   (d) be indeterminate because we cannot know what prices can be charged.

11. Compared to price and output in a competitive market, the monopolist
    (a) produces less and charges a higher price.
    (b) produces more and charges a lower price.
    (c) produces less and charges a lower price.
    (d) produces more and charges a higher price.

12. Assume that a profit-maximizing monopolist can sell 10 units of output for $15 each or 11 units of output for $14 each. The marginal revenue of the eleventh unit sold is
    (a) $14.
    (b) $15.
    (c) $4.
    (d) $154.

13. Natural barriers to entry
    (a) include patent laws and exclusive franchises.
    (b) most commonly arise through economies of scale.
    (c) result from unforeseen increases in long-run average cost.
    (d) imply that smaller firms have significantly lower average total costs than larger ones.

14. Unlike a competitive firm, a monopolist can
    (a) produce even if price is less than *AVC*.
    (b) continue to operate in the short run if total revenues are less than total variable costs.
    (c) continue to earn economic profits in the long run.
    (d) be assured of earning profits in the short run.

15. Price discrimination
    (a) tends to decrease the allocative inefficiency of monopoly.
    (b) will provide more total revenue to the firm than the profit-maximizing single price.
    (c) generally results in greater output than under single price monopoly.
    (d) includes all of the above.

Questions 16 to 18 refer to the diagram below, which shows a perfectly competitive market:

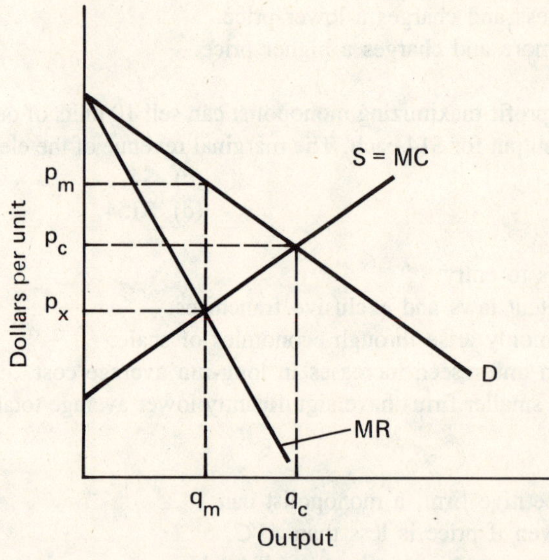

16. Equilibrium price and output for a perfectly competitive industry are
    (a) p_m and q_m.
    (b) p_m and q_c.
    (c) p_x and q_m.
    (d) p_c and q_c.

17. If the industry is cartelized, and a profit-maximizing output-restriction agreement is reached, output and price will become
    (a) q_c and p_m.
    (b) q_m and p_m.
    (c) q_c and p_c.
    (d) q_m and p_x.

18. Creating a cartel and reducing output can be profitable for this industry because
    (a) all units between q_c and q_m add less to total revenue than to total costs.
    (b) at output q_m, $MR = MC$.
    (c) at competitive equilibrium, the marginal revenue is less than price and marginal cost.
    (d) of all of the above.

19. Cartels tend to be unstable because
    (a) there is an incentive for individual firms to violate output quotas by expanding output.
    (b) they invariably reduce industry profits in the short run.
    (c) like monopolies, cartels produce more output than a competitive equilibrium can sustain.
    (d) individual firms have an incentive to cut back beyond the restrictions imposed by the cartel.

20. A competitive firm's equilibrium output occurs where market price (p) equals marginal cost (MC); a monopoly firm produces at an output where
    (a) $p < MC$.
    (b) $p = MC$.
    (c) $p > MC$.
    (d) The relationship of price to marginal cost is indeterminate for a monopoly.

Self-Test Key

Matching Concepts: 1–g; 2–c; 3–h; 4–f; 5–i; 6–b; 7–a; 8–d; 9–j; 10–e

Multiple-Choice Questions: 1–d; 2–c; 3–b; 4–c; 5–c; 6–a; 7–d; 8–b; 9–c; 10–a; 11–a; 12–c; 13–b; 14–c; 15–d; 16–d; 17–b; 18–d; 19–a; 20–c

Exercises

1. The diagram below shows the demand and unit cost situation of a monopolist.

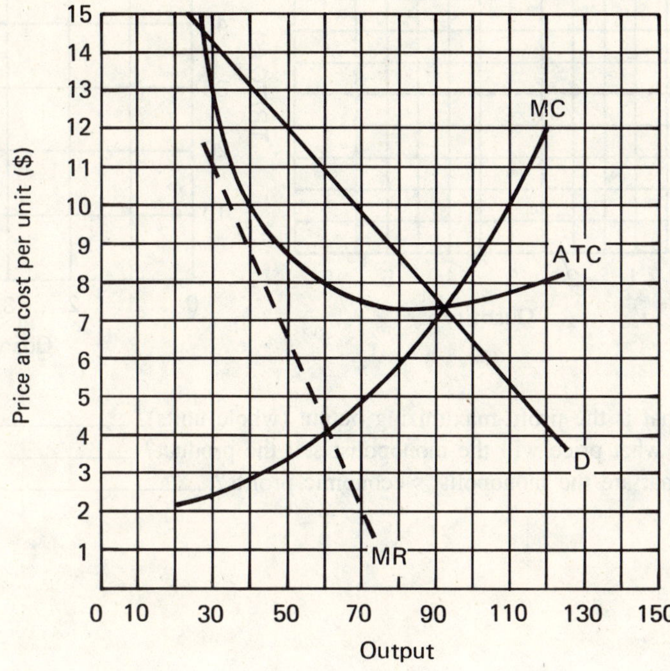

   (a) What is the output where the firm's profits are at a maximum? ______________
   (b) What will be the price at this output? ______________
   (c) What will be the total revenue at this output? ______________
   (d) What will be the total costs? ______________
   (e) What will be the economic profits? ______________
   (f) Within what range of output will there be at least *some* economic profit? ______________

2. The data below relate to a pure monopolistic firm and its product.
   (a) Calculate marginal cost (*MC*), marginal revenue (*MR*), total revenue (*TR*), and profit to complete the table.

Output	Total cost	Price	Quantity demanded	*MC*	*MR*	*TR*	Profit
0	$20	$20	0				
1	24	18	1				
2	27	16	2				
3	32	14	3				
4	39	12	4				
5	48	10	5				
6	59	8	6				

   (b) Plot average revenue (*AR*), *MR*, and *MC* in (i); *TC* and *TR* in (ii):

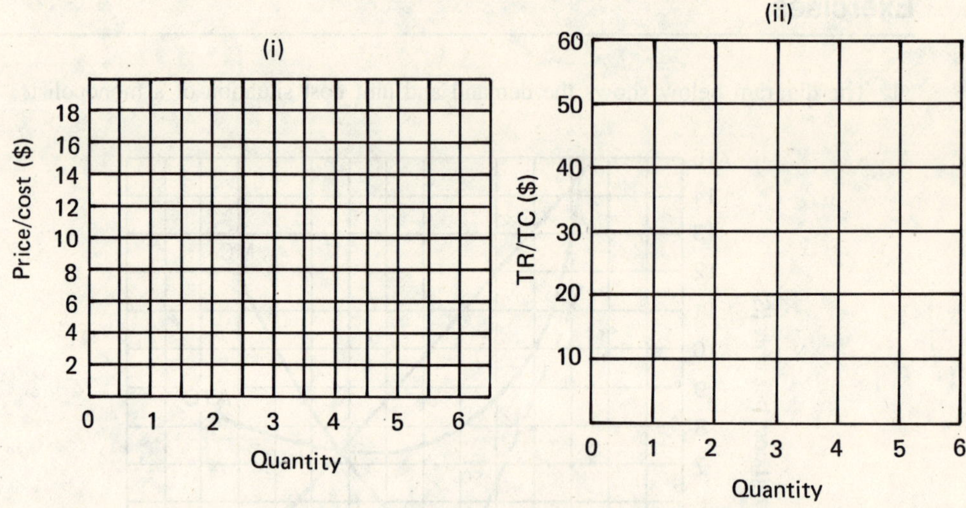

   (c) What is the profit-maximizing output (whole units)? ______________
   (d) At what price will the monopolist sell the product? ______________
   (e) What are the monopolist's economic profits? ______________

3. The diagram below shows the cost and revenue curves for a monopolist.

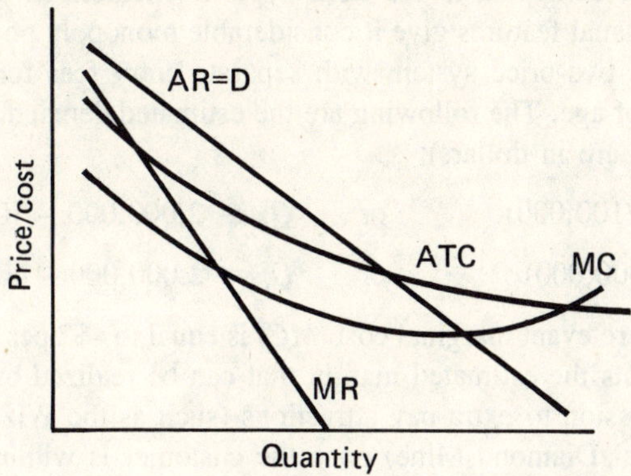

(a) Illustrate on the diagram the price the profit-maximizing monopolist will set and the quantity that will be sold. (Label these P_M and Q_M.)
(b) Indicate by vertical hatching, |||||||||| , monopoly profits.
(c) Suppose the monopolist, to be allocatively efficient, set price (*AR*) equal to marginal cost. Label the price P_E and the output Q_E. Would this output be sustainable in the long run? Explain with reference to the costs the monopolist faces in the diagram.

4. Assume that a unique amusement park has been developed based on *The Wizard of Oz* and designed to appeal to the same type of clientele as the Disney parks. Its location and unusual features give it considerable monopoly power. Its management is considering a two-price system with separate entry fees for adults and children under 15 years of age. The following are the estimated demand curves for customers per year (prices are in dollars):

$P_a = 20 - (Q_a/100{,}000)$ or $Q_a = 2{,}000{,}000 - 100{,}000P_a$

$P_c = 5 - (Q_c/400{,}000)$ or $Q_c = 2{,}000{,}000 - 400{,}000P_c$

Assume that the relevant marginal cost (*MC*) is equal to –$2 per person. The negative number represents the estimated margin that can be realized by the sale of refreshments and admission to extra-pay attractions (such as the Wizard's Inner Chamber and the Gnomes' Diamond Mine) once the customer is within the park.

Solve diagrammatically for the profit-maximizing prices on the graphs below. (*Hint:* The marginal revenue curves will cut the horizontal axes halfway between 0 and the quantity demanded.)

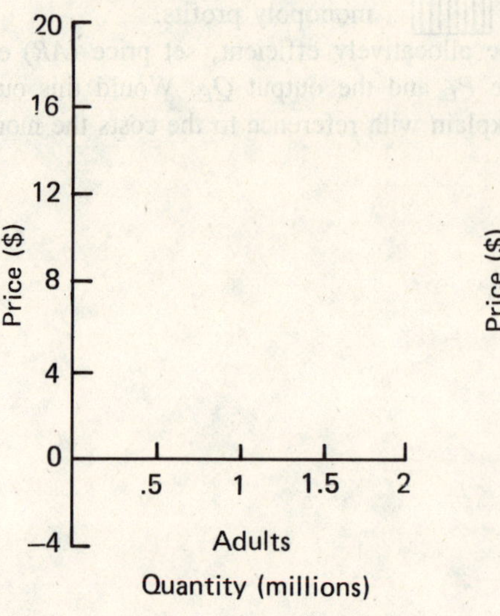

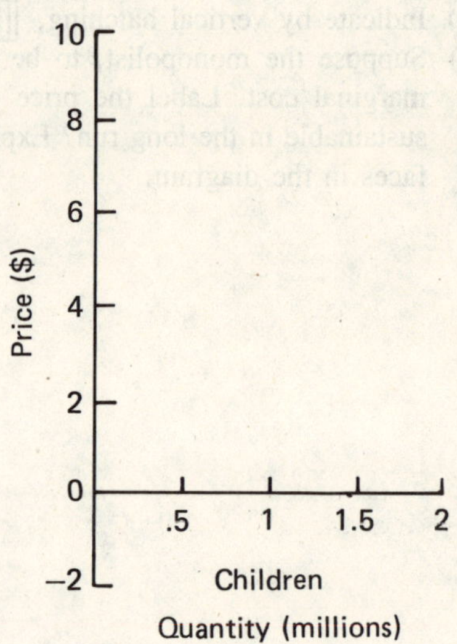

Short Problems

1. Some of the basic cost data for a monopolist are given in the following table.

Output	Total cost
0	40
5	50
10	65
15	90
20	130
25	190
30	275

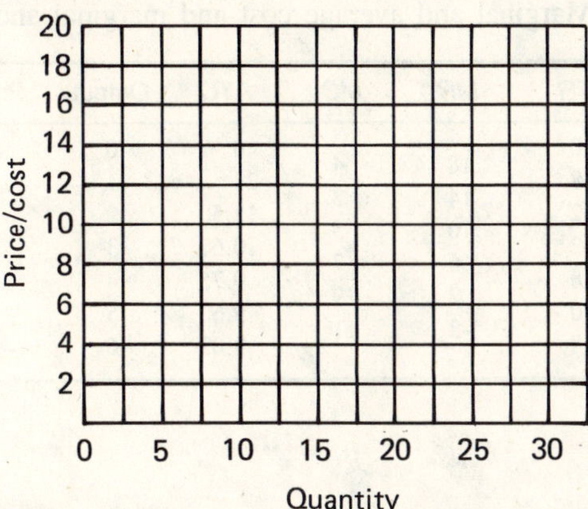

The demand schedule is given by $Q_d = 20 - 1.0P$, where Q_d is quantity demanded and P is average revenue or price.

(a) Compute and graph the average cost, marginal cost, average revenue, and marginal revenue schedules. (*Note:* The *MR* curve will intersect the horizontal axis at half the output of the demand curve intersection.)

(b) What approximately are the profit-making monopolist's profits? Show this by shading the area in the diagram you have completed.

(c) If the government imposed a tax equal to \$4 per unit of output, would the monopolist change its price and output? Why and in what way?

2. In the Oz amusement park (Exercise 5), take $MC = 0$ and solve for the profit-maximizing prices. (For comparison to the diagrammatic solution, convert demand equations to total revenue by multiplying by Q; obtain the *MR* equations by taking the first derivative and setting it equal to zero.)

3. Assume a monopoly with a demand curve of $P = \$50 - 0.001q$ and with $TC = \$100{,}000 + 10q - 0.0002q^2$ over the relevant range of output. Calculate the profit-maximizing quantity and price. (*Hint:* To do this expeditiously, convert demand curve into TR as a function of q, and set $MR = MC$. MC is the first derivative of total cost curve.)

Answers to the Exercises

1. (a) 60 (b) \$11 (c) \$660 (d) \$480 (e) \$180 (f) output; about 25 to 90 units; price is about \$14.75 to \$7.50

2. (a) Marginal and average cost and marginal and total revenue

TR	*MR*	*MC*	*ATC*	Output	Profit
0			0	0	–20
	18	4			
18			24	1	–6
	14	3			
32			13.50	2	5
	10	5			
42			10.67	3	10
	6	7			
48			9.75	4	9
	2	9			
50			9.60	5	2
	–2	11			
48			9.83	6	–11

(b)

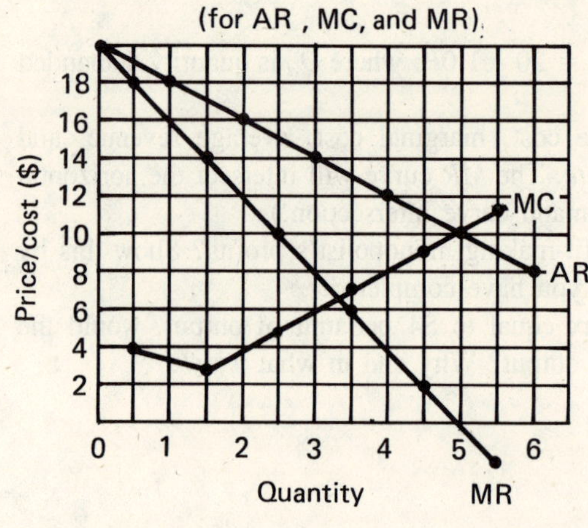

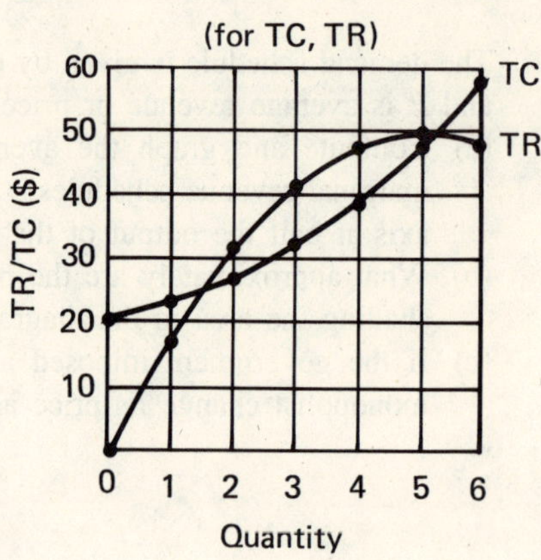

(c) 3 units
(d) \$14 (price to sell output where $MR = MC$)
(e) At 3 units of output, *TR* is \$42, *TC* is \$32, and profits are \$10.

3. (a) and (b)

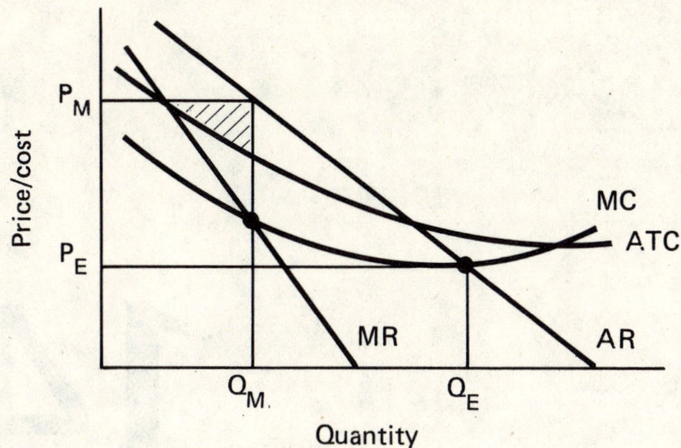

(c) No, it would not, because the *ATC* exceeds the price and business could not be sustained for long.

4. Adults: $p = \$9$; $q = 1{,}100{,}000$
Children: $p = \$1.50$; $q = 1{,}400{,}000$
Graphically:

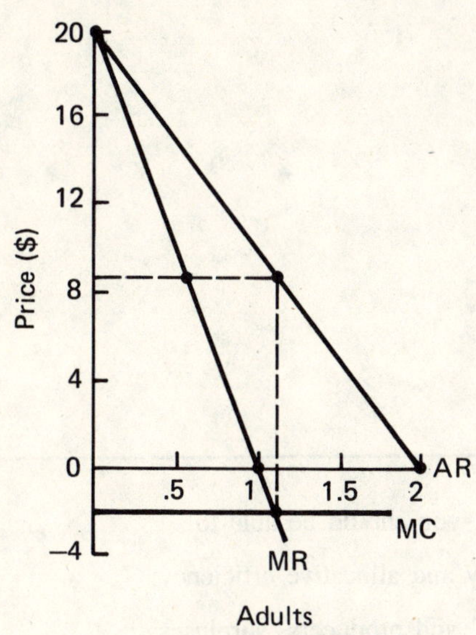

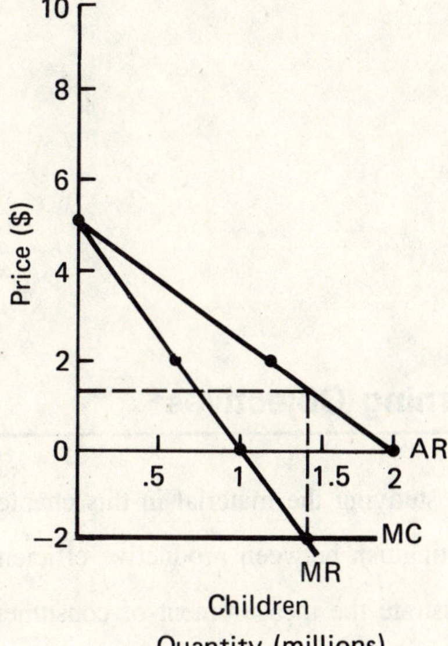

14

Competition and Monopoly Compared

Learning Objectives

After studying the material in this chapter, you should be able to

—distinguish between productive efficiency and allocative efficiency;

—illustrate the measurement of consumers' and producers' surpluses;

—explain how economies of scale and scope influence market structure;

—understand how in market structures other than perfect competition, firms tend to administer prices;

—explain how monopolistically competitive markets are characterized by product differentiation.

Review and Self-Test

Matching Concepts

_______ 1. economies of scope

_______ 2. productive efficiency

_______ 3. market structure characterized by product differentiation

_______ 4. effect of monopolization of a competitive industry if costs are unaltered

_______ 5. excess capacity

_______ 6. equality of price and marginal cost for all products

_______ 7. difference between revenue received for a commodity and market supply curve

_______ 8. consumers' surplus

_______ 9. price set by conscious decision of seller rather than by impersonal market forces

_______ 10. process of creative destruction

(a) condition for allocative efficiency

(b) monopolistic competition

(c) difference between market demand curve and amount paid for a commodity

(d) administered prices

(e) Schumpeter's term for replacement of one monopoly by another through innovation

(f) producers' surplus

(g) rise in price with fall in output

(h) advantage to large firms due to multiproduct production, large-scale distribution, etc.

(i) difference between output at which *ATC* is a minimum and actual equilibrium output

(j) production at lowest attainable cost for a particular level of output

Multiple-Choice Questions

1. Classical economists preferred perfect competition to monopoly because it fulfilled all but which one of the following basic goals?
   (a) consumer sovereignty
   (b) dispersion of economic power
   (c) virtual equality in income distribution
   (d) efficiency of resource allocation

2. As far as it affects consumer welfare, monopoly is potentially objectionable because
   (a) price = marginal revenue.
   (b) price > marginal cost.
   (c) marginal cost = marginal revenue.
   (d) marginal revenue > marginal cost.

3. Assuming that costs would be the same in an industry under either monopoly or competition, a monopoly will produce at a point where, compared with the competitive equilibrium,
   (a) output is larger and price is higher.
   (b) output is lower and price is higher.
   (c) output is lower but price is the same.
   (d) output is the same but price is higher.

Questions 4 to 6 refer to the diagram below:

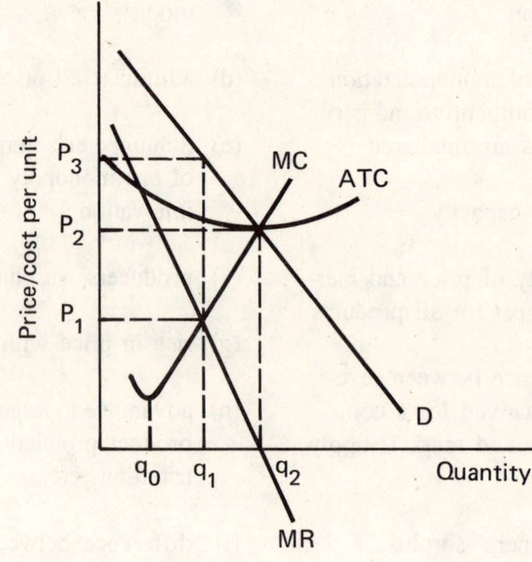

4. A long-run equilibrium described by the combination P_3 and q_1 is
   (a) compatible with any market structure.
   (b) an impossible long-run result.
   (c) Pareto-efficient.
   (d) compatible only with a single-price monopoly or a cartel.

5. A long-run competitive equilibrium (market) would tend to result in a price of
   (a) P_1.
   (b) P_2.
   (c) P_3.
   (d) impossible to predict with the information above

6. A monopoly firm would set its price equal to
   (a) P_1.
   (b) P_2.
   (c) P_3.
   (d) impossible to predict with the information above

7. The important difference between the assumptions for monopolistic competition and those for perfect competition is that monopolistic competitors
   (a) do not try to maximize profits.
   (b) worry about their influences on the market.
   (c) have an inelastic demand curve facing them.
   (d) sell similar but not identical products.

8. In the sense used in this chapter, administered prices are prices
   (a) set by government agencies.
   (b) determined by international forces.
   (c) that incorporate costs of administration in price-setting agencies.
   (d) set by individual firms, rather than in reaction to market forces.

Questions 9 to 12 refer to the diagram below:

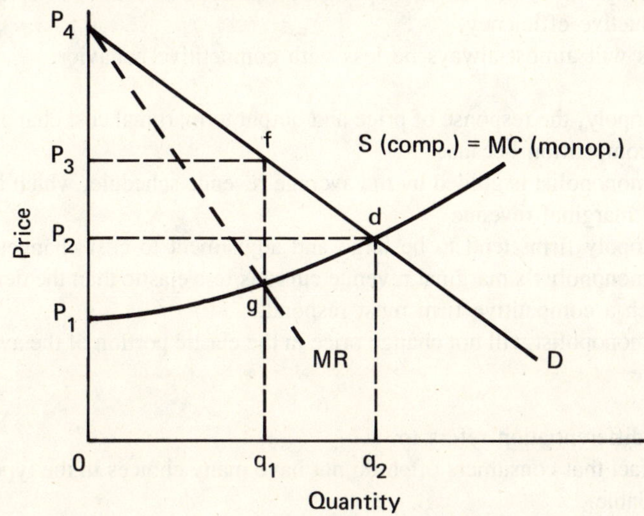

9. Allocative efficiency would be achieved in this market if the profit-maximizing output and price were
   (a) q_1 and p_3.
   (b) q_2 and p_2.
   (c) set where $MR = 0$.
   (d) q_1 and p_2.

10. If p_2 is the market price, producers' surplus is the area
   (a) p_1p_4d.
   (b) Op_2dq_2.
   (c) p_1p_2d.
   (d) Op_1dq_2.

11. If p_2 is the market price, consumers' surplus is the area
   (a) p_2p_4d.
   (b) p_1p_4d.
   (c) Op_4dq_2.
   (d) Op_2dq_2.

12. Reducing output from q_2 to q_1 and increasing the price from p_2 to p_3
   (a) reduces consumers' surplus by the amount *dfg*.
   (b) increases producers' surplus by the amount p_2p_1d.
   (c) reduces the total of consumers' and producers' surplus by the amount *dfg*.
   (d) has no effect on consumers' surplus.

13. The incentive to introduce cost-saving innovations
   (a) is not affected at all by market structure, barriers to entry, or difficulty of copying the innovation.
   (b) is less in monopoly than in competition because the monopolist has no incentive to reduce its costs.
   (c) is likely to be greater in monopoly than in competition because the monopolist can maintain economic profits in the long run.
   (d) is greater in competition than in monopoly according to economist Joseph A. Schumpeter.

14. A major difference between equilibrium in a competitive industry and monopoly is that
    (a) at competitive, but not monopolistic, equilibrium, $P = MC$, thus achieving allocative efficiency.
    (b) when minimum efficient scale (*MES*) is large, competitive behavior will lead to lower average costs.
    (c) at competitive, but not monopolistic, equilibrium, $MR = MC$, thus achieving productive efficiency.
    (d) costs will almost always be less with competitive behavior.

15. In a monopoly, the response of price and output to marginal cost changes will be less than in competition because
    (a) the monopolist is guided by the average revenue schedule, which is more elastic than marginal revenue.
    (b) monopoly firms tend to be large and adjustment to cost changes is slow.
    (c) the monopolist's marginal revenue curve is less elastic than the demand curve to which a competitive firm must respond.
    (d) the monopolist will not change price in the elastic portion of the average revenue curve.

16. Product differentiation refers to
    (a) the fact that consumers often do not have many choices in the types of products available.
    (b) a situation whereby firms have some control over price because they are not selling a homogeneous product.
    (c) an industry that produces more than one commodity group.
    (d) the degree by which a firm can change its output from one product to another.

17. An important prediction of monopolistic competition is that the long-run equilibrium output of the firm occurs at an output
    (a) where price exceeds average total cost.
    (b) less than the one at which average total cost is at a minimum.
    (c) less than the one at which average total cost equals average revenue.
    (d) less than the one at which marginal cost equals marginal revenue.

18. Productive efficiency refers to
    (a) producing at the minimum average cost of production.
    (b) producing what is demanded.
    (c) using resources to ensure that at least some demand for all products is satisfied.
    (d) producing the appropriate mix of products.

Answer questions 19 and 20 referring to the diagram below:

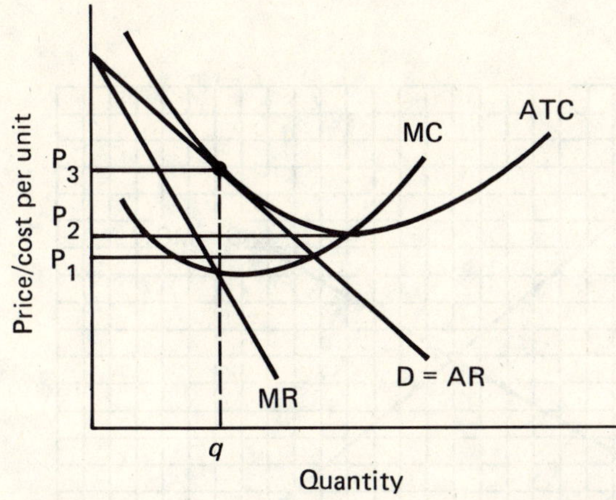

19. The firm in monopolistic competition will set its price equal to
    (a) P_1.
    (b) P_2.
    (c) P_3.
    (d) minimum MC.

20. The situation described by price P_3 and output q is
    (a) identical to perfect competition since there are no economic profits.
    (b) a long-run equilibrium in monopolistic competition.
    (c) unstable; new firms will enter the industry to eliminate economic profits.
    (d) Pareto-efficient.

Self-Test Key

Matching Concepts: 1–h; 2–j; 3–b; 4–g; 5–i; 6–a; 7–f; 8–c; 9–d; 10–e

Multiple-Choice Questions: 1–c; 2–b; 3–b; 4–d; 5–b; 6–c; 7–d; 8–d; 9–b; 10–c; 11–a; 12–c; 13–c; 14–a; 15–c; 16–b; 17–b; 18–a; 19–c; 20–b

Exercises

1.

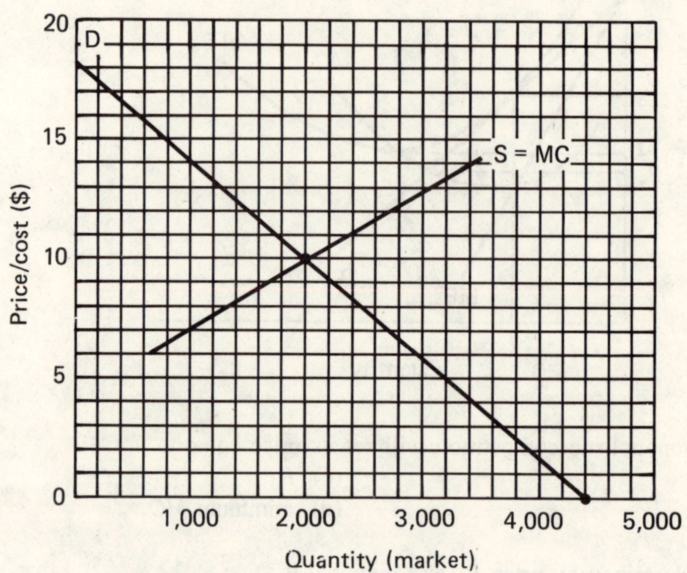

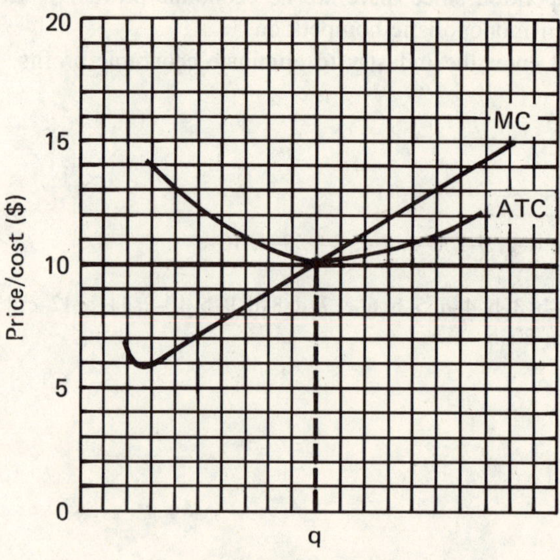

(a) In the market described above, if there are many buyers and sellers, the price will be _________ and quantity exchanged will be _________.

(b) If there is a profit-maximizing monopolist in this market, price will be approximately _________ and output will be approximately _________.

(c) In the case of the monopolist, by how much will price be in excess of minimum average total cost, assuming that the cost curves are the same in (a) and (b) and that $10 represents a long-run zero-profit competitive equilibrium? _________

2. The diagram below is for a competitive industry that has been monopolized. *AL* is the market demand curve and *AK* the marginal revenue curve. *EH* is the long-run supply curve for the industry and also the *LRAC* = *LRMC* for the monopolist. (There are no significant economies of scale or scope. It is a constant cost industry, and to change output the monopolist would simply shut down—or open—plants that had each previously been competitive firms.)

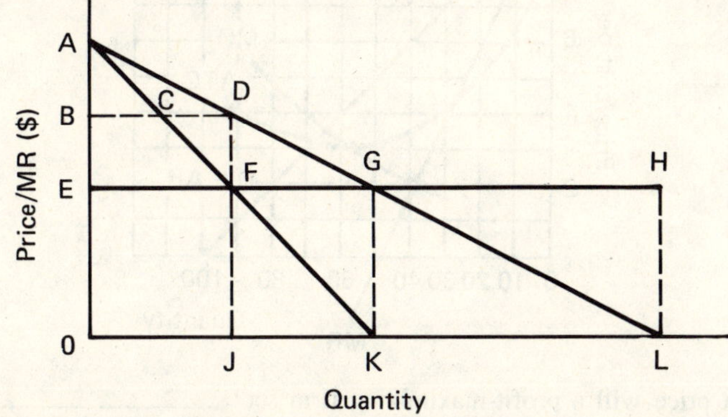

Predict the following:

(a) the competitive price ______ and output ______

(b) the amount of consumer surplus under competition ______

(c) the amount of economic profits under competition ______

(d) the monopolistic price ______ and output ______

(e) the amount of consumer surplus under monopoly ______

(f) the amount of economic profits under monopoly ______

(g) the deadweight allocative loss under monopoly ______

3. The figure below describes a firm in a monopolistically competitive industry characterized by easy entry, product differentiation, and a large number of firms.

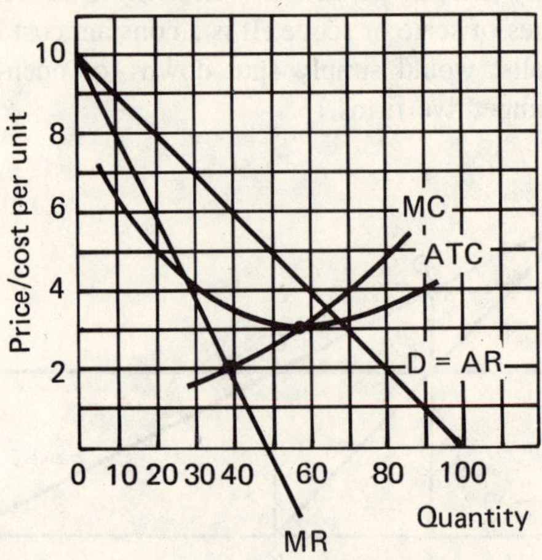

(a) What price will a profit-maximizing firm set? ____________

(b) What total economic profit will this firm receive? ____________

(c) Given that entry is relatively easy, is this a long-run equilibrium situation? Explain.

(d) Which curves will be affected and in which direction if the firm now increases its advertising expenditures by a given amount, causing increased sales?

(e) If new firms were attracted to this industry, what curves in the figure would be affected the most? Why? What would be the *main* consequence for this firm?

(f) Explain how the result in (e) illustrates the excess capacity theorem.

4. The diagrams below illustrate a perfectly competitive situation and a monopoly situation in a market. If marginal costs were to rise by one dollar per unit of output, illustrate that the price would rise by less and output would fall by less in the case of monopoly. Assume the monopolist charges a single price for its output. Explain your answer.

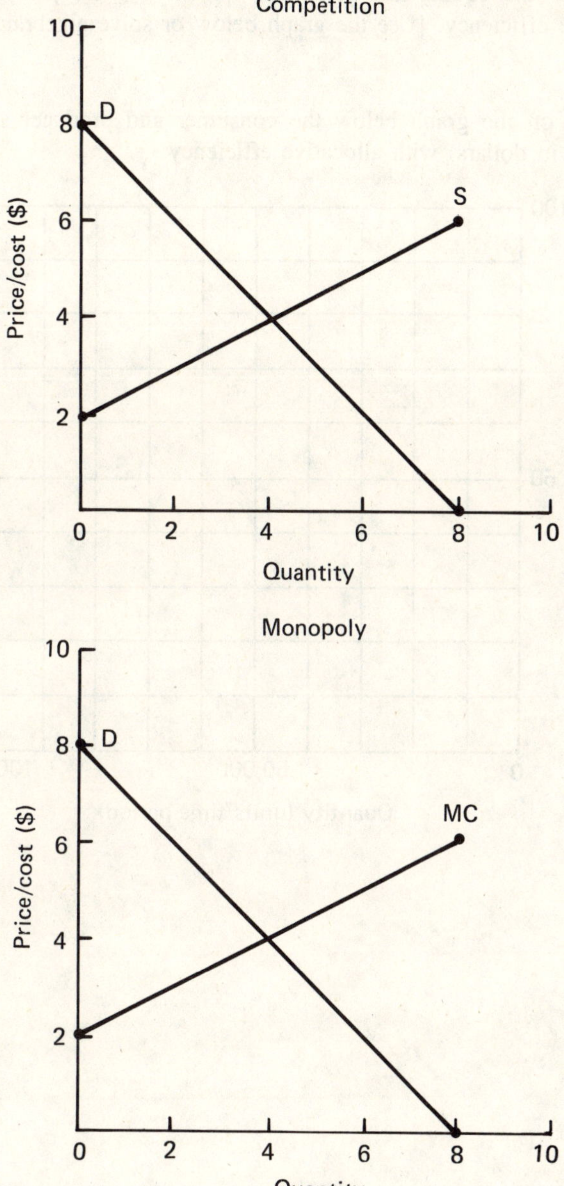

5. Assume a demand curve for a product is $Q_d = 90{,}000 - 1{,}000P$ with P (the price) expressed in dollars. In a competitive market the supply curve is $2{,}000P - 45{,}000$ (with the supply being zero at $P \leq \$22.50$). Remember, the competitive supply curve is the horizontal summation of the firm's marginal cost curves above the minimum average variable cost (here, \$22.50).
   (a) Determine the equilibrium price and quantity of the product necessary for allocative efficiency. [Use the graph below or solve algebraically.]

   (b) Illustrate on the graph below the consumer and producer surplus (total net benefits, in dollars) with allocative efficiency.

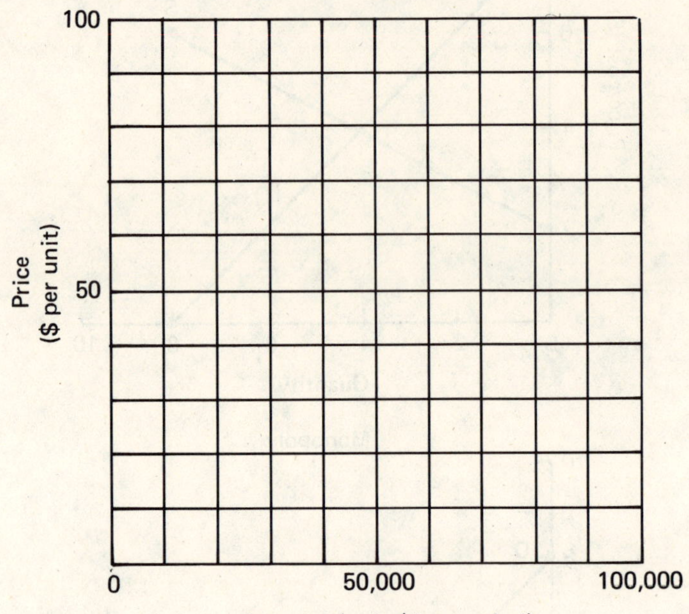

(c) Assume the product was supplied instead by a monopoly. Determine the quantity that will be supplied and market price and illustrate on the graph below the consumer and producer surplus. The counterpart of the competitive supply curve above is $MC = 22.5 + 0.0005Q$. [Note the graphic identity of MC in this graph to S in (b).]

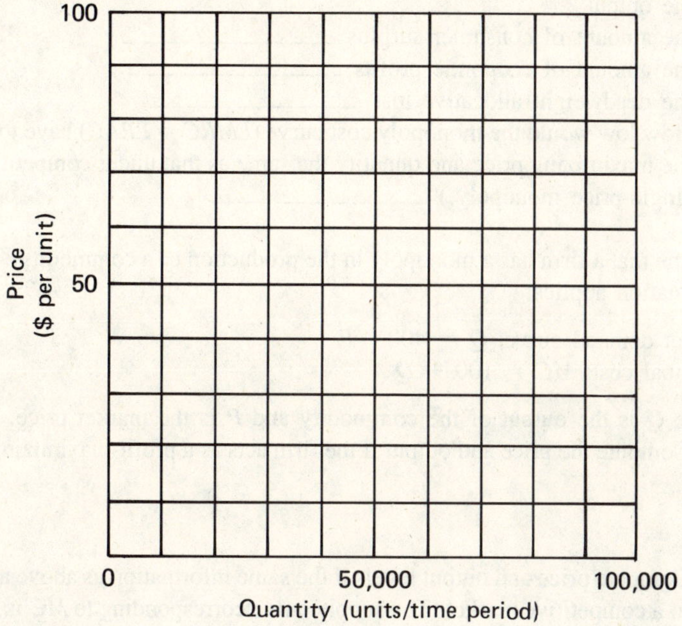

(d) Compare producer surplus, consumer surplus and total net benefits in (c) with those in (b).

Short Problems

1. (Refer to Exercise 2.) Assume a discriminating monopolist that could get the maximum price for each unit and answer the following:
   (a) the price range, from ______________ to ______________
   (b) the output ______________
   (c) the amount of consumer surplus ______________
   (d) the amount of economic profits ______________
   (e) the deadweight allocative loss ______________
   (f) How low would the monopoly cost curve ($LMRC = LRAC$) have to shift to make the maximizing price and quantity the same as that under competition? (Assume single-price monopoly.) ______________

2. Assume that a firm has a monopoly in the production of a commodity. The following information applies:

   Market demand curve: $Q = 400 - P$
   Marginal cost: $MC = 100 + Q$

   where Q is the output of the commodity and P is the market price.
   (a) Compute the price and output if the firm acts as a profit-maximizing monopolist.

   (b) Compute price and output levels if the same information as above applied instead to a competitive market. The supply curve corresponding to MC is $Q = P - 100$.

   (c) Compare your answers to (a) and (b).

3. (Refer to Exercise 5.)
   (a) Calculate the magnitude of total net benefits (in dollars) with allocative efficiency. Relate it to the consumers' surplus and producers' surplus in Exercise 5 (b), which assumes the product is produced and sold in a competitive market.

   (b) Compute the consumers' surplus and producers' surplus assuming this same product was supplied by a (single-price) monopoly.

   (c) Show that the producers' surplus is more while consumers' surplus and total net benefits are less when the market is monopolistic than when it is competitive.

Answers to the Exercises

1. (a) \$10; 2,000 units
   (b) \$13; 1,250 units (Obtain this answer by drawing the *MR* curve on the right diagram with a *y*-axis intercept of 18 and horizontal intercept of 2,250.
   (c) \$3

2. (a) *OE, OK* (b) *AEG* (c) zero (d) *OB, OJ* (e) *ABD* (f) *BDEF* (g) *DFG*

3. (a) \$6.00
   (b) (\$6.00 – \$3.50) × 40 = \$100.00
   (c) No. The entry of new firms will reduce profits.
   (d) *ATC* curve rises; *D* curve will shift rightward, with *MR* curve shifting accordingly. *MC* curve will be unchanged since, in this case, advertising is a fixed amount.
   (e) The average revenue (demand) and marginal revenue curves for this firm would shift leftward and profits would be reduced.
   (f) The leftward shift of the downward-sloping demand curve produces tangency with the delining part of *ATC*. This must be at less than capacity, which is defined as output at which *ATC* is minimum.

4. In the diagram illustrating monopoly, draw in *MR* by bisecting the horizontal intersect of demand. Equate *MR* to *MC* to determine price and output. Shift *MC* curve up by one. In the diagram illustrating competition, equate *S* = *D* to get price and output. Shift supply curve up by one. Visual inspection should show smaller responses in the case of monopoly. The rise in price under competition is from \$4.00 to \$4.67 or \$.67; in monopoly, it is from \$5.60 to \$6.00 or \$.40. Quantity reduction is smaller in absolute terms under monopoly.

5. (a) Set demand equal to supply and solve for price (45) and output (45,000). [See graph (i) below.]
   (b) Consumers' surplus is (a) and producers' surplus is (b) in graph (i).
   (c) On graph (ii) below, consumers' surplus is shown by the triangle *ehg*; producers' surplus is quadrangle, 22.5 *hgf*.
   (d) Under competitive conditions, consumers' surplus (*CS*) is more and producers' surplus (*PS*) is less, than with monopoly. For example, *CS* in (c) above is the area *ehg* in graph (ii), which is less than triangle (a) in graph (i).

   Net benefits (that is, consumers' surplus plus producers' surplus) are less with monopoly. The amount of the reduction (the so-called deadweight allocative loss) is shown by the triangle *ifg* in graph (ii).

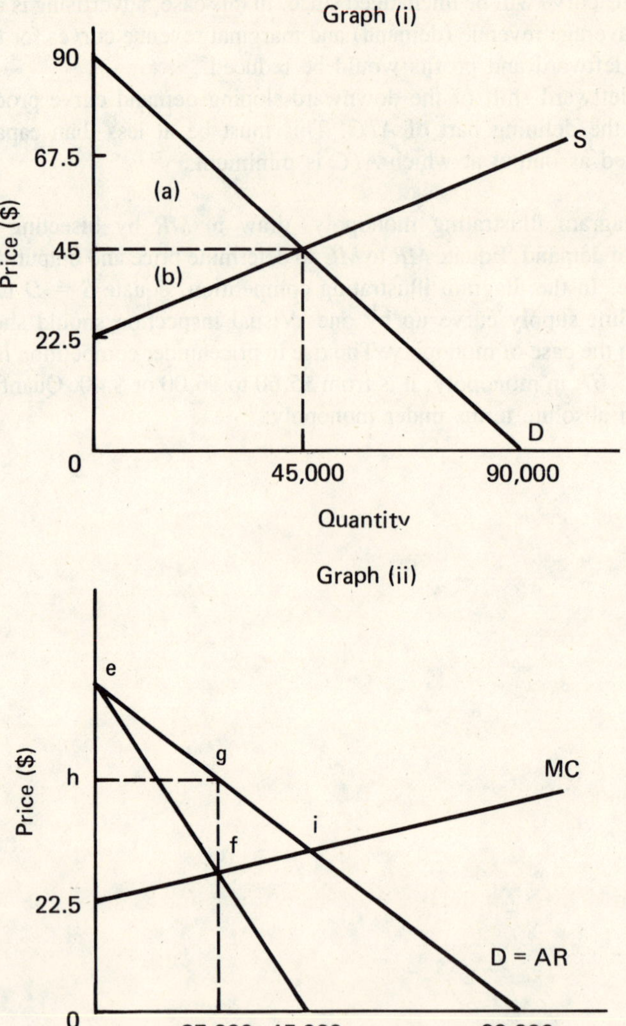

15

Oligopoly

Learning Objectives

Careful study of the material in this chapter should enable you to

—discuss the effects of OPEC cartelization;

—understand why saucer-shaped cost curves and high costs of changing administered prices cause relatively sticky prices for oligopolies in the short run;

—explain the hypothesis of qualified joint profit maximization;

—understand that oligopoly profits can persist in the long run because of barriers to entry, which may be natural or created;

—explain allocative inefficiency under oligopoly.

Review and Self-Test

Matching Concepts

_______ 1. reasons for OPEC "success"

_______ 2. major difficulty facing cartel over long run

_______ 3. conjectural variations

_______ 4. approximately constant *AVC* over extensive range of outputs

_______ 5. stickiness

_______ 6. tendency of oligopoly firms for maximum industry profits modified by each firm's attempts for larger share

_______ 7. example of created barrier to entry

_______ 8. $P = MC$

_______ 9. interdependence of decisions concerning price and output

_______ 10. maximum output attainable before average and marginal costs rise significantly

(a) saucer-shaped cost curve

(b) characteristic of oligopoly prices

(c) hypothesis of qualified joint profit maximization

(d) condition of allocative efficiency

(e) important characteristic governing behavior of oligopoly firms

(f) short-run inelasticity of demand; limitation of alternative supply of oil

(g) full-capacity output

(h) set of possible assumptions about rivals' reactions

(i) maintenance of output restriction by voluntary agreement

(j) brand proliferation

Multiple-Choice Questions

1. Which of the following were reasons for the "success" of the OPEC cartel from 1973 to 1985?
   (a) The member countries provided a large part of the world supply of oil.
   (b) World demand for oil was relatively inelastic in the short run.
   (c) Other oil-producing countries could not quickly increase their oil outputs in response to price increases.
   (d) All of the above are reasons.

2. A dilemma that faces all cartels and monopolies is that
   (a) government prosecution according to antitrust laws is inevitable.
   (b) the greater their short-run profits, the greater the incentive for market reactions that will reduce their profits in the long run.
   (c) they must continue to produce even if price is less than *AVC*.
   (d) there is a continuous incentive to restrict output to levels where $MR > MC$.

3. The text's explanation of "sticky" prices for oligopolists facing cyclical changes in demand stresses
   (a) the need to maintain barriers to entry.
   (b) saucer-shaped *AVC* curves and costs of price changes.
   (c) extensive product differentiation.
   (d) the excess capacity theorem.

4. Oligopolistic prices ordinarily change
   (a) whenever there are changes in costs of production.
   (b) with cyclical and seasonal fluctuations of demand.
   (c) in response to large unexpected shifts in demand.
   (d) for all of the above reasons.

5. The hypothesis of qualified joint profit maximization implies that
   (a) oligopolists openly set monopoly prices.
   (b) oligopolists tacitly agree to policies that will maximize collective profits.
   (c) oligopolists independently set prices.
   (d) the relative strength of tendencies toward and away from joint profit maximization varies among oligopolistic industries.

6. Firm-created barriers to entry include all but which of the following?
   (a) high prices relative to costs
   (b) credible threat of predatory pricing
   (c) high start-up costs, such as for advertising
   (d) brand proliferation

7. Economic profits can exist in an oligopolistic industry in the long run because of
   (a) natural barriers to entry.
   (b) barriers created by existing firms.
   (c) barriers created by government policy.
   (d) all of the above.

8. In an oligopolistic industry, joint profit maximizing by setting prices through tacit agreement is
   (a) more likely the fewer the number of firms.
   (b) more likely the less similar the products.
   (c) more likely when prices are falling than when they are rising.
   (d) invariably illegal under the antitrust laws.

9. A decision-making process referred to as conjectural variations
   (a) guarantees a constant price across all firms in an oligopoly.
   (b) applies only to duopoly.
   (c) involves consideration of how rivals will respond to price changes.
   (d) is used only in monopolistic competition.

10. An oligopoly is characterized by
    (a) a single dominant firm in the industry.
    (b) a formal agreement among firms on how much to produce and what price to charge.
    (c) relatively few firms, each with limited market power due to intense rivalry.
    (d) ease of entry by new firms.

11. Prices in an oligopolistic market are most likely to
    (a) change almost constantly.
    (b) be relatively sticky.
    (c) consistently increase, regardless of demand and supply considerations.
    (d) be even lower than competitive prices in the long run.

12. Firms that set administered prices at levels at or below marginal cost so as to deter new entrants are engaging in
    (a) predatory pricing.
    (b) marginal cost pricing.
    (c) efficiency pricing.
    (d) loss-minimizing pricing.

13. Restriction of output below the competitive level
    (a) leads to allocative inefficiency.
    (b) can lead to profits in the short run.
    (c) is the goal of joint profit maximizers, such as a cartel.
    (d) all of the above

14. The upper price limit for firms who collude to maximize their joint profits is
    (a) the competitive price.
    (b) the price for output where average cost is minimized.
    (c) the monopoly price, at the output where $MR = MC$.
    (d) the price where marginal revenue equals zero.

15. A duopoly is
    (a) a bilateral monopoly.
    (b) an industry containing only two firms.
    (c) a firm that has a monopoly in two different markets.
    (d) none of the above.

16. Holding price constant in the face of short-term fluctuations in demand
    (a) can never be profitable.
    (b) is a frequent occurrence in competitive markets.
    (c) can be expected only with U-shaped cost curves.
    (d) can be profitable if costs are stable over the range of output fluctuations.

17. The empirical evidence is now overwhelming that in manufacturing industries, the *AVC* and *MC* curves are
    (a) U-shaped.
    (b) saucer-shaped.
    (c) continuously declining.
    (d) continuously rising.

18. A firm might well prefer to build a plant with marginal and average costs flat over a relatively large range of output
    (a) if it anticipates fluctuating demand.
    (b) only if its costs at normal capacity are less than the costs of alternative plants.
    (c) if demand is expected to be fairly stable.
    (d) if its fixed factors are indivisible.

19. A Cournot-Nash equilibrium
    (a) results when each firm in an oligopoly assumes that the outputs of other firms are constant.
    (b) is an example of a cooperative equilibrium.
    (c) necessarily produces competitive price levels.
    (d) necessarily produces monopolistic price levels.

20. The text suggests that the relative stability of oil prices in the 1981–1985 period can be attributed primarily to
    (a) the ability of OPEC to control cheating among its members.
    (b) cooperation by non-OPEC members in maintaining price.
    (c) great increases in the demand for oil.
    (d) the acceptance during that time of greatly reduced output levels by Saudi Arabia.

Self-Test Key

Matching Concepts: 1–f; 2–i; 3–h; 4–a; 5–b; 6–c; 7–j; 8–d; 9–e; 10–g

Multiple-Choice Questions: 1–d; 2–b; 3–b; 4–c; 5–d; 6–a; 7–d; 8–a; 9–c; 10–c; 11–b; 12–a; 13–d; 14–c; 15–b; 16–d; 17–b; 18–a; 19–a; 20–d

Exercises

1. A firm has the choice of constructing a plant with either of the long-run average variable cost curves shown in the figure below.
   (a) If there was considerable uncertainty about demand for the product, which plant would the firm choose to build? Why?

   (b) What does the shape of AVC_1 suggest about the nature of the fixed factors in this plant?

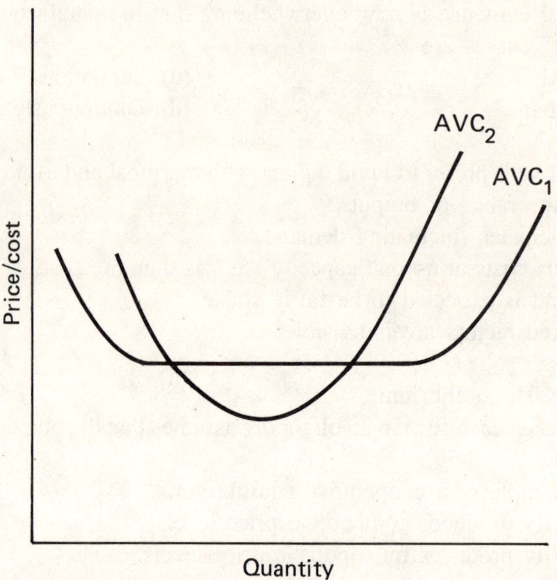

2. The saucer-shaped (flat) average cost curve discussed in the text can be estimated for the relevant range of output (where AVC is approximately equal to MC) by a total cost function in the form $TC = a + bq$ where $a = TFC$, $q =$ output, and $b = MC = AVC$.
   (a) Assume a firm's "normal" demand curve is estimated as $P = 50 - 0.01q$, so that $TR = 50q - 0.01q^2$, $MR = 50 - 0.02q$, and that $TC = \$25{,}000 + 10q$. What is the profit-maximizing price and quantity?

   (b) According to the "sticky price" hypothesis of oligopoly theory, what changes are likely in price and quantity as demand fluctuates over this range? Explain.

3. In the figure below, suppose that *D* is the demand curve for an oligopoly firm if all the firms in the industry act together, and that *d* is the demand curve for the firm when it alone in the industry varies its price. Assume that price is now at $2.

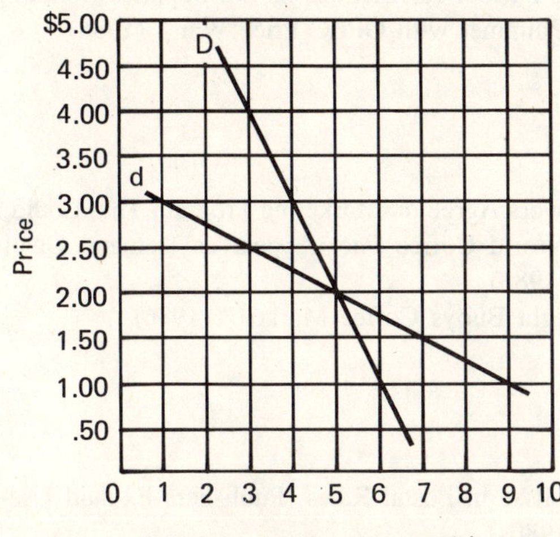

(a) If the firm lowers its price from $2.00 to $1.50 and no other firm does, its sales will go from ________________ to ________________, and total revenue will go from ________________ to ________________.

(b) If the firm lowers its price from $2.00 to $1.50 and every other firm does too, its sales will go from ________________ to ________________, and total revenue from ________________ to ________________.

(c) If the firm raises its price from $2.00 to $2.50 and no other firm does, its sales will go from ________________ to ________________, and its total revenue will go from ________________ to ________________.

(d) If the firm raises its price from $2.00 to $2.50 and every other firm does too, its revenue will go from ________________ to ________________.

(e) Assuming that this firm has a fairly level variable cost of about $.75 in the relevant range of output, under what circumstances, if any, would the manager consider raising the price? Lowering it?

(f) Does this situation encourage collusive action by the firms in the industry to raise prices together? ________________ To lower prices together? ________________

(g) Relate this exercise to the concept of *conjectural variations*.

4. Use economic analysis to discuss each of the following events described in newspaper headlines. Use supply and demand diagrams to the extent possible.
   (a) "The Prices of Petroleum Products Rise as OPEC Restricts Oil Supplies." (1974)
   "OPEC Plans Further Restrictions on Oil Supplies to Maintain Prices." (1983)
   "Oil Prices Plummet with OPEC Price War." (1986)

   (b) "Coffee Growers Agree on Marketing Program That Could Lift Prices." (1980)
   "Cracks in World Coffee Pact Appear as Demand Declines and Production Increases." (1983)
   "Brazil Drought Buoys Coffee Market." (1986)

   (c) "Spurred by Rise in Postal Rates, Publishers Expand Use of Private Delivery Systems." (1980s).

   (d) " 'Rent-A-Wreck' Used Car Rental Agency Competes with Hertz and Avis for Car Rentals." (1978)

Short Problems

1. Regulating New York City Taxicabs
Monopoly profits can be obtained by foreclosing entry into a market by legal means. Laws requiring a license to provide a service in a particular industry often cause this result.

An interesting example is the law requiring licensure of taxicabs in many U.S. cities. New York City passed such a law in 1937, freezing the number of taxicab licenses (medallions) at 11,797. Taxicabs without such medallions are not supposed to pick up persons who hail cabs from the street. Prior to the law, free entry of taxicabs had been allowed. In 1937, the price of taxicab medallions was near zero since existing cabs were "grandfathered": existing operators obtained a medallion by virtue of already being in the industry. New entrants had to purchase a medallion from an existing owner at whatever price the current owner charged. As demand rose, the market value of a medallion rose, reaching $100,000 in December 1985. About 1,600 medallions are traded every year, with banks often giving mortgages for their purchase.

Questions

(a) Use a graph to illustrate why the price of medallions has increased over time. Why is the increase in market price likely to continue?

(b) What does the market value of a medallion represent?

(c) What effect has the emergence of "gypsy" cabs in the city (cabs without medallions) had on the taxicab market and the market value of a medallion? How would unrestricted entry affect the market value of a medallion?

(d) In April 1985, New York's Mayor Koch proposed increasing the number of medallions by 10 percent of the existing number. Under the plan, they were to be made available by auction. Earlier, the mayor had proposed giving each medallion owner a second one to use or sell. Contrast these two plans.

(e) How might the licensing of taxicabs affect the quality of taxicab services, particularly with regulation of cab fares by the city and little or no price competition among cabs allowed?

2. (a) This problem refers back to Exercise 2 in which the firm's "normal" demand curve was estimated as $P = 50 - 0.01q$ and its $TC = \$25{,}000 + 10q$. The profit-maximizing price and quantity were estimated as $P = \$30$ and $q = 2{,}000$, respectively. Assume that short-run fluctuations in demand shift the demand as far to the right as $P = 60 - 0.01q$ and as far to the left as $P = 40 - 0.01q$.

Calculate the apparent profit consequences of maintaining the price of \$30 and altering quantity to the new demand situations. Contrast the result with that of setting new profit-maximizing prices appropriate to the shifted demands. [You should note that the profit consequences of a sticky price in this example are significant, but remember that several, or even many, price changes (instead of just one) would have to be made as the demand shifted back and forth. Also note that had the shift to the right been to $P = 50 - 0.005q$, which would have maintained the same demand elasticity at the \$30 price, \$30 would have remained the profit-maximizing price.]

(b) This example is like that for a firm in monopoly or monopolistic competition since the demand curves seem to assume that the firm's price can be set *ceteris paribus* (without changing anything else). What special attribute of oligopoly might also work toward stable or sticky prices in this situation?

Answers to the Exercises

1. (a) The firm would likely choose the plant with AVC_1. If demand were to vary considerably, the average cost of producing various quantities would not vary considerably, whereas with a plant characterized by AVC_2 costs, on average, could rise considerably if demand increased or decreased noticeably.
   (b) It suggests that the fixed factors are such that their rate of utilization can be varied so as to keep the variable to fixed factor ratio constant or close to constant.

2. (a) Set $MR = MC$ to find output: $50 - 0.02q = 10$; $q = 2{,}000$. Solve for p in the demand equation at $q = 2{,}000$: price equals $30.
   (b) Price will be constant; output will vary. The high costs of changing administered prices causes their stickiness.

3. These answers are approximate, depending on how you read the values on the horizontal axis.
   (a) from 5,000 to 7,000; from $10,000 to $10,500
   (b) from 5,000 to 5,500; from $10,000 to $8,250
   (c) from 5,000 to 3,000; from $10,000 to $7,500
   (d) from $10,000 to $11,250
   (e) It would raise price only if everyone else did; it would not lower it even without retaliation because additional revenue would be less than additional costs. For instance, at 6,000 units *MC* would equal $.75 but *MR* would be only $.50.
   (f) Yes, note answers to (d) and (e) that show some form of tacit collusion, such as price leadership would increase profits; no, note answers to (a) and (e) that indicate lower prices are unprofitable even when firm has a price advantage over competitors. In this example the decision to raise price or not depends upon the assumption made about other firms' response.
   (g) Conjectural variations refer to assumptions about rivals' behavior.

4. (a) leftward shifts of the supply curve in 1974 and 1983; rightward shift in 1986
   (b) restriction of supply in 1980 (cartel); demand shift leftward and supply rightward in 1983; supply curve shift leftward in 1986
   (c) movement up demand curve for postal services; demand for private delivery systems shifts rightward
   (d) provision of low-priced service finds niche in differentiated market; modest shift of demand to left for standard rental companies

16

Public Policies About Monopoly and Competition

Learning Objectives

After studying the material in this chapter, you should be able to

—outline the purposes of antitrust legislation;

—discuss the difficulties of public utility regulation;

—explain the mechanism and effects of destructive competition;

—understand that, while the main thrust of antitrust and regulatory policies has been the protection of competitive forces, regulation has also been used to protect firms from competition;

—discuss the purposes and progress of the deregulation movement.

Review and Self-Test

Matching Concepts

_______ 1. amended antitrust law forbidding unfair and deceptive acts of commerce

_______ 2. destructive competition

_______ 3. Clayton Antitrust Act

_______ 4. first federal antitrust law

_______ 5. natural monopoly

_______ 6. allowable investment on which a public utility is allowed a fair rate of return

_______ 7. protectionist policy of Interstate Commerce Commission

_______ 8. deregulation

_______ 9. Supreme Court interpretation that only unreasonable combinations of business in restraint of trade merited conviction under the Sherman Antitrust Act

_______ 10. practice whereby regulatory commissions determine allowable prices to maintain "fair" profit levels

(a) Sherman Antitrust Act

(b) industry where only a single firm can supply market demand efficiently

(c) rate base

(d) reduction of interference with private decision making

(e) Federal Trade Commission Act

(f) rule of reason

(g) law concerned with practices such as mergers and price discrimination that "may substantially lessen competition"

(h) rate of return regulation

(i) restriction of entry and setting minimum rates for trucking

(j) maintenance of long-run prices insufficient to cover long-run costs

Multiple-Choice Questions

1. Enforcement provisions of the Sherman Antitrust Act include all but which one of the following?
   (a) treble damages payable to private firms and individuals
   (b) jail sentences for guilty corporation executives
   (c) dissolution of an offending monopolist
   (d) public ownership of the violating firm

2. The original philosophy of regulating natural monopolies like public utilities
   (a) was to guarantee the consumer a low price.
   (b) involved government ownership of necessary enterprises.
   (c) was to achieve the advantages of large-scale production but prevent the monopolist from raising price and restricting output.
   (d) has been implemented with little difficulty over the years.

3. Mergers or acquisitions that may substantially lessen competition or tend to create a monopoly are prohibited by the
   (a) Sherman Antitrust Act.
   (b) Federal Trade Commission Act.
   (c) Clayton Antitrust Act, as amended by the Celler–Kefauver Act.
   (d) all of the above

4. From the public's standpoint, a "fair rate of return" on a utility investment
   (a) should mean approximately the current rate of return on alternatives of similar risk.
   (b) should be determined by historical costs.
   (c) can always be earned, provided prices are set high enough.
   (d) means what stockholders think is fair.

5. The larger the minimum efficient scale of firms, *ceteris paribus,*
   (a) the more likely a concentrated market structure will improve productive efficiency.
   (b) the greater the tendency toward a natural monopoly.
   (c) the greater the advantages of large-scale production.
   (d) all of the above

6. A natural monopoly
   (a) can occur only in the resources industry.
   (b) evolves over time through conglomerate mergers.
   (c) will tend to arise in industries with either scale or scope economies.
   (d) leads to higher costs and higher prices than large-group market structures.

7. Currently a major debate concerning regulation
   (a) applies primarily to public utilities rather than other business activity.
   (b) regards whether the benefits from certain regulations justify their costs.
   (c) concerns whether the United States should return to a strict laissez-faire regime.
   (d) is whether the government should assume ownership of most natural monopolies.

8. All but which one of the following is a problem for public utility regulation?
   (a) definition of costs
   (b) determining the allowable rate base
   (c) setting a fair return
   (d) determining the price and level of service provided by a natural monopoly

9. "Protectionist" policies by regulatory commissions
   (a) are aimed at protecting the consumer.
   (b) reflect concern of existing firms about potential competitors.
   (c) concern the trade-offs between domestic and foreign trade policy.
   (d) deal with work safety and environmental issues.

10. The imposition of "fair" rate of return legislation in an industry where a monopolist is currently earning economic profits should result in
    (a) an increase in price and decrease in output.
    (b) a decrease in both price and output.
    (c) a decrease in price and increase in output.
    (d) The answer cannot be determined with the information provided.

11. Even large conglomerate mergers are difficult to challenge under antitrust laws since
    (a) they are explicitly given antitrust exemptions.
    (b) the political influence of giant firms makes them difficult to prosecute.
    (c) their contribution to efficiency through economies of scope is so clear.
    (d) definable markets in which competition may be lessened are usually not involved.

12. Antitrust litigation under amended Section 7 of the Clayton Antitrust Act is most likely to require a definition of
    (a) the appropriate market.
    (b) what constitutes a fair price.
    (c) price discrimination.
    (d) all of the above.

13. Regulatory agencies do not generally force pricing according to allocative efficiency because
    (a) it would lead to excessive profits for the regulated firm.
    (b) the resulting output would be less than the output with average cost pricing.
    (c) the regulated firm could suffer losses unless subsidized by the government.
    (d) the price would exceed the price necessary for the company to earn a fair rate of return.

14. The notion of "necessary and prudent investments" has entered into regulatory rules because
    (a) by acquiring expensive capital goods, a regulated firm can expand its rate base, thereby justifying higher prices.
    (b) regulatory commissions have the tendency to make unsound investments.
    (c) regulated firms often curtail service to reduce costs.
    (d) public utilities would otherwise reduce their investments in useful capital equipment.

15. As compared to other firms that may have monopoly power, a natural monopoly
    (a) faces a demand curve that is inelastic throughout its entire output range.
    (b) has marginal and average costs that decline continuously over the entire range of industry demand.
    (c) is often the result of conglomerate mergers.
    (d) is likely to have a stranglehold on raw material sources.

16. The overall effect of antitrust policies at any time rests on
    (a) the nature of the antitrust laws themselves.
    (b) the courts' interpretation of the laws.
    (c) the vigor of bringing prosecutions by the government and by private plaintiffs.
    (d) all of the above.

17. Deregulation of the 1980s
    (a) was limited to eliminating close supervision of the airline, banking and telecommunications industries.
    (b) concerns the whole question of how much interference with private decision making is desirable.
    (c) focused on reversing the protectionist policies of regulatory commissions such as the ICC and FCC.
    (d) made destructive competition illegal.

18. There is a growing consensus that natural monopoly regulation by public utility regulatory commissions
    (a) has served effectively to protect consumers from natural monopolies.
    (b) has led to a maze of bureaucratic rules because of the adaptive behavior of regulated firms.
    (c) is concerned more with protecting firms from competition than with protection of the consumer from natural monopoly.
    (d) both (b) and (c)

Self-Test Key

Matching Concepts: 1–e; 2–j; 3–g; 4–a; 5–b; 6–c; 7–i; 8–d; 9–f; 10–h

Multiple-Choice Questions: 1–d; 2–c; 3–c; 4–a; 5–d; 6–c; 7–b; 8–d; 9–b; 10–c; 11–d; 12–a; 13–c; 14–a; 15–b; 16-d; 17-b; 18-d

Exercises

1. The diagram below illustrates a natural monopoly. The cost curves are long-run.

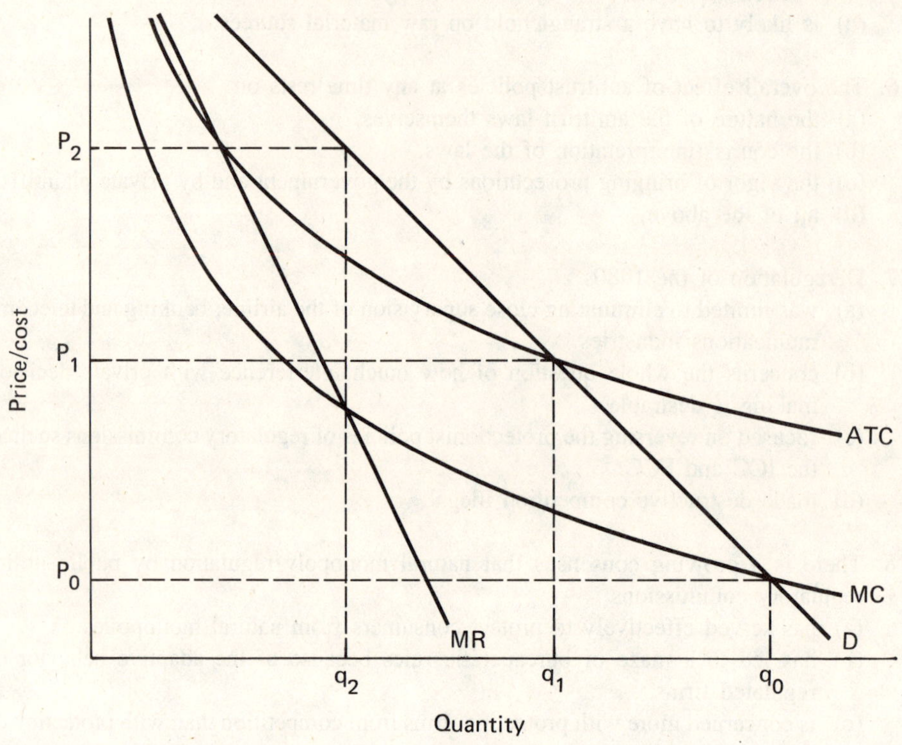

(a) Referring to the diagram above, explain what is meant by the term *natural monopoly*.

(b) The optimal single price for a monopolist would be ________________ at which output would be limited to ________________.

(c) Assume a regulatory commission attempted to set the price equal to *MC*, the result predicted for competitive markets. The price would be ________________ but output in the long-run would be ________________ since average revenue would be ________________ than average cost.

(d) The regulatory commission could set a price equal to average cost. This would result in output ________________. This would still be allocatively inefficient since consumers would still desire to purchase ________________ additional units at prices between ________________ and ________________ that are above *MC*.

(e) As was pointed out in Chapter 13, a price-discriminating monopolist could more nearly approach the output that met the competitive test of $P = MC$. In the extreme case where every unit was sold at the maximum price the consumer was willing to pay, an unregulated monopolist's output would be ________________ and all of the surplus over the cost of resources used would be (producer, consumer) surplus.

(f) A sophisticated regulatory commission could encourage expansion of output towards the competitive norm by following the rule that average revenue (i.e., average, rather than specific, prices) should approximately equal average costs but that the regulated firm could set different prices for separate segments of the market based on elasticity and marginal costs. Such regulation would permit output to exceed ________________ and to insure that most surplus would be (producer, consumer) surplus.

2. Indicate which antitrust law would seem most appropriate to use against the indicated violation:
   (a) a conspiracy to monopolize ________________
   (b) a horizontal merger of two very large firms ________________
   (c) unfair business practices ________________
   (d) secret price fixing agreements ________________
   (e) exclusive dealing and tying contracts ________________
   (f) price discrimination ________________

Short Problems

1. At Last, Mergers the Reagan Administration Didn't Like

"After six years, the Reagan Administration's antitrust watchdog found a merger it didn't like. In fact, it found two." (*Business Week,* July 7, 1986). The two mergers blocked by Federal Trade Commission (FTC) orders on June 20 were proposed purchases of Dr. Pepper Company by Coca-Cola for $470 million, and of the Seven-Up Company, owned by Philip Morris Inc., by PepsiCo for $380 million. The FTC actions followed by a day a temporary restraining order barring both mergers by a federal district judge in response to an antitrust complaint by Royal Crown.

The initial quote reflects the absence of a government action during the corporate takeover activity of the 1980s. It is true that most of the mergers were conglomerate like the Reynolds Industries' (tobacco plus food) purchase of Nabisco (food, particularly crackers) to form RJR, in which government action would have to make a dubious case on the lessening of potential competition. The large horizontal mergers in oil (Texaco–Getty for one) and steel (LTV–Republic) involved markets with much international competition.

Soda companies essentially produce the syrup and franchise independent bottlers to distribute the product (Coke had 350 bottlers). Both Pepsi and Coke were purchasing bottling companies however, and, with the mergers, would each distribute 30 percent of its total volume.

Market shares of the U.S. soda market in mid-1986 (as calculated by Montgomery Securities and published in *Beverage Digest*) were:

Coca Cola	40 percent	Royal Crown	4.6 percent
PepsiCo	28	Cadbury-Schweppes	3.7
Seven-Up	7	Other	10.2
Dr. Pepper	6.5		

(a) Calculate the two-firm and four-firm concentration ratios in mid-1986, and as they would have been after the mergers.

(b) Philip Morris immediately dropped its sale offer to PepsiCo (two weeks later, however, PepsiCo purchased Seven-Up's international division); Coca-Cola said it would legally challenge the FTC decision. Consider the government's case as to why these mergers "may substantially lessen competition" in the U.S. soda market. What defense might Coca-Cola make?

(c) Royal Crown, the third cola which had reversed a decline to increase its shipments by 10 percent in 1985, apparently felt the most threatened by the merger. Why?

(d) The Cadbury-Schweppes share of 3.7 percent mostly came from its earlier purchase of Canada Dry and Sunkist Orange from RJR–Nabisco. It combined the two leading producers of ginger ale. Should this merger have been challenged?

(e) Many economists distinguish antitrust actions from other forms of economic regulation, though the Reagan administration apparently has seen it as another undesirable form of government intervention in the free market. What is the distinction?

2. Price War in the Sky

In 1976 the Civil Aeronautics Board (CAB) regulated both prices and entry into the air passenger business. All major domestic routes were controlled by the same carriers (or merged successors) as pioneered the industry in the 1930s. Alfred Kahn, Cornell economist and head of the CAB, was committed to restoring competition to involve more than services (meals, attractive flight attendants, frequent flights, etc.) and some special discounts for charter airlines.

A first step was to allow charter airlines to compete on major routes as long as reservations were made 30 days in advance. This produced vigorous price competition on such routes as New York and Chicago to the West Coast and New York to Florida.

The next step was enactment of the Airline Deregulation Act in 1978. Airlines were free to set prices (popular with existing air carriers), and almost "automatic" entry into new routes was allowed (not so popular). New airlines such as People Express entered on a price basis, and existing regional airlines such as Allegheny (now US Air) expanded to major city routes. Between 1978 and 1983, vigorous price competition to the point of sporadic price wars and greatly reduced overall profits characterized this industry. One established carrier, Braniff, went bankrupt in 1982.

As of 1986, the airline industry was still fairly "unstable." Price competition remained very active, particularly along the major air routes, and several mergers had taken place among larger carriers (e.g., Texas Air and Eastern). In late 1986, People ran into financial difficulties and was taken over by Texas Air.

(a) Why was freer entry into the market (government regulation had been the main obstacle to entry), as well as freedom to set prices, probably necessary for vigorous price competition?

(b) How does past airline regulation illustrate what the text terms "protectionism" in government regulatory policies?

Answers to the Exercises

1. (a) One in which only one firm can supply demand with productive efficiency. In this diagram, economies of scale are so great relative to demand that most efficient plant size cannot be reached.
   (b) P_2; q_2 (c) P_0; zero; less (d) q_1; $q_0 - q_1$; P_1 and P_0 (e) q_1; producer (f) q_1; consumer.

2. (a) Sherman Antitrust Act, Sec. 2; (b) Clayton Antitrust Act, Sec. 7 (Cellar–Kefauver); (c) FTC Act, Sec. 5; (d) Sherman Antitrust Act, Sec. 1; (e) Clayton Antitrust Act, Sec. 3; (f) Clayton Antitrust Act, Sec. 2 (Robinson–Patman)

17

Who Runs the Firm and for What Ends?

Learning Objectives

After studying the material in this chapter, you should be able to

—explain the basic thesis of Galbraith's new industrial state and consider its merits;

—list several hypotheses concerning who really controls the modern corporation;

—distinguish the sales maximization and profit maximization theories from the nonmaximization theories of the behavior of firms;

—explain the evolutionary theory of firm behavior;

—recognize profits as an important driving force in the economy in all of the theories discussed.

Review and Self-Test

Matching Concepts

_______ 1. theory that firms operate cautiously in a gradually changing environment

_______ 2. "satisficing"

_______ 3. Ralph Nader

_______ 4. sales maximization hypothesis

_______ 5. J. K. Galbraith

_______ 6. pricing by average cost plus fixed markup

_______ 7. proxy fight

_______ 8. hypothesis of the separation of ownership from control

_______ 9. limiting factor for goals other than profit maximization

_______ 10. local profit maximizer

(a) full-cost pricing

(b) use of target levels of adequate performance instead of maximizing profits

(c) managerial control of firms that leads to different behavior than would stockholder control

(d) *The New Industrial State*

(e) struggle for control of corporation

(f) corporate emphasis on maximizing market share subject to profit constraint

(g) threat of a takeover bid

(h) leading spokesperson for consumerism

(i) maximization of profits within a firm's present range of commodities and markets

(j) evolutionary theory of the firm

Multiple-Choice Questions

1. A characteristic of most large modern U.S. corporations is that
   (a) the stockholders really run the business.
   (b) the board of directors really runs the business.
   (c) hired managers run the business.
   (d) the workers run the business.

2. A firm that acts according to the full-cost pricing hypothesis will
   (a) equate marginal revenue and marginal cost.
   (b) equate marginal revenue and full or average cost.
   (c) equate average revenue with full cost.
   (d) add a conventional markup to average cost at normal capacity.

3. Firms that behave according to the satisficing hypothesis will
   (a) not concern themselves with profit considerations.
   (b) strive to achieve certain target levels of profits rather than the maximum level attainable.
   (c) choose the unique output level corresponding with maximum profits.
   (d) seek to maximize consumer satisfaction rather than profits.

4. Recent "evolutionary" theories of firm behavior
   (a) stress tradition and gradual change in firms' decisions.
   (b) incorporate profit-maximizing assumptions.
   (c) emphasize dynamic and innovative elements.
   (d) suggest that firms react quickly to changing economic conditions.

5. The sales-maximizing hypothesis implies that
   (a) a firm will sell as many units as it can at a fixed price, regardless of resulting profits.
   (b) firms have no interest in profits, only in growth of sales.
   (c) a firm will sell additional units by reducing price to the point where $MR = MC$.
   (d) firms will seek to maximize their sales revenue, subject to a profit constraint.

6. Which of the following would be inconsistent with Galbraith's hypothesis of the "new industrial state"?
   (a) large advertising budgets for large corporations
   (b) interlocking directorships among large corporations
   (c) constraint of large firms by government policies
   (d) subversion of public institutions by corporate managers

7. The firm's goals, according to Simon's "satisficing" hypothesis, would not include
   (a) maintenance of market share.
   (b) achievement of a specified gain in sales.
   (c) attaining a target level of profits.
   (d) maximization of profits.

8. Which statement best describes Galbraith's "new industrial state"?
   (a) The federal government now has a great deal of control over U.S. corporations.
   (b) U.S. corporations are very responsive to the desires, needs, and best interests of the buying public.
   (c) Because of the power of unions and shareholders, U.S. industrial management has little real control.
   (d) The size and influence of large U.S. corporations give them great power over government, consumers, markets, and other institutions.

9. The recommended approach for testing theories about firm behavior is to
   (a) ask business management whether it maximizes profits, "satisfices," or maximizes sales.
   (b) abstract from reality as much as possible.
   (c) try to find evidence, facts, and figures to show what firms actually have done in what circumstances.
   (d) watch a business manager make a decision to see how it is done.

10. The central prediction of organization theory is that
   (a) the economy is becoming more centralized.
   (b) different decisions will result from different kinds of organizations.
   (c) corporations should decentralize decision making.
   (d) large organizations are more efficient than small ones.

11. The hypothesis of minority control
    (a) refers to affirmative action programs that have encouraged stock ownership by nonwhites.
    (b) recognizes that holders of much less than 51 percent of the stock may effectively select directors and managers.
    (c) holds that a minority of employees, the top managers, run the firm.
    (d) is seldom applicable.

12. The hypothesis of the separation of ownership from control
    (a) implies that the chief executive officer seldom is a stockholder.
    (b) is that managers effectively control decisions, leading to different behavior than would direct control by owners.
    (c) stresses the important role of government regulation in influencing management decisions.
    (d) is inconsistent with the sales maximization hypothesis of firms' behavior.

13. One thing generally agreed on even by opponents of Galbraith is that advertising
    (a) is essential to ensure the existence of corporations.
    (b) shifts demands among similar products.
    (c) causes major changes in peoples' values.
    (d) must be limited by government to only informing consumers.

14. A difference between maximizing and nonmaximizing theories of firm behavior is
    (a) the speed and magnitude, but not the general direction, of the response to changes in demand or cost conditions.
    (b) that firms are nonmaximizers because they have inadequate information to maximize profits.
    (c) that maximizing and nonmaximizing firms respond entirely differently to changes in economic conditions.
    (d) that maximizing firms all exhibit a great deal of inertia.

15. The use of corporate takeovers through tender bids that offer stockholders a premium for their shares
    (a) lends support to the hypothesis of minority control.
    (b) encourages sales maximization by managers.
    (c) limits the discretion of management to pursue goals other than profit maximization.
    (d) declined in the 1980s because of the aggressive antimerger stance of the Reagan administration.

16. Full-cost pricing can be reconciled with profit-maximization theory
    (a) if the markups are conventional and only rarely revised.
    (b) if the markup is applied to costs at the actual output.
    (c) if the markup is the profit-maximizing one for normal capacity output and price changes are costly.
    (d) It cannot be reconciled because of its failure to include marginal concepts.

Self-Test Key

Matching Concepts: 1–j; 2–b; 3–h; 4–f; 5–d; 6–a; 7–e; 8–c; 9–g; 10–i

Multiple-Choice Questions: 1–c; 2–d; 3–b; 4–a; 5–d; 6–c; 7–d; 8–d; 9–c; 10–b; 11–b; 12–b; 13–b; 14–a; 15–c; 16–c

Exercises

1. The diagram below represents demand and cost conditions for a firm.

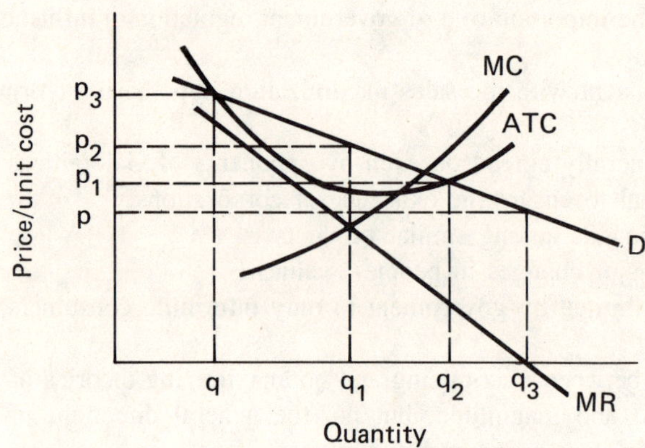

(a) What would be the choice of price and output for a profit maximizer? ________________

(b) What would be the range of price and output for a profit satisficer who is content to cover opportunity costs as a minimum? ________________

(c) What could be the price and output of a sales maximizer who is willing to accept losses for short periods (assume sufficient economies of scale so that *LRAC* will be less than p at q_3)? ________________

2. Assume that a firm is capable of making a reasonable projection of its profits (π) as it expands output (Q) and that this relationship is

$$\pi = 7Q - Q^2 - 6$$

(a) For values of Q = 1, 2, 3, 3½, 4, 5, and 6, plot the profits function on the graph.

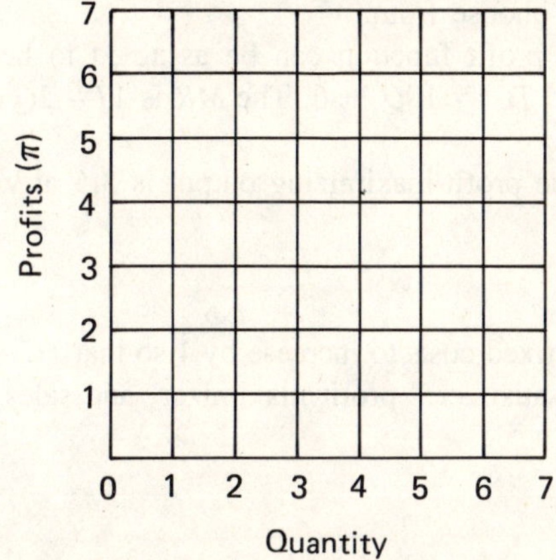

(b) If a "satisficing" firm has a profit target of 4, what ranges of output will that firm accept?

(c) What output is consistent with profit maximization?

(d) If the firm is a sales maximizer and the only constraint was to have profits of at least 1.0, approximately what output will it choose?

Short Problems

1. To suggest why economists tend to be unsatisfied with nonmaximizing models for price-output decisions, this problem extends the analysis of Exercise 2. In doing that exercise, you already should have noted that the "satisficing" firm has a rather wide range of outputs to choose from.

   Note that the profit function can be assumed to be the difference between $TR = 17Q - Q^2$ and $TC = 10Q + 6$. The MR is $17 - 2Q$ and the demand curve is $P = 17 - Q$.

   (a) Confirm that the profit-maximizing output is 3.5 at which the price is 13.5.

   (b) Now allow the fixed costs to increase by 1 so that $TC = 10Q + 7$. How are the decisions for "satisficer," profit maximizer, and sales maximizer altered?

   (c) Now change the cost function to $11Q + 6$ to test the effect of a change in marginal costs. You should get straightforward answers for the maximizers, but what about the "satisficer"? How might it resolve its dilemma?

   (d) Now assume the original cost conditions but with a favorable demand shift to $P = 17 - 0.5Q$ (which also increases the demand elasticity at every price). Work out the decisions for the maximizers. How might the profit "satisficer" deal with the wide range of choices that meet the criterion of profits of at least four?

Answers to the Exercises

1. (a) p_2 and q_1 (b) from p_3 and q to p_1 and q_2 (c) p and q_3

2. (a)

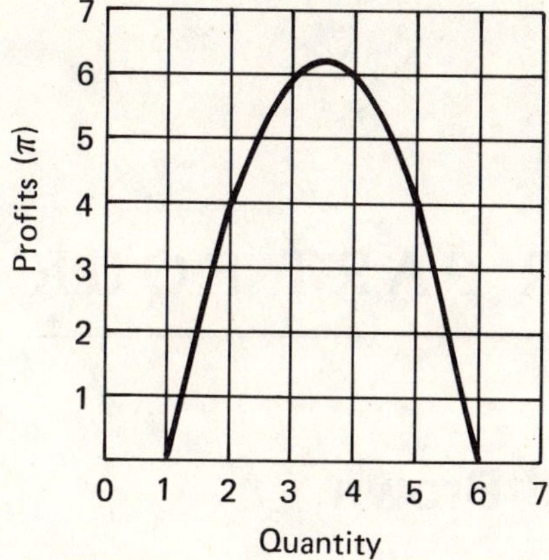

(b) $Q = 2$ to $Q = 5$
(c) 3½
(d) between $Q = 5$ and $Q = 6$

CASES FOR PART FOUR

CASE 10: Adams and Brown

Adams, Inc., and the Brown Company are 2 of 100 firms in the plastic-molding industry, in which equilibrium has been disturbed both by increases in demand and by new cost-saving techniques. Adams' costs reflect these. The current price for the product is \$.35.

Volume of output (in thousands of units)	Adams				Brown			
	Total cost	*AVC*	*ATC*	*MC*	Total cost	*AVC*	*ATC*	*MC*
100	\$100,000[a]	0.20	1.00	0.20	\$60,000[a]	0.30	0.60	0.30
200	120,000	0.20	0.60		90,000	0.30	0.45	
300	140,000				120,000			
400	160,000				150,000			
500	180,000				180,000			
600	200,000				210,000			0.40[b]
700	220,000				250,000	0.31	0.36	
800	240,000			0.30[b]	295,000			0.55
900	270,000	0.21	0.30		350,000	0.36	0.39	
1,000	310,000				N.A.			

[a]Adams' fixed costs are \$80,000; Brown's are \$30,000.
[b]Remember to associate *MC* with the midpoints of volume intervals.
N.A. = not attainable

Questions

1. Graph below the *ATC, AVC,* and *MC* functions for the two firms, with each firm's demand curve reflecting the \$.35 price. What output decision would you predict that Adams would make? ________ That Brown would make? ________

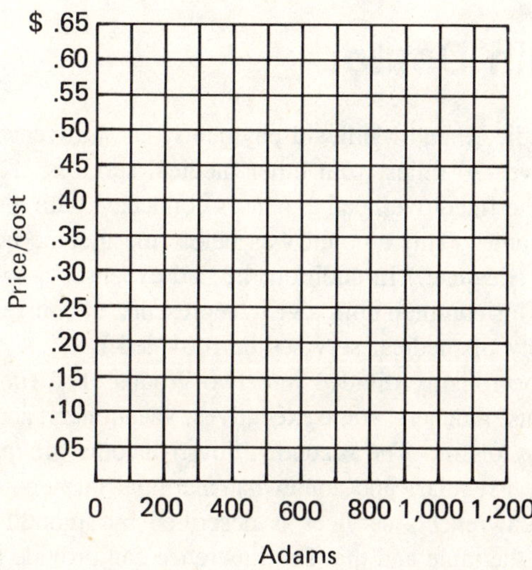

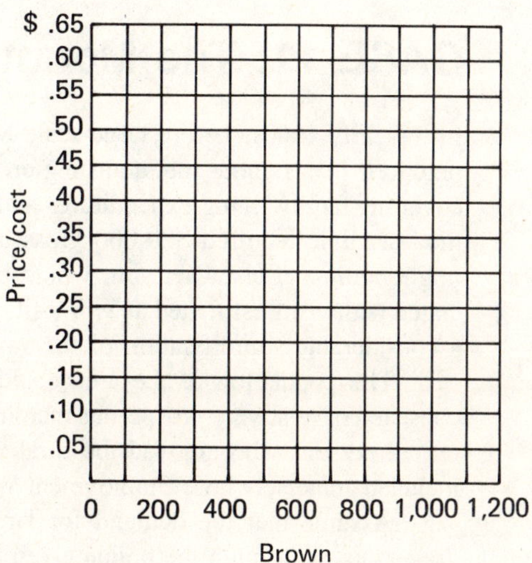

Output, in thousands of units

2. Assuming that 50 firms in the industry have costs identical to Adams and that 50 have costs identical to Brown, construct a short-run supply curve.

	Amount supplied		
Price[a]	Adams	Brown	Industry (50*A* + 50*B*)
\$.15	0	0	0
.20	800	0	40,000
.25			
.30			
.35			
.40			
.45			
.50			
.55			

[a]Treat each price as a shade above price listed.

3. Predict the long-run equilibrium price, assuming that the industry is one of constant costs and that the conditions of perfect competition regarding entry and exit are satisfied: ______________. What kind of adjustments will firms of the Adams type need to make? Firms of the Brown type?

CASE 11: The Mountain Doctor

In the early 1960s, before large-scale Medicare and Medicaid payments, Dr. Lawrence practiced in a remote mountain region over 50 miles from other medical services. To cover his family living expenditures and the fixed overhead expenses connected with his modest clinic required $20,000 gross income. (This amount was below the income he might command elsewhere but would be adequate.) In addition, he had expenses associated with visits estimated at $1 a visit. (This common unit, a visit, represents, of course, a considerable simplification of the variety of medical services he provided.)

The population of the area could be roughly divided into two groups. The first consisted of relatively prosperous merchants, ranchers, some executives, vacationers, and retired persons who enjoyed the rural way of life. The second, a lower-income group, included miners, whose employment was irregular, and somewhat marginal farmers.

Assume that the demand for Dr. Lawrence's services is described by smoothly drawn curves through the points given in the table and that Dr. Lawrence can provide a maximum of 5,000 visits per year.

Hypothetical demand schedule for Dr. Lawrence's services

Fee	Group I visits	Group II visits	Total visits
$25	300	0	300
20	500	0	500
15	700	200	900
10	900	800	1,700
5	1,100	2,000	3,100
0	1,300	3,700	5,000

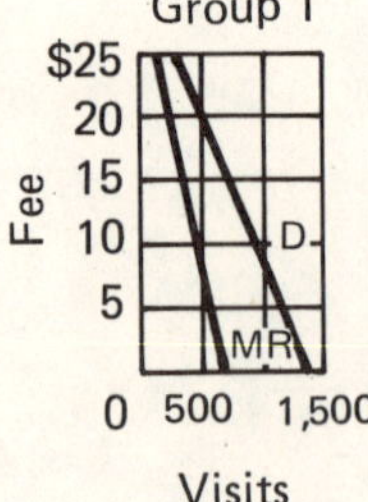

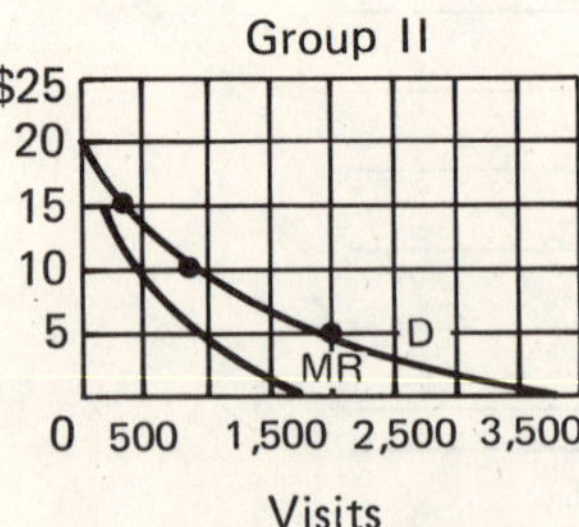

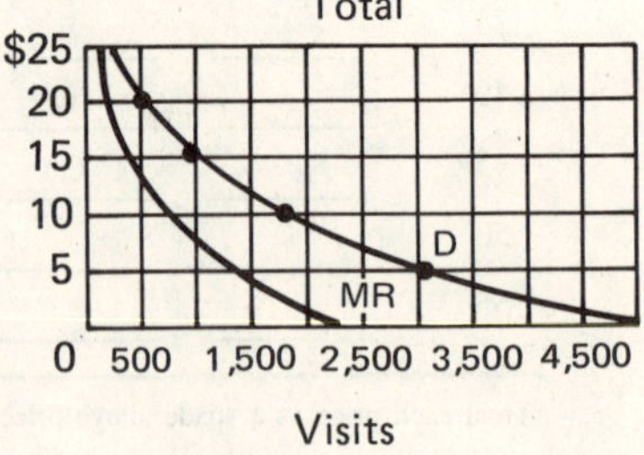

Note: The *MR* curves were plotted at interval midpoints as follows:
Group I: $12.50 at an output of 400, $2.50 at 600, –$7.50 at 800
Group II: $15.00 at 100, $8.33 at 500, $1.67 at 1,400
Total: $8.75 at 700, $4.38 at 1,300, –$1.07 at 2,400

Questions

1. Evaluate the following pricing alternatives by the criteria below. To size up Dr. Lawrence's problem draw the long-run average cost curve on the "total" graph, and to help in the evaluations draw the *MC* curve on all three diagrams.

		Price(s)	Output	*TR*	*TVC*	*TC*	*TR* – *TC*
(a) One-price system		______	______	______	______	______	______
(b) Two-price system							
I		______	______	______	______	xxx	xxx
II		______	______	______	______	xxx	xxx
Total		xxx	______	______	______	______	______
(c) Perfect price discrimination	from	______					
			______	______	______	______	______
	to	______					
		(approximate total revenue from area under total demand curve on graph)					

2. Recognizing that none of the alternatives above is fully possible, Dr. Lawrence would not have the perfect knowledge required for (c) and would find it professionally difficult to practice (a) and (b) without providing some free services and lower fees as well. What approach would you recommend?

3. Price discrimination in medical services probably has declined because of government programs.
   (a) Some communities have subsidized the building of a medical clinic. How would this affect Dr. Lawrence's problem?

   (b) How would the provision of government payments of minimum fees under Medicare (to the old) and Medicaid (to the poor) alter the demand and reduce the necessity for price discrimination?

CASE 12: Are Diamonds (Valuable) Forever?

In September 1982, less than two years after De Beers posted a record $2.8 billion in sales of diamonds and $1.1 billion in profits, *Fortune* ran an article entitled "De Beers and the Diamond Debacle." Another commentator, Edward J. Epstein, was more flamboyant, stating, "The cartel has lost control of the diamond market and the final collapse of diamonds is months not years away."

The economic issue was whether De Beers, as the dominant firm in an international cartel, the CSO or Central Selling Organization, could keep the quantity demanded and quantity supplied in equilibrium at prices far above the cost of production.

From the late nineteenth century, when De Beers controlled the only abundant source of diamonds in the "volcanic" pipes of South Africa, De Beers was successful in contracting to buy the output of new producers, mostly in neighboring countries. Demand grew quickly, largely because young U.S. males lived up to the expectation that intended brides should be furnished with bestoned rings as a demonstration both of depth of affection and financial competence.

Strategies for maintaining prices and profits varied with outside influences. It was necessary to shut down production for four years in the Great Depression and to stockpile the output of outside producers. A major postwar problem was the entry of Soviet supplies. While the Soviets were willing to sell through the CSO, by 1981 the Siberian mines were accounting for nearly one-quarter of the CSO supplies, a share that otherwise would have been available to African producers. A fortunate development was the successful introduction into Japan of the U.S. engagement ring. With the help of a massive De Beers advertising campaign, the proportion of Japanese brides receiving diamond rings increased from 5 percent in 1967 to 60 percent in 1977.

The cause of the proximate crisis in the 1980s was the arrival on a large-scale of the investor/speculator who fancied diamonds with their long record of gradual price appreciation as an appropriate source of profit during times of inflation. The price of a one-carat, quality diamond was bid up from its level of a few thousand dollars in the early 1970s to over $60,000 in 1980. This high price proved unsustainable since the profitability of holding diamonds depended on continued annual appreciation by at least as much as the high interest rates of the time. Despite the accumulation by De Beers of $1.4 billion dollars in diamond inventories and cutbacks in production, the price plummeted to the $8,000 to $18,000 range in the early 1980s and speculative demand, which represented about one-quarter of the total demand, became comatose. A new Australian discovery increased prospective supplies by 25 million carats a year. Fortunately for De Beers, most of the output promised to be in industrial diamonds and De Beers was able to contract for all but 5 percent of Australian diamond production.

In the early 1980s, De Beers was hopeful of increasing the market for the larger stones with advertising based on the slogan ". . . a diamond of a carat or more, there's only one in a million." (In 1981, the average diamond in an engagement ring weighed only 0.29 carats; it had been 25 percent bigger five years before.)

Fortune felt De Beers might have the resources to restore the status of the diamond as a precious stone whose value would gradually appreciate. In contrast, Epstein concluded that "as De Beers realizes it can no longer afford its multi-billion dollar illusion of scarcity, diamonds will be recognized for what they are—brilliant, glittering, and exceedingly common pebbles." The stock market of mid-1983 (when the Dow-Jones average was at a peak of about 1250) took the middle ground: De Beers stock was selling on the over-the-counter market at $9, well below its speculative peak of $12 but substantially over its 1982 low of $4.

Under the heading "Restored Luster," the *Wall Street Journal,* July 7, 1983, expressed guarded optimism for the De Beers-led cartel, though the production cuts were deep and painful. It felt the rough treatment of Zaire (who left the cartel) would keep other African producers in line. De Beers helped drive the prices of industrial diamonds (Zaire's specialty) down by two-thirds. It also speculated that the Soviet Union, a major independent producer, would opt for long-run price stability at high prices over independent action that would maximize production and possibly be more lucrative in the short run. Finally, De Beers had increased its own prices by modestly more than the CPI rise in 1973–1983 and never cut the official cartel price even during the speculative decline.[1]

[1]The quoted *Fortune* article was in the September 6, 1982, issue. The Epstein citations are from "Diamonds Are Not Forever," *Penthouse,* June 1983.

Questions

1. Contrast predictions of the monopolistic and competitive models for price and output of diamonds using demand, marginal revenue, and supply curves.

2. Show what happened to the demand for diamonds when speculators expected higher prices; what happened when it became clear that increases in prices produced by speculation could no longer be maintained?

3. How are each of the following likely to affect the success of the cartel in maintaining high prices for demands and achieving joint profit maximization: (a) the advent of worldwide prosperity; (b) new discoveries, particularly from non-South African sources; (c) the wide distribution of the cubic zirconia, which closely approximated the appearance of the diamond and sells at costume jewelry prices; (d) a boycott of diamonds by U.S. youth to protest South African racial policies?

4. The diamond cartel has been successful far longer than any other international cartel. How might the nature of the product help in maintaining the cartel? How might it eventually hurt?

5. How well De Beers has done in restoring the mystique of "a diamond is (valuable) forever" might be judged by comparing its present stock price relative to that of the Dow Jones with the figures given for mid-1983. Check it (you will find De Beers in the NASDAQ listings). In July 1986 with the Dow at 1900, the price of De Beers was 6½.

CASE 13: The Cigarette Industry: An Enduring and Beleaguered Oligopoly

A brief historical survey of the U.S. cigarette industry reveals the effects of modest product differentiation plus heavy advertising on market entry. In addition, it gives a perspective on brand and variety proliferation as added barriers to entry. The growth of the industry has been enormous, from sales of 14 billion cigarettes in 1912 to 400 billion cigarettes by 1950. After 1950, growth was slowed by medical findings and virtually ceased after approximating a level of 550 billion in the mid-1950s. The industry remained highly profitable during subsequent years in spite of TV advertising bans, required health warnings, and antismoking laws, though sales have receded recently from above to below 600 billion.

The Rise of the Big Three

The history of the modern cigarette industry began with the breaking up of the American Tobacco trust in 1913. Cigarettes accounted for only 6 percent of annual sales in an industry that stressed cigars, chewing tobacco, pipe tobacco, and snuff.

In 1913 one of the successor companies, Reynolds, with no cigarette brand of its own, chose a strategy of a mild blend (mostly of domestic tobaccos) in a standard package of 20 cigarettes advertised under the brand name *Camels*. Liggett and Myers quickly followed with the *Chesterfield* brand, and in 1917 the American Tobacco Company introduced *Lucky Strike*. A fourth company, P. Lorillard, made a modest entry in 1926 following the same strategy with its advertising campaign for *Old Golds*, financed by a $15 million bond issue. By 1931, sales of these four brands accounted for 97 percent of cigarette sales.

New Entrants During the Depression

In June, 1931, despite the Great Depression, the cigarette companies followed Reynolds' leadership and raised prices to enhance profit margins. This permitted a handful of small tobacco companies to temporarily gain over 20 percent of the market with the "10-cent" brands. One of these companies, Brown and Williamson, did well with *Wings* and then found permanent niches with *Raleighs*, which used premium coupons as a marketing device, and the mentholated Kools, that prospered in the later filter era.

The Phillip Morris company also was able to enter the market during this period, using skillful advertising and maintaining retailer prices. The larger companies retaliated against the 10-cent brands by using market clout to squeeze retail margins and keep prices of standard brands within 3 cents of the low-priced interlopers.

The low-priced brands did not survive the war and postwar prosperity. In 1947, six one-variety brands had over 95 percent of the market. Besides *Phillip Morris*, the other significant addition was American's *Pall Mall*, a king-sized brand that had the price appeal of an 85-mm length (standard length was 70 mm) and the quality appeal of greater smoothness by "traveling" the smoke farther.

The Filter Revolution

The era of one brand in a single variety ended in the 1950s with the filter revolution. The stimulus for change was the publication of test results in the early 1950s relating smoking to illness and death. Particularly convincing were prospective studies in which large samples of men were classified by smoking habits and other characteristics and were followed for several years to observe the time and cause of death. Heavy smokers were found to die from lung cancer at twenty times the rate of nonsmokers and to have death rates in their late forties and fifties comparable to nonsmokers seven to eight years older.

By 1959, five cigarette companies had seven filter brands with market shares of 2.5 percent or more. In total there were 16 varieties of 15 brands with at least this share that collectively had 86 percent of the market, a sharp contrast to the four brands with 97.1 percent in 1931 and the six with 95.3 percent in 1947.

American Tobacco was the one company that failed to establish a firm foothold in the filter market. *Pall Mall,* its king-sized entry, had replaced *Camels* as the number one cigarette and with its extra length to "travel the smoke farther" probably gave more protection to smokers than most filters of the time (which initially were little more than mouthpieces). The Federal Trade Commission had effectively banned advertising on health themes as potentially deceptive and worked out an industry agreement that allowed no firm to make tar and nicotine claims.

The Low-Tar Cigarettes

Further opportunities for splintering the possible product space came with changes in government policy stimulated by the Surgeon General's official recognition in 1964 of cigarette smoking as a health threat. American Tobacco with *Carlton* and Lorillard with *True* challenged the industry advertising code and made low-tar/nicotine claims. In the 1970s, when the government required all advertising to display the tar and nicotine content from standardized tests, the companies felt that representation in the low-tar segment of the market (less than 15 mm tar as measured by FTC tests) was essential. By the mid-1970s, an ultra-low low-tar segment of 6 mm or less emerged with several brands competing to be the lowest of all. The very small sales of the close-to-zero tar varieties were less important to the firms than providing a low-tar advertising theme that could help more flavorful varieties of the same brand. As the quality of filters improved, the added taste of menthol became more important and mentholated cigarettes added to the number of varieties.

New lengths, first of 100 mm and then of 120 mm, had both an economy ("more puffs") and style appeal. Industry merchandisers noted the appeal to women of these longer brands and produced even slimmer cigarettes of which *Virginia Slims* was the most successful with its advertising, "You've come a long way, baby," and the implication, "now you have equal rights to increase the probability of lung cancer." The industry recognized that with men decreasing their smoking, sales could be maintained only with increased smoking by women.

The cost of launching new brands is high and risks are great, even for an established firm and despite a ban on expensive television advertising. For example, *Real,* introduced by Reynolds, required a $40 million initial advertising outlay in 1977 to announce, "the natural cigarette is here; taste your first low-tar cigarettes with nothing artificial added." Perhaps $100 million later, in 1980, Reynolds withdrew *Real,* which had an unprofitable 0.25 percent of the market. The recent tendency has been to make each brand a separate product line encompassing numerous varieties (as many as eight or nine). Thus, in the early 1980s, American Tobacco added *Carlton 120s*; Brown and Williamson, an ultra-light version of *Kools*; Reynolds, a box in addition to a softpack for *Camel* filters, and *Salem Slims,* aimed at women.

The New Price Competition

The ability of the standard-priced brands to maintain and even enhance the margins of price over cost along with federal and state tax increases brought average retail prices to over $1.00 a pack by the mid-1980s. Liggett, with sales of its established brands dwindling, introduced "generic" cigarettes and in 1983 enjoyed the largest increase in sales as its generics, priced $.20 to .30 lower, took 4 percent of the market. Brown and Williamson introduced a generic cigarette of its own, cutting Liggett's share by about 1.5 percent. R. J. Reynolds introduced *Century* cigarettes in packs of 25, which in 1986 sold for the price of a pack of 20, and revamped its *Doral* brand to sell competitively with generics. Phillip Morris, with its market leadership threatened, repackaged its marginal *Players* brand into packs of 25 to compete with *Century,* and converted its unsuccessful ultra-low-tar *Cambridge* brand to a low-tar "branded generic." The market share of the low-priced generic segment exceeded 8 percent in 1986.

After Fifty Years

The same six firms that had established themselves by the end of the 1930s occupied virtually the whole market in 1986, but changes have been dramatic. Only Brown and Williamson (a subsidiary of a British tobacco firm) remained preponderantly a cigarette company. Of the original Big Three, only RJR–Nabisco (formerly Reynolds Tobacco) maintained its market position, but instead of one cigarette brand, *Camels,* it sold 41 varieties of 8 brands. The advertising of the *Marlboro* cowboy had taken Phillip Morris to a slight lead with over one-third of the market. The original *Phillip Morris* 70-mm cigarette had been replaced by a total of eleven cigarette brands and was supplemented by beverages, such as *Miller* and *Lite* beers, and foods. American Industries (originally American Tobacco) had fallen from being an occasional leader to a poor fourth, and Liggett, the third of the original Big Three, had lost its identity in a conglomerate (as had Lorillard) and, except for its precarious success with generic cigarettes, was fading from the industry. Consumers could choose among 200 varieties of some 45 brands with distinct price options as in the 1930s.

Questions

1. Why is large advertising expenditure more clearly a qualification to the joint profit maximization hypothesis in a mature market (the 1980s) than in a growing market (1920–1965)?

2. What additional difficulty for the entry of new firms is caused by extensive product proliferation? Why might even an existing oligopolist prefer to use an existing brand for a new variety?

3. For the established brands, price competition has been limited to such indirect forms as coupons and greater product length, or such temporary promotions as two for the price of one or one dollar off per carton. What inhibits more aggressive pricing on standard brands to prevent the inroads of generics and lower-priced brands?

4. How may the present state of demand for cigarettes help explain
   (a) the virtual elimination of a (preponderantly) tobacco company?

   (b) the emergence of a significant low-priced cigarette market segment?

CASE 14: Breakfast Cereals: A Shared Monopoly?

The Federal Trade Commission's complaint against cereal companies in 1972, with its proposed remedies of divestiture and royalty-free licensing of trademarks, was potentially ground breaking. The case was dropped in 1982, but the economic analysis of market structure and behavior is of interest as an indication of the difficulties of dealing with monopolistic tendencies in a market displaying strong rivalry.

Four companies were charged with "shared monopoly" of the ready-to-eat (RTE) cereal industry in 1972 by the FTC. In 1972, these producers accounted for 89 percent of RTE-cereal pound sales: Kellogg, with a market share of 45 percent; General Mills (which entered the business in 1928 by purchasing the company making Wheaties) was second with 21 percent; General Foods (Post) was third, with 16 percent; Quaker was fourth, with 9 percent. The suit against Quaker was dropped in 1978.

The FTC's allegations included "proliferation of brands," "artificial differentiation of product" through advertising to children, control of supermarket shelf-space "particularly by Kellogg," and exercise of monopoly power by failure to cut prices and by following price increases. Kellogg denied any monopolistic practices, said less than 20 percent of breakfast main dishes were cereals, and attributed its success to "bringing the housewife what she wants"; General Mills was not only "distressed" but "puzzled" by the FTC charge; General Foods was confident that the Post cereal business was good for the consuming public; Quaker Oats found it impossible to see how its 9 percent share (up from 3 percent) was a basis for a monopoly charge.

The economic analysis of a consultant to the FTC concluded that "the privately optimal entry-deterrence strategy involves high prices, brand proliferation and some degree of overspending on advertising."[1] Brand proliferation was the key because it split the cereals' "product space" into such small segments as to make it unlikely that a new entrant could achieve the 3 percent share needed for efficient production. Only 2 of the 80

[1]Richard Schmalensee, "Entry Deterrence in the Ready-to-eat Breakfast Cereal Industry," *The Bell Journal of Economics* (Autumn 1978), p. 313.

brands introduced in the 1950–1972 period ever achieved this level, but Kellogg felt a 0.7 percent share was the test of success for a leading firm.

Heavy advertising would reinforce product differentiation and reduce incentives of sellers for price competition. Increased advertising as a kind of fixed cost would discourage potential entrants. Low limit prices were not necessary as a deterrent to entry in addition to brand proliferation and advertising. They probably would not have been effective since, with the small group of firms involved, mutually beneficial postentry price rises might be expected by a potential entrant.

The one opportunity for entry came in the early 1970s when the established companies did not anticipate the growth of natural cereals to 10 percent of the market by mid-1974. Colgate, International Multifoods, Pillsbury, and Pet all entered, but only Pet hung on after the entry of the major cereal producers and a decline of this market segment in the late 1970s.

The Proposed Relief and Its Impact

There were four components to the relief proposed by the FTC, the first two of primary importance and novelty:

1. The creation of five new firms by divestiture of certain established brands and trademarks of the three defendants: three from Kellogg, one from General Foods, and one from General Mills. To avoid delays, existing shareholders would simply receive shares in the new companies.
2. The licensing of existing trademarks (and provision of needed formulae) to all nonrespondent firms willing to meet quality control standards. Similar licenses would be required after 5 years on new products. All would revert to originating firms after 20 years.

The other provisions were a ban on acquisitions to make divestiture effective and a prohibition on the supermarket shelf-space plans allegedly used by defendants.

Economist Richard Schmalensee felt that the "fall in concentration should directly increase price competition," particularly by weakening the tacit agreement that made major producers reluctant to engage in private label production. But "divestiture may not by itself constitute an adequate remedy."[2] Under licensing, copies of the largest RTE cereals are likely, with price competition eroding margins and forcing reductions in prices of other brands. The proposed divestiture would create a set of firms well situated to take out licenses, and the ability to take out licenses should enhance the viability of the new firms plus other outsiders who could gain a toehold by producing copies of leading brands.

Questions

1. What benefits does the public obtain from the strong rivalry in product and advertising competition by the cereal companies? What costs does the public pay? (Notice on your next trip to the supermarket the display and pricing of cereals.)

[2]Schmalensee, p. 322.

2. The number of different brands sold by the 6 leading producers increased from 26 in 1950 to 80 in 1973. How could brand proliferation be a barrier to entry?

3. The wide availability of distributor and generic brands typifies most supermarket products, yet in cereals they appear to be less common. What particular brands or types of cereals are likely to be introduced as generic cereals? Why?

4. "The remedies proposed are too drastic in terms of traditional American business customs to be justified." Explain your agreement or disagreement.

PART FIVE

The Distribution of Income

18

Factor Mobility and Factor Pricing

Learning Objectives

From the study of this chapter you should obtain

—a broad perspective on how equally (or unequally) income is distributed in the United States and how various economic functions are rewarded;

—an understanding of the key role of factor mobility in determining how rapidly or well a market system allocates resources;

—awareness of special conditions in the supply of various factors, particularly the importance of nonmonetary considerations in the choices of labor;

—an appreciation of dynamic and equilibrium differentials in compensation as influences on the allocation of resources;

—the recognition that economic rent refers to surpluses over necessary compensation rather than the payments landlords receive from tenants.

Review and Self-Test

Matching Concepts

_______ 1. nonmonetary advantage

_______ 2. functional distribution of income

_______ 3. differences in factor prices that lead to resource movements

_______ 4. reliance on "unearned increments" in land values for financing government expenditures

_______ 5. inelastic labor supply

_______ 6. quasi-rent

_______ 7. Lorenz curve

_______ 8. factor mobility

_______ 9. demand for factor of production

_______ 10. equilibrium differentials

_______ 11. payments to factors in excess of transfer earnings

_______ 12. use of factors to maximize advantage to owner

(a) hypothesis of equal net advantage

(b) long summer vacation

(c) graphic depiction of size distribution of income

(d) derived demand

(e) differences in factor prices that persist

(f) economic rents

(g) ease of transfer of factors between uses; a function of time

(h) single tax

(i) temporary rent for factor

(j) employee compensation, 77 percent; corporate profits, 8 percent; proprietors' income, 7 percent; interest, 6 percent; rent, 2 percent

(k) dynamic differentials

(l) low labor mobility

Multiple-Choice Questions

1. The functional distribution of income
   (a) emphasizes the function of income in attracting workers.
   (b) is concerned with income distribution by size.
   (c) can be graphically shown by a Lorenz curve.
   (d) shows the percentages of income received by major categories of factors of production.

2. Complete equality of income distribution would appear on a Lorenz curve as
   (a) a straight line.
   (b) a convex curve.
   (c) a concave curve.
   (d) It could not be shown.

3. The total demand for an input
   (a) is the mirror image of the supply.
   (b) is the sum of the derived demands for it in all its various uses.
   (c) cannot be determined in any meaningful sense.
   (d) is identical to supply, according to Say's law.

4. A highly mobile factor of production
   (a) is one that shifts easily between uses in response to small changes in incentives.
   (b) is one that must be highly compensated in order to change its use.
   (c) displays supply inelasticity in most uses.
   (d) is a particularly applicable concept for the short run.

5. Equilibrium differentials in factor prices may reflect
   (a) intrinsic differences in factor characteristics.
   (b) acquired differences in factor characteristics.
   (c) nonmonetary advantages in uses of the factor.
   (d) all of the above.

6. The hypothesis of equal net advantage essentially is an assumption
   (a) that factor owners maximize the monetary and nonmonetary advantages of the use of their factors.
   (b) that net pecuniary returns will be the same in every use.
   (c) that proper policy will stress equality of opportunity.
   (d) that the tennis net will have the same central height at Wimbledon and Forest Hills.

7. The share of functional income paid as employee compensation in the United States is in which of the following percentage ranges:
   (a) 35 to 50 percent
   (b) 50 to 65 percent
   (c) 65 to 80 percent
   (d) 80 to 100 percent

8. Partial recovery of the sunk cost of a depreciable capital asset with a single use represents
   (a) transfer earnings.
   (b) long-run economic profit.
   (c) quasi-rent.
   (d) misguided business policy.

9. For the lowest 20 percent in a size distribution of U.S. income, family income has been
   (a) only one-tenth of the average.
   (b) slightly less than one-quarter of the average.
   (c) almost one-half of the average.
   (d) over three-quarters of the average.

10. The policy proposal for a single tax on the economic rent of land was made by
    (a) Vilfredo Pareto.
    (b) Karl Marx.
    (c) Alfred Marshall.
    (d) Henry George.

11. Assume that Jimmy Connors is willing to continue on the professional tennis circuit as long as he earns $250,000 a year. If in a particular year his earnings are $600,000, his transfer earnings and economic rent are respectively
    (a) $250,000 and $350,000.
    (b) $600,000 and zero.
    (c) $350,000 and $250,000.
    (d) zero and $600,000.

12. Economic rent is
    (a) the income of a landlord.
    (b) earned only by factors in completely inelastic supply.
    (c) the excess of income over transfer earnings.
    (d) usually taxable under the income tax, whereas transfer earnings are not.

13. A dynamic differential in factor earnings
    (a) can exist in equilibrium.
    (b) will be more quickly eliminated if factor supply is inelastic rather than elastic.
    (c) will tend to cause movements of factors.
    (d) is greater the greater the mobility of the factor.

14. The need for the physical presence of the owner of the labor factor (the worker)
    (a) is comparable with that of owners of capital and land.
    (b) is not economically significant.
    (c) makes nonmonetary factors much more important for labor than for other factors.
    (d) has not been fully demonstrated.

15. In a free-market economy, teachers would get paid more than truck drivers
    (a) only if teachers were scarcer relative to demand.
    (b) only if teachers were smarter.
    (c) because they paid more for their education.
    (d) because of the nonmonetary advantages of teaching.

Self-Test Key

Matching Concepts: 1–b; 2–j; 3–k; 4–h; 5–l; 6–i; 7–c; 8–g; 9–d; 10–e; 11–f; 12–a

Multiple-Choice Questions: 1–d; 2–a; 3–b; 4–a; 5–d; 6–a; 7–c; 8–c; 9–b; 10–d; 11–a; 12–c; 13–c; 14–c; 15–a

Exercises

1. Apply the "laws" of demand and supply to the competitive factor market below by showing the changes in price and in total factor compensation (vertical shading for increase, horizontal shading for decrease).

   Case (a), following Figure 18-2 of text, has been completed for you.

(a) Increase in demand

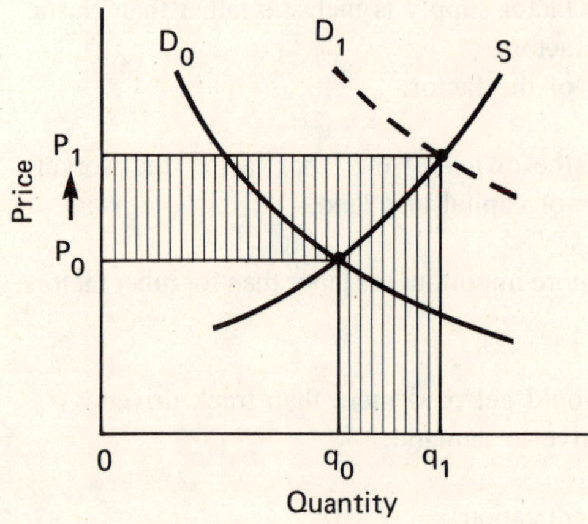

(b) Decrease in demand

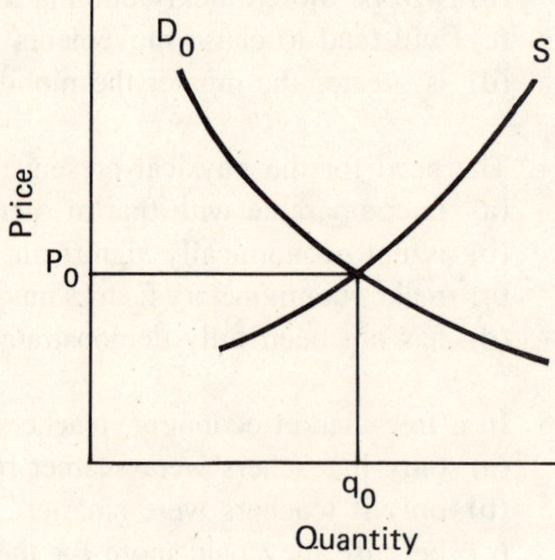

(c) Increase in supply

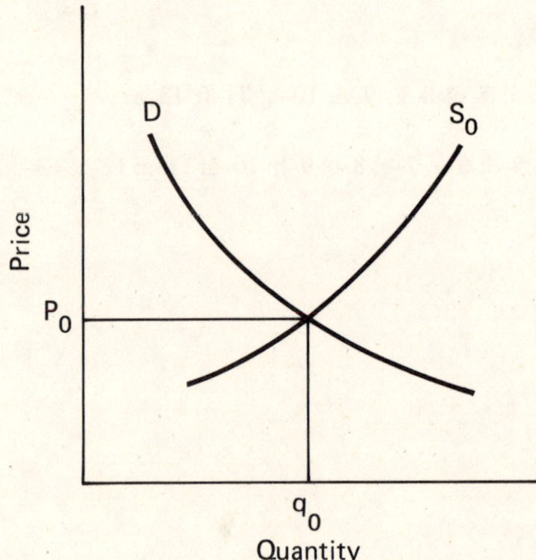

(d) Decrease in supply

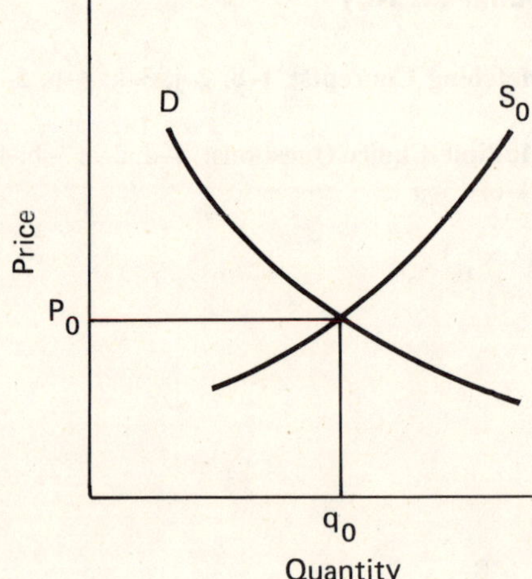

2. Table 18-3 of the text gives data on "Inequality in Family Income Distribution, 1983." The counterpart of this information for 1969 is as follows:
Lowest fifth, 5.6 percent; second fifth, 12.3 percent; middle fifth, 17.6 percent; fourth fifth, 23.4 percent; highest fifth, 41.1 percent; top 5 percent, 14.7 percent.
   (a) Fill in the cumulative income-population distribution of income for 1969 data in the table at the left below. The 1983 data are filled in to give you a model to follow.

Cumulative population (families)	*1983*	*1969*
	Percent of income	
0 percent	0.0	______
20 percent	4.7	______
40 percent	15.6	______
60 percent	32.7	______
80 percent	57.3	______
95 percent	84.2	______
100 percent	100.0	______

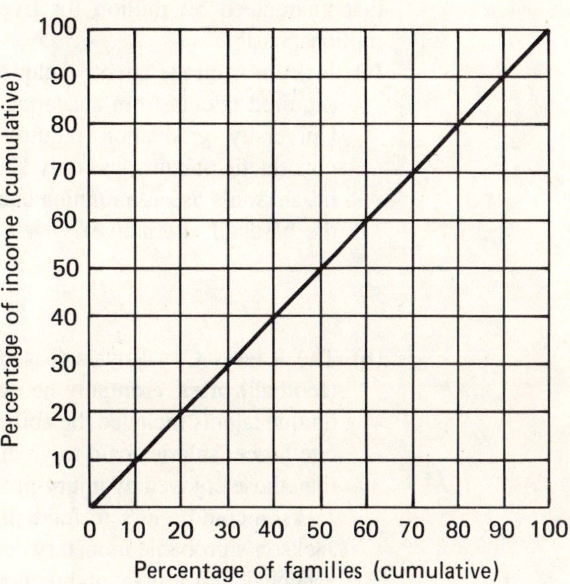

   (b) Plot the 1968 and 1983 data as Lorenz curves and shade in the area that indicates an increase in inequality.

   (c) Summarize this change toward inequality by completing this statement: In 1969 24.5 percent of income would have to be shifted from the top two-fifths of population to the bottom three-fifths to produce income equality; in 1983 ______ would have to be shifted.

3. Given that *DD* is the demand curve for commercial airplane pilots and *W* is the equilibrium monthly salary, draw in supply curves consistent with
   (a) all wages paid being transfer earnings.
   (b) all wages paid being economic rent.
   (c) half of wages being economic rent and half being transfer earnings.

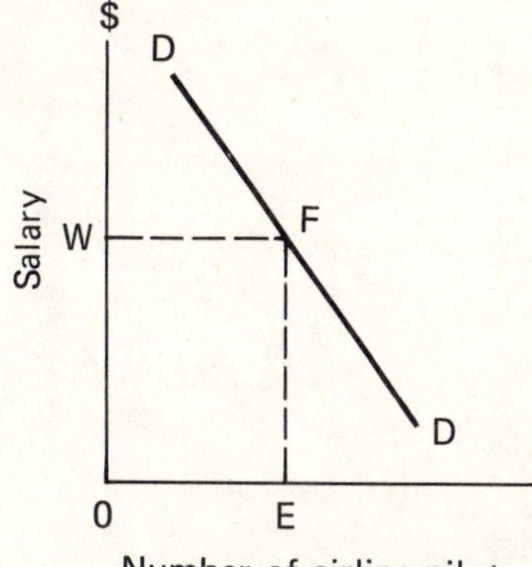

Short Problems

1. Bold Move, Bo (*Sports Illustrated*)

In the spring of 1986, Bo Jackson, the running back and winner of the Heisman trophy as the outstanding college football player in 1985, chose to sign a professional baseball contract at $200,000 for one year rather than a professional football contract that guaranteed $2 million for five years with bonus provisions that made $4.6 million possible.

(a) Jackson's unique talents included speed, power, and superb athletic ability. His acquired talents from academic training left him considerably short of Auburn University graduation requirements. Assume that his earning capacity in nonathletic pursuits was only $20,000 a year. How much economic surplus (rent) in Jackson's use as a running back is suggested by the football contract (disregard the baseball alternative)?

(b) The Kansas City Royals (baseball), did not meet the Tampa Bay Buccaneers' (football) offer, esentially because of great uncertainty as to whether Jackson's unique talents included the ability to hit major league curve balls. Baseball could cite higher salaries paid to great sluggers (about $2 million) over longer careers than those enjoyed by injury-prone running backs. Even allowing for the fact that Jackson could return to football in a subsequent year, an objective appraisal of Jackson's probable monetary compensation would seem to indicate that Jackson accepted a far less favorable monetary offer. Is such behavior consistent with the economic analysis of the behavior of labor in the chapter? Explain.

(c) (For sport fans) Assess Jackson's decision with the additional information you now have as time has passed.

2. The Two-earner Upper Middle Class and the Lorenz Curve

As reported in the June 27, 1980, *Wall Street Journal,* the Conference Board, a business research organization, estimates that the number of affluent households will increase three and a half times as rapidly as the total in the decade from 1980 to 1990. The criterion used is an income of $25,000 in 1978 dollars. The major reason is the expected continuation of the growth in households with two earners, itself a reflection of the increased participation rate of women in the paid work force. After World War II, it slowly but steadily increased until 1964 when it reached 38.7 percent (10 percent above prewar levels, and 2.2 percent above the war peak). From 1965 on, the increase was more rapid, and in the late 1970s the participation rate went up by more than 1 percent a year, reaching 51 percent in 1979. Even by 1974 the great majority of all households with over $25,000 of income had two income-earners. The 80 percent for that year represented a substantial increase from 65 percent in 1964 and just 57 percent in 1957.

The approximate percentage of households estimated for various income brackets (using 1978 dollars) is as follows:

	Percentage				Total
	$50,000+	$25 to 49,999	$15 to 24,999	Under $15,000	(millions)
1980	2	21	28	49	78
1985	3	24	28	45	88
1990	5	27	27	41	93

The share of personal income for each category is estimated for 1980 as 11 percent, 38 percent, 28 percent, and 23 percent; and in 1990 as 18 percent, 42 percent, 22 percent, and 18 percent, respectively.

Question

On the same diagram construct Lorenz curves for estimated 1980 and 1990 distributions of income. Do the estimates give a clear indication for either increasing equality or inequality?

Household Income	*Cumulative percentages of households*		*of income*	
	1980	1990	1980	1990
Under $15,000	____	____	____	____
$25,000 or less	____	____	____	____
$50,000 or less	____	____	____	____
All households	100	100	100	100

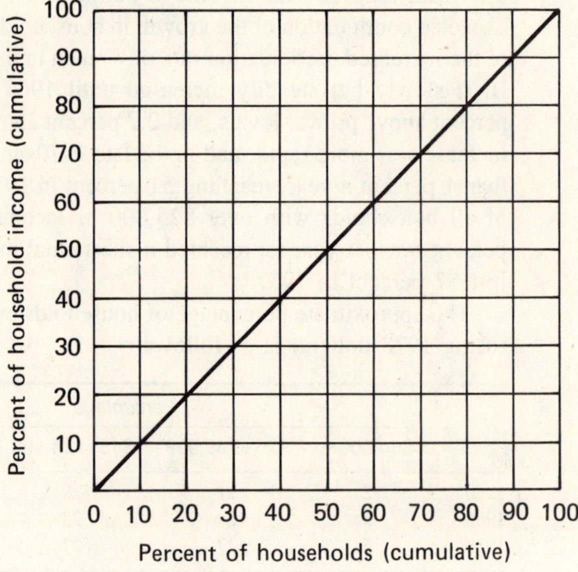

Answers to the Exercises

1.

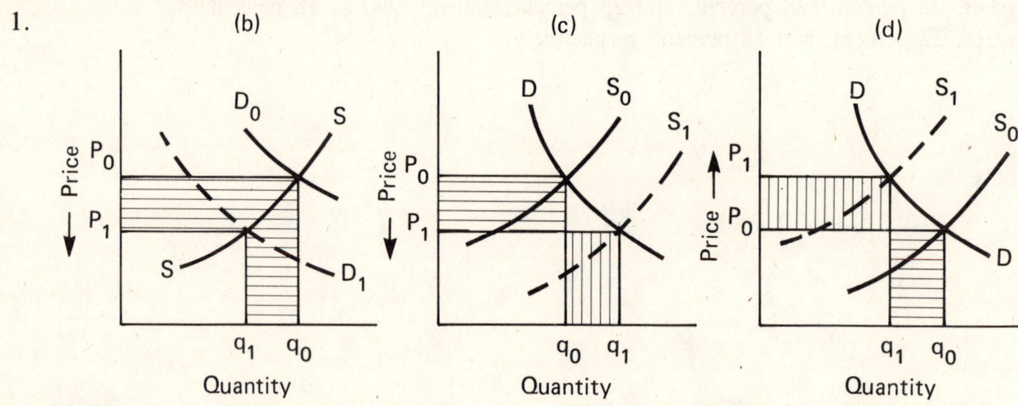

2. (a) The cumulative data for 1969: 20 percent, 5.6; 40 percent, 17.9; 60 percent, 35.5; 80 percent, 58.9; 95 percent, 85.3; 100 percent, 100

   (b) Your curves will have the abscissas 0, 20, 40, 60, 80, 95, and 100 with the ordinates as given in the table. The shaded area will be that between the higher 1969 curve and lower 1983 curve and will be a narrow crescent reaching its maximum width of 2.8 percent at 60 percent of the population.

   (c) 27.3 percent. The amount to be shifted is the maximum distance between the actual distribution and the 45° line of equality on the Lorenz graph. In both 1969 and 1983 the lower three quintiles receive less than 20 percent of income and the top two quintiles more, so this point comes at 60 percent of the population which receives only 32.7 percent of family income. 60 percent minus 32.7 percent equals 27.3 percent.

3. (a) horizontal supply curve at *W*
   (b) vertical supply curve at *E*
   (c) any of a number of supply curves dividing rectangle *OWFE* into two equal areas; diagonal straight line from *O* through *F* would be one

19

More on Factor Demand and Supply

Learning Concepts

From the study of this chapter you should obtain

—an understanding of the derived demand of factors of production based on the premise that firms will continue to hire only as long as the added revenue is greater than or equal to the added cost;

—an appreciation of the influence of market conditions on factor earnings and of the time dimension in the response of factor supplies;

—the recognition that investment in capital goods is profitable as long as the marginal efficiency of capital exceeds the interest rate.

Review and Self-Test

Matching Concepts

_______ 1. $MRP = w$

_______ 2. contribution to revenue by additional unit of variable factor

_______ 3. equilibrium condition for capital investment

_______ 4. $PV = A/i$, where A is annual income

_______ 5. substitution effect or income effect

_______ 6. 100 percent tax

_______ 7. supply of effort

_______ 8. net earnings of capital in a riskless investment

_______ 9. capital stock

_______ 10. gross returns to capital

(a) total number of hours a population is willing to work

(b) sum of pure returns to capital, risk premiums, economic profits, and depreciation

(c) tendencies to work more or to work less with rise in hourly wage

(d) marginal productivity theory of distribution

(e) capitalized value of a perpetual source of income

(f) *MRP*

(g) aggregate quantity of physical capital

(h) $MEC = i$

(i) cut in welfare by same amount as additional earnings

(j) pure returns to capital

Multiple-Choice Questions

1. The theory of factor prices in competitive markets says that
   (a) factors are paid what they are worth.
   (b) factor prices are determined by supply and demand.
   (c) factor prices depend on their cost of production.
   (d) equilibrium factor prices would differ even if all factors were identical and all payments were monetary.

2. Which of the following statements is *not* true about the demand for a factor of production?
   (a) It is more elastic the more elastic the demand for the final product.
   (b) It is more elastic in cases where technology dictates its use in fixed proportions with other factors.
   (c) It is less elastic the smaller a part it is of the total cost of the product.
   (d) The quantity demanded varies inversely with its price.

3. The marginal revenue product of a factor is
   (a) the amount added to revenue by the last unit hired of a factor.
   (b) total output divided by units of factors, multiplied by price.
   (c) less under competition than under monopoly, *ceteris paribus*.
   (d) always equal to its price.

4. The total supply of a factor of production for all uses
   (a) should be assumed as fixed.
   (b) can be expected to respond very quickly to economic forces.
   (c) is likely to be more responsive to economic forces the longer the time period.
   (d) is irrelevant since economics is concerned only with the supply to a particular use.

5. Cuts in income tax rates
   (a) are likely to induce for some a "substitution effect" of more work for leisure.
   (b) are likely to induce for others an "income effect" of less work since with higher after-tax wages more leisure is preferred.
   (c) probably have been a small net incentive for increasing the supply of effort.
   (d) all of the above

6. A capitalistic and communist society differ in that
   (a) capital goods are important only under capitalism.
   (b) no rental payments are charged for capital under communism.
   (c) payments for the use of capital generally go to the communist state rather than to private capitalists.
   (d) all of the above

7. When a firm uses its own funds instead of borrowing for investment purposes,
   (a) its economic costs are lower because it does not have to pay interest.
   (b) it should impute an interest rate to get a true picture of cost.
   (c) it means it cannot get a loan at the bank.
   (d) it does not have to worry about the rate of return on the investment.

8. Capital earns income because it is
   (a) productive.
   (b) expensive.
   (c) always cheaper to substitute capital for labor.
   (d) technically more efficient than labor.

9. Profits of a particular business could be at a rate less than the pure return on capital
   (a) if economic profits were negative.
   (b) if risks were unusually low.
   (c) never.
   (d) if most income had been paid out as dividends.

10. The present value of x dollars a year from now equals
    (a) xi.
    (b) $x(1 + i)$.
    (c) $x/(1 + i)$.
    (d) $(1 + i)/x$.

11. The higher the rate of interest, *ceteris paribus,*
    (a) the more profitable will any investment be.
    (b) the higher the rate of return on any investment must be for it to be profitable.
    (c) the greater the amount of borrowing by the federal government.
    (d) the greater the demand for investment funds.

12. The value of an income-earning asset
    (a) is the sum of all its income payments.
    (b) is the discounted present value of its expected future income stream.
    (c) is measured by its reproduction cost.
    (d) rises as interest rates rise.

13. If you borrow $300 and pay it back in 12 equal monthly installments of $28, the true rate of interest is about
    (a) 12 percent.
    (b) 6 percent.
    (c) 24 percent.
    (d) 10 percent.

14. The *MEC* curve shifts to the right as
    (a) capital is accumulated.
    (b) the interest rate drops.
    (c) technical knowledge increases.
    (d) households save more.

15. The opportunity cost of using capital includes all but which one of the following?
    (a) economic profits
    (b) the pure return on capital
    (c) risk premium
    (d) depreciation or user cost

16. An investment in human capital
    (a) is a contradiction in terms since capital applies only to plant and equipment.
    (b) confuses labor with capital.
    (c) applies to all investment since labor is used to build machines.
    (d) refers to resources devoted to increasing the productivity of people.

17. If the rate of interest goes from 4 percent to 5 percent, the present value of $200 paid annually and forever
    (a) declines by $500.
    (b) declines by $1,000.
    (c) increases by $2,000.
    (d) increases by $1,000.

18. If X equals the annual stream of net income from a machine into the indefinite future, P equals its purchase price, and i equals the interest rate, then a capital good should be purchased if
    (a) $X(i) = P$.
    (b) $X/P > i$.
    (c) $X/P < i$.
    (d) $X(P) = i$.

19. The marginal efficiency of capital schedule is negatively sloped because
    (a) of the "law" of diminishing returns.
    (b) the capital stock eventually wears out.
    (c) the price of additional output must be reduced to sell more of it.
    (d) real interest rates will inevitably be higher in the future.

The following three multiple-choice questions are illustrated in Exercise 1:

20. The marginal revenue product of a factor is
    (a) marginal revenue minus marginal cost.
    (b) marginal physical product times the units of factors used.
    (c) marginal revenue minus factor price.
    (d) marginal physical product times marginal revenue.

21. The "law" of diminishing returns
    (a) is not applicable in Exercise 1.
    (b) applies as soon as more than one unit of labor is employed.
    (c) is illustrated by the marginal product of the fifth and subsequent workers.
    (d) applies only to marginal revenue rather than actual output.

22. The marginal revenue product of a monopolistic firm (Case B) declines more rapidly than for a competitive firm (Case A) because
    (a) workers are apt to be less productive when they work for a monopoly.
    (b) the market demand for the product is less elastic.
    (c) the monopoly deliberately curtails output.
    (d) with the monopolist, marginal revenue declines as output increases, whereas the perfectly competitive firms's marginal revenue is constant.

Self-Test Key

Matching Concepts: 1–d; 2–f; 3–h; 4–e; 5–c; 6–i; 7–a; 8–j; 9–g; 10–b

Multiple-Choice Questions: 1–b; 2–b; 3–a; 4–c; 5–d; 6–c; 7–b; 8–a; 9–a; 10–c; 11–b; 12–b; 13–c; 14–c; 15–a; 16–d; 17–b; 18–b; 19–a; 20–d; 21–c; 22–d

Exercises

1. Suppose a firm can vary the number of employees and its output as shown. What will be the marginal physical product and the marginal revenue product of each additional worker? Note the differences between case A and case B. Fill in the table as necessary to answer the questions below. Assume that whole numbers of workers will be hired.

Total number of workers	Units of output per week		*Case A*		*Case B*	
		MPP	*MR*	*MRP*	*MR*	*MRP*
0	0	0	0	0	0	0
1	11	11	30	330	48	528
2	23	12	30	360	43	516
3	36	13	30	390	38	______
4	50	14	30	420	33	______
5	63	13	30	390	27	______
6	74	______	30	______	23	______
7	84	______	30	______	18	______
8	93	______	30	______	14	______
9	98	______	30	______	12	______

(a) If the market wage that this firm must pay is $250 per week, how many workers will the firm hire to maximize profits? Case A ______; case B ______
(b) If the wage rises to $300 per week, how many will the firm hire? Case A ______; case B ______
(c) If in case A the market price of the product rises to $40 and the wage is $300 per week, how many workers will be hired? ______

2. The marginal revenue productivity of a factor may depend on the costs saved by its substitution for another factor. In this exercise assume that a firm can accomplish a particular function by any of the following combinations of labor and capital. The costs involved are negligible enough so that the firm's output decision is not significantly affected:

Units of labor (worker-years)	Units of capital	*MRS*[a]	*MRP*[b] of labor (dollars)
0	100	-	-
1	60	40	$80,000
2	45	15	30,000
3	35	______	______
4	27	______	______
5	20	______	______
6	14	______	______
7	9	______	______
8	5	______	______
9	2	______	______
10	1	______	______

[a]Units of capital substituted for by additional units of labor.
[b]Assume the price of capital expressed as an annual cost (which, as discussed in Chapter 22, is a function of the price of the capital good, its economic life, and the interest rate) is $2,000 per unit of capital.

(a) If the market wage that the firm must pay is $15,000 a year, how many workers will be hired? ______________ (Assume worker-years are indivisible.) In conjunction with how many units of capital? ______________

(b) If wages had increased to $17,000 a year, how many workers would have been hired? ______________

(c) The firm's demand for labor would shift to the ______________ if the price of capital rose to $2,500 a unit, and at a wage of $17,000 it should result in the hiring of how many workers? ______________

3. (a) Just for practice, fill in the following blanks using the present value (*PV*) table, Table 19-1.

This many dollars	in *n* years	has this *PV*	at *i* rate of interest
10	5	______	6 percent
100	50	\$60.80	______
1,000	—	3.00	12 percent
______	6	4.56	14 percent

(b) More practice, this time with the annuity table, Table 19-2.

This many dollars	received each year for *n* years	has this *PV*	at *i* rate of interest
10	5	______	6 percent
100	50	\$3,919.60	______
1,000	—	8,304.00	12 percent
______	6	38.89	14 percent

(c) From Table 19-1, discover for yourself the famous Rule of ______________. The blank represents the number into which an interest rate (or any other rate of growth) is divided in order to get the number of years in which a magnitude will double at that rate of annual compound interest. What number belongs in the blank? (*Hint:* Find in each column the present value closest to 0.5; then multiply the associated year by the interest rate at the head of that column.)

4.(a) The MEC and Home Insulation

To illustrate how the *MEC* can decline as investment increases, consider this relationship between the insulation costs of a home (capital investment that practically speaking will last forever) and its annual heating costs.

1 Total insulation cost	2 Incremental insulation cost	3 Annual heating cost	4 Savings in heating	5 Estimated *MEC* (4 ÷ 2)
0		\$4,000		
\$ 5,000	______	2,500	______	______
10,000	______	1,600	______	______
15,000	______	1,200	______	______
20,000	______	1,000	______	______

What should the insulation investment be if (i) i = 13 percent? ______________

(ii) i = 6 percent? ______________

(b) My Son, the Doctor, Maybe

The senior Schmidts were considering with son Hermann whether he should go on to medical school or enter the family business. They estimated that if he went on to medical school (4 years), internship (1 year), and a residency for surgical training (4 years), the opportunity cost would be $25,000 a year—mostly for reduced earnings for the 9 years. It was estimated that from the tenth to the fortieth year, his earnings in medicine would exceed his business earnings by $25,000 a year. Mother Schmidt argued for the prestige of the M.D., but Father wanted assurance that this investment in Hermann capital would yield at least 6 percent. Would it? [*Hint:* To get the value of $1 from years 10 to 40, subtract the value of years 1 to 9 from the value of years 1 to 40 (Table 19-2).]

Table 19-1. Present Value of $1.00

$$PV = \left(\frac{1}{1 + i}\right)^n$$

Years hence (n)	1%	2%	4%	5%	6%	8%	10%	12%	14%	15%	16%	18%	20%	22%	24%	25%	26%	28%	30%	35%	40%	45%	50%
1	0.990	0.980	0.962	0.952	0.943	0.926	0.909	0.893	0.877	0.870	0.862	0.847	0.833	0.820	0.806	0.800	0.794	0.781	0.769	0.741	0.714	0.690	0.667
2	0.980	0.961	0.925	0.907	0.890	0.857	0.826	0.797	0.769	0.756	0.743	0.718	0.694	0.672	0.650	0.640	0.630	0.610	0.592	0.549	0.510	0.476	0.444
3	0.971	0.942	0.889	0.864	0.840	0.794	0.751	0.712	0.675	0.658	0.641	0.609	0.579	0.551	0.524	0.512	0.500	0.477	0.455	0.406	0.364	0.328	0.296
4	0.961	0.924	0.855	0.823	0.792	0.735	0.683	0.636	0.592	0.572	0.552	0.516	0.482	0.451	0.423	0.410	0.397	0.373	0.350	0.301	0.260	0.226	0.198
5	0.951	0.906	0.822	0.784	0.747	0.681	0.621	0.567	0.519	0.497	0.476	0.437	0.402	0.370	0.341	0.328	0.315	0.291	0.269	0.223	0.186	0.156	0.132
6	0.942	0.888	0.790	0.746	0.705	0.630	0.564	0.507	0.456	0.432	0.410	0.370	0.335	0.303	0.275	0.262	0.250	0.227	0.207	0.165	0.133	0.108	0.088
7	0.933	0.871	0.760	0.711	0.665	0.583	0.513	0.452	0.400	0.376	0.354	0.314	0.279	0.249	0.222	0.210	0.198	0.178	0.159	0.122	0.095	0.074	0.059
8	0.923	0.853	0.731	0.677	0.627	0.540	0.467	0.404	0.351	0.327	0.305	0.266	0.233	0.204	0.179	0.168	0.157	0.139	0.123	0.091	0.068	0.051	0.039
9	0.914	0.837	0.703	0.645	0.592	0.500	0.424	0.361	0.308	0.284	0.263	0.225	0.194	0.167	0.144	0.134	0.125	0.108	0.094	0.067	0.048	0.035	0.026
10	0.905	0.820	0.676	0.614	0.558	0.463	0.386	0.322	0.270	0.247	0.227	0.191	0.162	0.137	0.116	0.107	0.099	0.085	0.073	0.050	0.035	0.024	0.017
11	0.896	0.804	0.650	0.585	0.527	0.429	0.350	0.287	0.237	0.215	0.195	0.162	0.135	0.112	0.094	0.086	0.079	0.066	0.056	0.037	0.025	0.017	0.012
12	0.887	0.788	0.625	0.557	0.497	0.397	0.319	0.257	0.208	0.187	0.168	0.137	0.112	0.092	0.076	0.069	0.062	0.052	0.043	0.027	0.018	0.012	0.008
13	0.879	0.773	0.601	0.530	0.469	0.368	0.290	0.229	0.182	0.163	0.145	0.116	0.093	0.075	0.061	0.055	0.050	0.040	0.033	0.020	0.013	0.008	0.005
14	0.870	0.758	0.577	0.505	0.442	0.340	0.263	0.205	0.160	0.141	0.125	0.099	0.078	0.062	0.049	0.044	0.039	0.032	0.025	0.015	0.009	0.006	0.003
15	0.861	0.743	0.555	0.481	0.417	0.315	0.239	0.183	0.140	0.123	0.108	0.084	0.065	0.051	0.040	0.035	0.031	0.025	0.020	0.011	0.006	0.004	0.002
16	0.853	0.728	0.534	0.458	0.394	0.292	0.218	0.163	0.123	0.107	0.093	0.071	0.054	0.042	0.032	0.028	0.025	0.019	0.015	0.008	0.005	0.003	0.002
17	0.844	0.714	0.513	0.436	0.371	0.270	0.198	0.146	0.108	0.093	0.080	0.060	0.045	0.034	0.026	0.023	0.020	0.015	0.012	0.006	0.003	0.002	0.001
18	0.836	0.700	0.494	0.416	0.350	0.250	0.180	0.130	0.095	0.081	0.069	0.051	0.038	0.028	0.021	0.018	0.016	0.012	0.009	0.005	0.002	0.001	0.001
19	0.828	0.686	0.475	0.396	0.331	0.232	0.164	0.116	0.083	0.070	0.060	0.043	0.031	0.023	0.017	0.014	0.016	0.009	0.007	0.003	0.002	0.001	
20	0.820	0.673	0.456	0.377	0.312	0.215	0.149	0.104	0.073	0.061	0.051	0.037	0.026	0.019	0.014	0.012	0.010	0.007	0.005	0.002	0.001	0.001	
21	0.811	0.660	0.439	0.359	0.294	0.199	0.135	0.093	0.064	0.053	0.044	0.031	0.022	0.015	0.011	0.009	0.008	0.006	0.004	0.002	0.001		
22	0.803	0.647	0.422	0.342	0.278	0.184	0.123	0.083	0.056	0.046	0.038	0.026	0.018	0.013	0.009	0.007	0.006	0.004	0.003	0.001	0.001		
23	0.795	0.634	0.406	0.326	0.262	0.170	0.112	0.074	0.049	0.040	0.033	0.022	0.015	0.010	0.007	0.006	0.005	0.003	0.002	0.001			
24	0.788	0.622	0.390	0.310	0.247	0.158	0.102	0.066	0.043	0.035	0.028	0.019	0.013	0.008	0.006	0.005	0.004	0.003	0.002	0.001			
25	0.780	0.610	0.375	0.295	0.233	0.146	0.092	0.059	0.038	0.030	0.024	0.016	0.010	0.007	0.005	0.004	0.003	0.002	0.001	0.001			
26	0.772	0.598	0.361	0.281	0.220	0.135	0.084	0.053	0.033	0.026	0.021	0.014	0.009	0.006	0.004	0.003	0.002	0.002	0.001				
27	0.764	0.586	0.347	0.268	0.207	0.125	0.076	0.047	0.029	0.023	0.018	0.011	0.007	0.005	0.003	0.002	0.002	0.001	0.001				
28	0.757	0.574	0.333	0.255	0.196	0.116	0.069	0.042	0.026	0.020	0.016	0.010	0.006	0.004	0.002	0.002	0.002	0.001	0.001				
29	0.749	0.563	0.321	0.243	0.185	0.107	0.063	0.037	0.022	0.017	0.014	0.008	0.005	0.003	0.002	0.002	0.001	0.001	0.001				
30	0.742	0.552	0.308	0.231	0.174	0.099	0.057	0.033	0.020	0.015	0.012	0.007	0.004	0.003	0.002	0.001	0.001	0.001					
40	0.672	0.453	0.208	0.142	0.097	0.046	0.022	0.011	0.005	0.004	0.003	0.001	0.001										
50	0.608	0.372	0.141	0.087	0.054	0.021	0.009	0.003	0.001	0.001	0.001												

Table 19-2. Present Value of $1.00 Received Annually for *n* Years

$$PV = \left(\frac{1}{1+i}\right)^1 + \left(\frac{1}{1+i}\right)^2 + \cdots + \left(\frac{1}{1+i}\right)^n$$

Years (*n*)	1%	2%	4%	5%	6%	8%	10%	12%	14%	15%	16%	18%	20%	22%	24%	25%	26%	28%	30%	35%	40%	45%	50%
1	0.990	0.980	0.962	0.952	0.943	0.926	0.909	0.893	0.877	0.870	0.862	0.847	0.833	0.820	0.806	0.800	0.794	0.781	0.769	0.741	0.714	0.690	0.667
2	1.970	1.942	1.886	1.859	1.833	1.783	1.736	1.690	1.647	1.626	1.605	1.566	1.528	1.492	1.457	1.440	1.424	1.392	1.361	1.289	1.224	1.165	1.111
3	2.941	2.884	2.775	2.723	2.673	2.577	2.487	2.402	2.322	2.283	2.246	2.174	2.106	2.042	1.981	1.952	1.923	1.868	1.816	1.696	1.589	1.493	1.407
4	3.902	3.808	3.630	3.546	3.465	3.312	3.170	3.037	2.914	2.855	2.798	2.690	2.589	2.494	2.404	2.362	2.320	2.241	2.166	1.997	1.849	1.720	1.605
5	4.853	4.713	4.452	4.329	4.212	3.993	3.791	3.605	3.433	3.352	3.274	3.127	2.991	2.864	2.745	2.689	2.635	2.532	2.436	2.220	2.035	1.876	1.737
6	5.795	5.601	5.242	5.076	4.917	4.623	4.355	4.111	3.889	3.784	3.685	3.498	3.326	3.167	3.020	2.951	2.885	2.759	2.643	2.385	2.168	1.983	1.824
7	6.728	6.472	6.002	5.786	5.582	5.206	4.868	4.565	4.288	4.160	4.039	3.812	3.605	3.416	3.242	3.161	3.083	2.937	2.802	2.508	2.263	2.057	1.883
8	7.652	7.325	6.733	6.463	6.210	5.747	5.335	4.968	4.639	4.487	4.344	4.078	3.837	3.619	3.421	3.329	3.241	3.076	2.925	2.598	2.331	2.108	1.922
9	8.566	8.162	7.435	7.108	6.802	6.247	5.759	5.328	4.946	4.772	4.607	4.303	4.031	3.786	3.566	3.463	3.366	3.184	3.019	2.665	2.379	2.144	1.948
10	9.714	8.983	8.111	7.722	7.360	6.710	6.145	5.650	5.216	5.019	4.833	4.494	4.192	3.923	3.682	3.571	3.465	3.269	3.092	2.715	2.414	2.168	1.965
11	10.368	9.787	8.760	8.306	7.877	7.139	6.495	5.988	5.453	5.234	5.029	4.656	4.327	4.035	3.776	3.656	3.544	3.335	3.147	2.757	2.438	2.185	1.977
12	11.255	10.575	9.385	8.863	8.384	7.536	6.814	6.194	5.660	5.421	5.197	4.793	4.439	4.127	3.851	3.725	3.606	3.387	3.190	2.779	2.456	2.196	1.985
13	12.134	11.343	9.986	9.394	8.853	7.904	7.103	6.424	5.842	5.583	5.342	4.910	4.533	4.203	3.912	3.780	3.656	3.427	3.223	2.799	2.468	2.204	1.990
14	13.004	12.106	10.563	9.899	9.295	8.244	7.367	6.628	6.002	5.724	5.468	5.008	4.611	4.265	3.962	3.824	3.695	3.459	3.249	2.814	2.477	2.210	1.993
15	13.865	12.849	11.118	10.380	9.712	8.559	7.606	6.811	6.142	5.847	5.575	5.092	4.675	4.315	4.001	3.859	3.726	3.483	3.268	2.825	2.484	2.214	1.995
16	14.718	13.578	11.652	10.838	10.106	8.851	7.824	6.974	6.265	5.954	5.669	5.162	4.730	4.357	4.003	3.887	3.751	3.503	3.283	2.834	2.489	2.216	1.997
17	15.562	14.292	12.166	11.274	10.477	9.122	8.022	7.120	6.373	6.047	5.749	5.222	4.775	4.391	4.059	3.910	3.771	3.518	3.295	2.840	2.492	2.218	1.998
18	16.398	14.992	12.659	11.690	10.828	9.372	8.201	7.250	6.467	6.128	5.818	5.273	4.812	4.419	4.080	3.928	3.786	3.529	3.304	2.844	2.494	2.219	1.999
19	17.226	15.678	13.134	12.085	11.158	9.604	8.365	7.466	6.550	6.198	6.877	5.316	4.844	4.442	4.097	3.942	3.808	3.546	3.316	2.850	2.497	2.221	1.999
20	18.046	16.351	13.590	12.462	11.470	9.818	8.514	7.469	6.623	6.259	5.929	5.353	4.870	4.460	4.110	3.954	3.808	3.546	3.316	2.850	2.497	2.221	1.999
21	18.857	17.011	14.029	12.821	11.764	10.017	8.649	7.562	6.687	6.312	5.973	5.384	4.891	4.476	4.121	3.963	3.816	3.551	3.320	2.852	2.498	2.221	2.000
22	19.660	17.658	14.451	13.163	12.042	10.201	8.772	7.645	6.743	6.359	6.011	5.410	4.909	4.488	4.130	3.970	3.822	3.556	3.323	2.853	2.498	2.222	2.000
23	20.456	18.292	14.857	13.489	12.303	10.371	8.883	7.718	6.792	6.399	6.044	5.432	4.925	4.499	4.137	3.976	3.827	3.559	3.325	2.854	2.499	2.222	2.000
24	21.243	18.914	15.247	13.799	12.550	10.529	8.985	7.784	6.835	6.434	6.073	5.451	4.937	4.507	4.143	3.981	3.831	3.562	3.327	2.855	2.499	2.222	2.000
25	22.023	19.523	15.622	14.094	12.783	10.675	9.077	7.843	6.873	6.464	6.097	5.467	4.948	4.514	4.147	3.985	3.834	3.564	3.329	2.856	2.499	2.222	2.000
26	22.795	20.121	15.983	14.375	13.003	10.810	9.161	7.896	6.906	6.591	6.118	5.480	4.956	4.520	4.151	3.988	3.837	3.566	3.330	2.856	2.500	2.222	2.000
27	23.560	20.707	16.330	14.643	13.211	10.935	9.237	7.943	6.935	6.514	6.136	5.492	4.964	4.524	4.154	3.990	3.839	3.567	3.331	2.856	2.500	2.222	2.000
28	24.316	21.281	16.663	14.898	13.406	11.051	9.307	7.984	6.961	6.534	5.152	5.502	4.970	4.528	4.157	3.992	3.840	3.568	3.331	2.857	2.500	2.222	2.000
29	25.066	21.844	16.984	15.141	13.591	11.158	9.370	8.022	6.983	6.551	6.166	5.510	4.975	4.531	4.159	3.994	3.842	3.569	3.332	2.857	2.500	2.222	2.000
30	25.808	27.306	17.292	15.373	13.765	11.258	9.247	8.055	7.003	6.566	6.177	5.517	4.979	4.534	4.160	3.995	3.842	3.569	3.332	2.857	2.500	2.222	2.000
40	32.835	27.355	19.793	17.159	15.046	11.925	9.779	8.244	7.105	6.642	6.234	5.548	4.997	4.544	4.166	3.999	3.846	3.571	3.333	2.857	2.500	2.222	2.000
50	39.196	31.424	21.482	18.256	15.762	12.234	9.915	8.304	7.133	6.661	6.246	5.554	4.999	4.545	4.167	4.000	3.846	3.571	3.333	2.857	2.500	2.222	2.000

Short Problems

1. This problem is a more complex and realistic version of Exercise 1. First you will note that marginal revenues are \$10 greater than in Exercise 1 although the marginal revenue products are the same. It has been assumed that in order to produce each additional unit, \$10 worth of materials must be purchased so that *MRP* available for labor equals (*MR* – 10) (*MP*).

   The total output is ten times as great and the intervals given are for ten workers rather than one. The estimates for output are obtained from the continuous function $TP = 10X + 0.1X^2 - 0.001X^3$ (X = number of workers) and for the marginal revenue in case B from the demand curve $P = 60 - 0.02Q$. In case A (the price taker) $P = \$40$. The *MPP*s and *MR*s refer to the midpoints of the intervals (for example, the *MPP* of 13 is an estimate of that for the twenty-fifth worker, and its *MR* of 48 is that for the two hundred ninety-fifth unit of output). You will have to interpolate between the midpoints to estimate employment.

Total number of workers	Units of output per week	*MP*	*Case A*		*Case B*	
			MR	*MRP*	*MR*	*MRP*
0	0					
		11	\$40	\$330	\$58	528
10	110					
		12	\$40	\$360	\$53	516
20	230					
		13	\$40	\$390	\$48	
30	360					
		14	\$40	\$420	\$43	
40	500					
		13	\$40	\$390	\$37	
50	630					
			\$40		\$33	
60	740					
			\$40		\$28	
70	840					
			\$40		\$24	
80	930					
			\$40		\$22	
90	980					

   (a) If the market wage that this firm must pay is \$250 per week, how many workers will the firm hire to maximize profits? Case A ______________; case B ______________

   (b) If the wage rises to \$300 per week, how many will the firm hire? Case A ______________; case B ______________

   (c) If in case A the market price of the product rises to \$50 and the wage is \$300 per week, how many workers will be hired? ______________

   (d) (Optional) Confirm that the *MP* is about 13 and the *MR* about \$48 for the output of the twenty-fifth worker by taking the first derivative of the total product and total revenue equations. (Some smoothing has been done, so using the derivatives for other estimates may lead to modest discrepancies.)

2. Do this problem and you have a start on the subject of engineering economics. If the net *PV* of a given cash flow is greater than 0, the rate of return is greater than *i*, and the project is "go." Similarly, to find *r* (which you should recognize as the *MEC*), you find the *i* at which the net $PV = 0$.

The Acme Machine Shop is analyzing a proposal to purchase labor-saving equipment estimated to save $15,000 a year less $1,000 maintenance. It calculates a ten-year life and $10,000 salvage value for the $75,000 machine. It wishes a return of 14 percent per year before taxes. Should it invest? For this problem it is wise to set up a brief cash flow table. Then by using *PV* tables you can find whether the net present value of a project is positive or negative.

Year:	0	1 to 10	10
Cash flow:	–75,000	14,000	10,000

Calculate *r* to the nearest 0.1 percent by evaluating cash flows at 15 percent and interpolation.

3. **The U.S. Way of Life and The Fixed Payment Mortgage**

Part of the U.S. way of life has been home ownership financed by the fixed payment mortgage. Our tax laws reflect this favoritism: One does not have to pay taxes on the implicit income from the housing services provided by home ownership. In addition, one can subtract from taxable income the interest paid to finance this ownership.

As a basis for this problem, take an $80,000 house financed by an $8,000 down payment and a $72,000 mortgage. Assume three interest rates, 6 percent, 12 percent, and 15 percent, and a mortgage term of 30 years. To simplify calculations, use Table 19-2, rather than formulas, and annual, rather than monthly, payments (dividing by 12 will give you a tolerable estimate of the usual monthly payment). Six percent (or a little less) is a fair estimate of long-term pure interest rates plus a risk premium and an allowance for administrative cost. Twelve percent (a rate in 1983 that encouraged house building) and 15 percent (a rate in 1981 that discouraged house building) have inflationary expectations built into them—the lender wishes to be compensated for the decline in the real value of fixed payments due.

(a) What would be the annual payments under each interest rate? (*Hint:* Simply divide $72,000 by the appropriate annuity factor in Table 19-2 for the first part of the answer.)

(b) How much is still owed after 15 years under each interest rate? (*Hint:* Get *PV* of annual payments for the 15 years remaining from Table 19-2.)

(c) At what year end does one reduce initial debt to less than half under each interest rate? (*Hint:* Find year in which *PV* of remaining payments is less than $36,000.)

(d) How much interest does one pay over the life of the mortgage under each interest rate? (*Hint:* Simply subtract $72,000 from 30 times annual payment.)

(e) How does this problem help you understand why the housing market is considered to be very sensitive to interest rates?

(f) Why is it important if one takes out a mortgage at substantially over 6 percent that the right to pay off the debt early without substantial penalties be reserved?

Answers to the Exercises

1. Table: case A, *MRP*: 0, 330, 360, 390, 420, 390, 330, 300, 270, 150; case B, *MRP*: 0, 528, 516, 494, 462, 351, 253, 180, 126, 60
   (a) case A, 8: *MRP*(8) = \$270, *MRP*(9) = \$150
   case B, 6: *MRP*(6) = \$253, *MRP*(7) = \$180
   (b) case A, 7: *MRP*(7) = \$300
   case B, 5: *MRP*(5) = \$351
   (c) case A, 8: *MRP*(8) = \$360, *MRP*(9) = \$200

2. Table: *MRS*: 40, 15, 10, 8, 7, 6, 5, 4, 3, 1; *MRP*: \$2,000 multiplied by *MRS*
   (a) 4, 27 (b) 3 (c) right, 5

3. (a) \$7.47, 1 percent, 50, 10 (b) \$42.12, 1 percent, 50, 10 (c) 72

4. (a) Increments in insulation are all \$5,000: savings are \$1,500, \$900, \$400, \$200; thus estimated *MEC*s are 30 percent, 18 percent, 8 percent, and 4 percent.
   (i) \$10,000 (ii) \$15,000 (These answers would hold whether *MEC* is taken as a series of steps or plotted as midpoints of insulation cost intervals connected by straight lines.)
   (b) The rate of return is over 6 percent but is somewhat less than 8 percent as shown by the following calculations:
   At 6 percent, *NPV* = –(6.802)(\$25,000) + (15.046 – 6.802)(\$25,000) = \$36,050
   At 8 percent, *NPV* = –(6.247)(\$25,000) + (11.925 – 6.247)(\$25,000) = –\$14,225

20

Wages, Unions, and Discrimination

Learning Objectives

This is a chapter with some analysis, a section on union history and labor legislation, and considerable discussion of significant and controversial issues. After studying it you should be able to

—see the effects of labor market structure (competitive, seller's monopoly, and buyer's monopsony) on wages and employment levels;

—recognize the pros and cons of legislated minimum wages;

—have a microview of involuntary unemployment (or why labor markets may not set prices that equate demand and supply);

—develop an historical perspective on unionism and labor legislation;

—see how simple models can help you understand aspects of race and sex discrimination and the remedies proposed, including the idea of comparable worth.

Review and Self-Test

Matching Concepts

_______ 1. association of employees by skill or occupation	(a)	law limiting use of closed shop and providing for cooling-off period in strikes imperiling national health or safety
_______ 2. indirect discrimination	(b)	monopsony
_______ 3. state laws permitting nonunion employees in organized establishments	(c)	strike
_______ 4. union shop	(d)	arrangement where workers must join union after being hired
_______ 5. National Labor Relations (Wagner) Act	(e)	discrimination in employment
_______ 6. concerted refusal by employees, usually unionized, to work	(f)	right-to-work laws
_______ 7. industrial union	(g)	guarantee to most employees of the right to collective bargaining through unions
_______ 8. market dominated by one buyer	(h)	craft union
_______ 9. Taft-Hartley Act	(i)	inferior economic status for race or sex reflecting differences in aspiration, education, and experience because of past discrimination
_______ 10. refusal to hire or promote qualified people on grounds of race or sex	(j)	association of employees within an industry, regardless of skills
_______ 11. comparable worth	(k)	two-tier wage structure
_______ 12. dual pay arrangement with lower level for new workers	(l)	controversial method of dealing with indirect discrimination of occupational segregation

Multiple-Choice Questions

1. If a union sets wages above the competitive level in an industry, all but which one of the following will probably occur, *ceteris paribus?*
   (a) Employment in the industry will fall.
   (b) Those employed will earn higher wages than before.
   (c) A pool of unemployed labor will be created.
   (d) Labor will be substituted for capital.

2. If a group of workers or members of an occupation are able to reduce their numbers and prevent others from entering, in an otherwise competitive market,
   (a) it will still be necessary for them to bargain for any wage increases.
   (b) the antitrust laws may be used against them.
   (c) their wages will rise, *ceteris paribus*.
   (d) the individual members will benefit only if the demand curve for their services is inelastic.

3. Which of the following was *not* a general problem for U.S. union leadership during the 1970s and 1980s?
   (a) whether or not to strike for its demands
   (b) how to obtain legal recognition
   (c) what choice to make between higher wages and increased unemployment for its members
   (d) how to deal with technological displacement of its members

4. The right of workers in interstate commerce to organize and elect an exclusive bargaining agent was guaranteed by the
   (a) Taft-Hartley Act of 1948.
   (b) Nixon-Fulbright Act of 1955.
   (c) Wagner Act of 1935.
   (d) Clayton Act of 1914.

5. The failure of U.S. union membership to grow in recent years may reflect all but which of the following?
   (a) the growing proportion of workers in services rather than manufacturing
   (b) the restrictions on organizing activities imposed by provisions of the Webb-Pomerene Act of 1959
   (c) instances of labor leader corruption and irresponsible strikes
   (d) the previous unionization of the most obvious and most easily organized occupations

6. Pension rights for workers may help employers keep total costs down because
   (a) they are a form of piecework pay.
   (b) many workers choose not to accept them.
   (c) employers have ways to avoid providing them.
   (d) they may reduce labor turnover.

7. Which might you expect to be the *major* reason that northern union leaders have been eager to unionize southern industry?
   (a) concern about economic justice for all
   (b) concern about a tendency of northern firms to move south to find lower wage costs
   (c) concern about race relations
   (d) desire to winter in the South

8. An arrangement in which workers must join the union soon after employment is called
   (a) a union shop.
   (b) a closed shop.
   (c) an open shop.
   (d) a jurisdictional shop.

9. Which statement best sums up the text analysis of the influence of unions on the general wage level?
   (a) Union influence has been unimportant because, in the absence of unions, wages rise as labor productivity rises.
   (b) Labor's share of the national income has risen steadily since the 1930s because of union action.
   (c) The fact of higher wages in highly unionized industries such as steel and automobiles proves that unions have been the chief cause of higher wages in general.
   (d) Unions may have helped raise the wage level, but it is hard to tell by how much.

10. An employer may find that discrimination in employment against equally competent, skilled blacks is more profitable than nondiscrimination
    (a) because white workers must be paid more.
    (b) if the majority of the firm's workers and customers are prejudiced.
    (c) because whites are better workers.
    (d) if this employer is the only one practicing discrimination, in a market of unprejudiced customers.

11. It was quite common in the past that female elementary school teachers could be hired at much lower salaries than men, with the result that school boards saved taxpayers' dollars by hiring mostly women. This suggests all *but* which one of the following?
    (a) Single women, with lower living expenses than men with families, were willing to work for less than men.
    (b) Women were not as productive teachers as men.
    (c) The supply of female teachers was greater than that of male teachers.
    (d) There were far more women than men applying for teaching jobs in elementary schools.

12. The major difficulty in raising the economic status of blacks to equal that of whites is
    (a) rapidly raising the levels of motivation, education, and training of blacks.
    (b) passing laws requiring equality of treatment.
    (c) dealing with blatant, direct discrimination in hiring.
    (d) exaggerated, since approximate equality has been achieved.

13. Refer to the diagrams in Exercises 1 and 3 which follow. The rising supply curve with higher marginal labor cost for the purchasing firm indicates
    (a) a competitive labor market.
    (b) monopsony in the labor market.
    (c) a unionized labor market.
    (d) monopoly in the product market.

14. Empirical evidence and recent theory indicate that reasonably competitive labor markets
    (a) promptly set wages that equate current demand and current supply.
    (b) are unresponsive to long-lasting changes in demand.
    (c) are unlikely to make frequent wage adjustments to equate current demand and supply.
    (d) are unresponsive to long-lasting changes in supply.

15. The doctrine of "comparable worth" holds that
    (a) interoccupational pay differences may represent sex discrimination.
    (b) supply and demand should determine relative wages.
    (c) returns to capital and labor should be comparable.
    (d) differences in wages of males and females should be approximately the same across all occupations.

16. The objective of "two-tier" wage structures is
    (a) to pay different wages to men and women.
    (b) to lower labor costs while preserving higher wages for present employees.
    (c) to recognize difference in the intrinsic value of different jobs.
    (d) to make difficulties for the union.

Self-Test Key

Matching Concepts: 1–h; 2–i; 3–f; 4–d; 5–g; 6–c; 7–j; 8–b; 9–a; 10–e; 11–l; 12–k

Multiple-Choice Questions: 1–d; 2–c; 3–b; 4–c; 5–b; 6–d; 7–b; 8–a; 9–d; 10–b; 11–b; 12–a; 13–b; 14–c; 15–a; 16–b

Exercises

1. Referring to the diagram, which represents the labor market in an industry, answer the questions below.

(a) If a competitive labor market prevailed, the equilibrium wage would be___________________________, and the amount of employment would be ______________.

(b) If a wage-setting union enters this market and sets the rate at w_4, the amount of employment would be ___________________________, and the amount of surplus labor unemployed would be___________________________. How would the labor supply curve look? ______________

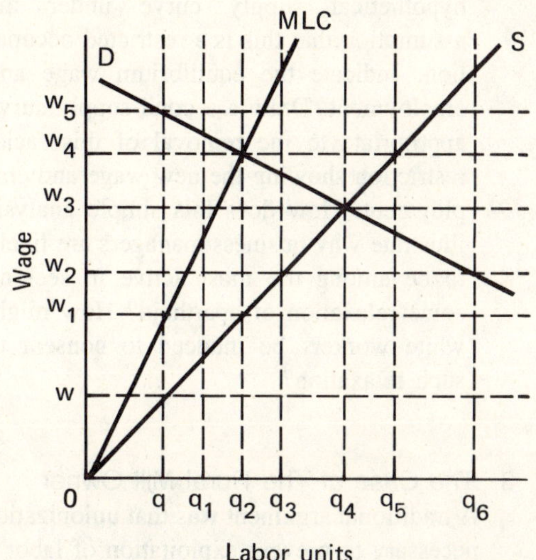

(c) Assume that this market consists of a single large firm hiring unorganized workers. If the firm hired q workers, it would have to pay all workers the wage ______________, but the marginal labor cost of the last person hired would be ______________. Because the marginal revenue product of the last person hired is equal to the amount ______________, there is an incentive for the firm to continue hiring to the amount ______________, at which the wage will be ______________, the marginal labor cost will be ______________, and the marginal revenue product will be ______________. Compare this with the result in (a).

(d) Suppose a union now organizes and tries to set a wage at w_4 at which employment would be ______________. The firm would probably successfully resist, because at w_4 there would be a large ______________ supply of workers. The union could eliminate this problem by setting the wage at ______________ where the employment, ______________, would be the same as under competition. (Actually, the solution in this bilateral monopoly case is indeterminate.)

(e) Suppose the labor supply is cut in half (at every wage) because of union or government restrictions. The competitive equilibrium would be a wage of ______________ and quantity employed of ______________.

2. One feature of apartheid in South Africa has been the restriction of many occupations to the 15 percent of population which is white. Take the given demand curve as one for a semiskilled occupation. Draw a hypothetical supply curve under the assumption that this is a restricted occupation. Indicate the equilibrium wage and employment. Draw a second supply curve appropriate to the removal of this racial restriction showing the new wage and employment. How does this simple analysis illustrate why business managers are likely to be among the most active in seeking some relaxation of apartheid? How might white workers be induced to consent to such relaxation?

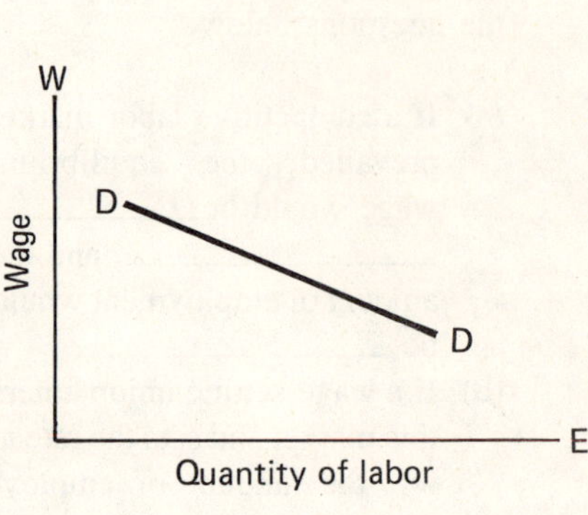

3. The Case of The Rural Mill Owner

A traditional argument was that unionization (and/or a legislated minimum wage) was necessary to prevent exploitation of labor by a monopsonistic firm. Not only would wages be raised, it was contended, but also employment would be increased.

Take the hypothetical case of Mr. Alfred Newman, whose mill was the only major employer in a rural county. Everyone available locally was on his payroll at the profit-maximizing wage ($2.40 per hour). He had decided not to expand output because he would have had to offer higher wages to attract workers from the next county. Then the United Textile Workers won a representation election and negotiated $3.00 as the wage in the mill.

(a) Show on the diagram what happens to the supply curve of labor with the new wage.

(b) What happens to the marginal cost of labor (*MLC*) curve?

(c) Where does the new *MLC* curve intersect the *D* curve for labor?

(d) If Newman wishes to maximize profits, how many people will he now employ? ______________

(e) Assume that the union gets a further raise; at what level will it reduce employment below the original level? ______________

(f) Assume that the minimum wage had been $2.30 (the legislated federal level in 1977) and the government now raises it to $3.00. Would your answers be the same as in (a) to (d)? Explain.

4. The text discussed comparable worth as a means of dealing with the indirect discrimination of occupational segregation, in which entry into many occupations, including highly paid professions and top administrative jobs, was virtually barred to women. The result was preponderantly female occupations, such as elementary school teaching and nursing, that frequently had lower wages than male-dominated occupations requiring roughly comparable skills, training, and responsibility.
   (a) Show the situation diagrammatically:

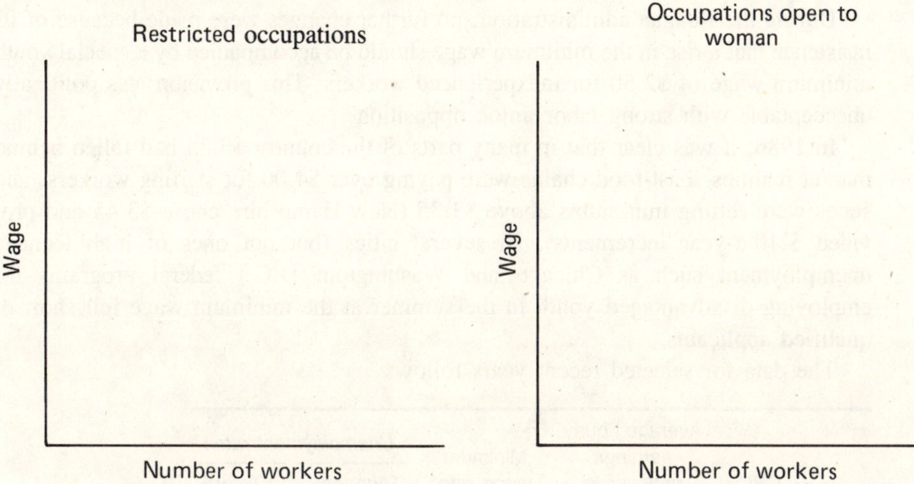

   (b) Why over time have some occupations open to women become almost exclusively female? For example, why was the schoolmaster (male) replaced by the school marm (female)?

   (c) Show diagrammatically what should happen as the barriers in restricted occupations are being broken down.
   (d) Assume that at a time when the wage in the previously restricted occupation (now 85 percent male, 15 percent female) still exceeds that of the preponderantly female occupation, the government invokes the doctrine of comparable worth and requires that the wage paid in the preponderantly female occupation be raised to that of the previously restricted occupation. Show the effect diagrammatically and comment on who are the winners and losers.

Short Problems

1. This problem is diagrammed in Exercise 1. The supply curve of labor is $w = q$; thus the total labor cost to the firm is $wq = q^2$ and the marginal labor cost is $2q$. The demand curve (marginal revenue product) is $w = \$1{,}000 - \frac{1}{2}q$.
   (a) The competitive wage and employment levels are ______ and ______, which correspond to ______ and ______ in Exercise 1.
   (b) The monopsonistic wage and employment levels are ______ and ______, which correspond to ______ and ______ in Exercise 1.
   (c) The excess supply of labor at a wage of \$800 would be ______, which corresponds to ______ in Exercise 1.

2. Toward a Minimal Minimum Wage?

In 1986, the minimum wage had remained at its 1981 level of $3.35 for over five years despite significant (but slowing) rises in the Consumer Price Index (CPI) and in average hourly earnings. In 1977, labor unions had argued that the $2.30 then in effect should be raised to 60 percent of the average wage in manufacturing ($5.58 at the time) to assure that a family of four would have income that would exceed the poverty level. The compromise was a series of steps that brought the minimum to $3.35 on January 1, 1981.

During the Reagan administration, no further changes were made because of its insistence that a rise in the minimum wage should be accompanied by a special youth minimum wage of $2.50 for inexperienced workers. This provision was politically unacceptable with strong labor union opposition.

In 1986, it was clear that in many parts of the country $3.35 had fallen behind market realities. Fast-food chains were paying over $4.00 for starting workers, and states were setting minimums above $3.35 (New Hampshire chose $3.45 and provided $.10-a-year increments). In several cities (but not ones of high teenage unemployment such as Chicago and Washington, D.C.) federal programs for employing disadvantaged youth in the summer at the minimum wage fell short of qualified applicants.

The data for selected recent years follow:

	CPI	Average hourly earnings nationwide	Minimum wage rate	*Unemployment rates* Teenage	Total
1956	81.4	$1.80	$ .75	11.1%	4.1%
1966	97.2	2.68	1.40	12.8	3.2
1976	170.5	4.86	2.30	19.0	7.7
1981	280.0	7.25	3.35	19.6	7.6
1985	319.9	8.58	3.35	18.6	7.1

Questions

(a) Compute the ratios of the legal minimum wage to the average wage.

(b) As of 1986 was the minimum wage still an effective minimum price?

(c) What is the economic and political compromise that seemed to be emerging on the minimum wage? In your answer, consider your answers to (a) and (b) and these questions. What economic effects was the administration concerned with? What were labor's concerns about the youth minimum? Is its past argument that the minimum wage should be high enough to keep a family of four above the poverty level (near $11,000) in the mid-1980s realistic?

Answers to the Exercises

1. (a) Ow_3; Oq_4
   (b) Oq_2; $Oq_5 - Oq_2$; horizontal at w_4 to supply curve
   (c) Ow, Ow_1; Ow_5; Oq_2, Ow_1, Ow_4, Ow_4. Wage is lower, employment is less than in (a).
   (d) Oq_2, excess; Ow_3, Oq_4
   (e) Ow_4, Oq_2

2. The supply curve shifts to the right (dramatically if training of "colored" and blacks is relatively easy), and *W* is lower and *E* higher. For the business this means a lowering of costs and a potential increase in profits. It also may be the only feasible way of expanding sales for a business operating in a small economy with few additional white workers available and with strong competition from foreign goods. The white workers would probably have to be guaranteed existing wages and normal increases or opportunities to transfer to equally desirable positions (a two-tier wage structure).

3. (a) It becomes a horizontal line at $3 up to quantity of 200 and then corresponds with *S* in diagram.
   (b) It coincides with new *S* curve up to 200 and then jumps to existing *MLC*.
   (c) at 200, $3
   (d) 200
   (e) above $4
   (f) yes, in this case where the $2.30 minimum was ineffective

4. (a)

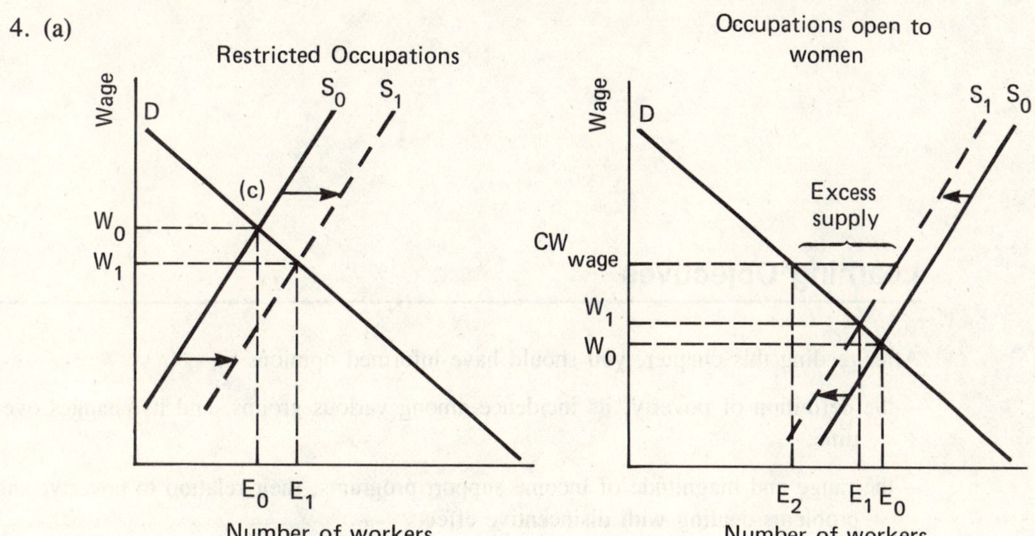

   (b) As women came into the labor force and lowered relative wages, men would find the opportunities of alternative employment much more desirable.
   (c) The supply shifts to the right in restricted occupation and to the left in open occupation as women leave it. The wage gap is narrowed.
   (d) The higher *CW* wage (equal to W_1 in the restricted occupation) in the open market benefits the job holders who remain. The clearest losers are the women (and men) who lost jobs $E_1 - E_2$. The public suffers also in having to pay a higher price for fewer services. The conflicting signals of a higher wage and the excess supply will increase involuntary unemployment.

21
The Problem of Poverty

Learning Objectives

After reading this chapter, you should have informed opinions on

—the definition of poverty, its incidence among various groups, and its changes over time;

—the range and magnitude of income support programs, their relation to poverty, and problems dealing with disincentive effects;

—the debate between those favoring "a war on poverty" and those concerned only with a minimal "safety net for the truly needy."

Review and Self-Test

Matching Concepts

_______ 1. largest income transfer program

_______ 2. poverty level

_______ 3. dollars needed to raise all to poverty level

_______ 4. Aid to Families of Dependent Children (AFDC)

_______ 5. 100 percent tax on earnings

_______ 6. in-kind benefit programs

_______ 7. Medicare

_______ 8. incidence of poverty

_______ 9. safety net

_______ 10. cash benefit program for aged, blind, and disabled

(a) poverty gap

(b) Supplementary Security Income (SSI)

(c) in-kind Social Security program

(d) Social Security (OASDI)

(e) percentage of population group below poverty level

(f) provision of minimum aid for "truly needy"

(g) reduction of welfare benefits by amount of earned income

(h) census calculation of minimum income to avoid poverty

(i) welfare program providing cash benefits

(j) food stamps and Medicaid

Multiple-Choice Questions

1. Under current definitions of the poverty level for the United States
   (a) more people were poor in 1973 than in 1983.
   (b) the problem can never be eliminated because poverty is entirely relative.
   (c) the majority of the world's people are poor.
   (d) most of the poor are nonwhite.

2. All but one of the statements below is a valid argument for putting public assistance programs on a national rather than a combined local-state-national basis.
   (a) Some states allow very inadequate benefits.
   (b) Some states and localities are less able to finance the present required fraction of the cost.
   (c) Uneven benefits result in poor people moving to more generous states.
   (d) Costs of living are not uniform nationwide.

3. The social welfare system in the United States does *not* provide
   (a) aid to needy mothers with small children.
   (b) payments for medical care for the poor.
   (c) a guaranteed minimum income to all needy.
   (d) unemployment compensation to those eligible.

4. The lower average income of black families
   (a) can be entirely accounted for by less education and less skill.
   (b) can be entirely accounted for by discrimination.
   (c) is attributable to disproportionate residence in the South.
   (d) is attributable partly to discrimination and partly to lower work qualifications and less capital per capita.

5. The poverty gap in recent years in the United States has been
   (a) roughly 1 percent of national income after taking into account money transfers.
   (b) nonexistent because of comprehensive welfare programs.
   (c) a good measure of income inequality.
   (d) around 11 percent for all families but higher for blacks.

6. Under present social security entitlements and taxes, the social security program
   (a) will run moderate surpluses until about the year 2015.
   (b) faces the immediate prospect of deficits.
   (c) can continue through the lifetimes of all now living without financing difficulties.
   (d) while all right now, will be in difficulty in the 1990s.

7. One population category in which blacks constitute a preponderant numerical majority is
   (a) those below the poverty level.
   (b) the persistently poor (nine years or more).
   (c) those not in the labor force.
   (d) those failing to complete high school.

8. Which one of these income support programs is means-tested?
   (a) Worker's Compensation
   (b) Social Security (OASDI)
   (c) the AFDC
   (d) Unemployment Compensation

9. The number and percentage of people with incomes below the poverty level
   (a) increased during President Reagan's first term.
   (b) decreased during President Reagan's first term.
   (c) was unreported during President Reagan's first term.
   (d) changed so little that no clear answer is possible.

10. Which one of these programs is not a means-tested welfare program?
    (a) the AFDC
    (b) Supplementary Security Income (SSI)
    (c) Medicaid
    (d) OASDI

11. The incidence of poverty is a measure of
    (a) the percentage of the population group below the poverty level.
    (b) the probability that a person randomly selected from the group will be below the poverty level.
    (c) the number of people below the poverty level.
    (d) both (a) and (b)

12. Which of the following is a positive statement about the problem of poverty?
    (a) Owing to disincentive effects, there is a conflict between short-run amelioration and long-run elimination of poverty.
    (b) Poverty programs should attempt to bring the poor to a decent standard of living.
    (c) Poverty policies should distinguish between the deserving and the undeserving poor.
    (d) Poverty and its elimination should be a compelling national concern.

13. A welfare program that reduces benefits by one dollar for each dollar earned can be said
    (a) to have no disincentive effects.
    (b) to embody a 100 percent marginal rate of taxation.
    (c) to be an example of "workfare."
    (d) to be illustrated by Medicare.

14. The "declaration" of "The War on Poverty" was made by President
    (a) Franklin D. Roosevelt
    (b) Lyndon Johnson
    (c) Richard Nixon
    (d) Ronald Reagan

15. Critics of the present measure of poverty level incomes have emphasized
    (a) that $10,000 for a family of four is outrageously high to be considered poor in the United States.
    (b) that benefits in-kind such as food stamps and Medicare are not included in income.
    (c) that illegal and unreported incomes can be significant and are not included.
    (d) both (b) and (c)

Self-Test Key

Matching Concepts: 1–d; 2–h; 3–a; 4–i; 5–g; 6–j; 7–c; 8–e; 9–f; 10–b

Multiple-Choice Questions: 1–c; 2–d; 3–c; 4–d; 5–a; 6–a; 7–b; 8–c; 9–a; 10–d; 11–d; 12–a; 13–b; 14–b; 15–d

Exercises

1. In a hypothetical economy with 20 million families, the poverty level is 1,000 piasters per year, with 5 million families below that level. The average family income of those below the poverty level is estimated at 300 piasters per year.
    (a) About how big is the poverty gap? ______________
    (b) What percentage of families is "in poverty"? ______________
    (c) Why would the percentage of persons "in poverty" almost certainly be greater than the percentage of families?

2. (a) Avoid thinking that poverty is primarily a black problem when looking at such incidence figures as 33.8 percent for black persons and 11.5 percent for white persons in 1984. The number of persons in 1984 classified as black were 28.1 million and the number as white 200 million. Therefore, using the number of people involved as the measure of the magnitude of the problem, the conclusion is that poverty is essentially a ______________ problem, since ______________ million white persons were poor, substantially more than double the ______________ million poor blacks.

   (b) In one increasing group the numerical magnitude of blacks in poverty approaches that of whites, "families with female householder." Such families typically are those with mother and child(ren), with husband-father absent. The incidence of poverty is high: 28 percent for whites and 54 percent for blacks in 1983 (this is after cash welfare benefits under the AFDC program). In 1981, of the 21.6 million white persons in poverty, 5.6 million persons, including 3.1 million children, lived in these families. Of the 9.2 million blacks below the poverty line, 5.2 million, also including 3.1 million children, lived in these families. 4.3 million other white children and 1.1 million other black children were also classified as poor.

      (i) Compare the proportions of poor blacks and poor black children to the proportion of poor whites and poor white children that are accounted for within this population category.

      (ii) What must be true about the relative prevalence of black and white female householder families? (See Short problem 2 for more on this.)

3. Refer to Table 21-4 in the text. The census figures, which do not estimate the value of in-kind benefits in determining the percentage of persons under the poverty level, are: 1965, 17.3; 1980, 13.0; 1983, 15.2.

   (a) How do the large increases from 1965 to 1980 for in-kind benefits, such as food stamps, influence the figures? Is there evidence of change after 1980?

   (b) How could a proponent of the war against poverty make a case from these figures?

   (c) What refutation could those who wished reductions in welfare programs make?

Short Problems

1. Lotteries: A Chance to Be Rich

Big winners in 1983 state lotteries included an announced "$4 million" winner in New York's Lotto game. The winner was to receive annual installments of $194,000 for 21 years. Another player (a retired steel worker whose wife was a waitress), who chose six numbers correctly, won a North American lottery record of "$8.8 million" in the Pennsylvania Lotto game in late July 1983. The jackpot was to be paid in 21 equal annual installments of $420,000 each.

Typically, states pay out 40 percent of total receipts in winnings with the rest split between administrative/sales costs and revenue for the state. Critics have pointed out that many lottery players are poor and that the states are raising revenue from people least able to pay. Others fault poor participants for misuse of their limited incomes (including welfare payments) in gambling.

(a) Should a poor family be criticized for spending $2 a week on lottery tickets?

(b) What is the present pre-tax value of the winnings above (assume i = 8 percent)? What is the after-tax value at a tax rate of 50 percent? At a rate of 25 percent?

2. Some Problems Are Very Difficult

Exercise 2 showed that the majority of poor black persons and almost three-quarters of poor black children were in female-householder families. In sharp contrast, in another family category, married with both spouses working, the black/white income ratio was rapidly narrowing from 77.2 percent in 1974 to 84.3 percent in 1983 as blacks increased their participation in professional and administrative occupations.

Accompanying the growth of the female-householder family has been a dramatic drop in black male employment, particularly among the youth. Only 60 percent of black males between 19 and 24 were employed in 1984, as compared with 71 percent in 1969, according to a study "The Black Youth Employment Crisis" by the National Bureau of Economic Research (NBER). The study found a willingness to work at wages comparable to whites but less ability to obtain work, and a greater proportion (32 percent) who considered crime a more lucrative alternative than legal employment. The NBER study found that the current welfare system is apparently doing little to correct joblessness. For black youths (aged 19–21) with the same family income, unemployment was 28 percent for those in private housing with no welfare, 44 percent with welfare, and 52 percent with welfare and living in public housing projects.

(a) How may the facts in this problem help explain how "persistent poverty (nine years or more)" was found to be preponderantly black? Consider the long-run implications.

(b) The theme of the study was that a "broad range of public and private activities" are needed, along with a strong job market, to inspire black youth employment? Do you have suggestions, particularly ones that draw on your study of economics?

Answers to the Exercises

1. (a) 3.5 billion piasters (b) 25 percent (c) Families with more dependent children are likely to be in poverty.

2. (a) white; 23 million; 9.5 million.
   (b) (i) about 57 percent of the poor blacks and 74 percent of poor black children; about 26 percent of the poor whites and 42 percent of poor white children
   (ii) It must be much greater since the incidence of poverty is about double for blacks who constitute only one-eighth of the population and yet have over 90 percent as many poor in this category. We can make this rough approximation: $(1/8 \cdot 2)\ x = 0.93$, so $x = 3.7$. This estimate that the proportion of female householders is 3.7 higher among black than white families is close to the actual data: 47 percent of black families were in the category as compared with 14 percent of white families.

3. (a) In 1965, in-kind benefits reduced the poverty percentage by only an additional 0.5 percent; by 1980, the additional reduction was 2.6 percent. The lower 1983 reduction of 2.2 percent could reflect Reagan administration curtailments.
   (b) Poverty was not reduced by the growth from 1965 to 1980 and increased with higher unemployment in 1983. Government transfers made a material difference and cut the poverty rate by more than half in 1980.
   (c) A reason that market incomes alone did not reduce poverty was that welfare dependence reduced earned income. Reduced welfare expenditures and lower taxes should be relied on to increase the growth rate and reduce the poverty rate.

CASES FOR PART FIVE

CASE 15: "The Average Guy Takes It on the Chin" (After 1973)

The sexism in the title, which is taken from the *New York Times,* July 13, 1986, reflects the prominence given to this table analyzing the great reduction in wages and salary prospects of the average thirty-year-old male worker after 1973. The data represent real earnings expressed in 1984 dollars.

Age 30 in	Average earnings age 30	Average earnings age 40	Percentage change age 30 to age 40
1949	$11,924	$19,475	+63
1959	$17,188	$25,627	+49
1973	$23,580	$23,395	−1
1983	$17,520	—	—

Source: U.S. Bureau of Labor Statistics as cited in study by Professor Frank S. Levy, University of Maryland.

The apparent conclusion, which we will modify a little, was that a male becoming thirty from the years 1949 to 1959 could expect large increases in real earnings. For those reaching 30 in 1973, it has been a struggle to maintain real earnings. Males attaining the age of 30 in 1983 earned only slightly more than their counterparts did more than two decades before. The problem is closely related to the lagging rise in worker productivity. The table on the following page relates percentage changes in the earnings above (columns 1 to 3) to percentage changes in total and nonfarm productivity (columns 4 and 5), and includes corresponding percentage changes in real compensation per hour (columns 6 and 7) with percentage increases in real weekly earnings for private, nonagricultural, nonsupervisory workers (column 8).

Percentage Changes in Real Earnings, Productivity and Compensation

	(1)	(2)	(3)	(4)	(5)	(6)	(7)	(8)
	Earnings (%)			Productivity (%)		Compensation (%)		Earnings (%)
				Total	Nonfarm	Total	Nonfarm	Private,
	M 30	M 40	M 30 to 40	bus.	bus.	business	business	nonfarm
1949–1959	44	NA	63	41	29	43	37	28
1959–1969	NA	31	49	31	27	33	28	16
1973–1983	–26	NA	–1	7	6	1.5	1.5	–14

The relationship between changes in productivity and in real compensation are clear, and the great decline in the rate of increase of labor productivity corresponds with the poor earnings performance between 1973–1983. Note that real compensation, which includes earnings, business contributions to social security, pensions, and other fringe benefits, did rise slightly in the 1973–1983 period. (Real compensation did not rise on a per worker basis since hours worked dropped about 5 percent.) There is no necessity that labor compensation go up exactly with productivity (this would imply that shares of labor and capital remained constant). There is even less reason that the earnings of different groups should exactly reflect overall productivity trends. Other market forces also affect earnings.

The economic malaise of 1973–1986 extends to virtually all other income series that depend primarily on labor income. The economy improved enough in 1984 to take the income of full-time female workers above 1973 levels and to 64.3 percent of the average of full-time male workers. Males, in contrast, were only at 90 percent of 1973 levels (when female income was only 56.8 percent of the male figure). But in 1985 and 1986 growth rates dropped to lower levels and elements of the traditional U.S. dream of being better off than one's parents and more prosperous in middle-age than in youth seemed less probable.

The real income series that did increase from 1973 to 1983 was disposable income per capita which went up by 10 percent, a pallid showing compared with the 42 percent it rose from 1963 to 1973. It extended its gain by another 6 percent through 1985. The reasons for its rise in the face of the decline in earnings are instructive.

First, in deflating current dollar income figures to get real income, the series used the implicit price deflator for personal consumption, which in 1983 stood at 2.14 times its 1973 level instead of the 2.20 for the consumer price index (CPI), which is used in calculating real earnings figures. In 1983, the CPI was revised to eliminate what was considered an upward bias in the way it handled housing expenditures, and it can be argued that real earnings data for 1983 as compared with 1973 are understated by close to 3 percent.

Second, the labor supply and the number actually employed increased significantly relative to the total population, which is the divisor for arriving at per capita figures. The underlying factors behind the increase of the labor supply were the maturing of the offspring of the baby boom (1947 to about 1967) into a working-age population, and the acceleration of the postwar trend toward female participation in the labor force, which took the proportion from 44.4 percent in 1973 to 54.7 percent in 1984 (these percentages are for females 20 years and over). This increase in the female labor supply added both to unemployment and employment as indicated in the table below. The first three columns give percentages of the noninstitutional population 16 years and over. Column 4 is total employment, and column 5 represents the percentage employed of the total U.S. population. (Resident armed forces members are included in both population and employment.)

	(1) Labor force participation (percent)	(2) Unemployment rate (percent)	(3) Employed (1)–(2)	(4) Employment (000's)	(5) (4) divided by U.S. pop. (percent)
1973	61.3	4.8	56.5	86,838	41.0
1983	64.4	9.5	54.9	102,510	43.7
1985	65.1	7.1	58.0	108,256	45.3

Third, disposable personal income includes payments for fringe benefits that are not part of earnings figures. More importantly, it includes income from ownership of assets. For persons there was a more than fourfold increase in personal interest payments from $93.3 billion in 1973 to $385.7 billion in 1983, as nominal interest rates increased. Finally, it includes transfer payments, the most important being social security. (This is not double counting—both the employer and employee contributions are deducted before arriving at disposable personal income.)

Fourth, the Reagan administration tax cut in 1983 reduced the income tax deduction from personal income by about 2 percent. [Actually, in 1983, the income tax deduction was somewhat higher (14.5 percent) than that in 1973 (13.8 percent) but without the tax cut it would have been 16.5 percent.]

Questions

1. The closest to being Mr. Average Guy is the man who was thirty years old in 1973 and forty years old in 1983 (in the sense that his earnings were close to the median for all male full-time workers). In what sense had he taken it "on the chin"?

2. Consider the economic position of the male "baby boomer" who attained age 30 in 1983. What economic factors could have made his earning position so much worse than that of Mr. Average Guy who was 30 in 1973?

3. The salary data are given in constant 1984 dollars. Convert the earnings data in the first table to current dollars using these values for the CPI (1967 = 100): 1949, 71.4; 1959, 87.3; 1969, 109.8; 1973, 133.1; 1983, 298.4; 1984, 311.1. (*Hint:* First convert the CPI so that 1984 = 1 by dividing all figures by 311.1. Then multiply earnings by the index expressed in decimal form that you have calculated.) Comment briefly on the results.

4. Real disposable income per capita did rise more than the rise in labor productivity during the period 1973–1983. Can it do so in the future? Explain.

CASE 16: Are the Rich Getting Richer?

In July 1986 summaries of two "wealth" studies were published in the press. One, by Congress' Joint Economic Committee, concentrated on the size distribution of net wealth in 1983. Its findings were of high and increasing concentration as the following table indicates.

	Percentage of households	Range of net assets (millions of dollars)	*Percentage of net assets held* 1983	1963
Super-rich	0.5	2.5 and up	35.1	25
Very-rich	0.5	1.4 to 2.5	6.7	7
Rich	9.0	0.2 to 1.4	29.9	33
Everyone else	90.0	negative to 0.2	28.3	35

Notes: 1. Total net assets were estimated at $10.7 trillion.
2. The total number of households was estimated to be 84 million.
3. Fifty percent of the assets of "everyone else" was in real estate (mostly in owned houses; only 20 percent of the top 1 percent were in real estate).
4. The top 1 percent owned 67 percent of all unincorporated business assets and 60 percent of individually owned stock in 1983. Business assets for the super-rich rose from $206 billion in 1962 to $1.9 trillion in 1983. For "everyone else," they rose from $206 to $214 billion.

The second study, by the U.S. Bureau of the Census, used a larger sample in 1984. Its concern was the association of net asset holdings with demographic and economic characteristics. Its definition of net assets (similar to the study above) included: real estate (41 percent), automobiles (6 percent), financial and business assets (51 percent), less debt. The finding given most attention was the racial and ethnic division of assets. These can be summarized as follows:

	Percentage of households with net assets >$100,000	Median holding of assets	Percentage of households with net assets <$0
White	26	$39,135	8.4
Hispanic	8.2	4,913	23.9
Black	3.9	3,398	30.5

The age distribution of wealth was also striking. Householders 35 or under had a median net worth of $5,764 (median annual income, $19,152) and those 55 to 64 had a median net worth of $73,664 (median annual income, $21,864).

Questions

1. (a) Compare the equality of the distribution of wealth with the distribution of income in the United States (summarized in text Chapter 18).

   (b) Compare the disparity in wealth and income between black and white households (median household income in 1984 for blacks was $13,476; for whites, $23,647).

   (c) Why may wealth be so much more unequally distributed than income?

2. U.S. Representative Obey, a Democrat, said the figures in the first table are "proof that the rich get richer," and if "wealth is power then most Americans have less power in the 1980s than the 1960s." U.S. Representative Lundgren, a Republican, termed this conclusion farfetched since the studies omitted the value of pensions and social security benefits, "two of the greatest accumulations of wealth in the middle class."

   (a) Let us concentrate on social security. In 1986, the top payment a recipient could receive at 65 was about $9,000 a year, plus 50 percent of this amount for a spouse aged 65. Assume these payments continued for 15 years (they are indexed for inflation) and that the real interest rate is 6 percent. What would the present value of social security be to the couple at age 65?

   (b) By fiscal 1983, social security payments, including Medicare, totalled about $235 billion (in fiscal 1987 they were estimated at $282 billion). In 1962, social security payments were only $14.3 billion, which would amount to about $43 billion in 1983 prices. Capitalize the $235 and $43 billion at 6 percent interest to get an estimate of the wealth that would be needed to generate these annual income flows, and compare these amounts with the totals for net assets, $10.6 trillion in 1983 and $5.9 trillion in 1962 (both figures expressed in 1983 dollars).

   (c) Consider the opposing positions of Obey and Lundgren on the significance of the shift in the concentration on net asset holdings between 1962 to 1987. Keep in mind that social security payments increase far less than in proportion to past annual earnings.

3. The young, particularly recent college graduates, tend to be poor in terms of wealth.
   (a) Take $20,000, roughly the average earnings per employee (110 million of them) in 1985, and compute the present value at 6 percent for a 40-year working life. The market value of capital assets that constitute wealth is determined by the stream of future earnings; to what extent can this present value of labor earnings be considered wealth?

   (b) The supervisor of the census bureau's study stated "that wealth is as important a gauge of family prosperity as income." Would you agree?

   (c) Social security is a negative holding of wealth for a 35-year-old worker. Show this by discounting this income stream: $1,500 of social security taxes on earnings for 30 years; then $8,000 a year of social security benefits for about 20 years.

CASE 17: Who Gets the Economic Surplus in Professional Baseball and Football?

The economic surplus referred to is the excess of revenue that can be obtained by employing special talents of young men for playing games rather than working. For example, in 1985, the revenues of the clubs that make up the National Football League have been estimated at $780 million. About 1,400 players worth perhaps $25,000 each in other occupations represent the primary resource. Much of the revenue must be used for other factors such as stadia, shoulder pads, administrators, and urinalyses. This case is concerned with economic rents that remain for the players and the profits left for the clubs.

Some operating results for football (1985) and baseball (1984) are given in the following table:

	National Football League, 1985	Major league baseball, 1984
Estimated total revenues	$870 million	$625 million
Shared revenues from national TV	$420 million	$180 million
Number of clubs	28	26
Average number of players per club	50	27
Total players in leagues	1,400	700
Estimated total profits of clubs	$70 million	$28 million
Estimated range of value for clubs (1986)	$50 to 90 million	$26 to 100 million
Estimated total value of clubs (1986)	$1.85 billion	$1.05 billion
Average salary per player	$193,000	$360,000

Sources: Fortune, August 4, 1986; *Business Week*, August 12, 1985.

It could be argued that the total profits of the clubs are underestimated because of generous tax deductions and benefits for other businesses, but seven of the baseball teams had significant operating losses. The salary figures clearly underestimate the total compensation to players which include generous pensions and the opportunity for substantial income from endorsements, speeches, and so on. Two generalizations are justified: first, baseball players have made about double the average salaries of football players; second, the NFL football clubs as a group have been more profitable, with their franchises worth collectively more.

Both football clubs and baseball clubs have been attempting to control recent escalations in player salary levels. For football, a doubling in the average level of salaries between 1981 and 1985 was associated with bidding competition with the United States Football League. Its major threat in 1986 was an antitrust suit for $1.3 billion in damages. The USFL charged that the TV contracts the NFL had with all three major networks represented monopolization.

Even if the NFL won the suit its annual TV payments seemed likely to be reduced by $60 million or more because of losses by the networks on their football programs. The NFL clubs significantly reduced their offers to the newly drafted players in 1986 since the USFL (with only eight clubs remaining) had little need or financial strength to compete for additional players.

No baseball clubs made offers to free agents in 1986. The rapid escalation in baseball salaries had begun with the negotiation of free agency and salary arbitration clauses in 1976 that is discussed below.

The following contrasts between professional baseball and football can be helpful in explaining why in baseball economic surpluses have tended to go more to the players, and in football more to the clubs:

1. Revenue Sharing In the NFL the bulk of total revenue is from national TV, which all teams share equally. Gate revenue is split fairly evenly: 60 percent to the home team, 40 percent to the visitor (except revenue from luxury sky boxes, classified as real estate income). In major league baseball, national TV receipts, while split equally, are relatively small. Visiting teams get little of the gate and none of the local TV receipts. These vary enormously with the size of the metropolitan population, and with the recent performance of the team.

2. Free Agency and Arbitration Both football and baseball confront unions strong enough to conduct strikes in the 1980s. Neither union can negotiate specific wages because of the disparity in talents between stars and run-of-the-mill players. Following an arbitrator's decision in 1975 that a player who played out the option year in his contract could deal with any club, the Baseball Players' Association negotiated an agreement that allowed players to become free agents after six years and to appeal contract disputes to binding arbitration after two years. The arbitration clause served to disseminate the gains achieved by free agents throughout the wage structure. Football's free agency clause accomplished little since the team hiring a free agent player had to compensate that player's team with high draft choices reflecting the salary paid.

3. The Draft and Player Training It was the universities that pointed the way to the potential profitability of weekly gladitorial spectacles, and it is not surprising that professional football has seen fit to work out mutually advantageous arrangements with the college sports industry. The NFL will employ young men only after the four years when their class is scheduled to graduate. It then will draft them with the selection order in the reverse order of league standings. By so doing, football avoids the significant costs that baseball undertakes with a draft system that reaches down to the high school level where talent appraisal is uncertain and there are thousands of high school and other youth teams. Baseball also maintains a significant minor league system. The universities have not let professional football down: Their attendees have been intensively well trained, and the system has proved flexible enough to minimize discrimination against those prospects who lack academic competence and motivation. Critics have pointed out that annually a few thousand potential professionals are being turned out without much but football skills to fill about 200 positions.

4. Unlimited Substitution After World War II football took a dramatic turn toward economic specialization in permitting unlimited substitution, in effect more than doubling manpower requirements by having separate offensive and defensive elevens plus such narrow functional specialists as kickers. This presumably improved the quality of the spectacle and on the amateur level increased possibilities for participation. More traditional baseball stuck to the principle that a player must both offend and defend (except for the designated hitter allowed by the American League).

5. Evaluation of Performance Part of the fascination of baseball is that it is really an individual game in the guise of a team sport and so the statistics that it generates, such as earned-run-averages and runs-batted-in, are public evidence of individual performance. The numbers that football generates are fewer and more suspect. The percentage completions by a quarterback are not only a function of his skill but of the line blocking and receiver surehandedness and elusiveness. Numbers for many football players, the linesmen, are virtually nonexistent.

Questions

1. Estimate the economic rents received by baseball and football players using an opportunity cost of $25,000 per year.

2. Use the economic concepts of marginal revenue productivity and qualified joint profit maximization to explain why football has been more profitable for the clubs and baseball more rewarding for the players.

3. Three competing leagues have challenged the NFL in the post-World War II period while none have reached the operational state in baseball. What encourages entry into football?

4. The arbitration process in baseball has been recommended for wider application in labor disputes. The arbitrator must choose either the last offer of the club or the last offer of the player with no splitting of the difference. The arbitrator's choice then becomes the settlement. Consider the merits and drawbacks of this procedure.

PART SIX

The Market Economy: Problems and Policies

22

Benefits and Costs of Government Intervention

Learning Objectives

After studying the material in this chapter, you should be able to

—explain how the market system coordinates the allocation of resources;

—explain the role of windfall profits;

—distinguish between private valuations and social valuations of benefits and costs;

—identify the major causes of market failure and of government failure;

—define the term "externalities" and identify methods for internalizing them;

—explain why it is not usually economically efficient to completely eliminate pollution and other undesirable externalities.

Review and Self-Test

Matching Concepts

_______ 1. market signal for additional resources to enter an industry

_______ 2. situation in which markets do not achieve best possible outcome

_______ 3. externalities

_______ 4. ocean fish, particularly those beyond the 200-mile limit

_______ 5. benefit of government intervention

_______ 6. part of net private benefit

_______ 7. key concept in judging economic efficiency

_______ 8. effluent charge

_______ 9. decrease in growth because of regulatory activities

_______ 10. example of government "failure"

(a) net social benefit

(b) per unit tax on producer for polluting activity

(c) government insistence on inefficient methods of pollution control

(d) cost of government intervention

(e) windfall profits

(f) market failure

(g) the difference between a unit of output's contribution to a firm's revenues and the firm's costs

(h) common-property resource

(i) decrease in market failure

(j) effects of a transaction on parties not directly involved

Multiple-Choice Questions

1. The likely result in a market system if government taxed away all windfall profits would be
   (a) a quicker shift of resources from declining to expanding markets.
   (b) the removal of the most important driving force for allocating resources.
   (c) improved market signals and responses.
   (d) increased information about temporary shortages and surpluses.

2. One of the most important features of a free-market economy is that
   (a) it generally responds quickly and automatically to changing demand-and-supply conditions.
   (b) prices are kept stable and low.
   (c) it solves the economic problem of scarcity and ensures abundance for all.
   (d) market systems automatically compel payment for collective consumption goods like national defense.

3. If there are negative externalities (external costs) associated with an activity and that activity is being carried out until net private benefits equal zero,
   (a) that activity should be subsidized.
   (b) net social benefits for the last unit will still be positive.
   (c) private costs exceed social costs.
   (d) output should be restricted.

4. A positive externality would probably result from
   (a) a discharge of a toxic waste into the Hudson River.
   (b) a newly painted house.
   (c) the dumping of wastes on an outgoing tide.
   (d) cigarette smoking.

5. A firm currently emitting harmful pollutants would have an incentive to reduce polluting discharges if
   (a) it were to be penalized by a pollution tax per unit of discharge.
   (b) it were to receive a tax credit for investments it makes in pollution control.
   (c) legal standing is given to private citizens to sue the firm for damages.
   (d) all of the above

6. A market is operating most efficiently if
   (a) total social cost is minimized.
   (b) total private benefit is maximized.
   (c) net social benefit is maximized.
   (d) the excess of private benefits over social cost is maximized.

7. Which of the following is the best example of a collective consumption good?
   (a) a home's solar heat collector
   (b) a pencil
   (c) a television broadcast
   (d) a fire extinguisher in a rural home.

8. A market economy is unlikely to provide a sufficient amount of a collective good like national defense because
   (a) national defense does not benefit individuals sufficiently.
   (b) private firms will provide national defense less efficiently than the government.
   (c) consumers are poorly informed about the benefits of national defense.
   (d) it is impossible to withhold national defense from persons who do not pay for it.

9. Which one of the following is *not* an argument for increased reliance on markets for allocating resources?
   (a) The market system coordinates economic activity automatically.
   (b) With competitive markets, price will tend to equal minimum average total costs of production.
   (c) Markets function best when external costs are associated with consumption or production of a commodity.
   (d) Market forces tend to automatically correct disequilibrium situations.

10. In order to achieve the optimal level of government intervention,
    (a) costs of enforcing government rules must be zero.
    (b) expected benefits from government intervention should be compared with expected costs.
    (c) ideal government performance should be compared with ideal market performance.
    (d) government intervention should proceed until negative externalities are entirely eliminated.

11. If pollution abatement becomes increasingly expensive with increasing levels of abatement,
    (a) the optimal level of pollution is not likely to be the minimum attainable.
    (b) the optimal level of pollution reduction will depend on the benefits from pollution abatement as well as the costs.
    (c) optimal pollution will not be zero pollution.
    (d) all of the above

12. If a ton of newspaper costs $350 to produce and in the process causes $10 worth of damage to the environment,
    (a) the private cost is $360 per ton.
    (b) the social cost is $10 per ton and the private cost is $350 per ton.
    (c) the private cost is $350 per ton and the social cost is $340 per ton.
    (d) the social and private costs per ton are $360 and $350, respectively.

13. A New York City resident who drives her car to work rather than take the subway
    (a) is maximizing private utility.
    (b) is likely to be creating an externality.
    (c) creates a situation in which social cost is likely to exceed private cost.
    (d) all of the above

14. The presence of external costs that make the marginal net social benefit negative implies that
    (a) private output exceeds the socially optimal output.
    (b) private output is less than the socially optimal output.
    (c) private output corresponds with the socially optimal output.
    (d) none of the above

15. An effluent tax or charge based on marginal pollution damages would
    (a) provide an incentive to expand output and increase external costs.
    (b) be inequitable to consumers of the product.
    (c) encourage the polluter to reduce pollutant emissions.
    (d) always entirely eliminate pollution.

16. Moral hazard refers to a situation in which
    (a) managers of firms pursue their own goals and not those of the firm.
    (b) values differ among sellers of products and services.
    (c) government intervention is required to internalize an externality.
    (d) in a two-person transaction, one person has information not available to the other and acts to increase aggregate risk.

17. If production of steel generates external costs, private efficiency in the production of steel will result in
    (a) too much steel at too high a price.
    (b) too little steel at too low a price.
    (c) too much steel at too low a price.
    (d) the socially efficient amount of steel, but at too low a price.

18. Which of the following are tools that the government can use to alter the workings of a market economy?
    (a) public provision of goods and services
    (b) redistribution of income by public expenditures and taxes
    (c) adoption of rules and regulations constraining market activities
    (d) all of the above

Self-Test Key

Matching Concepts: 1–e; 2–f; 3–j; 4–h; 5–i; 6–g; 7–a; 8–b; 9–d; 10–c

Multiple-Choice Questions: 1–b; 2–a; 3–d; 4–b; 5–d; 6–c; 7–c; 8–d; 9–c; 10–b; 11–d; 12–d; 13–d; 14–a; 15–c; 16–d; 17–c; 18–d

Exercises

1. Suppose that installing an antipollution device adds $10 to the cost of making each unit of a product at every level of output. Other things being equal,
    (a) Marginal cost will ____________________.
    (b) Average cost will ____________________.
    (c) The supply curve will ____________________.
    (d) Short-run equilibrium price will ____________________, but by less than ____________________.
    (e) Short-run equilibrium output will ____________________.

2. The following schedule shows (a) how the cost of production increases as a pulp and paper firm expands output and (b) the effect of pollution from the firm on commercial fishing in the area.

Output (tons/week)	Total private cost (dollars)	Value of fishing loss due to pollution (dollars)
0	$ 0	$ 0
1	500	100
2	550	225
3	620	365
4	710	515
5	820	675
6	1,050	845
7	1,350	1,025

(a) Complete the table below and graph your results.

Output (tons/week)	Average private cost (*APC*)	Marginal private cost (*MPC*)	Average social cost (*ASC*)	Marginal social cost (*MSC*)

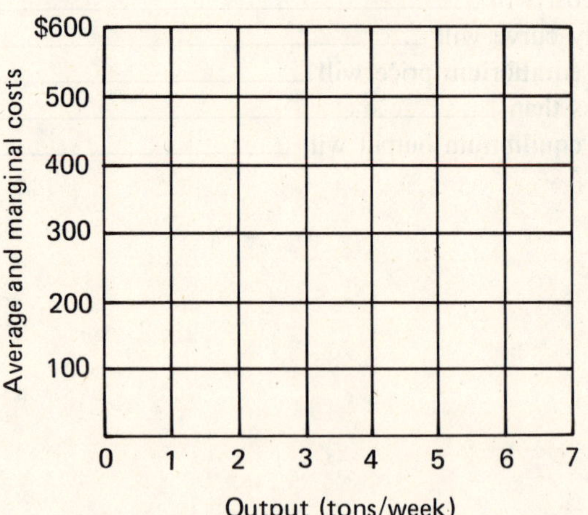

(b) If the firm were producing four tons of output per week, how much revenue would be required to cover its private costs? How much revenue would be required to cover the social costs?

(c) Assume a perfectly competitive market for this firm's product (paper) and that this firm's private costs of production are typical for the industry. Predict the long-run equilibrium price and the output for this firm. (Assume no pollution controls.)

(d) Assume now that firms in this industry are required either to pay compensation for the negative externalities or incur abatement costs to eliminate them. The industry price would be (higher, the same, lower) and the output (less, same, greater). This firm's ability to survive would depend on the long-run equilibrium price for paper being at least ________________, or on it being able to keep the total of negative externalities and costs of abatement at levels as (low, high) as those of its competitors.

3. The graph at right illustrates the situation for a firm that is producing a good that imposes external costs on neighboring residences. Marginal revenues to the firm are shown by the line *AB*; *PMC* represents the marginal costs to the firm; *MD* represents the external costs resulting from production. Label the graph as needed to answer the questions.

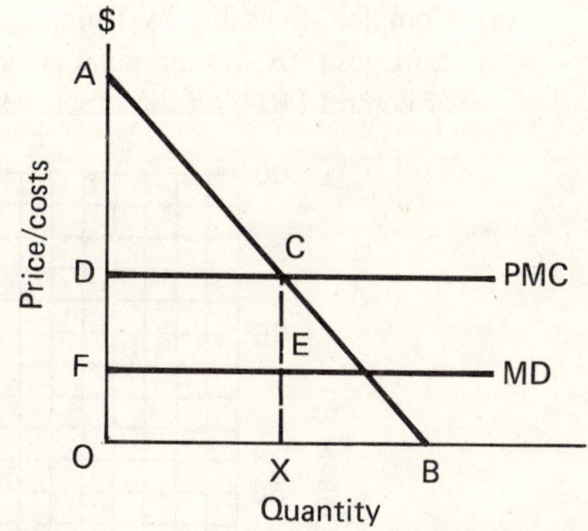

(a) Explain why output *X* is the private optimum (profit-maximizing) output for the firm.

(b) Draw the social marginal cost curve on the graph.

(c) The total external cost of producing quantity *X* is indicated by area ________________.

(d) Indicate on the graph the socially optimal output level as *Z*.

(e) The additional external costs from producing *X* instead of *Z* is equal to the area ________________.

(f) The additional private costs from producing *X* instead of *Z* is equal to the area ________________.

(g) Explain why there will be a net gain in welfare (that is, net social benefits will be positive) in reducing output from *X* to *Z*.

(h) What per unit tax on output could be levied to provide the incentive for the firm to produce output level *Z* instead of *X*?

4. The following table shows the dollar value of damages that might result from the indicated levels of SO_2 pollution associated with production of electricity (in lbs of SO_2 per million Btu). The table also shows the costs of reducing discharges of pollution from their existing level of 3 lbs per million Btu.

(1) Quantity of SO_2 emissions controlled (lbs per million Btu)	(2) Monetary value of damages (dollars)	(3) Marginal value of damages (dollars)	(4) Cost of pollution control (dollars)	(5) Marginal costs of control (dollars)
0	$150		$ 0	
1	90		25	
2	40		75	
3	0		175	

(a) Complete the table by filling in columns 3 and 5. Plot the marginal value of damages (*MB*, for marginal benefits of pollution control) and the marginal costs of control (*MC*) on the graph below. Plot *MB* and *MC* at each unit of control.

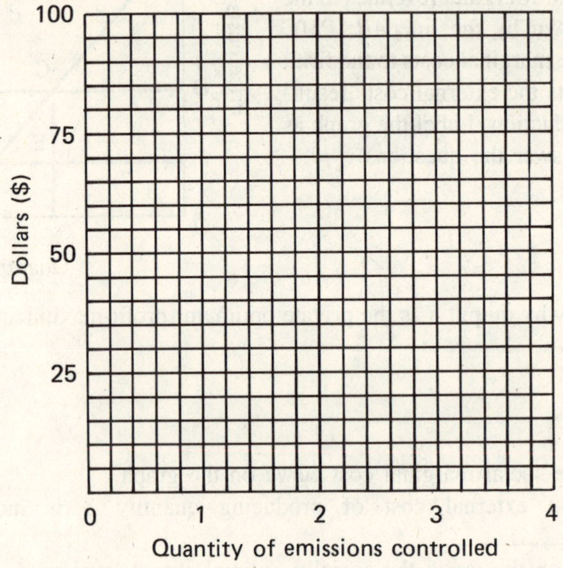

(b) Should emissions be reduced from their current level of 3 lbs per million Btu? Explain.

(c) What is the optimal level of pollution (control)? Explain.

(d) Suppose the dollar value of damages were to double at every level of pollution. What would be the optimal level of pollution?

Short Problems

1. Suppose the demand function for a commodity is $q = 90 - P$ and the marginal cost of supplying it is $MC = 1q$, where P is the commodity's price (in dollars), MC is the marginal cost (in dollars), and q is the quantity demanded or supplied in a given time period.

   Answer the following questions. (It might help to review Exercise 5 in Chapter 14 before attempting to make the necessary calculations.) Use the graph below.

   (a) Determine the equilibrium price and quantity with an efficient allocation.

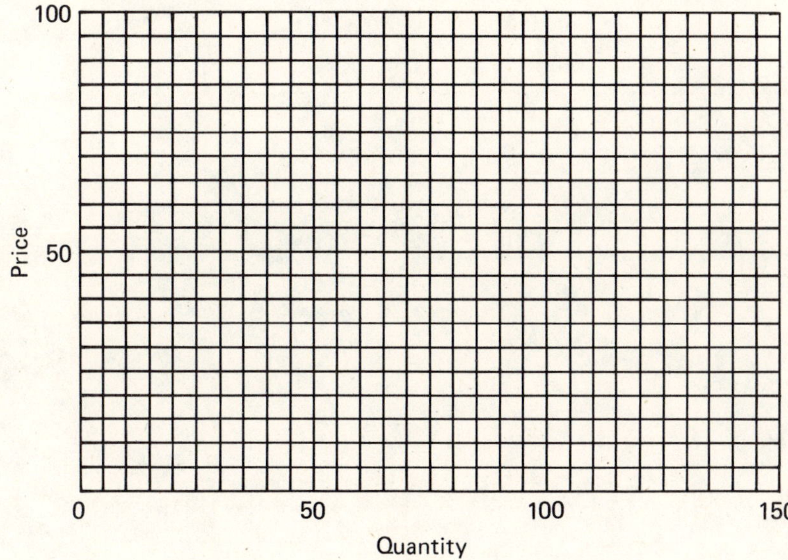

   (b) Calculate the magnitude of the consumer surplus, the producer surplus, and the net benefits in dollars.

   (c) Suppose the government imposes a price ceiling of \$30. Calculate the quantities demanded and supplied and the net benefits with the price ceiling.

   (d) Compare the consumer surplus, producer surplus, and net benefits in (c) with their respective amounts in an efficient allocation.

2. Suppose the demand function ($q = 90 - P$) and marginal cost function ($MC = 1q$) apply in a market with a single-firm pure monopoly.
   (a) Compute the equilibrium price and quantity. Use the graph on page 279.

   (b) Compute the net benefits, consumer surplus, and producer surplus under monopoly and compare with their respective amounts if there is a price ceiling of $30.

3. Assume that five firms located along a river discharge the amount of wastes into the river shown in the table below and that an environmental authority wishes to reduce the discharges to one-half their current level. Several policies for achieving the reduction in emissions are being considered. Costs of controlling pollution for each firm are also shown in the table. Assume that all costs are variable costs, and that they reflect costs of pollution control equipment, changing the production process or input mix to reduce emissions, or other methods for reducing discharges.

Firm	Weekly units discharged	Marginal costs of pollution control (dollars per unit)
A	100	$ 2
B	200	5
C	300	10
D	300	8
E	300	4

(a) One option is for the government to require all firms to cut back their discharge levels by 50 percent. Calculate the costs to the firms of this policy.

(b) An alternative regulatory policy would require all firms to institute a specific treatment procedure. Explain why this would likely result in higher costs to the firms than the uniform percentage cutback.

(c) Assume now that the pollution control authority wishes to levy a per unit effluent charge or fee on each firm's discharges to provide an incentive for them to reduce their discharges. What per unit fee would achieve the 50 percent cutback in discharges? What would be the pollution control expenditures of the firms with this policy? Are there advantages of an effluent fee compared to the policies in (a) or (b)? Are there disadvantages?

(d) The pollution control authority is also considering an effluent permit system whereby a limited number of permits to discharge effluents would be allocated, with the price of the permits determined by demand and supply. In this case, 600 permits (each corresponding with a unit of allowable discharge) would be issued. What is the likely market price for a permit? Compare this policy with the effluent fee.

Answers to the Exercises

1. (a) rise by \$10 (b) rise by \$10 (c) shift to left (d) rise, less than \$10 (e) decline
2. (a)

Output (tons/week)	*APC*	*MPC*	*ASC*	*MSC*
0				
	\$500			\$600
1	\$500		\$600	
		50		175
2	275		387.50	
		70		210
3	206.67		328.33	
		90		240
4	177.50		306.25	
		110		270
5	164		299	
		230		400
6	175		315.83	
		300		480
7	192.86		339.29	

(b) \$710 (per ton price of \$177.50); \$1,225 (per ton price of \$306.25)
(c) \$164; 5 tons/week
(d) higher; less; \$299 (the lowest average social cost); low

3.

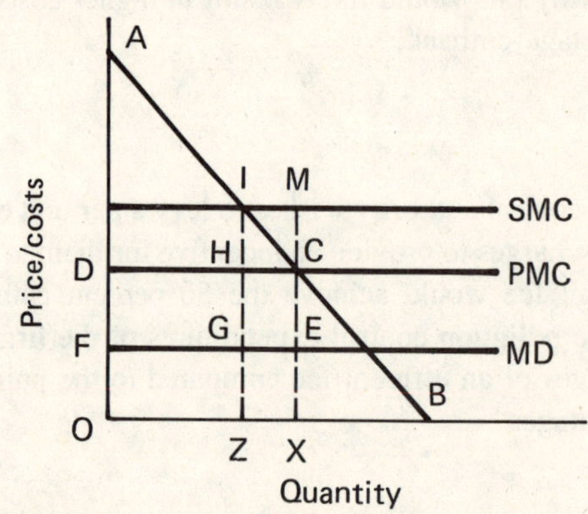

(a) output *X* maximizes net private benefit ($MR = PMC$)
(b) graph above: $SMC = PMC + MD$
(c) *OFEX*
(d) on graph
(e) *ZGEX*
(f) *ZXCH*
(g) Reducing output from *X* to *Z* will decrease social costs by $ZHCX + ZGEX$, but decrease revenues to the firm by a lesser amount, *ZICX*. The triangle, *IMC*, represents the net gain.
(h) tax of *FO*, equal to marginal damages.

4. (a) Marginal benefits of control (in reduced damages): 60,50,40 for the first, second, and third units of *PC*. Marginal costs of control: 25,50,100

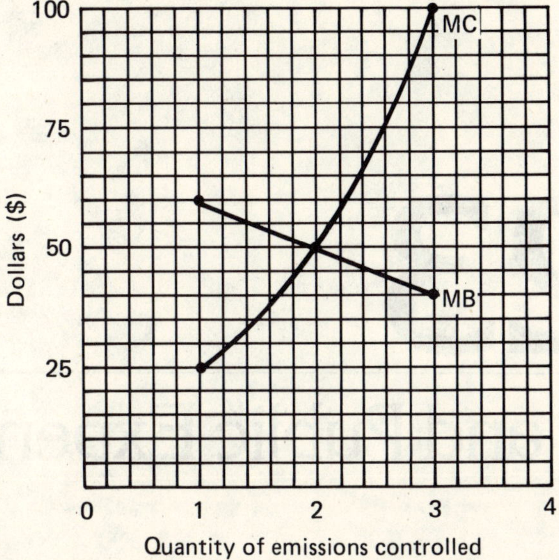

(b) Yes. Incremental benefits of pollution control are the corresponding reduction in damages. The marginal benefits of the first 1 lb of SO_2 removed would be \$60; the marginal costs of control would be only \$25.

(c) The optimal level of pollution control would be 2 lbs per million Btu (or an allowable emissions rate of 1 lb of SO_2 per million Btu). Reducing pollution to that level maximizes the net benefits of control.

(d) Zero.

23

Taxation and Public Expenditure

Learning Objectives

Careful study of the material in this chapter should allow you to

—explain the meaning of progressive and regressive taxes;

—define the term tax incidence;

—explain the role of transfer payments to individuals and grants-in-aid to state and local governments;

—identify the major economic sources of the urban crisis;

—discuss the issues in debates about the relative merit of public and private expenditures and about the desirable size of government.

Review and Self-Test

Matching Concepts

_______ 1. comprehensive income taxation (CIT)

_______ 2. decreasing ratio of taxes to income with increased income

_______ 3. marginal tax rate

_______ 4. tax system that provides payments to low-income households

_______ 5. tax incidence

_______ 6. tax assessed as a percentage of the value of a commodity

_______ 7. excise tax

_______ 8. consumption taxation

_______ 9. grants to state and local governments for specified types of expenditures

_______ 10. revenue sharing

_______ 11. progressive tax

_______ 12. Laffer curve

(a) fraction of an additional dollar of income that is paid in taxes

(b) location of the ultimate burden of a tax

(c) tax on the sale of a specific commodity

(d) taxation of a household on its income minus saving

(e) general purpose federal grants to state and local governments

(f) negative income tax

(g) regressive tax

(h) categorical grants-in-aid

(i) *ad valorem* tax

(j) increasing ratio of taxes to income with increased income

(k) relation of revenue yield to tax rate

(l) levies on a substantially expanded tax base

Multiple-Choice Questions

1. A tax that takes the same amount from everyone, regardless of income, is
   (a) regressive.
   (b) progressive.
   (c) not fair at all.
   (d) proportional to the benefit received.

2. The judgment concerning whether a tax is regressive, proportional, or progressive is based on a comparison of the amount of tax with the
   (a) tax base.
   (b) value of the item being taxed.
   (c) taxpayer's income.
   (d) distribution of income.

3. Comprehensive income taxation
   (a) requires different tax rates for income received from different sources.
   (b) refers to reducing the gap between taxable income and total income.
   (c) requires a fixed flat-rate tax.
   (d) would probably lead to higher marginal and average tax rates than an equivalent-yield tax with deductions and exemptions.

4. Property taxes generally
   (a) fall entirely on the homeowner or landlord.
   (b) are less likely to be shifted in the long run than in the short run.
   (c) fall on renters as well as homeowners and landlords.
   (d) are borne entirely by the occupant of a house.

5. The marginal rate of taxation of a progressive income tax is necessarily
   (a) the same as the average rate.
   (b) less than the average rate.
   (c) more than the average rate.
   (d) higher the lower the income.

6. A marginal rate of 50 percent on a taxable income of $200,000
   (a) means that the average person with $200,000 of income pays $100,000 in taxes.
   (b) has no effect whatever because of exemptions, deductions, and tax avoidance.
   (c) signifies the collection of $.50 on each additional dollar of income for a person in the $200,000 tax bracket.
   (d) always applies to capital gains as well as to dividend income.

7. The text suggests that the overall U.S. tax structure is nearly proportional, at least below the top brackets, inasmuch as state and local taxes are
   (a) proportional.
   (b) intolerable.
   (c) about the same as federal.
   (d) regressive in total.

8. A negative income tax of the type described in the text would have the advantage of
   (a) reducing the progressivity of the tax structure.
   (b) guaranteeing a minimum income to the poor with less red tape and with increased work incentives.
   (c) penalizing those with large families.
   (d) keeping recipients out of the labor force where they would cause unemployment.

9. Tax "incidence" indicates
   (a) who actually bears the final burden of the tax.
   (b) who pays the tax to the federal Treasury.
   (c) the progressivity of the tax.
   (d) whether or not the tax is fair.

10. The more elastic the demand for a commodity on which a specific excise was levied, *ceteris paribus,*
    (a) the greater the after-tax price increase.
    (b) the less the reduction in the quantity produced.
    (c) the more elastic the associated supply curve.
    (d) the less the after-tax price increase.

11. Proponents of the Laffer curve idea argue that
    (a) tax yields will increase proportionally with tax rates.
    (b) the relationship between tax yields and tax rates are unpredictable.
    (c) revenues will first decrease and then increase as tax rates are increased.
    (d) revenues will increase with rising tax rates to a maximum after which higher rates reduce tax yields.

12. The largest single component of government expenditure is
    (a) federal grants-in-aid.
    (b) national defense.
    (c) transfer payments to persons.
    (d) education.

13. Which of the following is *not* thought to be associated with the "urban crisis"?
    (a) heavy reliance of state and local governments on property, sales, and excise taxes
    (b) relatively lower unit costs for state and local government output compared with other sectors of the economy
    (c) increased demand for police, health, and welfare services
    (d) selective migration of residents from central cities to suburbs

14. Economic analysis suggests that for a given government activity,
    (a) the value of total benefits should equal total costs.
    (b) expenditure should be expanded until marginal benefit exceeds marginal cost.
    (c) expenditure should be expanded as long as marginal benefit exceeds marginal cost.
    (d) private benefits should equal social costs.

Questions 15 and 16 refer to the diagram below.

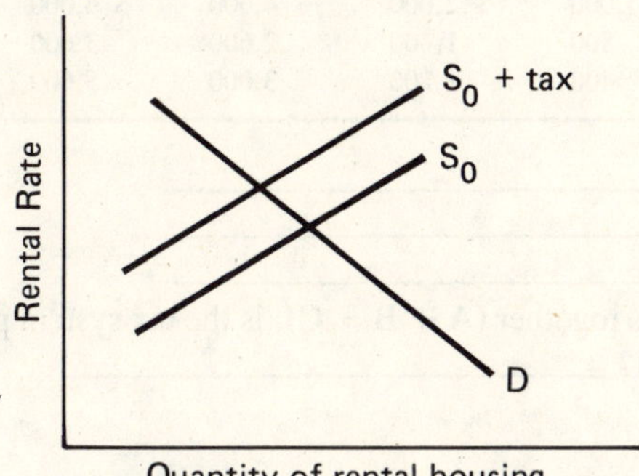

15. A tax on landlords in the market described in the diagram
    (a) would be paid entirely by landlords.
    (b) would be paid entirely by renters.
    (c) would be shared by landlords and tenants.
    (d) would produce a leftward shift in the demand schedule.

16. In the situation described by the diagram,
    (a) the amount of rental housing demanded remains the same before and after the tax.
    (b) the quality of rental housing would improve.
    (c) the quantity of rental housing demanded would fall.
    (d) the quantity of rental housing that landlords would be willing to supply does not change.

Self-Test Key

Matching Concepts: 1–l; 2–g; 3–a; 4–f; 5–b; 6–i; 7–c; 8–d; 9–h; 10–e; 11–j; 12–k

Multiple-Choice Questions: 1–a; 2–c; 3–b; 4–c; 5–c; 6–c; 7–d; 8–b; 9–a; 10–d; 11–d; 12–c; 13–b; 14–c; 15–c; 16–c

Exercises

1. (a) The table below shows the amount of tax paid by individuals in four different income categories. For each of the three taxes, A, B, and C, indicate whether the tax is proportional, regressive, or progressive.

Amount of Tax Paid by Income Level

	Income Level			
Tax	$10,000	$20,000	$40,000	$60,000
A	$ 1,000	$ 2,000	$ 4,000	$ 6,000
B	800	1,400	2,600	3,600
C	400	1,200	3,000	5,600

Tax A is ______________________.
Tax B is ______________________.
Tax C is ______________________.

(b) Taking all taxes together (A + B + C), is the tax system progressive, regressive, or proportional? ______________________

2. (a) Suppose that a negative income tax provides $5,000 guaranteed income for a family and a 50 percent marginal tax rate on earnings. Complete the table.

(A) Before-tax earnings	(B) Income tax (–$5,000 + 0.5A)	(C) After-tax income (A – B)
$ 0	–$5,000	$5,000
2,000	–$4,000	____
5,000	____	$7,500
7,000	____	____
10,000	____	____

(b) The following version of the negative income tax was part of a 1970 experiment.

A man with a family of five earns $96 a week in income and receives $10.75 a week in cash from the government; if his earnings fall to $50, he will receive $43 a week from the government, and if he earns nothing, he will receive $78 a week from the government.

Calculate the implicit marginal rate of taxation.

Earnings	Change in earnings	Cash transfer	Change in cash transfer	Marginal rate of taxation
$ 0		$78.00		
	____		____	____
50		43.00		
	____		____	____
96		10.75		

3. The three diagrams below represent three different market situations with respect to the supply and demand for rental accommodation in the short run. Assume that a property tax of equal yield is imposed in all three situations.

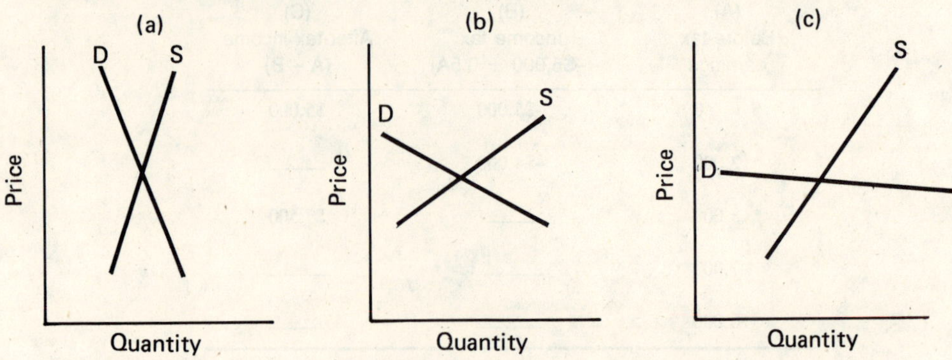

(a) In which market situation will the landlord bear most of the tax burden? Explain.

(b) In which market situation is there the smallest change in the quantity of rental accommodations? Why is this the case?

(c) Suppose that in case B rent controls had "fixed" rent or price at the original equilibrium, pretax rate. Is the tax burden shouldered by the landlord in case B altered because of the existence of rent control?

4. Sophia Hollingsworth has become eligible for tax-free unemployment benefits of $100 a week. She now has the opportunity of a near-minimum wage job for $150 subject to 6 percent social security and 15 percent income tax rates. Commuting expenses necessary for the job are estimated at $20. Show that the effective marginal rate of "taxation" for Sophia is over 100 percent if she accepts the new position.

Short Problems

1. The Saving Canadians

   In the late 1970s Canadians were saving between 9 and 22 percent of household income after taxes, while U.S. residents were saving between 3 and 6 percent. The *Wall Street Journal* (August 8, 1980) observed that part of the difference was due to tax policy.

   Canada exempted the first $1,000 of income in interest on savings accounts; it also did not limit the interest savings banks could pay on ordinary accounts. (U.S. restrictions on interest are scheduled to be phased out by 1986.) Savings interest was fully taxable in the United States through 1980 (in 1981, $200 of interest per person could be tax free).

   Compare the real after-tax income received and effective tax rate on real income from $1,000 additional savings for the M. Leafs (Canadian) and W. Stars (U.S.). Both are considering whether to add the money to their savings accounts or to spend it on vacation trips. The inflation rate is 8 percent in each country. The Leafs can get 10 percent interest, the Stars 5 percent.

2. In each of the following versions of a 1970 experiment with negative income tax alternatives, calculate the marginal rate of taxation:
   (a) A family of four receives a negative tax of $3,300 with zero earnings, and nothing with earnings of $6,600. ________
   (b) A man earning $100.00 a week with a family of six is given $28.50 negative tax a week; if his income drops to zero, he will receive $58.50. ________

Answers to the Exercises

1. (a) Tax A is proportional; tax B is regressive; tax C is progressive.
   (b) For each income group the tax rates are: 22 percent for $10,000, 23 percent for $20,000, 24 percent for $40,000, and 25.3 percent for $60,000. The tax system is slightly progressive.

2. (a) column B: –$5,000; –$4,000; –$2,500; –$1,500; 0
   column C: $5,000; $6,000; $7,500; $8,500; $10,000
   (b)
   $$MRT = \frac{\Delta T}{\Delta Y} = \frac{43 - 10.75}{46} \text{ or } \frac{35}{50} = 0.70$$

3. (a) Situation C. Demand is very elastic, and quantity of accommodation would decline significantly with little rise in price.
   (b) Situation A. Demand is inelastic and does not respond significantly to the higher price.
   (c) In the short run the landlord would shoulder *all* the tax.

4. The additional income of $150.00 is more than offset by $22.50 of income taxes, $9.00 in social security, $100.00 of lost unemployment compensation, and $20.00 commuting. $151.50/150.00 = 101 percent.

CASES FOR PART SIX

CASE 18: Acid from the Skies

"Acid rain" is the name given to air pollution caused by burning fossil fuels in industry (utilities, smelters), home heating, and motor vehicles. Discharges of sulfur and nitrogen oxides are changed chemically in the atmosphere to sulfates and nitrates and fall to the earth, often far from their point of origin, as acidic rain, snow, fog, or dust. Acid rain has been found to destroy fresh-water life in some lakes and streams, particularly in the eastern United States and Canada. There is debate about whether it damages forests and threatens human health.

The areas receiving the largest amounts of acidic deposition in eastern North America are directly downwind from concentrated emissions in the midwestern areas of the continent. The underlying geological composition of many of these areas is characterized by little buffering capacity, making them particularly susceptible to elevated levels of acidic pollutants.

The potential effects of acid rain include acidification of surface waters and ground waters, acidification and release of metals from soils, reduction in forest productivity, damage to agricultural crops, deterioration of buildings, statues, and metal structures, and contamination of drinking water supplies. In New York's Adirondack Mountains, significant losses of fish life have been documented (at least 25 percent of ponded brook trout water is already devoid of fish as a result of acid rain, and another 25 percent is predicted to be void of life by 1990).

Although some lakes are known to be naturally acidic, others have become significantly more acidic over the past several decades, primarily because of increased use of fossil fuels over the period. The Clean Air Act of 1970 indirectly contributed to the problem with its emphasis on reducing local levels of sulfur and nitrogen oxides. Emitters were able to meet the more stringent emission standards by increasing the height of newly constructed smokestacks. This solved the local sulfur oxide problem at the expense of downwind regions. Residents of the northeastern United States complain that they must impose harsh pollution controls on their own industries to compensate for the incoming pollutants from the Midwest. But officials of Ohio and Illinois, states that both mine high-sulfur coal and burn it in their power plants, say that they don't see the effects of acid rain in their states, that their citizens should not be forced to pay to clean up someone else's air, and that their citizens need the jobs of mining the high-sulfur fuel.

Several bills have recently been introduced in Congress aimed at controlling acid rain, but as of July 1986, none had passed. The states of New York, New Hampshire, and Massachusetts enacted legislation in 1986 to curtail sulfur dioxide emissions. The Canadian province of Ontario also announced in 1986 a program to sharply curtail sulfur dioxide emissions from its four biggest industrial sources.

Questions

1. Consider first the problem of firms emitting sulfur and nitrogen oxides. What is the element of "market failure"? Explain.

2. Consider next the government intervention that was meant to correct the market imperfection. Would you also characterize it as being a "failure"?

3. If you were a government official from a Midwestern state, what would your position probably be with respect to the acid rain problem? What if you were from the Northeast? Use the externality concept to explain the basis of these viewpoints.

4. Consider the problem of acid rain from a *national* standpoint, rather than from a particular region's point of view. Identify and discuss some possible solutions.

5. Main economic issues in legislation considered by Congress concern the costs of controlling acid rain and who would bear the costs. Most bills have called for a sulfur dioxide emissions standard of 1.2 lbs per million Btus, with a goal of reducing annual emissions nationwide by 10 million tons. Among the plans being considered was one which forced the 50 largest sources to reduce emissions by the use of smokestack scrubbing equipment, whether they burned high- or low-sulfur coal. According to this plan, 90 percent of the costs would be subsidized from a fund created by levying on all electricity consumers one-tenth of a cent fee for each kilowatt hour of electricity used. Critically examine this plan.

CASE 19: Taxing the Cigarette Habit in the Most Profitable Way

In 1982 cigarettes were taxed by states at rates ranging from $.02 to $.03 on a pack of 20 in the three "tobacco" states of Kentucky, Virginia, and North Carolina, to a range of $.21 to $.25 in eight states. (Hawaii was the only state to levy an *ad valorem* tax, 40 percent of the wholesale price, and would be another high-tax state.)

New Hampshire was about average with a $.12 per-pack tax but nonetheless had by far the highest per capita sales of cigarettes: 240 packs in 1982 as compared to a national average of 131 packs. Tax rates in 1982 and 1983 are shown in the following table.

		Cigarette Tax	
State	Population	1982	1983
Maine	1,133,000	$.21	$.26
Massachusetts[a]	5,773,000	.21	.26
Vermont	516,000	.12	proposed .17
New Hampshire	936,000	.12	proposed .17

[a]Over 2,600,000 lived in 3 counties bordering New Hampshire; about 210,000 in the counties bordering Vermont.

As indicated in the table, two of the three states surrounding New Hampshire were high-tax states. At the start of 1983 the United States raised the federal tax from $.08 to $.16 (it had been unchanged since World War II). Massachusetts and Maine raised their taxes shortly afterwards. In July 1983, New Hampshire raised its tax to $.17, to take effect only after Vermont made the same raise (which it did in August 1983).

A leading New Hampshire industry was tourism. In addition there were many vacation homes owned by out-of-staters. Its fiscal system had a number of peculiarities:

1. The state was fiftieth in tax revenues per capita in 1980. The state and local governments together spent less per capita on education than all but two other states and tied Maine for the bottom spot on health and hospital expenditures. Only on highways did New Hampshire spend more than the average per capita.
2. Its revenue-raising methods were different, since it was the only state within which more than half the tax revenues (60 percent) were property taxes. It also pioneered the state lottery and had a state-owned liquor monopoly with aggressive pricing policies and with most stores located near the state's borders.

   In face of a nationwide decline in alcohol sales, New Hampshire reported an increase in fiscal 1986 and increased its advertising budget by 35 percent to $358,000. It was almost political death in New Hampshire to talk of broad-based sales or income taxes, but the state had the highest gasoline tax in the nation and a hefty impost on meals and rooms (7 percent). The only income tax was on interest and dividends, with interest from New Hampshire savings accounts exempted.

Questions

1. The U.S. Treasury assumed that its $.08 tax on cigarettes would decrease the quantity of cigarettes sold by 4 percent. (Assume initial retail price of cigarettes was $.80 a pack and quantity sold was 30 billion packs.)
   (a) Approximately what elasticity of demand for cigarettes does the Treasury estimate imply?

   (b) By how much would federal tax receipts increase?

   (c) Explain why the cigarette tax is regressive.

   (d) Why are raises in cigarette taxes considered acceptable in a country that relies heavily on income taxation?

2. (a) New Hampshire apparently considers "the best tax" to be one paid by an "out-of-stater." How is this illustrated in their tax system generally, and particularly in their approach to cigarette taxation?

   (b) What drawbacks (if any) do you see in the New Hampshire fiscal approach? Consider particularly the heavy reliance by towns on the property tax with the state too strapped to give much aid.

3. (a) The demand for cigarettes in New Hampshire is much more elastic than that assumed by the U.S. Treasury for the country. Why?

   (b) Assess New Hampshire's cigarette tax policy in 1983. Consider whether it should have left the tax at $.12, raised it to $.17 (whether Vermont's went up or not), or gone along with Maine and Massachusetts to $.26. Assume that consumption in New Hampshire would have been equal to the national average if there were no price advantage and that about half the difference in consumption represents sales to transients who stock up seasonally and about half are sales to regular out-of-state shoppers. (A diagram showing tax incidence would be helpful—assume the supply curves are horizontal.)

   (c) Why can Massachusetts gain revenue by its higher taxes (Rhode Island and Connecticut have even higher taxes) rather than meeting New Hampshire's prices?

CASE 20: Government Regulation of Worker Safety: Valuing Human Lives

In June 1986, the Occupational Safety and Health Administration (OSHA) issued new rules designed to cut the amount of asbestos in the workplace by 90 percent. OSHA said the new exposure levels would eliminate nine-tenths of the deaths caused by asbestos. The Environmental Protection Agency (EPA) has estimated that exposure to asbestos causes 3,300 to 12,000 deaths a year from cancer and other diseases. The OSHA rules, aimed at protecting workers who are already exposed to asbestos, require that companies train employees on the dangers of asbestos and provide information on safe work practices. OSHA estimated that the new rules would cost the affected industries $460 million annually.

Questions

1. Why would government regulation of workplace safety, such as rules to reduce employee exposure to asbestos, be appropriate (or necessary) in a market economy?

2. (a) Why would OSHA choose a goal of 90 percent reduction of the amount of asbestos when they presumably are aware that medical evidence definitely links exposure to asbestos with cancer? Why not eliminate all deaths from asbestos if it is possible to do so?

   (b) Could there be an economic rationale for a particular goal of reduction, whether 90 percent or some other amount such as 75 percent or 100 percent? Explain.

3. Knowing that the new regulations were to cost about $460 million annually, what do the OSHA rules imply about the value placed on each life to be saved? (Use the EPA figures above to calculate your answer.)

4. Putting a price tag on the value of a human life is a common activity among courts, life insurance companies, and federal government agencies.
   (a) Is this necessary? What are the ethical and moral considerations in doing so?

   (b) The underlying reason for valuing lives involves questions of risk and whether the prevailing levels of risk should be reduced to "acceptable" levels. What should be the basis for determining the value of human life in this context?

CASE 21: The Tax Reform Act of 1986

The most conspicuous features of the Tax Reform Act of 1986 are the reductions in the tax rates and in the number of tax brackets in both the personal and corporate income taxes. The personal income tax was changed from fourteen brackets with tax rates from 11 percent to 50 percent to two basic rates: 15 percent for taxable incomes up to $29,750, and 28 percent for that income over $29,750 (married couples filing jointly). Five corporate income tax brackets were reduced to three: the most important was 34 percent for incomes of over $75,000—a reduction from the previous high of 46 percent. Tax bills are never quite so simple; both taxes have an alternative minimum tax rate of 20 percent applicable to some incomes receiving tax preferences, and the personal income tax has a higher effective rate (33 percent) beginning at taxable income of $71,900 ($41,000 for a single taxpayer).

The other touted features of the personal income tax reductions were scheduled increases in personal exemptions and in standard deductions, both designed to remove below-poverty-level families from the tax rolls. The personal exemption for each dependent was scheduled to increase from $1,080 to $1,900 in 1987, and to $2,000 in 1989 (with indexing to CPI thereafter). The standard deduction remains at $3,670 for joint filers in 1987 (but indexed for 1986 inflation) and rises to $5,000 in 1989.

To achieve these reductions in income tax rates, the following preferences were done away with (corporations suffered more since $120 to 125 billion in taxes were shifted to them from individuals):

1. Deductibility of interest on consumer loans, other than for interest on home mortgages, was repealed; also those for state and local sales taxes, for political contributions, for 10 percent of the earned income of the second working spouse, and for many miscellaneous deductions.

2. The exclusion from income of 60 percent of capital gains was abolished. This represented one prong on the attack of tax shelters that aimed at converting ordinary income into the lightly taxed capital gains. The second prong was to largely abolish the deduction of passive losses (depreciation on real estate, for example) against ordinary income (salaries, medical fees, etc.).

3. The most substantial reductions of corporate tax preferences were the abolishing of the 10 percent investment tax credit and a sharp curtailment of the very rapid depreciation permitted on factory and office buildings. The minimum corporate tax of 20 percent applicable to most forms of sheltered income was a key provision on shifting taxes to corporations.

Questions

1. One contribution of the tax reform bill was to remove below-poverty families from the role of income taxpayers. Show how a family of four with a 1986 poverty-level income of $11,000 would be removed from the tax lists.

2. A second effect of the tax reform would be to limit the income tax bite on the very rich to 28 percent, down from 70 percent at the start of the Reagan administration. What might be responsible for such an apparently dramatic reform?

3. (a) Some tax preferences are almost untouchable, for example, the tax-exempt status of state and local bonds. The best the reform could do was to curb such bonds issued for nongovernmental purposes (such as aid to industrial projects).

   (b) Some deductions were very hard to touch such as the Industrial Retirement Account (IRA) which allowed the deduction of up to $2,000 a year against taxable income as well as the nontaxability of interest and dividends on funds in IRAs. The reform was to maintain the nontaxability of capital income from IRAs but to rule out the nontaxability of contributions for persons with employer-pension plans or high incomes.

   Consider the support for these preferences and the effects of the modifications.

4. An argument for the lower tax rates was that a greater total supply of effort and capital would be forthcoming. Many economists would suggest that the contributions to allocative efficiency could be more significant. Discuss these positions.

PART SEVEN

National Income and Fiscal Policy

24

An Introduction to Macroeconomics

Learning Objectives

From this, the first chapter on macroeconomics, you should become familiar with

—the concern of macroeconomics with the overall flow of income in the economy and with the aggregate data that describe it;

—the definition and measurement of key macro variables such as the labor force, unemployment, the gross national product, and the price level;

—the broad changes over the past half-century in these macro variables;

—aggregate supply and aggregate demand as analytic concepts for the simultaneous determination of price and output levels.

Review and Self-Test

Matching Concepts

____ 1. nominal GNP

____ 2. real GNP

____ 3. possible GNP with productive resources fully employed

____ 4. GNP gap

____ 5. unemployment rate

____ 6. aggregate demand curve

____ 7. relationship between desired output and the price level

____ 8. coexistence of high rates of unemployment and high rates of inflation

____ 9. supply shock

____ 10. shift in aggregate demand curve

____ 11. full employment

____ 12. long-run economic growth

(a) demand shock

(b) potential GNP minus actual GNP

(c) relationship between desired expenditures and the price level

(d) condition when the only unemployment is frictional

(e) GNP estimated with current prices

(f) potential GNP

(g) unemployment expressed as a percentage of labor force

(h) GNP estimated with base year prices

(i) aggregate supply curve

(j) shift in aggregate supply curve

(k) trend increase in real GNP

(l) stagflation

Multiple-Choice Questions

1. The primary emphasis that distinguishes microeconomics and macroeconomics is that
   (a) macroeconomics concerns the causes of relative price changes.
   (b) microeconomics concerns broad aggregates such as the behavior of the price level.
   (c) macroeconomics deals with the overall behavior of the whole economy.
   (d) microeconomics is concerned primarily with the causes of unemployment and inflation.

2. The *Economic Report of the President* estimated the average CPI to be 315.5 in December 1984 and 327.4 in December 1985. The annual rate of inflation was approximately
   (a) 11 percent.
   (b) 3.8 percent.
   (c) 327 percent.
   (d) minus 11 percent.

3. Changes in real GNP reflect only output changes, whereas changes in nominal GNP reflect
   (a) only price changes.
   (b) only output changes.
   (c) changes both in total output and in market prices.
   (d) neither price nor output changes.

4. Cyclical patterns of economic activity are most readily visible in which of the following indicators?
   (a) the GNP gap
   (b) nominal GNP
   (c) the GNP deflator
   (d) potential GNP

5. The downward-sloping aggregate demand curve means that, *ceteris paribus,*
   (a) the higher the price level, the greater the quantity of output demanded.
   (b) the lower the price level, the smaller the total quantity demanded.
   (c) there is a direct positive relationship between the price level and the total quantity of output demanded.
   (d) the higher the price level, the smaller the total output demanded.

6. The GNP price deflator differs from the CPI in that
   (a) it is not concerned with price changes in consumer goods.
   (b) it is less comprehensive than the CPI.
   (c) it uses quantities purchased for each current year rather than fixed-quantity weights.
   (d) it is more widely used for labor contracts and social security adjustments.

7. If aggregate demand increases and the economy is operating along a constant (upward-sloping) *SRAS,*
   (a) the effect will be felt only on the price level.
   (b) both the price level and total output will increase.
   (c) only total output will be affected.
   (d) both the price level and total output will decrease.

8. The supply shocks of the mid-1970s in the United States
   (a) coupled with aggregate demand increases to cause the price level and total output to fall.
   (b) exerted little effect on economic activity.
   (c) coupled with aggregate demand shifts to bring about falling output and a rising price level.
   (d) induced both output and the price level to rise.

9. One reason the aggregate demand curve slopes downward is that
   (a) a rise in the price level causes a surplus of money that drives interest rates up and thus discourages interest-sensitive expenditures.
   (b) a fall in the price level creates a shortage of money that drives interest rates up and thus encourages exports.
   (c) an increase in output causes interest rates to fall and aggregate expenditures to rise.
   (d) a rise in the price level creates a shortage of money that drives interest rates up and thus discourages interest-sensitive expenditures.

10. The GNP gap measures the difference between
    (a) nominal and real GNP.
    (b) potential national income and the national income that is actually produced.
    (c) output and employment.
    (d) the aggregate demand curve and the aggregate supply curve.

11. Unforeseen inflation
    (a) benefits borrowers and injures lenders.
    (b) benefits lenders and injures borrowers.
    (c) hurts everyone.
    (d) has precisely the opposite effects of anticipated inflation.

12. Indexing in macroeconomics refers to
    (a) techniques for constructing index numbers.
    (b) the filling up of the last pages of an economics textbook.
    (c) alphabetizing the acronyms for government regulatory agencies.
    (d) linking the payments under terms of a contract to changes in the price level.

13. The course of the price level since World War II can be described
    (a) by yearly fluctuations around an essentially unchanging plateau.
    (b) as trending generally upward at a consistent 3 to 4 percent a year.
    (c) as showing a distinct upward trend with a higher magnitude of change from the early 1970s through the early 1980s.
    (d) as showing no consistent pattern.

The following three questions involve the exercises.

14. (Refer to Exercise 1.) The effect of using the total labor force (including armed services) rather than the civilian labor force in calculating unemployment and labor force participations rates
    (a) increases both rates.
    (b) reduces both rates.
    (c) increases unemployment rate, reduces participation rate.
    (d) reduces unemployment rate, increases participation rate.

15. (Refer to Exercise 2.) The rate of increase in nominal GNP will be approximately equal to
    (a) the difference between the rates of increase in real GNP and the price level.
    (b) the sums of the rate of increase in real GNP and the price level.
    (c) the difference between the rates of increase of the price level and real GNP.
    (d) none of the above since nominal GNP is related only to potential GNP.

16. (Refer to Exercise 3.) If both aggregate demand and *SRAS* increase as in 3(c), we can predict
    (a) an increase in real output but uncertain effects on price level.
    (b) an increase in price level but uncertain effects on real output.
    (c) increases in both real output and the price level.
    (d) decreases in both real output and the price level.

Self-Test Key

Matching Concepts: 1–e; 2–h; 3–f; 4–b; 5–g; 6–c; 7–i; 8–l; 9–j; 10–a; 11–d; 12–k

Multiple-Choice Questions: 1–c; 2–b; 3–c; 4–a; 5–d; 6–c; 7–b; 8–c; 9–d; 10–b; 11–a; 12–d; 13–c; 14–d; 15–b; 16–a

Exercises

1. (a) In 1983 the federal government started reporting its unemployment rate as a percentage of the total labor force (including the armed forces) rather than as a percentage of the civilian labor force. Compute the unemployment rate as a percentage of the total labor force for the years in the table below.

	Resident armed forces (millions)	Civilian labor force (millions)	Unemployed (millions)	*Unemployment rate (percent)*	
				Civilian	Total
1972	1.81	87.03	4.88	5.6	____
1977	1.66	99.01	6.99	7.1	____
1982	1.67	110.20	10.68	9.7	____
1985	1.71	116.23	8.31	7.2	____

(b) Work out the total labor force participation rates (labor force as percent of noninstitutional population) that would recognize the resident armed forces as part of the labor force. The noninstitutional population (all persons 16 or over not in prison, mental hospitals, etc.) was (in millions): 1972, 146.74; 1977, 161.17; 1982, 174.45; 1985, 178.21.

(c) What did these changes in labor force and participation rates represent in terms of the *SRAS* curve?

2.

	Nominal or current dollar GNP (billions)	Real or constant dollar GNP (billions 1982 $'s)	Price deflator for GNP (1982 = 100)
1972	$____	$2,609	46.5
1977	1,991	2,959	____
1982	3,166	____	100.0
1985	3,993	3,574	____

(a) Fill in the blanks in the above table.

(b) Estimate percentage growth in real GNP from 1972 to 1977 ________; from 1977 to 1982 ________; from 1982 to 1985 ________.

(c) What was the 10-year annual growth rate for 1972 to 1982 (approximate) in nominal GNP ________; in real GNP ________; in the price deflator ________? [*Hint:* 1972/1982 = $1/(1 + i)^{10}$.] See Table 19-1 in Study Guide for values of $1/(1 + r)^n$ to solve for r.

(d) Add the rate of increase in the price level to that in real GNP to approximate the rate of growth in nominal GNP from 1972 to 1982. ________________

(e) In 1985 the nominal GNP was 3993, the GNP in 1982 dollars was 3,574, so the GNP deflator was ________. Calculate the annual rate of growth from 1982 to 1985 in nominal GNP, price deflator, and real GNP. Compare with the results in (c).

3. In this exercise you are asked to assess the impact of each of the events below on *AD* and *SRAS*. Show the shifts in the curves graphically and predict the effects on the price level and real national income. Use + for an increase, – for a decrease, 0 for unchanged, and U for uncertain. We are dealing with general equilibrium rather than product markets, so a single event is more likely to affect both demand and supply. For example, in (a) the wage increases represent both a decrease in *SRAS* and a probable increase in *AD*.

	AD	*SRAS*	Price level	Real national income
(a) General wage increases in the 1970s as workers tried to get ahead of inflation				
(b) The Reagan program of increased defense expenditure				
(c) The 5–10–10 percent cuts in personal income taxes from 1981 through 1983				
(d) The serious crop failures and OPEC oil production cutbacks of 1973–1974				

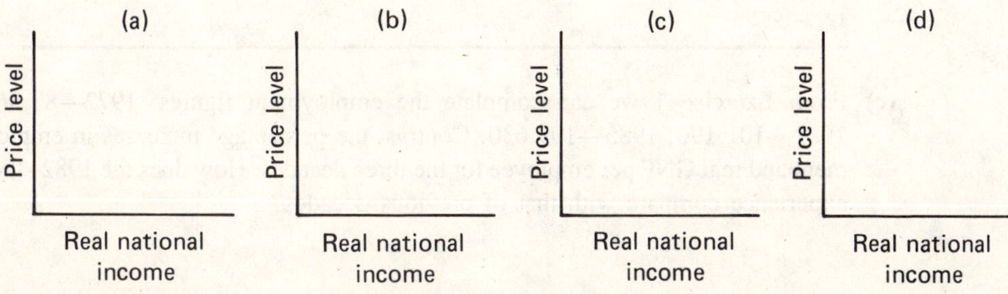

4. Box 24-1 of the text on "understanding annual rates" dealt with hypothetical 1984–1986 CPI data. Here are actual CPI data for these years (1967 = 100).

Date	CPI	Date	CPI
1984	311.1	Dec. 1985	327.4
Dec. 1984	315.5	May 1986	326.3
1985	322.2	June 1986	327.3
Nov. 1985	326.6		

Work out the *annual* percent change in the price level:
(a) From 1984 to 1985 ______
(b) From December 1984 to December 1985 ______
(c) From November 1985 to May 1986 (6 months) ______
(d) From November 1985 to December 1985 ______
(e) From May 1986 to June 1986 ______
Comment briefly on the usefulness of each measure.

Short Problem

This problem refers back to Exercises 1 and 2 for data on 1972, 1982, and 1985. The additional figures for 1952 and 1962 are given below.

	Nominal GNP (billions of dollars)	Real GNP (billions 1982 dollars)	GNP price deflator (1982 = 100)	Total employment (including resident armed forces)
1952	352	______	25.5	62,636
1962	575	1799	______	68,739

(a) Fill in the blanks above.
(b) Contrast the 10-year percentage increases in nominal GNP, real GNP, and price deflator for GNP in the 1952–1962, 1962–1972, and 1972–1982 periods. In what sense was the 1982–1985 period a throwback to the fifties and sixties?

	Percentage increases in				
	Nominal GNP	Price deflator	Real GNP	Employment	Real GNP/ employee
1952–1962					
1962–1972					
1972–1982					

(c) From Exercise 1 we can complete the employment figures: 1972—83,960; 1982—101,190; 1985—109,630. Contrast the percentage increases in employment and real GNP per employee for the three decades. How does the 1982–1985 experience compare with that of previous decades?

Answers to the Exercises

1. (a) 5.5; 6.9; 9.5; 7.0 (small difference but a more accurate measure with a volunteer army)
   (b) 1972, 60.5 percent; 1977, 62.5 percent; 1982, 64.1 percent; 1985, 66.2 percent
   (c) increased supply (rightward shift in *SRAS*)

2. (a) 1972, 1,213; 1977, 67.3; 1982, 3,166; 1985, 111.7
   (b) 1972–1977, 13.4 percent; 1977–1982, 7.0 percent; 1982–85, 12.9 percent
   (c) $1/(1 + r)^{10} = 0.383$, $r \approx 10$ percent; $2{,}609/3{,}166 = 0.824$, $r \approx 2$ percent; $46.5/100 = 0.465$, $r \approx 8$ percent
   (d) 8 percent + 2 percent = 10 percent
   (e) 111.7. $1/(1 + r)^3 = 3{,}166/3{,}993 = 0.793$, $r \approx 8$ percent; $100/11.7 = 0.895$, $r \approx$ 4 percent; $3{,}166/3{,}574 = 0.886$, $r \approx 3.9$ percent. The real rate of growth is about double and the rate of price increase about half. Since these three years were ones of economic recovery from the trough of 1982, it would be dangerous to conclude that real growth near 4 percent represents a trend for the future.

3.

	AD	*SRAS*	Price level	Output
(a)	+	–	+	U
(b)	+	0	+	+
(c)	+	+	U	+
(d)	0	–	+	–

Note: In (d), it is true that income of farmers and oil producers was increased because of inelastic demand and thus *AD* could increase. The shift in supply was much more pronounced, making 0 answer acceptable. Output almost certainly would (and did) drop.

4. (a) 11.1/311.1 = 3.6 percent
   (b) 11.9/315.5 = 3.8 percent
   (c) −0.3/326.6 = −0.1 percent × 2 = −0.2 percent
   (d) 0.8/326.6 = 0.24 percent × 12 = 2.9 percent, or $(1.0024)^{12} - 1 = 2.9$ percent
   (e) 1/326.3 = 0.31 percent × 12 = 3.7 percent, or $(1.0031)^{12} - 1 = 3.8$ percent
   Comment: (a) best for plotting annual time series; (b) has merit of recency for year-to-year changes but is subject to irregularities in terminal observations; (c) more recent, more subject to the irregularities of (b): (d) and (e) monthly estimates most recent, but can be quite fluctuating. Note change in (d) answer from (c) answer.

25

Measuring Macroeconomic Variables

Learning Objectives

After studying these concepts for measuring national output you should have

—an understanding of the use of price indices to convert nominal (current dollar) income into real (constant dollar) income;

—a recognition of the equality between measurements of final expenditures on newly produced goods and services, income generated by their production, and output representing value added by sectors;

—a knowledge of the definition, use, and limitations of each of the major income and product concepts, such as gross national product and personal income;

—an overall perception of the national income accounts as a well-articulated system.

Review and Self-Test

Matching Concepts

______ 1. consumption expenditures	(a)	GNP = GNE = $C^a + I^a + G^a + (X^a - M^a)$
______ 2. expenditure on goods used for the production of future goods	(b)	GNP deflator
	(c)	series expressed in base year prices
______ 3. transfer payments	(d)	investment
______ 4. the value of net exports	(e)	$(X^a - M^a)$
______ 5. total market value of all final goods and services produced	(f)	disposable income
	(g)	method that accounts for final output by the various claims to its value
______ 6. factor-income approach to measuring national income	(h)	outlays on goods and services for current consumption
______ 7. personal income		
______ 8. amount of current income after personal income taxes	(i)	payments to households for other than current factor services
	(j)	income received by individuals, before taxes
______ 9. constant dollar figures		
______ 10. index number used to adjust current GNP for price level changes		

Multiple-Choice Questions

1. The GNP, as measured, understates the total production of goods and services for all but which of the following reasons?
   (a) No allowances are included for the services of owner-occupied homes.
   (b) Illegal activities are ruled out of the GNP estimate.
   (c) Legal production in the "underground economy" is not reported for income tax purposes.
   (d) Nonmarketed services of housewives or househusbands are not included.

2. Value added in production is equal to
   (a) purchases from other firms.
   (b) profits.
   (c) total sales revenues.
   (d) total sales revenues minus purchases from other firms.

3. Which of the following would *not* be included in measures of the consumption component of aggregate expenditure?
   (a) expenditures for new houses
   (b) expenditures for services
   (c) expenditures for durable goods, such as automobiles
   (d) expenditures for nondurable goods, such as fresh food

4. A manager concerned with forecasting sales of a consumer product would probably use
   (a) GNP.
   (b) NNP.
   (c) personal income.
   (d) disposable personal income.

5. The difference between GNP and NNP is
   (a) depreciation.
   (b) total taxes paid to governments.
   (c) net exports.
   (d) personal savings.

6. The factor-payments approach to measuring gross or net national product
   (a) usually results in a higher value for total national income than results from the income-expenditure approach.
   (b) must add indirect business taxes to payments to factors of production.
   (c) will be most accurate if resource markets are reasonably competitive.
   (d) includes only profits retained by firms.

7. GNP can be measured in all but which one of the following ways?
   (a) by the flow of goods produced for final demand
   (b) by the payments made to purchase this flow of goods
   (c) by adding all money transactions in the economy
   (d) by the value of payments made to factors of production

8. Which of the following is *not* a direct part of the total of final goods included in the GNP as currently measured?
   (a) transfer items
   (b) goods sold to government
   (c) new capital goods
   (d) additions to inventories

9. Disposable income is
   (a) the same as personal income.
   (b) income that is used only for consumption.
   (c) personal income remaining after income taxes.
   (d) exclusive of social security payments or welfare.

10. Estimating final output (gross domestic product) by adding the sales of all firms
   (a) will overstate total output because it double counts the output of intermediate goods.
   (b) provides the same value as net national income.
   (c) is a measure of income accruing to U.S. residents.
   (d) is equivalent to GNP minus net exports.

11. If GNP in current pesetas in 1980 was 500 billion p, while GNP in constant (1970) pesetas was 200 billion p in 1980,
    (a) real GNP doubled over the decade 1970–1980.
    (b) the price level more than doubled over the decade.
    (c) real income declined slightly over the decade.
    (d) it is impossible to estimate what happened to prices over the decade.

12. If nominal GNP rises from $2,000 billion to $2,300 billion and the GNP deflator rises from 125 to 150,
    (a) real GNP has risen.
    (b) real GNP has fallen.
    (c) real GNP is unchanged.
    (d) everyone is worse off.

13. As a measure of human economic welfare, GNP may be inadequate because
    (a) it overstates the value of work that does not pass through the market.
    (b) it does not count investment in consumer durable goods.
    (c) it does not account for changes in leisure over the years.
    (d) it ignores the purchase of goods by foreign firms.

14. Which of the following is *not* included in measures of GNP?
    (a) the amount a firm spent on a new factory
    (b) the amount a family spent on a new Volkswagen made in Pennsylvania
    (c) the amount a person spent on five shares of GM stock
    (d) the amount a firm increased its inventories

15. The frequently used national income measures are GNP, disposable personal income (DPI), personal income (PI), net national income at factor prices (NNI), and net national product at market prices (NNP). Which of the following are in the correct order of magnitude?
    (a) GNP, NNI, DPI
    (b) PI, DPI, NNP
    (c) NNI, GNP, PI
    (d) GNP, NNI, NNP

Self-Test Key

Matching Concepts: 1–h; 2–d; 3–i; 4–e; 5–a; 6–g; 7–j; 8–f; 9–c; 10–b

Multiple-Choice Questions: 1–a; 2–d; 3–a; 4–d; 5–a; 6–b; 7–c; 8–a; 9–c; 10–a; 11–b; 12–b; 13–c; 14–c; 15–a

Exercises

1. (a) Identify the items below according to the following code referring to U.S. national income accounts:

C Consumption	*M* Imports
I Investment (domestic)	*X* Exports
G Government expenditure	*N* None of the above

   ______ 1. A student gets a haircut from a self-employed barber.
   ______ 2. The barber buys some new clippers from the Short-Cut Clipper Company.
   ______ 3. Out of each day's revenue, the barber sets aside $5 in his piggy-bank.
   ______ 4. IBM replaces an old plant with a new, bigger one.
   ______ 5. Endicott employs more teachers in its public schools.
   ______ 6. Out of after-tax profits of $40,000, the Short-Cut Clipper Company pays dividends of $25,000.
   ______ 7. Ethiopia buys tractors from the International Harvester Company's Peoria plant.
   ______ 8. U.S. tourists go to Quebec and stay at the Chateau Frontenac.
   ______ 9. Susan Jones buys a motorcycle from a friend.
   ______ 10. The Blandings build their dream house.

   (b) Which of the ten items would be included in the output expenditures approach to measuring GNP?

2. GNP expressed in constant 1982 dollars has been estimated as $716.6 billion in 1939, $2,608.5 billion in 1972, and $3,166.0 in 1982. The implicit price deflators for GNP were estimated as 12.7 in 1939 and 46.5 in 1972 (1982 = 100).

   (a) Real GNP was ______ times as large in 1982 as in 1939, and the price level was ______ times higher than in 1939. The nominal GNP of ______ in 1982 compared with the nominal GNP of ______ in 1939 and was ______ times as great. (Calculate the nominal GNPs by multiplying the constant GNP in dollars by the deflators expressed as decimals, and note that the final blank can be filled in either by the product of the first two blanks or by the ratio of 1982 nominal GNP to 1939 nominal GNP.)

   (b) The preliminary estimate of 1985 GNP expressed in 1982 dollars was $3,573.5 billion. By what percentage had real GNP increased since 1982?

3. Estimating National Income

The following are statistics for the country of Eastern Utopia for 1986 in current millions of dollars:

Government expenditures	$150
Consumption	325
Gross investment	70
Capital consumption allowance	25
Government transfer payments	60
Social security taxes paid by individuals	30
Personal income taxes	110
Net exports	75
Undistributed business profits (retained earnings)	45
Indirect business taxes (sales, real estate, etc.)	20

Compute each of the following related measures of national income, and explain the aspect of national output upon which each focuses.

(a) gross national product (GNP)

(b) net national product (NNP)

(c) national income (NNI)

(d) personal income (PI)

(e) disposable income (DI)

4. We can disaggregate nominal GNPs to establish what proportion represented each broad class of final expenditure, and we find:

	Percentage					
	GNP	*C*	*I*	*G*	*X*	*M*
1939	100	73.7	10.2	14.9	5.0	3.8
1982	100	64.5	13.8	21.2	11.4	10.9
1985	100	64.7	16.8	20.4	9.3	11.2

(a) What statement can be made about our economic interdependency with the rest of the world in 1982 as compared with 1939? What change occurred by 1985?

(b) To arrive at 100 percent of GNP, which component above must be subtracted and why?

(c) Outside of foreign trade, what changes took place in the composition of GNP?

Short Problems

1. The very small and simple country of *XYZ* decided to prepare a consumer price index. The consumer expenditures survey showed the following pattern of expenditures for year 1 of their newly adopted calendar. *X, Y,* and *Z* are the three inhabitants and *A* and *B* the only products.

Consumer Expenditures

	X	Y	Z	Total
Product *A*	2	4	12	18
Product *B*	9	6	3	18
Total	11	10	15	36

Prices of A and B

	Year 1	Year 2	Year 3
P_A	2	4	6
P_B	3	2	1

Prepare price indexes for *XYZ* and for *X, Y,* and *Z* separately using fixed quantity weights based on the consumer expenditure of year 1.

Consumer Price Index

Year	*XYZ*	*X*	*Y*	*Z*
1	100	100	100	100
2				
3				

Would the *XYZ* price index have been helpful to its inhabitants in judging the amount of *ZU* needed to maintain fixed consumption patterns? Why does the U.S. CPI have more relevance? What caution does this exercise suggest for using it?

2. Listed below are 20 categories of the national income accounts with preliminary estimates for 1985 (in billions of dollars). Eleven of them taken together will add up to GNP by the gross national expenditures approach. Five of them combined will equal national income (NNI) by adding up the factor incomes generated in production. Four of them represent necessary adjustments to reconcile the GNP and NNI totals. A fifth adjustment, the statistical discrepancy, is listed in question a; when two different sets of data are used to measure the same concept (GNP), a modest statistical discrepancy lends veracity.

Business transfer payments	19.3	Nondurable goods	912.5
Capital consumption allowances with adjustment	438.2	Other federal government expenditures	91.9
Compensation of employees	2372.7	Plant and equipment	475.7
Corporate profits	299.0	Proprietors' income	242.4
Durable consumption goods	360.8	Rental income of persons	14.0
Exports	370.4	Residential construction	185.6
Imports	444.8	Services	1308.6
Increase in business inventories	9.1	State & local government expenditures	460.7
Indirect business taxes	328.5	Subsidies less surpluses of government enterprises	9.9
National defense	262.0		
Net interest received	287.7		

(a) Use the data above to work out GNP, NNP, and NNI:

Consumption (____ + ____ + ____) + GPDI (____ + ____ + ____) + net exports (____ – ____) + government expenditures (____ + ____ + ____) = GNP (____) – (____) = NNP (____) – (____ + ____) + (____) – statistical discrepancy, 0.6 = NNI (____) = (____ + ____ + ____ + ____ + ____)

(b) Discuss the conceptual and practical reasons why indirect business taxes, business transfer payments, and surplus of government enterprises are deducted from NNP and government subsidies are added to arrive at national income.

Answers to the Exercises

1. (a) 1–C; 2–I; 3–N; 4–I; 5–G; 6–N; 7–X; 8–C and M; 9–N; 10–I
   (b) 1, 2, 4, 5, 7, 8 (actually no effect, both addition and deduction), 10.

2. (a) 4.42; 7.81; $3,166; $91.1; 34.8
   (b) In 1982 prices, 1982 GNP was $3166.0, so the percentage increase over the period is 12.9.

3. (a) $620 ($C + I + G + X - M$); focuses on market value of total output
   (b) $595 (GNP – CCA); net value of output after allowance for depreciation of capital stock
   (c) $575 (NNP – IBT); net earned incomes (factor prices)
   (d) $560 (NNI – UBP – SST + GTP); income received by persons before PIT
   (e) $450 (personal income – PIT); after-tax income of persons

4. (a) It is substantially greater since exports have more than doubled as a proportion of GNP and imports have almost tripled. By 1985 net exports are significantly negative.
   (b) M or imports since these represent parts of final expenditures that are not part of U.S. output.
   (c) In 1982, the proportion of expenditures by government has gone up by almost one-half, or 6.3 percent, and investment by over one-third, or 3.6 percent. These are compensated for by a drop of 9.2 percent in consumption with the balance accounted for by a reduction in the proportion of net exports. The major increase in I is to be expected in good times.

26

National Income and Aggregate Demand

Learning Objectives

Careful study of the material in this chapter should enable you to

—understand that national income is demand-determined under the assumption of a fixed price level along a horizontal (Keynesian) *SRAS*;

—explain the difference between actual and desired expenditures;

—relate changes in disposable income to changes in consumption and saving through the marginal propensities to consume and spend;

—explain and also show graphically the determination of equilibrium national income as the level at which desired aggregate expenditure equals national income.

Review and Self-Test

Matching Concepts

____ 1. desired aggregate expenditure function

____ 2. cause of shifts in the consumption function

____ 3. income not consumed

____ 4. consumption function

____ 5. change in desired consumption expenditure over change in disposable income

____ 6. 45° line from the origin

____ 7. change in desired saving over change in disposable income

____ 8. condition for equilibrium national income

____ 9. final response to aggregate desired expenditure greater than current output

____ 10. final response to current output greater than aggregate desired expenditure

____ 11. net export function

____ 12. Keynesian *SRAS*

(a) desired aggregate expenditure equal to national income

(b) locus of points where desired aggregate expenditure equals national income

(c) marginal propensity to consume (*MPC*)

(d) changes in wealth

(e) fall in national income

(f) relationship of national income and total amount of desired expenditures

(g) marginal propensity to save (*MPS*)

(h) rise in national income

(i) saving

(j) relationship between consumption and disposable income

(k) horizontal line assuming fixed price level

(l) relationship of desired $X - M$ to national income

Multiple-Choice Questions

1. The Keynesian short-run aggregate supply curve discussed in this chapter applies to situations where
   (a) current national income is below potential national income and the price level is constant.
   (b) the price level is rising.
   (c) firms respond to cyclical demand changes by holding output constant and changing prices.
   (d) firms are producing at levels beyond their normal capacity.

2. Which of the following is *not* a component of aggregate expenditure?
   (a) investment in plant and equipment
   (b) government expenditure on goods
   (c) personal taxes
   (d) exports

3. We generally assume that desired consumption expenditure is
   (a) a function of net exports.
   (b) an autonomous expenditure.
   (c) an unimportant component of aggregate desired expenditure.
   (d) a function of households' disposable income.

4. The theory of national income determination deals with
   (a) the desired levels of the components of aggregate expenditure.
   (b) the actual levels of the components of aggregate expenditure.
   (c) the desired level of only consumption and investment expenditure.
   (d) the actual level of only consumption and investment expenditure.

5. An *MPC* of less than 1 means that an increase in current disposable income would cause desired consumption expenditures to
   (a) rise by less than the full increase in disposable income.
   (b) fall slightly because the increase in income will increase savings.
   (c) rise by the full increase in disposable income.
   (d) stay the same because the *MPS* is also less than 1.

6. The average propensity to consume out of disposable income is defined as
   (a) the ratio of total consumption expenditure to total national income.
   (b) the ratio of total consumption expenditure to total disposable income.
   (c) the ratio of the change in consumption to total disposable income.
   (d) $\Delta C/\Delta Y$.

7. If the marginal propensity to save out of disposable income is 0.25, then the *MPC* is
   (a) 0.25. (c) 1.0.
   (b) 0.75. (d) 0.33.

8. If $Y_d = 0.8Y$ and consumption was 80 percent of disposable income, then the marginal propensity to consume out of national income would be
   (a) 0.8. (c) 1.0.
   (b) 0.2. (d) 0.64.

9. The aggregate expenditure function is a relationship between
   (a) actual real expenditure and real national income.
   (b) desired real expenditure and nominal national income.
   (c) actual nominal expenditure and nominal national income.
   (d) desired real expenditure and real national income.

10. The slope of the aggregate expenditure function is mostly accurately represented by
   (a) the marginal propensity to save ($\Delta S/\Delta Y_d$).
   (b) the marginal propensity to consume ($\Delta C/\Delta Y_d$).
   (c) the marginal propensity to spend ($\Delta AE/\Delta Y$).
   (d) none of the above

11. At a level of national income where aggregate desired expenditure falls short of total output, there will be a tendency for
    (a) national income to rise.
    (b) national income to fall.
    (c) national income to remain constant.
    (d) fairly widespread shortages of goods to develop.

12. Given a Keynesian *SRAS* curve, if aggregate desired expenditure exceeds total output, we would expect
    (a) inventories to rise, and then production, employment, and income to rise.
    (b) inventories to fall, and then production, employment, and income to fall.
    (c) inventories to rise, and then production, employment, and income to fall.
    (d) inventories to fall, and then production, employment, and income to rise.

13. An increase in household wealth is predicted
    (a) to lower the consumption function.
    (b) to raise the consumption function.
    (c) to have no effect on consumption.
    (d) (a), (b), or (c) depending on the magnitude of the change.

14. National income will be at an equilibrium level
    (a) when aggregate desired expenditure equals actual current output.
    (b) when all of it is sold, including inventories.
    (c) only when there is full employment.
    (d) only when net exports equal net domestic expenditures.

The following multiple-choice questions refer to Exercise 3:

15. According to the diagram, the marginal propensity to spend is
    (a) two-thirds and constant.
    (b) less than one, but variable according to the level of national income.
    (c) one-third and constant.
    (d) always equal to the average propensity to spend.

16. If GNP were actually 300, desired aggregate expenditure would equal 400, and
    (a) the average propensity to spend is 0.75.
    (b) the average propensity to spend is two-thirds.
    (c) the average propensity to spend is less than the marginal propensity to spend.
    (d) the average propensity to spend is four-thirds.

Self-Test Key

Matching Concepts: 1–f; 2–d; 3–i; 4–j; 5–c; 6–b; 7–g; 8–a; 9–h; 10–e; 11–l; 12–k

Multiple-Choice Questions: 1–a; 2–c; 3–d; 4–a; 5–a; 6–b; 7–b; 8–d; 9–d; 10–c; 11–b; 12–d; 13–b; 14–a; 15–a; 16–d

Exercises

1. Assume that line C on the graph is a consumption function.

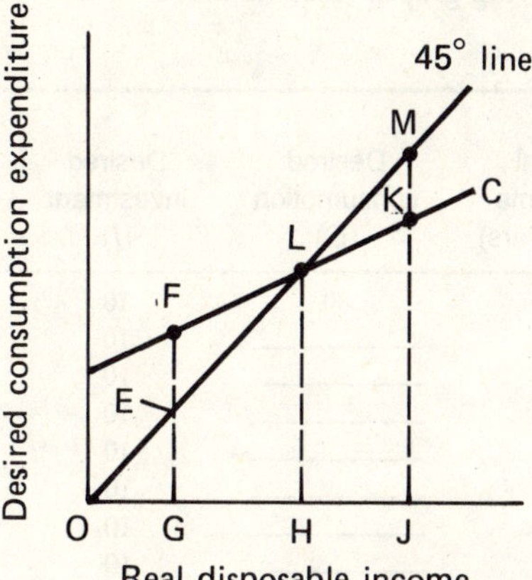

   (a) The break-even level of income is ________________.
   (b) At the break-even level of income, the numerical value of the average propensity to consume (APC) is ________________. As real disposable income rises, the APC is (falling/rising/constant).
   (c) MPC equals the slope of the line ________________. It shows that in this case, the proportion of an increase in income spent on increased consumption is (increasing/constant/decreasing).
   (d) At income OJ, savings = ____________; at OG, savings = ____________.

2. In the consumption function described by the equation $C = 300 + 0.9Y_d$,
   (a) MPC out of Y_d = ________________.
   (b) at disposable income of zero, C = ________________.
   (c) the MPC is (rising/falling/constant) as disposable income rises.
   (d) the break-even level of income ($C = Y_d$) is ________________.

3. Answer the following questions from the graph:

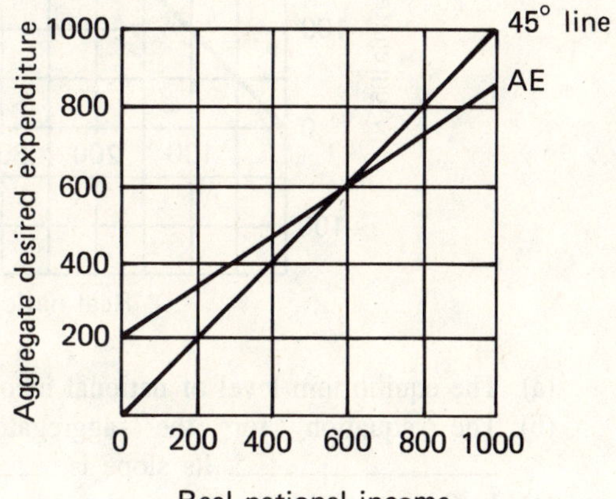

   (a) When national income is 0, desired aggregate expenditure is ________________.
   (b) When national income is 600, desired aggregate expenditure is ________________.
   (c) If actual national income was 300, desired aggregate expenditure would be (less/greater) than income, and hence output and national income are likely to (expand/contract).
   (d) If actual national income was 1,000, desired aggregate expenditure would be (less/greater) than national income, and hence output and national income are likely to (expand/contract).
   (e) In this case, the marginal propensity not to spend is ________________.
   (f) The equilibrium level of national income is ________________.

4. The following table shows what the various components of desired spending would be at each level of national income. Fill in the blanks of the table, and plot the data on the following graph. Assume that $C = 80 + 0.6Y$, $(X - M) = 40 - 0.1Y$, $G = 20$, and $I = 10$.

Level of real national income (billions of dollars)	Desired consumption (C)	Desired investment (I)	Desired government expenditure (G)	Desired net exports ($X - M$)	Aggregate desired expenditure
0	80	10	20	40	150
100	______	10	20	______	______
200	______	10	20	______	______
250	______	10	20	______	______
300	______	10	20	______	______
400	______	10	20	______	______
450	______	10	20	______	______
500	______	10	20	______	______

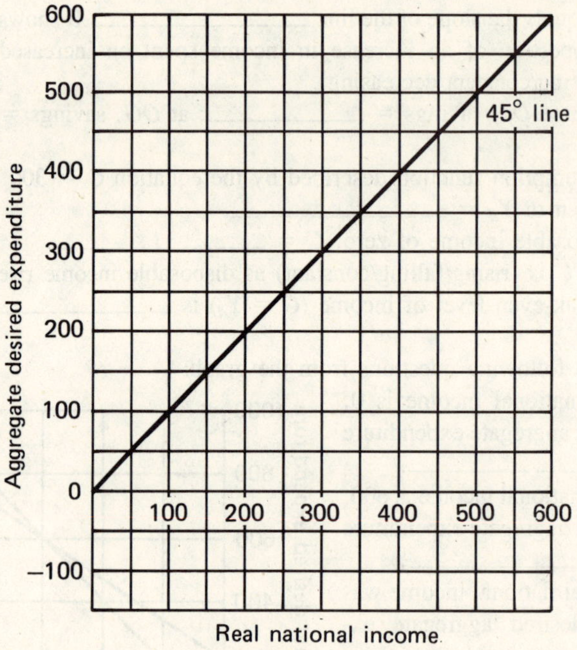

(a) The equilibrium level of national income would be ______________.

(b) The equation for the aggregate desired expenditure function is ______________. Its slope is ______________. Explain.

(c) In this example, the marginal propensity to spend on domestic production is ______________.

(d) Suppose that desired consumption expenditures increase by $50 billion at each level of national income. The equation for the consumption function would become ______________, and the equilibrium level of national income would become ______________.

Short Problems

1. An Algebraic Determination of Equilibrium National Income in the Simple Keynesian Model

You are given the following information about desired expenditures in an economy:

Equation 1: the consumption function $C = 100 + 0.7Y_d$
Equation 2: the relationship between Y and Y_d $Y_d = 0.8Y$
Equation 3: desired investment expenditures $I = 56$
Equation 4: desired net export expenditures $(X - M) = 10 - 0.1Y$
Equation 5: desired government expenditures $G = 50$

(a) Referring to the consumption function, what does the coefficient 0.7 mean?

(b) What components of aggregate expenditure depend on national income?

(c) Aggregate expenditure is the algebraic sum of the components. Derive *AE*.

(d) Equilibrium national income is where $Y = AE$. This is the expression for the 45° line. Equate your expression for *AE* in part (c) with *Y*. Solve for *Y*.

(e) Derive the marginal propensity to spend. (*Hint:* Substitute values for *Y* equal to 100 and 200 into the algebraic expression for *AE* and then calculate ΔY and ΔAE.)

2. The Determination of Equilibrium Income

The purpose of this problem is to work through algebraically the determination of equilibrium income for a simple economy smaller than (but similar to) that of the United States.

The households in this economy behave simply. They wish to spend 90 percent of disposable income (Y_d) on consumption (one-eighteenth of this, or 5 percent of Y_d, goes for imports). The government (federal, state, and local) would like to collect 30 percent of GNP, or Y, in taxes. It purchases $200 billion of goods and services including $15 billion of purchases abroad, the latter largely related to defense and brushfire wars. It also transfers $60 billion to persons for social security, welfare, veterans' benefits, and the like; these can be treated as negative taxes, so net taxes are $T_n = 0.3Y - 60$ (billion dollars).

Gross desired investment is $125 billion, of which $5 billion is for foreign equipment and components. Much of the financing comes from earnings retained by firms, which amount to 10 percent of GNP.

Desired exports are $40 billion. Assume the price level is constant and that the national income levels below are all below potential national income.

(a) First, examine Y_d, which will determine desired household consumption and saving. What is the equation for desired consumption? Desired savings by households?

(b) Fill in the following table (you will find it desirable to work out M as a function of Y first):

Real national income	Desired (*C*)	Desired (*I*)	Desired (*X* – *M*)	Desired (*G*)	Aggregate desired expenditure (*AE*)
0					
300					
500					
700					
900					

(c) On the graph plot *AE, C, I, G,* and (*X* – *M*).

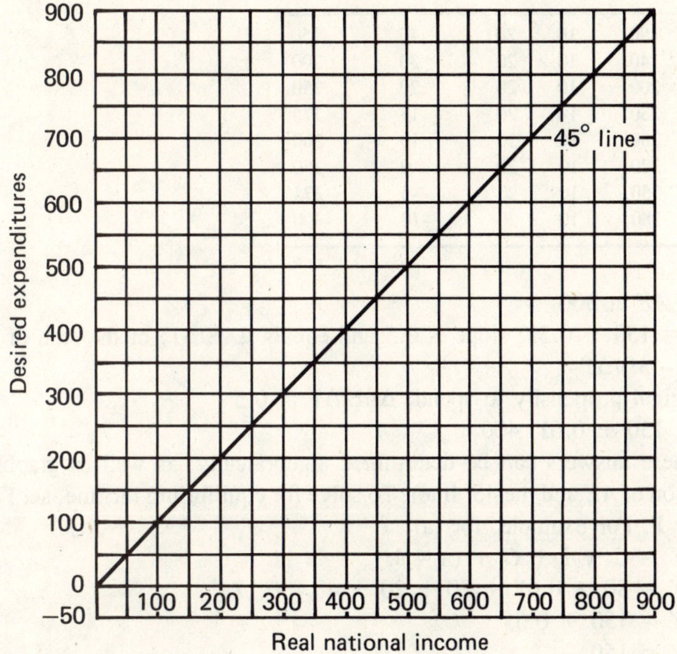

(d) What does the vertical distance between *C* and the 45° line represent? What does the vertical distance between *AE* and *C* represent?

(e) What is the equilibrium level of real national income?

Answers to the Exercises

1. (a) *OH*
   (b) unity (*LH*/*OH*); falling
   (c) *C*; constant
   (d) *KM*; –*EF*

2. (a) 0.9 (b) 300 (c) constant (d) 3,000

3. (a) 200 (b) 600 (c) greater; expand (d) less; contract (e) 2/3 (f) 600

4.

Y	C	I	G	$(X - M)$	AE
0	80	10	20	40	150
100	140	10	20	30	200
200	200	10	20	20	250
250	230	10	20	15	275
300	260	10	20	10	300
400	320	10	20	0	350
450	350	10	20	–5	375
500	380	10	20	–10	400

(a) $Y = AE$ at 300

(b) $AE = 150 + 0.5Y$; slope is 0.5 and equals $\Delta AE/\Delta Y$, or the sum of $\Delta C/\Delta Y + \Delta(X - M)/\Delta Y$

(c) marginal propensity to spend, $\Delta AE/\Delta Y = 0.5$

(d) $C = 130 + 0.6Y$; 400

Note: These answers can be determined algebraically, as well as graphically (the intersection of AE and the 45° line). To solve for equilibrium income, set $Y = AE$ and solve for Y. For example, for (a),

$$Y = C + I + G + (X - M)$$
$$Y = 80 + 0.6Y + 10 + 20 + 40 - 0.1Y$$
$$Y = 150 + 0.5Y$$
$$0.5Y = 150$$
$$Y = 300$$

27

Changes in National Income I: The Role of Aggregate Demand

Learning Objectives

After studying the material in this chapter, you should be able to

—distinguish movement along the desired aggregate expenditure function from shifts and recognize that a shift in the AE function may involve a change of slope;

—list causes of changes in equilibrium national income;

—explain why the magnitude of change in national income resulting from a given change in autonomous expenditure depends on the marginal propensity to spend;

—distinguish between the aggregate desired expenditure function (*AE*) and the aggregate demand curve (*AD*);

—explain how changes in autonomous expenditure shift the *AE* and the *AD* curves and why the change in real output will be less with a positively sloped aggregate supply curve.

Review and Self-Test

Matching Concepts

_______ 1. marginal propensity to spend

_______ 2. effect of a rise in tax rates

_______ 3. increase in household's desire to spend at each level of disposable income

_______ 4. function relating equilibrium levels of national income to price levels

_______ 5. reduction in equilibrium real national income

_______ 6. multiplier

_______ 7. reciprocal of the multiplier

_______ 8. situation in which the multiplier effect is dampened due to a price level change

_______ 9. *AE* curve

_______ 10. ΔA

(a) aggregate demand curve (*AD*)

(b) positively sloped aggregate supply curve

(c) expenditure change related to a change in income

(d) marginal propensity not to spend

(e) increase in aggregate desired expenditure function

(f) effect of a rise in the price level, other things being equal

(g) relation between a change in autonomous expenditure and the resulting change in real national income

(h) decrease in aggregate desired expenditure function

(i) change in autonomous expenditure

(j) locus of desired expenditure for each level of national income at given price level

Multiple-Choice Questions

1. Movement along a desired aggregate expenditure function
   (a) represents a change in prices at every level of national income.
   (b) causes a change in the equilibrium level of national income.
   (c) represents induced changes in desired expenditure caused by changes in national income.
   (d) has no effect on the level of national income.

2. Increases in the equilibrium level of national income are predicted to be caused by increases in
   (a) imports.
   (b) tax rates.
   (c) desired autonomous expenditures.
   (d) personal saving.

3. The multiplier measures
   (a) the magnitude of changes in equilibrium national income in response to changes in autonomous expenditures.
   (b) the rise in expenditures caused by a change in national income.
   (c) the marginal propensity to spend.
   (d) the amount of time it takes to move from one equilibrium to another.

4. The greater the value of the marginal propensity to spend out of national income,
   (a) the greater the value of the marginal propensity not to spend.
   (b) the smaller the value of the multiplier.
   (c) the flatter the aggregate expenditure curve.
   (d) the steeper the aggregate expenditure curve.

5. Which of the following is the correct expression for the simple multiplier?
   (a) $K = 1/(1 - z)$, where z is the marginal propensity to spend out of national income.
   (b) $K = 1/(1 + z)$, where z is the marginal propensity to spend out of national income.
   (c) $K = \Delta A/\Delta Y$, where ΔA is the change in autonomous expenditure and Y is real national income.
   (d) $K = 1/z$, where z is the marginal propensity to spend out of national income.

6. If the marginal propensity not to spend is 0.2, the multiplier is
   (a) equal to the marginal propensity to spend.
   (b) 2.0.
   (c) 5.0.
   (d) 1.25.

7. Assuming a horizontal aggregate supply curve and a marginal propensity not to spend of 0.25, an increase in autonomous expenditure of $1 billion should increase equilibrium national income by
   (a) $250 million.
   (b) $1 billion.
   (c) $25 billion.
   (d) $4 billion.

8. If all of any increase in income were either saved, spent on imports, or taxed away, the multiplier would be
   (a) infinity.
   (b) 1.
   (c) 0.
   (d) –1.

9. When the *SRAS* curve is positively sloped, the multiplier associated with a given change in autonomous expenditure
   (a) is larger than the simple multiplier for a given price level.
   (b) is the same as the simple multiplier for a given price level.
   (c) is smaller than the simple multiplier for a given price level.
   (d) is offset by the change in real national income.

10. The aggregate demand curve illustrates
    (a) levels of equilibrium real national income that correspond with given price levels.
    (b) all of the price levels corresponding with a constant equilibrium income.
    (c) all of the equilibrium real national income levels corresponding with a particular price level.
    (d) alternative levels of aggregate expenditure and their corresponding levels of real national income.

11. Movement along an aggregate demand curve
    (a) results from a shift in the aggregate desired expenditure function at a given price level.
    (b) shows the response of equilibrium real national income to a change in price level.
    (c) occurs when desired expenditure differs from current output.
    (d) results from movement along an aggregate desired expenditure function.

12. If an economy is operating on the upward-sloping portion of the short-run aggregate supply curve, an increase in aggregate demand will
    (a) increase the price level but not real national income.
    (b) increase real national income, but not the price level.
    (c) increase neither real national income nor the price level.
    (d) increase both real national income and the price level.

13. Increases in national income can be caused by all but which of the following, other things being equal?
    (a) increased government expenditures on national defense
    (b) increased exports of personal computers
    (c) an increase in consumer spending on recreational equipment
    (d) increased purchases of savings bonds by the public

14. Decreases in national income can be caused by decreases in all but which of the following, other things equal?
    (a) exports
    (b) the propensity to consume
    (c) tax rates
    (d) investment

15. Which of the following would likely increase national income by the *greatest* extent?
    (a) a $25 billion increase in government expenditures on highway maintenance
    (b) a $25 billion increase in government transfer payments
    (c) a $25 billion decrease in personal income-tax revenues
    (d) a $25 billion decrease in business savings

Questions 16 to 20 refer to the following diagrams:

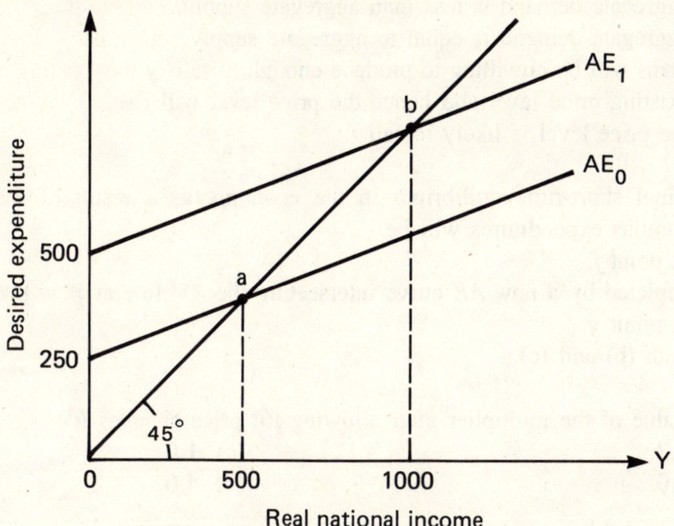

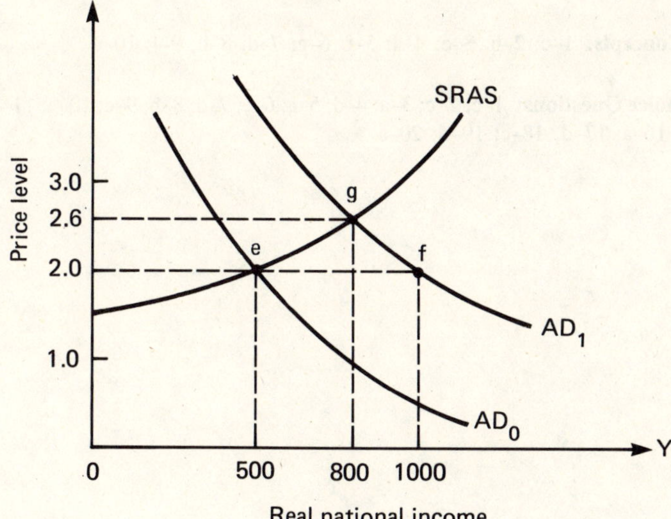

16. According to the curves labeled AE_0 and AD_0, the equilibrium levels of price and real national income are, respectively,
    (a) 2.0 and 500.
    (b) 2.6 and 800.
    (c) 2.0 and 1,000.
    (d) none of the above

17. If the AE curve shifts from AE_0 to AE_1, we can say that
    (a) autonomous expenditures must have increased by 250.
    (b) the aggregate demand curve shifts to the right so that $Y = 1{,}000$ at the price level 2.0.
    (c) the shift in the AD curve will raise the price level, shifting the AE curve downward from AE_1.
    (d) all of the above

18. Given the curves *SRAS* and AD_1 and a price level of 2.0,
    (a) aggregate demand is less than aggregate supply.
    (b) aggregate demand is equal to aggregate supply.
    (c) firms will be unwilling to produce enough to satisfy the existing demand at the existing price level and hence the price level will rise.
    (d) the price level is likely to fall.

19. The final short-run equilibrium in the economy as a result of the increase in autonomous expenditures will be
    (a) at point *f*.
    (b) depicted by a new *AE* curve intersecting the 45° line at $Y = 800$.
    (c) at point *g*.
    (d) both (b) and (c)

20. The value of the multiplier after allowing for price changes is
    (a) 1.2.
    (b) 2.0.
    (c) 1.0.
    (d) 4.0.

Self-Test Key

Matching Concepts: 1–c; 2–h; 3–e; 4–a; 5–f; 6–g; 7–d; 8–b; 9–j; 10–i

Multiple-Choice Questions: 1–c; 2–c; 3–a; 4–d; 5–a; 6–c; 7–d; 8–b; 9–c; 10–a; 11–b; 12–d; 13–d; 14–c; 15–a; 16–a; 17–d; 18–c; 19–d; 20–a

Exercises

1. Show graphically each of the following occurrences with *AE* functions and indicate the direction of change in the equilibrium level of national income. Assume constant price level.
   (a) A decrease in personal income tax rates.
   (b) Additional federal government expenditures of $30 billion per year to strengthen conventional armed forces.
   (c) An increase in the percentage spent for recreational equipment from income that would otherwise have been saved.
   (d) An increase in exports to Japan because of fewer Japanese import restrictions.
   (e) An increase in households' purchases of U.S. savings bonds with no change in consumption expenditures.

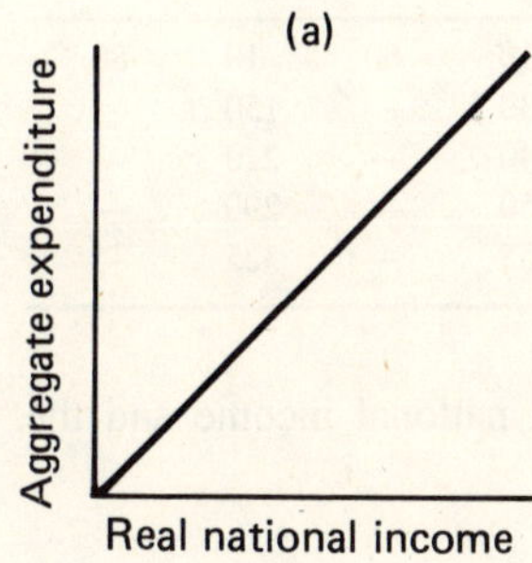

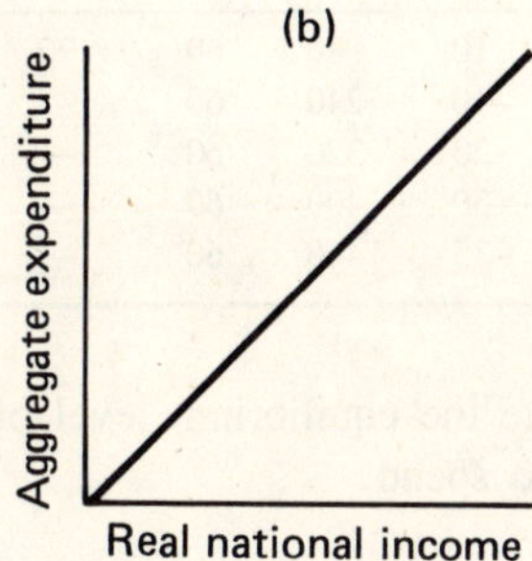

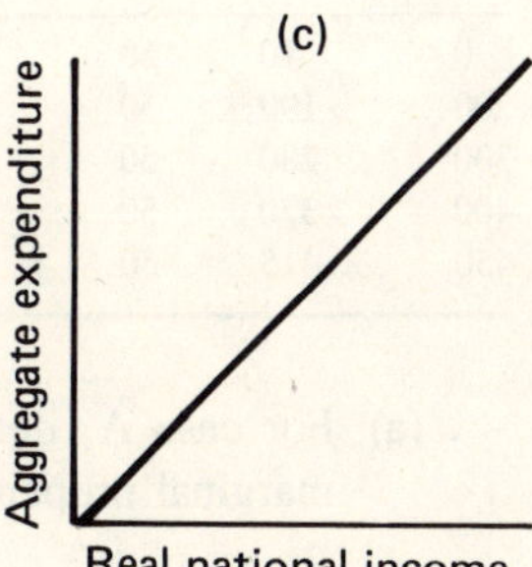

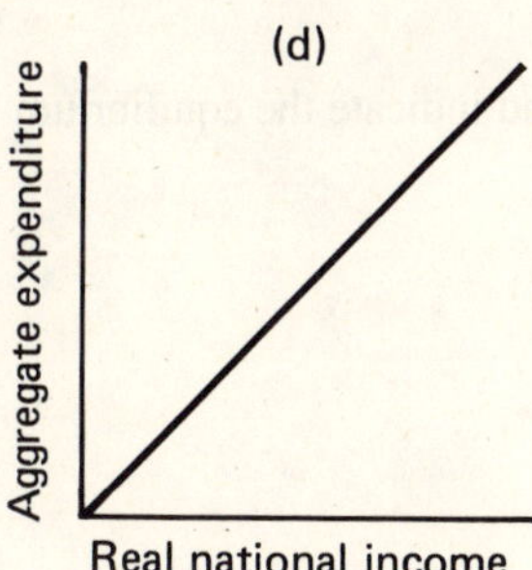

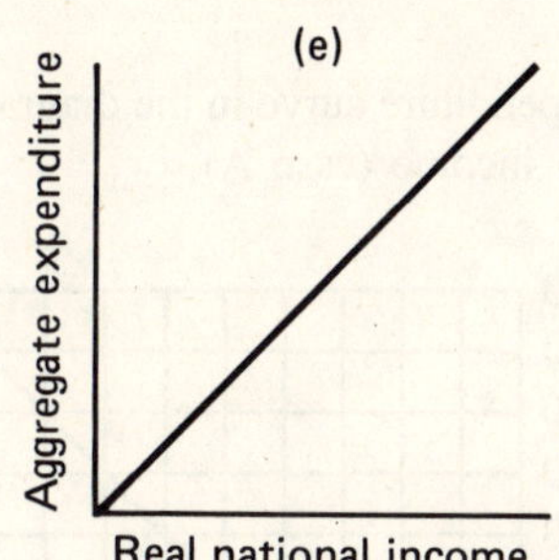

2. (a) If *MPC* out of disposable income is 0.90, and if disposable income is 60 percent of national income, the marginal propensity to spend is ________________.
(b) The marginal propensity not to spend is therefore ________________.
(c) The simple multiplier would be about ________________.
(d) This simple multiplier for real output would be (increased, reduced) if the *SRAS* were positively sloped.

3. You are given the following information about an economy. The data labeled case A represent the initial situation in the economy. Assume the price level is constant for all levels of real national income (*Y*). Case B is dealt with in questions (c) through (g), case C in (h) and (i), and case D in Short problem 1.

	Case A					Case B		Case C		Case D	
Y	*C*	*I*	*G*	*(X – M)*	*AE*	*I*	*AE*	*(X – M)*	*AE*	*C*	*AE*
0	10	50	10	10	80	60	90	–10	60	10	80
200	190	50	10	–10	240	60	—	–30	—	150	—
300	280	50	10	–20	320	60	—	–40	—	220	—
400	370	50	10	–30	400	60	—	–50	—	290	—
450	415	50	10	–35	440	60	—	–55	—	325	—

(a) For case A, determine the equilibrium level of real national income and the marginal propensity to spend.

(b) Plot the aggregate expenditure curve in the diagram and indicate the equilibrium level of real national income (case A).

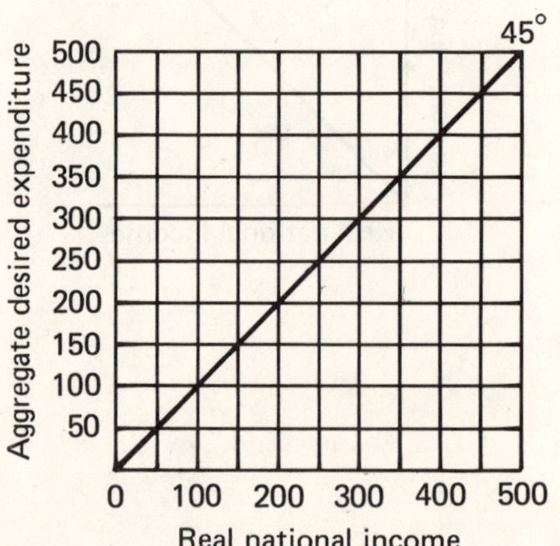

(c) Now assume that a change occurs in the economy such that case B holds. Case B is identical to case A except that investment at every level of *Y* increases from 50 to 60. Fill in the missing values for *AE* and plot the new aggregate expenditure curve in the diagram above. What has happened to the aggregate expenditure curve? (Compare case A with case B.)

(d) Using the *AE* curve for case B, what is the value of desired *AE* at a level of national income of 400? What do you predict will happen to the equilibrium level of national income in this situation? Explain.

(e) What is the equilibrium level of national income for case B? What has been the total change in equilibrium national income (ΔY) between cases A and B? Calculate the ratio $\Delta Y/\Delta I$ to determine the value of the multiplier.

(f) Calculate the value of the marginal propensity to spend (denoted as *z* in the text) for case B. Using the formula, $K = 1/(1 - z)$, confirm your answer for the value of the multiplier in part (e).

(g) The total change in income is composed of two parts: the change in the autonomous component of *AE* (ΔA), which in this case is ΔI; and the *induced* change in aggregate expenditure (ΔN). What is the value for ΔN? What was the change in consumption? The change in $(X - M)$?

(h) In case C, exports at every level of national income fall by 20. Fill in the missing values of *AE*. What is the new equilibrium level of national income? What is the marginal propensity to spend?

(i) Comparing case A with case C, what is the total change in *Y*? Calculate the value of the multiplier. Calculate the change in ΔA [the autonomous shift in $(X - M)$] and in ΔN.

4. Return to Exercise 4 in Chapter 26. Recall that initially $C = 80 + 0.6Y$, $G = 20$, $I = 10$, $X - M = 40 - 0.1Y$, and $AE = 150 + 0.5Y$. Equilibrium national income was \$300 billion.
   (a) The marginal propensity to spend is ________________.
   (b) The marginal propensity not to spend is ________________.
   (c) The multiplier is ________________.
   (d) Suppose that *G* spending now rises by \$20, *ceteris paribus*. The *AE* schedule will rise by ________________. (Draw it on the graph in Chapter 26.)
   (e) The multiplier indicates that the new equilibrium level of real national income will be ________________.

5. Suppose that the economy behaves as follows: Whenever national income rises (falls) by $1, disposable income rises (falls) by $.90, induced consumption expenditure on domestically produced goods and services rises (falls) by $.80, and induced import expenditures and savings each rise (fall) by $.05.
   (a) What is this economy's marginal propensity to spend out of national income?

   (b) Now suppose that autonomous expenditure decreases because the federal government decides to spend $4 million less on national defense. National income initially *falls* by $4 million. But that is not the end of the process. In the table below, fill in the values for the decreases in disposable income and expenditure for three rounds.

	Decreases in Y_d (thousands of dollars per year)	Decreases in aggregate expenditure (thousands of dollars per year)
Assumed decrease in government expenditure per year		$4000.0
Second round (decrease in Y_d and expenditure)	$3600.0	3200.0
Third round (decrease in Y_d and expenditure)	2880.0	______
Fourth round (decrease in Y_d and expenditure)	______	______
Fifth round (decrease in Y_d and expenditure)	______	______
Sum of first five rounds		______

   (c) Using the formula $\Delta Y = K \cdot \Delta A$, where ΔA is –4 million and K is the value of the multiplier, calculate the final change in national income (ΔY).

Short Problems

1. Assume that case A in Exercise 3 in this chapter is the initial situation but that factors in the economy change such that case D applies. Case D is identical to case A except that the desired consumption schedule has changed.
   (a) Calculate the marginal propensities to consume out of national income for both cases and indicate the nature of the behavioral change between the two cases.

   (b) Fill in the missing values of *AE* for case D. Plot the new aggregate expenditure curve in the diagram for Exercise 3(b) and compare it with that for case A.
   (c) Calculate the marginal propensity to spend for case D and compare it with that of case A. Calculate the multiplier value and compare it with the multiplier for case A.

   (d) What is the equilibrium value of national income for case D?

2. You are given the following equations:

Equation 1: the consumption function	$C = 30 + 0.9Y_d$
Equation 2: the relationship between Y and Y_d	$Y_d = 0.8Y$
Equation 3: desired investment expenditures	$I = 40$
Equation 4: desired government expenditures	$G = 20$
Equation 5: desired net export expenditures	$(X - M) = 20 - 0.12Y$
Equation 6: the *AE* expenditure identity	$AE = C + I + G + (X - M)$
Equation 7: the equilibrium national income condition	$AE = Y$

(a) Substitute Equation 2 into Equation 1 and solve for C in terms of Y. Call this Equation 8.

(b) Substitute Equations 8, 3, 4, and 5 into the right-hand side of Equation 6. What is the value of the slope of the *AE* function ($\Delta AE/\Delta Y$)? [This is the marginal propensity to spend.]

(c) Using Equation 7, solve for the equilibrium level of Y.

(d) Now suppose that the federal government raised the personal income-tax rate such that Equation 2 changed to $Y_d = 0.689Y$. Call this Equation 9.

(i) Substitute Equation 9 into Equation 1 and solve for C in terms of Y. Call this Equation 10.

(ii) Substitute Equations 10, 3, 4, and 5 into the right-hand side of Equation 6. What is the slope of this *AE* function? Compare it with the value you obtained for part (b).

(iii) Using Equation 7 and the new expression for the aggregate expenditure function, solve for the equilibrium level of Y. Compare this with your answer to part (c).

(e) Calculate and compare the value of the simple multiplier before and after the tax rate increase.

Answers to the Exercises

1. (a), (c) (b), (d)

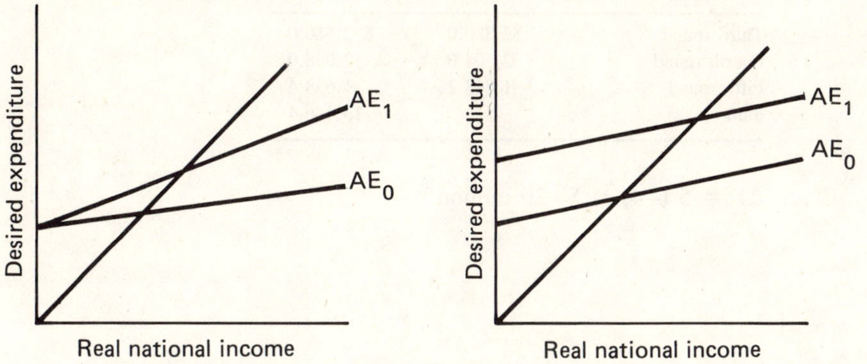

(e) no change in *AE* function or national income

2. (a) 0.54 (b) 0.46 (c) 1/0.46, or 2.17 (d) reduced

3. (a) *AE* = *Y* at 400. The marginal propensity to spend is 0.80 and is constant (ΔAE = 160, ΔY = 200, $\Delta AE/\Delta Y$ = 0.80).
   (b) The *AE* curve has an intercept value of 80 on the vertical axis, a slope of 0.80, and intersects the 45° line at an income level of 400.
   (c) *AE:* 90, 250, 330, 410, 450. The *AE* curve shifts vertically upward by 10 in a parallel fashion.
   (d) *AE* = 410 when *Y* = 400. Since *AE* is greater than real national income, real national income and employment will rise.
   (e) *AE* = *Y* at 450. The change in income is 50 and $\Delta Y/\Delta I$ = 5. The value of the multiplier is 5.
   (f) The marginal propensity to spend is 0.80. The marginal propensity not to spend is 0.20. The multiplier is 1/0.20 = 5.
   (g) Since the total change in income is 50 and ΔI = 10, the value of ΔN is 40. The value 40 is composed of ΔC = 45 and $\Delta(X - M)$ = –5.
   (h) *AE:* 60, 220, 300, 380, 420. Equilibrium is *Y* = 300. The marginal propensity to spend remains at 0.80.
   (i) *Y* fell by 100. The multiplier is $\Delta Y/\Delta(X - M)$ = –100/–20 = 5. The change in income was distributed –10 for (*X* – *M*) and –90 for *C*. The change in autonomous (*X* – *M*) was –20, but since *Y* fell, (*X* – *M*) only fell by –10. The ΔN of 80 is thus comprised of –90 for consumption plus 10 for (*X* – *M*).

4. (a) 0.5 (b) 0.5 (c) 1/0.5 = 2 (d) 20 (at each level of income) (e) $340

5. (a) The marginal propensity to spend out of national income is 0.80.

(b)

	ΔY_d	ΔAE
Third round	$2,880.0	$ 2,560.0
Fourth round	2,304.0	2,048.0
Fifth round	1,843.2	1,638.4
Sum		13,446.4

(c) $\Delta Y = 5\ (-4) = \$-20$ million

28

Changes in National Income II: The Role of Aggregate Supply

Learning Concepts

After studying the material in this chapter, you should be able to

—explain the increasing positive slope of the *SRAS* curve;

—recognize the asymmetry of rapid input price rises to eliminate inflationary gaps and sluggish wage reductions to reduce recessionary gaps;

—combine aggregate demand and aggregate supply in the analysis of changes in real national income and the price level;

—relate "supply-side economics" and the analysis of this chapter.

Review and Self-Test

Matching Concepts

_______ 1. increased prices of inputs

_______ 2. combination of falling real output and rising price level

_______ 3. rightward shift of *SRAS* curve

_______ 4. leftward shift of *SRAS* curve

_______ 5. decrease in tax rates to increase potential national income

_______ 6. *LRAS* curve

_______ 7. increased productivity of inputs

_______ 8. rapid response to inflationary gap; sluggish response to recessionary gap

_______ 9. attribute of "sticky wages"

_______ 10. role of aggregate demand with vertical *LRAS*

(a) cause of a rightward shift in *SRAS* curve

(b) cause of a leftward shift in *SRAS* curve

(c) asymmetry of aggregate supply

(d) automatic response to recessionary gap

(e) determination of the price level

(f) stagflation

(g) major policy recommendation of supply-side economics

(h) automatic response to an inflationary gap

(i) vertical line at level of potential output

(j) weak effect of unemployment on labor prices

Multiple-Choice Questions

1. The positive slope of the short-run aggregate supply (*SRAS*) curve indicates that
   (a) the price level and real national income are negatively related.
   (b) a higher price level is associated with a higher level of real national income.
   (c) final output prices and input costs are negatively related.
   (d) there is no association between real national income and the price level in the short run.

2. The increasing slope of the *SRAS* curve has which one of the following important consequences?
   (a) Below potential national income, changes in output are accompanied by relatively small changes in the price level.
   (b) Above potential national income, changes in real income are accompanied by relatively small changes in the price level.
   (c) Below potential national income, changes in real income are accompanied by relatively large changes in the price level.
   (d) Above potential national income, changes in output are accompanied by relatively large increases in factor productivity.

Questions 3 through 7 refer to the diagram below.

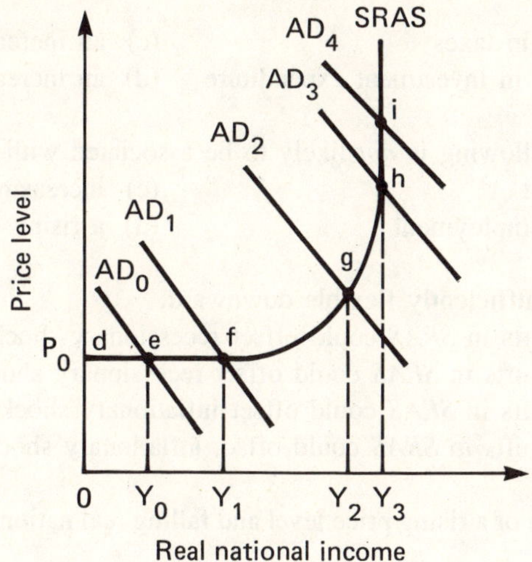

3. The Keynesian range of the *SRAS* curve is defined by the line segment
   (a) *df*.
   (b) *fh*.
   (c) *hi*.
   (d) *fi*.

4. A shift of the aggregate demand curve in the Keynesian (flat) portion of the *SRAS* curve will
   (a) cause a change in the price level but not in real national income.
   (b) cause changes in both real national income and the price level.
   (c) lead to a change in real national income predicted by the simple multiplier.
   (d) none of the above

5. Assuming the aggregate demand curve shifts from AD_1 to AD_2,
   (a) nominal output increases but real output is constant.
   (b) it is likely that unemployment will increase.
   (c) prices and real national income will both increase.
   (d) a recessionary gap will be opened.

6. At point *i*,
   (a) the economy is at or very near its capacity constraints.
   (b) any further increase in aggregate demand leads to a sharp rise in the price level.
   (c) the multiplier is nearly zero.
   (d) all of the above

7. Assume (for this question) that in the diagram above Y_2 represents potential real national income. A shift in aggregate demand from AD_2 to AD_4 can be predicted to
   (a) produce a stable equilibrium with national income at Y_3.
   (b) induce a rightward shift in the *SRAS* curve.
   (c) induce a leftward shift in the *SRAS* as factor prices rise.
   (d) lead to a contractionary shock.

8. From an initial real national income level with nearly full employment and stable prices, which of the following could cause an inflationary shock, other things being equal?
   (a) an increase in taxes
   (b) a sharp rise in investment expenditure
   (c) an increase in imports
   (d) an increase in desired saving

9. Which of the following is *not* likely to be associated with an inflationary gap?
   (a) rising output
   (b) increasing employment
   (c) increasing unemployment
   (d) a rising price level

10. If wages were sufficiently flexible downward,
    (a) leftward shifts in *SRAS* could offset recessionary shocks.
    (b) rightward shifts in *SRAS* could offset recessionary shocks.
    (c) leftward shifts in *SRAS* could offset inflationary shocks.
    (d) rightward shifts in *SRAS* could offset inflationary shocks.

11. The combination of a rising price level and falling real national income can be caused by
    (a) aggregate demand shifts along a given *SRAS* curve.
    (b) the automatic adjustment mechanism of a deflationary shock.
    (c) rightward shifts in the *LRAS* curve.
    (d) leftward shifts in the *SRAS* curve along a constant *AD* curve.

12. The vertical long-run aggregate supply curve shows that, given full adjustment of input prices,
    (a) potential real national income is compatible with any price level.
    (b) output is determined solely by the level of aggregate demand.
    (c) equilibrium real national income is indeterminate.
    (d) the price level is determined solely by aggregate supply.

13. The primary purpose of the tax incentives recommended by supply-side economists was to
    (a) decrease aggregate demand.
    (b) decrease aggregate supply.
    (c) decrease both aggregate demand and aggregate supply.
    (d) increase potential real national income.

14. The *SRAS* curve will shift in response to a change in all but which one of the following?
    (a) factor prices
    (b) productivity of inputs
    (c) the price level
    (d) factor supplies that change factor prices

15. An initial effect of the decreases in tax rates that were presented as supply-side measures was
    (a) to shift the aggregate demand curve to the right.
    (b) to shift the aggregate demand curve to the left.
    (c) to leave the aggregate demand curve unaffected.
    (d) to increase tax receipts.

16. With a vertical *LRAS* curve, the role of aggregate demand is to determine
    (a) actual output.
    (b) potential output.
    (c) the price level.
    (d) both the price level and actual output.

Self-Test Key

Matching Concepts: 1–b; 2–f; 3–d; 4–h; 5–g; 6–i; 7–a; 8–c; 9–j; 10–e

Multiple-Choice Questions: 1–b; 2–a; 3–a; 4–c; 5–c; 6–d; 7–c; 8–b; 9–c; 10–b; 11–d; 12–a; 13–d; 14–c; 15–a; 16–c

Exercises

1. Illustrate the following events and predict the effect of each on the price level and on real national income. In each case, draw a graph with the axes as below and label the aggregate demand curve *AD*, the short-run aggregate supply curve *SRAS*, and (when applicable) the long-run aggregate supply curve *LRAS*.
   (a) an increase in *AD* in the Keynesian (flat) range of the *SRAS* curve
   Effect:______
   (b) an increase in the costs of inputs (assume constant *AD*)
   Effect:______
   (c) an increase in *AD* in the intermediate range of the *SRAS*
   Effect:______
   (d) an increase in *AD* in the classical portion of the *SRAS*
   Effect:______
   (e) an increase in potential national income (assume constant *AD*)
   Effect:______
   (f) demand-shock inflation
   Effect:______

Price level

Real national income

(a) (b) (c)

(d) (e) (f)

2. For each of the following changes, indicate the response in terms of a shift in or movement along the aggregate demand curve or the short-run aggregate supply curve and the effect on real national income and the price level. In all cases, assume a short-run time period. Indicate shifts in the curves by "S" and movement along the curves by "A." In the last two columns, indicate increases as "+," decreases as "–," and no change as "0."

Event	Aggregate demand curve	*SRAS* curve	Real national income	Price level
(a) an increase in labor productivity due to technological change				
(b) an increase in the prices of inputs used by many firms				
(c) a boom in investment spending, starting from a position of full employment				
(d) a major reduction in investment expenditure (assume flexible wages and start from full employment)				

3. An economy has an *SRAS* function given by $P = 1 + 0.01Y$, which is presented below in schedule form, where *P* is the price level and *Y* is the level of real national income. The long-run aggregate supply curve is vertical at a real national income level of 1,000. Two schedules for the *AD* curve are presented below, with case I being the initial situation.

SRAS		*LRAS*		*AD* Case I		*AD* Case II	
Y	*P*	*Y*	*P*	*Y*	*P*	*Y*	*P*
0	1.0	1,000	1.0	0	111	0	116.5
500	6.0	1,000	6.0	500	61	500	66.5
1,000	11.0	1,000	11.0	1,000	11	1,000	16.5
1,050	11.5	1,000	11.5	1,050	6	1,050	11.5

(a) Taking case I for the *AD* curve, what are the equilibrium levels of *P* and *Y*? What is the value of the GNP gap?

(b) Assume that the *AD* curve shifts upward, represented by case II. If the *SRAS* curve does not change immediately, what are the new short-run equilibrium values for *P* and *Y*? What type of gap exists and what is its magnitude?

(c) Given the shift of the *AD* curve, what do you predict will happen in the long-run to the equilibrium levels of *P* and *Y*? What will happen to the short-run GNP gap?

(d) Explain what is likely to happen to the *SRAS* curve in the long run and rewrite the algebraic expression for it assuming the slope of the *SRAS* curve does not change.

Short Problem

The aggregate demand curve is given by the expression $P = 40 - 2Y$, and the aggregate supply curve is given by the following:

(i) $P = 20$ for $0 \leq Y \leq 30$*

(ii) $P = 5 + 0.5Y$ for $30 \leq Y \leq 50$

(iii) $Y = 50$ for $P \geq 30$

(a) Plot the *AD* curve in the diagram and carefully indicate the intercept values. Label the curve AD_0.

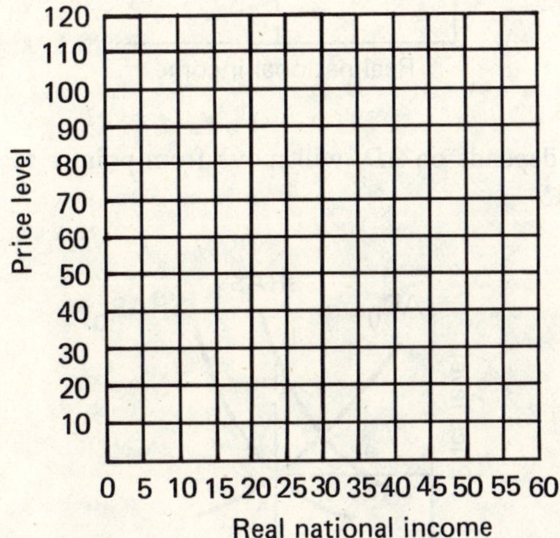

(b) Plot the *AS* curve in the diagram. Indicate the Keynesian, intermediate, and classical ranges.

(c) Referring to the diagram, what are the equilibrium levels of *P* and *Y*? Prove algebraically that the intersection of equation (i) and the *AD* expression yields these equilibrium values.

(d) Suppose the expression for the *AD* curve became $P = 80 - 2Y$. Plot this expression in the diagram (label it AD_1) and discuss the changes that occurred to the equilibrium values of *P* and *Y*.

(e) Suppose the *AD* expression became $P = 105 - 2Y$. Plot this relationship (AD_2) and determine the equilibrium levels of *P* and *Y*.

(f) What would be the significance of shifts in the *AD* to the right of $P = 130 - 2Y$? How could this inflationary gap be eliminated?

*$0 \leq Y \leq 30$ means national income has the range greater than or equal to zero but less than or equal to 30.

Answers to the Exercises

1. (a) price level constant; real GNP increases

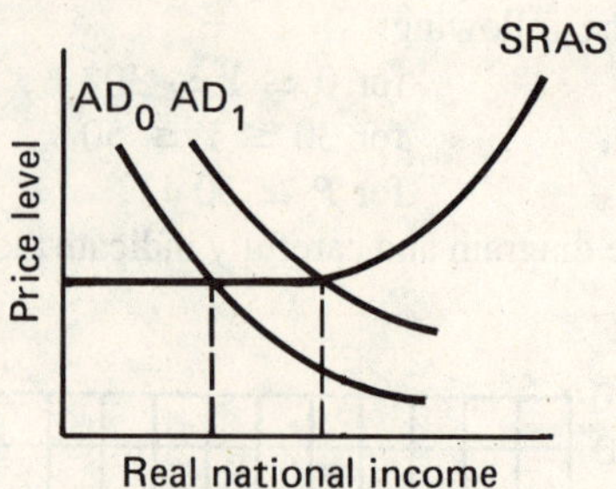

(b) actual effect depends on *AD*; will move from point *e* to somewhere on the *ab* range of *SRAS*

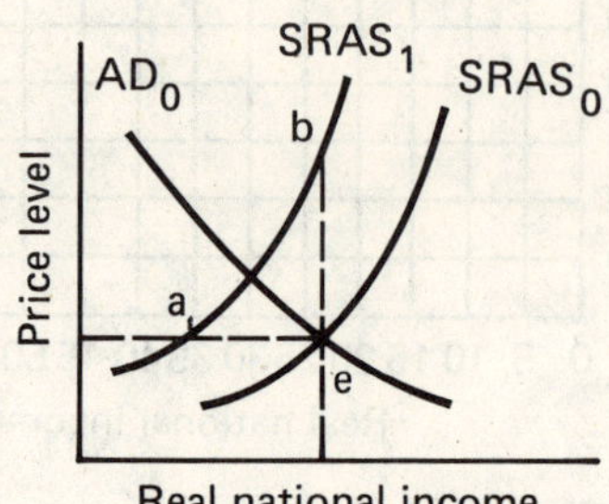

(c) price level increases; real national income increases

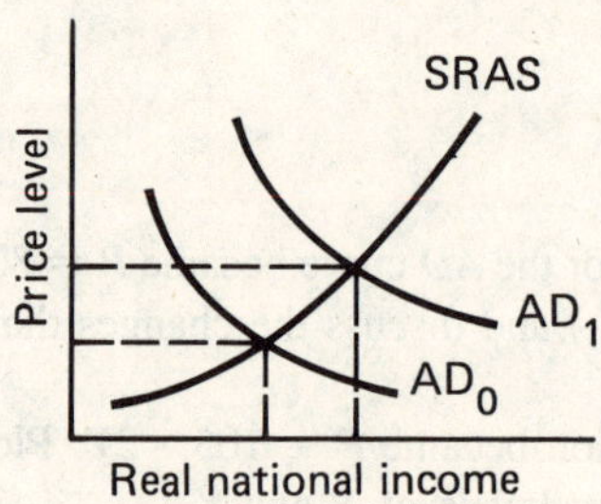

(d) price level increases; real national income virtually constant

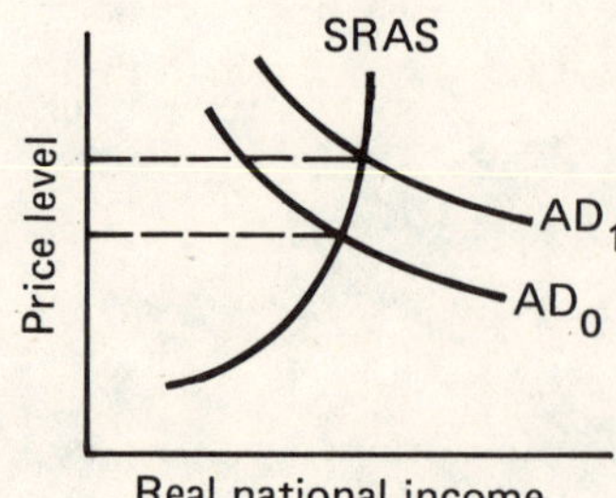

(e) price level decreases; real national income increases

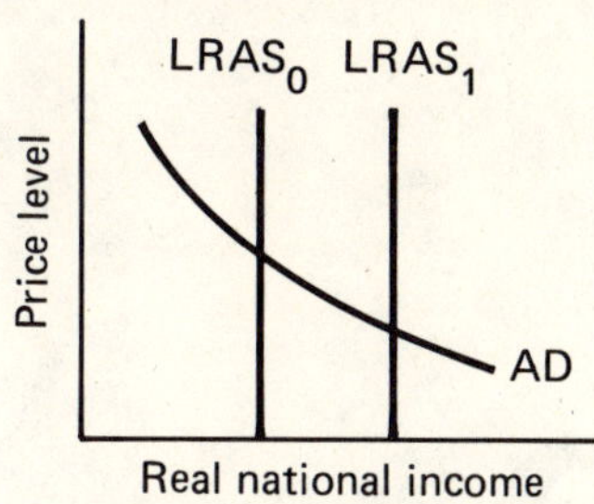

(f) price level increases; output effect depends on relative magnitude of *AD* and *SRAS* shifts

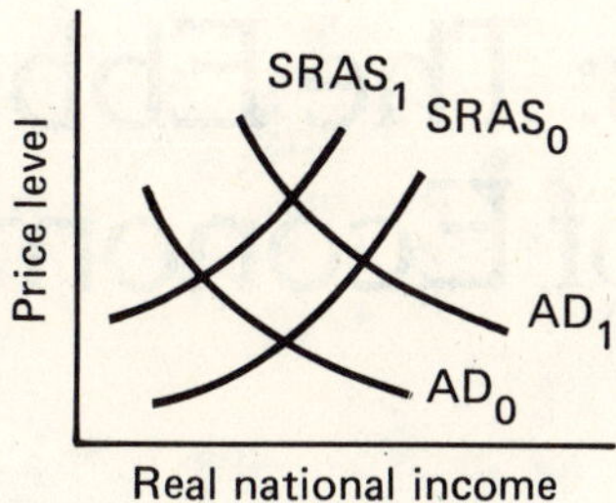

2. (a) A, S, +, –; (b) A, S, –, +; (c) S, A (then S), 0, +; (d) S, A (then S), 0, – (In cases C and D, induced shifts in supply follow to eliminate inflationary and recessionary gaps.)

3. (a) The equilibrium levels are $P = 11$ and $Y = 1,000$. The GNP gap is 0.
   (b) The new equilibrium levels are $P = 11.5$ and $Y = 1,050$. The GNP gap is a negative value (–50). This is known as an inflationary gap of 50.
   (c) In the long run, potential national income will be restored at $Y = 1,000$. According to the *AD* curve (case II), $Y = 1,000$ is associated with a price level of 16.5. Since the *LRAS* curve is vertical at $Y = 1,000$, the *SRAS* curve will intersect the new *AD* curve at $Y = 1,000$ and $P = 16.5$. The short-run inflationary gap will be eliminated in the long run with a rise in the price level.
   (d) The *SRAS* curve shifts upward and intersects the *AD* curve and the *LRAS* curve at $P = 16.5$ and $Y = 1,000$. The new algebraic expression for the *SRAS* function is $P = 6.5 + 0.01Y$. Notice that when $Y = 1,000$, $P = 16.5$, which are the equilibrium values in the long run.

29

Business Cycles: The Ebb and Flow of Economic Activity

Learning Objectives

Careful study of the material in this chapter should enable you to

—describe the phases of business cycles;

—explain how fluctuations in GNP are related to shifts in aggregate demand and aggregate supply curves;

—understand the influence of the interest rate on investment and how the accelerator theory works;

—recognize the multiple causes of fluctuations in economic activity.

Review and Self-Test

Matching Concepts

_______ 1. business cycles

_______ 2. major element in fluctuations of U.S. national income

_______ 3. consumption

_______ 4. cause of counter-cyclical shift in consumption

_______ 5. investment in inventories

_______ 6. investment in plant and equipment

_______ 7. relationship of investment to the rate of change in national income

_______ 8. reason for multiple rates of interest

_______ 9. downswing in the level of economic activity

_______ 10. combination of the multiplier and the accelerator

(a) largest single component of aggregate expenditures

(b) largest component of domestic investment

(c) more or less regular fluctuations in the level of economic activity

(d) the accelerator

(e) recession

(f) cause of cumulative fluctuations in economic activity

(g) smallest but most volatile component of investment

(h) investment expenditure

(i) differences in risk

(j) increase in transfer payments as national income falls

Multiple-Choice Questions

1. There is a consensus among students of economic fluctuations that
   (a) there is a common pattern of variation that pervades most economic series.
   (b) there is little difference from cycle to cycle in duration and in amplitude.
   (c) there are few, if any, differences among economic series in their particular patterns of fluctuation.
   (d) there are factors at work causing the economy to display continual long-term fluctuations around its short-term rising growth trend.

2. The largest component of aggregate expenditure in the United States is
   (a) consumption.
   (b) government expenditure.
   (c) net exports.
   (d) investment expenditure.

3. Which of the following would tend to shift the consumption function upward?
   (a) Real interest rates increase.
   (b) Prices are expected to fall in the future.
   (c) Income is redistributed from households with high marginal propensities to consume to households with low ones.
   (d) Government lowers income tax rates.

4. If government transfer payments fall when national income expands, it can be said that these payments are
   (a) countercyclical since they will rise relative to GNP when GNP is rising.
   (b) procyclical since they fall relative to GNP when GNP is rising.
   (c) countercyclical since they fall relative to GNP when GNP is rising.
   (d) inconsistent with an upward-sloping consumption function.

5. History shows that investment in the United States has
   (a) been quite stable but a small fraction of GNP.
   (b) fluctuated a great deal compared with other components of aggregate demand.
   (c) usually been about 25 percent of GNP.
   (d) never fallen below the amount needed for replacement.

6. If you were measuring the total amount of investment expenditure, which of the following would you *not* include?
   (a) purchases of stocks and bonds
   (b) changes in inventories
   (c) new residential construction
   (d) business fixed investment

7. Other things being equal, investment in inventories tends to vary
   (a) positively with production and sales, negatively with interest rates.
   (b) negatively with production and sales, negatively with interest rates.
   (c) positively with production and sales, positively with interest rates.
   (d) negatively with production and sales, positively with interest rates.

8. Other things being equal, investment in residential construction tends to vary
   (a) negatively with changes in average household income, positively with interest rates.
   (b) positively with changes in average household income, negatively with interest rates.
   (c) positively with both average household income and interest rates.
   (d) negatively with both average household income and interest rates.

9. The amount of investment spending by firms
   (a) is influenced by profit expectations and interest rates.
   (b) seems to be entirely random.
   (c) has little effect on the economy.
   (d) is quite stable and predictable.

10. Desired investment spending in an economy will usually
    (a) rise as national income falls.
    (b) rise as interest rates fall.
    (c) remain unaffected by changes in interest rates.
    (d) remain unaffected by changes in national income.

11. According to the accelerator theory, investment is a function of
    (a) the level of national income.
    (b) profits.
    (c) the rate of change of national income.
    (d) savings.

12. The multiplier and accelerator effects operating together
    (a) tend to cancel out.
    (b) help to explain why movements of the economy tend to acquire momentum.
    (c) make the amplitude of cycles less than they otherwise would be.
    (d) tend to keep growth going perpetually.

13. Imagine an economy that has been in a recovery following a depression. In its initial stages, it should be characterized by all but which of the following?
    (a) increases in aggregate demand
    (b) rising incomes
    (c) increased inflation
    (d) favorable business and consumer expectations

14. A trough is characterized by
    (a) high unemployment of labor.
    (b) large amounts of unused production capacity.
    (c) low business profits and pessimistic expectations about future profits.
    (d) all of the above.

15. The upper turning point will *not* include which one of the following?
    (a) a high degree of utilization of existing capacity
    (b) a high unemployment rate
    (c) shortages of certain key raw materials
    (d) shortages of labor in certain key skill categories

16. If for every one unit of output produced, three units of capital are required, then
    (a) the capital-output ratio is one-third.
    (b) the capital-output ratio is three.
    (c) six units of capital are required to produce three units of output.
    (d) capital must cost more, relative to labor, per unit of output.

17. The accelerator theory assumes
    (a) an increasing capital-output ratio, therefore capital deepening.
    (b) an increasing capital-output ratio, therefore capital widening.
    (c) a fixed capital-output ratio, therefore capital deepening.
    (d) a fixed capital-output ratio, therefore capital widening.

18. You pay $8 interest for a $100 loan for one year, during which the annual rate of inflation is 5 percent. The real rate of interest is about
    (a) 8 percent.
    (b) 3 percent.
    (c) 13 percent.
    (d) none of the above.

19. The difference between real and nominal rates of interest is that
    (a) real rates measure the actual money payments while nominal rates are theoretical.
    (b) nominal rates exceed real rates by the rate of inflation.
    (c) real rates take into account differences in risk and costs of administration.
    (d) nominal rates are quoted without taking into account special fees associated with the loan.

20. Exercise 3 implies that the desired stock of inventories held will be higher
    (a) the higher the sales of the firm and the lower the rate of interest.
    (b) the lower the sales of the firm and the higher the rate of interest.
    (c) the higher the sales of both the firm and the rate of interest.
    (d) the lower the sales of both the firm and the rate of interest.

Self-Test Key

Matching Concepts: 1–c; 2–h; 3–a; 4–j; 5–g; 6–b; 7–d; 8–i; 9–e; 10–f

Multiple-Choice Questions: 1–a; 2–a; 3–d; 4–c; 5–b; 6–a; 7–a; 8–b; 9–a; 10–b; 11–c; 12–b; 13–c; 14–d; 15–b; 16–b; 17–d; 18–b; 19–b; 20–a

Exercises

1. Illustrating the Accelerator Principle

The table below shows the hypothetical situation for a firm that requires one machine for every 1,000 units of product it turns out annually. As it increases its output and sales in response to changing demand, show how its investment will be affected. Replacement for depreciation is one machine per year throughout. Complete the table and answer the questions.

Year	Annual output (units)	Units of capital needed	Additional machines required	Replacement machines	Total machines to be purchased
1	10,000	10	0	1	1
2	10,000	______	______	1	______
3	11,000	______	______	1	______
4	12,000	______	______	1	______
5	15,000	______	______	1	______
6	17,000	______	______	1	______
7	18,000	______	______	1	______
8	18,000	______	______	1	______

(a) Between years 2 and 5, annual output increased by ______ percent.

(b) In the same period, total investment spending by this firm increased by ______ percent.

(c) Plot the cyclical fluctuation in desired investment on the diagram below.

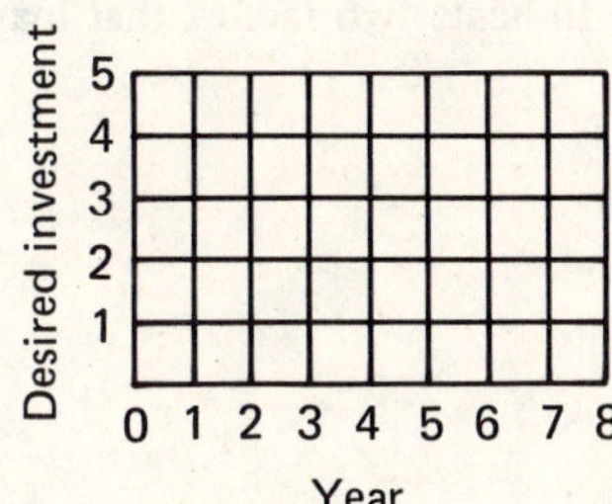

2. The following two schedules relate desired capital stock to the interest rate.

Schedule A		*Schedule B*	
Capital stock	Interest rate (percent)	Capital stock	Interest rate (percent)
100	20	150	20
200	18	250	18
300	14	350	14
400	8	450	8
500	1	550	1

(a) Inspect both schedules. Does a negative or positive relationship exist between the desired capital stock and the rate of interest?

(b) Assuming schedule A applies, if the current rate of interest falls from 20 percent to 18 percent, what is the change in the desired capital stock? Desired investment? Would firms necessarily be able to achieve this level of investment in the current time period?

(c) Suppose that the schedule given by A suddenly changed to that given by schedule B. With a current interest rate of 14 percent, what is the new magnitude of the desired capital stock? Does the change in the schedule imply new desired investment activity? Indicate two factors that may have caused the schedule to change.

3. Economic Indicators

All economic and business series do not fluctuate in exact synchronization. Some series called "leading" indicators fairly consistently turn down before the upper turning point (peak) and up before the lower turning point (trough) of real national income (GNP). Others, the "lagging" indicators, turn down after the peaks and up after the troughs. More general measures, such as the index of industrial production, are termed "roughly coincident" since their turning points coincide with the "business cycle."

Your first task in this exercise is to classify each of the eight indicators as leading (L), lagging (G), or roughly coincident (C). You should end up with four L's, two G's, and two C's, and have a reason for each of your selections.

Your second task is to complete the diagram to the right by showing a prototype leading series above and lagging series below the illustrative coincident series.

_______ (a) Common stock prices (index of S&P 500)

_______ (b) New building permits

_______ (c) Personal income less transfer payments

_______ (d) Nonagricultural employment

_______ (e) Ratio of consumer installment debt to personal income

_______ (f) Inventory/sales ratio in constant dollars

_______ (g) Vendor performances (percent of companies receiving slower deliveries)

_______ (h) Contracts and orders for plant and equipment

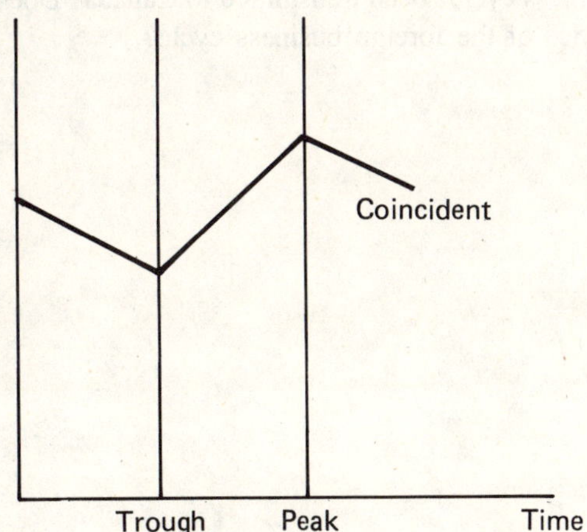

4. For Canada and the United Kingdom, exports comprise a larger share of GNP than for the United States. For example, approximately 30 percent of Canada's GNP is comprised of exports, making Canada's economy activity critically dependent on foreigners' willingness to buy Canadian goods and services, and allowing cycles in foreign economic activity to be transmitted to Canada. A major determinant of foreign imports is their national income, which itself can display cyclical activity.

   You are given the following hypothetical relationship between foreign income and Canadian exports. Assume that the export multiplier on Canadian GNP is 2.

Year	Foreign GNP	Canadian exports	Change in Canadian GNP
1	100	10	____
2	150	15	+10
3	200	20	____
4	180	18	____
5	100	10	____
6	100	10	____

(a) Determine the relationship between foreign GNP and Canadian exports. List some factors that explain why foreign income levels might determine Canadian exports.

(b) Assume that exports change between two years and the multiplier process works itself through by the end of the second year. On this basis, fill in the missing values for the change in the Canadian GNP.

(c) Has a "business cycle" been transmitted to Canada? Does it have the same basic characteristics of the foreign business cycle?

Short Problem

In forecasting economic activity, the prediction of cyclical turning points is of such great interest that the government publishes the monthly *Business Conditions Digest*. This publication traces the fluctuations of *hundreds* of economic series including an index of twelve leading indicators. Below are the values of this index from 1979 to 1982. This period includes all four turning points in the business cycle between 1975 and 1986. The months classified as upper turning points are marked P (for peak), and the lower turning points are marked T (for trough).

Month	1979	1980	1981	1982
January	142.6	138.4P	135.2	135.1
February	142.3	134.1	134.2	135.7
March	143.2	131.1	135.8	134.7
April	140.3	125.6	137.3	136.0
May	141.4	122.2	136.0	136.2
June	141.6	123.7	135.2	135.5
July	141.2	128.0T	134.8P	136.2
August	140.1	130.6	134.1	136.1
September	140.1	135.0	130.7	137.5
October	137.2	136.0	128.3	138.6
November	135.6	137.6	128.2	139.4T
December	135.2	136.4	127.1	140.9

(a) Use the rule of thumb that three successive declines in the leading index forecast an upper turning point and three successive rises forecast a lower turning point. In what month would you be forecasting each turning point, allowing a month for the data to become available?

(b) Assess your success as a forecaster using this rule. Would you have done better on the basis of a single month or a two-month advance or decline?

(c) You will almost certainly conclude that examining leading series can be modestly helpful but that more is needed than a single index. You may wish to analyze the cyclical situation at the time you are taking this course. *Business Conditions Digest* is a good starting point.

Answers to the Exercises

1.

Year	Units of capital needed	New machines required	Replacement machines	Total machines to be purchased
1	10	0	1	1
2	10	0	1	1
3	11	1	1	2
4	12	1	1	2
5	15	3	1	4
6	17	2	1	3
7	18	1	1	2
8	18	0	1	1

(a) 50 percent
(b) 300 percent

(c)

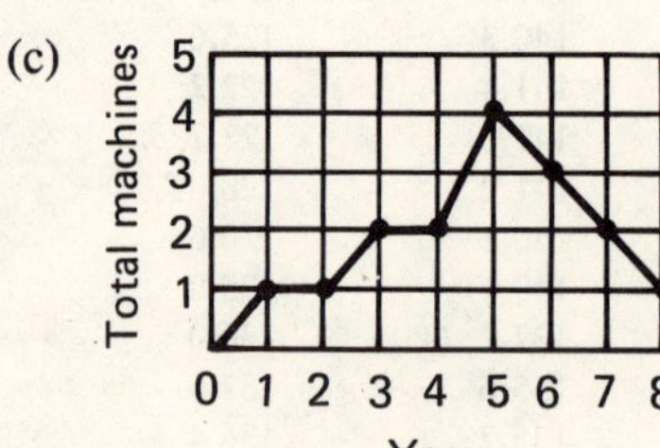

2. (a) negative
(b) Desired capital stock increases from 100 to 200. Desired investment is 100. It depends on the availability of capital goods from capital-producing firms.
(c) Desired capital is 350. Yes, desired investment increases by 50. Profit expectations may have improved because of new innovations, or there are more optimistic forecasts about future sales.

3. (a) L, prices are determined by expectation of future returns.
(b) L, most permits lead to future buildings.
(c) C, represents household income from productive activity.
(d) C, good measure of economic activity.
(e) G, continues to increase after personal income drops (or decrease with rise in income).
(f) G, continues to increase after sales drop (or decrease with rise in sales).
(g) L, deliveries speed up as companies exhaust backlog.
(h) L, orders lead to future activity.

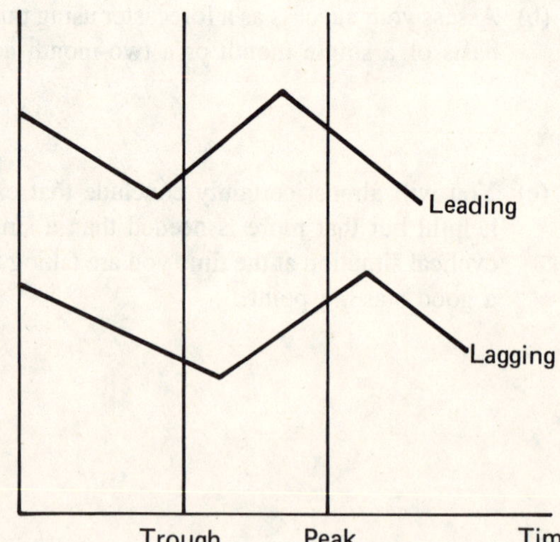

4. (a) Canadian exports are positively related to foreign GNP. It appears that exports are 10 percent of foreign income. Foreign households will tend to buy more Canadian products when their incomes rise; foreign firms require more Canadian-produced inputs in order to expand their production.
   (b) Year 3: Δ in Canadian GNP = 2 × 5 = 10
   Year 4: Δ in Canadian GNP = 2 × (–2) = –4
   Year 5: Δ in Canadian GNP = 2 × (–8) = –16
   Year 6: Δ in Canadian GNP = 0
   (c) Clearly, a business cycle has been transmitted from abroad. The cycles of both economies are similar; they peak and trough in similar fashions.

30

Fiscal Policy

Learning Objectives

Careful study of this chapter should enable you to

—describe the underlying principles of fiscal policy to remove inflationary and recessionary gaps;

—explain the difference between discretionary fiscal policy and automatic stabilizers and why policy must be reversible to be effective;

—understand why changes in the stance of fiscal policy are best judged by looking at changes in the high-employment budget surplus;

—distinguish the Keynesian and conservative views concerning the role and importance of budget deficits and the size of the national debt;

—explain why a government policy to always keep the budget balanced may actually have destabilizing effects on the economy.

Review and Self-Test

Matching Concepts

_______ 1. use of government expenditure and tax policies to affect aggregate expenditures	(a)	probable contractionary pressure on national income
_______ 2. budget deficit	(b)	balanced budget multiplier
_______ 3. effect of a budget surplus	(c)	built-in stabilizers
_______ 4. measurement of effect of balanced change in government expenditures and taxes	(d)	excess of government's expenditures over revenues
_______ 5. fine tuning	(e)	use of fiscal policy to remove minor fluctuations of GNP from full-employment level
_______ 6. automatic adjustments in taxes and government expenditures	(f)	permanent income hypothesis
_______ 7. discretionary fiscal policy	(g)	deliberate changes in government taxes and expenditures to alter aggregate demand
_______ 8. high-employment surplus	(h)	accentuated swings in national income
_______ 9. theory emphasizing importance of expected lifetime income as the determinant of consumption	(i)	fiscal policy
_______ 10. likely effect of annually balanced budget	(j)	estimate of government tax revenues minus expenditures if full employment were attained
_______ 11. Gramm–Rudman–Hollings	(k)	reduction of short-run income by attempts to increase saving
_______ 12. paradox of debt	(l)	legislation aimed at eliminating federal deficits by 1991

Multiple-Choice Questions

1. Fiscal policy refers to
   (a) government's attempt to regulate prices.
   (b) budget results that change pro-cyclically.
   (c) the use of tax, expenditure, and debt management policies to reach desired levels of national income.
   (d) government's attempt to have receipts exactly equal to expenditures.

2. An increase in the government's budget deficit, assuming private expenditure functions do not shift,
   (a) is an example of contractionary fiscal policy.
   (b) would be an appropriate policy for closing an inflationary gap.
   (c) will shift the aggregate demand curve to the right.
   (d) will have no effect on aggregate demand.

3. If there is currently an inflationary gap, an appropriate fiscal policy would be to
   (a) increase taxes.
   (b) increase government spending.
   (c) decrease taxes.
   (d) increase transfer payments.

4. Candidate Reagan proposed a cut in personal income tax rates and an increase in real defense spending. In the short run the execution of these proposals under President Reagan tended to
   (a) reduce aggregate supply, causing prices to rise.
   (b) increase aggregate demand, thus increasing national income.
   (c) reduce aggregate demand, decreasing national income.
   (d) have uncertain effects since policies contradict each other.

5. The Reagan administration argued for
   (a) fiscal policy as a stabilization tool.
   (b) the necessity that more resources be allocated to defense.
   (c) the position that lower marginal rates of taxation would increase factor supplies.
   (d) both (b) and (c)

6. Consider an increase in government purchases of $X, a tax cut of $X, and a balanced budget increase in expenditure of $X as alternative policies. Which will probably yield the largest increase in national income?
   (a) the expenditure increase
   (b) the tax cut
   (c) the balanced budget increase
   (d) They will all increase the GNP by $X times the multiplier.

7. A "high-employment surplus" means that
   (a) there will be surplus aggregate demand at high-employment levels of national income.
   (b) the government's budget will be in surplus at any level of national income.
   (c) the government's tax revenues will exceed its expenditures at high-employment national income.
   (d) there will be a surplus of output at high-employment levels of national income.

8. The balanced budget multiplier
   (a) is larger than the multiplier for government expenditures.
   (b) applies when additional tax receipts are equal to additional government expenditures.
   (c) is the same as the multiplier for government expenditures.
   (d) is the same as the multiplier for tax changes.

9. An increase in income tax rates (assuming other expenditure functions are constant) will lead to all but which one of the following?
   (a) an increase in the high-employment budget surplus
   (b) a decrease in the value of the multiplier
   (c) a movement along the aggregate demand function
   (d) a reduction in the equilibrium level of national income

10. Which of the following is *not* a built-in stabilizer in the economy?
   (a) steeply progressive tax rates
   (b) government expenditures that vary directly with the level of national income
   (c) the farm support program
   (d) social security payments and unemployment insurance

11. Built-in stabilizers tend to
   (a) stimulate inflations.
   (b) prolong recessions.
   (c) reduce cyclical fluctuations.
   (d) stabilize income but destabilize prices and employment.

12. Which of the following would give the *best* measure of the stance of current fiscal policy?
   (a) tax rates alone
   (b) the size of the government budget's current deficit or surplus
   (c) changes in the high-employment budget surplus
   (d) the relation between tax revenues and government expenditures

13. Fiscal policy in the early 1980s
   (a) concentrated on precise fine tuning of the economy at acceptable levels of employment and inflation.
   (b) was primarily concerned with reducing the size of the public debt.
   (c) stressed relatively large cuts in personal income tax rates.
   (d) reverted back to pump priming to stimulate the economy.

14. An annually balanced federal government budget
   (a) is an idea supported by most economists because it would be easy to achieve.
   (b) would have greater potential for a built-in stability than one with deficits during slumps and surpluses during booms.
   (c) is feasible from a political standpoint and desirable from an economic one.
   (d) would avoid the inflationary consequences of chronic budget deficits, but at the cost of destabilizing the economy.

15. An attempt to reduce the national debt
   (a) would be an appropriate policy for attempting to cure a recession.
   (b) requires a budget surplus and therefore would have a deflationary effect, *ceteris paribus*.
   (c) would cause aggregate demand to rise by an amount equal to the debt reduction.
   (d) transfers money from bondholders to taxpayers.

16. If the government increases personal income tax revenues and its purchases of goods and services by the same amount, the most likely effect is
    (a) a net decrease in aggregate expenditures.
    (b) a net increase in aggregate expenditures.
    (c) aggregate expenditures would remain unchanged.
    (d) an increase in the balanced budget multiplier.

17. The Gramm–Rudman–Hollings Act of 1985
    (a) aimed at an annually balanced budget by 1991.
    (b) required the immediate balancing of the budget.
    (c) specifically ruled out tax increases to balance the budget.
    (d) established the framework for a cyclically balanced budget.

18. All but which of the following make it difficult to use discretionary fiscal policy?
    (a) the time delay in legislating and implementing tax and expenditure changes
    (b) the limited impact of temporary changes in tax rates
    (c) the difficulty of quickly reversing policies to compensate for changes in private decisions
    (d) the undesirability of having any government deficits

19. Endogenous changes in the government's actual budget balance due to changes in national income
    (a) are shown by shifts in the budget surplus function.
    (b) result from policy-induced changes in tax rates or expenditures.
    (c) are shown by movements along the budget surplus function.
    (d) cause shifts of the aggregate demand curve.

Questions 20 and 21 refer to the appendix.

20. The permanent-income and life-cycle hypotheses are consistent with an average propensity to consume out of current income
    (a) that does not vary with current income.
    (b) that varies inversely with current income.
    (c) that varies directly with current income.
    (d) that has no relationship at all with current income.

21. The inflation adjustment to government's debt service payments
    (a) holds that the real component of government interest paid on debt is not a true transfer to bondholders.
    (b) holds that the inflation premium paid as part of government debt service is offset by the decline in the real value of government debt.
    (c) is made before the government issues its annual figures on receipts, expenditures, and debt.
    (d) all of the above

Self-Test Key

Matching Concepts: 1–i; 2–d; 3–a; 4–b; 5–e; 6–c; 7–g; 8–j; 9–f; 10–h; 11–l; 12–k

Multiple-Choice Questions: 1–c; 2–c; 3–a; 4–b; 5–d; 6–a; 7–c; 8–b; 9–c; 10–b; 11–c; 12–c; 13–c; 14–d; 15–b; 16–b; 17–a; 18–d; 19–c; 20–b; 21–b

Exercises

1. Below is a graph of an aggregate expenditure function for a hypothetical economy showing an estimated high-employment national income of 400. A horizontal *SRAS* is assumed.

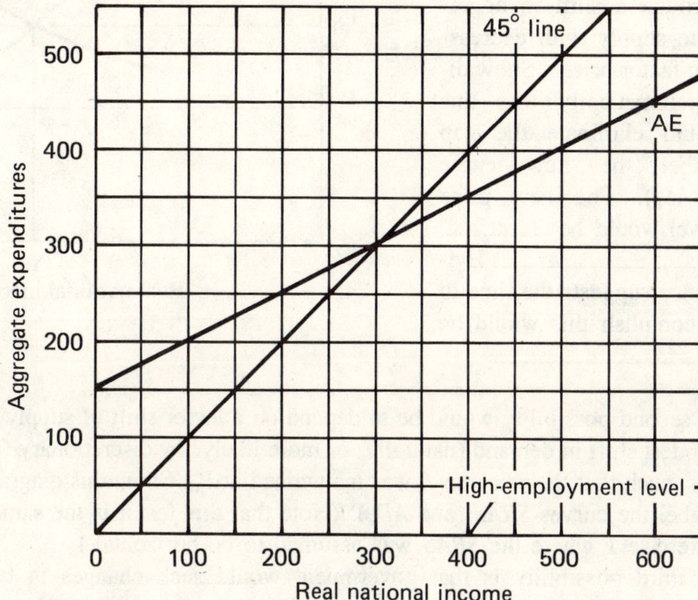

(a) What will be the actual national income level in equilibrium? ________________

(b) The recessionary gap is ________________.

(c) How much of an increase in aggregate expenditure would be needed to eliminate the recessionary gap? ____________

(d) Explain why your answer to (c) is different from your answer to (b).

(e) What fiscal policy measures would be appropriate in this situation?

(f) Note that for any planned budget balance, the actual budget deficit or surplus of the government depends on the national income that is actually produced. As output—and incomes—rise, tax revenues tend to (rise/remain unchanged/fall), while government transfer payments tend to (rise/remain unchanged/fall).

(g) Explain how a government's budget that was planned to generate a high-employment surplus might end up with an actual deficit.

(h) Draw in a new *AE* curve showing the elimination of the recessionary gap through the use of fiscal policy.

2. (a) Assume a persistent (inflationary, recessionary) gap as shown by the diagram to the right.

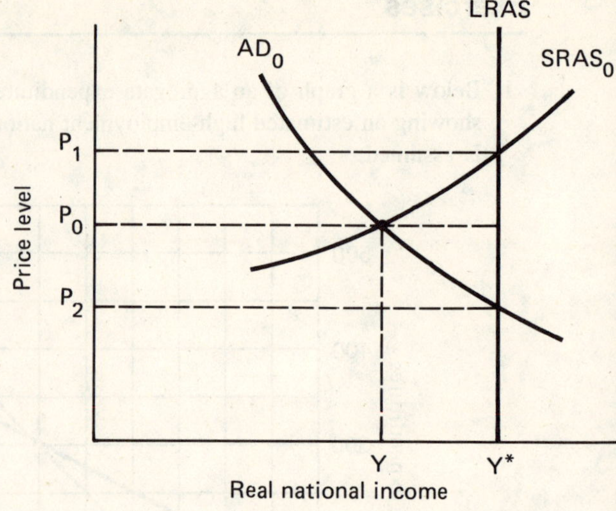

(b) One possible way of eliminating the gap is through a shift in aggregate supply with decreasing factor prices. Show diagrammatically that this could eliminate the gap (label the new curve $SRAS_b$). The new price level would be ________________________. Evidence suggests the time to accomplish this would be ________________.

(c) A second possibility would be to depend on a lesser shift of supply and have a modest shift in demand (naturally, or more likely, by discretionary fiscal stimulus) such that the price level was maintained at P_0. Show this diagrammatically (label the curves $SRAS_c$ and AD_c). (Note that this result is the same as that in Exercise 1 where the *SRAS* was assumed to be horizontal.)

(d) A third possibility is that government would seek changes in taxes and/or expenditures that would rapidly bring the economy to full employment. Show this diagrammatically (label the curve AD_d).

(e) One risk of this policy is that a(n) ________________ gap would be created if private expenditures returned to more normal levels.

3. Assume that a hypothetical economy is currently at an equilibrium national income level of $1,000 billion, but the high-employment national income is $1,200 billion. Assume the government's budget is currently in balance at $200 billion and the marginal propensity to spend is 0.75.

(a) The recessionary gap is ________________.

(b) The value of the multiplier is ________________.

(c) Aggregate expenditures would have to be (increased/decreased) by ________________ billion to eliminate the (inflationary/recessionary) gap.

(d) The government could attempt to eliminate the gap by holding taxes constant and (increasing/decreasing) expenditures by ________________ billion.

(e) Alternatively, the government could attempt to eliminate the gap by holding expenditures constant and (increasing/decreasing) its tax receipts by ________________ billion.

(f) As a third policy option, the government could propose a balanced budget (increase/decrease) of ________________ billion.

4. Assume that the government's initial net tax function (taxes − transfers) is $T_n = 0.19Y$ and that government expenditures are \$725 billion. Over a three-year period, the government cuts taxes so that the net tax function becomes $T_n = 0.16Y$. Increases, mostly for defense, bring expenditures on goods and services to G = \$800 billion. Figures are in constant dollars of the final year. Your first task is to calculate and plot the initial and final budget surplus functions. All figures are in billions of dollars.

Y	Initial budget surplus	Final budget surplus
3,200		
3,500[a]		
4,000[b]		
4,200[c]		
4,500		

[a]Initial actual income level
[b]Initial high-employment and final actual income level
[c]Final high-employment income level

(a) The initial budget surplus was ________; the final actual budget surplus was ________.
(b) The initial high-employment budget surplus was ________; the final high-employment budget surplus was ________.
(c) The shift of the budget surplus function represents the assumption of a (more, less) expansionary stance by the government as can best be measured by the decrease in the (actual, high employment) budget surplus of ________.

5. The events in Exercise 4 are a rough approximation of those taking place in the United States between 1982 and 1985. The government expenditures and surpluses resemble those of all U.S. governments (including state and local which were running increasing surpluses during the period) expressed in constant 1985 dollars.

The price level rose by about 12 percent between the initial and the last period. Describe these events using plausible *AD*, *SRAS*, and *LRAS* curves and indicate whether the initial recessionary gap has been altered during the period.

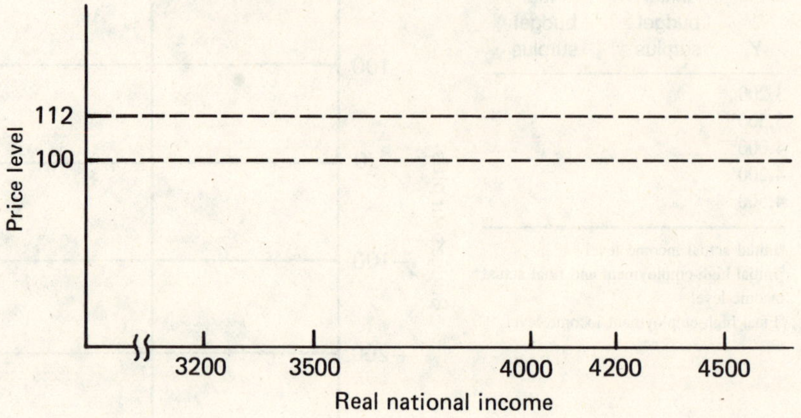

Short Problems

1. Assume that the hypothetical economy in Exercise 3 is currently producing an equilibrium GNP of $1,250 billion. All other assumptions remain the same as in the introduction to Exercise 3.
   (a) Aggregate expenditures would have to be (increased/decreased) by ________________ billion to eliminate the (inflationary/recessionary) gap.
   (b) The government could attempt to eliminate the gap by holding taxes constant and (increasing/decreasing) expenditures by ________________ billion.
   (c) The government could also attempt to eliminate the gap by holding its expenditures constant and (increasing/decreasing) its tax receipts by ________________.
   (d) Finally, as a third option, the government could propose a balanced budget (increase/decrease) of ________________.
   (e) Explain why the change in government expenditures required to eliminate the gap would be less than the required change in taxes.

2. Concern about the Increased Federal Debt/GNP Ratio?

Refer to text Figure 30-6 that shows two measures of the relative importance of the national debt: the ratio of debt to GNP, and the ratio of net interest paid to GNP. Note that the two series give conflicting pictures as to changes in recent years: the debt ratio is relatively constant after 1972 with a sharp rise after 1981; the interest ratio rose rapidly after 1972 with some rounding off after 1982.

To understand this difference, concentrate on fiscal year 1981 during which the debt rose from $914.3 billion to $1,003.9 billion. It dropped as a percentage of GNP from 34.3 percent of the 1980 GNP of $2667.6 billion to 33.65 percent of the 1981 GNP of $2986.2 billion. Fiscal year 1981 was essentially one of recovery; but with the onset of recession in July, the GNP price deflator rose by 9.4 percent.

(a) Estimate the increase in real debt (constant 1980 dollars) by dividing the $1,003.9 billion by 1.094 and compare with the increase in nominal debt.

(b) Estimate the 1981 real GNP (in constant 1980 dollars) in the same fashion and note that the debt/GNP ratio is the same for 1981 whether current or constant dollars are used.

Relating the flow of net interest to GNP raises more complex issues about the measurement of government deficits. This ratio rose in 1981 since the net interest/debt ratio increased from 5.7 to 6.8 percent, but in both 1980 and 1981 it was exceeded by price increases of 9.3 and 9.4 percent (as measured by the GNP deflator). The effective interest rate paid by the government was negative as the net interest payments paid to bondholders as a group were less than the erosion of the real value of their securities. (Some bondholders did better since the government had to pay over 14 percent interest on some newly issued securities in 1981.)

By 1985, the situation changed dramatically with the interest/debt ratio at 7.1 percent and the annual price increase only 3 percent.

(c) In 1985, the debt/GNP ratio had increased to about 46 percent.

(i) Should this in itself be of concern?

(ii) In contrast to 1945, when private indebtedness was at historically low levels relative to GNP, mortgage debts, consumer credit, and corporate debt-equity ratios were at or near relative peaks in 1985. How might this add to concerns?

(iii) Foreigners held about 12 percent of the government debt and foreign private investment in the United States had just passed U.S. investment abroad. How does this modify present and future problems of debt management?

Answers to the Exercises

1. (a) 300
   (b) 100
   (c) 50
   (d) The injection is multiplied by 2 by subsequent rounds of respending.
   (e) tax cut or increased government spending or both
   (f) rise, fall
   (g) There may have been an unexpected decline in national income, which would both lower tax revenues and increase government expenditures and transfer payments.
   (h) Your new *AE* curve should be shifted upward by 50 at each level of real national income.

2. (a) recessionary (Y Y^*)
   (b) P_2 (see $SRAS_b$); very long
   (c) and (d) on diagram
   (e) inflationary

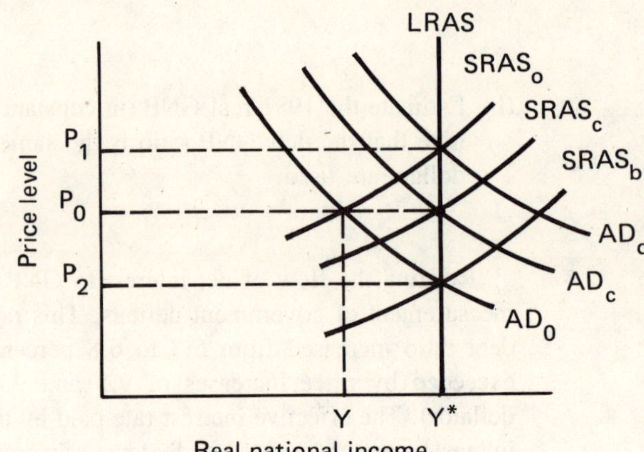

3. (a) \$200 billion (b) 4 (c) increased, \$50, recessionary (d) increasing, \$50 (e) decreasing, \$66.66 (f) increase, \$200

4.

Y	IBS	FBS
3,200	−117	−288
3,500	−60	−240
4,000	35	−160
4,200	73	−128
4,500	130	−80

On the diagram, the initial budget surplus line will intercept the O line at *Y* of 3,816 with slope of 0.19. The final budget line runs from (3,200, −288) to (4,500, −80) with a slope of 0.16.

(a) −60, −160
(b) 95, −128
(c) high employment, −163 (from 35 to −128)

5. The most plausible is modest shifts in *LRAS* and *SRAS* (lower prices on raw materials, etc.) and large shift in *AD* with changed fiscal stance outlined in Exercise 4. The recessionary gap has been reduced from 500 to 200 (Y_0Y_0* to Y_1Y_1*).

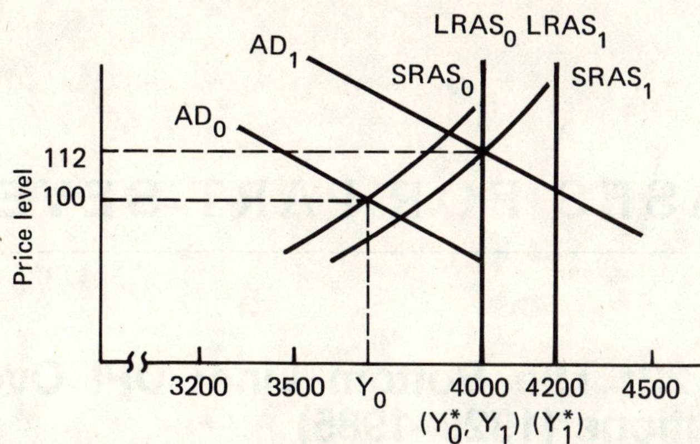

CASES FOR PART SEVEN

CASE 22: The Bottom Line: DPI Over Three Generations (1929–1985)

A current cliché is that what counts is the bottom line (presumably a reference to net income after taxes for a corporation). Its household counterpart could be considered the DPI (disposable personal income), although a purist could insist that at least necessary survival expenses should be deducted. Certainly politicians in the 1980s were talking about cutting personal income taxes, perhaps the fastest way of increasing DPI.

DPI is probably the most widely used of the national income concepts as a tool for forecasting consumer sales (using the measured income elasticities of Chapter 5).

The purpose of this problem is to allow you to see the sources of DPI for your grandparents and parents in their youth. Data are included for 1929, 1957, and 1985. One problem of comparability is the changing value of the dollar. You should be able to see how the applicable consumer price index was calculated from current- and constant-dollar GNP. The data are from the *Economic Report of the President* (1986).

	1929	1957	1985
DPI (billions)—current dollars	81.7	313.9	2,801.1
DPI (billions)—1982 dollars	498.6	1,012.1	2,509.0
DPI (per capita)–current dollars	671.0	1,833	11,727
DPI (per capita)—1982 dollars	4,091.0	5,909.0	10,504
Price index (1982 = 100)	16.4	31.0	111.6
Population (millions)	121.8	172.0	238.9
Employment (millions)	47.8	68.9	115.2
Population aged 16 and under (millions)	38.5	54.8	55.4

The following data give components and the disposition of DPI for these years, given as rounded-off percentages of personal income. Personal incomes were $84.3 billion, $356.3 billion, and $3,294.2 billion in the three years, respectively. Subcategories are in parentheses.

	1929	1957	1985		1929	1957	1985
Wages and salaries	60	67	60	Transfer payments	2	6	15
(commodity production)	(25)	(29)	(18)	(Social Security)	(0)	(1)	(8)
(in distribution)	(19)	(17)	(14)	(other)	(2)	(5)	(7)
(in services)	(10)	(9)	(16)	Less: personal contribution			
(in government)	(6)	(12)	(11)	to social security	–0	–2	–5
Other labor income	1	3	6	Personal income	100	100	100
Proprietors' income	17	14	7	Less: personal income taxes	–3	–11	–15
(farm)	(7)	(3)	(1)	Disposable personal income	97	89	85
(nonfarm)	(10)	(11)	(6)	Interest on consumer debt[a]	2	2	3
Property income	21	12	16	Consumer expenditure[a]	94	92	92
(rental)	(6)	(4)	(0)	Personal saving[a]	4	6	5
(dividends)	(7)	(3)	(2)				
(interest)	(8)	(5)	(14)				

[a]Percentages are of DPI.

Questions

1. The changes in total current-dollar DPI between 1929 and 1957 and between 1957 and 1985 can be resolved into three components: the change in real per capita DPI, the change in population, and the change in price level. What was the relative importance of each of these changes from 1929 to 1957 and from 1957 to 1985? Use the following format as an aid in working this out:

   (Population ratio 57/29 ______) × (Real per capita DPI ratio 57/29 ______)
   × (Price ratio 57/29 ______) = Current dollars DPI ratio 57/29 ______
   (Population ratio 85/57 ______) × (Real per capita DPI ratio 85/57 ______)
   × (Price ratio 85/57 ______) = Current dollars DPI ratio 85/57 ______

2. Real per capita DPI can rise for two reasons: income per employee can rise, and the proportion of the population employed can increase. Make the necessary computations to complete the table below and comment on the importance of each factor in explaining the rise in real DPI.

	(1) *Real DPI/ employment*	*(2)* *Employment/ population*		*(1) × (2) = Real DPI*		
1929	______	______	57/29	______	______	______
1957	______	______	85/57	______	______	______
1984	______	______				

3. What were the most significant changes in composition of DPI between 1929 and 1957 and between 1957 and 1985? What are current and future issues that you see for the composition and continued growth of per capita DPI?

CASE 23: Multipliers and the Marginal Propensity Not to Spend

The simple multiplier is defined as $1/(1 - z)$ where z is the marginal propensity to spend out of national income so that $(1 - z)$ is the marginal propensity not to spend. It is used to estimate the change in national income (ΔY) that will result from a change in autonomous expenditures (ΔA), by the relationship $\Delta Y = K \cdot \Delta A$ in which K is the multiplier. The concern of this case is to reconcile the apparently high multiplier suggested by consumption functions (with low marginal propensities to save) with a multiplier of about two that is more applicable to the U.S. economy. The method is to examine models of economies of increasing complexity in which the gaps between national income and disposable income become wider.

Economy A: Closed, Ungoverned, Without Business Savings

In this economy all income is disposable ($Y = Y_d$). Assume a marginal propensity to consume 0.9 out of income received by households for this and all subsequent models.

$1 - z =$ ________________ and the multiplier is ________________.

Economy B: Closed, Ungoverned, with Business Savings

In this economy it is assumed that firms do not distribute all of their income. Assume that business savings are $0.1Y$ so only $0.9Y$ is disposable income to households.

$1 - z =$ ________________ and the multiplier is ________________.

Economy C: Closed, Governed, with Business Savings

With government, another gap between Y_d and Y in the form of taxes is introduced. Whether such taxes are directly on personal income or not, they are usually related to income. With government transfer payments treated as negative taxes, we define T_n (net taxes) as taxes minus transfers and assume $T_n = 0.25Y$. Y_d now equals $Y - 0.1Y - 0.25Y$.

$1 - z =$ ________________ and the multiplier is ________________.

Economy D: Open, Governed with Business Savings

With trade opened up to foreign countries, not all expenditures will be made on domestically produced commodities. Assume that imports (M) $= 0.10Y$, and that the other deductions from Y still hold.

$1 - z =$ ________________ and the multiplier becomes ________________.

CASE 24: Investment Expenditures and Fluctuations in Economic Activity

The purpose of this case is to explore the relationship between investment and fluctuations in economic activity, and variability in the value of the multiplier.

The data in the table below are expressed in billions of 1982 dollars. The deltas (Δ) represent changes from the average of the year before: ΔGNP, gross national product; ΔGPDI, gross private domestic investment; ΔG, government expenditures on goods and services; and ΔX, exports. ΔA, autonomous expenditures, refers to the sum of ΔGPDI, ΔG, and ΔX which have been treated as the primary "autonomous" categories in previous chapters. The data are for the United States and are taken from the *Economic Report of the President, 1986*.

The use of average annual data dampens peaks and troughs since turning points can be designated for particular months: the upper turning points (peaks) were November 1973, January 1980, and July 1981; the lower turning points (troughs) were November 1970, March 1975, July 1980, and November 1982.

Year	(1) GNP	(2) ΔGNP	(3) GPDI	(4) ΔGPDI	(5) ΔX	(6) ΔG	(7) ΔA
1970	2416	—	382	—	—	—	______
1971	2485	69	419	37	1	–6	______
1972	2609	124	465	46	16	4	______
1973	2744	135	521	56	47	–6	______
1974	2729	–15	481	–40	27	8	______
1975	2695	–34	383	–98	–9	8	______
1976	2827	132	454	71	14	–1	______
1977	2959	132	521	67	8	9	______
1978	3115	156	577	56	31	15	______
1979	3192	77	575	–2	44	5	______
1980	3187	–5	509	–66	32	12	______
1981	3249	62	546	37	4	9	______
1982	3166	–83	447	–99	–31	12	______
1983	3278	112	503	56	–13	6	______
1984	3492	214	661	158	22	28	______
1985	3574	82	651	–10	–11	39	______

Questions

1. Concentrate on columns 2 and 4. What general relationships do you note between changes in real GNP and GPDI, in direction and in magnitude? To what extent can these be simply explained?

2. Measure the relative volatility of GNP and GPDI by establishing the range for each between the greatest percentage annual rise and decline for each. Why should this great difference exist?

3. In columns 5 and 6 are the changes in the other categories of autonomous expenditures: ΔG, government expenditures on goods and services, which had a maximum percentage increase of 5.8 percent from 1984 to 1985, and a maximum decline of 1.1 percent from 1970 to 1971; and ΔX, much more volatile with a 24.18 percent rise from 1972 to 1973 (with the booming grain exports) and a 1981–1982 decline of 7.9 percent. Sum columns 4, 5, and 6 to arrive at the total change (ΔA) in these autonomous expenditure categories.

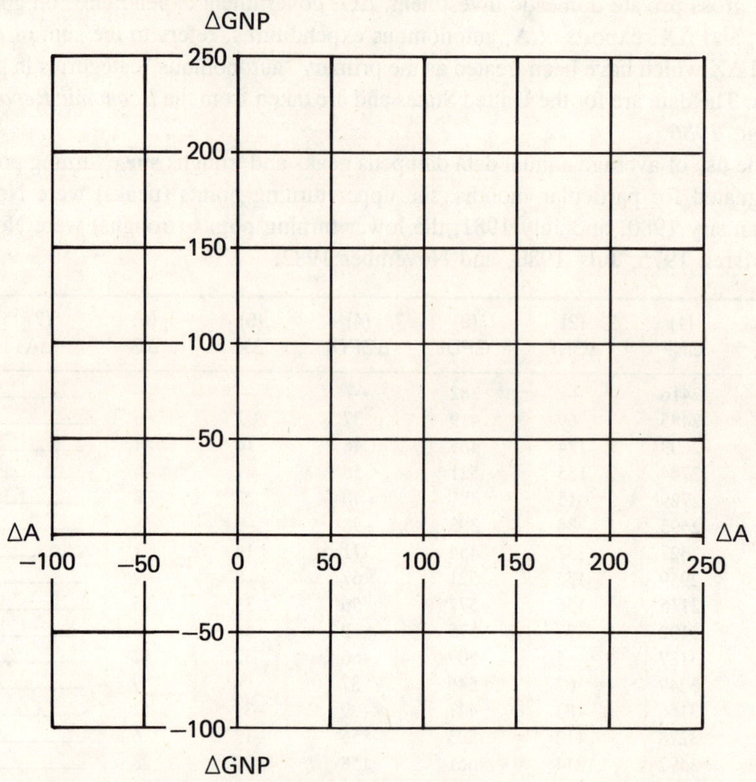

4. Plot the data from column 2 (ΔGNP) against column 7 (ΔA) as a scatter diagram. Draw a diagonal through the origin with a slope of +2. What could you conclude about the multiplier from your diagram?

5. From the diagram it can be seen that three of the years displayed multipliers of far less than 2 (1975, 1982, 1985).
   (a) In the recovery year of 1984 imports had a record increase of $88 billion. How would this affect the multiplier?

   (b) In the trough years of 1975 and 1982 transfer income showed unusually large increases. What aspect of fiscal policy does this illustrate?

CASE 25: How a Fiscal Shot in the Arm Would Work

This case represents a slice of economic history that remains relevant both for its similarities and its contrasts with the 1980s. The text analyzes the 1964 situation graphically in Box 30-4, which should serve as a reference.

Macroeconomic problems were less acute in the early 1960s: "creeping inflation" of a little over 1 percent a year in a period of wage-price guidelines and unemployment in the 5 to 6 percent range. The comparable figures in the late seventies and early eighties were double-digit inflation and unemployment of 5.5 to 7.5 percent. The biggest contrast, however, was in economic growth. Productivity in the late Eisenhower and Kennedy years was increasing by more than 3 percent a year while from 1978–1981 its annual change averaged close to zero. The arguments used by President Reagan for the personal income tax cut amounting to an average 23 percent over three years and the accelerated capital recovery system (ACRS) for business stressed lower marginal rates of taxation as incentives for increasing productivity and output.

Here is how the CEA in its *Economic Report* of 1964 described the way the gap of almost $30 billion between actual and potential national income would be closed by the 1964 tax cut. (Personal income tax rates were cut across the board from brackets of 18 to 91 percent to 14 to 70 percent. Corporate profit tax rates were cut from 30 to 22 percent of the first $25,000 and from 52 to 48 percent of the excess over $25,000.)

> The process by which an $11.1 billion tax cut can add as much as $30 billion to total demand has been frequently described and needs only to be summarized briefly here.
>
> If the new proposed personal income tax rates were in full effect today, disposable after-tax incomes of consumers would be approximately $8.8 billion higher than they are, at present levels of pretax incomes. In addition, if the lower corporate tax rates were now in effect, after-tax profits would be about $2.3 billion higher. Based on past dividend practice, one can assume that corporate dividends received by individuals (after deducting personal income taxes on such dividends) would then be more than $1 billion higher, giving a total increment of consumer after-tax incomes—at present levels of production—of about $10 billion.
>
> Since consumer spending on current output has remained close to 93 percent of disposable income in each of the past dozen years, one can safely project that consumer spending would rise by about 93 percent of the rise in disposable incomes, or by over $9 billion.
>
> But this is far from the end of the matter. The higher production of consumer goods to meet this extra spending would mean extra employment, higher payrolls, higher profits, and higher farm and professional and service incomes. This added purchasing power would generate still further increases in spending and incomes in an endless, but rapidly diminishing, chain. The initial rise of $9 billion, plus this extra consumption spending and extra output of consumer goods would add over $18 billion to our annual GNP—not just once, but year-in and year-out, since this is a permanent, not a one-shot, tax cut. We can summarize this continuing process by saying that a "multiplier" of approximately 2 has been applied to the direct increment of consumption spending.
>
> But that is not the end of the matter either. For the higher volume of sales, the higher productivity associated with fuller use of existing capacity and the lower tax rates on corporate profits also provided by the tax bill would increase after-tax profits, and especially the rate of expected after-tax profit on investment in new facilities. Adding to this the financial incentives embodied in last year's tax changes, which are yet to have their full effect, one can expect a substantial induced rise in business plant and equipment spending, and a rise in the rate of inventory investment. Further, higher consumer incomes will stimulate extra residential construction; and the higher revenues that state and local gov-

> ernments will receive under existing tax rates will prompt a rise in their investment in schools, roads, and urban facilities. The exact amount of each of these increases is hard to estimate with precision. But it is reasonable to estimate their sum as in the range of $5 to $7 billion. This extra spending would also be subject to a multiplier of 2 as incomes rose and consumer spending increased. Thus there would be a further expansion of $10 to $14 billion in GNP to add to the $18 billion or so from the consumption factor alone. The total addition to GNP would match rather closely the estimated $30 billion gap.

The tax cut worked very much as predicted. Later, inflationary difficulties came from the second shot in the arm, an increase of over $28 billion from 1965 to 1968 in federal defense expenditures mostly reflecting escalation of the Vietnam war.

Questions

1. Write the equation for the CEA's marginal propensity to consume out of disposable income.

2. The CEA assumes that the marginal propensity not to spend was what fraction of incremental incomes?

3. How could a reduction of corporate income tax rates result in an increase of disposable personal income?

4. Total increase in disposable income predicted from the tax cut is ________________. Total increase in consumer spending predicted initially from the tax cut is ________________. When multiplied it would add how much to national income? ________________

5. For what reason does the CEA also predict a rise in investment to occur?

6. Why does the CEA expect state and local governments to increase their spending?

7. Total anticipated increases from questions 5 and 6, when multiplied, are predicted to add how much to national income? ________________

8. Total rise in national income predicted from the tax cut is ________________.

9. Compare the situation in 1964 with that in 1981 (when the Reagan tax cuts were initiated), citing similarities and differences.

PART EIGHT

Money, Banking, and Monetary Policy

31

The Nature of Money and Monetary Institutions

Learning Objectives

Careful study of the material in this chapter should enable you to

—distinguish among the various functions of money;

—explain the historical development of fractionally backed paper money and fiat money;

—explain the process by which the banking system can create deposits, given an initial injection of new bank reserves;

—recognize a spectrum of liquid asset holdings and distinguish among various definitions of the money supply.

Review and Self-Test

Matching Concepts

_______ 1. expansion of loans

_______ 2. currency, demand deposits, and other checkable deposits

_______ 3. excess reserves

_______ 4. money's roles

_______ 5. interest-bearing deposits transferable by check

_______ 6. Gresham's law

_______ 7. liquid asset not generally accepted as a medium of exchange

_______ 8. Federal Reserve notes

_______ 9. form of money that involves transfers between banks

_______ 10. reserve requirements of less than 100 percent

(a) fiat money constituting most U.S. currency

(b) fractional reserve banking system

(c) driving of "good" money from circulation by "bad" money

(d) narrowest definition of money supply (M1)

(e) near money

(f) reserves permitting loans by commercial banks to create money

(g) automatic transfer and NOW accounts

(h) deposit money

(i) functions of a medium of exchange, store of value, and unit of account

(j) method by which commercial banks "create" deposits and thus increase the money supply

Multiple-Choice Questions

1. Which one of the following characteristics is unnecessary for money to serve as an efficient medium of exchange?
   (a) general acceptability
   (b) convertibility into precious metals
   (c) high value for its weight
   (d) divisibility

2. "Debasing" the coinage had the effect of
   (a) increasing the money supply, resulting in inflation.
   (b) reducing the price level.
   (c) increasing the purchasing power of each coin.
   (d) reducing aggregate demand.

3. A requirement for a gold standard was that
   (a) the price level be stable.
   (b) there be no paper money.
   (c) paper money be convertible into gold at a fixed price.
   (d) gold coinage be 100 percent of the money supply.

4. The value of money depends primarily on
   (a) the gold backing of the currency alone.
   (b) the gold backing of both currency and deposits.
   (c) its purchasing power.
   (d) who issues it.

5. Demand deposits are
   (a) part of M1.
   (b) part of M2.
   (c) part of M3.
   (d) all of the above

6. The most widely used form of money in the United States (measured by transaction dollars)
   (a) takes the form of demand and other checkable deposits.
   (b) is paper money with the status of legal tender.
   (c) is paper money that is valuable despite the fact that it is not legal tender.
   (d) is near money, such as time deposits and certificates of deposit.

7. The commercial banking system is distinct from investment banking in that it
   (a) lends the savings of the public to borrowers.
   (b) pays interest on funds deposited with it.
   (c) is subject to some government regulation.
   (d) creates and destroys money.

8. A commercial bank is able to create money by
   (a) printing it.
   (b) creating a demand deposit as it extends a new loan.
   (c) maintaining reserves.
   (d) issuing checks to its depositors.

9. The required reserves of a bank that is a member of the Federal Reserve System
   (a) are listed among the bank's liabilities.
   (b) consist of cash in its vault.
   (c) are kept at correspondent banks.
   (d) consist of cash in the vault and deposits in the Federal Reserve banks.

10. The process of creation of deposit money by commercial banks
    (a) is possible because of fractional reserve requirements.
    (b) is consciously undertaken by each bank.
    (c) always occurs if there are excess reserves.
    (d) permits only small, gradual changes in the supply of money.

11. For a monopoly bank with a required reserve ratio of 0.20, an additional deposit of $1,000 could result in a total increase in loans of
    (a) $5,000.
    (b) $1,000.
    (c) $4,000.
    (d) $8,000.

12. Suppose you cash a check for $500 at your bank and hold currency as a personal reserve. If the required reserve ratio is 0.20, what is the potential total effect on the money supply?
    (a) +$2,500
    (b) –$500
    (c) The money supply will not change.
    (d) –$2,000

13. One way that time deposits differ from demand deposits is that
    (a) advance warning must always be given before withdrawing money from time deposits.
    (b) time deposits are not considered very liquid assets.
    (c) demand deposits earn interest; time deposits do not.
    (d) time deposits usually cannot be drawn on by personal check (except for NOW accounts).

14. A government bond could fill one function of money by acting as a
    (a) medium of exchange.
    (b) store of wealth.
    (c) unit of account.
    (d) hedge against inflation.

15. The major components of the M1 measure of the U.S. money supply are
    (a) currency.
    (b) currency, demand deposits, and other checkable deposits.
    (c) currency, demand deposits, and all time deposits.
    (d) currency, demand deposits, and near money.

16. The definitions of M_2 and M_3 do not include
    (a) certificates of deposit (CDs).
    (b) savings accounts.
    (c) money market deposit accounts (MMDAs).
    (d) government securities maturing within one year.

17. A rise of the Consumer Price Index from 300 to 330 would change the store of value represented by $1,000 in currency to
    (a) $1,100.
    (b) $700.
    (c) $910.
    (d) $1,000 (no change).

18. If one dollar is added to a bank's reserves, and the required reserve ratio is 0.20, the money supply can eventually be increased by several dollars because
    (a) the bank can use its new reserves to purchase government bonds that it can then sell to the public for a profit.
    (b) the bank can make $.80 in new loans; this will create new reserves of $.80 in another bank, which in turn can lend $.64, and so on.
    (c) the bank can create $5 of new deposit money by making loans.
    (d) the bank can issue new loans of $4, which creates excess reserves for other banks.

Self-Test Key

Matching Concepts: 1–j; 2–d; 3–f; 4–i; 5–g; 6–c; 7–e; 8–a; 9–h; 10–b

Multiple-Choice Questions: 1–b; 2–a; 3–c; 4–c; 5–d; 6–a; 7–d; 8–b; 9–d; 10–a; 11–c; 12–d; 13–d; 14–b; 15–b; 16–d; 17–c; 18–b

Exercises

1. Indicate which of the three functions of money is demonstrated in the following transactions. Use the appropriate number: medium of exchange (1); store of value (2); unit of account (3).
   (a) Farmer Brown puts cash in a mattress. ______
   (b) Storekeeper Brown adds up the total sales for the day. ______
   (c) Banker Brown uses some of the bank's reserves to buy government bonds. ______
   (d) Traveling salesperson Brown uses a credit card to buy gas for the car. ______
   (e) The Browns buy a good oriental rug with the thought that it will keep its value for a long time. ______

2. Suppose that the reserve ratio is 0.20 and that a commercial bank has reserves of $22 million, loans of $88 million, and demand deposits of $110 million. The bank is a member of the Federal Reserve System.
   (a) Excess reserves are $______.
   (b) This bank, being a single bank in a multibank system, can safely lend an additional $______.
   Assume now that the Fed lowers the required reserve ratio to 0.15.
   (c) This bank, being a single bank in a multibank system, can safely lend an additional ______.
   (d) If this were a monopoly bank, it could safely lend up to a maximum in new loans of ______.
   (e) In either case, it is now possible for the money supply to increase by a total of ______.

3. Which of the following might be regarded as "money," which as "near money," and which as neither? Briefly explain your answers.
   (a) a share of stock in General Motors ______
   (b) the ounce of gold in a 1986 American $50 gold coin ______
   (c) a $2 Federal Reserve note ______
   (d) a bank note dated 1867 ______
   (e) one pound of prime northern duck down ______
   (f) a savings account ______
   (g) a U.S. Treasury bill for $10,000 due in one month ______

4. Arrange the following items on the proper side of the balance sheet below.

(a) demand deposits	$5,000,000
(b) time deposits	1,000,000
(c) cash in vault	60,000
(d) reserve deposits with Federal Reserve	1,000,000
(e) loans to public	4,000,000
(f) security holdings: U.S. government, state, municipal, and other	1,500,000
(g) banking house and fixtures	500,000
(h) capital and surplus	550,000
(i) other liabilities	500,000
(j) borrowing from other banks	10,000

Assets	*Liabilities*

5. We use T-accounts (abbreviated balance sheets) to show changes in a bank's reserves, loans, and deposits. Make the entries on the T-account below, using + and – signs to show increase and decrease, for each of the following independent events. Under the column labeled M_s, indicate whether the money supply has increased (+), decreased (–), or remained unchanged (U).

	Assets	*Liabilities*	M_s
(a) You cash a check for $100 at your bank.	Reserves: Loans and securities:	Deposits:	
(b) A commercial bank sells $10,000 of government bonds in the market to replenish its reserves.	Reserves: Loans and securities:	Deposits:	
(c) A commercial bank makes a loan of $5,000 to a local business and credits its checking account.	Reserves: Loans and securities:	Deposits:	
(d) A member bank borrows $50,000 from its Federal Reserve bank to restore reserves to the required level.	Reserves: Loans and securities:	Deposits: Borrowing:	
(e) A business uses $5,000 of its demand deposit to pay off a loan from the same bank.	Reserves: Loans and securities:	Deposits:	
(f) A member bank orders $5,000 in currency from the Federal Reserve Bank.	Reserves: Loans and securities:	Deposits:	

Short Problems

1. Are MMDAs and MMFs Money?

Money market mutual funds (MMFs) originated in the mutual fund industry in 1973 and spread to other nonbank financial institutions such as stockbrokers. The rapid growth in money market funds serving individuals occurred between 1977 (assets: $2.4 billion) and 1981 (assets: $150.6 billion). In December 1985, total assets in funds serving individuals were $175.8 billion.*

Commercial and savings banks gained permission to offer MMDAs (money market deposit accounts) in 1982. They grew explosively from $43.2 billion in December 1982 to $509 billion in December 1985.

A comparison of typical rules and terms is as follows:

	MMFs	MMDAs
Accounts denominated in	Shares valued at $1	Dollar amounts
Initial investment	$500 to $2,500	$2,500
Minimum balance for full interest	None	$2,500
Federal deposit insurance	No	Yes
Investment fee charge	0.5 percent annually on balance	None specified
Checking restrictions	$100 minimum (no withdrawals on last two weeks' deposits)	Three per month (but no limit on transfers to other accounts or cash)

The MMFs have typically paid a fraction of a percent greater interest than the MMDAs and the rates paid are typically the same as those in other short-term financial markets less a charge of about 0.5 percent to cover the investment fee and other expenses. For practical purposes, each MMF share has been equivalent to $1 since capital losses or gains on their very short-run investments such as commercial paper have been negligible.

Questions

(a) What prevents MMDAs and MMFs from being primary money (M1)?

(b) What features of money do they clearly possess (that make them M2)?

(c) Why may MMDAs have done so well in competition with MMFs? (Think of how you might arrange your own future liquidity.)

*Text Table 31-9 lists this category as money market mutual balances (MMMBs).

2. The purpose of this problem, for which text Table 31-9 is a good reference, is to familiarize you with the variety of money-like instruments and with current monetary jargon. Label each item M1, M2, M3, or L (liquid assets). Use only one label even though an M1 item would also be in each broader category.

(a) overnight RPs	______	(e) traveler's checks	______
(b) OCDs	______	(f) commercial paper	______
(c) MMDAs	______	(g) demand deposits	______
(d) institutional MMMFs	______	(h) currency	______

Answers to the Exercises

1. (a) 2 (b) 3 (c) 1 (d) 3 now; 1 when debt is repaid
   (e) 1; and the rug serves as function 2

2. (a) 0 (b) 0 (c) \$5.5 million (d) \$5.5/.15 = \$36.7 million (e) \$36.7 million

3. (a) neither, but a relatively liquid asset subject to price fluctuations
   (b) neither, because of nominal fixed denomination, but readily convertible to money and considered by many a superior store of value in inflationary times
   (c) money
   (d) neither; once money, but now a collector's item
   (e) neither, but it clearly has market value
   (f) close to money, and many regard time deposits as money (see M2 definition)
   (g) near money (highly liquid included in "L," a broader definition of liquidity than M3)

4. Assets: (c), (d), (e), (f), (g); total = \$7,060,000
   Liabilities: (a), (b), (h), (i), (j); total = \$7,060,000

5. (a) reserves, –100; deposits, –100; M_s, U
   (b) securities, –10,000; reserves, +10,000; M_s, U
   (c) loans, +5,000; deposits, +5,000; M_s, +
   (d) borrowing, +50,000; reserves, +50,000; M_s, U
   (e) deposits, –5,000; loans, –5,000; M_s, –
   (f) total reserves unchanged; cash in vault; +5,000; reserve deposits with Federal Reserve bank, –5,000; M_s, U

32

The Role of Money in Macroeconomics

Learning Objectives

Careful study of the material in this chapter should enable you to

—explain the demand for money (liquidity preference) as a function of interest rates, income, and the price level;

—distinguish between real and nominal money balances;

—recognize the three stages in transmitting the effects of money supply changes to aggregate demand: monetary equilibrium to the interest rate to investment expenditures to aggregate demand;

—explain why the effectiveness of monetary and fiscal policies depends on the liquidity preference and marginal efficiency of investment elasticities.

Review and Self-Test

Matching Concepts

______ 1. quantity of money demanded

______ 2. desire for holding money balances because of the nonsynchronization of payments and receipts

______ 3. speculative motive

______ 4. function relating demand for money to the rate of interest

______ 5. monetary equilibrium

______ 6. effect of excess demand for money in monetary market

______ 7. a rise in the price level that raises the demand for money

______ 8. final effect of decrease in money supply

______ 9. inelastic *LP* function and elastic *MEI* function

______ 10. elastic *LP* function and inelastic *MEI* function

______ 11. validation of inflation

(a) increase of money supply at same rate as price level in presence of inflationary gap

(b) rise in interest rates

(c) liquidity preference

(d) reason for negative relation between price level and equilibrium real GNP

(e) factors that give fiscal policy a large effect on aggregate demand

(f) money balances people wish to hold

(g) decrease in aggregate demand

(h) desire for holding money balances that varies inversely with interest rates

(i) equality of demand and supply of money

(j) factors that give monetary policy a large effect on aggregate demand

(k) transactions motive

Multiple-Choice Questions

1. If the current price of a long-term bond falls, the yield (effective rate of interest) on the bond will
   (a) fall.
   (b) rise.
   (c) equal the new price of the bond.
   (d) not be affected.

2. The amount of money held for transactions balances will
   (a) vary in the same direction as national income measured in current prices.
   (b) vary in the same direction as interest rates.
   (c) vary inversely with the value of national income.
   (d) be larger with shorter intervals between paydays.

3. Precautionary balances would be expected to increase if
   (a) business conditions were to become much less certain.
   (b) interest rates increased.
   (c) people were expecting securities prices to rise.
   (d) prices and incomes fell.

4. The speculative motive for desiring to hold money balances
   (a) applies to bonds, but not to other interest-earning assets.
   (b) varies directly with national income.
   (c) assumes that the opportunity cost of holding cash balances is zero.
   (d) is based on the expectation that interest rates will rise, lowering the price of securities.

5. If there is an excess supply of money, households and firms will
   (a) sell bonds and add to their holdings of money, thereby causing the interest rate to fall.
   (b) purchase bonds and reduce their holdings of money, thereby causing the interest rate to rise.
   (c) purchase bonds and reduce their holdings of money, thereby causing the price of bonds to rise and interest rates to fall.
   (d) purchase bonds and reduce their holdings of money, thereby causing the price of bonds to fall.

6. A fall in the interest rate will cause
   (a) a shift in the *MEI* function to the left.
   (b) a shift in the *MEI* function to the right.
   (c) a movement down the *MEI* function.
   (d) a movement up the *MEI* function.

7. Changes in interest rates caused by monetary disequilibrium
   (a) are usually of little consequence in influencing economic activity.
   (b) provide the link between changes in the money supply and changes in aggregate demand.
   (c) cause the liquidity preference function to shift, thus affecting desired investment expenditures.
   (d) cause a change in the money supply, thereby affecting interest-sensitive expenditures.

8. The movement from excess demand for money balances to monetary equilibrium
   (a) tends to increase aggregate demand.
   (b) has an unpredictable effect on aggregate demand.
   (c) tends to decrease aggregate demand.
   (d) will have no effect on aggregate demand.

9. If the Fed creates monetary disequilibrium by supplying more reserves to banks,
   (a) interest rates will fall and aggregate expenditures rise, tending to increase aggregate demand.
   (b) interest rates will rise and aggregate expenditures fall, tending to decrease aggregate demand.
   (c) interest rates will be unaffected but desired consumption expenditures will rise, causing an increase in aggregate demand.
   (d) no effect on aggregate demand is to be expected.

10. A given change in the money supply will exert a larger effect on national income
    (a) the more elastic the *LP* function and the more inelastic the *MEI* function.
    (b) the more elastic both the *LP* and the *MEI* functions are.
    (c) the more inelastic both the *LP* and the *MEI* functions are.
    (d) the more inelastic the *LP* function and the more elastic the *MEI* function.

11. A decrease in the money supply will cause the
    (a) *AE* function to shift upward.
    (b) *LP* function to shift leftward.
    (c) *AD* and *AE* functions to shift downward.
    (d) *AE* function to shift downward, but the *AD* curve will be unaffected.

12. A rise in the price level, other things being equal, will tend to shift the aggregate expenditure function downward because of
    (a) reduced demand for money balances.
    (b) a rise in the demand for money balances which increases interest rates.
    (c) an excess supply of money balances which decreases interest rates.
    (d) the fact that interest rates will fall.

13. The monetary adjustment mechanism will eliminate an inflationary gap by
    (a) raising interest rates, reducing desired expenditure, and increasing aggregate expenditure.
    (b) lowering interest rates, increasing desired expenditure, and increasing aggregate expenditure.
    (c) raising interest rates, reducing desired expenditure, and moving leftward along the aggregate demand curve.
    (d) raising interest rates, reducing desired expenditure, and shifting the aggregate demand curve.

14. An implication of the monetary adjustment mechanism is that
    (a) an inflation will tend to accelerate regardless of changes in the supply of money.
    (b) deflationary and inflationary gaps will cancel each other over the long run.
    (c) an inflation will tend to be self-correcting unless the money supply increases as fast as prices rise.
    (d) price level changes cause automatic changes in the money supply.

15. The present value of any asset maturing at some future date
    (a) is negatively related to the interest rate.
    (b) is positively related to the interest rate.
    (c) depends entirely on the maturity date rather than the interest rate.
    (d) will be greater for a later maturity date, other things equal.

16. The *MEI* function is a relation between interest rates and
    (a) the capital stock.
    (b) desired investment expenditure.
    (c) real national income at which $AE = Y$.
    (d) the quantity of money demanded.

17. The crowding-out effect will be smaller
    (a) the steeper the *MEI* curve and the flatter the *LP* curve.
    (b) the flatter the *MEI* curve and the steeper the *LP* curve.
    (c) the flatter both the *LP* and *MEI* curves.
    (d) the steeper both the *LP* and *MEI* curves.

Appendix

18. With a contractionary fiscal policy, the
    (a) *IS* curve shifts to the right.
    (b) *LM* curve shifts to the right.
    (c) *LM* curve shifts to the left.
    (d) *IS* curve shifts to the left.

19. If the money supply increases, the
    (a) *LM* curve shifts to the left.
    (b) *LM* curve shifts to the right.
    (c) *IS* curve shifts to the left.
    (d) *IS* curve shifts to the right.

20. For a given *LM* curve, if the *IS* curve shifts to the right
    (a) interest rates and real national income will fall.
    (b) interest rates will rise, real national income will fall.
    (c) interest rates and real national income will rise.
    (d) the money supply will rise causing interest rates to fall but real national income to rise.

Self-Test Key

Matching Concepts: 1–f; 2–k; 3–h; 4–c; 5–i; 6–b; 7–d; 8–g; 9–j; 10–e; 11–a

Multiple-Choice Questions: 1–b; 2–a; 3–a; 4–d; 5–c; 6–c; 7–b; 8–c; 9–a; 10–d; 11–c; 12–b; 13–c; 14–c; 15–a; 16–b; 17–a; 18–d; 19–b; 20–c

Exercises

1. Below are three hypothetical liquidity preference (*LP*) curves representing the demand for money balances at various rates of interest, other things being equal.

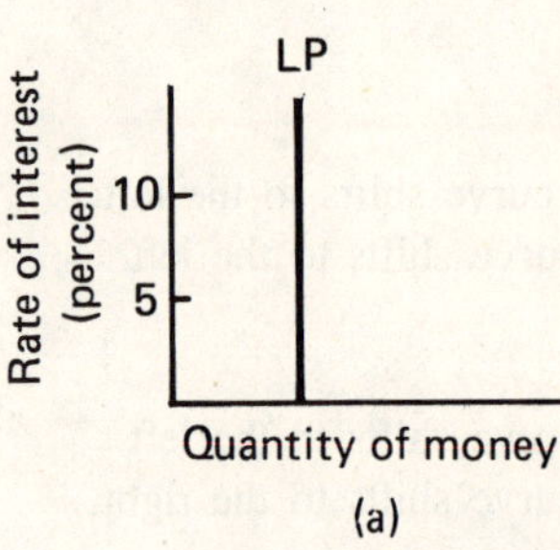

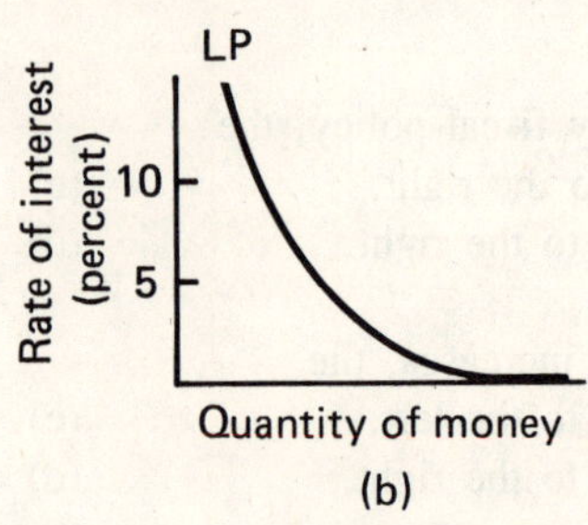

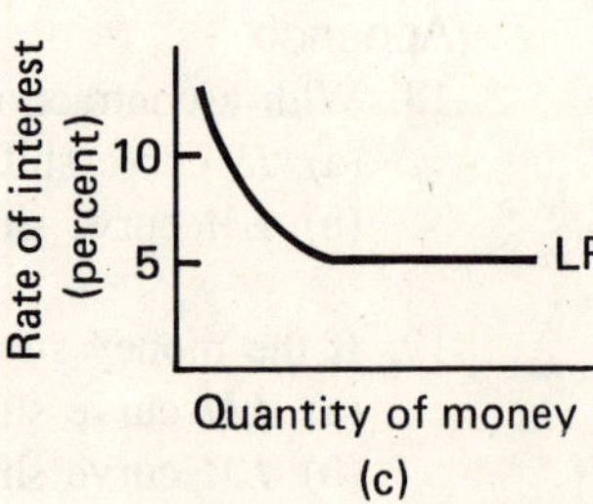

   (a) Which curve could best represent the transactions demand for money? _______
   (b) Which curve seems to ignore the transactions demand for money? _______
   (c) Which curve could best represent willingness to convert cash into securities at small increases in interest rates, when $i > 5$ percent? _______ when $i < 5$ percent? _______
   (d) Which curve shows no apparent relationship to the rate of interest? _______ What is the position of this curve related to? _______
   (e) If the central authorities wished to force interest rates to low levels, which curve would thwart them? _______

2. Explain and illustrate graphically each of the following:
   (a) Monetary disequilibrium: Illustrate an excess demand for money and predict the effect on interest rates.

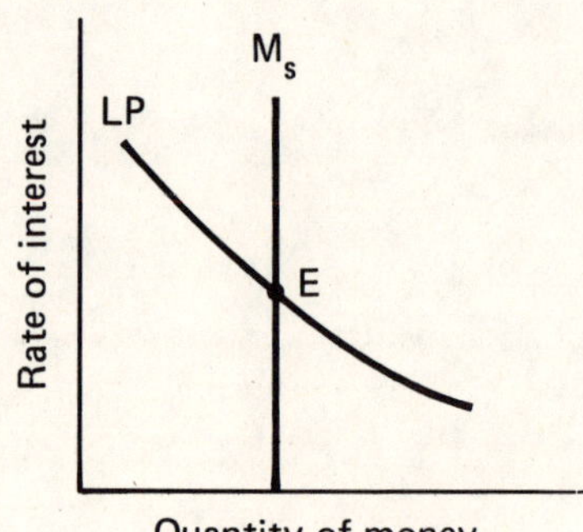

(b) Monetary disequilibrium: Illustrate an excess supply of money and predict the effect on interest rates.

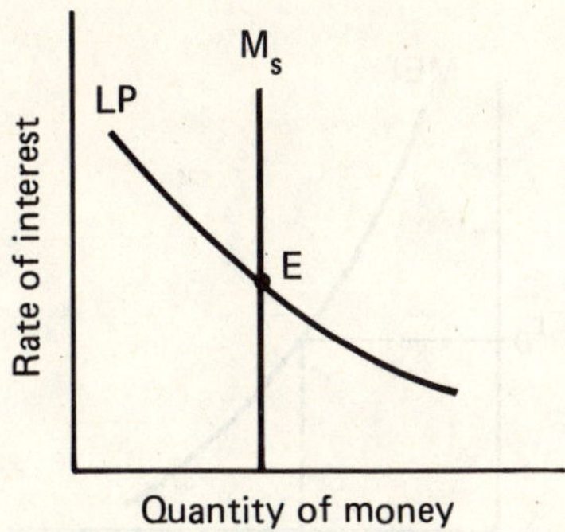

(c) Predict the effect of an increase in the money supply (by the Fed) on the rate of interest and desired investment expenditure. Initial equilibrium is M_0, r_0, E_0, and I_0.

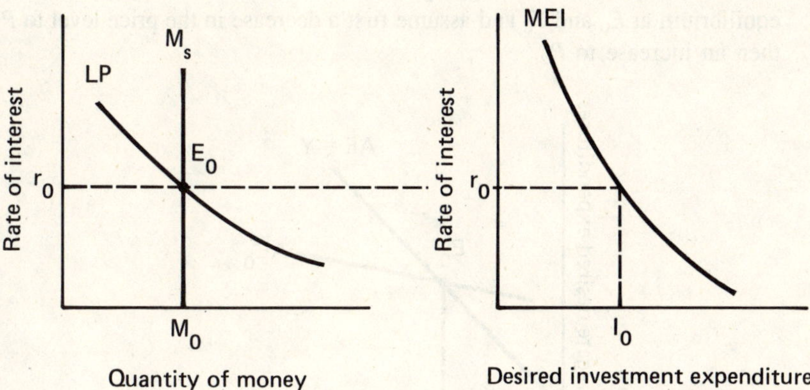

(d) Show the effect of an increase in desired expenditure on the equilibrium level of real national income. Initial equilibrium is E_0 on both diagrams.

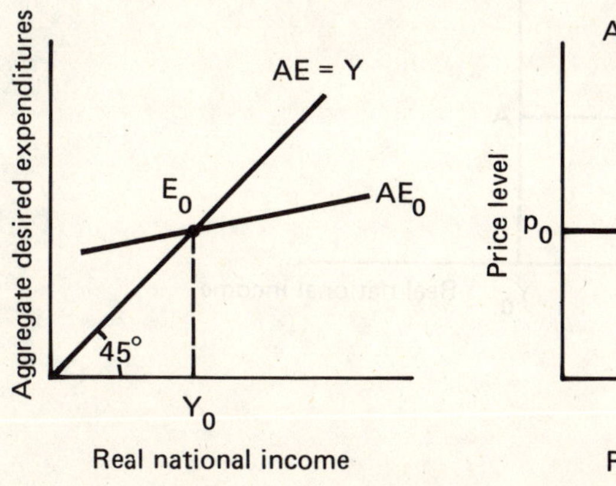

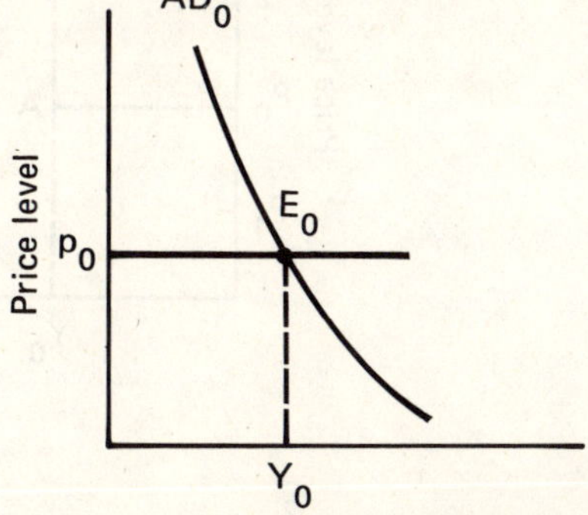

(e) Show the effect of an increase in the price level, *ceteris paribus*, on the rate of interest and investment expenditure. Start from equilibrium at E_0, r_0, and I_0.

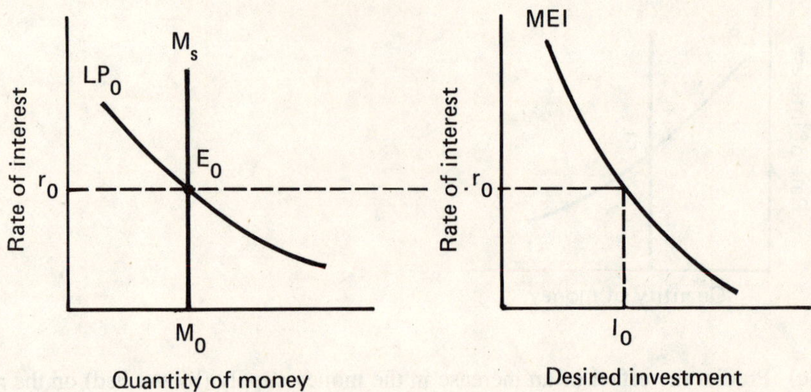

(f) Show and explain how the aggregate demand curve (*AD*) is derived. Start from equilibrium at E_0 and Y_0 and assume first a decrease in the price level to P_1 and then an increase to P_2.

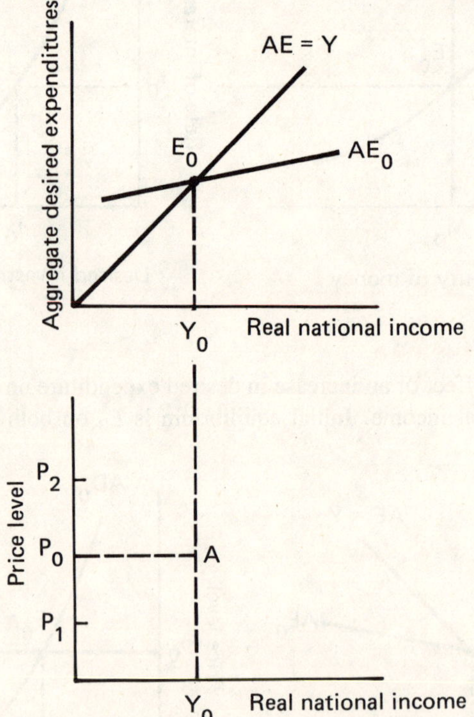

3. Here are two hypothetical marginal efficiency of investment curves.
   (a) With which schedule, MEI_1 or MEI_2, would a reduction in rates of interest encourage a greater amount of additional investment? ________
   (b) Which schedule would better represent the views of those who believe that the amount of investment is not affected very much by changes in rates of interest? ________

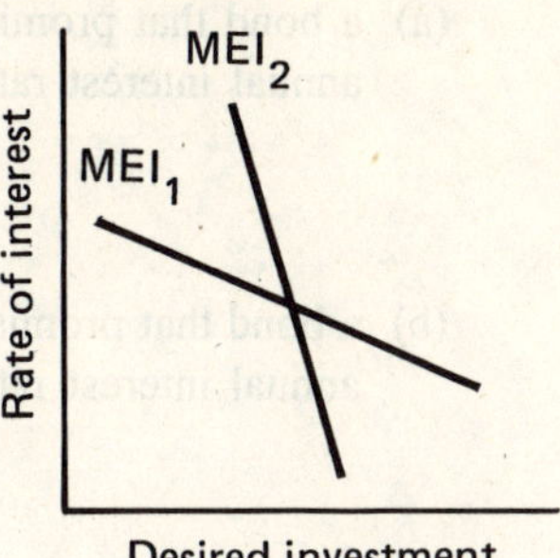

4. Calculate the present value for each of the following assets:
   (a) a bond that promises to pay $100 3 years from now and which has a constant annual interest rate of 2 percent

   (b) a bond that promises to pay $100 two years from now and which has a constant annual interest rate of 6 percent

   (c) a perpetuity that pays $100 a year and which has an interest rate of 17 percent

   (d) an investment that pays $100 after one year, $150 after two years, and $80 after three years and which has an annual interest rate of 10 percent

5.

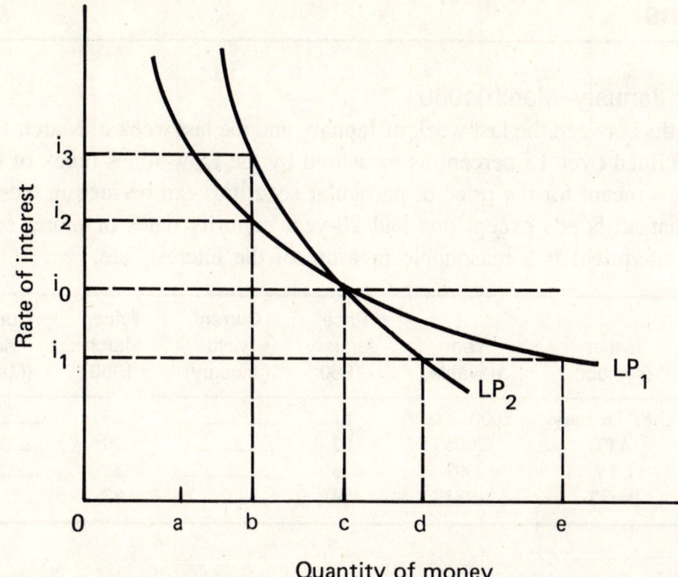

(a) (i) For which *LP* function do specified changes in the money supply have the greatest effect on the interest rate? ______

(ii) If i_0 is taken as the initial interest rate, what supply of money would be needed to produce i_1 for LP_2? ______ For LP_1? ______

(iii) If the money supply is cut from *oc* to *ob*, what will be the interest rate for LP_2? ______ For LP_1? ______

(b) Which *LP* curve does the text associate with the monetarist view? ______ With the Keynesian view? ______

(c) Consider the transactions, precautionary and speculative motives for holding money to explain the downward slopes of the alternative *LP* functions shown. Do LP_2 and LP_1 place a different emphasis on these motives?

Short Problems

1. A Bond Bust: January–March 1980

In the two months between the last week of January and the last week of March 1980, bond prices declined over 15 percent as measured by the Dow-Jones index of bond prices. What this meant for the price of particular securities can be seen in the table below. Note that all bonds except one had 20-year maturity dates or more, so the current yield (rate/price) is a reasonable measure of the interest rate.

Rate (dollars per year)	Issuer (symbol)	Year payable	Price, January 1980	Current yield (January)	Price, March 1980	Current yield (March)
8.25	U.S. Treasury	2000–2005	81	______	67	______
8.80	ATT	2005	82	______	70	______
11.00	LTV	2007	76	______	58	______
3.50	PacTT	1981	89	______	87	______

Key economic circumstances associated with this "bond bust" were an increase in the rate of inflation with the CPI rising in the first quarter at about a 20 percent annual rate as compared with under 13 percent for 1979, and substantial monetary restraint; the money supply (Ml) declined by 3.8 percent in the first quarter of 1980.

Questions

(a) (i) What were the changes in interest rates received on these particular bonds? Approximate them by filling in the current yield column.

(ii) Why are these current yields good approximations of interest received for the first three bonds and very poor ones for the Pacific T & T bond? How does this illustrate the chapter's statement that "the longer the term to maturity the greater the change in bond price for a given change in the interest rate"?

(b) What effect would the increase in the rate of inflation have on the transactions demand for money? Combined with a slight decline in the supply of money, show the probable effect on interest rates (and bond prices) diagrammatically.

(c) According to *Fortune* (July 14, 1980), "the Spring of 1980 will long be remembered as the time the U.S. economy fell off a cliff." It referred to the 9 to 10 percent annual rate of decline in national income that took place in the second quarter. Is such a real decline in income following a sharp rise in interest rates consistent with the discussion of this chapter? Is it consistent with the fact that total new borrowing by all sectors (households, corporations, and government) dropped from 16 to 8 percent of GNP in the second quarter of 1980?

(d) During the first few months of 1980 the financial press made frequent references to the "high liquidity," "large cash positions," and "many uncommitted funds" of large institutional investors. This liquidity meant that they chose near-money and short-term assets such as treasury certificates and certificates of deposit that were yielding high interest for days, weeks, or months, not years. Why should the "speculative demand" for money be increased by the perceptions of higher inflation rates and the probability of monetary restraint?

2. The Crowding-Out Effect

Suppose that the federal government decides to increase its expenditures by $500 million permanently. The price level and foreign exchange rates are assumed constant. The marginal propensity to spend is 0.5, potential national income is $151 billion, and current equilibrium national income is $150 billion.

(a) What is the size of the recessionary gap?

(b) The government assumes that the interest rate will not change due to its policy change. If this assumption is correct, will the increase in G eliminate the gap?

(c) In fact, suppose that the demand for money equation is given by the expression $D_M = 0.8Y - 2i$, where Y stands for national income and i represents the level of the interest rate (in percentage terms). If the current money supply is $100 billion and $Y = 150$, solve for the level of i assuming the money market is in equilibrium.

(d) If the government's policy raised real national income to $151 billion, what would be the effect on the level of the interest rate?

(e) Suppose you know that every increase in the interest rate of 0.1 decreased desired investment expenditures by $125 million. Given your answer to part (d), what is the total effect on desired investment expenditures?

(f) Instead of the relationship given in (e), suppose that for every increase in the interest rate of 0.1, investment expenditure fell by $25 million. Given your answer to part (d), what is the total effect on desired investment expenditure now?

(g) What is the extent of the crowding-out effect in part (e). Part (f)? Which result is most likely to reflect the monetarist view?

3. (Assumes reading of Appendix to Chapter 32.) The advantage of the *LM–IS* analysis is that the curves together show the one combination of real national income and interest rate that satisfy both the goods market equilibrium and the monetary equilibrium simultaneously.
   (a) To illustrate: show the effect of the increase in the money supply on national income using *LM–IS* analysis [this is the event taken up in Exercise 2(c) and 2(d)].
   (b) Now go back to Exercise 2(c) and consider what the increase in national income shown above would do to the *LP* curve; consider how this would have modified your prediction about desired investment and real income [in 2(d)].

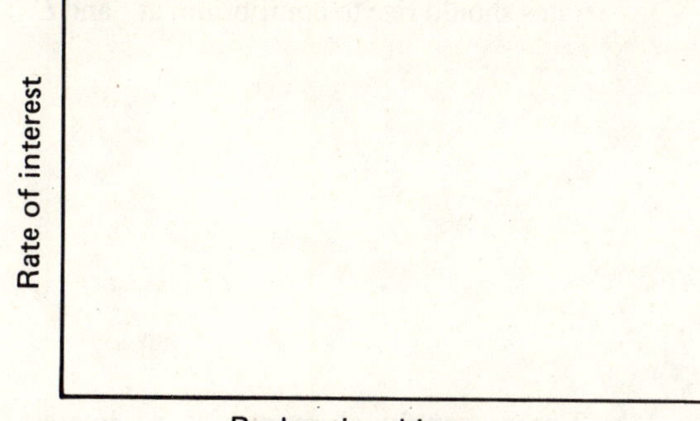

   (c) (i) Which approach more precisely predicts results when there is feedback between events in the monetary and goods markets? ______________
   (ii) Which approach more clearly shows the steps by which a result is reached while being qualitatively accurate in its predictions? ______________

Answers to the Exercises

1. (a) a (b) c (c) c, b (d) a; national income (e) c

2. (a) Excess demand for money at r_0; interest rates should rise to equilibrium at r and E.

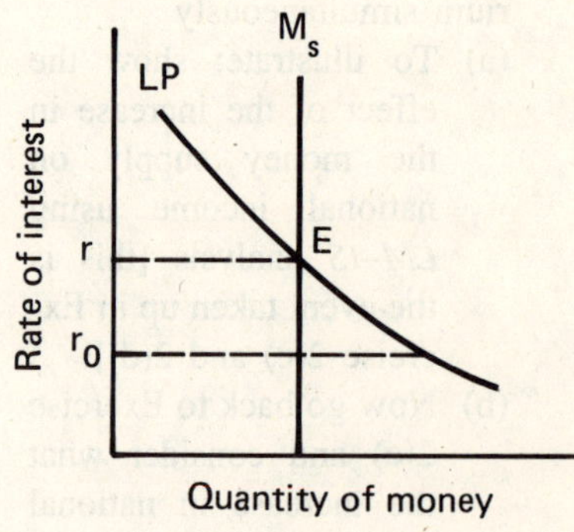

(b) Excess supply of money at r_0; interest rates should fall to equilibrium at r and E.

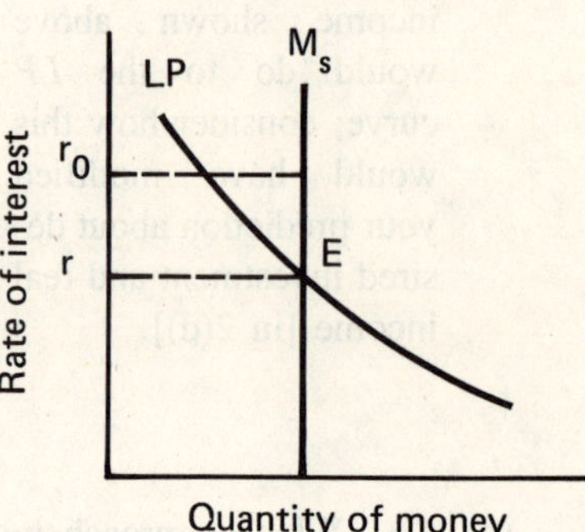

(c) Interest rate drops from r_0 to r_1; investment expenditures rise from I_0 to I_1.

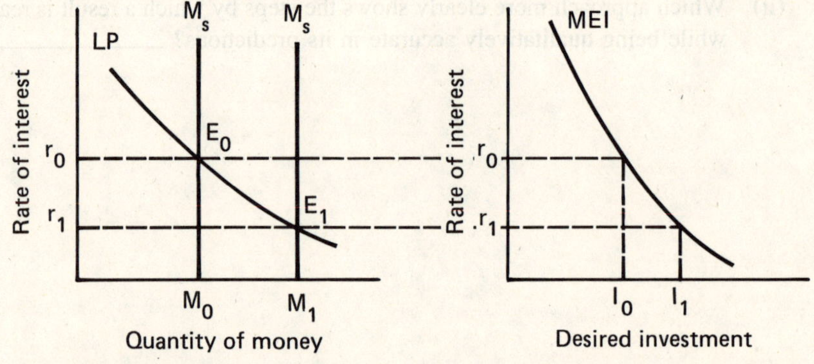

(d) Upward shift in AE caused by more desired expenditure, also shifting AD outward; equilibrium income rises from Y_0 to Y_1.

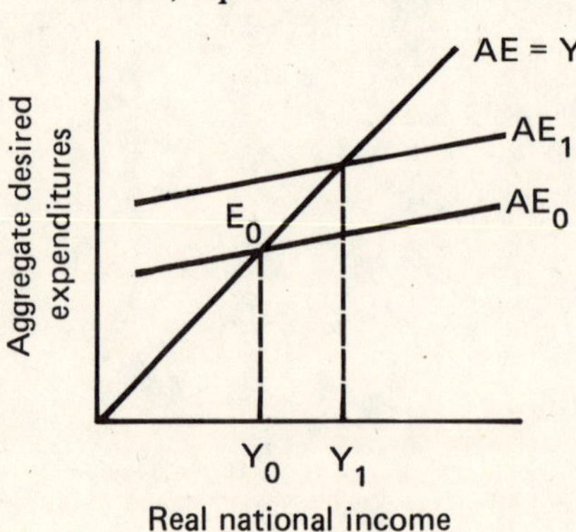

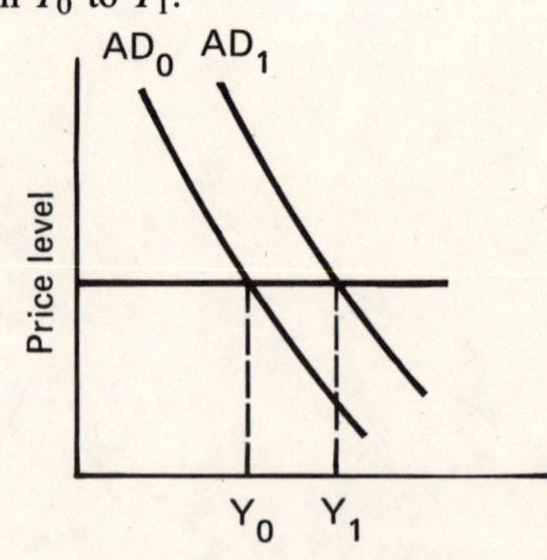

(e) An increase in the price level increases demand for money (for transactions purposes primarily) from LP_0 to LP_1; this raises interest rates from r_0 to r_1 and lowers investment from I_0 to I_1.

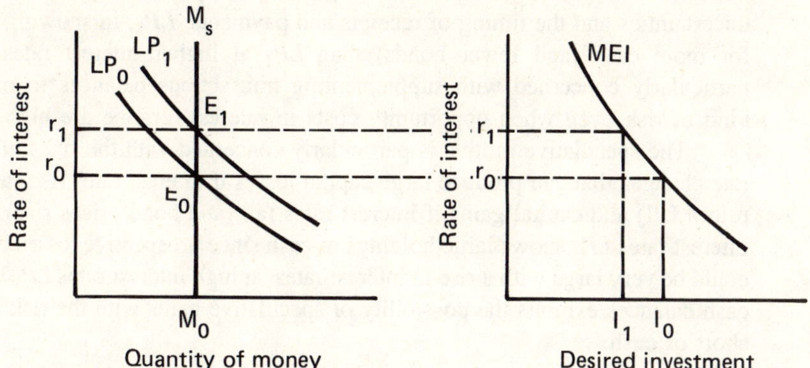

(f) A decrease in the price level to p_1 increases the desired level of aggregate expenditure from AE to AE_1, raising equilibrium income to Y_1 and to point B on AD curve. An increase in price level to p_2 shifts AE_0 to AE_2, with equilibrium income to Y_2, yielding point C on AD. Connecting the points generates an AD curve.

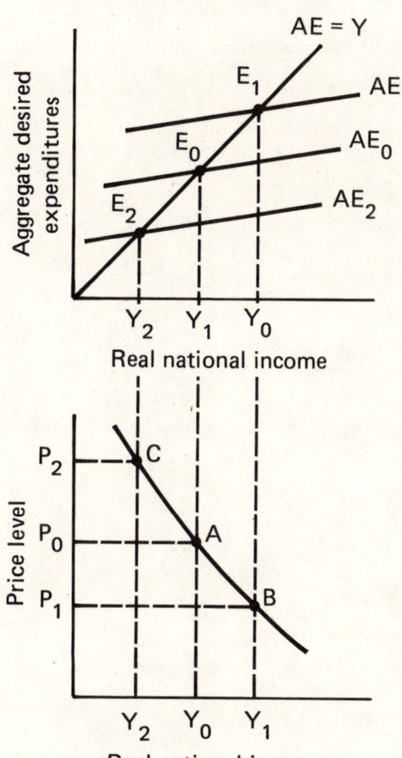

3. (a) MEI_1 (b) MEI_2

4. (a) PV = $\$100/(1 + 0.02)^3 = \$94.23$
(b) PV = $\$100/(1 + 0.06)^2 = \$89$
(c) PV = $\$100/0.17 = \$588.24$
(d) PV = $\$100/(1.10) + \$150/(1.10)^2 + \$80/(1.10)^3$
PV = $\$90.91 + \$123.97 + \$60.11 = \$274.99$

5. (a) (i) LP_2 (ii) *od*; *oe*; (iii) i_3; i_2
   (b) LP_2; LP_1
   (c) Both curves suggest that *oa* is minimum needed to satisfy the motive for transactions balances. The precautionary motive is particularly concerned with uncertainties and the timing of receipts and payments. LP_2, in showing a desire for more cash (and fewer bonds) than LP_1 at higher interest rates, seems particularly concerned with supplementing transactions balances to meet this kind of risk even when opportunity costs in interest forgone are high.

   The speculative motive is particularly concerned with the risks of interest rate changes that can produce large capital losses if interest rates rise (and bond prices fall) and capital gains if interest rates fall (and bond prices rise). At low interest rates LP_1 shows large holdings of cash since prospective losses on bonds could be very large with a rise in interest rates; at high interest rates LP_1 with low cash balances exhibits the possibility of speculative gains with the risk of being short of cash.

33

Monetary Policy

Learning Objectives

Careful study of the material in this chapter should enable you to

—understand the functions of a central bank;

—describe the policy instruments of the Federal Reserve system: open market operations, the discount rate, and reserve requirements;

—analyze the impact of changes in these three major policy instruments of the Fed;

—explain the distinctions among policy variables, policy instruments, and intermediate targets;

—recognize the advantages and drawbacks of monetary rules and targets.

Review and Self-Test

Matching Concepts

______ 1. major monetary policy variables

______ 2. instrumental variables

______ 3. group within the Fed that actually determines day-to-day monetary policy

______ 4. purchase of bonds by the Fed

______ 5. sale of government securities by the Fed

______ 6. expansion of the money supply at a constant rate

______ 7. Trcasury-Federal Reserve accord (1951)

______ 8. discount rate

______ 9. fraction of demand and time deposits that a commercial bank must hold in reserve

______ 10. removal of regulations limiting interest rates on deposits

______ 11. margin requirements

______ 12. unborrowed reserves greater than legal minimum

(a) contractionary monetary policy

(b) Depositary Institutions Deregulation and Monetary Control Act of 1980

(c) national income, unemployment, and the price level

(d) rate of interest at which the Fed will lend reserves to member banks

(e) only selective credit control in use in 1987

(f) interest rates, money supply, monetary base (reserves)

(g) expansionary monetary policy

(h) Federal Open Market Committee (FOMC)

(i) monetary rule

(j) reserve requirements

(k) position for expansion of deposit money by banks

(l) discontinuance of practice of supporting prices of government bonds

Multiple-Choice Questions

1. Policy variables
   (a) are tools used by the Fed to alter the money supply.
   (b) usually include some level of national income as an ultimate objective.
   (c) are most often controlled by changes in reserve requirements by the Fed.
   (d) must receive congressional approval, although the Fed usually acts independently of both the legislative and executive branches of government.

2. Which of the following statements is *not* true?
   (a) A specified level of national income is a policy variable.
   (b) The money supply is an instrumental variable.
   (c) The rate of interest may be either an instrumental variable or a policy variable.
   (d) The money supply may be either an instrumental variable or a policy variable.

3. If the Fed wishes to pursue an expansionary monetary policy, it can
   (a) buy bonds on the open market, thus contracting reserves of commercial banks and causing interest rates to rise.
   (b) sell bonds on the open market, thus expanding reserves of commercial banks and causing interest rates to fall.
   (c) buy bonds on the open market, thus expanding commercial bank reserves and causing interest rates to fall.
   (d) sell bonds on the open market, thus contracting reserves of commercial banks and causing interest rates to rise.

4. Open-market operations are
   (a) used by the Fed regularly to meet seasonal, cyclical, and erratic fluctuations in the banks' need for reserves.
   (b) changes in the discount rate charged by the Fed for loans to member banks.
   (c) conducted primarily in order to make a profit for the Fed.
   (d) not very effective as a means of influencing the supply of money and credit.

5. An increase in the required reserve ratio has the effect of
   (a) reducing total reserves.
   (b) reducing the multiple by which the money supply can expand.
   (c) increasing excess reserves.
   (d) enabling the banks to reduce borrowings from the Fed.

6. If the central bank purchases government securities in financial markets,
   (a) commercial bank reserves will increase.
   (b) the money supply can increase only by the value of the purchase.
   (c) commercial bank reserves will decrease.
   (d) interest rates will tend to rise.

7. Suppose the Fed believes that there is too much inflationary pressure in the economy. Its contractionary policy should include
   (a) the purchase of government bonds on the open market.
   (b) forcing the U.S. Treasury to buy more government securities.
   (c) the sale of government bonds on the open market.
   (d) a decrease in reserve requirements.

8. Which one of the following cannot be used by the Fed to alter the money supply?
   (a) open-market operations
   (b) changes in the discount rate
   (c) changes in the required reserve ratio
   (d) changes in tax rates

9. The discount rate is
   (a) changed almost daily by the Fed in response to market conditions.
   (b) the rate of interest at which the Fed will lend to its member banks.
   (c) the rate of interest at which the Fed will lend to large companies.
   (d) required by law to be higher than the prime rate.

10. Generally recognized as a sign of a policy favoring tighter money is a
    (a) reduction of the required reserve ratio.
    (b) rise in government bond purchases by the Fed.
    (c) rise in the money supply.
    (d) rise in the discount rate.

11. Which of the following is *least* likely to have an expansionary effect on the economy, other things being equal?
    (a) a decrease in the discount rate
    (b) purchase of government securities by the Fed
    (c) an increase in the demand for money
    (d) a decrease in the required reserve ratio

12. One way that monetary policy deliberately tries to influence the economy is by
    (a) directly affecting income.
    (b) making it harder (more costly) or easier (less costly) to borrow money.
    (c) changing the velocity of money.
    (d) directly affecting the price level.

13. Since World War II, monetary policy has
    (a) unquestionably been contractionary throughout most of the period.
    (b) not ordinarily been used in an attempt to counteract fluctuations in rates of unemployment and inflation.
    (c) been characterized by some critics as being destabilizing, rather than contributing to economic stability.
    (d) has never really focused on the money supply as an instrumental variable.

14. The long-term upward trend in the rate of monetary expansion since the mid-1950s accompanied by a similar rising trend in the price level
    (a) proves that the monetary expansion caused the recent U.S. inflation.
    (b) proves only that monetary expansion passively reacted to the U.S. inflation during the period.
    (c) leads to the conclusion that the supply of money has no effect on the price level.
    (d) leads to an unmistakable correlation between the rate of monetary expansion and the rate of inflation, but does not prove causation.

15. There is general agreement among economists that
    (a) rapid changes in the money supply have significant effects on aggregate demand.
    (b) monetary policy should be given a minor role relative to fiscal policy in stabilizing economic activity.
    (c) control of the money supply is a sufficient means for controlling inflation.
    (d) changes in the money supply are the only cause of inflation.

16. Over two-thirds of the Federal Reserve Bank's assets are
    (a) gold certificates.
    (b) U.S. government securities.
    (c) loans to commercial banks.
    (d) none of the above

17. The overwhelming proportion of Federal Reserve Bank liabilities consists of
    (a) Federal Reserve notes and deposits of the U.S. Treasury.
    (b) deposits of the U.S. Treasury and deposits of member bank reserves.
    (c) liabilities other than the three categories in (a) and (b).
    (d) Federal Reserve notes and deposits of member bank reserves.

18. The negative real interest rates in the late 1970s
    (a) represented a response to expansionary policies by the Fed accompanied by a decrease in the demand for money.
    (b) accompanied a contractionary monetary policy with slow growth in M1.
    (c) reflected the low rate of inflation at the time.
    (d) can be taken as a red herring since negative interest rates of any kind are a logical impossibility.

19. In late 1979 and 1980 (as cited in Exercise 4) the Fed switched to
    (a) a monetary growth target and was able to temper fluctuations in interest rates.
    (b) a monetary growth target that accepted sharp rises and greater fluctuations in interest rates.
    (c) an interest rate target that aimed at relatively stable rates.
    (d) interest rate targets with substantial volatility.

20. A contractionary monetary policy, assuming money demand is unchanged, will cause
    (a) a decrease in interest rates and the money stock.
    (b) a decrease in interest rates and increase in the money stock.
    (c) an increase in interest rates and decrease in the money stock.
    (d) an increase in both interest rates and the money stock.

Self-Test Key

Matching Concepts: 1–c; 2–f; 3–h; 4–g; 5–a; 6–i; 7–l; 8–d; 9–j; 10–b; 11–e; 12–k

Multiple-Choice Questions: 1–b; 2–d; 3–c; 4–a; 5–b; 6–a; 7–c; 8–d; 9–b; 10–d; 11–c; 12–b; 13–c; 14–d; 15–a; 16–b; 17–d; 18–a; 19–b; 20–c

Exercises

1. List the major policy instruments available to the Fed and describe briefly how each could be used to increase or decrease the money supply.

	Policy Instrument	*Increase Money Supply*	*Decrease Money Supply*
(a)			
(b)			
(c)			

2. Use the graphs to illustrate the effects of the following central bank monetary policies and answer the questions.

   (a) The Fed sells government securities:

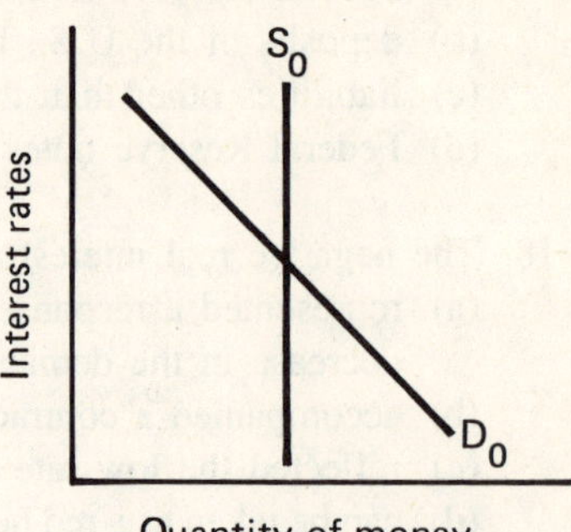

   Total reserves will (increase/decrease).
   The money supply curve should shift to the
   ________________.
   This policy is (expansionary/contractionary).
   Interest rates will tend to
   ________________.

   (b) The Fed reduces the required reserve ratio for member banks:

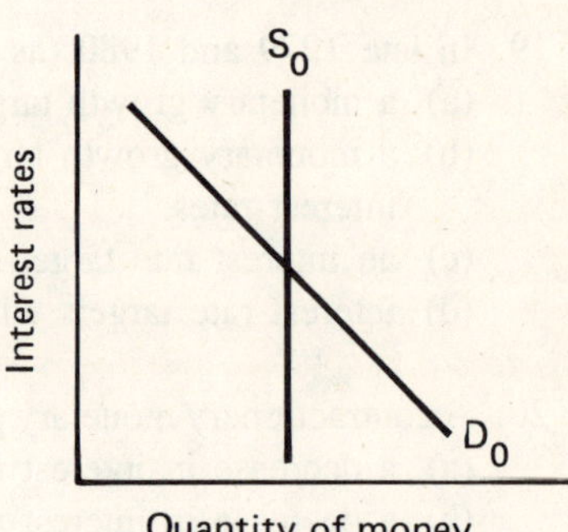

   Excess reserves will (increase/decrease).
   The money supply curve should shift to the
   ________________.
   This policy is (expansionary/contractionary).
   Interest rates will tend to
   ________________.

3. The Fed decides to purchase \$100 million of U.S. government securities from the nonbank public. Show the effect of this on the banking system. (Be sure to use + and – to indicate changes.) Assume that the public holds all their money in bank deposits.

   (a) *Federal Reserve* *All member banks*

Assets	Liabilities
Securities:	Member bank reserves:

Assets	Liabilities
Reserves:	Demand deposits:

   (b) If the reserve ratio is 20 percent, it is now possible for demand deposits to increase by a total of ________________ (including the original increase).

   (c) Will the money supply necessarily increase by this amount?

4. Suppose that commercial banks sell government securities worth $5 million in the bond market. Show the changes that would occur on the T-accounts involved if (a) the bonds are bought by the public and (b) the bonds are bought by the Fed in open-market operations.

(a)

All member banks

Reserves:	Deposits:
Securities:	

Federal Reserve

Securities:	Reserve deposits of member banks:

(b)

All member banks

Reserves:	Deposits:
Securities:	

Federal Reserve

Securities:	Reserve deposits of member banks:

(c) Consider the expansionary or contractionary effects of each event.

5. "On October 6 (1979) the Federal Reserve announced a major shift in its technique for implementing monetary policy. Previously it had attempted to control the expansion of the monetary aggregates by adopting a target for the Federal Funds rate (the interest on reserves the banks lend to one another overnight). Under the new approach the object of open-market operations would be to supply the volume of bank reserves consistent with desired rates of monetary growth. The Federal Reserve also raised the discount rate to 12 percent and established a marginal reserve requirement of 8 percent on increases in the total of managed liabilities of member banks." (*Economic Report of the President, 1980*)

   The *Economic Report* also stated that "bringing an end to inflation must remain the top priority of economic policy" (consumer prices had risen at a 12.7 percent rate in 1979). The annual rate of growth in M1 was brought down to 3.1 percent in the last quarter (from 7.1 percent), bringing it within the target range for 1979.

   (a) Use text Table 33-4 as a guide to complete the following:

	Prior to October 6, 1979	After October 6, 1979
(i) Operating regime		
(ii) Policy instrument(s)		
(iii) Intermediate target(s)		
(iv) Policy variables		

   (b) Before October 6, the Fed had attempted to keep interest changes to 1/2 percent or less a month, and had found that M1 increased out of the target range. Why may such interest rate targets be incompatible with control of the money supply?

   (c) (i) The "top priority" was to control inflation. Can monetary policy be so selective that only the price level is affected? Explain briefly.

   (ii) In view of your answer to (c)(i), is it surprising that the economy peaked in January 1980 and went into recession (the federal budget moved into a high-employment surplus in the second half of 1979)? Explain.

   (d) The primary target on which the Fed's policy instruments work directly is ________________. To slow down monetary growth, how would the Fed alter its open market operations?

   (e) Outline briefly how the other two instruments used in the fall of 1979 would work on reserves and the money supply.

Short Problems

1. M1s Hot Streak

"M1s hot streak" was noted by Milton Friedman in an article in the September 18, 1986 *Wall Street Journal*. From the second quarter of 1981 through the third quarter of 1985, the quarterly changes in M1 two-quarters before closely coincided with quarterly changes in the GNP.

	(1) Nominal GNP (billions)	(2) M1 previous December (billions, daily average)	(3) Estimated velocity (V) (1 ÷ 2)
1982	$3166	$442	______
1983	3402	481	______
1984	3775	528	______
1985	3993	559	______

(a) We can see the basis for his findings without dealing with a multitude of figures by working out the velocity using annual GNP data and the M1 of the December of the previous year (to deal with probable lags). Show that V is remarkably constant using the figures above.

(b) Friedman's major point was that this relationship "gave Keynesians the bad idea" of "fine-tuning" the economy. He stated that this "hot streak" was highly exceptional; the data before 1981 and in 1986 were highly erratic (from mid-1985 to mid-1986 M1 was increasing at annual rates averaging 13 percent while GNP was increasing at little over 4 percent). Why might one get the idea that discretionary monetary policy could be effective from the almost constant M1 velocity calculated in the table above?

(c) Friedman concludes, "I remain convinced of a fundamental tenet of monetarism: Money is too important to be left to the central bankers." What is the alternative suggested by the monetarists?

2. The choice of which definition of the money supply to use as an intermediate target is important. The table gives data for 25 years on M1 and the more inclusive M2 (billions outstanding in December of the previous year) and nominal GNP in billions.

	GNP	M1	GNP/M1	M2	GNP/M2
1960	$ 515	$141		$ 298	
1965	705	170	______	459	______
1970	1015	206	______	590	______
1975	1598	278	______	908	______
1980	2732	389	______	1498	______
1985	3993	559	______	2372	______

(a) If the criterion for choice was long-run stability in relationship with nominal GNP, which measure would be preferred? Explain.

(b) The short-run stability of M1 in relation to GNP in the early 1980s was explored in Short problem 1. How might the dropping of the restriction against the paying of interest on checkable deposits help explain stability of the GNP/M1 ratio after 1980 (and its actual drop in 1986)?

Answers to the Exercises

1.

Policy instrument	*Increase money supply*	*Decrease money supply*
(a) open market operations	Buy government bonds and create reserves.	Sell government bonds and reduce reserves.
(b) discount rate	Reduce rate and encourage banks to borrow reserves.	Increase rates and encourage banks to repay borrowed reserves.
(c) reserve requirements	Lower required percentages, creating excess reserves.	Raise required percentages so that banks must curtail deposit liabilities.

2. (a) decrease; left; contractionary; rise
   (b) increase; right; expansionary; fall

3. (a)

Federal Reserve	
Securities: +100	Member-bank reserves: +100

All member banks	
Reserves: +100	Demand deposits: +100

(b) $500 million

(c) It depends on whether banks are willing and able to lend their excess reserves.

4. (a)

All member banks	
Reserves: no change Securities: −5	Deposits: −5

Federal Reserve	
no change in assets	no change in liabilities

(b)

All member banks	
Reserves: +5 Securities: −5	Deposits: no change

Federal Reserve	
Securities: +5	Reserve deposits: +5

(c) Policy (a) is neutral. While deposits are down by $5 million, the banks can be expected to make loans and create deposits of $5 million. Policy (b) is expansionary. On the basis of $5 million in additional reserves, the banking system can extend loans and create deposits of $25 million.

5. (a)

	Prior to October 6, 1979	After October 6, 1979
(i)	interest rate targeting (or, arguably, monetary targeting: interest rate control)	monetary targeting: base control
(ii)	open-market operations	open-market operations, discount rate, reserve requirements
(iii)	interest rates (federal funds)	money supply
(iv)	nominal national income	price level (control inflation, but must accept effects on real national income as well)

(b) To keep interest rate changes low in times of substantial inflation required more increases in money than targeted.

(c) (i) By influencing *AD*, monetary policy can reduce nominal national income including its price component but also its real component.

(ii) No, with the restrictive monetary policy, especially given fiscal restraint, a turndown in real national income was likely (and contributed to President Carter's political problems).

(d) The member bank reserve component of the monetary base; it would sell more government bonds and purchase fewer over time.

(e) The higher discount rate discouraged bank borrowings of added reserves and thus their ability to expand loans and the money supply. The marginal reserve requirement would increase required reserves for banks most prone to expand the money supply.

CASES FOR PART EIGHT

CASE 26: Did the Silver Make the Quarter Valuable?

Before 1873[1] and after 1965, the silver bullion in a silver dollar was worth $1.00 or more. Between those years, it dropped to as low as $.22. In the late 1950s and 1960s, it became apparent that the demand for silver for both coinage and industrial uses was increasing far more rapidly than the newly mined supplies (silver is largely a by-product of other mining). The world price was maintained first at $.906 and then at $1.293 an ounce, first through purchases of excess supplies and then through sales by the U.S. Treasury.

In 1963, the retirement of U.S. silver certificates was begun. These certificates were paper money backed by 371¼ grains of silver bullion, the same as in a silver dollar. In 1968, the right to receive bullion for a silver certificate was repealed and most silver coins disappeared either into private hoards or into Treasury stocks. The Coinage Act of July 1965 authorized cupronickel quarters and dimes and a 40 percent silver half-dollar. The Coinage Act of 1970 permitted cupronickel half-dollars and dollars. The only paper money that circulated after 1965 were Federal Reserve notes.

Price of Silver and the Cost-of-Living Index in Selected Years

Year(s)	Price Per Ounce (cents)	Value of Silver in Silver Dollar (cents)	Cost-of-Living Index (1957–1959 = 100)
1929	53	41	59.7
1932	25	20	47.6
1940[a]	71.1	55	48.8
	(35)	(27)	
1951–1961[a]	90.6	70	90.5–104.2
1965	129.3	100	109.9
1968 (approx. range)	190–235	147–178	121.5

[a]The 71.1 cent price was the U.S. government support price for newly mined domestic silver. The $.35 price was the world market price. From 1951 to 1961, the world price corresponded approximately to the postwar government support price.

[1]After 1873 with the enormous silver discoveries in the U.S. west, it was no longer possible to maintain bimetalism in this country and it chose the gold standard. A burning political issue for western debtors and miners in the late nineteenth century was the free coinage of silver at a value of one-sixteenth of gold which, if permitted, would have dramatically expanded the money supply.

Foresighted hoarders of silver certificates were able to exchange them for silver bullion before June 1968 at 129.3 cents an ounce and sell it at higher prices. Premiums received by silver coin holders would reflect anticipated scarcity values for collections, for illegal melting down of coins, or for speculation on the eventual legalization of the recovery of the silver from coins (done at the end of 1970).

The most dramatic price action in silver came in 1979 and 1980. In August 1979 silver sold for just under $9 an ounce but was being accumulated in tremendous quantities by the Hunts and others. As the price rose above $20.00 in early 1980, silverware, jewelry, and coins came onto the market in great volume and, in an emergency order, the commodities exchanges suspended futures trading except for the purpose of liquidating speculative positions. The price peaked at $50.00 and in a few days crashed to $10.80. In August 1980 silver sold for $16.00 an ounce. (The Hunts reputedly still held 63 million ounces and predicted silver should sell at $125.00 an ounce, one-fifth the price of gold, on the grounds that the silver supply got used up industrially while almost all the gold ever mined is still around.) Silver coinage was resumed in 1986 (see question 4 below).

Questions

1. Did the fluctuations in the value of silver in coins and for backing silver certificates have any direct correspondence with the value of this money from 1929 to 1961? What gave value to silver money in this period? Was Gresham's law applicable?

2. Comment on this quotation: "By 1965 silver became just too valuable to use as coins." In 1965, in those countries regularly reporting, industrial demand totaled 275 million ounces and was increasing by 5 percent a year. Reported world newly minted supply was 275 million ounces and not increasing at current prices. Corresponding coinage demand (mostly U.S.) was 300 million ounces a year.

3. (a) Why would production as a by-product lead to accentuated price fluctuations? (Over 75 percent of all silver is produced by primarily base-metal mines, particularly copper, lead, and zinc.)

   (b) What can make the short-run supply of silver somewhat elastic (at least for historically high prices)?

4. In 1986 a one-ounce silver bullion coin with legal tender status at a face value of $1 was issued. Its announcement coincided with that for four gold pieces ranging in denomination from $5 to $50 and in weight from 0.1 to 1 ounce. These coins were to be sold by the government at modest margins (3 to 9 percent) over bullion price (then about $420 for gold and $6 for silver). The government expected additional profit by selling limited mintage "proof" versions to coin collectors at much higher prices. The 1986 leader in gold bullion coins in the U.S. market (estimated annual sales about $1 billion) was Canada's Maple Leaf.
   (a) Contrast the function of the new silver dollar with that of the quarter before 1965.

   (b) What special service in minting these coins does the government provide for its citizens that could not be met by private bullion dealers?

   (c) Does the introduction of gold and silver bullion coins contribute to the public interest?

CASE 27: A Bond Boom: May 1984 to May 1986

The bond bust of Short problem 1 in Chapter 32 was an early sharp dip on the roller coaster bond prices took in the early 1980s until a two-year climb after May to June of 1984.

The table below traces the boom in bond prices after May 1984 by showing the decline in interest rates the U.S. government attached to new issuances of 30-year bonds. It also shows the prices per $100 of principal value and the yields to maturity of these bonds on September 21, 1986. (Information for current dates is available to you in newspapers carrying comprehensive business sections.) The price data is the annual rate of change for the implicit GNP deflator for the quarter before the issuance of the bonds.

Issue date	Rate	Price (September 21, 1986)[a]	Yield (September 21, 1986)	Increase in price level (percent)[b,c]	Estimated real interest rate (percent)
May 1984	13¼	$146.28	8.53	5.0	______
November 1984	11¾	$134.6	8.37	3.8	______
August 1985	10⅝	$125.4	8.31	3.3	______
February 1986	9¼	$113.14	8.04	3.3	______
May 1986	7¼	$ 94.7	7.74	2.5	______

[a]Bond prices after the decimal points are in thirty-seconds, not hundredths.
[b]Intermediate bond series show the same rate decline: August 1984, 12½; February 1985, 11; November 1985, 9⅞.
[c]The price level increase dropped to 1.8 percent for the second quarter of 1986.

Questions

1. The yield to maturity is a better measure of the desirability of alternative bond investments than the current yield. To illustrate its calculation, take the February 1986 bond which promises annual payments of $9.25 for thirty years and $100 principal in the thirtieth year. The yield is that interest rate, *i*, that equates the price to the present value of these future payments.

   For September 21, 1986, this equation can be set up as follows (the use of 30 years is a simplification with negligible effect on the results):

   $$\text{Price} = \text{PV of 30 annual interest payments} + \text{PV of principal}$$
   $$\$112.33 = 9.25/(1 + i) + \cdots + 9.25/(1 + i)^{30} + \$100/(1 + i)^{30}$$

   Test this equality for an interest rate of 8 percent. Table 19-1 in *Study Guide*, will give you the value of $1/(1 + r)^{30}$, and Table 19-2 the sum of $1/(1 + r) + \cdots + 1/(1 + r)^{30}$. You should find that the sum of the present values is slightly over the price and conclude that the yield is slightly over 8 percent (as indicated above).

2. (a) In September 1981, the yields on long-term government securities reached an all-time peak of over 15 percent. Estimate the prices of a U.S. bond with an 8.25 percent rate (cited in Short problem 1) for September 1981 and September 1986. Assume its remaining life was 20 years in 1981 and use 15 percent for 1981 and 8 percent for 1986 as the proper discount rates.

   (b) From these calculations and the data about the bond boom, would you conclude that investments in long-term U.S. treasuries were a nonspeculative, risk-free investment from 1980 to 1986?

   (c) How does the evidence of this case fit with "speculative motive" for holding cash balances?

3. Estimate the decline in real interest rates from May 1984 to May 1986 by deducting the percentage of price increase at the time from the stated rates. How might the decline in both nominal and real rates be related to the following?
   (a) a 5.8 percent growth in M1 in 1984, followed by double-digit annual growth rates from May 1985 to September 1986, with the annual growth up to 13.3 percent over the last twelve months

   (b) a supply "shock" in the early months of 1986 in the form of a cut in crude oil prices of over 50 percent

   (c) a slowdown in the growth of real GNP, which after annual growth rates of 6.5 percent in 1983 and 11.4 percent and 5.1 percent in the first two quarters of 1984 dropped to rates averaging just over 2 percent for the rest of 1984, 1985, and the first half of 1986

4. This bond boom can be considered over because almost a half-year after long-term bonds reached peaks in April 1986 their prices were somewhat lower. In the table above, this is shown by the $94 7/32 price as compared to the May 1986 issuance price that can be assumed to have been $100. In contrast, short-term interest rates continued to decline as the Fed cut the discount rate three times from 7 to 5.5 percent. The interest rate on treasury bills of three-month maturity dropped from 6.10 to 5.25 percent.
   (a) Why might the increasing spread of long-term over short-term interest rates reflect rising fears of inflation?

   (b) Why might this relative rise in long-term rates be frustrating to the Fed in a time of weak economic growth and excess capacity?

PART NINE

Issues and Controversies

34

Inflation

Learning Objectives

After studying the material in this chapter you should be able to

—distinguish between temporary and sustained inflation;

—list several reasons for aggregate supply and demand shocks and explain how they cause inflation;

—explain why continued money supply expansion is necessary to sustain inflation;

—understand the role of expectations of inflation in continuing inflation;

—explain how changes in wage costs cause shifts in the *SRAS* curve;

—understand the basis for the acceleration of inflation and the conditions for sustaining a constant inflation rate.

Review and Self-Test

Matching Concepts

______ 1. monetary accommodation	(a) restrictive monetary policy leading to a recessionary gap
______ 2. pure expectational inflation	(b) monetary validation
______ 3. possible reaction of the Fed to demand shock	(c) constant rate of inflation at full employment national income
______ 4. demand inflation	(d) Phillips curve
______ 5. natural rate of unemployment	(e) possible reaction of the Fed to supply shock
______ 6. equilibrium inflation	(f) direct government influence on wages and prices
______ 7. relation between rate of change of wages and unemployment rate	(g) theory that inflation rate responds to persistent recessionary or inflationary gaps
______ 8. incomes policies	(h) increase in price level due to excess demand
______ 9. mechanism for stopping an entrenched inflation	(i) increase in price level due to anticipated inflation
______ 10. acceleration hypothesis	(j) amount of unemployment corresponding with potential national income

Multiple-Choice Questions

1. For an increase in the price level to be sustained,
   (a) there must be a series of supply shocks rather than a single one.
   (b) supply or demand shocks must be accompanied by increases in the money supply.
   (c) both demand and supply shocks must occur simultaneously.
   (d) it is only necessary that expectations of inflation cause a wage-price spiral.

2. Wage-cost push inflation emanating from labor markets is a type of
   (a) inflation caused by demand shocks.
   (b) equilibrium
   (c) recurring supply shock inflation.
   (d) none of the above.

3. All but which of the following will result with monetary validation of a single demand shock?
   (a) The AD curve shifts rightward, fueled by monetary policy.
   (b) Wages will rise, causing the *SRAS* curve to shift leftward.
   (c) The price level will rise.
   (d) Real national income will fall.

4. If an isolated supply shock is not accommodated by monetary policy, the consequence will be
   (a) a rise in output.
   (b) accelerated inflation.
   (c) another supply shock.
   (d) creation or expansion of a recessionary gap.

5. Which one of the following would be the least important factor in causing continued inflation?
   (a) increases in the money supply
   (b) wage increases
   (c) increasing profit margins
   (d) expectational forces

6. Which one of the following statements is correct?
   (a) An ever-increasing money supply is necessary for an ever-continuing inflation.
   (b) A decrease in the money supply is necessary to halt continuing inflation.
   (c) Monetary accommodation is an effective way to prevent supply shocks from causing a sustained inflation.
   (d) Monetary validation is an effective way to control inflation caused by demand shocks.

7. The percentage of unemployment that exists when national income is at its potential (high-employment) level is called
   (a) frictional unemployment.
   (b) structural unemployment.
   (c) inertial unemployment.
   (d) the natural rate of unemployment.

8. Which one of the following could not be the initiating cause of demand shock inflation?
   (a) an increase in the money supply
   (b) a change in autonomous expenditure
   (c) increased costs for imports
   (d) an increase in government spending

9. Sustaining a steady rate of inflation with full employment
   (a) is impossible.
   (b) is possible only when the expected rate of inflation is zero.
   (c) is possible when wages rise due to expectations of inflation and these expectations are being fulfilled.
   (d) will result if random supply shocks dampen the effect of wage increases.

10. According to the acceleration hypothesis, when there is an inflationary gap and monetary validation,
    (a) inflation expectations will moderate, bringing the inflation under control.
    (b) the rate of inflation will tend to increase.
    (c) output will be held below its potential so that a recessionary gap occurs.
    (d) the rate of inflation will remain unchanged.

Questions 11 to 13 refer to the following diagram:

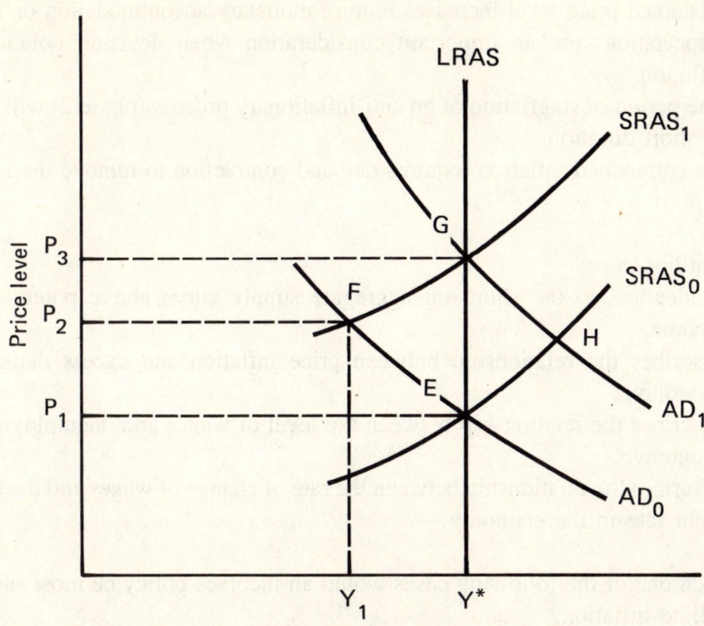

11. Starting from equilibrium at point *E*, if a supply shock shifts the *SRAS* curve from $SRAS_0$ to $SRAS_1$ and there is no monetary accommodation,
    (a) the recessionary gap puts downward pressure on wages and prices, slowly shifting *SRAS* back downward to $SRAS_0$.
    (b) aggregate demand will increase from AD_0 to AD_1.
    (c) the final equilibrium will be at point *G*.
    (d) the final equilibrium will be at point *F*.

12. Starting from equilibrium at point *E*, if the short-run aggregate supply curve shifts from $SRAS_0$ to $SRAS_1$ and there is complete monetary accommodation,
    (a) real national income would temporarily fall to Y_1, then be restabilized at Y^*.
    (b) the aggregate demand curve would shift to the right to pass through point *G*.
    (c) the price level will rise.
    (d) all of the above

13. Starting from an equilibrium at point *E*, if the aggregate demand curve shifts from AD_0 to AD_1 and there is no monetary validation,
    (a) equilibrium will be established at point *F*.
    (b) the price level will first rise to P_3, then fall back to P_1.
    (c) the price level will increase to P_3.
    (d) *SRAS* stays constant at $SRAS_0$.

14. Keynesians and monetarists would agree on all but which one of the statements below about inflation?
    (a) Sustained price level increases require monetary accommodation or validation.
    (b) Expectations are an important consideration when devising policies to curb inflation.
    (c) The period of stagflation of an anti-inflationary process (phase 2) will usually be of short duration.
    (d) An entrenched inflation requires demand contraction to remove the inflationary gap.

15. The Phillips curve
    (a) is identical to the short-run aggregate supply curve above potential national income.
    (b) describes the relationship between price inflation and excess demand in the economy.
    (c) describes the relationship between the level of wages and unemployment in the economy.
    (d) describes the relationship between the rate of change of wages and the unemployment rate in the economy.

16. In which one of the following cases would an incomes policy be most successful in controlling inflation?
    (a) in conjunction with an expansionary monetary policy, to break an entrenched inflation
    (b) in conjunction with a contractionary monetary policy, to break an entrenched inflation
    (c) alone, as a permanent solution to a demand inflation
    (d) alone, as a well-publicized substitute for contractionary monetary and fiscal policies

17. Which of the following would contribute to rising wage rates and leftward shifts of the *SRAS* curves?
    (a) inflationary gaps
    (b) expectations of inflation
    (c) positive random shocks
    (d) all of the above

18. If the Fed ceases to validate an entrenched inflation, we would expect
    (a) a supply shock because interest rates rise.
    (b) a persistent inflationary gap.
    (c) stagflation until inflationary expectations are reversed.
    (d) a fall in the price level.

Self-Test Key

Matching Concepts: 1–e; 2–i; 3–b; 4–h; 5–j; 6–c; 7–d; 8–f; 9–a; 10–g

Multiple-Choice Questions: 1–b; 2–c; 3–d; 4–d; 5–c; 6–a; 7–d; 8–c; 9–c; 10–b; 11–a; 12–d; 13–c; 14–c; 15–d; 16–b; 17–d; 18–c

Exercises

1. Briefly explain and also illustrate on the graphs the following:
   (a) monetary accommodation of a single supply shock

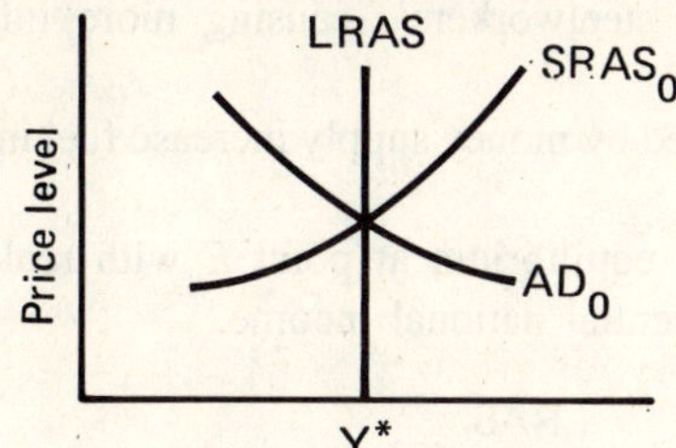

   (b) a single supply shock with no monetary accommodation

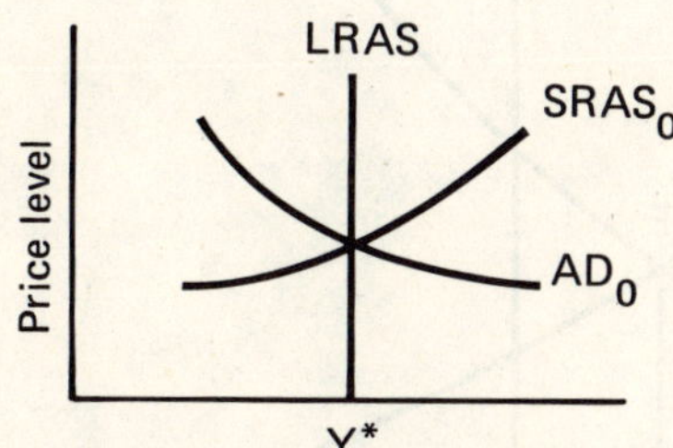

   (c) a demand shock with no monetary validation

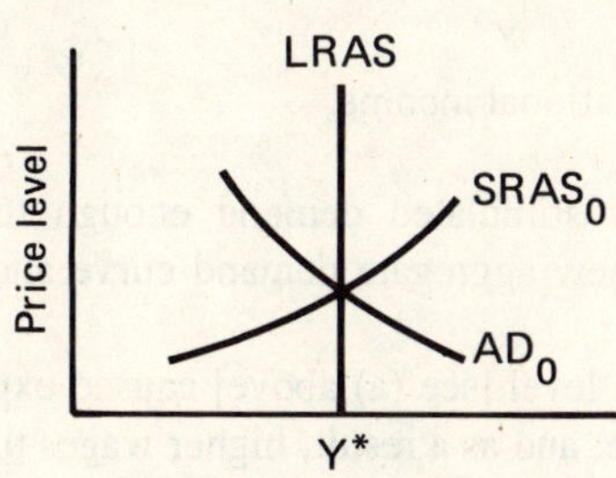

   (d) a validated demand-shock inflation

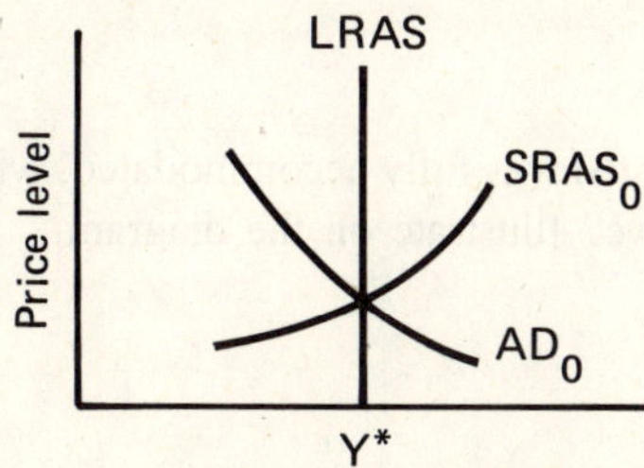

2. To what source (or sources) of inflation do the following statements refer?
   (a) "Prices jump in response to price increases for imported oil."
   (b) "Persistent budget deficits at high employment levels are a major cause of inflation."
   (c) "CPI rise in September blamed on grain shortage."
   (d) "Autoworkers' wage increases top steelworkers', causing more inflationary pressure."
   (e) "Increased arms expenditures followed by money supply increase fuel inflation."

3. The diagram below illustrates an initial equilibrium at point *E* with real national income Y_0 and price level P_0. Y^* is potential national income.

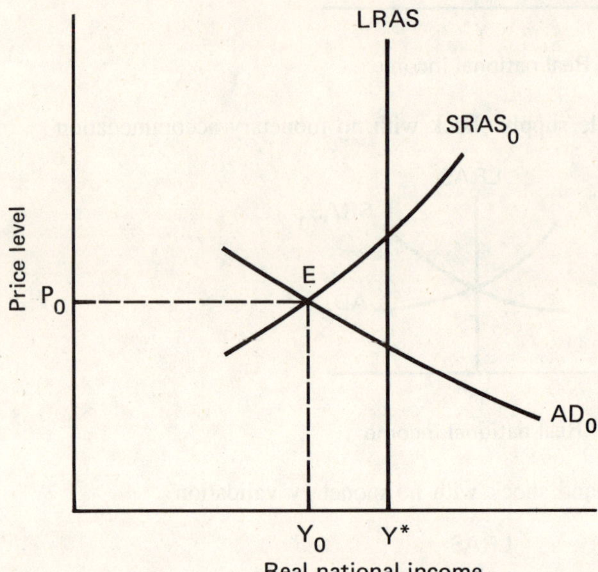

   (a) If an increase in the money supply stimulated demand enough to achieve potential national income, draw the new aggregate demand curve and indicate the new price level.
   (b) Suppose the resulting rise in the price level [see (a) above] caused expectations that inflation would occur in the future, and as a result, higher wages throughout the economy occurred. Show on the diagram what would happen to the *SRAS* curve. What will be the immediate consequence for real national income and the price level?

   (c) If the supply shock which occurred in (b) was fully accommodated, what would happen to the aggregate demand curve? Illustrate on the diagram.

4. The Phillips curve relates the rate of change in wages to the level of unemployment. As Box 34-3 in the text relates, most countries exhibited fairly stable Phillips curves during the 1960s. On the graph below, plot the percentage changes in wages in current dollars and the unemployment rates for the 1960s, indicating the year beside each point plotted. Fit a curve to the results.

Year	Average unemployment rate	Rate of change in wages
1960	5.5	2.4
1961	6.7	2.4
1962	5.5	4.0
1963	5.7	3.0
1964	5.2	3.2
1965	4.5	4.5
1966	3.8	3.5
1967	3.8	3.1
1968	3.6	5.8
1969	3.5	6.4

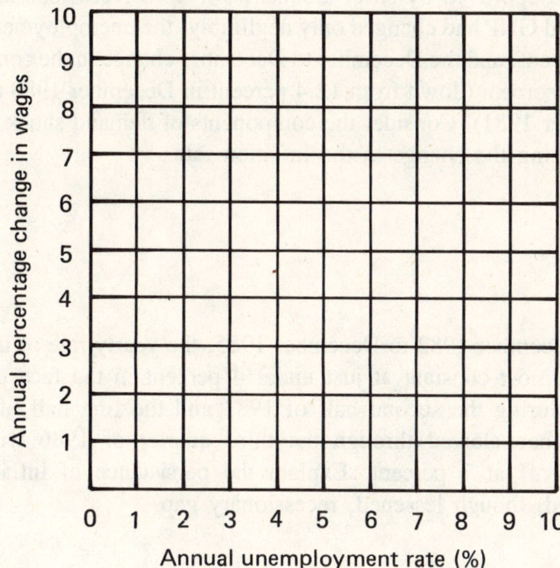

5. (a) In 1979, inflation reached double-digit figures (year-to-year, 11.3 percent; December 1978 to December 1979, 13.3 percent). It had previously done so in 1974 after the oil and grain price rises. The immediate impetus was the more than doubling of oil prices. The proximate cause of the rise of inflation to double-digit levels represented a ______ shock. It could be diagrammatically represented by a ______ shift in the *SRAS* curve.

(b) After the 1974–1975 recession, civilian unemployment had failed to fall below 5.7 percent. Nonetheless, the year-to-year rises in prices were: 1976, 5.8 percent; 1977, 6.5 percent; 1978, 7.7 percent. The economy was apparently operating with a (recessionary, inflationary) gap and much of the continuing inflation could be classified as ______________. Its effects would be to shift the ______________ curve ______________.

(c) Real short-term interest rates in the late 1970s were negative, which would indicate that the monetary authorities were ______________ the inflation. This monetary policy would tend to shift the ______________ curve to the ______________.

(d) Under chairman Paul Volcker, the Fed switched to a generally restrictive monetary policy in October 1979 (though with more changes in the money supply than would be approved by strict monetarists). Two recessions later, at the end of 1982, real GNP had changed only negligibly, the unemployment rate had risen to 10.6 percent, and the December to December change in the consumer price index was 3.9 percent (down from 12.4 percent in December 1980 and 8.9 percent in December 1981). Consider the components of demand shock and core inflation in analyzing the change in the inflation rate.

(e) From December 1982 to December 1985, the yearly rate of increase in the CPI stayed almost constant at just under 4 percent in the face of rapid economic growth during the second half of 1983 and the first half of 1984. Economic growth then slowed through the third quarter of 1986 with unemployment leveling off at 7 percent. Explain the persistence of inflation in face of a continued, though lessened, recessionary gap.

(f) After a sharp drop in energy prices beginning in January 1986, the rate of inflation slowed markedly. Changes in the CPI were small and even negative for several monthly periods; the producers' price index was distinctly negative (–2 percent, on an annual basis), as it is influenced more than the CPI by dropping commodity prices.

The Fed's monetary policy became easier, with four cuts in the discount rate and accelerating increases in M1. Why would forecasts of inflation for the period remain in the 3 to 4 percent range?

Short Problem

(Refer to Exercise 4.) By the early 1970s, the rate of wage and price inflation associated with any given level of unemployment began to rise in comparison with the 1960s. Use the data given to confirm this statement (use the graph in Exercise 4). Explain why the curve shifted over the 1970–1985 period.

Year	Average unemploy-ment rate	Annual rate of increases in wages
1970	4.9	4.6
1971	5.9	6.2
1972	5.6	7.5
1973	4.9	6.2
1974	5.6	6.4
1975	8.5	5.7
1976	7.7	7.3
1977	7.0	7.7
1978	6.0	7.8
1979	5.8	8.0
1980	7.1	6.9
1981	7.6	8.5
1982	9.7	4.7
1983	9.6	5.0
1984	7.5	4.8
1985	7.2	2.4

Answers to the Exercises

1. (a) Monetary accommodation of a single supply shock causes costs, the price level, and the money supply all to move in the same direction. The supply shock is represented in the leftward shift of the *SRAS* curve; monetary accommodation shifts the *AD* curve rightward. Equilibrium shifts from E_0 to E_2.

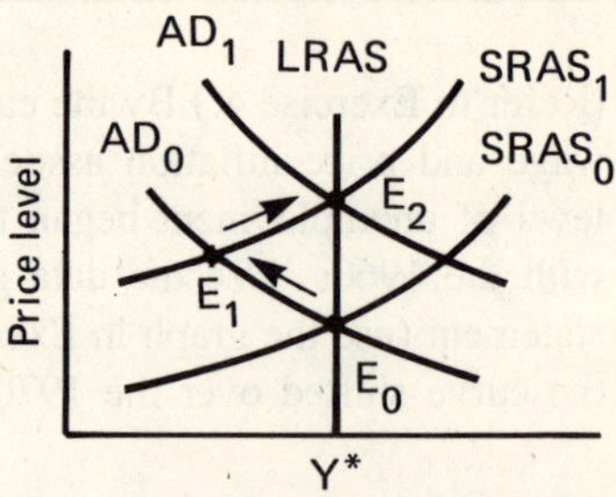

(b) The supply curve shifts to the left as a result of the supply shock; but without monetary accommodation, unemployment puts downward pressure on wages and costs, shifting the *SRAS* curve back to $SRAS_0$.

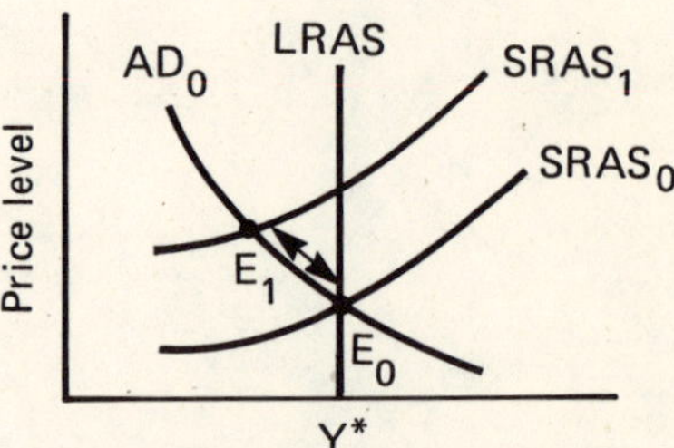

(c) The demand shock shifts the *AD* curve and creates an inflationary gap; this causes wages to rise, shifting the *SRAS* curve to the left. The monetary adjustment mechanism causes movement along the *AD* curve with the rise in price level eliminating the inflationary gap (at E_2).

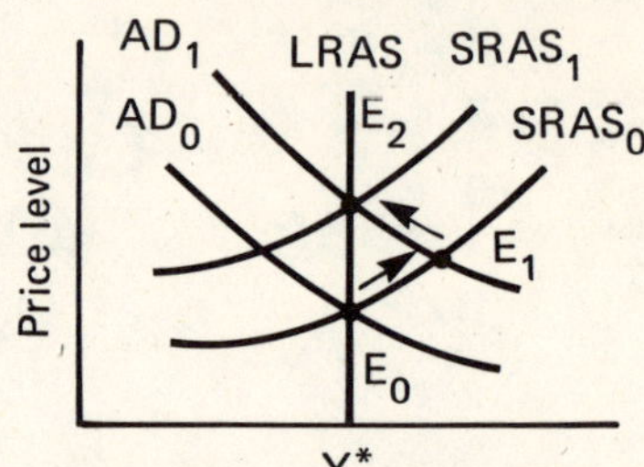

(d) The adjustment process in (c) is frustrated with monetary validation; increases in the money supply shift the *AD* curve to the right and the inflation is sustained. The economy moves along the vertical path indicated by the arrow.

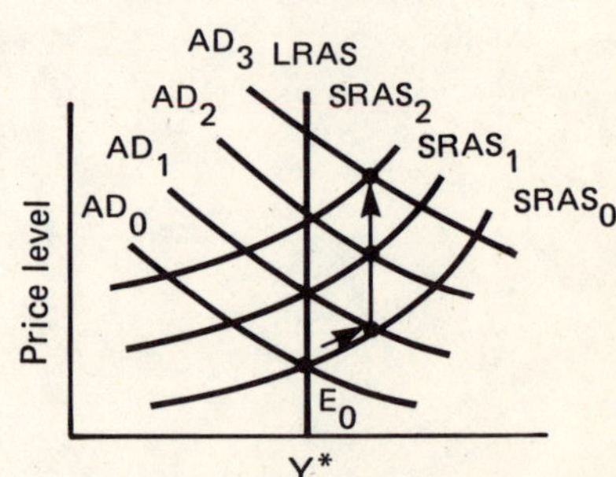

2. (a) supply shock (b) demand shock (c) supply shock (d) wage-cost push inflation (e) monetary validation of a demand shock

3. (a) The new *AD* curve is AD_1 and the price level is P_1. (See diagram below.)
   (b) The *SRAS* would shift to the left, for example, $SRAS_1$ in the diagram below, and the price level would rise further (along AD_1) to P_2. Real national income would decline to Y_1.
   (c) The aggregate demand curve would shift to AD_2. (See diagram.)

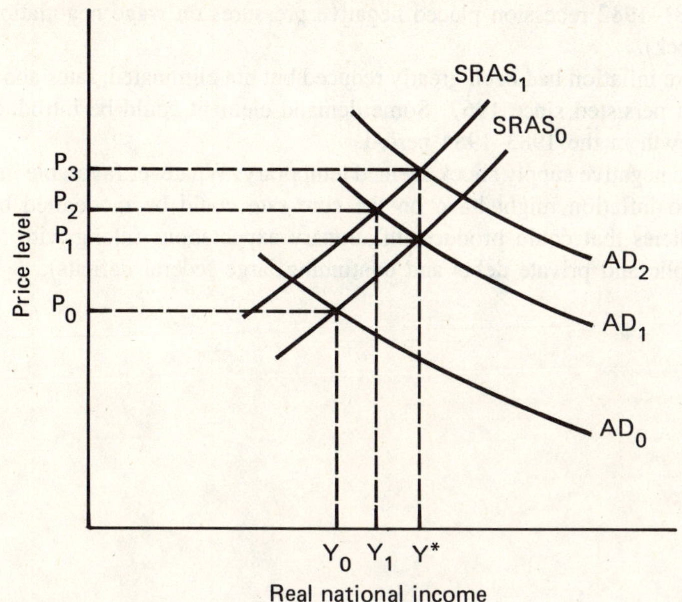

4. Note the fairly constant trade-off in the graph below:

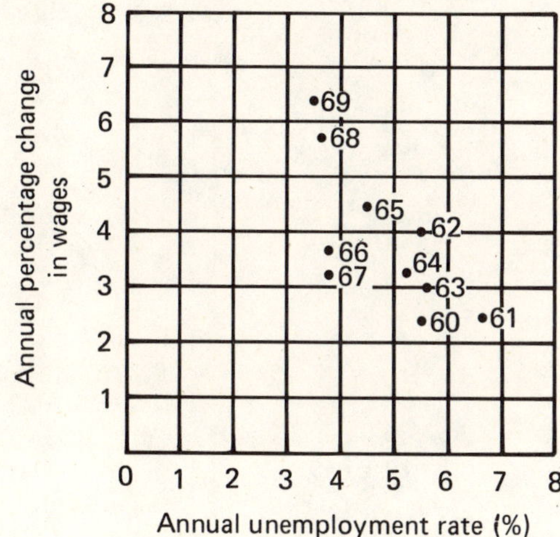

5. (a) supply shock; leftward
   (b) recessionary; expectational or core; *SRAS*; to the left (gradually)
   (c) validating; aggregate demand; right
   (d) The first task was to contain the supply-shock inflation and to prevent it from establishing itself as part of expectational inflation which constituted the bulk of continuing inflation with a recessionary gap in 1979. The sharpness of the 1981–1982 recession placed negative pressures on wage negotiations (demand shock).
   (e) Core inflation had been greatly reduced but not eliminated; rates above 3 percent had persisted since 1967. Some demand element could be introduced in rapid growth in the 1983–1984 period.
   (f) The negative supply shock seemed temporary. Whatever favorable influences the zero inflation might have on the core rate could be moderated by monetary policies that could produce inflationary expectations (along with related large public and private debts and continuing large federal deficits).

35

Employment and Unemployment

Learning Objectives

Careful study of the material in this chapter should enable you to

—distinguish voluntary from involuntary unemployment;

—define frictional, structural, deficient-demand, real-wage, and search unemployment and indicate their relative importance in the current U.S. economy;

—describe the effects of demographic and structural changes on unemployment.

Review and Self-Test

Matching Concepts

_______ 1. natural rate of unemployment

_______ 2. frictional unemployment

_______ 3. unemployment caused by mismatch between available and required resource inputs

_______ 4. deficient-demand unemployment

_______ 5. search unemployment

_______ 6. appropriate policy for reducing deficient-demand unemployment

_______ 7. appropriate policy for reducing structural unemployment

_______ 8. discouraged workers

_______ 9. measure of unemployed persons as a percentage of labor force

_______ 10. real product wage

(a) type of unemployment associated with recessionary gap

(b) unemployment rate

(c) type of voluntary frictional unemployment

(d) job retraining programs and relocation incentives

(e) nonmeasured unemployment

(f) unemployment associated with normal turnover of labor

(g) expansionary monetary and/or fiscal policy

(h) structural unemployment

(i) real cost to the employer of hiring a worker

(j) sum of frictional plus structural unemployment

Multiple-Choice Questions

1. Voluntary unemployment
   (a) occurs when there is a job available but the unemployed person is unwilling to accept it at the going wage rate.
   (b) is of more concern to policy-makers than involuntary unemployment.
   (c) increases substantially during a deep recession.
   (d) occurs when a person is willing to accept a job at the going wage rate but no such job can be found.

2. Unemployment that occurs as a result of the normal turnover of the labor force as people move from job to job is called
   (a) involuntary unemployment.
   (b) structural unemployment.
   (c) search unemployment.
   (d) frictional unemployment.

3. The existence of structural unemployment means that
   (a) there is an inadequate number of jobs in the economy.
   (b) real wages are too high across the whole economy.
   (c) the building trades workers are suffering from high unemployment rates.
   (d) the composition of the demand for labor does not match the composition of the available supply.

4. Search unemployment
   (a) is a form of voluntary frictional unemployment.
   (b) will tend to increase with more generous unemployment insurance benefits.
   (c) occurs when members of the labor force look for more suitable jobs.
   (d) all of the above

5. The unemployment that exists when there is a recessionary gap is called
   (a) structural unemployment.
   (b) deficient-demand unemployment.
   (c) frictional unemployment.
   (d) real-wage unemployment.

6. To say that the labor force is currently "fully employed" means that
   (a) there is zero unemployment.
   (b) any person desiring a job has one.
   (c) all unemployment is frictional or structural.
   (d) the natural rate of unemployment is zero.

7. Which one of the following causes of unemployment is likely to vary most with cyclical changes in economic activity?
   (a) real-wage unemployment
   (b) structural unemployment
   (c) deficient-demand unemployment
   (d) frictional unemployment

8. After 1970, the level of unemployment in the United States that would persist if deficient demand were removed
   (a) has risen.
   (b) has fallen.
   (c) has remained unchanged.
   (d) has fluctuated substantially.

9. Which of the following is *not* correct?
   (a) Unemployment insurance encourages voluntary and search unemployment.
   (b) It is not possible to reduce unemployment to zero.
   (c) Frictional unemployment is inevitable.
   (d) A rise in real product wages will reduce unemployment, other things being equal.

10. Which one of the following statements concerning demographic characteristics and unemployment rates is incorrect?
    (a) Young and inexperienced workers have higher unemployment rates than experienced workers.
    (b) Over the last 15 years there has been a large increase in the number of households with more than one income earner.
    (c) An increasing percentage of households with two earners tends to increase search unemployment.
    (d) An increasing number of inexperienced workers in the labor force decreases frictional and structural unemployment.

11. An appropriate policy for reducing structural unemployment would be
   (a) an income tax cut.
   (b) an increase in the minimum wage.
   (c) an increase in the money supply.
   (d) programs for retraining and relocating idle workers.

12. The unemployment rate is defined as
   (a) the ratio of unemployed to employed workers.
   (b) the percentage of the adult population who are unemployed.
   (c) the percentage of the labor force who are unemployed and are actively searching for a job.
   (d) the percentage of the unemployed who are collecting unemployment compensation.

13. Zero unemployment is impossible to attain because, at minimum, there will always be
   (a) deficient-demand unemployment.
   (b) frictional unemployment.
   (c) classical unemployment.
   (d) real-wage unemployment.

14. The real product wage is defined as
   (a) the marginal product of labor times the real-wage rate.
   (b) the nominal cost of labor to the employer (excluding any taxes or fringe benefits) divided by the CPI.
   (c) the nominal cost of labor to the employer (including taxes and fringe benefits) divided by the CPI.
   (d) the nominal cost of labor to the employer (including payroll taxes and fringe benefits) divided by the value of output of labor in the same time period.

15. The measured unemployment figure may underestimate the actual number of unemployed because
   (a) it includes people who have voluntarily withdrawn from the labor force.
   (b) part-time workers are not included as members of the labor force.
   (c) it does not include discouraged workers who have voluntarily withdrawn from the labor force.
   (d) it excludes those who are actively searching for work but who are unable to find work.

16. Voluntary frictional unemployment is also known as
   (a) structural unemployment.
   (b) deficient-demand unemployment.
   (c) search unemployment.
   (d) real-wage unemployment.

17. Deficient-demand unemployment exists when
   (a) frictional and structural unemployment is zero.
   (b) real national income exceeds potential income.
   (c) the real wage is too high across the whole economy.
   (d) there is a recessionary gap.

18. Which one of the following has *not* been an important factor in causing structural unemployment over the past 15 years?
   (a) inappropriate monetary and fiscal policies
   (b) rapidly changing technology
   (c) certain input price shocks
   (d) changing composition of the labor force

19. A rise in the real product wage will, other things being equal, cause all but which of the following?
    (a) Some firms will no longer be able to cover their variable costs and will shut down.
    (b) Unemployment will increase.
    (c) New labor-intensive plants will be built.
    (d) Investment in new, more capital-intensive plant and equipment will be undertaken in the long run.

Self-Test Key

Matching Concepts: 1–j; 2–f; 3–h; 4–a; 5–c; 6–g; 7–d; 8–e; 9–b; 10–i

Multiple-Choice Questions: 1–a; 2–d; 3–d; 4–d; 5–b; 6–c; 7–c; 8–a; 9–d; 10–d; 11–d; 12–c; 13–b; 14–d; 15–c; 16–c; 17–d; 18–a; 19–c

Exercises

1. Classify the following situations as frictional unemployment, structural unemployment, search unemployment, real-wage unemployment, or demand-deficient unemployment, and briefly explain your choice:
   (a) An auto assembly worker is laid off because auto sales decrease with a slowdown in economic activity.

   (b) Firms lay off workers when real-wage costs increase because of costlier fringe benefit payments.

   (c) An accountant refuses a job offer and decides to look for another job with a higher rate of compensation.

   (d) A social worker is laid off because the government has reduced funding for social services programs.

   (e) A salesperson in Chicago is laid off when a toy manufacturing firm relocates in Denver.

   (f) Stenographers are laid off as firms introduce word-processing equipment into their offices.

2. The following diagram depicts the demand and supply curves of labor in a particular industry. We assume that both curves depend on the real product wage rate. The current real product wage is RPW_0.

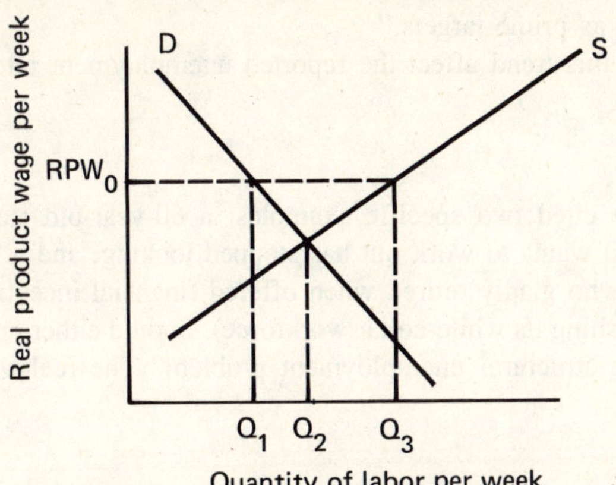

(a) What factors (elements) are included in the real product wage?

(b) Given the current real product wage, what situation exists in this labor market?

(c) What might be predicted for this industry?

3. What specific types of government policies would you recommend for each of the following causes of unemployment? Explain.
(a) structural unemployment

(b) deficient-demand unemployment

(c) frictional unemployment

(d) real-wage unemployment

4. Under the headline, "Alarming Surge in Prematurely Jobless," the *New York Times* (October 13, 1986) reported that only 67 percent of men aged 55 to 64 were in the labor force in 1986 (as compared with 72 percent in 1980 and 83 percent in 1970). The *Times* cited the "restructuring of American industry" as the biggest factor with "older workers as prime targets."
   (a) How does this trend affect the reported unemployment rate?

   (b) The article cited two specific examples: a 60-year-old steelworker who was laid-off and wants to work but has stopped looking, and a 57-year-old Amoco executive who gladly retired when offered financial incentives (as a means of Amoco slashing its white-collar workforce). Should either or both be considered part of the structural unemployment problem? The real-wage unemployment problem?

   (c) What effects might the continuation of this trend (approximately a 1 percent decline per year) have on potential and per capita national income?

Short Problem

(Refer to Exercise 1.) Interpret the following newspaper headlines in terms of (a) the type of unemployment and (b) what government policy would be appropriate for the problem.
(a) "Robots to replace half of auto workers by 1990."

(b) "High interest rates cripple local housing industry."

(c) "College graduates, unable to find suitable jobs, drive taxis and wait on tables."

(d) "Jobs shift from the Midwest to Northeast."

Answers to the Exercises

1. (a) Demand-deficient because of the slowdown in economic activity
   (b) Real-wage unemployment; increased real-wage costs have forced firms to lay off workers, perhaps through plant shutdowns.
   (c) Search or voluntary frictional unemployment; the accountant refused a job because of the expectation of finding another job with a higher rate of remuneration.
   (d) Frictional if short term; structural if the social worker is unable to find work after a prolonged search
   (e) Frictional if short term; structural if the person cannot find work in Chicago or refused to move to Denver
   (f) Structural; stenographers may have to undergo retraining in order to acquire skills required by word-processing equipment or other types of occupations. It would be frictional if the stenographers could find office work elsewhere.

2. (a) As the textbook explains, the nominal costs include wages, fringe benefits, and payroll taxes or other taxes (per week in this problem). The nominal cost is then divided by the firm's revenue product for labor per week.
   (b) Unemployment equal to $Q_3 - Q_1$ exists in this industry. The disequilibrium suggests a recent shift to the left in demand, a strong union, or both.
   (c) With as many unemployed as employed workers, there is a strong possibility that some employers would seek to lower wages (by negotiating "givebacks"). Alternatives are raising productivity of workers or higher product prices.

3. (a) retraining and relocation grants to make movement of labor easier; policies to improve information about existing and (possibly) future employment opportunities
   (b) expansionary fiscal and monetary policies
   (c) increased information about employment opportunities; decreased unemployment compensation to raise the cost of staying unemployed
   (d) cuts in real wages while aggregate demand is increased, possibly aided with an incomes policy

4. (a) There is no direct effect on the number of unemployed (the numerator) but the labor force (denominator) is reduced, so that the reported unemployment percentage could increase slightly. However, insofar as unemployed younger or female workers are substituted for the "prematurely jobless," the rate would drop.
   (b) Narrowly, one could argue that since these "prematurely jobless" are not technically measured as unemployed, "neither" is the answer. Broadly, one could argue that both retirements were of high-wage employees affected by structural changes, so "both" is the answer.

   Many will prefer the middle ground and argue that involuntary retirement placed the steelworker in the "discouraged worker" class and that the steelworker's plight reflected too high a real wage.
   (c) The loss of skilled, experienced workers will reduce potential and per capita income. Until the mid-eighties, the accessions of baby-boom and women workers increased the percentage participation in the labor force, masking this effect. One might reasonably expect that the rate of decline will diminish and then reverse itself as the population ages (aided by public policy modifications in retirement benefits).

36

Economic Growth

Learning Objectives

After reading this chapter you should have a better understanding of

—the cumulative nature of growth;

—factors that affect economic growth;

—the emphasis of contemporary theory on growth-by-learning (including technical innovation and a better-educated labor force) rather than the classical emphasis on capital accumulation;

—the costs, including the loss of current consumption, as compared with benefits of economic growth;

—the difficulty of maintaining growth rates in the face of resource and environmental constraints.

Review and Self-Test

Matching Concepts

______	1. *The Limits to Growth*	(a) improvement requiring investment
______	2. measure of increase in a nation's living standard	(b) quality of human and physical capital as major source of recent economic growth
______	3. output produced per unit of input	(c) outward shift in the *MEC* schedule
______	4. lower rate of current consumption	(d) pioneering presentation of "doomsday" model
______	5. creation of new investment opportunities	(e) productivity
		(f) classical view of economic growth
______	6. decrease in the marginal efficiency of capital	(g) growth in per capita output
______	7. embodied technical change	(h) gradual exhaustion of investment opportunities (world without learning)
______	8. increased output through innovation, without additional capital	(i) primary cost of growth
		(j) disembodied technical change
______	9. gradual slowing of growth with exhaustion of investment opportunities	
______	10. contemporary view of economic growth	

Multiple-Choice Questions

1. Economic growth is best defined as
   (a) a rise in real national income as unemployment is reduced.
   (b) an increase in the current level of real national income.
   (c) a rise in potential national income due to increases in factor supplies or in the productivity of factors.
   (d) an increase in investment and the capital stock.

2. Output per unit of input is likely to increase if, other things being equal,
   (a) the size of the labor force increases.
   (b) health improvements increase longevity for (only) the nonworking aged population.
   (c) better machinery and training are available for workers.
   (d) wages increase.

3. Theories of economic growth concentrate on
   (a) the effects of investment on raising potential real national income.
   (b) the effects of investment on aggregate demand in the short run.
   (c) cyclical fluctuations of actual national income around potential national income.
   (d) reductions in structural unemployment over time.

4. In the long run, an increase in saving, other things being equal, is likely to
   (a) cause the aggregate demand curve to shift to the left.
   (b) cause real national income to fall.
   (c) increase economic growth because more investment expenditure can be financed from these funds.
   (d) demonstrate the "paradox of thrift" phenomenon.

5. According to the "rule of 72," a growth in the population of 2 percent per year means that population will be double in approximately
   (a) 2 years.
   (b) 36 years.
   (c) 72 years.
   (d) 50 years.

6. The marginal efficiency of capital curve
   (a) relates the stock of capital to the productivity of an additional unit of capital.
   (b) is generally assumed to be downward sloping as a consequence of the law of diminishing returns.
   (c) relates the stock of capital to the efficiency of investment.
   (d) both (a) and (b)

7. Economic growth theories that assume "no learning" predict that
   (a) the capital-output ratio will be falling through time.
   (b) the marginal efficiency of capital increases for successive increments in the capital stock.
   (c) more and more investment opportunities appear through time.
   (d) output per unit of capital falls through time.

8. With technical change and new knowledge,
   (a) diminishing returns to additional investment will cause the capital-output ratio to fall.
   (b) the marginal efficiency of the capital curve will become horizontal.
   (c) the marginal efficiency of the capital curve will shift to the left.
   (d) the marginal efficiency of the capital curve will shift outward over time.

9. Classical theories of economic growth
   (a) predicted a declining return on capital.
   (b) predicted an increasing return on capital.
   (c) predicted a constant return on capital.
   (d) had no prediction for the rate of return on capital.

10. The major difference between the earlier classical theory of economic growth and the contemporary view is that
    (a) contemporary economists place much more importance on the quantity of labor than do classical economists.
    (b) classical economists ignored the role of capital accumulation.
    (c) contemporary economists emphasize the creation of investment opportunities rather than simply the exploitation of existing opportunities.
    (d) classical economists emphasized the role of international trade in economic growth.

11. An embodied technical change is one that
    (a) improves the quality of labor.
    (b) involves changes in the form of capital goods in use.
    (c) is concerned with techniques of managerial control.
    (d) is exogenous to the economic system.

12. Suppose two countries have the same per capita output. Country A has an annual economic growth rate of 6 percent while Country B grows at 3 percent a year. Country A will have a per capita output four times as large as Country B's in
    (a) 12 years.
    (b) 24 years.
    (c) 36 years.
    (d) 48 years.

13. An increase in the rate of economic growth
    (a) will usually require a reduction in the proportion of current national income consumed.
    (b) will usually result from an increase in consumption.
    (c) is often the result of increased investment in physical capital alone.
    (d) will be aided by high interest rates.

14. The text concludes that the predictions of "doomsday" models
    (a) have proved totally incorrect and should be ignored.
    (b) were correct until the early 1900s but are now incorrect because of technological change.
    (c) place too much weight on a gradual reduction in the rate of population growth to be valid in the present world.
    (d) may be avoidable in the future with technological advances, but the problem of timing is crucial.

15. The "rule of 72" for an annual compounded growth rate
    (a) gives the doubling time by multiplying 72 times the growth rate.
    (b) suggests that growth will cease after 72 years.
    (c) refers to the public policy toward optimal growth first formulated in 1972.
    (d) gives the doubling time in years if 72 is divided by the growth rate.

16. The most important benefit of economic growth historically has been its role in
    (a) redistributing income among people.
    (b) raising living standards.
    (c) helping countries defend themselves.
    (d) providing for the employment of scarce resources.

17. Which one of the following has played the largest role in the economic growth of North America since 1900, according to recent studies?
    (a) increases in the quantity of raw materials
    (b) increases in the size of the labor force due to population growth
    (c) improvements in the quality of capital, human as well as physical
    (d) increases in the quantity of capital

18. For the economy as a whole, the primary opportunity cost of economic growth is
    (a) borne by future generations whose living standards will be reduced.
    (b) the natural resource shortages that result from economic growth.
    (c) the reduction in living standards for the current generation of consumers.
    (d) the increased poverty that inevitably results from economic growth.

Self-Test Key

Matching Concepts: 1–d; 2–g; 3–e; 4–i; 5–c; 6–h; 7–a; 8–j; 9–f; 10–b

Multiple-Choice Questions: 1–c; 2–c; 3–a; 4–c; 5–b; 6–d; 7–d; 8–d; 9–a; 10–c; 11–b; 12–d; 13–a; 14–d; 15–d; 16–b; 17–c; 18–c

Exercises

1. Assume that the productivity of labor increases by 2.5 percent a year, the labor force increases by 1.75 percent a year, hours worked per member of the labor force decline by 0.25 percent a year, and population increases by 1 percent a year. Predict:
   (a) the annual increase in real GNP

   (b) the annual increase in GNP per capita

   (c) the number of years to double real GNP

   (d) the number of years to double GNP per capita

2. Designate how each of the following factors would probably affect standards of living as measured by real consumption per capita, now and a few years from now. Use a (+) for an increase, a (–) for a decrease, and (U) for no change or too uncertain to call (first dash is for current effect, second dash for future effect). Assume other things remain constant and full employment of resources.
   (a) an increase in the birthrate _______ _______
   (b) a decrease in current saving _______ _______
   (c) a technological innovation reducing input requirements _______ _______
   (d) an increase in current expenditures for technical education financed by increased taxes _______ _______
   (e) a decrease in the working life span of the labor force _______ _______
   (f) an increase in labor force participation _______ _______

3.

	1953	1969	1985
Real GNP (in 1982 dollars)	$1,435	2,423	3,574
Labor productivity index (1977 = 100)	57.7	87.7	105.3
Unemployment rate (percent)	2.9	3.5	7.2

(a) Contrast the percentage increases in real GNP and in labor productivity for these two sixteen-year periods.

Growth emphasizes the increase in *potential* national income. Make these assumptions: inflationary gaps of 2 percent for 1953 and 1 percent for 1969, and a recessionary gap of 6 percent for 1985.

(b) (i) Contrast diagrammatically the situation in 1953 with that of 1985 using *LRAS*, *AD*, and *SRAS* curves.

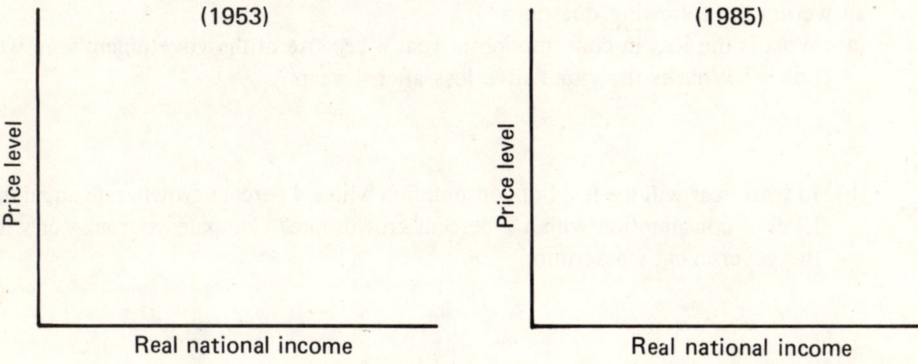

(ii) Calculate and compare the percentage increases in potential national income from 1953 to 1969 and from 1969 to 1985 modifying the GNP figures in (a) for the assumptions in (b).

4. The Opportunity Costs of Growth

Suppose that the national income of an economy was 100 in year 0 and consumption expenditure was 85 percent and investment expenditure was 15 percent. The growth of real national income on an annual basis is expected to be 2 percent. The current government urges the citizens of this nation to pursue policies to increase the growth rate to 4 percent on an annual basis. Its economic forecasters suggest that by reducing consumption to 70 percent (increasing saving by 15 percent), and increasing investment expenditure to a level of 30 percent that: (1) consumption expenditure 7 years hence will be equal to that level of consumption without these policies (with the economy growing at 2 percent) and (2) the aggregate level of consumption in 20 years would be *double* the level associated with a 2 percent growth.

Annual level of consumption

In year	2 percent growth	4 percent growth	Cumulative loss or gain
0	85.0	70.0	(15.0)
1	86.7	72.9	(28.8)
2	88.5	75.8	(41.5)
3	90.3	78.9	(52.9)
4	92.1	82.1	(62.9)
7	97.8	92.6	(83.3)
8	99.7	96.4	(86.6)
9	101.8	100.3	(88.1)
10	103.8	104.4	(87.5)
17	119.4	138.2	(14.9)
18	121.8	143.8	7.1
20	126.8	155.8	61.5
30	154.9	232.4	
40	189.2	346.7	
50	231.1	517.2	

Note: Parentheses denote a loss.

Your task is to confirm the accuracy of the government's economic forecasts by answering the following questions:

(a) What is the loss in consumption in year 4 because of the government's growth policy? What is the cumulative loss after 4 years?

(b) In what year will the level of consumption with a 4 percent growth rate equal the level of consumption with a 2 percent growth rate? Compare your answer with the government's assertion.

(c) In what year does this economy recoup all of the cumulative losses in forgone consumption?

(d) Is the government's assertion that this society will double its consumption level in 20 years correct?

Short Problems

1. Refer to Exercise 1 which gives numbers appropriate for the U.S. in the late 1960s and early 1970s. More appropriate numbers for the future would be 2 percent annual increases in the productivity of labor, an increase in the labor force of 1 percent per year, a decline of 0.3 percent in hours worked per year per member of the work force, and a population increase of 0.7 percent per year. Calculate:
   (a) the annual increase in real GNP ______
   (b) the annual increase in output per capita (of total population) ______
   (c) the number of years to double real GNP ______
   (d) the number of years to double output per capita ______

2. (Refer to Exercise 3.) Consider that in 1973 real GNP was $2,744 billion and the productivity index was 95.9. Assume that actual GNP was equal to potential national income. Estimate the annual rates of growth in potential national income and for productivity in the three periods 1953 to 1969, 1969 to 1973, and 1973 to 1985. [To illustrate a method: 1953/1969 potential national income ratio was 1406/2399 = 0.5861. From the PV Table 19-1 in the Study Guide in row 16, this falls between 2 and 4 percent. By interpolation, we can estimate the rate of growth as 4 percent – (52/194) (2 percent) or somewhat below 3.5 percent. We can confirm the figure as 3.4 percent by calculating $0.1/(1.034)^{16} = 0.586$.]

   Use your calculations to judge whether 1969 or 1973 is the best year to separate a fast growth period from a slow growth period.

Answers to the Exercises

1. (a) 4 percent (2.5 + 1.75 – 0.25) [Precise formulation is: (1.025)(1.0175)(0.9975) = 1.0403, thus 4.03 percent.]
   (b) 3 percent (4 percent – 1 percent)
   (c) 18 = 72/4
   (d) 24 = 72/3

2. (a) (–) (U) increases number of nonworking dependents in population now
   (b) (+) (–) current increase in consumption; reduction in future output
   (c) (U) (+) current effect depends on investment required if "embodied"
   (d) (–) (+) contribution to intangible capital, increasing production in future
   (e) (–) (–) reduces proportion of productive population; immediate effect may be negligible so "U" could be entered
   (f) (+) (+) more producers for given population

3. (a) 68.9 percent, compared to 47.5 percent for real GNP
52.0 percent, compared to 20.1 percent for labor productivity
The increase in real GNP was significantly lower in the 1969–1985 period, and in contrast with the 1953–1969 period more than half the increase reflected increases in labor inputs. The productivity increase was less than 48 percent of what it had been in 1953–1969.
(b) (i)

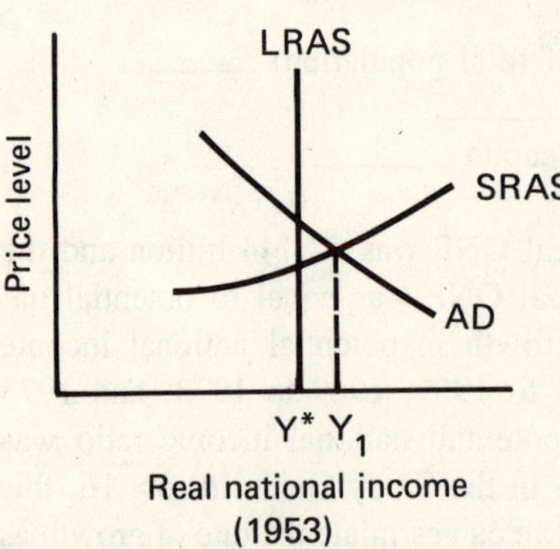

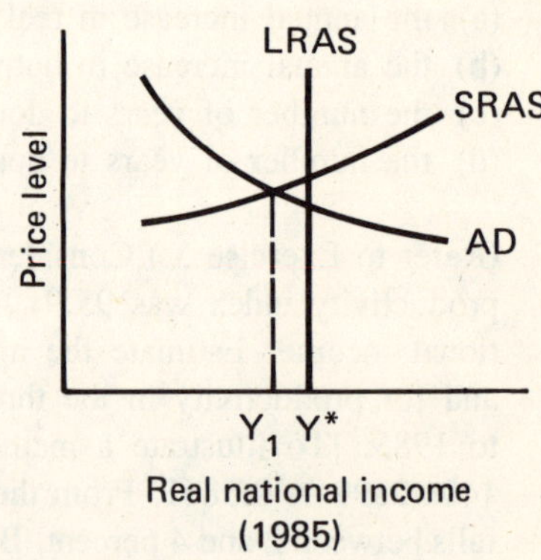

(b) (ii) 2399/1406 – 1 = 70.6 percent; 3802/2399 – 1 = 58.5. Growth was clearly less in the 1969–1985 period, but by a smaller percentage than the estimate in (a).

4. (a) The loss in consumption is 10 (92.1 – 82.1); 62.9 is the cumulative loss.
(b) According to the schedule, C (4 percent growth) will equal C (2 percent growth) sometime in years 9 and 10. This is substantially longer than suggested by the government.
(c) Sometime between the seventeenth and eighteenth years.
(d) No; it is much later. According to the schedule, C (4 percent growth) is double C (2 percent growth) in approximately 45 years.

Note to students: You may think that government forecasters are complete dolts after answers to (b) and (d), particularly if you find you cannot replicate these figures using $(1 + i)^n$. They apparently have used continuous compounding tables rather than annual compounding. Government officials could claim they had been misquoted. Clearly in the seventh year, consumption could be raised to equal that from 2 percent growth. In the twentieth year, consumption could more than double year 0 consumption.

37

Macroeconomic Controversies

Learning Objectives

After studying the material in this chapter, you should be able to

—recognize that the purpose of this chapter is to contrast extreme policy positions;

—explain the noninterventionist positions toward policies concerned with full employment, stable prices, and satisfactory growth;

—explain the interventionists' positions on these same macroeconomic policies;

—contrast these polar positions on policies, underlying assumptions, and particular recommendations;

—recognize that the noninterventionist is also called "conservative" and frequently "monetarist" and that the interventionist is frequently termed "Keynesian."

Review and Self-Test

Matching Concepts

______ 1. necessary condition for slowing inflation

______ 2. tax-related incomes policy (TIPS)

______ 3. the *k*-percent rule

______ 4. monetarist view of cyclical changes in money supply

______ 5. examples of interventionist policy prescriptions

______ 6. post-Keynesian diagnosis of inflation

______ 7. general weakness of discretionary policy, emphasized by conservatives

______ 8. implication of monetarist view of "microbehavior"

______ 9. implication of Keynesian view of "microbehavior"

______ 10. amount of unemployment occurring at full employment, due to frictional and structural causes

(a) temporary nature of departures from full-employment, market-clearing equilibrium

(b) inclusion of wage-cost push theory

(c) fluctuations in money supply as cause of fluctuations in national income

(d) natural rate of unemployment

(e) monetary restraint to prevent rapid increases in aggregate demand

(f) discretionary stabilization policies, tax incentives, subsidies

(g) guide for targeting a stable path of money supply changes

(h) involuntary departures from full-employment equilibrium considered frequent and long lasting

(i) long and variable lags

(j) post-Keynesian prescription to control inflation

Multiple-Choice Questions

1. Those who advocate that macroeconomic goals can be achieved satisfactorily if the free market is left on its own have been classified as
   (a) Keynesians.
   (b) conservatives.
   (c) post-Keynesians.
   (d) neo-mercantilists.

2. In the view of the monetarist group of economists,
   (a) changes in the money supply should be made often as a countercyclical tool.
   (b) interest rates have very little effect on spending.
   (c) the economy will not recover by itself from recessions.
   (d) fluctuations in the money supply cause fluctuations in nominal national income.

3. Keynesians argue that most cyclical fluctuations result from
   (a) variations in the rate of growth of the money supply.
   (b) changes in government expenditures.
   (c) variations in investment expenditure.
   (d) fluctuations in the stock market.

4. Which one of the following would not represent a monetarist's view of the causes of cyclical fluctuations in the economy?
   (a) A major cause of the severity of the depression of the 1930s was a large decline in the money supply between 1929 and 1933.
   (b) Inflationary gaps and rapid inflation are the result of excessive expansion of the money supply.
   (c) Fluctuations in the money supply cause fluctuations in national income.
   (d) Inflationary gaps created by excess demand will automatically cause an increase in the money supply.

5. The economists called Keynesians in this chapter
   (a) do not agree with Keynes that investment spending is important in causing fluctuations in national income.
   (b) believe that fiscal policy is always a more effective stabilization tool than monetary policy.
   (c) are opposed entirely to the use of monetary policy.
   (d) generally have less faith in the economy's self-correcting mechanisms than do monetarists.

6. Keynesians
   (a) believe that a recessionary gap will not be self-eliminating in the short run because prices do not adjust downward very rapidly.
   (b) do not believe there is any correlation between changes in the money supply and changes in national income.
   (c) do not believe that fluctuations in national income can cause fluctuations in the money supply.
   (d) all of the above

7. According to the new classical theory, active use of monetary policy to stabilize the economy leads to
   (a) confusion about absolute and relative prices.
   (b) mistakes in the public's production and price decisions.
   (c) increased fluctuations in aggregate output.
   (d) (a) which leads to (b) which leads to (c).

8. With reference to the causes of inflation, an accurate statement of a difference between monetarists and Keynesians is that
   (a) monetarists emphasize that short-run, supply shock-induced inflation requires active government intervention to arrest the inflation.
   (b) monetarists believe that all inflations are caused by excessive monetary expansion and would not occur without it.
   (c) Keynesians accept the need for a stable growth in the money supply and argue against government intervention to curb inflation.
   (d) Keynesians believe that inflation is largely due to excessive growth in the money supply.

9. According to the theory of the Lucas aggregate supply curve, if the ratio of actual to expected inflation declines,
   (a) national income will fall.
   (b) the aggregate supply curve will shift left.
   (c) the aggregate supply curve will shift right.
   (d) an inflationary gap will be created.

10. The *k*-percent rule
    (a) is supported by both monetarists and Keynesians.
    (b) calls for money supply to grow at a constant rate even when there are short-run fluctuations in the demand for money.
    (c) calls for the money supply to expand and contract as the GNP expands and contracts, respectively.
    (d) is equivalent to the central bank following an interest rate target policy.

11. The *k*-percent rule as advocated by conservatives usually provides that the money supply should be increased steadily at the same rate of increase as
    (a) the price level.
    (b) aggregate demand.
    (c) potential real national income.
    (d) interest rates.

12. Stable, preannounced money supply targets
    (a) are the best approach to interest rate stability.
    (b) are consistent with discretionary monetary policy.
    (c) permit the use of once-and-for-all monetary expansion.
    (d) can induce speculative behavior by bondholders.

13. The micro model on which Keynesian economics is based consists of
    (a) perfectly competitive markets and an excess supply of labor.
    (b) perfectly competitive markets through which changes in demand are transmitted rapidly.
    (c) imperfect markets but flexible prices.
    (d) imperfect markets and fairly rigid prices.

14. A major distinction between post-Keynesians and other interventionists is
    (a) the post-Keynesians' emphasis on monetary factors as the cause of most macroeconomic problems.
    (b) that other interventionists place most blame for the inflation of the late 1970s on expansionary fiscal policy.
    (c) the post-Keynesians' emphasis on wage-cost push as an important factor in the 1970s and early 1980s' inflation.
    (d) the contrast in their views regarding the necessity of monetary restraint for controlling inflation.

15. An important component of the micro model of monetarists is that
    (a) unemployment is involuntary.
    (b) firms respond to changes in demand mainly by changing output and employment rather than prices.
    (c) prices are inflexible.
    (d) the automatic adjustment mechanism of markets works efficiently.

Self-Test Key

Matching Concepts: 1–e; 2–j; 3–g; 4–c; 5–f; 6–b; 7–i; 8–a; 9–h; 10–d

Multiple-Choice Questions: 1–b; 2–d; 3–c; 4–d; 5–d; 6–a; 7–d; 8–b; 9–a; 10–b; 11–c; 12–d; 13–d; 14–c; 15–d

Exercises

1. Using your judgment from how the text develops the opposing positions, insert an M for monetarist or a K for Keynesian after the statements below.
   (a) The demand for money is quite sensitive to interest rates. _______
   (b) Changes in the money supply are the primary cause of fluctuations in the level of national income. _______
   (c) National income can be influenced strongly by monetary policy, but only weakly by fiscal policy. _______
   (d) Investment spending is much more responsive to profit expectations than to changes in interest rates. _______
   (e) Changes in the money supply may be a response to, rather than the cause of, changes in GNP and the price level. _______
   (f) Fiscal policy works only to the extent that it affects the supply of money. _______
   (g) An activist countercyclical government policy is needed to achieve economic stability. _______
   (h) Contraction of the money supply raises interest rates, but the small rise in interest rates only moderately affects expenditures on plant and equipment. _______
   (i) Monetary policy is uncertain, variable, powerful, and lagged in its effects; therefore it should be as neutral as possible. _______
   (j) Fiscal policy has very general effects on the economy, whereas monetary policy affects primarily interest rates and therefore has its major effect on housing and small businesses. _______
   (k) Private sector expenditures would be relatively stable without the interference of erratic fiscal and monetary policy. _______
   (l) Cyclical fluctuations in economic activity are largely due to fluctuations in private sector expenditures. _______

2. The data below pertain to the U.S. economy for the 1975–1985 period.

	Percentage change in		
Year	Money Supply (M1)	Consumer Price Index (CPI)	Nominal GNP
1975	4.9	7.0	8.5
1976	6.6	4.8	11.5
1977	8.1	6.8	11.7
1978	8.3	9.0	13.0
1979	7.2	13.3	11.5
1980	6.6	12.4	8.9
1981	6.5	8.9	11.7
1982	8.8	3.9	3.7
1983	9.8	3.8	7.4
1984	5.8	4.0	11.0
1985	11.9	3.8	5.8

(a) In graph (a), plot the percentage change in the money supply as a solid line and the percentage change in the CPI as a broken line.

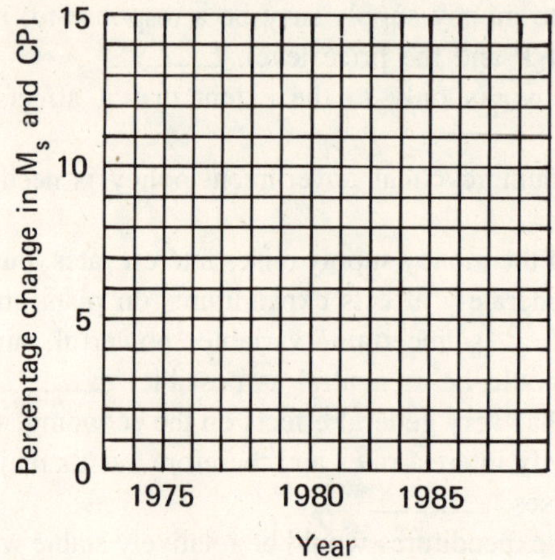

(b) In graph (b), plot the percentage change in the money supply as a solid line and the percentage change in nominal GNP as a broken line.

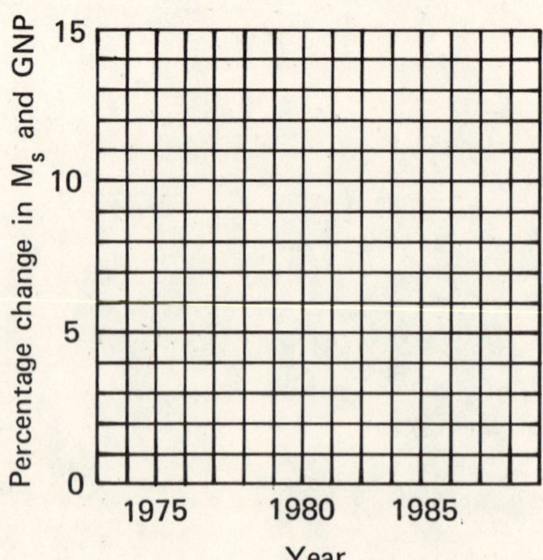

(c) Would it be possible to argue the monetarists' position on the Keynesian position on the basis of the data you have plotted? Explain.

Answers to the Exercises

1. (a) K (b) M (c) M (d) K (e) K (f) M (g) K (h) K (i) M (j) K (k) M (l) K
2. (a): graph (a) (b): graph (b)

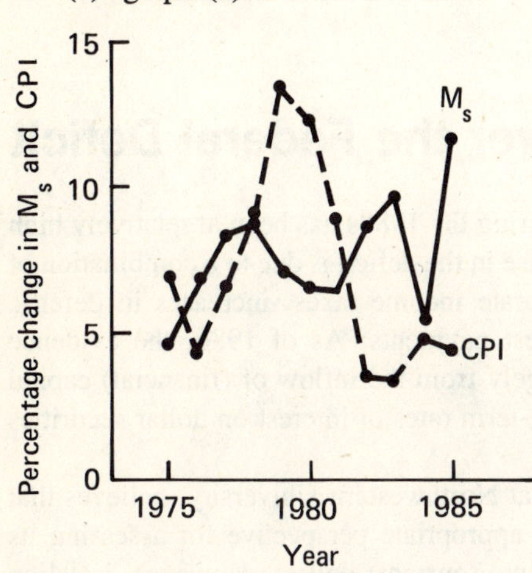

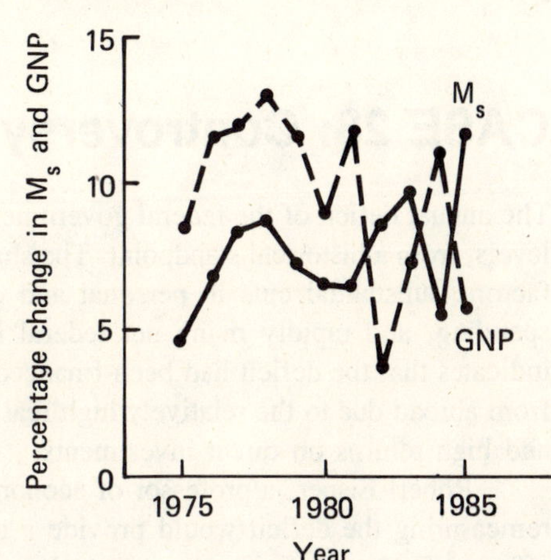

(c) With reference to graph (a), monetarists would argue that the money supply increase in the period 1975–1978 was associated with rising inflation, and the money supply decrease from 1978–1981 reduced inflation, both with a lag (that is, the change in inflation followed the change in the money supply). In graph (b), the two series again move together in a rough way from 1975 to 1980 that is not inconsistent with the Keynesian position.

However, a simple graphical description of this sort cannot be used to say much that is meaningful about the cause and effect among the money supply, nominal GNP, and the price level. It is suggestive of the difficulties of proving one (or refuting the other) theory.

CASES FOR PART NINE

CASE 28: Controversy over the Federal Deficit

The annual deficit of the federal government during the 1980s has been at relatively high levels, from a historical standpoint. The sharp rise in the deficit is due to a combination of factors: substantial cuts in personal and corporate income taxes, increases in defense spending, and rapidly rising net federal interest payments. As of 1986, the evidence indicates that the deficit had been financed largely from the inflow of (financial) capital from abroad due to the relatively high real long-term rates of interest on dollar securities and high returns on direct investments.

Robert Eisner, a professor of economics at Northwestern University, believes that remeasuring the deficit would provide a more appropriate perspective for assessing its effects.[1] Today, deficits are measured in nominal (current) dollars. However, inflation decreases the real value of debt already held by the public and thus the real obligations of the government. Eisner argues that if the federal government kept its books like a business by maintaining a capital account and adjusting the value of its assets and liabilities for inflation, actual deficits would be substantially different than those currently reported. In fact, use of Eisner's measurements converts the reported deficits of the late 1970s to actual surpluses, largely due to high rates of inflation lowering the real value of government debt. Eisner contends that inflation-adjusted deficits or surpluses are also more appropriate indicators of the expansionary and contractionary nature of fiscal policy than nominal deficits or surpluses.

To illustrate the inflation adjustment, assume an individual who has a portfolio of government securities with a market value of $104,000 at the start of the year. The price level rises by 4 percent leading to real value of $100,000 (104,000/1.04) at the end of the year, *ceteris paribus*. The difference of $4,000, "an inflation tax," represents both a reduction of purchasing power to the individual and of the real obligation of government. Thus, an outstanding debt of $1.04 trillion would require a $40 billion downward adjustment of the federal deficit (with 4 percent inflation), according to Eisner's inflation adjustment.

On the facing page are the data with the Eisner adjustments for the period 1980–1982 and for 1984. The term surplus is used with the negative signs indicating deficits.

[1]"The real surplus or deficit may be viewed as essentially the sum of three components: (1) the nominal surplus or deficit as currently measured (at actual or high employment levels); (2) an adjustment for changes in the market value of government finances and liabilities due to changes in interest rates; and (3) an adjustment for changes in real value due to changing general price levels incident to inflation." Robert Eisner, *How Real is the Federal Deficit,* Free Press, 1986.

	(1) Actual surplus	(2) Added surplus at full employment	(3) FE Surp./ GNP	(4) Inflation adjustment	(5) Interest adjustment	(6) Adjusted FE surplus	(7) Column 6/ GNP
1980	−61	44	−.65	55	14	52	1.97
1981	−64	61	−.11	50	−4	43	1.45
1982	−148	117	−1.06	33	−63	−61	−2.01
1984	−176	84	−2.51	42	−21	−71	−1.92

Notes:

Column 1: Billions of dollars (as are columns 2, 4, 5, and 6), taken from National Income Accounts.

Column 2: The estimated reduction in the deficit if the unemployment rate had been 5.1% instead of 7.1, 7.6, 9.5, and 7.4% for these four years.

Column 3: (1–2)/GNP; the traditional measure of budgetary restraint for which Eisner is suggesting adjustments.

Column 4: Eisner's inflation adjustment; December to December rates of change in CPI were 12.4, 8.9, 3.9, and 4.0 for the four years.

Column 5: Eisner's interest adjustment; large 1982 figure reflects drop from 13.7 to 9.9 percent for interest rate on 3-year governments.

Column 6: 1 + 2 + 4 + 5; absolute amount of Eisner adjusted measure which he expresses as a percent of GNP as given in column 7.

Column 7: Eisner measure suggested as alternative to column 3.

Eisner contends that his adjusted measures of the high- or full-employment budget surplus illuminate the switch from a "very high surplus in 1981 to a very high deficit in 1982," leading to rapid expansion of the economy in 1983 and 1984. Similarly in the 1977–1980 period, the failure to see that "fiscal policy was not stimulative" (by not recognizing "the substantial inflation-adjusted surpluses") contributed significantly to the 1981–1983 recession.

Questions

1. Why have many economists preferred the full-employment measure of the federal government surplus or deficit to the actual deficit for judging the economic impact of the federal government budget?

2. How could inflation and rising interest rates make this measure of budget balance overestimate the stimulative effects of a full-employment government deficit (considering the effects on the wealth of the public). How does Eisner adjust for this over-estimation?

3. Eisner emphasizes the stimulative switch in fiscal policy from 1981 to 1982. How much does it amount to as a percentage of GNP? Nonetheless, 1982 was a year of steady decline until November. What could Eisner reply?

4. Critics have argued that using Eisner's inflation-adjusted measure as a target for a "balanced" budget in times of rising prices would be destabilizing. Explain.

5. Consider the suggestion of Paul Wonnacott, professor of economics at the University of Maryland and one of the critics mentioned in question 4. Under the circumstances of 1986 with an actual deficit of more than $200 billion, he proposed an interim goal for the deficit of 5 percent of the national debt of about $2 trillion. The 5 percent is the sum of the long-run growth trend and a comfortable inflation rate of 1–2 percent. How would this meet the concern about the long-run burden of the debt?

6. Is there a standard for a deficit that would be "proper" for all circumstances? Consider the standard set by the Gramm-Rudman-Hollings bill.

CASE 29: Are the Worst Problems with High Unemployment Almost Over?

A case can be made that the problems of structural unemployment became particularly great in the 1970s and early 1980s but will decrease in the late 1980s.

Starting in the mid-1960s, the total labor force increased at a much more rapid rate for two reasons: a great increase in the number of 16- to 20-year-olds and increased participation by women. That the number of teenage accessions to the work force decreased in the 1980s is an established demographic fact, as indicated by the last column of the following table. That the increase in women's participation will slow up is not so certain. In terms of the chapter, "structural unemployment occurs when adjustments do not occur fast enough." If adjustments in terms of the absorption of new workers take place at a constant, absolute, or percentage pace, times of rapid expansion in the labor force will be times of higher unemployment levels.

Year	Noninstitutional population (16 years and older)	Total labor force	*Civilian labor force*			*Labor force participation rates[a] (percent)*				Children born 15 years before
						Male		Female		
			Civilians employed	Civilians unemployed	Percent unemployed	White	Black	White	Black	
1960	117.2	71.4	65.8	3.9	5.5	83.4	N.A.	36.5	N.A.	2.9
1965	126.5	76.4	71.1	3.4	4.5	80.8	N.A.	38.1	N.A.	3.6
1970	137.1	84.9	78.7	4.1	4.9	80.0	N.A.	42.6	N.A.	4.1
1975	153.2	95.4	85.8	7.9	8.5	78.7	70.9	45.9	48.8	4.3
1980	167.7	108.5	99.3	7.6	7.1	78.2	70.3	51.2	53.1	3.8
1985	178.2	117.2	107.2	8.3	7.2	77.0	70.8	54.1	56.5	3.1

Figures are in millions except where noted.

[a]The greatest increases in female participation have been in the 20–24 and 25–34 age brackets. The greatest decreases in male participation rates have been in the 55–64 and over-65 age brackets.

Questions

1. Compute the changes in total labor force and in civilian employment for the period from 1960 through 1985. Did unemployment during the 1970s reflect slower growth in jobs or more rapid increases in the labor force? What about 1980–1985?

	ΔLabor force	Percent change	ΔCivilian employment	Percent change
1960–1965				
1965–1970				
1970–1975				
1975–1980				
1980–1985				

2. (a) The labor force participation rate for married women increased from 30 percent in 1960 to over 50 percent in 1985. How might this affect search unemployment?

   (b) Would you expect measured GNP to be affected as more married women move into the labor force? Explain.

3. (a) There has been a dramatic rise in years of schooling for all groups in the labor force over the past 20 years. For example, in 1960, 60 percent of 25- to 29-year-olds had 4 years of high school and 11 percent had attended college for 4 years. In 1980, the percentages had risen to 85 and 23 percent, respectively. How should this affect structural unemployment?

   (b) What data from the table support the hypothesis that there should be a lower unemployment rate in the late 1980s than in the 1970s?

4. As the share of young people in the labor force continues to decline sharply over the next decade, what is the likely effect on the natural rate of unemployment? What are the implications for macroeconomic policy, other things equal?

CASE 30: Legislating Macroeconomic Goals

The U.S. Congress has played a major role in establishing a legal framework for the government's macroeconomic policy. The first major piece of legislation was the Employment Act of 1946, which gave the federal government statutory responsibility to promote full employment and price stability. In 1978 the government's responsibility was more clearly specified with the Full Employment and Balanced Growth Act, popularly known as the Humphrey-Hawkins Act. This act established specific numerical objectives for employment and price stability, as shown in the table below. The unemployment rate was to be reduced to 4 percent by 1983; at the same time, the rate of inflation was to be reduced to zero by 1988, with an interim target of 3 percent in 1983. The timetable for achieving these specific objectives was extended by President Carter in 1980 as shown by the figures in the second row.

Other than calling for improved coordination of stabilization policy among the executive branch, the Congress, and the federal monetary authorities, the Humphrey-Hawkins Act made no specific recommendations for policy changes to meet the specified objectives.

	Year									
	1979	1980	1981	1982	1983	1984	1985	1986	1987	1988
Unemployment rate[a]										
Humphrey-Hawkins goal	6.2	6.2	5.4	4.6	4.0	4.0	4.0	4.0	4.0	4.0
Economic Report (1980)	—	7.5	7.3	6.5	5.6	4.8	4.0	—	—	—
Economic Report (1983)	—	—	—	—	10.7*	9.9*	8.9	8.1	7.3	6.5
Actual	5.8	7.0	7.5	9.5	9.5	7.4	7.1	—	—	—
Inflation rate[b]										
Humphrey-Hawkins goal	7.5	6.4	5.2	4.1	3.0	—	—	—	—	—
Economic Report (1980)	—	10.7	8.7	7.9	7.2	6.5	5.8	—	—	—
Economic Report (1983)	—	—	—	—	4.9*	4.6*	4.6	4.6	4.5	4.4
Actual	13.3	12.4	8.9	3.9	3.8	4.0	3.8	—	—	—

[a]Annual percentage of labor force.
[b]December to December change in CPI.
*These figures were subsequently revised in July 1983 to 9 percent and 8 percent for unemployment and 4.6 percent and 5 percent for inflation, respectively.

Questions

1. Does the historical record suggest that the goals of 4 percent unemployment and 0 percent inflation are realistic?

2. In what years were interim goals for either unemployment or inflation achieved? When this occurred, what happened to achievement of other goals?

3. The *Economic Report of the President* (1983) suggested that the four-point program of the Reagan administration, "reducing the growth of Federal outlays, taxes, regulation, and the money supply," constituted the best approach for attaining the goals of the Humphrey-Hawkins Act. Is this an interventionist or noninterventionist program? Do its projections suggest that it will achieve the specific goals of the act? What nonlisted objective is probably its most important aim?

4. What are the elements of a program an interventionist might propose?

5. Track the actual performance by filling in the "actual" rows in the exhibit from the latest *Economic Report, Economic Indicators,* or the *Survey of Current Business.*

PART TEN

International Trade and Finance

38

The Gains from Trade

Learning Objectives

After studying the material in this chapter, you should recognize that

—international trade among countries involves basically the same principles of exchange that occur among individuals;

—the gains from trade arise from specialization by nations in production of goods for which they have a comparative advantage;

—comparative advantage arises from differences in opportunity costs of producing particular goods and can be acquired as well as depending on resource endowments;

—the terms of trade are the ratio of export to import prices.

Review and Self-Test

Matching Concepts

_______ 1. absence of trade

_______ 2. greater production of a commodity from equal quantity of resources

_______ 3. gains from trade

_______ 4. comparative advantage

_______ 5. generalized basis for gains from trade

_______ 6. learning by doing

_______ 7. quantity of domestic goods needed to obtain a unit of imported goods

_______ 8. index of terms of trade

_______ 9. economies of scale

_______ 10. determinants of comparative advantage, according to classical economists

(a) increased availability of goods and services from specialization and trade

(b) differences in opportunity costs of products among nations

(c) greater efficiency resulting from work experience

(d) absolute advantage

(e) terms of trade

(f) self-sufficiency and lower standards of living

(g) greater absolute advantage in producing *X* than in producing *Y*

(h) import prices divided by export prices expressed as a percentage

(i) natural resource endowments

(j) advantage of specialization, especially for small countries

Multiple-Choice Questions

1. A country is relatively more efficient than another in producing a good if
   (a) it produces it more cheaply in terms of other goods not produced.
   (b) it produces it at lower money cost.
   (c) it has lower wage levels.
   (d) there are economies of scale available.

2. Which of these statements represents the least appropriate use of the concept of opportunity cost?
   (a) Exports can be thought of as the opportunity cost of imports.
   (b) The opportunity cost of product *B* is the amount of product *A* that could be produced with the same resources.
   (c) The opportunity cost of increased output may be measured by the utility of leisure given up to produce the output.
   (d) The opportunity cost of producing *C* is the sum of its real and monetary costs.

3. Through trade nations
   (a) can effectively consume at levels beyond their production possibilities frontiers.
   (b) will be limited in their consumption to points on the production possibilities frontier.
   (c) will not alter their previous production patterns.
   (d) are more likely to be confined to choices inside their production possibilities frontiers.

4. The doctrine of comparative advantage says that there are gains from international trade
   (a) only if both comparative and absolute advantage are present in both countries.
   (b) if opportunity costs are the same in the countries involved.
   (c) only if there are economies of scale available.
   (d) if countries specialize in the production of goods in which they are relatively more efficient.

5. Tweedledum has a comparative advantage over Tweedledee in planting as compared with harvesting. Therefore,
   (a) Tweedledum must have an absolute advantage over Tweedledee in planting.
   (b) Tweedledum must have a comparative advantage over Tweedledee in harvesting.
   (c) Tweedledee must have an absolute advantage over Tweedledum in planting.
   (d) Tweedledee must have a comparative advantage over Tweedledum in harvesting.

6. Suppose an equal quantity of resources could produce in Japan two radios and four cameras and in the United States one radio and two cameras.
   (a) The United States should export cameras to Japan and import radios.
   (b) The United States should export radios and import cameras.
   (c) Japan will be able to undersell the United States in both commodities, whatever the exchange rate.
   (d) There is no basis for mutually advantageous trade between the United States and Japan in cameras and radios.

7. Inaugurating trade with nations whose wage levels are much lower
   (a) will necessarily lower the real wages in the high-wage nation.
   (b) will probably raise per capita real income in both countries.
   (c) may help political relationships but does not contribute economically.
   (d) will lower the real wages in low-wage nations.

8. A country would welcome an improvement in its terms of trade because
   (a) it can then export more.
   (b) its exchange rate will rise.
   (c) the cost of acquiring its imports will fall.
   (d) it now becomes cheaper to produce the same goods at home instead of importing them.

9. For a country with one important exported commodity (such as coffee or oil)
   (a) a rise in its price in international markets will improve the country's terms of trade.
   (b) a fall in its price will improve the terms of trade.
   (c) its terms of trade will be unaffected by a change in its price.
   (d) a rise in its price will be helpful to the terms of trade and balance of payments only if world demand for it is elastic.

10. The several-fold rise in the price of oil in the 1970s meant that the United States
   (a) could export less of its resources in exchange for oil imports.
   (b) had to export more of its resources to pay for oil imports.
   (c) had to export the same amount of resources to pay for oil imports.
   (d) faced only monetary rather than real costs.

11. The concept of dynamic comparative advantage is best described by
   (a) the importance of natural resource endowments.
   (b) dwindling of resources over time, as with British coal and U.S. oil.
   (c) emphasizing human capital as a resource and the ability to innovate and develop skills.
   (d) all of the above

12. A rise of export prices as compared with import prices is considered a favorable change in the terms of trade since
   (a) one can make more exports per unit of imports.
   (b) jobs in export industries are likely to be created.
   (c) jobs in import-substitute industries are increased.
   (d) one can acquire more imports per unit of exports.

13. The gains of trade can be best approximated
   (a) by the increase in world output with trade as compared to without trade.
   (b) by the incidence of favorable terms of trade.
   (c) by comparing nations' standards of living with the percentage of their output exported.
   (d) by comparing nations' standards of living with the percentage of their consumption imported.

14. The gains to less-developed nations from trade
   (a) are limited because their underdevelopment rules out the possibility of absolute advantage.
   (b) are limited because of their dependence on agriculture.
   (c) can be enhanced by economies of scale from specialization.
   (d) will necessarily be eliminated by unfavorable terms of trade.

15. The terms of trade refer to
   (a) specific trade agreements between two countries.
   (b) the ratio of opportunity costs within a country.
   (c) the quantity of domestic goods that must be exported to obtain a unit of imported goods.
   (d) the inverse of the opportunity costs between two products in a given country.

16. In Exercise 1, Japan has a comparative advantage in cameras
   (a) in (a), (b), and (c).
   (b) in case (a) only.
   (c) in cases (a) and (c).
   (d) in none of the cases.

Self-Test Key

Matching Concepts: 1–f; 2–d; 3–a; 4–g; 5–b; 6–c; 7–e; 8–h; 9–j; 10–i

Multiple-Choice Questions: 1–a; 2–d; 3–a; 4–d; 5–d; 6–d; 7–b; 8–c; 9–a; 10–b; 11–c; 12–d; 13–a; 14–c; 15–c; 16–b

Exercises

1. For each of the situations below, determine which commodity each country should specialize in and trade:

(a) One unit of resources can produce: The opportunity costs are:

	Radios	Cameras		1 Radio	1 Camera
Japan	2	4	Japan	______	______
Korea	3	1	Korea	______	______

Japan should specialize in the production of ______________.
South Korea should specialize in the production of ______________.

(b) One unit of resources can produce: The opportunity costs are:

	Radios	Cameras		1 Radio	1 Camera
Japan	2	4	Japan	______	______
Korea	1	3	Korea	______	______

Japan should specialize in the production of ______________.
South Korea should specialize in the production of ______________.

(c) One unit of resources can produce: The opportunity costs are:

	Radios	Cameras		1 Radio	1 Camera
Japan	2	4	Japan	______	______
Korea	1	2	Korea	______	______

Japan should specialize in the production of ______________.
South Korea should specialize in the production of ______________.

(d) Explain briefly the differences in (a) through (c). Can a nation as technologically advanced as Japan gain from trading with other countries with lower wage levels?

2. Assume that Liechtenstein (L) and Andorra (A), with equal (and very few) resources, can produce the following (in addition to postage stamps):

	Grapes	or	Wool
Liechtenstein	100,000 kilos		100,000 kilos
Andorra	50,000 kilos		100,000 kilos

(a) Before trade, L produces 50,000 kilos of each and A produces 25,000 of grapes and 50,000 of wool. Show that trade has the potential of increasing total consumption for the two countries.

(b) A has a comparative advantage in ______________ and L has a comparative advantage in ______________.

(c) The opportunity cost of grapes in terms of wool is ______________ in A and ______________ in L. Therefore the terms of trade will be between ______________ and ______________.

3. Countries A and B are both currently producing both watches and dairy products. If country A gives up the opportunity to produce 100 pounds of dairy products for each watch it makes, and B could produce 1 watch at a cost of 200 pounds of dairy products:
   (a) The opportunity cost of making watches (in terms of dairy products) is lower in country ________.
   (b) The opportunity cost of making dairy products (in terms of watches) is lower in country ________.
   (c) So country B should specialize in ________ and let country A produce ________.
   (d) The terms of trade (the price of one product in terms of the other) would be somewhere between ________ and ________ pounds of dairy products for 1 watch.

4. (a) The impact of the two supply shocks on oil prices in 1973–1974 and in 1978–1980 can be traced in the U.S. terms of trade. Do this in the table below in which 1972 is taken as the base year of the implicit price deflators. Remember to divide the export price index by the import price index and multiply by 100. Round to the nearest percent. (See Short problem 1 for subsequent developments.)

Year	Export prices	Import prices	Oil imports (billions of dollars)	Terms of trade
1972	100	100	\$ 4.7	100
1974	135	165	26.6	________
1978	173	214	42.3	________
1980	213	289	79.3	________

   (b) What does the change in terms of trade signify for the amount of exports needed to pay for imports?

   (c) The change was blunted in the 1972–1974 period by a world grain shortage that took U.S. agriculture exports from \$9.5 billion to \$22.4 billion. How would this event enter the calculation of the terms of trade index?

Short Problems

1. (a) (See Exercise 4.) The year 1980 turned out to be a low point in the U.S. terms of trade. Oil prices softened (and broke sharply in 1986); the government chose a new base year, 1982, for the export and import price indexes. Oil imports dropped from 31.7 percent of total U.S. imports in 1980 to 14.7 percent in 1985.

	Export prices	Import prices	Oil imports (billions of dollars)	Terms of trade
1980	90	96	79.3	______
1982	100	100	61.2	100
1985	103	96	48	______

(a) Calculate terms of trade for 1980 and 1985 on the basis of 1982 as 100. Go back to Exercise 4 and approximate what 1972 would have been with a 1982 base.

(b) We can infer that substantial economizing took place in the use of imported oil between 1972 and 1982 by contrasting the rise in the import index using 1972 fixed-quantity weights with that using 1982 fixed-quantity weights. With the approximate tripling of oil prices between 1978 and 1980, the rise in the import price index was from 210 to 304 (1972 weights) and from 71 to 96 (1982 weights). Explain this result. (Note: The implicit price deflators use the quantities of the current year.)

(c) From mid-1985 to mid-1986 the price of petroleum was approximately halved. Predict the effect on the U.S. terms of trade.

2. Below are assumed production patterns with respect to wheat and wool for Canada and New Zealand. (This problem is a variant of Exercises 1 to 3 above.)

	One unit of resources will produce	
	Wheat (bu)	Wool (kg)
Canada	10	2
New Zealand	12	6

(a) Do these data suggest the existence of absolute advantage or comparative advantage? ________

(b) What is the opportunity cost of wheat, in terms of wool, for each country? Canada ________ New Zealand ________

(c) Is a gain from trade possible? Why?

(d) Will trade take place if the world price for wheat is $3 and that for wool $8? Explain.

Answers to the Exercises

1. (a) Japan: 1 radio costs 2 cameras; 1 camera costs ½ radio.
   Korea: 1 radio costs ⅓ camera; 1 camera costs 3 radios.
   Japan should produce cameras. Korea should produce radios.

   (b) Japan: 1 radio costs 2 cameras; 1 camera costs ½ radio.
   Korea: 1 radio costs 3 cameras; 1 camera costs ⅓ radio.
   Japan should produce radios. Korea should produce cameras.

   (c) Japan: 1 radio costs 2 cameras; 1 camera costs ½ radio.
   Korea: 1 radio costs 2 cameras; 1 camera costs ½ radio.
   Japan should produce both and Korea should produce both. There would be no gains from trade.

   (d) In case (a), Japan has absolute (and comparative) advantage in producing cameras, Korea in radios.
   In case (b), Japan has absolute advantage in producing both commodities but a comparative advantage only in radios; Korea has comparative advantage in cameras.
   In case (c), relative costs are the same in *both* countries for the two commodities. There are no potential gains from trade.
   Yes, Japan can gain from trade, because opportunity costs *within* each country determine whether such gains exist.

2. (a) If L specialized in grapes and A in wool, 100,000 kilos of wool and 100,000 kilos of grapes would be available for consumption, greater than the present total of 100,000 wool and 75,000 grapes. A possible exchange would be 50,000 of A's wool for 35,000 of L's grapes. Both countries would have more grapes to consume.
   (b) A, wool; L, grapes
   (c) A, 2; L, 1; terms between 1/1 and 2/1 (price of grapes over price of wool). At 1/1 all gains go to Andorra; at 2/1 all gains go to Liechtenstein.

3. (a) A (b) B (c) dairy products, watches (d) 100, 200

4. (a) Terms of trade index: 1974, 82; 1976, 81; 1980, 74
   (b) More exports are required by roughly 1/.74 – 1 = 35 percent over the entire period.
   (c) The sharp rise in the export price index to 135 would have been significantly influenced by higher grain prices.

39

Barriers to Free Trade

Learning Objectives

Careful study of the material in this chapter should give you a better understanding of

—the benefits and costs of expanding international trade;

—fallacious arguments for free trade and protectionism;

—the pressures for and prospects of a reversal of the trend toward freer trade in the last half century;

—the vital importance of trade for many nations and the significant lowering of U.S. living standards if there was a large shift toward self-sufficiency.

Review and Self-Test

Matching Concepts

_______ 1. dumping

_______ 2. absence of restrictions on importing and exporting

_______ 3. use of trade barriers to reduce imports of domestically produced products

_______ 4. valid reason for protecting domestic industry

_______ 5. voluntary export restriction (VER)

_______ 6. General Agreement on Tariffs and Trade (GATT)

_______ 7. import quotas

_______ 8. European Community

_______ 9. trigger prices

_______ 10. tariff

_______ 11. countervailing duties

_______ 12. free trade association

(a) free trade

(b) potential economies of scale

(c) nontariff barriers to trade

(d) a customs union without uniform external tariffs

(e) extensive common market

(f) minimum prices for imports

(g) periodic meetings to arrange mutually advantageous cuts in tariffs

(h) tax applied on imports

(i) protectionism

(j) charging lower prices abroad than at home

(k) negotiated quota

(l) U.S. tariffs on subsidized imports that damage U.S. industry

Multiple-Choice Questions

1. The principle of comparative advantage indicates that
   (a) free trade is invariably best.
   (b) free trade is hardly ever best.
   (c) self-sufficiency is almost always preferable to free trade.
   (d) trade with mutual gain is possible so long as relative cost differences exist.

2. For immediate effects on the domestic standard of living, a country should
   (a) welcome cheap imports.
   (b) try to expand exports.
   (c) impose tariffs to keep out foreign competition.
   (d) try to be self-sufficient.

3. Canadians who feel that more protectionism is worth a cut in living standards for national identity or independent cultural development are
   (a) irrational.
   (b) irrational if the costs of doing so are significant.
   (c) not aware of the principle of comparative advantage.
   (d) making value judgments that cannot be directly refuted by the classical case for free trade.

4. The infant industry argument for tariffs
   (a) is recognized as incorrect because protection often extends beyond infancy.
   (b) is recognized as incorrect because it is present and not future comparative advantages that should be considered.
   (c) is recognized as theoretically sound if economies of scale and learning are available.
   (d) says that industries should be protected in poor countries to provide for the welfare of infants there.

5. Which of the following would be the least valid reason for imposing a tariff?
   (a) to protect an infant industry that will eventually be competitive
   (b) to diversify the economy
   (c) to maximize worldwide real income
   (d) to maintain a vital but high-cost defense industry

6. The "buy American" argument for tariffs
   (a) is economically valid.
   (b) states that dollars spent on foreign goods will be used for U.S. exports.
   (c) should be recognized as usually being fallacious.
   (d) is a defense of tariffs as revenue-raising measures.

7. Lower wages in countries other than the United States
   (a) create unfair competition for U.S. labor.
   (b) mean that those countries cannot gain from trade with the United States.
   (c) mean that U.S. costs are bound to be higher.
   (d) may reflect lower labor productivity and higher unit costs abroad.

8. European nations with substantial tariffs on coffee (the United States has none) appear to
   (a) be motivated by protectionism.
   (b) have found a convenient way to raise revenue.
   (c) be unaware of the principle of comparative advantage.
   (d) have worsened their terms of trade.

9. A general increase of import duties by a nation during a time of unemployment
   (a) will not produce any short-run increase of income and employment.
   (b) should prove a very substantial stimulus to employment.
   (c) would have the same effect on the allocation of resources as an export subsidy.
   (d) would have a mild expansionary effect on the economy provided others do not fully retaliate.

10. The gains from the removal of tariff barriers within the Common Market have been estimated to be
    (a) very large.
    (b) negative.
    (c) significant though modest.
    (d) zero.

11. The European Community (EC)
    (a) is an example of a completely free-trading area, externally as well as internally.
    (b) was intended to allow the free movement of labor, capital, and goods among its members.
    (c) now includes all of Europe.
    (d) has completely fixed exchange rates among its currencies and in relation to others.

12. After World War II, the United States
    (a) reversed what had usually been a protectionist position in favor of lower tariffs.
    (b) continued its long tradition of free trade.
    (c) found it necessary to increase tariffs generally as foreign nations caught up on technology.
    (d) continued to protect high U.S. wages with high tariffs.

13. Countervailing duties are attempts to maintain "a level playing ground" by
    (a) retaliating against foreign tariffs.
    (b) raising or lowering tariffs multilatcrally.
    (c) establishing a common tariff wall around a customs union.
    (d) assessing tariffs that will offset foreign government subsidies.

14. A long established free-trade association has been
    (a) the European Community (EC).
    (b) the European Free Trade Association (EFTA).
    (c) between the United States and Canada.
    (d) the Southeast Asia Treaty Organization (SEATO).

15. The Kennedy round and the Tokyo round were
    (a) negotiations to deal with Japan's exports to the United States, particularly of automobiles.
    (b) attempts to persuade Japan to relax unfair trade practices on imports.
    (c) agreements under the General Agreement on Tariffs and Trade (GATT).
    (d) bilateral discussions concerned with the security and economic development of Southeast Asia.

Self-Test Key

Matching Concepts: 1–j; 2–a; 3–i; 4–b; 5–k; 6–g; 7–c; 8–e; 9–f; 10–h; 11–l; 12–d

Multiple-Choice Questions: 1–d; 2–a; 3–d; 4–c; 5–c; 6–c; 7–d; 8–b; 9–d; 10–c; 11–b; 12–a; 13–d; 14–b; 15–c

Exercises

1. Listed below are short paraphrases of pro- and anti-tariff arguments that the text suggests are fallacious. Give a brief refutation of each paraphrase. (Your words may not necessarily be the same as the suggested answers but still be to the point.)
   (a) Trade is exploitation.

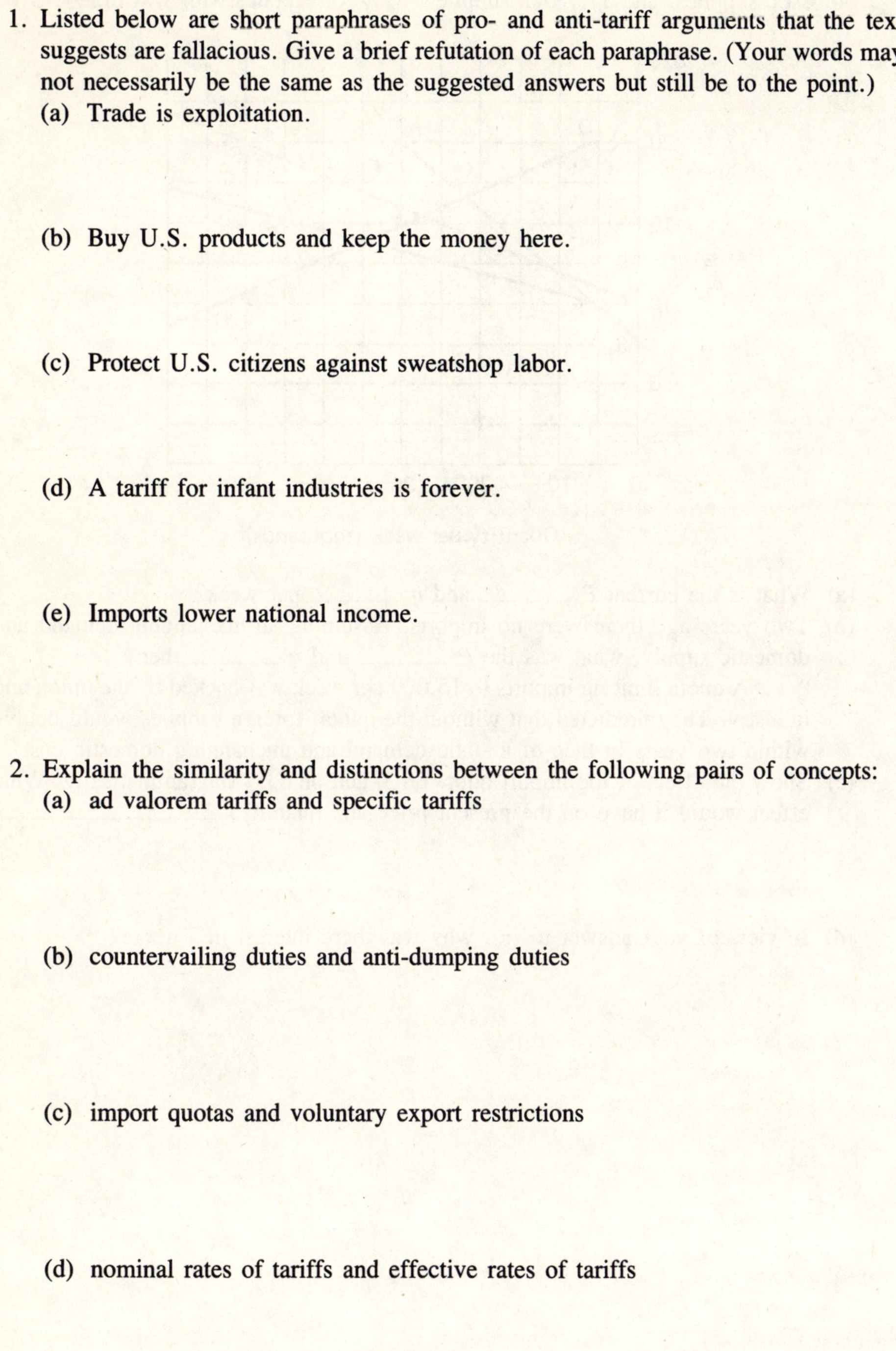

   (b) Buy U.S. products and keep the money here.

   (c) Protect U.S. citizens against sweatshop labor.

   (d) A tariff for infant industries is forever.

   (e) Imports lower national income.

2. Explain the similarity and distinctions between the following pairs of concepts:
   (a) ad valorem tariffs and specific tariffs

   (b) countervailing duties and anti-dumping duties

   (c) import quotas and voluntary export restrictions

   (d) nominal rates of tariffs and effective rates of tariffs

3. Foreign suppliers had been making rapid inroads into the market for product *X* as shown on the diagram in which S_f represents foreign supplies to the U.S. market, S_d domestic supplies, and S_{d+f} total supplied. S_{d+f} corresponds with S_f with $P < \$10$.

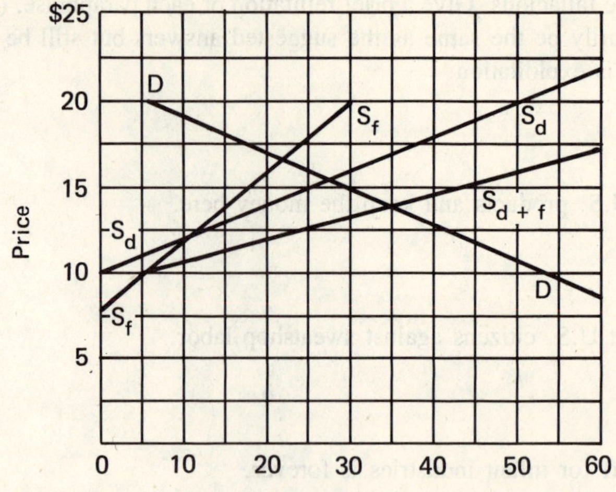

(a) What is the current *P* ______ and *q* ______ per week?

(b) Two years ago there were no imports. Assuming an unchanging demand and domestic supply, what was the *P* ______ and *q* ______ then?

A quota limiting imports to 15,000 per week was backed by the union and industry. They predicted that without the quota, foreign supplies would double within two years in face of a static demand and unchanging domestic cost.

(c) Show the effect of the import quota on S_f and on S_{d+f} diagrammatically. What effect would it have on the present price and quantity? ______

(d) In view of your answer to (c), why was there interest in a quota?

4. The following hypothetical quotation is from a union official: "We are not opposed to imports so long as they do not destroy jobs. It seems nonsensical to me, however, that last year when the overall unemployment rate was 7.5 percent, we destroyed another 100,000 jobs by allowing the importation of cheap goods from abroad."
   (a) Would a higher tariff on a particular imported product reduce the overall unemployment rate? Explain.

   (b) Would such a tariff reduce the unemployment rate in the domestic industry that competes with the imported product?

   (c) Would such a tariff "destroy" jobs in other industries? Elaborate.

5. Show that import restrictions may raise, leave unchanged, or lower the price exporters (to the importing country) receive. Situations (a) and (b) are those in Box 39-1 of the text and (c) illustrates the point the text makes as to how a substantial importing country can improve its terms of trade through a tariff. In each situation, imports are to be restricted to q_1. Complete the diagrams to show the new price, P_1, that would be received by exporters.

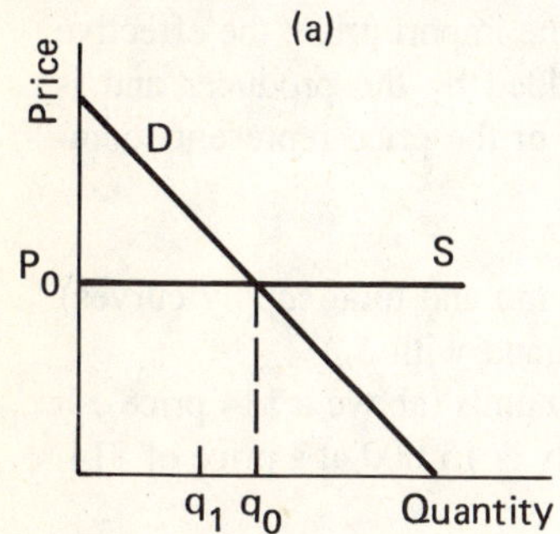

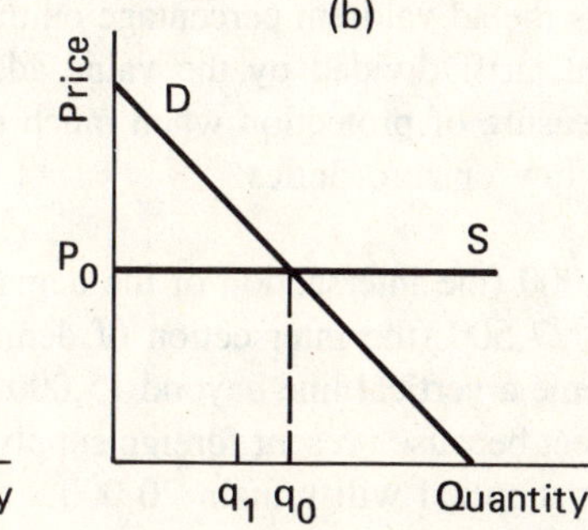

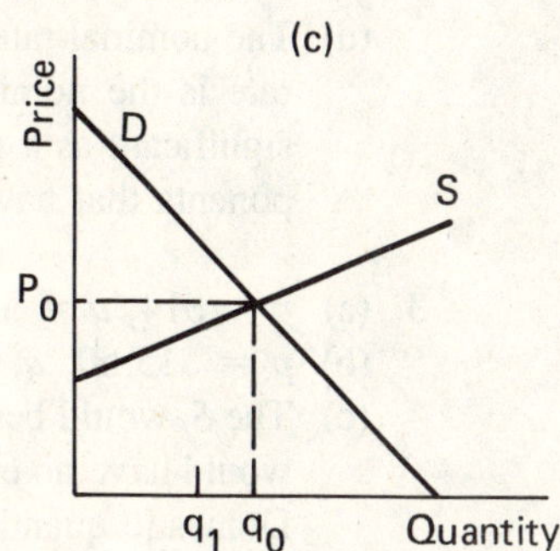

Short Problems

1. (Refer to Exercise 3.) Assume the foreign quantity supplied is doubled at each price, unchanging demand, and no shift in domestic supply. Predict the following:
   (a) p, q, and domestic production if quota is established

   (b) p, q, and domestic production if no quota is established

2. An option that has been seriously considered by the United States is the imposition of a tariff on imported oil. Consider briefly its probable effects on the following:
(a) U.S. tax revenues
(b) U.S. oil imports
(c) U.S. oil production
(d) U.S. terms of trade
(e) U.S. price of gasoline
(f) U.S. petrochemical industry

Answers to the Exercises

1. (a) When opportunity cost ratios differ, both partners can have more goods by trade.
(b) Dollars abroad represent purchasing power for U.S. goods just as dollars at home do.
(c) Cheaper imports mean more goods for U.S. workers.
(d) Whether tariffs remain or not, the real costs of production, and thus resources required, have been reduced as the infant industry developed.
(e) Imports are the only way in which resources used for exports can be recovered.

2. (a) Both represent duties on imports. Ad valorem represents a percentage of import price; specific represents a money amount per unit of product.
(b) Both represent attempts "at a level playing field" for U.S. and foreign firms; countervailing duties are designed to offset foreign subsidies, anti-dumping duties at price discrimination, i.e., lower prices in U.S. markets than in domestic markets.
(c) Both represent quantity limitations on imports into the United States. Voluntary export restrictions are negotiated with leading exporting countries (such as Japan with automobiles).
(d) The nominal rate is the ad valorem percentage on the import price; the effective rate is the nominal tariff divided by the value added by the producer and is significant as a measure of protection when much of the price represents components that have low or zero duties.

3. (a) p = \$14, q = 35,000 (the intersection of the demand and total supply curves)
(b) p = \$15.50, q = 27,500 (the intersection of demand with S_d)
(c) The S_f would become a vertical line beyond 15,000 units (above a \$14 price). It would have no effect because present foreign supply is 15,000 at a price of \$14. Domestic quantity supplied will remain 20,000.
(d) The protection is against expected future foreign increases.

4. (a) Probably not in the long run. Higher tariffs may reduce real income and even raise the overall unemployment rate if U.S. exports are reduced.
(b) Yes, the particular industry would ordinarily be helped by increased sales and/or higher prices.
(c) It could. The immediate effect would be to reduce foreigners' dollar holdings and domestic exports. Retaliation could later occur, reducing exports further.

5. (a) (b) (c)

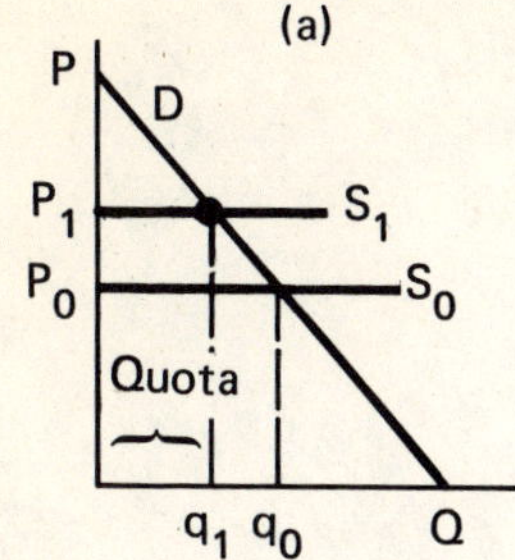

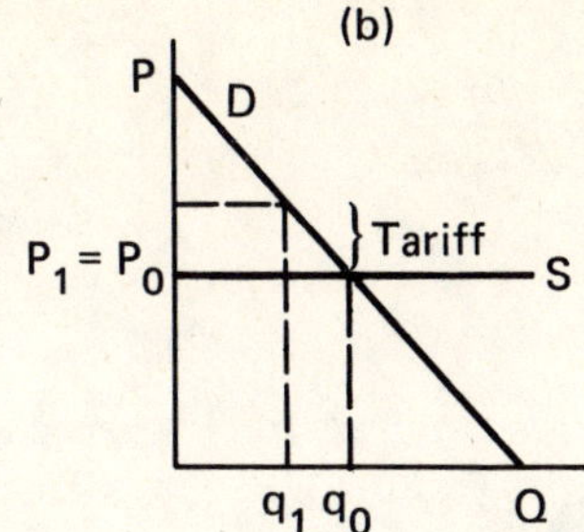

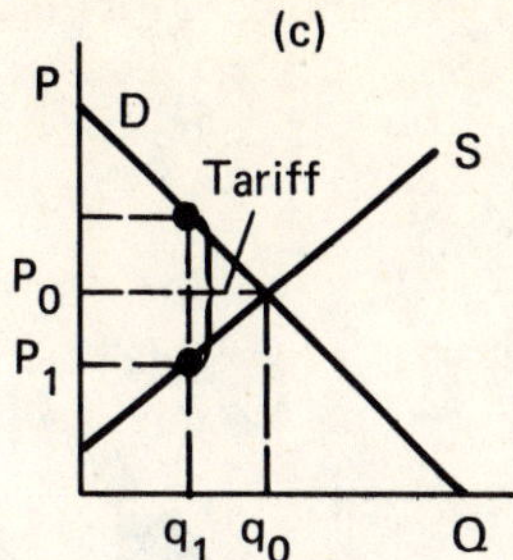

With the same demands and q_1's, prices to the consumer will rise by the same amount [$P_0 P_1$ in (a)], but note the difference in the price received by producers.

40

Exchange Rates and the Balance of Payments

Learning Objectives

After studying the material in this chapter, you should recognize

—the appropriateness of demand and supply analysis in determining exchange rates;

—the variety of transactions that lead to demand for and supply of foreign exchange;

—the significance of trade imbalances and capital account surpluses and deficits while the overall balance of payments is always equal to zero;

—the role of exchange rate changes in international economic adjustments.

Review and Self-Test

Matching Concepts

_______ 1. foreign exchange rates

_______ 2. record of a nation's payments and receipts of foreign exchange

_______ 3. balance of merchandise trade

_______ 4. surplus on current account

_______ 5. cause of loss in official reserves

_______ 6. greater inflation in the United States than elsewhere

_______ 7. managed flexibility

_______ 8. floating exchange rate

_______ 9. downward revision of a nation's monetary unit relative to foreign money

_______ 10. fixed exchange rates

_______ 11. surplus on capital account

_______ 12. direct investment

(a) ownership of controlling interest in foreign firm

(b) balance-of-payments deficit

(c) modification by central bank action of floating exchange rate

(d) balance-of-payments statement

(e) devaluation or depreciation

(f) exchange rate system in general use from World War II to early 1970s

(g) prices for purchase or sale of foreign currencies

(h) price of currency determined by forces of supply and demand

(i) cause of depreciation of the U.S. dollar

(j) excess in value of exports over imports (services and unilateral transfers included)

(k) value of export goods minus value of import goods

(l) counterpart to deficit on current account

Multiple-Choice Questions

1. In the exchange market between dollars and pounds sterling, a demander of dollars is also a
   (a) supplier of dollars.
   (b) supplier of pounds.
   (c) demander of pounds.
   (d) demander of gold.

2. A dollar price of $.40 for the mark can be expressed as a mark price for dollars of
   (a) 2.5.
   (b) 0.50.
   (c) an indeterminate amount, because all currencies are quoted only in dollars.
   (d) 0.25.

3. Arbitrage operations in the foreign exchange markets are
   (a) any transactions in foreign exchanges.
   (b) transactions involving currencies other than dollars or pounds.
   (c) transactions among central banking authorities.
   (d) foreign exchange transactions that seek gains from discrepancies in exchange rates.

4. Which of the following statements is true about the balance of payments?
   (a) Current account debits must equal current account credits.
   (b) Visibles must equal invisibles.
   (c) Total debits must equal total credits.
   (d) Desired payments must equal actual payments.

5. Exports of U.S. goods are on the same side (credit) of the U.S. accounts as
   (a) U.S. investment abroad.
   (b) U.S. government aid to underdeveloped countries.
   (c) the money spent on travel in Europe by U.S. tourists.
   (d) investment by British people in U.S. stocks.

6. A loan to Jordan accompanied by U.S. deliveries of $2 million in military equipment to them leads to which of the following in the balance of payments?
   (a) a $2 million credit in the U.S. current account
   (b) a $2 million debit in the U.S. capital account
   (c) both (a) and (b)
   (d) no record because the transaction was of military equipment

7. If the Fed wishes to intervene to prevent depreciation of the dollar in the foreign exchange market, it could
   (a) lower the discount rate.
   (b) purchase pounds from the Bank of England.
   (c) sell U.S. securities on the open market.
   (d) find none of the above measures appropriate.

8. If the price of the Canadian dollar is allowed to fluctuate, and U.S. citizens wish to buy fewer Canadian goods, *ceteris paribus,* it will take
   (a) more U.S. dollars to buy a Canadian dollar than before.
   (b) the same number of Canadian dollars to buy a U.S. dollar as before.
   (c) fewer Canadian dollars to buy a U.S. dollar than before.
   (d) more Canadian dollars to buy a U.S. dollar than before.

9. Suppose the U.S. demand for Canadian dollars is 50 billion Canadian dollars per year at an exchange rate of $.70 for a Canadian dollar and 40 billion Canadian dollars a year at an exchange rate of $.80. The elasticity of demand is
   (a) inelastic (< 1).
   (b) approximately unit elasticity (= 1).
   (c) moderately elastic (≈1.6).
   (d) very elastic (> 2).

10. The current account includes all but which of the following transactions?
   (a) merchandise exports and imports
   (b) unilateral transfers
   (c) short-run capital transfers
   (d) invisibles

11. A system of fixed exchange rates
   (a) needs no government intervention in the currency market.
   (b) usually results in balance-of-payments deficits and surpluses.
   (c) was only possible under the gold standard.
   (d) creates additional uncertainties for importers.

12. Increased preferences of U.S. consumers for Japanese cars would
   (a) shift the supply-of-dollars curve to the left and lead to an appreciation in the value of the yen.
   (b) shift the demand-for-dollars curve to the left and lead to a depreciation in the value of the dollar.
   (c) shift the demand-for-dollars curve to the right and lead to an appreciation in the value of the yen.
   (d) shift the supply-of-dollars curve to the right and lead to a depreciation in the value of the dollar.

13. An "overall" balance-of-payments deficit or surplus
   (a) refers to the balance on all accounts.
   (b) refers to the balance on all accounts excluding official financing (reserves).
   (c) refers to the balance of trade.
   (d) refers to the differences between capital inflows and capital outflows.

14. The "overall" imbalances referred to in Question 13
   (a) are logically impossible because debits must equal credits.
   (b) will be eliminated if exchange rates are completely free to vary.
   (c) would not exist under firmly fixed rates.
   (d) have been created by the abandonment of the gold standard.

15. The $100 billion plus current account deficits that the United States incurred during the mid-1980s
   (a) had counterparts in capital account surpluses (inflows).
   (b) were responsible for the United States becoming a net debtor nation.
   (c) were largely accounted for by deficits in merchandise trade.
   (d) all of the above

The following questions refer to Exercise 4.

16. In this two-nation model, the analysis could have used the quantity of dollars on the horizontal axis and
   (a) the vertical axis would be the dollar price for pounds, but the demand-and-supply curves would remain the same.
   (b) the vertical axis would be the pound price of dollars, but the demand-and-supply curves would remain the same.
   (c) the vertical axis would be the dollar price for pounds, demand would be converted to supply, and supply to demand.
   (d) the vertical axis would be the pound price for dollars, demand would be converted to supply, and supply to demand.

17. The equilibrium price would then be expressed as
   (a) £ .435.
   (b) £ .417.
   (c) $2.30.
   (d) $2.40.

Self-Test Key

Matching Concepts: 1–g; 2–d; 3–k; 4–j; 5–b; 6–i; 7–c; 8–h; 9–e; 10–f; 11–l; 12–a

Multiple-Choice Questions: 1–b; 2–a; 3–d; 4–c; 5–d; 6–c; 7–c; 8–d; 9–c; 10–c; 11–b; 12–d; 13–b; 14–b; 15–d; 16–d; 17–a

Exercises

1. The exchange rate between the Canadian dollar and other currencies has been free to fluctuate since the mid-1960s. Most other countries have more recently let the values of their currencies float. For each of the following (in some cases hypothetical) events, indicate whether the value of the Canadian dollar in terms of the U.S. dollar will tend to appreciate, depreciate, or remain unchanged. Explain your answer briefly.
   (a) Montreal hosts the 1976 Summer Olympics.

   (b) The rate of inflation in Canada increases relative to the U.S. inflation rate.

   (c) Investors in Quebec purchase substantial real estate in nearby New England and New York.

   (d) A consortium of U.S. oil companies constructs a pipeline in Canada to transport natural gas to the United States.

   (e) Short-term interest rates rise in the United States relative to those in Canada.

   (f) New York State and New England utilities contract to buy electricity from Canada's James River hydroelectric facility.

2. In this exercise "the current account" is considered for the years 1982 and 1984 when the balance switched from near zero to the $100 billion negative range for the United States. (In Exercise 3 you will be asked to relate the significant changes to economic events. Table 40-2 of the text presents data for 1985.)

(a) The two largest numerical items in a summary breakdown of U.S. current account transactions are (in billions of dollars as are all subsequent figures):

	1982	1984
Merchandise exports	$211	$220
Merchandise imports	248	334
Balance on merchandise (+ or –)	______	______

Complete the table. The negative signs indicate that people in the United States demanded (more/less) foreign exchange than was supplied by foreigners in these transactions for (visibles/invisibles). This balance is available with about a month's lag and is popularly called the balance of trade, a misleading term since the exports and imports of ______________ are not included.

(b) The balance on goods and services is the conceptual counterpart of net exports ($X - M$) in national income and product accounts. This is most easily calculated by starting from the overall balance in the current account:

	1982	1984
Balance on current account	$–8	$–107
Less unilateral transfers	–8	– 11
Balance on goods and services	______	______

(i) The unilateral transfers consist of government grants, pensions to expatriates, remittances to the family in the old country, and so on. Why should these be excluded from calculations of the national income?

(ii) Unilateral transfers now constitute such a trivial percentage of international transactions that the balance on current account is often referred to as the equivalent of $X - M$. In 1949, the heyday of the Marshall plan to rebuild war-torn Europe, grants were almost one-half of merchandise exports. Comment on this "solution" for financing real goods flows.

(c) The other way for calculating the balance on goods and services is to enumerate the invisibles. The largest category is capital services, so investment income and receipts are enumerated separately; the others are on a net basis ($X - M$). Net military transactions include *visibles* (excluded from the merchandise accounts) as well as *invisibles*. Confirm that the same balance on goods and services is reached by this method:

	1982	1984
Investment income (receipts)	$ 85	$ 88
Investment income (payments)	−55	−69
Net military transactions	0	− 2
Net travel and transportation	− 1	− 9
Other services, net ($X - M$)	8	10
Net services	______	______
Balance on merchandise		
Balance on goods and services	______	______

3. (a) From the data in Exercise 2, enter the changes between 1982 and 1984 in the following balance of payments accounts and confirm that they account for the bulk of the change in the current account deficit.

   1. Merchandise imports _______
   2. Investment income payments
   3. Net travel and transportation receipts _______
   4. Current account deficit _______

   These economic events also characterized the 1982–1984 period:

   5. A rapid increase in real GNP at an annual rate of over 6 percent from the cyclical low at the end of 1982.
   6. A substantial appreciation of the dollar (about 30 percent) in foreign exchange markets.
   7. A more than $100-billion-dollar increase in the annual federal government deficit from 1981 to 1984.
   8. A rise in short-term interest rates on U.S. treasury bills from 7.8 to 10.5 percent (about 3 percent higher on long terms) while annual consumer price changes were about 4 percent.

   (b) From the list of eight in part (a), briefly explain the relationships between the following:

   (i) 1 (or 3) to 5

   (ii) 3 (or 1) to 6

   (iii) 2 to 4

   (iv) 7 (and 5) to 8

   (v) 8 to 6

4. Assume that the bank of England is trying to maintain a fixed rate of about £ 1 = $2.40. Given demand and supply curves as shown on the graph, will it have to buy or to sell pounds to maintain the price? _______
About how many? _______
What is the existing equilibrium exchange rate? _______
How would this exchange rate be expressed as pounds per dollar? _______

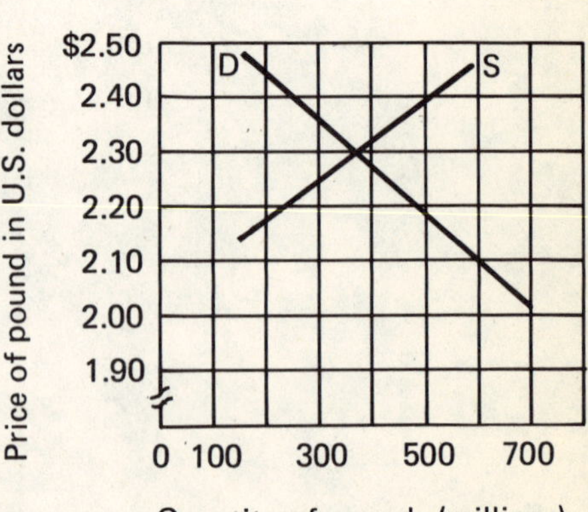

Short Problems

1. (Refer to Exercise 4.)
   (a) Show the same situation with the quantity expressed as dollars and the price as pounds per dollar. Provide suitable axis designations and grid.

   (b) Would the bank have to be prepared to buy or sell dollars to maintain the specified exchange rate? ______ About how many? ______ What would eventually limit the ability of the Bank of England to maintain the rate of approximately £ .4167 per dollar? ______

   (c) The last time the equilibrium rate was about £ .435 per dollar ($2.30 per pound) was in 1980. In the first half of 1983 the rate varied from $1.49 to $1.58 per pound or £ ______ to £ ______ per dollar. A special factor was the drop in oil prices in 1982–1983 (Britain was an exporter of North Sea oil). How would this change the exchange rate? What is the current exchange rate (consult the financial section of a newspaper)?

2. **The New Position of the United States as International Debtor**

In 1984, the net international investment position of the United States dropped from a reported $106.2 billion to $28.2 billion. The United States faced the prospect of being a net debtor, a situation it had not experienced since World War I. The balance on the U.S. current account was –$107 billion.

(a) The U.S. current account balance in the first three quarters of 1985 was estimated as –$24, –$28, and –$30 billion. In what quarter can we be quite certain that the United States achieved its debtor position? Explain.

(b) From 1982 (when U.S. net investment was at its peak) to 1984, U.S. assets abroad increased from $839 to $915 billion while foreign assets in the United States increased from $692 to $886 billion. Does the switch to international debtor position reflect a withdrawal from the U.S. position abroad or a capital inflow into the United States? Explain briefly.

(c) Below is a ten-year comparison in private direct, portfolio, and U.S. security holdings by foreigners. Between 1974 and 1984, U.S. prices about doubled, so changes in real flows can be roughly identified. Figures are in billions of dollars.

	1974	1984
U.S. direct investment abroad	$110	$231
Foreign direct investment in United States	25	160
U.S. holdings of foreign corporate securities	28	90
Foreign holdings of U.S. corporate securities	22	128
Foreign holdings of U.S. treasury securities	2	57

Comment on these patterns, including in your analysis the distinction between direct and portfolio investments.

(d) Net investment income for the United States reached a peak of $34 billion in 1981 with $86 billion in receipts and $52 billion in payments. How will this change with a continuation of $100 billion-plus deficits in the current account into the late 1980s? What is eventually likely to limit this process?

Answers to the Exercises

1. (a) Appreciate; visitors exchange their currency for the Canadian dollar.
   (b) Depreciate; U.S. goods become relatively cheaper, stimulating imports by Canadians and reducing Canadian exports.
   (c) Depreciate; capital outflow requires U.S. dollars.
   (d) Appreciate; investment funds shift from the United States to Canada.
   (e) Depreciate; Canadian capital should be attracted to the United States.
   (f) Probably unchanged until time of delivery, then appreciation because of increased exports

2. (a) –\$37; –\$114; more; visibles; invisibles or services
   (b) 0; –\$96; national income is defined as that received from current *productive* activity. By advancing foreign exchange (dollars) as a gift, Europe obtained the real goods needed to restore productive capacity without incurring future debt repayment problems. The U.S. interest was both humanitarian and military (the "Cold War" had begun).
   (c) 1982: –\$37 (merchandise deficit) + 37 (net services) = 0; 1984: –\$114 (merchandise deficit) + 18 (net services) = –\$96. The answers are the same as (b).

3. (a) 1. –\$86 billion 2. –\$14 billion 3. –\$8 billion 4. –\$99 billion
   The changes (1, 2, 3) total –\$108 billion; the +\$9 billion for exports and offsetting minor changes take care of the difference (between \$108 and \$99).
   (b) (i) We would expect imports, including invisibles such as travel, to increase with a rise in real national income and have considered M as a function of Y in our models.
   (ii) Foreign goods have become cheaper relative to domestic goods when the dollar buys more foreign exchange. Expenditures would rise if the elasticity of demand is greater than one. The travel in item (iii) would almost certainly have an increased negative component because of the probability that the demand for foreign travel is elastic. In addition, as a net item it also includes price effects that affect foreign tourism to the United States.
   (iii) The current account deficits had, as their counterpart, capital inflows into the United States, which increased foreign investment and the income from it.
   (iv) The deficit itself required substantial borrowing as did the booming economy (stimulated by an expansive fiscal policy of tax cuts and increased defense spending).
   (v) The high real interest rates stimulated a demand for dollars to invest in the United States. At the same time, the appreciation of the dollar kept downward pressure on prices because of cheaper imports and increased the spread of nominal interest rates over the inflation rate.

4. Buy; ≈ £ 250 million; \$2.30; £ .435

41

Alternative Exchange Rate Systems

Learning Objectives

After reading this chapter you should be able to

—explain the mechanism of the gold standard, the gold exchange standard with adjustable pegs (Bretton Woods system), and floating exchange rates accompanied by some government intervention;

—recognize problems arising under various monetary systems and the need for international cooperation in meeting them;

—explain the role of the International Monetary Fund (IMF);

—understand the significant differences between fixed and flexible exchange rate systems.

Review and Self-Test

Matching Concepts

______ 1. system in which exchange rates among national currencies were fixed in terms of gold	(a) negotiated devaluation of the dollar	
	(b) lending institution concerned with bridging short-term deficits	
______ 2. adjustment mechanism under the gold standard	(c) foreign exchange reserves	
	(d) supplementary reserve assets created by the IMF	
______ 3. Smithsonian Agreement		
______ 4. exchange rates fixed in the short term but adjustable if necessary	(e) exchange rates determined by demand and supply but with substantial intervention by central authorities	
______ 5. International Monetary Fund	(f) fall in the domestic price level of a deficit country	
______ 6. gold, key currencies, and SDRs	(g) accumulated payments surpluses of major oil producers	
______ 7. Special Drawing Rights (SDRs)	(h) gold standard	
______ 8. speculative crises	(i) major problem with an adjustable peg system	
______ 9. petrodollars	(j) explanation of long-run changes in foreign exchange rates	
______ 10. managed ("dirty") float		
	(k) Bretton Woods system	
______ 11. purchasing power parity hypothesis	(l) competitive devaluation	
______ 12. beggar-thy-neighbor policy		

Multiple-Choice Questions

1. Under the gold standard
   (a) exchange rates fluctuated frequently.
   (b) equilibrium was produced by changes in fixed exchange rates.
   (c) crises of confidence were met quickly despite the small amount of gold relative to claims on it.
   (d) equilibrium was supposed to be reached by changes in domestic price levels.

2. During the monetary crisis and the depression of the 1930s
   (a) most countries stayed on the gold standard despite difficulties.
   (b) competitive currency devaluations were frequent.
   (c) U.S. tariff policy became less protectionist.
   (d) international trade was stimulated because of the low prices.

3. Under the Bretton Woods agreement
   (a) most countries returned to the gold standard.
   (b) countries were given almost complete freedom to let their currencies float.
   (c) exchange rates were tied to the U.S. dollar.
   (d) gold was completely abandoned as an international means of payment.

4. The Bretton Woods system
   (a) ultimately proved unworkable because of exchange rates that remained in disequilibrium.
   (b) failed, because under it the United States ended up with all the gold.
   (c) created uncertainties and reduced the volume of world trade.
   (d) made currency devaluation by a nation illegal.

5. Postwar international developments included all of the following except
   (a) the dollar shortage confronting war-torn countries that needed U.S. goods.
   (b) the dollar surplus Europe and Japan accumulated as they recovered.
   (c) prompt upward adjustments of undervalued currencies.
   (d) considerable international cooperation to maintain stable exchange rates.

6. Destabilizing speculation occurs when
   (a) lower exchange rates increase the quantity of a currency demanded.
   (b) higher exchange rates increase the quantity of a currency supplied.
   (c) there is no expectation that fixed exchange rates will be changed.
   (d) a change in exchange rates leads to expectation of further changes in the same direction.

7. Special Drawing Rights are
   (a) supplementary reserves with the IMF, which member countries can use to finance balance-of-payments deficits.
   (b) demand deposits that central banks hold in the World Bank.
   (c) special credits given to importers in IMF countries.
   (d) long-term reserves available to member countries in return for gold.

8. Floating exchange rates
   (a) require the support of large monetary reserves.
   (b) describe the fluctuations around fixed rates permitted by IMF rules.
   (c) are necessarily destabilizing.
   (d) are determined in international exchange markets by demand and supply.

9. The "dirty" or managed float of currencies means that
   (a) currencies are officially pegged, but a large black market exists.
   (b) the official price at which gold is being sold is allowed to fluctuate.
   (c) currencies are officially floating but are being directly influenced occasionally by central bank policies.
   (d) currency speculation and monetary crises are even worse than under a fixed exchange rate regime.

10. Under the international monetary arrangements of the 1980s, gold
    (a) was effectively demonetized.
    (b) appreciated steadily in value without major fluctuations.
    (c) remained an important component of international reserves (the largest with current market values used in its valuation).
    (d) became the most frequently used asset in settling international payments.

11. The causes of the appreciation of the U.S. dollar from 1980 through 1984 included
    (a) more restrictive monetary policy.
    (b) high interest rates relative to the rest of the world.
    (c) low inflation.
    (d) (a), (b), and (c), which were closely interrelated.

12. Effects of the U.S. dollar's appreciation (and its slow depreciation after the first quarter of 1985) were
    (a) current account surpluses and reduced protectionist pressures.
    (b) current account surpluses and increased protectionist pressures.
    (c) current account deficits and reduced protectionist pressures.
    (d) current account deficits and increased protectionist pressures.

13. The status of the United States in 1986 as a net debtor came about with
    (a) the withdrawal by U.S. corporations and individuals of their investments abroad.
    (b) the wave of defaults that wiped out the foreign loans of U.S. banks.
    (c) direct loans from foreign governments to allow the United States to increase military expenditure.
    (d) large capital inflows that accompanied current account deficits.

14. According to the purchasing power parity hypothesis, if domestic inflation in country A exceeded that in country B by 10 percent, the price of B's currency expressed in A's currency
    (a) should increase by about 10 percent.
    (b) should decrease by about 10 percent.
    (c) should not change since inflation rates are domestic only.
    (d) cannot be predicted because of the inapplicability of PPP.

15. From 1967 to 1982 prices in the United States rose by 190 percent, while prices in France rose by 273.5 percent. If the exchange rate in 1967 for the franc was $.2032, purchasing power parity would indicate a rate in 1982 of
    (a) (290/373.5)(0.2032).
    (b) (190/273.5)(0.2032).
    (c) (373.5/290)(0.2032).
    (d) (273.5/190)(0.2032).

Self-Test Key

Matching Concepts: 1–h; 2–f; 3–a; 4–k; 5–b; 6–c; 7–d; 8–i; 9–g; 10–e; 11–j; 12–l

Multiple-Choice Questions: 1–d; 2–b; 3–c; 4–a; 5–c; 6–d; 7–a; 8–d; 9–c; 10–c; 11–d; 12–d; 13–d; 14–a; 15–a

Exercises

1. Briefly answer each of the following:
   (a) Under what circumstances would devaluation of one country's currency lead to an increase in domestic employment?

   (b) Explain why there might be more speculation under an adjustable peg system than with fluctuating exchange rates.

   (c) Under the adjustable peg system of the 1950s and 1960s, why couldn't the United States devalue the dollar as other countries devalued their currencies?

   (d) Which of the international monetary systems to date—the gold standard, the Bretton Woods system, or fluctuating exchange rates—tends to allow more flexibility in domestic monetary and fiscal policies? Explain.

2. Indicate which characteristics apply to each of the three following monetary arrangements by entering X's:

	Gold standard	Bretton Woods system	Current monetary arrangements
International Monetary Fund			
Fixed gold content for dollar			
Fluctuating exchange rate for dollar			
Special Drawing Rights			
Dollar convertible to gold in United States			
(a) at fixed price			
(b) at fluctuating price			
Adjustable peg			
"Dirty" float			
Free market for gold			
Fixed exchange rate			

3. The purchasing power parity hypothesis predicts that over the long run exchange rates will reflect relative rates of domestic inflation. Test this hypothesis for the period 1967–1982 (1982 data are the average of the second and third quarters).

	United States	France	United Kingdom
1982 CPI (1967 = 100)	289.1	373.5	517.8
Exchange rates (in U.S. cents), 1967		20.32	275.0
Exchange rates (in U.S. cents), 1982		15.17	175.2

(a) Predicted exchange rate, 1982 (U.S.CPI/foreign CPI)(1967 exchange rate) _____ _____

(b) Does the purchasing power parity hypothesis "predict" well in these cases? (See text Figure 41-2 for probable cause of U.K. discrepancy.)

4. (a) Test the purchasing power parity hypothesis of exchange rates using 1982 as a base for the first quarter of 1985, a peak for the dollar (figures for 1982 are in Exercise 3).

	United States	France	United Kingdom
First quarter, 1985 CPI	315.2	456.1	582.9
Predicted exchange rate for first quarter of 1985		_____	_____

(b) Assess the effectiveness of the hypothesis given that the average rate of exchange for the French franc was $.10050 and that for the pound was $.11152 in the first quarter of 1985.

(c) The U.S. economy in 1983 and 1984 was characterized by high interest rates, low inflation, an increase in real GNP of over 6 percent a year, a low savings rate, and moderately restrictive monetary policy. How would these be related to the foreign exchange rates and the deviations from the purchasing power parity hypothesis?

(d) Why was the dollar considered by some to be overvalued in 1985? What primary benefits and problems did this overvaluation cause for the United States?

Short Problem

"I Don't Give a (expletive deleted) about the Lira"

The title quote is President Nixon's reply to an observation about possible currency speculation in a taped conversation with H. R. Haldeman (June 23, 1972). The President found international monetary issues "too complicated" and uninteresting: "Only George Schultz [the economist and Secretary of the Treasury] and people like that think it's great. . . . There's no votes in it, Bob." Nonetheless, his administration led the world's switch from the Bretton Woods system of fixed exchange rates to floating rates.

In 1986 George Schultz was Secretary of State and the United States was somewhat concerned about the lira and far more about the yen. The table below gives the foreign exchange prices for the two leading trading partners of the United States (Canada and Japan), the strongest economy of the European Community (West Germany), and for Italy. The rates are given in U.S. cents to avoid extra zeros for the yen and lira. The reasons for the dates chosen and the inclusion of the Federal Reserve indexes are given in the questions.

	Canada (Dollar)	Japan (Yen)	W. Germany (Mark)	Italy (Lira)	Federal Reserve indexes[a] Nominal	Federal Reserve indexes[a] Real
1969	92.86	0.2790	25.49	0.1594	122.4	NA
1973 (March)	100.33	0.3819	35.55	0.1760	100.0	100.0
1980	85.53	0.4431	55.09	0.1169	87.4	84.8
1985 (first quarter)	73.88	0.3884	30.73	0.0495	156.5	144.2
1986 (10/27)	72.10	0.6219	48.87	0.0707	N.A.	110.4 (July)

[a]The Federal Reserve indexes are the Multilateral Trade-Weighted Value of the U.S. dollar. The real indexes have been adjusted by changes in consumer prices.

Source: Economic Report of the President, 1986, Federal Reserve Bulletin: the *New York Times.*

Questions

(a) 1969 was the last year in which the fixed exchange rates of Bretton Woods were reasonably effective. March 1973 turned out to be the first month of reasonably flexible exchange rates. (The appendix of Chapter 41 tells of the events between.) What clear evidence does the table give to indicate that the U.S. dollar was overvalued in 1969? What two currencies were clearly undervalued in 1969? Why didn't the United States simply devalue the dollar in 1969?

(b) 1979 and 1980 were the low points for the dollar, with U.S. inflation accelerating to double-digit levels. How can we recognize this from the data? For which two countries would we hypothesize that inflation was even more of a problem than for the United States?

(c) From knowledge gained previously in the course, what events turned the dollar around in 1980? What evidence is there of "exchange rate overshooting" in the 1985 figures?

(d) The first substantial evidence of the effect of the dollar's weakening on the U.S. current account deficit came with the publication of the balance on merchandise account figures for August 1986 which showed a reduction of imports from $35.7 billion in July to $30.9 billion. Critics suggested a reason for the small response to higher prices for foreign exchange was that the Federal Reserve indexes exaggerated the weakening of the dollar by including too few trading partners and using inaccurate weighting.

(i) What should happen to the large deficits in the current account with a weaker dollar?

(ii) How do the data for Canada illustrate one point of the criticism of the index (Mexico and Brazil are more extreme examples of this point)? How does the noninclusion in the Federal Reserve index of South Korea and Taiwan, leading exporters to the United States who peg their currencies to the dollar, also help explain the slow reaction of the U.S. current account to an apparently weaker dollar?

(e) You have a chance to see whether the adjustment in flexible exchange rates has continued and whether it has contributed to the resolution of the U.S. trade deficit. The sources for the data have been given.

Answers to the Exercises

1. (a) Domestic employment would increase if other countries do not competitively devalue their currencies, the demand for the country's exports and imports is sufficiently elastic, and if trade barriers are not erected by other countries in retaliation.

(b) Under fixed exchange rates, even with an adjustable peg, people who doubt the ability of central authorities to maintain the current exchange rate may reduce their holdings of the currency and force devaluation (or increase their holdings and force revaluation).

(c) Many other countries had based their domestic currency on the U.S. dollar. The value of their currencies would move automatically with the dollar, leaving the dollar no cheaper than before (except in terms of gold).

(d) There is greater independence with fluctuating exchange rates, because domestic authorities need not be so concerned with altering the money supply to maintain the exchange rate or with the effects of fiscal policy on imports and, to a lesser extent, on exports.

2.

	Gold standard	Bretton Woods system	Current monetary arrangements
International Monetary Fund		X	X
Effective fixed gold content for dollar	X	X	
Fluctuating exchange rate for dollar			X
Special Drawing Rights		X	X
Dollar convertible to gold in United States			
(a) at fixed price	X		
(b) at fluctuating price			X
Adjustable peg		X	
"Dirty" float			X
Free market for gold			X
Fixed exchange rate	X	X	

3. (a) for franc, (289.1/373.5)(20.32) = 15.73
for pound, (289.1/517.8)(275.0) = 153.5

(b) The prediction for the franc (within 4 percent) is very good. The accuracy probably reflects overvaluations of both franc and dollar in 1967 (see the short problem that follows) and the discrepancy the then higher overvaluation for the franc (see Case 34).

The pound prediction is tolerable (within 15 percent); the discrepancy reflects the still strong export position of the United Kingdom in oil.

4. (a) for franc

$$\left(\frac{315.2}{289.1} \div \frac{456.1}{373.5}\right) \times 15.17 = (109.0/122.1) \times 15.17 = 13.55$$

for pound

$$\left(\frac{315.2}{289.1} \div \frac{582.9}{517.8}\right) \times 175.2 = (109.0/112.6) \times 175.2 = 169.6$$

(b) The prediction for the franc is 30 percent higher than actual and for the pound over 50 percent higher than actual. The hypothesis that disparities in realized domestic inflation rates are the major explanations of variations in exchange rates clearly did not hold for this relatively short, extremely atypical period.

(c) The high interest rates, bolstered on the supply side by low savings and restrictive monetary policy and on the demand side by government borrowing and private investment needs, were the stimuli for enormous capital inflows into the United States. The strong dollar contributed to low inflation which in turn kept *real* interest rates high.

(d) Essentially because its foreign exchange value was above that indicated by the purchasing power parity hypothesis. The primary benefit was the present ability to obtain foreign goods cheaply and to finance much of our government and private investment expenditures by foreign loans. The current problem was loss of jobs in export and import-substitute industries plus the prospect of increasing costs to service the foreign-held debt.

CASES FOR PART TEN

CASE 31: Breaking Through the Production-Possibilities Frontier with Trade

In each of the cases below, assume a two-nation, two-product model in which no trade is currently taking place. The two nations, Austerity and Bacchanalia, henceforth referred to as A and B, make their production and consumption choices between products X and Y. Assume that both nations have identical patterns of tastes and preferences and that they are such that, when the products are equal in price, equal quantities will be consumed. In each situation, after trade commences, assume that the prices are equal and that the consumption of X and the consumption of Y will be equal in each country. In situation 5, the equality is at a higher level in Austerity. Perfect competition is assumed in product markets.

In each of the graphs below, you are given the production possibilities frontier and the price and quantity produced and consumed before trade (indicated by the dots). The before-trade relative prices (P_x/P_y) are given by the slope of the production possibilities curve. Show the amount that will be produced and consumed by each country after trade when $P_x = P_y$. Note that when trade does take place, each nation in its consumption will have broken through its production possibilities frontier. For questions on absolute advantage you should assume the same quantities of factors in each country.

Complete the table below on the before-trade conditions as you work with each case.

Before-trade conditions	1	2 (and 2a)	3	4	5
Opportunity cost of X (in terms of Y) in country A[a]	1/2				25/36
Opportunity cost of X (in terms of Y) in country B[a]		1			36/25
P_x/P_y in country A			1		
P_x/P_y in country B				8/5	

[a]At existing production levels

Situation 1

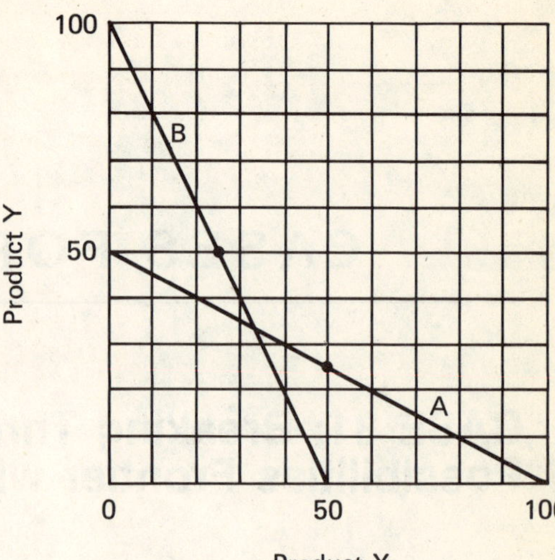

1. A has an absolute advantage in the production of ________.
   B has an absolute advantage in the production of ________.
   Therefore A has a comparative advantage in the production of ________ and is at a comparative disadvantage in the production of ________.
2. With the opening of trade, A will produce ________ units of product ________; B will produce ________ units of product ________.
   With $P_x = P_y$, A will export ________ units of product ________ and import ________ units of product ________.
3. Both countries will have gained because A can now consume ________ more units of ________ and B ________ more units of ________ each, while P_x/P_y is greater than before in country ________ and less than before in country ________.

Situations 2 and 2a

4. In situation 2, there (is/is not) an absolute advantage for either; there (is/is not) a comparative advantage for either.

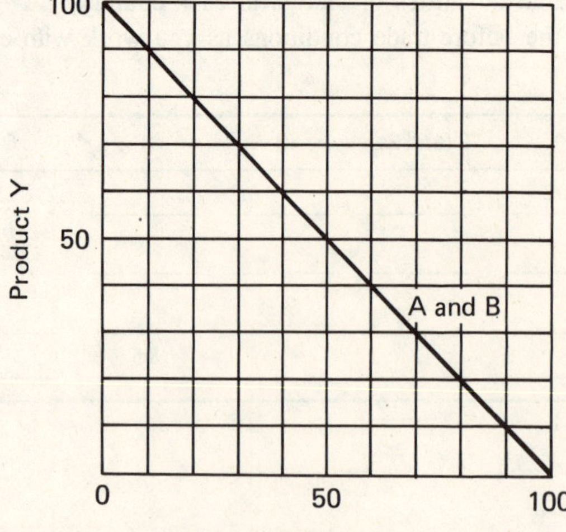

5. In situation 2a, country A has a(n) ________________ advantage in both products. It has no ________________ advantage because opportunity costs are the ________________, as reflected in relative prices of the products, which are ________________. There (will/will not) be trade.

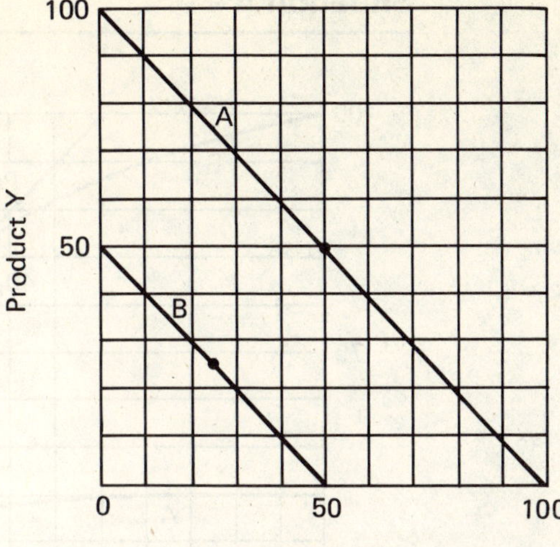

Situation 3

6. This case differs from Case 2, where opportunity costs were constant, because when either country expands its production of *X* or *Y* units it encounters ________________ opportunity costs for that product in terms of the other. If trade is opened up, it therefore will pay one country, say A, to ________________ in the output of *X*, and the other country, say B, to ________________ in the output of *Y*.
7. With such specialization, A will establish a comparative advantage in *X* and B in *Y*, and with $P_X = P_Y$, A will export ________________ units of *X* in exchange for ________________ units of *Y*. Both countries will be at consumption levels beyond their ________________ and will have gained by trade ________________ units of each commodity.

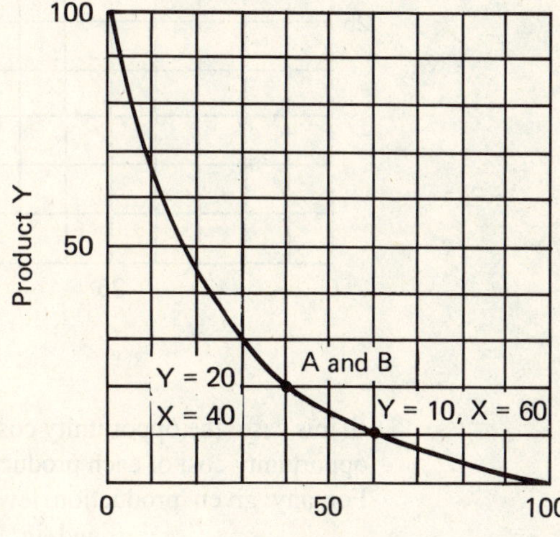

Situation 4

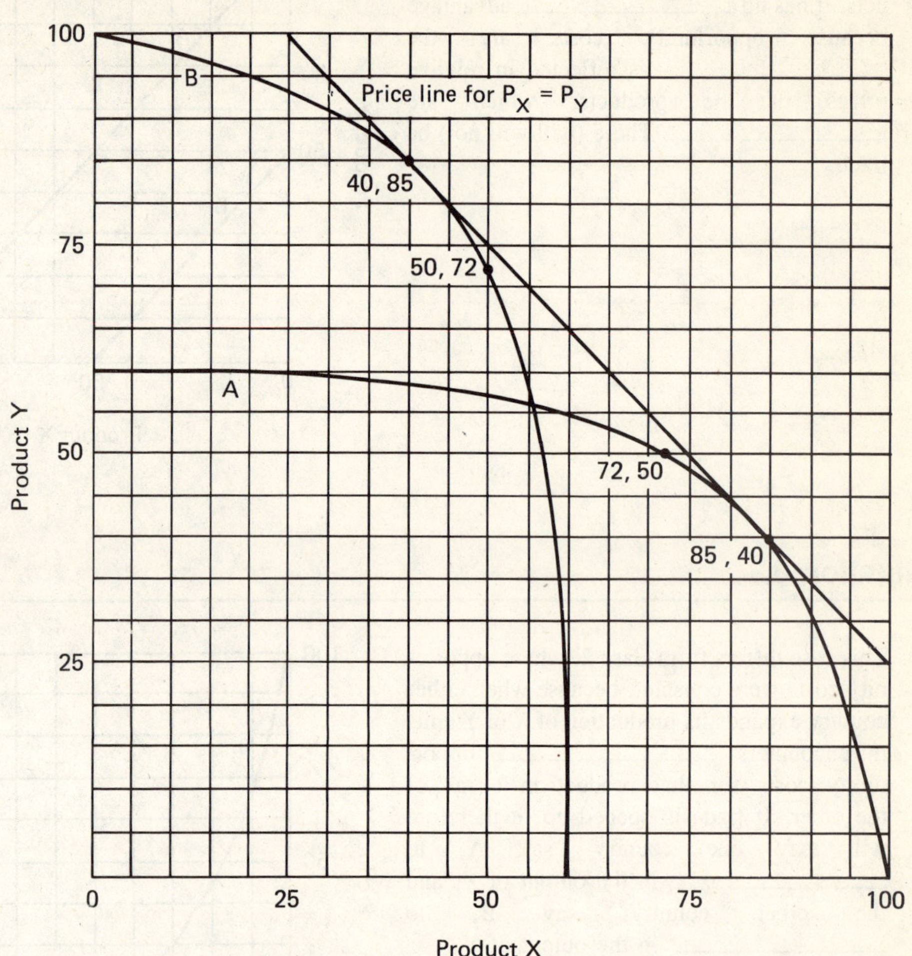

8. In this case, the opportunity costs vary with the production level. In each country, the opportunity cost of each product becomes ______________, as more is produced. For any given production level, the opportunity costs in A are less for product ______________, and in B for product ______________. Thus the comparative advantage in A is for product ______________ and in B for product ______________.

9. Even with trade complete, specialization will not occur because the opportunity costs become very ______________ as all resources are devoted to the output of one good. 1, 2, and 4 can be termed as cases of constant costs, 3 as one of decreasing costs, and this case as one of ______________ costs.

10. Trade can take place at $P_X = P_Y$ because in country A at before-trade consumption levels the opportunity cost of producing more X is ______________ than $1Y$, and in country B the opportunity cost of producing more Y is ______________ than $1X$. Thus A will ______________ its production of X from 72 to 85, where the opportunity cost is ______________ Y, and B will increase its production of Y from 72 to 85, where the opportunity cost is ______________ X.

11. Total production of X for both countries together is now ______________, instead of the before-trade ______________. Total production of Y is likewise ______________, instead of the before-trade ______________.

12. To achieve the equal consumption of both commodities called for by the demand assumptions, A will export ______________ in return for ______________. This new consumption point can be found on the graph on the price line with the slope of –1, which is ______________ to the production possibilities frontiers at the points of after-trade ______________.

Situation 5

13. A has ______________ advantages in production of both X and Y, but B has a(n) ______________ advantage in the production of Y.

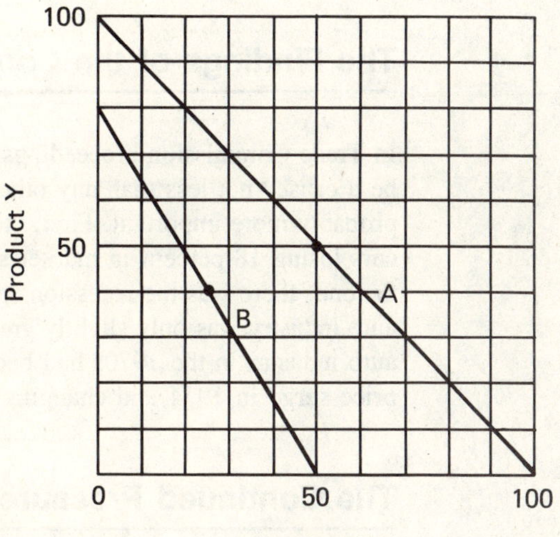

14. At an after-trade P_X/P_Y of 1, which is less than B's before-trade price ratio of 8:5 (reflecting the opportunity costs), the producers in B will choose to specialize in the production of ______________. By exporting 40 units of Y in return for ______________ units of X, B can consume ______________ X and ______________ Y, a gain of ______________ X.

15. If country A chooses to produce 90 of X and 10 of Y, it will be able to (increase/maintain) its before-trade consumption.

Note: You may be concerned about why the gains of trade go entirely to B. This reflects the assumption both of perfect competition and of the particular demand conditions that allowed P_Y to continue to equal P_X. For A to gain, it would be necessary that the after-trade price ratio be more favorable for product X, in which it has the comparative advantage. The complexities of this problem of price determination belong in a more advanced course in international trade, but you should recognize this much: If country A can keep the price ratio of $X:Y$ just below 8:5, B's producers will still find it profitable to offer Y in trade because trading for X will be cheaper than producing it. One way of accomplishing this would be for A to place a tariff on product Y of almost 60 percent (37.5/62.5). B could then get only 0.625X instead of 1X for each unit of Y, and most of the gains from trade would go to A.

CASE 32: Continued Protection for the Automobile Industry?

Since the spring of 1981, Japan has imposed "voluntary" quotas on their exports of automobiles to the United States. The initial annual quota was 1,680,000 cars per year, a drop of 175,000 cars from 1980 but enough to constitute 27.8 percent of the market in the deep recession year of 1982. The number of cars was increased to 2,300,000, about 21 percent of cars sold in the United States in 1986.

The Pressures for Protectionism

The quotation marks around "voluntary" are well advised. Quotas have been preferred to other protectionist legislation. In 1980 the Coalition of Auto Component and Supply Workers, joined by the United Auto Workers (UAW) and Ford Motor Company, petitioned the U.S. International Trade Commission for relief. They estimated that 650,000 auto supply workers and 325,000 auto assembly workers had lost their jobs since 1978. The auto companies had losses of $4 billion in the first half of 1980; Chrysler's survival was aided by $1.5 billion in loans and guarantees by the government. The policy desired was to raise the existing tariff from 2 to 20 percent and to impose an annual quota of 1,600,000 on cars imported in the United States (except those from Canada whose industry has been united with that in the United States with tariff-free arrangements).

The Findings of the Commission Staff

In Trade Commission proceedings a finding of "substantial injury" requires that imports be a cause "not less than any other." The staff report found two other causes that were probably more important. First, "the abrupt change in the price of gasoline" led to large cars losing 18 percent in market share, while imports gained only 10 percent in share. Second, there was the recession (plus high interest rates); the loss of employment in the auto industry was only slightly greater than in previous recessions. In addition, the U.S. auto industry in the 1970s had been slow to gear up for smaller cars despite a gasoline price surge in 1974 and changing consumer preferences.

The Continued Pressure for More Protection

As the United States swung from a current account surplus to deficit in the 1980s, pressure continued for more stringent protection. Ford continued to argue for tariffs. In 1983, the UAW and Chrysler pressed for a domestic content bill in which U.S. and foreign auto companies would be required to have specified percentages of domestic content, that is value-added in the United States. When the requirements would have reached their peak in 1987, a company selling over 900,000 cars would need 90 percent domestic content, with the percentage dropping to zero for companies selling fewer than 100,000 cars.

The Impact of the Quotas

The U.S. International Trade Commission in the spring of 1985 estimated some effects of the quotas:

U.S. auto buyers paid $15.7 billion more for cars from mid-1981 to 1984.

Japan could have sold 998,000 more cars in the United States in 1984 (the quota was then 1,995,000).

U.S. car prices averaged $659 higher in 1984 and Japanese cars $1,300 more than they would have without restraints.

U.S. car companies had become moderately more efficient, with hours of labor input per car dropping from 222 hours in 1982 to 199 in 1984.

Japanese manufacturers were increasingly switching from sub-compact cars to compact and luxury cars.

Average hourly wages rose in the auto industry from $10.52 in 1979 to $15.33 in the first half of 1984 (45 percent) as compared with a rise from $6.70 to $9.11 for all manufacturing (35 percent). The CPI increase was about 48 percent.

200,000 fewer workers were employed than in 1979 as compared with 244,000 fewer had there been no quotas.

The Improved Position of the U.S. Industry in the Mid-1980s

Until the first quarter of 1985, the Japanese producers had benefited from the stronger dollar, which bought an average of 225 yen in 1980 and 257 in early 1985. This ratio rapidly dropped to the 150–165 range in the fall of 1986. The president of Nissan stated, "at 180, we will be in the red" (*Fortune,* March 31, 1986). Effects were to push the Japanese to raise relative prices and switch into selling more expensive models, opening up the lower end of the market to the Koreans (Hyundai was a conspicuous 1986 success) and to U.S. automakers importing cheaper cars and parts.

Honda had established itself as the fourth substantial automaker and other Japanese makers were entering the United States as manufacturers. Joint arrangements with U.S. manufacturers had become common. The Toyota–General Motors joint venture to build the Saturn was perhaps the best known.

The business press, often critical in the past of auto management, observed increased managerial efficiency to some extent guided by the Japanese. Even General Motors, the laggard in competitive progress among the Big 3, received praise. "GM is tougher than you think. It has finally begun to conquer its own bloated bureaucracy" (*Fortune,* November 10, 1986). Some progress had been made in catching up to imported cars in product quality and reliability. *Consumer Reports,* in its 1985 auto issue, cited nine Ford and two Chrysler models in addition to a raft of imports as "competent and fairly trouble-free." Ford and Chrysler were making significant profits. Ford reported a 30 percent return on equity in four quarters of the 1983–1984 boom, a return reminiscent of GM's cyclical highs in the 1950s and 1960s. General Motors, however, announced a major cutback in November 1986.

Questions

1. Consider as alternatives the economic merits and demerits of (a) no added protection, (b) the "voluntary" quota, (c) a significant tariff increase (such as the 2 to 20 percent proposal), and (d) "domestic content" legislation as a policy for 1980 to 1985.

2. Assess the costs and benefits of the policy actually followed.

3. Consider whether, under the special conditions of the early 1980s, some protection was justified by an argument akin to that for an "infant industry." Would this argument be justified in 1986?

4. What protection is being given the industry at the time you are reading this case? What would you recommend as appropriate?

CASE 33: Le Franc à $.20255 et la Gloire de la France

Since March 1973, the world's monetary system has been one of flexible foreign exchange rates, sometimes termed a "dirty float" to take into account the intervention of central banks. The inclusion of this case (written originally in 1969 for the second edition of this book) is to illustrate the problems under the Bretton Woods regime with its fixed rates and adjustable pegs, and to test predictions made at that time. In the late 1980s, some favored a return to a fixed rate system and it is worthwhile to illustrate some of the problems of such a system.

In late November 1968, the central bank and treasury authorities of the ten leading financial and trading nations of the West gathered to meet the third major financial crisis within a year. In late 1967 Great Britain had reduced the exchange rate of the pound (£) from $2.80 to $2.40; in early 1968 the United States halted a speculative rise in the price of gold by getting an agreement that the gold to be used in foreign-exchange transactions would be limited to existing gold holdings. Now the question was whether the exchange rates of the deutschemark and the franc should be altered, the mark upward and the franc downward. The immediate problem was a dramatic increase in the demand for marks largely from holders of francs, and a dramatic inflow of francs and other Western currencies amounting to an estimated $2 billion into Germany within a few days. Most of this represented speculation of an impending change in the exchange rates.

Behind the crisis were both long-term and short-term causes. The major long-term factor was the remarkable economic recovery of West Germany from World War II and its ability to maintain relatively stable prices. This led to persistent and increasing surpluses in its balance of trade and increases in its foreign-exchange reserves. After the mark was revalued upward by 5 percent to its current rate of $.25 in 1961 (an increase inadequate to correct the mark's undervaluation in the eyes of many economists), West Germany's average consumer price increases were limited to 2.6 percent per year through 1967, the lowest rate of increase in Western Europe.

Though one might trace many long-run factors as contributing to France's problems (for example a relatively sluggish growth in productivity), the rapid deterioration in its financial position started in May 1968. Student and worker demonstrations were followed by widespread strikes and general elections that gave the Gaullists a great parliamentary majority but committed them to substantially higher wage levels. Money wages rose 10 percent in two months and the cost of living 6 percent in three months. Reserves dropped from almost $7 billion in April to a little over $4 billion in October and by more than a billion more in November as speculators anticipated a devaluation.

A few days before the closing of the European foreign-exchange markets, de Gaulle called French devaluation "the worst of absurdities." Words of this kind were quite standard for government officials before changes in exchange rates, since to announce that a change is a possibility would only increase destabilizing speculation. De Gaulle's commitment was probably strengthened by his concept of the glory of France and by a history of French devaluations associated with war and with relatively unstable governments; the last took place in 1958. De Gaulle's government's substitution of a new franc equal in value to 100 former francs had the effect of making the dollar value of the franc a more traditional \$.20255 instead of \$.0020255.

Probably most of the participants and observing economists would have favored an upward revaluation of the mark along with some devaluation of the franc to meet the crisis. Such a solution would have taken some pressure off the pound and dollar, still considered overvalued by many. While the German Bundesbank seemed favorable, the West German government would not consider this solution. The German economics minister is reported to have stated, "It is quite unacceptable that we Germans should correct mistakes made by other countries in their own houses."

One day it seemed to be established that France would devalue the franc without German revaluation. The next day de Gaulle said "non" and exhorted the French people to sacrifice immediate economic gains. He spoke of the threat of "odious speculators" and stated that the decision not to devalue was made in order to avoid rewarding "those who gambled on our decline."

What was done?

1. Two billion in foreign exchange was loaned to France by the leading Western countries in addition to almost one billion available from the International Monetary Fund.
2. Germany reduced the tax rebate rate on exports by 4 percent, decreased the general tax on imports from 11 to 7 percent, and placed restrictions on nonresident speculative bank accounts. It estimated that these measures would reduce its surplus on current accounts by about \$1.5 billion or 40 percent of the current amount.
3. France imposed controls on exchanges of francs for foreign currency, reduced taxes on exporters, proposed wage and price controls, and cut the proposed government deficit by about five billion francs.

Questions

1. Calculate the mark price for a franc and the franc price of the mark from the official dollar prices in 1969.

2. What were the underlying factors that made the fixed rate between mark and franc no longer appropriate?

3. What were the political and economic difficulties of "adjusting the peg"? For Germany? For France?

4. You have more of a time perspective to assess what in late 1968 looked like a patchwork solution. Check this prediction with the following data (also see Exercises 3 and 4 and the Short problem in Chapter 41): "The value of the mark will rise relative to the franc and quite probably relative to the pound and dollar as well."

   The dollar prices of the franc and mark averaged $.1815 and $.2877 in 1971, the year of the Smithsonian agreement, and were $.2219 and $.3555 in March 1973, the month following the final abandonment of fixed rates.

PART ELEVEN

Economic Growth and Comparative Systems

42

Growth and the Less-Developed Countries

Learning Objectives

After studying this chapter, you should be able to

—grasp the scope of the growth problem: About one-fourth of the world's population still exists at a bare subsistence level and three-fourths are poor by U.S. standards;

—identify barriers to development;

—explain the roles of infrastructure and planning in development;

—explain the types of development strategies open to the less-developed countries (LDCs);

—distinguish between wealth creation and wealth transfers in the growth of LDCs.

Review and Self-Test

Matching Concepts

_______ 1. development gap

_______ 2. population growth, resource limitations, and inefficient use of resources

_______ 3. critical minimum effort

_______ 4. resources such as roads, postal service, and water supply to support economic development

_______ 5. allocative inefficiency

_______ 6. production at a point inside the production possibilities boundary

_______ 7. sources of investment capital

_______ 8. development through expansion in all sectors of the economy

_______ 9. unbalanced growth to stress exports

_______ 10. policy of encouraging domestic industry by restricting imports

(a) strategy for import-substitution industry (ISI)

(b) infrastructure

(c) symptom of *x*-inefficiency

(d) balanced growth

(e) domestic savings; loans, investments, or contributions from abroad

(f) emphasis on industry with comparative advantage

(g) discrepancy between standards of living in the LDCs and developed countries

(h) use of society's scarce resources to produce the wrong goods and services

(i) raising capital required for increases in per capita income

(j) potential barriers to economic development

Multiple-Choice Questions

1. A Lorenz curve showing the world's distribution of income as compared to the Lorenz curve showing the distribution of income in the United States would be:
   (a) closer to the diagonal line.
   (b) farther from the diagonal line.
   (c) at the diagonal line.
   (d) in approximately the same position.

2. Increases in real GDP in LDCs do not necessarily lead to economic advancement
   (a) if prices rise faster than GDP growth.
   (b) if population growth exceeds real GDP growth.
   (c) if capital cannot be accumulated at the same time.
   (d) all of the above

3. Which of the following is *not* among the barriers to economic development of particular countries?
   (a) population growth
   (b) international trade
   (c) inefficient use of resources
   (d) insufficient natural resources

4. LDCs that have adopted production technology used in more-developed countries
   (a) have enjoyed almost uniform success in terms of substantial short-run increases in per capita GDP.
   (b) usually find that the same techniques prove less productive than in developed countries.
   (c) always spend large sums on research and development.
   (d) usually find that the same techniques are more productive than in developed countries.

5. A major problem with educational expenditures for an LDC is that
   (a) education does not contribute to productive capacity.
   (b) cultural traditions are usually hostile to education.
   (c) no resources are available for education.
   (d) the contribution of education to economic development is realized only in the long run.

6. Public health advances in an underdeveloped country are most likely to
   (a) increase per capita income.
   (b) increase the rate of population growth.
   (c) be very expensive to bring about.
   (d) be self-defeating because the death rate from famine will rise equivalently.

7. The proposals for a New International Economic Order (NIEO) included all but which one of the following proposals?
   (a) preferential tariff and quota treatment of LDCs' exports
   (b) marketing boards to reduce output and raise prices for LDCs' primary product exports
   (c) the elimination of capitalistic institutions in the LDCs
   (d) renegotiation and possible cancellation of the external debt of LDCs

8. It is usually important that developing countries improve their agricultural output because
   (a) agricultural surpluses will be needed to feed a growing population.
   (b) population is apt to be growing rapidly.
   (c) agricultural products may be exported to help pay for needed imports.
   (d) all of the above

9. A major problem with the import substitution industry strategy is
   (a) the difficulty of initial implementation.
   (b) shortage of foreign exchange.
   (c) the fostering of inefficient industries.
   (d) high levels of employment in the LDCs.

10. One of the arguments for specializing in the production of a few commodities is that
    (a) it will insulate the economy from the vagaries of foreign trade.
    (b) it will enable citizens to exercise a wide variety of talents in their work.
    (c) it can lead to more rapid growth in the short run.
    (d) diversification is always more expensive in the long run.

11. In an LDC, *x*-inefficiency might well be caused by
    (a) the economy being on the wrong place on the production possibility boundary.
    (b) unemployment.
    (c) malnutrition of the labor force.
    (d) market imperfections preventing resources from moving to their most valuable uses.

12. The vicious circle of poverty
    (a) describes an income-consumption process which cannot generate sufficient savings to raise the capital stock.
    (b) applies to countries which borrow from abroad and spend the proceeds on consumer goods.
    (c) is a result of failure of policies in LDCs to hold population growth to 0 percent.
    (d) describes a situation where any savings out of domestic income are invested abroad, lowering the domestic rate of capital accumulation.

13. Heavy reliance on expanding agricultural production in LDCs is to be avoided, according to some experts, because
    (a) such reliance would suggest little need to educate the population.
    (b) it would be difficult to sell the surplus at any price.
    (c) it frequently requires subsidization of both agricultural production and consumption.
    (d) per dollar of factor input, the value of manufacturing output is greater than agricultural output.

14. In raising capital for development, an LDC would be inclined to prefer foreign borrowing over domestic saving because
    (a) there is less reduction in living standards in the future.
    (b) of the political disadvantages of foreign ownership of business firms.
    (c) less current consumption must be forgone.
    (d) of the interest which must be paid.

15. The "green revolution" refers to
    (a) recent inflows of U.S. dollars to various Asian countries.
    (b) the dramatic growth in food exports to certain less-developed countries.
    (c) recent increases in agricultural productivity in certain less-developed countries, resulting from advances in technology.
    (d) the policy of changing the emphasis in less-developed countries from agriculture to manufacturing.

Self-Test Key

Matching Concepts: 1–g; 2–j; 3–i; 4–b; 5–h; 6–c; 7–e; 8–d; 9–f; 10–a

Multiple-Choice Questions: 1–b; 2–b; 3–b; 4–b; 5–d; 6–b; 7–c; 8–d; 9–c; 10–c; 11–c; 12–a; 13–c; 14–c; 15–c

Exercises

1. Why may the gap between the rich and poor countries grow larger, even if both have the same rate of growth? Consider the following example. Use the "rule of 72," recognizing that for continuous compounding, as in population growth, the doubling time is the number 72 divided by the annual percentage rate. GDP is gross domestic product.

	Country A	Country B	Difference
Year *X*, GDP per capita	$10,000	$500	______
Annual rate of growth, real GDP per capita (percent)	3	3	______
Year *X* + 1, real GDP per capita	______	______	______
Year *X* + 24, real GDP per capita	______	______	______

2. Use the "rule of 72" for the following (assume annual compounding):
   (a) If real GDP is rising at a steady rate of 4 percent, it will be doubled in how many years? ______________
   If the population is rising steadily at 3 percent per year, it will double itself in how many years? ______________
   In how many years, then, will real GDP per capita be doubled in this example?
   ____
   (b) It was predicted in 1971 that at current rates of increase the population of the less-developed countries would double itself by the year 1996. What would have been the approximate annual rate of increase in population in these countries?
   ____
   (c) In the early 1980s, the population growth rate in the poorest LDCs was 2.4 percent annually. At this rate, population of the LDCs will double in ______________ years.

3. Briefly explain the advantage and drawbacks of the following development policies:
   (a) a policy of agricultural development
   (b) a specialization in a single commodity
   (c) development of import substitution industries
   (d) industrialization to compete in world markets

4. You should recognize the similarities of the diagram below to Figure 42-4 of the text, which presented a production possibility boundary between good A and good B in a less-developed country.

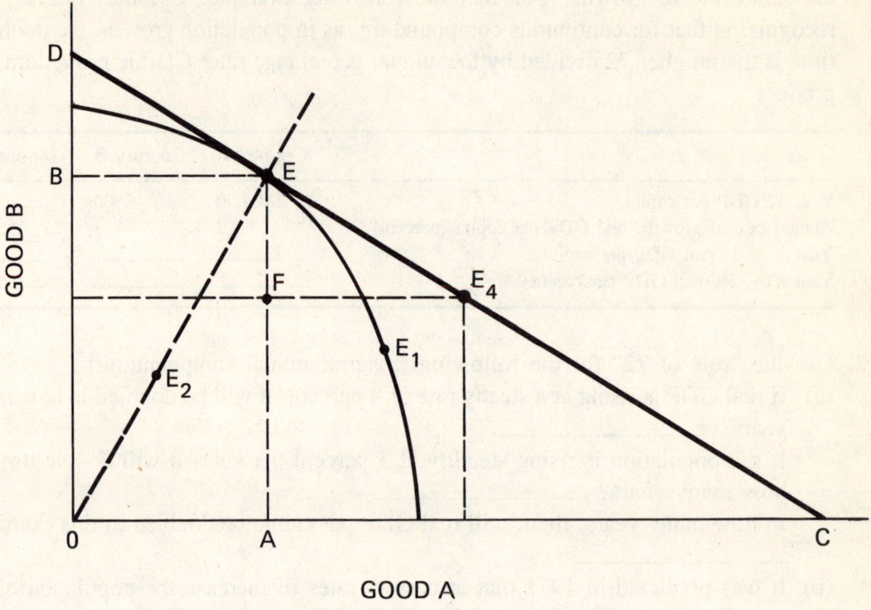

(a) Production at E_2 illustrates ________________, which for an LDC could be caused by

(b) Production at E_1 illustrates ________________, which could be roughly defined

(c) As the new president of an LDC elected on a platform of improving the standard of living of a poor people, you wish to move from E_1 (you are fortunate in having no x-inefficiency) to E_4. This, of course, is impossible under the past regime's policy of self-sufficiency in production. Why?

(d) The new president recognizes that the opportunity cost of producing a unit of B rather than A was given by the thicker line tanget to E with a slope of ________, which represents the world price ratio ________. To preserve traditional production patterns the country had excluded imports of A by means of a substantial tariff. Draw in the line at E_1 that shows this high domestic ratio of P_A/P_B.

(e) The president's solution was to remove the tariff on good A. Guided by relative world prices, the country produced ________ of good B and ________ of good A. It achieved consumption at point E_4 by exporting ________ of good B and importing ________ of good A.

(f) Despite some dissatisfaction from former producers of *A* who made an unsuccessful attempt at a military coup, the president was re-elected because standards of living clearly improved. How do we know this?

(g) In this case a strategy of ________________ proved superior to one of ________________.

Short Problem

Before doing this problem it would be helpful to make the projections in Exercises 1 and 2.

The following information is provided:

Column 1: 1979 per capita GNP expressed in 1978 dollars
Column 2: Annual percentage population growth (for a representative date, 1980)
Column 3: Annual percentage growth in GNP, 1970–1979 (in 1978 dollars)

	(1)	(2)	(3)	(4)	(5)	(6)	(7)	(8)
Kenya	$ 335	4.0	6.0	______	______	______	______	______
Nepal	$ 115	2.5	2.5	______	______	______	______	______
Taiwan	$1,600	1.5	9.8	______	______	______	______	______
United States	$9,900	1.0	3.3	______	______	______	______	______

Calculate the following:

Column 4: Per capita real GNP growth [approximated by (3) – (2)]
Column 5: 1980 change in per capita GNP [(1) – (4)]
Column 6: 1980 change in "GNP gap" with United States [United States (5) – "other" (5)]
Column 7: Years needed to reach $5,000 GNP [Formula: $P(1 + r)^t = \$5,000$, about half of United States GNP, where *P* is column (1) and *r* is column (4)]
Column 8: Years to catch up with United States (only applicable to Taiwan; determine the *t* that will equalize values of real GNP for United States and Taiwan)

Check the accuracy of these projections in the international section of the *Statistical Abstract of the United States*.

Answers to the Exercises

1.

	Country A	Country B	Difference
Year X	$10,000	$ 500	$ 9,500
Year $X + 1$	10,300	515	9,785
Year $X + 24$	20,000	1000	19,000

2. (a) 18; 24; 72
   (b) 3 percent
   (c) 30 years

3. (a) Advantages: It meets the fundamental need of its population and may allow a surplus for export; technical training requirements are low.
   Disadvantages: Agricultural populations tend to grow more rapidly; in the past agricultural commodities have faced worsening terms of trade, attempts for rapid modernization use up capital, unemployment of agricultural labor is likely.
   (b) Advantages: Stresses specialization in commodity with greatest comparative advantage and leads to highest immediate growth and standard of living.
   Disadvantages: Subjects country to short-term fluctuations in demand and supply and long-term secular risk of resource exhaustion or technological obsolescence.
   (c) Advantages: Easy to start by establishing tariff, leads to diversification.
   Disadvantages: Greater risks of inefficiency and of favoring manufacturing incomes over agricultural. Serious problem of finding enough industries where potential inefficiencies are not too great because of scale and know-how required.
   (d) Advantages: More likely to choose industry with potential of comparative advantage, world market permits efficient scale.
   Disadvantages: World competition tough, success may be followed by protection from customers.

4. (a) x-inefficiency; illiteracy, poor health, lack of skills, cultural attitudes, etc. (actually any barrier to productive efficiency)
   (b) allocative inefficiency; using resources, however, efficiently to make the undesired quantities of products
   (c) E_4 is outside of the production possibilities boundary.
   (d) OD/OC; P_A/P_B; line tangent to boundary of point E_1
   (e) OB, OA; EF, FE_4
   (f) At E_4 more of both products are available than at E_1. (Note that any combination on DC is a consumption possibility and that with good A's lower price less of good B may be consumed than at E_1.)
   (g) Specialization and trade; import substitution

43

Comparative Economic Systems: The Economies of China and the USSR

Learning Objectives

After reading this chapter, which contrasts the two largest "command" economies with each other and with "market" economies, you should be able to

—recognize that every real economy is "mixed" but that the differences can be substantial;

—appreciate the significant changes that can take place within a system, with China as a prime example;

—understand how market economies may do better in the microeconomic criteria relating to efficient allocation of resources while command economies may do better on the macroeconomic policy variables of unemployment and price stability;

—know something more about the economic systems of the Soviet Union and China.

Review and Self-Test

Matching Concepts

_______ 1. free-market economy

_______ 2. centralized allocation decisions

_______ 3. socialism

_______ 4. traditional command-type, centrally planned economy

_______ 5. the Great Leap Forward

_______ 6. little used source of revenue in the Soviet Union

_______ 7. Gosplan

_______ 8. pragmatic strategy for balanced development introduced by Chou En-lai

_______ 9. economic sector for which controls have been relaxed in both China and the Soviet Union

_______ 10. important component of consumer prices in the Soviet Union

(a) command system of decision making

(b) the Four Modernizations

(c) turnover tax

(d) public ownership of productive assets

(e) the overall planning agency of the Soviet Union

(f) characterized by private firms and private households interacting in markets

(g) Soviet economy

(h) an unsuccessful attempt to mobilize Chinese labor for industry and agriculture

(i) personal income tax

(j) agriculture

Multiple-Choice Questions

1. All types of economic systems can be said to
   (a) operate primarily for private profit.
   (b) operate to favor a wealthy few.
   (c) reward only the hard worker.
   (d) face the basic problem of scarcity relative to wants.

2. All types of economic systems must
   (a) have a mechanism for making choices about production.
   (b) have a price system that is flexible and responsive to demand.
   (c) do away with large fortunes and inherited wealth if economic growth is desired.
   (d) have centralized planning or nothing gets done.

3. The ownership and operation by the government of the United States of a major railroad network
   (a) means that the United States is a socialist country.
   (b) guarantees better service than if the railroad were privately owned.
   (c) is an example of the mixture of ownership patterns so common in the world.
   (d) is very unusual among Western capitalist countries.

4. Socialism has meant
   (a) centralized planning and control of all production.
   (b) state ownership of most of the means of production.
   (c) no freedom to choose an occupation.
   (d) to each according to his or her need, from each according to his or her ability.

5. The Soviet Union has achieved rapid growth since 1928 primarily by
   (a) borrowing capital from other countries.
   (b) putting everybody to work efficiently.
   (c) investing heavily and restraining consumption.
   (d) centralized, efficient planning that eliminated surpluses and shortages.

6. It is probably fair to say that the standard of living in the Soviet Union
   (a) is much higher than it used to be.
   (b) is as high as that of the United States, but different.
   (c) is about 25 percent of that of the United States.
   (d) has been increased by the relatively large amounts of expenditures on armaments and space exploration.

7. The five-year plan is used in the Soviet Union
   (a) to indicate what and how much each firm will produce.
   (b) to establish growth guidelines and priorities.
   (c) to enforce rigid quotas and targets for each industry.
   (d) only as window dressing to be ignored in practice.

8. Which of the following is *not* true of the price system in the Soviet Union?
   (a) Some prices of agricultural produce from private plots are set by supply and demand.
   (b) Wage rates recognize the need for incentives to induce greater output.
   (c) Prices contain high or low taxes to influence consumption deliberately.
   (d) Prices fluctuate frequently to reflect market conditions.

9. Turnover taxes in the Soviet Union are
   (a) used contracyclically to affect aggregate demand.
   (b) used as direct anti-inflationary measures.
   (c) used both to regulate consumption and as a source of investment capital.
   (d) more regressive than a general sales tax.

10. It is believed that (at least in the past) capital was used inefficiently in the Soviet Union because
    (a) it was so scarce.
    (b) their engineers were so poorly trained.
    (c) interest rates were set too high.
    (d) the cost of capital was not recognized.

11. Profits (that is, revenue exceeding cost) in the Soviet Union
    (a) are divided up by the workers.
    (b) are partly used for investment by the firm and partly turned over to the state.
    (c) are forbidden by law.
    (d) cannot exist because production is not for profit.

12. The Chinese authorities in the late 1970s and 1980s have stressed
    (a) the need to be self-sufficient domestically.
    (b) the collectivization of agriculture.
    (c) integration of cooperatives' activities with state activities.
    (d) increased reliance on material incentives in both agriculture and industry.

13. The most serious of the following problems for a socialist, command type of system is probably
    (a) economic depression.
    (b) economic growth.
    (c) inflation.
    (d) efficient production and distribution.

14. Of the following, the freedom that is *least* available to the Chinese citizen is
    (a) the right to become a small entrepreneur.
    (b) the right to raise food on private plots.
    (c) the right to join cooperatives.
    (d) the right to migrate to different places and different jobs.

15. The rate of per capita economic growth in China as compared with other predominantly Chinese countries (Taiwan, Singapore, and Hong Kong)
    (a) has been lower but substantial.
    (b) has been significantly higher.
    (c) has been about the same.
    (d) has been so much lower that a closer comparison would be with Burma or Bangladesh.

16. In China, state control of the nature and amount of consumption occurs through its control of
    (a) income distribution.
    (b) prices.
    (c) ration tickets for some goods.
    (d) all of the above

Self-Test Key

Matching Concepts: 1–f; 2–a; 3–d; 4–g; 5–h; 6–i; 7–e; 8–b; 9–j; 10–c

Multiple-Choice Questions: 1–d; 2–a; 3–c; 4–b; 5–c; 6–a; 7–b; 8–d; 9–c; 10–d; 11–b; 12–d; 13–d; 14–d; 15–a; 16–d

Exercise

Compare how the economies of the United States, China, and the Soviet Union would attempt to achieve each of the following:

(a) avoid a shortage of coffee in the face of a bad harvest

(b) increase the rate of economic growth

(c) produce more Pepsi Cola and less Coca Cola

(d) redistribute income from rich to poor

(e) achieve full employment of resources

(f) improve the level of air quality

Short Problem

Consider the following numerical picture of three countries who together comprise more than 30 percent of the world's land area. To what extent might the differences be attributed to the economic system (S), to the stage of economic development (D), or to neither (N)?

	United States	China	Soviet Union	Category and brief explanation
Area (thousands of square miles)	3,615	3,707	8,649	
Population (millions)	232.3	1,008	265.5	
Per capita GNP (1982 in 1981 dollars)	12,482	630	5,991	
Percentage growth rate 1975–1982, annual average (in per capita GNP)	1.5	5.9	1.5	
Crude steel production (million metric tons)	67.7	37.2	148.9	
Telephones (per 100 people)	79	0.4	9.3	
Newspapers (daily, per 1,000)	382	(NA)	396	
Military expenditures (percent of GNP)	5.2	8.8	15.0	

Note: These data are from the Comparative International Statistics section of the *Statistical Abstract of the United States,* 1985–1986.

Answers to the Exercises

(a) The United States has relied on higher prices. The Soviet Union uses planned quotas (probably rationing in this case). The response in China depends on whether coffee is one of the goods whose price is controlled and the extent to which it is available in private markets. It would likely be rationed if its price is officially controlled.

(b) The United States may use stabilization policies to lower interest rates and thereby encourage investment, or tax policies such as the investment tax credit, but the decision to innovate and to save and invest is essentially made by private individuals. The Soviet Union would simply divert resources from current consumption to capital investment. In China, decisions about major investments and about input prices and many output prices are left to the state, thus limiting the discretion of individual enterprises.

(c) In the United States this would occur with a shift in demand from Coke to Pepsi that would increase the profitability of Pepsi as compared to Coke. The Soviet Union would plan a shift of resources from Coca Cola to Pepsi Cola production. In China, if the prices of Pepsi and Coke are officially controlled, the prices would be altered and ration tickets issued to achieve the desired result.

(d) The United States uses the tax system and transfer payments. The Soviet Union uses the turnover tax and sets wage rates. China might relax its strict controls over internal migration to allow population to migrate from rural areas to urban areas.

(e) The United States aims for full employment with macroeconomic policies. The Soviet Union achieves full employment by setting production quotas to use the entire labor force or by diverting surplus labor from rural areas where it is underemployed. In China, officially there is no unemployment. Every person of working age is assigned to a job or is classified as "waiting for assignment." This leads to underemployment in rural areas by restrictions on migration that prevent people from leaving rural villages.

(f) In both systems, incentives to preserve environmental quality are lacking because air is treated as common property. Soviet officials would (if so inclined), plan to devote resources to pollution control. Government policy to improve environmental quality in the United States usually involves either regulations or economic incentives. The very rapid expansion in China would have to be reduced by directives and resources devoted to pollution control if air quality is to be improved.

CASES FOR PART ELEVEN

CASE 34: The Hesitant MDCs and the Aspiring LDCs

In September 1980 a special session of the United Nations General Assembly failed to agree on guidelines that would govern future economic negotiations between the LDCs and the more-developed nations (MDCs) on measures designed to aid the development of the LDCs. The developing nations had set a growth target of a 7 percent annual increase in their total output. They outlined a strategy for development that closely followed the Declaration for a New International Order discussed in the chapter. It specified that 0.7 percent of the developed countries' annual output should be granted as foreign aid, supported cartel arrangements to push up the prices of raw materials sold by the developing world, and suggested reduction of trade barriers for exports of the LDCs.

The detailed negotiations on such goals were to be left to specialized forums like the International Monetary Fund which the LDCs hoped would become a source of development funds through the issuance of SDRs. The voting power in the International Monetary Fund (as well as in the World Bank) is weighted by contributions of exchange and capital. Thus the poorer nations wished that a body organized like the United Nations General Assembly should have ultimate authority on the arrangements made and that this body (the "conference") should review recommendations with the view of reaching agreement. To protect the richer nations, conference decisions would be reached by a "consensus." However, this was not satisfactory to the United States, West Germany, and the United Kingdom. A spokesperson for the LDCs from India complained that a few nations had blocked an accord in order to "maintain their entrenched position."

In fact, from 1975 to 1983 the growth of the domestic product of LDCs exceeded that of the developed countries (see Table 42-2 in the text). However, real GDP per capita growth rates have been slower for the LDCs because of more rapid population growth.

The engine of growth, according to the noted development economist W. Arthur Lewis, was the significant increase in real world trade (8 percent per annum) fueled by the accelerating growth of imports by the rapidly growing MDCs. But in the late 1970s and early 1980s slower growth in the MDCs cut the growth in real world trade to 4 percent. To remedy this, Lewis envisioned the possibility of LDCs increasing trade among themselves with more advanced LDCs acting as capital equipment sources. Another possibility would be for the MDCs to allow the LDCs a greater share of MDC markets for manufactured goods.[1]

[1]W. Arthur Lewis, "The Slowing Down of the Engine of Growth," *American Economic Review* (September 1980), pp. 555–564. This is a revision of his Nobel Prize lecture of 1979.

Questions

1. Why is the ability to import from the developed nations so important for the development of LDCs? How would each of the LDCs' proposals (for income transfers, commodity cartels, and reduced trade barriers) contribute to that ability?

2. U.S. economic grants to developing nations declined in 1980 to about 0.2 percent of U.S. output rather than the 0.7 percent requested by the LDCs. Yet U.S. economic aid in the late 1940s (mostly to Western Europe) approximated 2 percent of GNP and exceeded 0.5 percent in the early 1960s. What could be reasons that such aid has become so politically unpopular?

3. One disappointment to the MDCs was the failure of LDC proposals to emphasize the problems resulting from OPEC price policies of the late 1970s, when huge debts had been incurred by the LDCs to meet oil import needs. What might explain the reluctance of LDCs to call for price restraint by the OPEC?

4. How would the combination of high inflation and high unemployment rates in the MDCs increase the resistance to LDC proposals? Why could leading MDCs be reluctant to give a General Assembly type "conference" a leading role in LDC–MDC negotiations?

5. What effects were the U.S. fiscal and balance of payments positions in the mid-1980s likely to have on the LDCs' prospects? (Federal deficits were in the $200 billion range; current account deficits and capital inflows were over $100 billion.)

CASE 35: A Little Adam Smith in the Little Red Book

Significant departures from past communist practice have been occurring in both China and Poland over the last decade. While changes have also been taking place in other countries, the Chinese and Polish examples provide interesting cases of the contrasting directions and practices possible under "socialism."

In China the approach outlined at a 1980 meeting of the National People's Congress was toward giving factory managers of state enterprises greater discretion and toward measuring performance by enterprise profits rather than production quotas alone. The greater discretion was to extend to the purchase of raw materials and to the selling of products. Factories were to be allowed to keep significant shares of profit for their own expansion. Peking, however, was hesitant to lift controls on prices. Fox Butterfield in the *New York Times* (September 7, 1980) raised the question, "Will China's millions of conservative bureaucrats, many from peasant backgrounds with their education confined to Mao's revolutionary maxims (in the "Little Red Book"), willingly put the reforms into practice?"

At approximately the same time hundreds of thousands of striking workers in Poland forced reforms that struck directly at the Leninist doctrine that the Communist party represented the workers and that Communist unions do not strike. The concessions gained included the right to organize unions independent of the Party and the legal right of such unions to strike, as well as promises of reduced censorship and restraint on free speech. Ironically, part of the workers' unrest was created by higher food prices that had resulted from the pressures from Western creditors. In order to get loan extensions, the Polish regime had agreed to withdraw food subsidies that eroded the government's ability to meet its debt obligations. One of the effects of the strike was to require the lowering of these prices from levels that had more accurately reflected true market conditions.

Questions

1. Why should independent labor unions be seen as a major challenge to Communist ideology? (Clearly there were tensions between Solidarity and the Communist authorities in the 1980s.)

2. Is the use of market incentives incompatible with socialist institutions? Why might a centralized communist system be reluctant to allow "free" markets?

3. What do you think of "convergence" theories which suggest that practices in capitalist and communist countries are becoming increasingly similar?

4. What effect do you suppose these policies will have on long-term economic growth in China and Poland?